To Sue

Warm Wishes

Sandra.

HANDBOOK OF GENDERED CAREERS IN MANAGEMENT

This book is dedicated to our families:
Stuart, Ian, Ian, Jacob, Alex James, Libby, Penny, Rosie and Jamie

Handbook of Gendered Careers in Management

Getting In, Getting On, Getting Out

Edited by

Adelina M. Broadbridge

Stirling Management School, University of Stirling, UK

Sandra L. Fielden

Manchester Business School, University of Manchester, UK

Cheltenham, UK • Northampton, MA, USA

© Adelina M. Broadbridge and Sandra L. Fielden 2015

All rights reserved. No part of this publication may be reproduced, stored in a retrieval system or transmitted in any form or by any means, electronic, mechanical or photocopying, recording, or otherwise without the prior permission of the publisher.

Published by
Edward Elgar Publishing Limited
The Lypiatts
15 Lansdown Road
Cheltenham
Glos GL50 2JA
UK

Edward Elgar Publishing, Inc.
William Pratt House
9 Dewey Court
Northampton
Massachusetts 01060
USA

A catalogue record for this book
is available from the British Library

Library of Congress Control Number: 2014954958

This book is available electronically in the Elgaronline
Business subject collection
DOI 10.4337/9781782547709

ISBN 978 1 78254 768 6 (cased)
ISBN 978 1 78254 770 9 (eBook)

Typeset by Servis Filmsetting Ltd, Stockport, Cheshire
Printed and bound in Great Britain by T.J. International Ltd, Padstow

Contents

List of figures	viii
List of tables	ix
List of contributors	x

Introduction　　　　　　　　　　　　　　　　　　　　　　　1
Adelina M. Broadbridge and Sandra L. Fielden

PART 1　GETTING IN

1　Education and career counselling　　　　　　　　　　　15
　Lori D. Paris and Diane L. Decker

2　The internship class: subjectivity and inequalities – gender,
　race and class　　　　　　　　　　　　　　　　　　　　30
　Elaine Swan

3　Understanding and researching 'choice' in women's career
　trajectories　　　　　　　　　　　　　　　　　　　　　44
　Patricia Lewis and Ruth Simpson

4　Gender scripts as access codes to management positions　61
　Edeltraud Hanappi-Egger

5　Gendered understanding of recruitment processes:
　applications and résumés　　　　　　　　　　　　　　　74
　Ulla Hytti

6　Presumed incompetent: perceived lack of fit and gender bias
　in recruitment and selection　　　　　　　　　　　　　90
　Madeline E. Heilman, Francesca Manzi and Susanne Braun

7　Talking yourself into work: insights from sociolinguistics
　about gender and the employment interview　　　　　105
　Mary Barrett

8　'This is just the way it is': executive search and gendered
　careers　　　　　　　　　　　　　　　　　　　　　　123
　Charlotte Holgersson and Janne Tienari

vi *Handbook of gendered careers in management*

9 Inclusion and exclusion processes in the executive search business: an intersectional approach 140
Regine Bendl, Helga Eberherr and Angelika Schmidt

10 Breaking down barriers 158
Susan M. Adams

PART 2 GETTING ON

11 Theories of vertical segregation in feminized occupations: rethinking dominant perspectives and making use of Bourdieu 179
Kate Huppatz

12 Women's beliefs about breaking glass ceilings 194
Paul Smith

13 Risk aversion among women: reality or simply 'doing gender'? 208
Mary Shapiro, Susan Hass, Sylvia Maxfield and Vipin Gupta

14 Pursuing, doing and reviewing mentoring relationships 225
Jane L. Fowler

15 Women managers, careers and organizations 243
Viki Holton

16 How some women achieve success 258
Adelina M. Broadbridge

17 Creating and sustaining positive careers for women: a closer look at organizational context 275
Janet L. Kottke and Mark D. Agars

18 Women and leadership 290
Linda L. Carli

19 'Woman as a project': key issues for women who want to get on 305
Sharon Mavin, Jannine Williams, Patricia Bryans and Nicola Patterson

20 Women on boards in Australia: achieving real change or more of the same? 322
Alison Sheridan, Anne Ross-Smith and Linley Lord

21 Global career challenges for women crossing international borders 341
Yehuda Baruch and Cristina Reis

22	Pursuing partnerships: flexible work arrangements in US accounting and law firms *Leslie A. Levin, Mary Mattis, Andrea Tsentides and Jill Choate Beier*	357
23	Back to the future: a gendered analysis of 'getting on' in the professional services firm *Savita Kumra*	374
24	What's 'woman's work'? Work–family interface among women entrepreneurs in Italy *Silvia De Simone and Vincenza Priola*	390

PART 3 GETTING OUT

25	Playing, quitting or changing the game? A discussion of women managers' responses to organizational conditions *Yvonne Due Billing*	411
26	Encore careers: motivating factors for career exit and rebirth *Wendy Marcinkus Murphy and Elizabeth Hamilton Volpe*	425
27	Senior women, work–life balance and the decision to quit: a generational perspective *Deirdre A. Anderson and Susan Vinnicombe*	445
28	Exploring the career decisions of professional women with dependent children *Helen M. Woolnough and Jane Redshaw*	460
29	Retirement – a new beginning or the beginning of the end? *Adelina M. Broadbridge and Agneta Moulettes*	474
30	Transitioning with Grace: women's post-retirement needs and adjustment *Rachel A. August*	490

Index   507

Figures

4.1	Gender scripts and managerial identity	69
9.1	Modalities of inclusion and exclusion in the executive search process	143
10.1	Working in concert to break down women's career barriers	169
12.1	Women's beliefs about glass ceilings: a four-factor model	196
12.2	Relationships between women's glass ceiling beliefs and subjective success	200
14.1	A conceptual framework for mentoring: pursue, do, and review	227
19.1	Woman as a project: key issues for women who want to get on	317
20.1	AICD monitoring of women's representation on boards	331
21.1	The push-pull model for expatriation – women's perspective	343
21.2	Traditional and new expatriate career paths	351
22.1	Initiatives aimed at female advancement	364
22.2	Trends in retention/advancement of females	365
26.1	Factors motivating encore careers	429

Tables

3.1	Researching 'choice' in women's careers	57
5.1	Background information of the applicants	79
14.1	Mentoring functions performed by mentors to assist their mentees with personal, professional and career development	235
15.1	Career development support received	249
20.1	Representation of women board directors (WBD)	324
20.2	Compliance with reporting	328
20.3	Women's representation across different levels of organization	329
20.4	Female ASX200 board appointments 2010, 2012	332
20.5	Female pathways to ASX200 board appointments 2010, 2012	332
22.1	Women law students and associates	368
24.1	Research participants	395
27.1	Number of women partners by generation and parental status	450
29.1	Demographic background of the respondents	479

Contributors

Susan M. Adams is Professor of Management and Senior Director, Center for Women and Business at Bentley University, Massachusetts, USA. Her research and consulting focus on changes needed for business success with rewarding careers for employees. Her current studies concentrate on eliminating career barriers that women face and the careers, lives and leadership styles of successful women and CEOs. At Bentley, she teaches leadership, organization theory and management consulting courses to undergraduate, MBA, PhD and executive classes. She has served on and chaired boards of companies and non-profit organizations. Adams is a former Chair of the Management Consulting and Careers Divisions of the Academy of Management, a member of the American Psychological Association and member of the Society for Human Resource Management. Her PhD in Management is from the Georgia Institute of Technology.

Mark D. Agars is a Professor of Psychology and Director of the Institute for Child Development and Family Relations at California State University, San Bernardino. He earned his PhD in Industrial and Organizational Psychology from Penn State University in 1999. Mark's primary research and writing interests are in gender and diversity issues in the workplace with an emphasis on women's advancement, diversity management, and the work–family interface. His most recent research in this area has focused on the work and family challenges of the working poor, their implications for individual and family health, and the development of novel and efficacious organizational solutions.

Deirdre A. Anderson is Director of the Executive MBA and Senior Lecturer in Organizational Behaviour at the Cranfield International Centre for Women Leaders in the UK. Her research interests include flexibility, work and family, gendered careers and the challenges faced by senior professionals in meeting demands from both the work and non-work domains. In all her work she seeks to increase awareness of diversity and inclusion, challenging the often-unconscious processes that can limit individual actions and organizational practices. Deirdre is a member of the British Psychological Society, the British Academy of Management and the Work and Families Researchers Network. Before taking up academic research and teaching, Deirdre spent over 15 years as an independent business psychology consultant with an emphasis on assessment and personal development.

Rachel A. August is a Professor of Psychology at California State University, Sacramento (CSUS) in California, USA. Her background is in industrial-organizational psychology and qualitative research. She regularly teaches in the areas of qualitative research methods, statistics, and graduate and undergraduate organizational psychology. She conducts ongoing research in the areas of women's later-life career development, retirement, and the work–family interface. As a result of those activities, she has published in numerous journals, presented at national and international conferences, and written two book chapters. Professor August offers her students innovative learning and research experiences by creating curricula based on service–learning partnerships. Her most recent teaching and research endeavours involve long-term collaborative partnerships with a local middle school, a public agency aimed at improving the health and well-being of financially disadvantaged seniors, and a continuing care retirement community. Prior to Sacramento State, she worked in market research with a public utility company and in human resources with a large retailer.

Mary Barrett is a Professor of Management at the School of Management and Marketing at the University of Wollongong, New South Wales, Australia, where she teaches management, especially human resource management and business communication. Mary's original training was in foreign languages and literature and her academic career began in that field. Following a Fulbright Postdoctoral Fellowship at the University of California, Berkeley, and an MBA, Mary re-entered academia as a management academic. Mary's research interests and publications focus on communication issues at work (which allows her to apply her training in languages and linguistics to the workplace), gender issues in management and entrepreneurship, and family business.

Yehuda Baruch is a Professor of Management and Research Director of the Southampton Business School at the University of Southampton, UK. He formerly worked at Rouen Business School, France, UEA Norwich, UK, University of Texas at Arlington, George Mason University, USA, University of Canterbury, New Zealand, and London Business School. His research interests and writing have been extensive and wide ranging, with particular focus on careers and global HRM, including over 110 refereed papers, in journals including *Journal of Management, Human Resource Management, Journal of Vocational Behavior, Human Relations,* and *Organization Studies,* five books and over 40 chapters. He is former

Editor of *Group & Organization Management* and former Chair, Careers Division, Academy of Management.

Jill Choate Beier is an Assistant Professor at Marymount Manhattan College (MMC), USA, teaching courses in accounting, business law and income taxation. Her research interests focus on the areas of trusts and estates law and income, estate and gift taxation. In addition to her teaching responsibilities, Professor Beier acts as the Faculty Advisor and Coach to the MMC Mock Trial Team and involves her students in community service work by coordinating MMC's participation in the Volunteer Income Tax Assistance programme. Professor Beier is very active in the New York State Bar Association and is currently the Chair of the Estate and Trust Administration Committee. Ms Beier earned a BBA in Finance from the University of North Texas, an MBA from Fordham University Graduate School of Business (concentration in Professional Accounting), a JD from Touro Law School and an LLM in Taxation from New York University School of Law.

Regine Bendl is Associate Professor at the Institute for Gender and Diversity in Organizations, WU Vienna, Department of Management. She carries out research on gender and diversity management, subtexts and queer perspectives in organization theory. An author and editor of numerous books, her writings have been published in *Gender Work and Organization*, *Journal of Management and Organization*, *British Journal of Management*, *Gender in Management: An International Journal*, *European Journal of International Management*, and *Equality, Diversity and Inclusion – An International Journal*. She has received a number of professional awards, including the Käthe Leichter Award for Women's and Gender Studies 2006, a Best Paper Award EURAM 2007 (stream gender equality and diversity in management) and an Emerald Highly Recommended Paper Award 2009. She edits *Equality, Diversity and Inclusion: An International Journal* and *Diversitas – Zeitschrift für Managing Diversity und Diversity Studies* and is an editorial board member of *Gender in Management: An International Journal* and the *British Journal of Management* as well as Associate Editor of *Gender Work & Organization*.

Yvonne Due Billing works at the University of Copenhagen (Reader in Sociology), Denmark. She holds a PhD in Sociology from the University of Lund (Sweden) and a PhD in business administration from Copenhagen Business School. She is Associate Editor for the journal *Gender, Work & Organization* and editorial member for the journals *Organization* and *Leadership*. Yvonne Due Billing is the author of many books and articles within the area of gender, work, organization and leadership, including

Understanding Gender and Organizations (Sage, 1997, 2nd edition 2009), *Gender, Managers and Organizations* (De Gruyter, 1994), 'Beyond Body-counting' (in *Gender, Identity and the Culture of Organizations*, Routledge, 2002), 'Questioning the Notion of Feminine Leadership' (*Gender, Work & Organization*) all with co-author Mats Alvesson, with whom she has also adopted two smart girls from Hanoi (Vietnam).

Susanne Braun is a Postdoctoral Researcher at the Center for Leadership and People Management (Ludwig-Maximilians-Universität) and at the Chair of Research and Science Management (Technische Universität) in Munich, Germany. She received a graduate degree in psychology with a major in organizational psychology from the University of Münster in 2007 and a PhD degree from Ludwig-Maximilians-Universität in 2011. Subsequently, she was a Visiting Scholar at New York University and University of California in Berkeley. Her major research interests include leadership and diversity, with a particular focus on the impact of gender stereotypes on evaluations of women in management, the impact of leadership on trust and performance in teams as well as leadership development. She also conducts leadership and teamwork training in business and academic settings.

Adelina M. Broadbridge is a Senior Lecturer and Director of Learning and Teaching in the Stirling Management School, University of Stirling, UK. Her main research interests, and focus of her PhD, are around the broad area of gendered management careers. Much of her work has concentrated on the UK retail industry where she has interviewed a diverse range of people from undergraduate students and their perceptions of a career in retailing, to managers' experiences within the retail sector (including not-for-profit retailing) as well as the careers of retail directors. She has also researched issues connected with stress, age and work–life balance. She additionally has conducted various research with Generation Y undergraduates and graduates and their perceptions and experiences of the initial stages of their careers. She has published in numerous journals and presented her work at a range of national and international conferences. Adelina is the Editor of *Gender in Management: An International Journal*, an editorial board member of *Equality, Diversity and Inclusion: An International Journal* and co-track Chair of the Gender in Management stream at the British Academy of Management Conference. She has devised and delivered programmes on personal and professional development for women working in the higher education sector.

Patricia Bryans is Reader in Leadership and Management at the University of Sunderland, UK. Her research focuses on gender issues of leadership, the experiences of women managers, media representations of women leaders, and leadership education. She is particularly interested in innovative methods for enhancing the teaching of qualitative research methods. Her work has been published in journals including *Management Learning*, *Gender in Management*, *Gender and Education*, *Qualitative Research in Organizations and Management*, *Futures Journal* and the *Journal of Workplace Learning*. She has presented papers at international conferences in the UK and Europe, authored and co-authored several book chapters and with Sharon Mavin received the Outstanding Article of the Year Award by the journal *Women in Management Review* for their article 'Gender on the Agenda in Management Education'. Trish has designed and delivered management development programmes for many organizations, particularly in the public sector. She is an experienced executive coach.

Linda L. Carli, a social psychologist, has taught at Wellesley College, USA, since 1991. An authority on gender discrimination and the challenges faced by professional women, she is the author (with Alice Eagly) of *Through the Labyrinth: The Truth About How Women Become Leaders* (Harvard Business School Press, 2007), published in conjunction with the Center for Public Leadership at the Kennedy School of Government. The book received the 2008 Distinguished Publication Award from the Association of Women in Psychology; an article based on the book received a McKinsey Award as the second most significant article published in the *Harvard Business Review* in 2007. In 2001, she co-edited a volume of the *Journal of Social Issues* that focused on women leaders. Her research on the effects of gender on women's leadership, group interaction, communication, influence, and reactions to adversity, has resulted in more than 100 scholarly articles, book chapters, and presentations.

Silvia De Simone is a Senior Researcher in Work and Organizational Psychology and teaches human resource management (HRM) at the University of Cagliari (Faculty of Human Sciences) in Italy. She is the coordinator of the Masters in HRM at Cagliari University. Her research interests focus on work–family interface, diversity and equality at the workplace, well-being at work, occupational health, safety and stress.

Diane L. Decker is a retired Assistant Professor of Management at California State University, Bakersfield. She received her Master of Human Resources and Industrial Relations from the University of Oregon. Her areas of interests are general and human resource management, and the effects of gender on leadership.

Helga Eberherr holds a PhD in Sociology and is a Senior Researcher and Lecturer at the Institute for Gender and Diversity in Organizations, WU

Vienna, Department for Management. She studied sociology, political science and gender studies at the University of Vienna, Austria and at the Université Paris Diderot, France and received a postgraduate diploma in sociology from the Vienna Institute for Advanced Studies, Austria. She was appointed a Marshall Plan Awardee for a visiting research fellowship at the University of California Berkeley, USA in 2010. Her main areas of research are in the fields of gendered organization and diversity studies, intersectionality, (re)production of inequalities, theory of social practices, ageing, and methodology.

Sandra L. Fielden, PhD, is a Senior Lecturer in Organizational Psychology in the Manchester Business School at the University of Manchester. She is well known globally for her work as Editor of the Emerald journal *Gender in Management: An International Journal* over the last ten years, and has been awarded Editor of the Year 2002, 2005 and for Outstanding Service in 2010. She has published two books and numerous chapters in the area of women's entrepreneurship and her current research interests include gender and ethnic entrepreneurship, gender in management, coaching and mentoring, sexual harassment and evaluation studies.

Jane L. Fowler, PhD, works in the School of Human Services and Social Work at Griffith University in Queensland, Australia. She is an inaugural Fellow of the Higher Education Research and Development Society of Australia and a member of the Australian Psychological Society. Jane's two main areas of research are healthy and productive workplaces and effective learning and teaching practices. A particular focus of her research is mentoring – investigating the relationship between mentee and mentor. She has designed, implemented, and evaluated mentoring programmes for organizations in Australia and internationally, including the FBI in West Virginia. Jane has been the recipient of an Australian Award for University Teaching.

Vipin Gupta is Associate Dean, MBA Director, Co-director of the Global Management Center, and Professor of Management at the California State University, San Bernardino. He has been a Japan Foundation fellow, and a Research Scholar at the University of Tokyo. He is a recipient of the Society for Industrial and Organizational Psychology's M. Scott Myers Award for Applied Research 2005. His research focuses on culture, sustainable and comparative strategy and management, organizational and technological transformations, emerging markets, entrepreneurial and women's leadership, and family business models. He has authored or edited 16 books, including the seminal GLOBE book on culture and leadership in 62 societies, 11 books on family business models in different cultures, and a strategy textbook. He has published more than 150 articles, and has presented at conferences and seminars in over 40 nations. He received his PhD from the Wharton School of the University of Pennsylvania.

Edeltraud Hanappi-Egger holds a PhD in Computer Science and is Full Professor for Gender and Diversity in Organizations. She was Head of the Department of Management at Vienna University of Economics and Business (WU). She was guest researcher at several international research institutions (recently at McGill University). Since 2008 she has been a member of the University Board of the Graz University of Technology and of the 'Young Faculty' of the Austrian Academy of Sciences. In 2014 she got the Jean Monnet Chair for 'Gendered Inequalities and Classism in Europe' from the European Commission. Edeltraud has published more than 350 articles, books and book chapters on gender and diversity, organization studies and diversity management.

Susan Hass is currently Professor of Management at the Simmons College School of Management, Boston, MA, USA, where she was previously Associate Dean. Her current research interests focus on risk, fraud, governance and ethics and their overlay on the successful execution of strategy in organizations of all types. Hass consults and coaches executives at international organizations on these topics and has presented her work at many national and international conferences. Hass was lead investigator on a grant from the Research Foundation of the Institute of Internal Auditors studying the global state of the internal audit profession. Aside from numerous academic journal articles resulting from the database created by this research, she co-authored the book, *A Global Summary of the Common Body of Knowledge (CBOK)* 2006 summarizing the state of the internal auditing profession worldwide. Hass is a graduate of Boston University and Harvard Business School.

Madeline E. Heilman is Professor of Psychology at New York University where for over 20 years she served as Coordinator of the Industrial/ Organizational Psychology programme. After receiving her PhD from Columbia University, she spent eight years as a member of the faculty at Yale's School of Organization and Management. She also spent the 1998–99 academic year as a Visiting Professor at Columbia University's Graduate School of Business. An author and co-author of over 70 published articles, she has been on the editorial boards of the *Journal of Conflict Resolution*, *Organization Dynamics*, *Journal of Applied Behavioral Science, Organizational Behavior and Human Decision Processes* and the *Academy of Management Review*. Professor Heilman currently serves on the board of the *Journal of Applied Psychology*. Her research has focused on sex bias in work settings, the dynamics of stereotyping and the unintended consequences of preferential selection processes.

Charlotte Holgersson is Researcher at the Department of Industrial Economics and Management at KTH Royal Institute of Technology in Stockholm, Sweden. Her research is located in the intersection between organization and management studies and gender studies. One of her main empirical concerns has been the perpetuation of men's dominance in top positions in organizations. She defended her doctoral thesis on the recruitment of managing directors and the concept of homosociality in 2003 at the Stockholm School of Economics. She is also interested in processes of change and several of her research projects focus on gender equality and diversity practices in organizations.

Viki Holton is a Research Fellow at Ashridge Business School, UK. She specializes in diversity and issues about women managers. She also has researched on a broad range of business and management issues including management effectiveness, career development, learning, teams, HR and leadership development. Viki regularly presents at conferences and her current research projects include women as leaders in the Higher Education sector. She was an early member and supporter of the European Women's Management Development Network – as a Board member and for a number of years edited the network's newsletter. Her publications include a book, co-authored with Fiona Dent, *Women in Business: Navigating Career Success* (Palgrave Macmillan, 2012).

Kate Huppatz is a Senior Lecturer in Sociology in the School of Social Sciences and Psychology at the University of Western Sydney, Australia. Her research explores gender and social class practices, inequalities and relationships. Her recent projects have examined the relations between gender, social class, occupations and mothering. Her publications include the books: *The Good Mother: Contemporary Motherhoods in Australia* (with Susan Goodwin, 2010), *Gender Capital at Work: Intersections of Femininity, Masculinity, Class and Occupation* (2012) and *Identity and Belonging* (with Mary Hawkins and Amie Matthews, forthcoming). Kate is Book Review Editor for the *Journal of Sociology* and is a member of the Institute for Culture and Society and the Sexualities and Genders Research Network at UWS.

Ulla Hytti is a Professor in Entrepreneurship in the Turku School of Economics at the University of Turku, Finland. Her research interests include entrepreneurial identities, entrepreneurial careers, entrepreneurship education and gender in the context of family firms and innovation.

She was a guest co-editor in a Special Issue on Gender and Innovation for the *International Journal of Gender and Entrepreneurship* in 2013, and she is currently co-editing a *Research Handbook on Gender and Innovation* for Edward Elgar (together with G. Alsos and E. Ljunggren). Ulla Hytti is also an Associate Editor in the *Journal of Small Business Management*, and on the Editorial Board for the *International Journal of Entrepreneurship and Innovation*. She has published articles in academic books and in entrepreneurship and management, such as *Gender in Management, International Journal of Human Resource Management, International Journal of Manpower*, and *International Journal of Entrepreneurial Behaviour and Research*.

Janet L. Kottke is Professor of Psychology at California State University, San Bernardino, where she founded the Master's programme in industrial and organizational psychology. Her primary scholarly works are in diversity, measurement and pedagogy. Currently, she is investigating the glass cliff phenomenon with a special focus on the underlying mechanisms of stereotyping the leadership characteristics of men and women. She has consulted with and for public and private organizations on organizational structure, human resource practices, and programme evaluation.

Savita Kumra is a Senior Lecturer at Brunel Business School, UK. Savita completed her doctorate at Cranfield School of Management in the UK and is co-track Chair of the Gender in Management track at the British Academy of Management, Associate Editor of *Gender, Work & Organization* and an Editorial Board Member of *Gender in Management: An International Journal*. She is also International Research Fellow in the Novak Druce Centre for Professional Service Firms at the Said Business School, University of Oxford. Savita has recently edited the *Oxford Handbook of Gender in Organizations* with colleagues Ruth Simpson and Ron Burke and has also published a textbook with Oxford University Press with colleague Simonetta Manfredi, *Managing Equality and Diversity: Theory and Practice*, which won the CMI Management and Leadership Textbook of the year in 2013. She has published in *British Journal of Management, Gender, Work & Organization, Journal of Business Ethics* and *Gender in Management: An International Journal*.

Leslie A. Levin is an Associate Professor of Business at Marymount Manhattan College, USA, teaching courses in advertising, marketing, and consumer behaviour. Her research interests include women in management, and religious imagery in advertising. Prior to her academic career, she worked in product management and marketing at the former Burson-Marsteller public relations agency, Lever Brothers, Bristol-Myers, and Catalyst, a non-profit organization working with women and management. She currently consults for several non-profit organizations. Dr Levin earned her BA from Goucher College, MBA from Columbia Business School, and PhD in Hispanic Studies from Brown University, USA.

Patricia Lewis is a Reader in Management at Kent Business School, University of Kent. Her current research interests include postfeminism and organization studies, gender and entrepreneurship and entrepreneurial identity. She has published in a range of journals including *Gender, Work & Organization, International Journal of Management Reviews, British Journal of Management, Work, Employment and Society, Human Relations* and *Journal of Business Ethics*.

Linley Lord is an Associate Professor and the Chair of the Academic Board at Curtin University. She holds a Doctor of Business Administration from Curtin University, Western Australia. She is also the Academic Director for the Curtin Leadership Centre and the Director of the Maureen Bickley Centre for Women in Leadership (MBC) at Curtin's Graduate School of Business. The MBC was established in March 2008 within the Curtin Graduate School of Business to promote and enable the increased representation of women in leadership roles. Linley's current research interests include women in STEM (science, technology, engineering and maths) careers, women's experience in leadership roles, new models of leadership, and women on boards (corporate and university boards). She is a member of the Chamber of Minerals and Energy (WA) Women in Resources Reference Group. In addition she has been a sessional member of the Western Australian State Administrative Tribunal since its inception in 2005.

Francesca Manzi is a Social Psychology doctoral student at New York University, where she works with Dr Madeline Heilman. After receiving her undergraduate Degree in Psychology with a concentration in organizational psychology from Universidad Católica de Chile, she was project coordinator at MIDE UC (the Measurement Center at Universidad Católica de Chile). She joined the Social Psychology programme in 2012. Her main research interests include gender stereotypes and the effects of gender-based expectations on evaluations of women and men, particularly in the context of gender-incongruent roles and domains.

Mary Mattis is the Director of the Institutional Review Board (IRB) of the New York City Department of Education, the largest school system in the USA. The IRB reviews over 400 proposals annually, ensuring that research conducted in NYC public schools meets professional standards for the treatment of human subjects, research design and ethical practices. During 14 years at Catalyst, she provided leadership for research, advisory services and the Information Center, authored a number of Catalyst's seminal research reports and worked with Fortune 500 companies and top US firms to identify best practices for recruiting, retaining and advancing women in business and the professions. She has authored numerous publications on the status of women in US business organizations, women's representation on corporate boards, workplace flexibility, and women's entrepreneurship. Prior to joining the NYC Department of Education, she was the Senior Officer for Evaluation and Research at the Wallace Foundation.

Sharon Mavin is Professor of Organization and HRM, Northumbria University, UK. Her research interests focus upon doing gender well and differently; women's intra-gender relations, micro-violence and management careers; leadership, identity and emotion work; gendered media representations; friendship, competition and ambition in management and leadership. Sharon is a Fellow of the British Academy of Management, Visiting Professor to Cranfield University collaborating with Professor Sue Vinnicombe. Sharon is currently working with Gina Grandy on abjection and respectable femininity and with Jannine Williams, Trish Bryans and Nicola Patterson exploring senior women's experiences of relations with other women at work. She is Associate Editor of the *International Journal of Management Reviews*, co-editor of *Gender in Management: An International Journal*, has authored and co-authored several book chapters and has recent publications in the *British Journal of Management*, *Gender Work & Organization*, *Organization*, *International Journal of Management Reviews*, *Human Resource Development Review*, *Qualitative Research in Organisations and Management* and *Gender in Management: An International Journal*.

Sylvia Maxfield has experience in both the academic and business worlds and she has become a specialist in the global economy, financial crises and corporate social responsibility. Before becoming Dean of the Providence College School of Business in the USA, she was MBA Director and Professor of Management at Simmons College. In business, Dr Maxfield was Vice President and Senior Sovereign Credit Analyst at the Wall Street firm of Lehman Brothers. At Yale for ten years, Dr Maxfield held joint faculty appointments in Management and Political Science and directed the Master's programme in International Relations. She has published several dozen books and articles about the interface of politics, society and financial markets and has translated her research for non-academic audiences through publication in the business press. She is a graduate of Cornell's School of Arts and Sciences and earned her MA and PhD degrees at Harvard University. She has served on several boards for non-profits operating in the fields of inter-American relations and education innovation and in numerous university leadership capacities.

Agneta Moulettes received her PhD from the School of Economics and Business Administration, Lund University in Sweden and is currently working as an Assistant Professor at the Department of Strategic Communication. She takes a special interest in post-colonial perspectives mainly to expose the dark side of culture and gender issues related to immigration. Her current research focuses on labour market intermediaries' role in integrating immigrants into the Swedish labour market and older workers' career opportunities and attitudes to retirement. She has published in *Journal of Multicultural Discourses*, *Gender in Management* and *Management Learning* and received an Emerald Highly Recommended Paper Award for her article 'The Absence of Women's Voices in Hofstede's *Culture's Consequences*: A Postcolonial Reading' in 2007.

Wendy Marcinkus Murphy, PhD, is an Associate Professor of Management at Babson College. Her research is at the intersection of careers, mentoring, and work–life issues, with particular attention to non-traditional developmental relationships and learning. She has published her work in a wide range of journals, including *Human Resource Management*, *Gender in Management*, *Group & Organization Management*, *Journal of Management*, and the *Journal of Vocational Behavior*, among others. Her new book with Dr Kathy Kram, *Strategic Relationships at Work: Creating Your Circle of Mentors, Sponsors, and Peers* (2014), bridges mentoring scholarship and practice.

Lori D. Paris is an Associate Professor of Management at California State University, Bakersfield. She received her doctorate from New Mexico State University. Her areas of interest and teaching are leadership, gender, international leadership, organizational behaviour, and strategic management. Dr Paris has received awards for best paper from the Academy of Management and San José Global Leadership Advancement Center for her dissertation and paper, 'The Effects of Gender and Culture on Implicit Leadership Theories: A Cross-cultural Study'.

Nicola Patterson is Senior Lecturer in Leadership and Management Development at Newcastle Business School, Northumbria University UK. Her research interests focus on leadership, gender, entrepreneurship and small business. Nicola is currently working on an empirical project exploring senior women's experiences of relations with other women at work, as well as researching disabled female entrepreneurs and nascent entrepreneurs. Nicola has previously published papers in the *International Small Business Journal*, *Gender in Management: An International Journal* and *European Journal of Training and Development* as well as co-authoring a book chapter on diversity.

Vincenza (Cinzia) Priola, PhD, is a Senior Lecturer in Organisation Studies at The Open University Business School in the UK. Her research interests focus mainly around issues of employee and managerial identities, gender, sexuality, diversity and inclusion in the workplace and how the concepts of brand and branding are experienced within organizations. Her book *Branded Lives: The Production and Consumption of Meaning at Work* (co-edited with Matthew Brannan and Elisabeth Parsons, 2011) is published by Edward Elgar. She is an associate editor of *Gender Work and Organization* and her latest work has been published in *Organization Studies*, *British Journal of Management* and *Gender Work and Organization*.

Jane Redshaw is a Senior Lecturer in Psychology and Society in the School of Social, Psychological and Communication Studies at Leeds Beckett University, UK. Her research interests are in women in management, the impact of children on women's career development and the effects of parent–child interaction on language development. Before moving to Leeds Beckett University Jane was based at the Medical Research Council, Child Psychiatry Unit, Institute of Psychiatry, University of London. During this time Jane conducted research into interactions between parents and children and how these influence language development, particularly in twins. She has also published numerous texts.

Cristina Reis is currently developing her research activities at ReisCenter. com. She is Associate Professor of Management and taught in the United States as well as in European countries namely in Austria, Finland, Germany and Portugal. Dr Reis has several academic publications in the *Social Responsibility Journal*, *Social Business*, *Tamara Journal for Critical Organization Inquiry* and others. Dr Reis is the author of *Careers and Talent Management: A Critical Perspective* (forthcoming) and *Men Working as Managers in a European Multinational Company* (2004). She is co-editor of *Careers Without Borders* (2013).

Anne Ross-Smith is Associate Dean, Curriculum and Quality Assurance, and Professor of Management Learning in the Faculty of Business and Economics at Macquarie University, New South Wales, Australia. She holds a PhD in Management from Macquarie University. Her major research areas are women in leadership, and gender and organization theory and organizational change and sustainability. In recent years, she has been researching the role of women on corporate boards in Australia and internationally. Anne was project leader in a team from Macquarie University that undertook the 2010 EOWA (Equal Opportunity for Women in the Workplace) Census on Women and Leadership. She is an Associate Editor of *Gender, Work & Organization* and a frequent reviewer for top-ranked journals in this field. Over the last decade, Anne has assisted organizations in creating environments that support women in leadership positions. She frequently advises women on leadership development and strategies for building and developing their careers and was awarded a University of Technology Sydney Human Rights Award for her work in this area.

Angelika Schmidt is Associate Professor, Institute for Change Management and Management Development, WU Vienna, Department for Management. Her research focuses on issues of employment relations, HR strategies, work–life boundaries and gender issues. Her articles have been published in *Journal of Managerial Psychology, Gender, Work & Organization, Management Revue, European Journal of International Management, Equality, Diversity and Inclusion – An International Journal*, and *British Journal of Management*.

Mary Shapiro holds the Diane K. Trust Professorship for Leadership Development, and teaches undergraduates, graduates, and executives at Simmons College School of Management in Boston, MA. She specializes in team building and leadership, communication across diverse stakeholders, and strategic career management. She researches and publishes in the areas of women, their careers, their risk-taking, and their use of power. Shapiro co-authored two books on interviewing and career management; developed 'Communication Styles Diagnostic', an online tool that has been used by thousands of managers to improve their effectiveness with individuals and teams; and in 2014 published *The HBS Guide to Leading Teams* with Harvard Business School Press. Shapiro consults with Fortune 500 companies, private institutions, non-profits and boards to create strategic plans, launch teams, and intervene in teams in crises. She serves as First Chair on the Board of the Girl Scouts of Eastern Massachusetts (GSEM).

Alison Sheridan is Professor of Management in the UNE Business School at the University of New England. She has been teaching and researching on women in paid work, including their representation on boards, for more than 20 years. She has held a number of board roles, is a graduate of the Australian Institute of Company Directors (GAICD), and a Life Fellow of the Australian and New Zealand Academy of Management (FANZAM). She was an elected member of the ANZAM Executive for seven years, including President (2008).

Ruth Simpson is Professor of Management at Brunel Business School. Her research interests include gender and emotions, gender and management education and gender and careers. She has published in *Human Relations*, *British Journal of Management*, *Management Learning*, *Work, Employment and Society*, and *Organization*. Authored and co-authored books include *Gendering Emotions in Organizations* (2007), *Men in Caring Occupations* (2009) and *Dirty Work: Concepts and Identities* (2012).

Paul Smith is an Honorary Fellow of the Australian Institute of Business Wellbeing at the Sydney Business School. He was a Lecturer in the School of Psychology at the University of Wollongong from 2004–13. Currently he runs his own business, Peak Potential, and specializes in resilience training and psychological testing. His interest in glass ceilings stems from his career as a corporate trainer, presenting workshops for private and government organizations. He has given speeches at many conferences for women including the Australian Local Government Women's Association and the Australasian Women's Firefighting Association. His research has been published in *Gender in Management: An International Journal*, *Career Development International* and the *Journal of Happiness Studies*. He is the author of two books on positive psychology, *How to Have an Outstanding Life* and *1001 Questions to Change Your Life*.

Elaine Swan is an organizational studies feminist and critical race theorist at the University of Technology, Sydney. Author of the books *Worked Up Selves: Personal Development Workers, Self-Work and Therapeutic Cultures* (2009), *Gender and Diversity in Management: A Concise Introduction* (2008 with Caroline Gatrell) and *Food Pedagogies* (2015 with Rick Flowers) she is interested in how informal and formal pedagogies produce gendered and racialized inequalities. With Rick Flowers, she convened a research programme about 'Everyday, Cultural and Public Pedagogies' at the University of Technology, Sydney. To this end, she collaborates with Flowers researching food pedagogies such as ethnic neighbourhood food tours, multicultural festivals, food activism and food social enterprises with a particular focus on intercultural learning. Drawing on this research, they are writing a book entitled *Multiculturalism as Work* and papers on ethnic food tourism and embodiment, and culinary ethnicism and digital multiculturalism.

Janne Tienari is Professor of Organizations and Management at Aalto University, School of Business, Finland. He also works as Guest Professor at Stockholm University, School of Business, Sweden. Tienari's research and teaching interests include gender and diversity, managing multinational corporations, strategy work, and cross-cultural management and communication. His latest passion is to understand management, new generations and the future. He has published in journals such as the *Academy of Management Review*, *Organization Science*, *Organization Studies*, *Journal of Management Studies*, *Human Relations*, *British Journal of Management*, *Organization*, and *Journal of Management Inquiry*.

Andrea Tsentides is an Assistant Professor of Accounting at Marymount Manhattan College in New York where she teaches accounting and auditing. A Fulbright scholarship recipient, she studied Economics Management with minors in Psychology and Spanish at Ohio Wesleyan University, graduating summa cum laude. She received her MBA with a concentration in Accounting from Baruch College, Zicklin School of Business (New York) and became a Certified Public Accountant in the State of New York. Her research interests include accounting education, audit firm culture, women in the profession, and factors affecting audit quality such as personality traits, group dynamics and organizational structure. She has professional work experience in a number of organizations, including a Big Four accounting firm.

Susan Vinnicombe, CBE, is a Professor of Women and Leadership, Director of the Cranfield International Centre for Women Leaders, UK and Deloitte Ellen Gabriel Endowed Chair in Women's Leadership, Simmons College, Boston, USA. Her particular research interests are gender diversity on corporate boards, women's leadership styles, and the issues involved in women developing their managerial careers. Her Research Centre at Cranfield University is unique in Europe with its focus on women leaders and its annual Female FTSE Report is regarded as the premier research resource on women directors in the UK. Susan has been elected as Fellow of the British Academy of Management and has been honoured by The International Alliance of Women (TIAW), which has named Susan as a recipient of the TIAW World of Difference 100 Award 2013, which recognizes those who have made a significant contribution to the economic empowerment of women. Susan is a member of the Davies Steering Committee and Vice Patron of the charity Working Families. Susan was awarded an OBE in the Queen's New Year's Honours List in 2005 and a CBE in the Queen's Birthday Honours List in 2014 for 'Services to Diversity'.

Elizabeth Hamilton Volpe, PhD, is an Associate Professor of Management at Roger Williams University, USA. Her research focuses on relationships in organizations, women's careers, and the work–life interface, with a particular interest in understanding how the integration of social networks and identity serve to influence women's career and work choices. She has published her work in journals including *Journal of Organizational Behavior*, *Gender in Management*, *Group & Organization Management* and *Journal of Occupational Health Psychology*.

Jannine Williams is Lecturer in HRM and Organizational Behaviour at Bradford University School of Management, Bradford University, UK. Her research interests encompass processes of organizing; categories of social relations and constructions of difference, particularly disability and gender; women's intra-gender relations and friendship at work; gendered media representations and career studies with a focus upon career boundaries. Jannine is currently working with Sharon Mavin, Trish Bryans and Nicola Patterson on an empirical project exploring senior women's experiences of relations with other women at work. She is also working with Alan Roulstone on disabled managers and career boundaries, and Nicola Patterson on disabled female entrepreneurs. Jannine has co-edited a book *Deaf Students in Higher Education: Current Research and Practice* (2007), has co-authored several book chapters and has published in the *British Journal of Management*, *International Journal of Management Reviews*, *Studies in Higher Education*, *Disability & Society* and *Human Resource Development Review*.

Helen M. Woolnough is a Senior Lecturer in Psychology in the School of Social, Psychological and Communication Studies at Leeds Beckett University, UK. She is also a Chartered Psychologist and an Associate Fellow of the British Psychological Society. Her research interests are in women in management, diversity at work, mothers in the workplace and mentoring. Helen conducted the evaluation of the highly successful 'Challenging Perceptions' programme, a career and personal development programme for female mental health nurses, commissioned by the NHS Leadership Centre. She has worked on numerous applied research projects both within the public and private sector in the field of equality and diversity at work including European-funded research into career development and good practice in the retail sector and Black Asian and Minority Ethnic (BAME) women's experiences of sexual harassment in the workforce. Helen has published numerous academic and practitioner texts.

Introduction
Adelina M. Broadbridge and Sandra L. Fielden

The position of women in management has been a topic of discussion for the past five decades and the purpose of this book is to take stock of current thinking, practice, ideas and developments, and to consider the future directions in the field of gendered careers in management. In 2000, men had higher tertiary attainment rates than women but by 2011 the situation was reversed (*University World News*, 2013). *University World News* (2013) also reports that women are more likely to hold a tertiary qualification than men in most OECD countries (Organisation for Economic Co-operation and Development). Hence one might expect that their position in the management hierarchies would have changed to reflect this. Although women have made substantial strides in middle management posts, and despite long-standing sex equality legislation in the UK, the USA and across Europe, women continue to be under-represented at the higher levels of management. For example, in the USA women represent only 15.9 per cent of board membership of Fortune 500 companies (Mulligan-Ferry et al., 2014) and in the UK women hold only 13.3 per cent of board membership of FTSE 250 companies (Sealy and Vinnicombe, 2013). Although the number of women on UK FTSE 100 boards has almost doubled in the last decade, from 8.6 per cent to 17.3 per cent (Sealy et al., 2008; Sealy and Vinnicombe, 2013), the ratio of women holding executive directorships compared to non-executive directorships has fallen, from 16.8 per cent in 2008 to 9.3 per cent in 2013. This means that, while there are greater numbers of women on boards, they have become less powerful. This evidence also suggests that despite numerous women being in pipeline positions (Sealy and Vinnicombe, 2013) they do not appear to be making it to the boards in sufficient quantities to make a difference.

The industry sector in which women have made the greatest advancement globally is in retail and consumer product companies, with women holding 18.4 per cent of board positions, which is 3.4 per cent higher than the Fortune Global 200 companies (Corporate Women Directors International, 2013). Nearly 80 per cent of the top retail and consumer product companies have at least one woman director, which is 3.5 per cent higher than Fortune Global 200 companies, 6.8 per cent higher than FTSE 250 companies (Sealy and Vinnicombe, 2013) and 20 per cent higher than Fortune 500 companies

(Mulligan-Ferry et al., 2014). Furthermore, 4.2 per cent of the top retail and consumer product companies have a woman CEO, compared to 3.0 per cent for the FTSE 100, 3.2 per cent for the FTSE 250 and 3.3 per cent for the Fortune 500 (ibid.). Given that women continue to experience occupational segregation, women are over-represented in service sector industries such as retail and under-represented in sectors such as manufacturing and construction (Davidson and Burke, 2011).

BARRIERS TO WOMEN'S ADVANCEMENT

Since the 1970s, research has explored the countless barriers women face in progressing their managerial careers and many of these issues are discussed throughout the chapters in this handbook. The barriers women face can be individual (for example, lack of confidence, assertiveness, ambition and competitiveness) and/or institutional (for example, recruitment processes, networks, organizational cultures) (Broughton and Miller, 2009; Davidson and Burke, 2011). The notion that effective and/or successful management is assumed to be consistent with characteristics traditionally valued in men and reflects organizational male cultural norms and hegemonic masculinity (Schein, 1975, 2001; Kanter, 1977; Kerfoot and Knights, 1993; Wajcman, 1996, 1998) is still apparent in the twenty-first century (Collinson and Hearn, 2000; Jackson, 2001; Mavin, 2009; Billing, 2011; Powell, 2012; Berry and Bell, 2012; Neale and White, 2014; Sang et al., 2014), and the established ideas about managerial behaviour and work norms remain (Carli and Eagly, 2011). Others (for example, Acker, 1990; Alvesson and Billing, 2009) have pointed out that many people believe that organizations are gender neutral but what is represented as gender neutral is in fact a masculine perspective and way of working. It is simply that this has become so instilled in cultural norms it is accepted as the norm, thus other behaviours (including those of many women) are seen as deviant or abnormal. Therefore, the established ideas about managerial behaviour and work norms remain (Carli and Eagly, 2011).

Issues of sex stereotyping and the widely shared beliefs about the attributes possessed by women and men and their acceptance in managerial positions continue to be highlighted. Women managers and leaders assert that women continue to be treated less favourably than men (Eagly and Carli, 2007; Powell, 2012). Even when women perform identically to men they are perceived as less competent than their male counterparts (Heilmann, 2001; Prime et al., 2008), and the ideal worker is still regarded as masculine (Benschop and Doorewaard, 2012). Further, women in senior positions are highly scrutinized in a way that does not apply to men (Ryan and Haslam, 2005; Eagly and Carli, 2007). A recent report showed that 59 per cent of women believed that the culture of their organization is male dominated, while just 42 per cent thought opportunities to advance are fair and equal between men and women in their workplace (Opportunity Now, 2014).

In addition to working in inhospitable organizational cultures and being more harshly evaluated, women continue to face myriad barriers in organizational life today. For example, they are less likely than men to be given challenging high-profile assignments; receive less feedback on their performance; receive less training; have less access to networks and mentors or sponsors; suffer from harassment; have inadequate career opportunities; suffer from gender-based stereotypes; experience tensions between private and work life; have less confidence; and are too self-critical (Oakley, 2000; Wellington et al., 2003; Agars, 2004; Broadbridge, 2008, 2009; Wood, 2009; Catalyst, 2010; Vanderbroek, 2010; Kumra, 2010; Sealy and Singh, 2010; Silva, 2012; Holgersson, 2013). Many women continue to be pigeonholed and segmented into certain types of roles (Bolton and Muzio, 2007), and this can be to their detriment particularly when broad and general management experiences are crucial to getting executive positions (Maineiro, 1994).

Moreover, Barsh and Yee (2012) identified four categories of barriers still persistent for women: structural, lifestyle, institutional mind-sets and individual mind-sets. For example, they found that structural barriers made it harder for women to access the networks of powerful executives and to nurture sponsor relationships. In addition, with regard to lifestyle, while both women and men were found to be primary breadwinners, only the women were also found to be the primary caregivers. Coupled with this, Barsh and Yee found only 3 per cent of managers working part-time, and less than 1 per cent of the senior executives working part-time, which they assert makes it a particularly difficult balance for mothers. Moreover, as successful executives were men and acted like men, institutional mind-sets expected women to also behave like men. They also argued that when leaders pay attention to differences between women and men, their responses are stereotyped and therefore may be limiting for women. They commented that one leader told them: 'For one opening, we had an employee who was highly qualified – she was running operations in Asia. However, we didn't ask her if she would be interested in the position, since she was pregnant and we assumed that she wouldn't want to move' (p. 7). With regard to individual mind-sets they discovered that some successful women sometimes blamed themselves for being held back, and proposed that they should have developed sponsors earlier.

Broadbridge and Simpson (2011) provided an overview of some of the reflections from the past 25 years of gender in management research, and speculated on the future developments. Their work showed how Kanter (1977) highlighted the problems women faced as 'token managers' and how stereotypical attributes were assigned to women by men. They also underscored how various institutional processes and experiences of women and men have worked to 'close ranks' against women in organizations. The women's voice literature recognized gender differences and the need to listen to women's accounts and experiences, while the feminization of management thesis highlighted women's strengths and particular contribution to organizations (Fondas, 1997). More recently, there has been a move towards seeing gender as a process or 'doing' (Acker, 1992; West and Zimmerman, 2001), which involves the (re)creation, negotiation and maintenance of difference in specific social and institutional contexts.

APPROACH TO THIS BOOK

This book provides an international overview of the current perspectives in the field of gendered careers in management, bringing together the foremost scholars in the field. It covers a wide range of pertinent issues that impact on the beginning of gendered managerial careers (Part 1: Getting In) such as education, recruitment and choice; the progress of gendered managerial careers (Part 2: Getting On) such as career phases, succession planning and mentoring; and what comes after gendered managerial careers (Part 3: Getting Out) such as recalibration of career patterns, transition and retirement.

Part 1: Getting In

The authors in the first part of the book 'Getting In' discuss the issues that can continue to hinder women gaining access to organizations. The section begins with Lori Paris and Diane Decker looking at the issues that women need to understand and manage in order to 'get in' to management careers. They focus on the curricula provided by business schools and explore how educators can support women students as they embark on their careers. Internships are the subject of Elaine Swan's chapter, which explores the inequalities in this first career step. She highlights how these generally unpaid 'opportunities' are increasingly being mis-sold as having many career and developmental benefits they do not always deliver, with the best opportunities afforded to those from privileged backgrounds.

Patricia Lewis and Ruth Simpson uncover the notions of 'choice' in women's careers, arguing that it is not as simple as Hakim (2000) asserts. They present the notion of 'choice feminism', which emphasizes individual action and choice, and highlight some of the criticisms of Hakim's preference theory. For example, they argue that there is a need to locate choice within its particular cultural domain, and explain why it is necessary to fully understand how and why choice frames career understandings and career experiences.

Edeltraud Hanappi-Egger explains how organizations are gendered spaces that establish and reproduce gendered regimes. She examines the role of male-oriented 'gender scripts' as a structural framework for organizational practices and shows how they are silently accepted and reproduced, thus serving to undermine career women. These, she argues, can lead to biased recruiting and promotion policies for management positions, which need to be critically examined and changed if change is to occur.

Ulla Hytii also continues the theme of using scripts and emphasizes how gender practices are played out in the context of recruitment. Her research demonstrates how gender plays an important role in recruiters' evaluations, disclosing how gendering is done in nuanced and subtle ways rather than it being overt.

Madeline Heilman, Francesca Manzi and Susanne Braun use the 'lack of fit' model to demonstrate how gender-based expectations result in different interpretations of the same behaviour and how stereotypes are reinforced. They continue to examine how these 'lack of fit' perceptions can be alleviated within the selection process.

Mary Barrett's chapter examines linguistic research into gender and language and she focuses on how meaning is constructed in a conversation and how these can lead to various judgements by interviewers. She re-examines Campbell and Roberts's (2007) research on interviews, taking a gender perspective.

In the following two chapters, the executive search process (that is, headhunting) is scrutinized. Charlotte Holgersson and Janne Tienari highlight how these people can act as gatekeepers and can help to endorse the position of white men in business. They indicate how executive search processes can serve to reproduce norms and expectations of a specific gendered management ideal. They reveal that the exclusion of women is not owing to the overt discrimination of women but to the active inclusion of a particular type of man. Regine Bendl, Helga Eberherr and Angelika Schmidt's chapter also discloses that executive search consultants reproduce male dominance in and through their practices. They recommend the introduction of diversity management as an organizational practice in executive management search firms, which should consider areas other than just gender.

Susan Adams's chapter rounds off this part of the book and her focus is on how to overcome gender-related barriers from a change management perspective. She points to how societal expectations and organizations still cater for men's way of working, and how difficult it is to activate changes.

Part 2: Getting On

The authors in the second part of the book 'Getting On' discuss the issues that can continue to hinder women developing their careers. It begins with Kate Huppatz's chapter, which reviews the dominant theoretical perspectives that have attempted to explain vertical segregation, and in particular she draws on Bourdieu's triad of concepts (habitus, capital and field) and her own research, and argues that a Bourdieusian analysis allows for a consideration of the ways in which social class complicates vertical segregation.

This is followed by Paul Smith's chapter looking at women's own views and beliefs of the barriers to their own career progression. He utilizes the Career Pathways Survey, which examines a diverse range of variables related to the glass ceiling for women at all stages of career advancement.

Mary Shapiro, Susan Hass, Sylvia Maxfield and Vipin Gupta look at the impact of risk-taking on women's career advancement, exploring the theory that taking fewer risks may indeed be a major cause of 'glass ceilings' in career ladders. They propose some best practices from women who have successfully managed risk to the benefit of their careers and their organizations.

Mentoring is consistently recognized as one way in which women can overcome the barriers to success and in the next chapter Jane Fowler looks at some of the main aspects to consider when pursuing, doing and reviewing mentoring. Her chapter also offers practical guidelines for both the mentor and mentee to consider to achieve mentoring goals.

Viki Holton focuses on what helps drive women's careers and the challenges they face. Support from bosses and being given challenging assignments early on drive their careers. The barriers women can face include combining work and family commitments, lack of career support and feedback, gaining the right experience and support from others, including networking and mentoring.

Adelina Broadbridge looks at UK retail companies and particularly focuses on those women who have succeeded in gaining high positions in their companies (a sector in which women are most likely to progress). This was attributed to self-efficacy, and the acquisition of human and social capital.

Janet Kottke and Mark Agars focus on how career success is defined, how it is perceived and the role of organizations in facilitating or inhibiting women's career progression. They discuss how the definition of career success can be varied and unique, but are able to identify the issues that challenge women in maintaining successful careers.

The issue of women and leadership is picked up in the next chapter by Linda Carli, who explores how gender affects opportunities for leadership and the factors that inhibit such opportunities. These include the competing demands of career and family, gender stereotyping and discrimination, gender and leadership styles and the structure and culture of organizations.

Sharon Mavin, Jannine Williams, Patricia Bryans and Nicola Patterson then look at how women have broken through the glass ceiling to achieve senior leadership positions in predominately 'think manager–think male' environments. They theorize six emergent themes to support women who want to get on as managers and leaders in organizations.

This is followed by Alison Sheridan, Anne Ross-Smith and Linley Lord's appraisal of the actions that have been taken by major institutions in Australia to increase women's access to corporate boards. One of their conclusions is that women should develop specialist knowledge in a particular industry sector to help them achieve board positions.

The issue of global careers is explored by Yehuda Baruch and Cristina Reis who focus on the push-pull model, kaleidoscope and intelligent career models to analyse expatriate women engaging in corporate executive careers. They highlight that women are likely to encounter greater and more complex hurdles than men. They argue that expatriation and repatriation can facilitate future career success but warn that there are also associated risks and that they can also pose threats to career success.

This is followed by Leslie Levin, Mary Mattis, Andrea Tsentides and Jill Choate Beier's chapter looking at women's experiences of promotion in US accounting and law firms, focusing on the availability, use and experiences of flexible work arrangements (FWAs). They claim that women's recruitment, retention and advancement, as well as use of FWAs, have been quite different in law firms than in accounting firms.

Savita Kumra then explores women's progression in professional service firms (which include law, accounting, banking and consultancy). She gives consideration to a wide range of theories to explain women's lack of progress, and comments on how little numerical progress has been made for women moving into senior positions in professional service firms.

This part of the book is concluded with a chapter by Silvia De Simone and Vincenza Priola, who focus on women entrepreneurs in Italy and the unique problems that arise from self-employment. They particularly focus on how women manage the demands of their work with those of their family and whether these are seen as opportunities or constraints.

8   *Handbook of gendered careers in management*

Part 3: Getting Out

The final part of this book 'Getting Out' looks at the issues women face when leaving their managerial careers. Yvonne Due Billing examines how women respond to the conditions in their organizations. She argues that organizations still tend to support the notion of the ideal worker but is hopeful that the de-masculinization of leadership and weakening of the traditional norms in management will eventually have an effect.

Then Wendy Marcinkus Murphy and Elizabeth Hamilton Volpe examine the benefits of encore careers in revitalizing working life. Their chapter demonstrates how the 'golden years' do not have to be spent in careers that no longer provide the key elements required by long-term managers and look at why people leave management careers in order to pursue careers that are more fulfilling and rewarding, investigating the role of factors such as fun and novelty.

Deirdre Anderson and Susan Vinnicombe look at senior women's work–life balance and their decision to leave large organizations. Their analysis was by age and whether the women fell into the Baby Boomer generation or Generation X. They found that the search for balance remained significant for all the women.

Helen Woolnough and Jane Redshaw look at how the support offered (social, organizational and family) to managerial and professional women in terms of reconciling their work and home life impacts on their career decisions. In particular, they consider how that support impedes women's ability to return to full-time employment.

Adelina Broadbridge and Agneta Moulettes explore what retirement means to contemporary women about to, or having recently, retired. They were able to deduce that not everyone approaches retirement in the same way, especially before they retire. They conclude that attitudes to retirement are not a straightforward process and, for some, can be lengthy and complex.

In the last chapter and taking a resource-based perspective, Rachel August examines women's post-retirement needs, well-being and adjustments. She identifies that adjustment may not mean the same things to all people and may be a somewhat relative concept by nature. She concludes by arguing that retirement is neither a discrete event nor static moment in women's lives.

And finally, we are grateful to all the authors for their contributions to this book. They responded to the reviewers' comments promptly and professionally, and this contributed to our enjoyment of putting the book together and it has been a pleasure working with them.

REFERENCES

Acker, J. (1990), 'Hierarchies, jobs, bodies: a theory of gendered organizations', *Gender & Society*, **4**(2), 139–58.
Acker, J. (1992), 'Gendering organizational theory', in A.J. Mills and P. Tancred (eds), *Gendering Organizational Analysis*, Newbury Park, CA: Sage, pp. 248–60.
Agars, M.D. (2004), 'Reconsidering the impact of gender stereotypes on the advancement of women in organizations', *Psychology of Women Quarterly*, **28**(2), 103–11.
Alvesson, M. and Y.D. Billing (2009), *Understanding Gender and Organizations*, London: Sage.
Barsh, J. and L. Yee (2012), *Unlocking the Full Potential of Women at Work*, McKinsey & Company, accessed 24 November 2014 at http://www.krus.nu/Global/J%C3%A4mst% C3%A4lld%20Karri%C3%A4r/Unlocking_full_potential_of_women_at_work%20(2).pdf.
Benschop, Y. and H. Doorewaard (2012), 'Gender subtext revisited', *Equality, Diversity and Inclusion: An International Journal*, **31**(3), 225–35.
Berry, D. and M.P. Bell (2012), 'Inequality in organizations: stereotyping, discrimination, and labor law exclusions', *Equality, Diversity and Inclusion: An International Journal*, **31**(3), 236–48.
Billing, Y.D. (2011), 'Are women victims of a male norm phantom in management?', *Gender, Work & Organization*, **18**(3), 298–317.
Bolton, S.C. and D. Muzio (2007), 'Can't live with 'em; can't live without 'em: gendered segmentation in the legal profession', *Sociology*, **41**(1), 47–64.
Broadbridge, A. (2008), 'Senior careers in retailing: an exploration of male and female executives' career facilitators and barriers', *Gender in Management: An International Journal*, **23**(1), 11–35.
Broadbridge, A. (2009), 'Sacrificing personal or professional life? A gender perspective on the accounts of retail managers', *International Review of Retail, Distribution and Consumer Research*, **19**(3), 289–311.
Broadbridge, A. and R. Simpson (2011), '25 years on: reflecting on the past and looking to the future in gender and management research', *British Journal of Management*, **22**(3), 470–83.
Broughton, A. and L. Miller (2009), *Encouraging Women into Senior Management Positions: How Coaching Can Help*, Research Report No. 462, Brighton: Institute for Employment Studies.
Campbell, S. and C. Roberts (2007), 'Migration, ethnicity and competing discourses in the job interview: synthesizing the institutional and the personal', *Discourse & Society*, **18**(3), 243–71.
Carli, L. and A. Eagly (2011), 'Gender and leadership', in A. Bryman, D.L. Collinson, K. Grint, M. Uhl-Bien and B. Jackson (eds), *The SAGE Handbook of Leadership*, London: Sage, pp. 103–17.
Catalyst (2010), 'Women in management, global comparison', accessed 15 March 2010 at http://www.catalyst.org.
Collinson, D.L. and J. Hearn (2000), 'Critical studies on men, masculinities and managements', in M.J. Davidson and R. Burke (eds), *Women in Management: Current Research Issues: Vol. II*, London: Sage, pp. 263–78.
Corporate Women Directors International (2013), *CWDI Report on Women Directors of Top Retail and Consumer Product Companies Globally*, Washington, DC: CWDI.
Davidson, M.J. and R. Burke (2011) (eds), *Women in Management Worldwide: Progress and Prospects*, Farnham, UK: Gower.
Eagly, A. and L. Carli (2007), *Through the Labyrinth: The Truth About How Women Become Leaders*, Boston, MA: Harvard Business School Press.
Fondas, N. (1997), 'Feminization unveiled: management qualities in contemporary writings', *Academy of Management Review*, **22**(1), 257–82.
Hakim, C. (2000), *Work–Lifestyle Choices in the 21st Century*, Oxford: Oxford University Press.

Heilman, M.E. (2001), 'Description and prescription: how gender stereotypes prevent women's ascent up the organizational ladder', *Journal of Social Issues*, **67**(4), 657–74.

Holgersson, C. (2013), 'Recruiting managing directors: doing homosociality', *Gender, Work and Organization*, **20**(4), 454–66.

Jackson, J.C. (2001), 'Women middle managers' perception of the glass ceiling', *Women in Management Review*, **16**(1), 30–41.

Kanter, R.M. (1977), *Men and Women of the Corporation*, New York: Basic Books.

Kerfoot, D. and D. Knights (1993), 'Management, masculinity and manipulation: from paternalism to corporate strategy in financial services in Britain', *Journal of Management Studies*, **30**(4), 659–77.

Kumra, S. (2010), 'The social construction of merit in a professional services firm: what is in and who is out?', British Academy of Management Annual Conference, Sheffield, UK, 14–16 September.

Mainiero, L.A. (1994), 'Getting anointed for advancement: the case of executive women', *Academy of Management Perspectives*, **8**(2), 53–64.

Mavin, S. (2009), 'Gender stereotypes and assumptions: popular culture constructions of women leaders', presentation at Women as Leaders, Gender in Management Special Interest Group Seminar Series, 20 November 2009, London.

Mulligan-Ferry, L., M.J. Bartkiewicz, R. Soares, A. Singh and I. Winkleman (2014), *2013 Catalyst Census: Financial Post 500 Women Board Directors*, New York: Catalyst.

Neale, J. and K. White (2014), 'Australian university management, gender and life course issues', *Equality, Diversity and Inclusion: An International Journal*, **33**(4), 384–95.

Oakley, J.G. (2000), 'Gender-based barriers to senior management positions: understanding the scarcity of female CEOs', *Journal of Business Ethics*, **27**(4), 321–34.

Opportunity Now (2014), *Project 28–40: The Report*, London: Opportunity Now.

Powell, G.N. (2012), 'Six ways of seeing the elephant: the intersection of sex, gender, and leadership', *Gender in Management: An International Journal*, **27**(2), 119–41.

Prime, J., K. Jonsen, N. Carter and M.L. Maznevski (2008), 'Managers' perceptions of women and men leaders: a cross-cultural comparison', *International Journal of Cross Cultural Management*, **8**(2), 171–210.

Ryan, M.K. and S.A. Haslam (2005), 'The glass cliff: evidence that women are over-represented in precarious leadership positions', *British Journal of Management*, **16**(2), 81–90.

Sang, K.J.C., A.R.J. Dainty and S.G. Ison (2014), 'Gender in the UK architectural profession: (re)producing and challenging hegemonic masculinity', *Work, Employment & Society*, **28**(2), 247–64.

Schein, V.E. (1975), 'Relationships between sex roles stereotypes and requisite management characteristics', *Journal of Applied Psychology*, **60**(3), 340–44.

Schein, V.E. (2001), 'A global look at psychological barriers in management', *Journal of Social Issues*, **57**(4), 675–88.

Sealy, R. and V. Singh (2010), 'The importance of role models and demographic context for senior women's work identity development', *International Journal of Management Reviews*, **12**(3), 284–30.

Sealy, R. and S. Vinnicombe (2013), *The Female FTSE Board Report 2013*, London: Cranfield University.

Sealy, R., S. Vinnicombe and V. Singh (2008), *The Female FTSE Board Report 2008*, London: Cranfield University.

Silva-Flores, J. (2012), 'Gender and the construction of dominant, hegemonic and oppositional femininities', *Gender and Education*, **24**(3), 353–54.

University World News (2013), 'Women tops in higher education but still earn less', *University World News*, 29 June 2013, Issue No. 278, accessed 25 July 2014 at http://www.universityworldnews.com/article.php?story=20130628104730556.

Vanderbroeck, P. (2010), 'The traps that keep women from reaching the top and how to avoid them', *Journal of Management Development*, **29**(9), 764–70.

Wajcman, J. (1996), 'Women and men managers: careers and equal opportunities',

in R. Crompton, D. Gallie and K. Purcell (eds), *Changing Forms of Employment: Organisations, Skills and Gender*, London: Routledge, pp. 259–77.
Wajcman, J. (1998), *Managing Like a Man*, Cambridge, UK: Polity Press.
Wellington, S., M. Brumit Kropf and P.R. Gerkovich (2003), 'What's holding women back?', *Harvard Business Review*, **81**(6), 18–19.
West, C. and D.H. Zimmerman (2002), 'Doing gender', in S. Fenstermaker and C. West (eds), *Doing Gender, Doing Difference*, London: Routledge, pp. 3–24.
Wood, G. (2009), 'Revisiting women managers and organisational acceptance', *Gender in Management: An International Journal*, **24**(8), 615–31.

PART 1

GETTING IN

1. Education and career counselling
Lori D. Paris and Diane L. Decker

A recent study of university students' perceptions of successful male and female managers found that the 'male as manager' stereotype is alive and well (Paris and Decker, 2012). Over 50 years of research has been conducted on gender issues in management and very little has changed. Facebook's Chief Operating Officer, Sheryl Sandberg, further drives this point home in an address to an audience at Harvard Business School. According to Sandberg (2013), 'if current trends continue, fifteen years from today, about one-third of the women [in this audience] will be working full-time and almost all of you will be working for the guy you are sitting next to. . . . If you want the outcome to be different, you will have to do something about it' (pp. 65–6). Currently, women comprise over 58 per cent and 60 per cent of US undergraduate and Master's degree students respectively (US Department of Education, 2012). The number of women in higher education has also increased worldwide (Becker et al., 2010). Women have an increasing presence in mid-level leadership positions, academia and entrepreneurial start-ups, and are working side by side with men in classrooms and businesses around the world, yet are faced with a persistent 'male as manager' stereotype to overcome as women work to obtain upper-level management positions (Paris and Decker, 2012). Given that women have a significant presence in business and business education, they comprise only 4.2 per cent of the Fortune 500, 4.5 per cent of the Fortune 1000 and 15 per cent of the top executives worldwide (Catalyst, 2012). As educators, how do we explain to over half of our student body that their chance of obtaining an upper-level management position is less than 15 per cent?

The lack of women in management is a global problem, though in some countries women fare a few percentage points better when it comes to obtaining upper-level management positions (ibid.). Trends around the world demonstrate that the gap between the perception of men and women as successful managers remains persistent (Schein, 1973, 1975, 1994; Brenner et al., 1989; Schein et al., 1989; Schein and Mueller, 1992; Heilman et al., 2004; Gorman, 2005; Duehr and Bono, 2006; Powell, 2012). Gender inequities appear early in a woman's career. According to Silva and Carter (2011) problems for women begin with their very first job after graduation and increased levels of education for both men and women compounds the problem. The more education received, the greater the gap in starting salaries in favour of men (Compton, 2007). Women usually start from behind when it comes to pay and hierarchical position, after which the gap continues to widen. To address gender inequities, business schools have added diversity studies to the curriculum, to create awareness of the problems that women face as leaders and to challenge traditional 'male as manager' schemas in an attempt to move towards a more inclusive model of leadership.

Cognitive research has demonstrated that an individual's schema may change over time, based upon exposure to counter-stereotypical information (Spence, 1984; Fiske and Taylor, 1991; Mackie et al., 1992) or an intervention (Duehr and Bono, 2006). Ideally, one would think that diversity awareness in formal business education programmes should serve as an intervening force and provide individuals with counter-stereotypic information, prompting a reorganization or shift in schema (ibid.). Schools around the world accredited by the Association to Advance Collegiate Schools of Business (AACSB) are required to include diversity education in the curriculum (Moore and Yakhou, 2006). Based upon the theoretical underpinnings of Lord and Maher's (1991) recognition-based processes model (Baumgardner et al., 1991), Paris and Decker (2012) hypothesized that students with greater familiarity of managerial role and managerial attributes would demonstrate fewer gender stereotypes of 'male as manager' than individuals who have not received formal business education. The hypothesis was not supported and according to the study, the greater the familiarity with the leader role the greater the 'pro-male bias'. Furthermore, the findings indicated that the female business education students stereotyped the managerial role with a 'pro-male bias' to a greater degree than their non-business student counterparts. Clearly, something is wrong with the current path that formal business education programmes are taking. As educators, we are preparing students for that critical first job, the one that helps to set their trajectory. We must be a solution to the problem by taking a more active role in ensuring that business schools focus on the current realities that female business students face as they enter the workforce, which will benefit the male business students as well (Simpson and Ituma, 2007).

In this chapter, we have identified knowledge, skills and abilities that benefit all students, but are of particular importance to female students. We address communication and the role it plays in perceived negotiations, connections as in fostering networks and mentoring relationships, and increasing competency-based self-efficacy of the female business student population as these areas are critical for women to understand and manage in order to 'Get In' and attain the job that they deserve. Most likely, communication, connections and competencies cause difficulties for women due to their lack of prominence in the curriculum of many business schools (ibid.). In this chapter, we suggest strategies for educators in an attempt to provide our female students with career management tools and knowledge that they can utilize as they embark on successful and satisfying careers.

CURRICULUM

According to the above study by Paris and Decker (2012), business schools appear to be negatively impacting the perceptions of women as managers. One explanation is that business schools and instructors use materials based upon traditional managerial research and paradigms, which include very little gender diversity (Sullivan and Buttner, 1992; Bryans and Mavin, 2003; Simpson, 2006) to the degree expected by AACSB. A review of contemporary business education materials by the current authors indicated that women are largely absent from popular business and management textbooks and the organizational research upon which these texts are written. Bryans and Mavin (2003) also noted that popular books used in MBA programmes are heavily male dominated. While it is impractical and naive to believe that instructors will be able to follow all of the current research on women in management and integrate this information into their coursework, it is imperative that organizational issues pertaining to women's success in the workplace be addressed at both a course and programmatic level to ensure success for all students. For instance, what knowledge, skills, and abilities do female students need to open doors to better employment opportunities? We discuss some subject areas in the next sections that can provide these knowledge, skills and abilities.

COMMUNICATION

Communication, specifically oral communication, is one of the top skills that employers deem necessary for new graduates to possess (Shuayto, 2013). Communication affects an individual's career from the moment of hire and increases in importance as the individual climbs the corporate ladder (Gallois et al., 1992; Jahnke, 2011). Images of confidence and credibility are developed almost exclusively through communication patterns and behaviour (Brownell, 1993). In job interviews, applicants using a dominant or assertive communication style received higher competency ratings, more favourable applicant impressions, and a greater desire to hire from the interviewer (Juodvalkis et al., 2003), while non-assertive applicants were viewed as less confident and socially incompetent (Gallois et al., 1992).

In studies of leadership effectiveness, there are few real differences between male and female leaders' style and behaviours (Eagly and Johnson, 1990), with the exception of communication differences (Bass, 1990). Female speech patterns differ from men significantly and in ways that make women appear powerless in the work environment (Brownell, 1993). For instance, women are more likely to use qualifying phrases, such as 'I think' or 'I feel', couch statements as questions, speak with an upward inflection that makes statements sound like questions, ask permission, apologize, use minimizing words, not answer the question, talk too fast or too softly, and use a naturally higher pitch that makes women sound childlike and incompetent (Frankel, 2004). Women also tend to use inclusive strategies in the workplace and are concerned with letting others have the opportunity to speak versus expressing their own opinion. Women have a challenge when it comes to communication. When they use gender-inappropriate communication behaviour (dominant behaviour), they improve their overall impression; however, they decrease their likeability and appear less social (Juodvalkis et al., 2003). While we want all students to communicate with integrity, honesty, and authenticity (Buckingham, 2012), we want them to be successful. To help female students with communication, their presentations should be carefully monitored to recognize and correct for some of the traditional, gender-based communication patterns mentioned above. Educators can also use oral presentation as a tool to help female students recognize and correct passive forms of communication.

In the future, diversity and globalization may eventually challenge traditional patterns of communication, with effectiveness being measured by an individual's ability to vacillate between stereotypically male or female communications as required by the context and/or situation (Fisher, 1999; Wood, 2003). Currently, however, most cultures still value an aggressive, linear, direct, and sequential communication style, one that is considered more conducive to a male's style of communication than to a female's (Gentile, 1998).

A critical area where communication skills play an important part is in negotiations. Women have been 'marked' with a stereotypical female negotiating style, such as, being nice, as problem solvers and as builders of relationships, which may be described as cooperative negotiating, while men have been granted the descriptors of aggressive, confrontational and less personal, which may fit the distributive negotiating style (Halpern and Parks, 1996; Lewicki et al., 2007). These tendencies are ingrained from an early age and unconsciously impact our activities, such as communication, negotiation, and value. Studies indicate that women feel a great deal of apprehension when negotiating starting salaries (Small et al., 2003) and lower self-efficacy, as they perceive that they are not as competent and deserve to earn less than men (Lagace, 2003). 'The combination of lower expectations and misinformation about their worth may contribute greatly to women receiving less when negotiating salary' (Barkacs and Standifird, 2008, pp. 4–5) and perhaps why they experience negotiating apprehension. To take this negative perception out of salary negotiations, women need to study the information on the range of salary for the particular position as well as the benefits available and decide not to just take the first offer, but an offer that supports what skills and talents they bring to the company. Women coming to the negotiation table armed with current salary and benefit information and recognizing their value to the company, should be able to negotiate starting salaries comparable to the men. In a study where graduating MBA women had relatively good information about the industry standards, they were able to negotiate salaries that were no different than their male counterparts. In situations where the salary information available was relatively poor, there was a 10 per cent salary difference between males and females (Bowles et al., 2005). Another study conducted on women in single-sex higher education institutions found that women received significantly lower salary offers than their peers from coed academic institutions (Belliveau, 2005).

Negotiations may also need to be framed differently for women than for men. Instead of entering into negotiations with an adversarial mindset, they may be more effective entering with a protective, team orientation. For example, when women understand that they are negotiating not only for themselves, but also for others, they tend to negotiate more confidently. One study showed that women negotiated for higher wages or resources when they believed that they were negotiating for others versus when they were negotiating solely for themselves (Bowles et al., 2005). When women are negotiating for salary, they need to remember that they and their entire family benefit from the outcome of the negotiation (ibid.). To neutralize gender difference in negotiations women should be taught to anticipate gender-related triggers, do their homework, and understand and anticipate the context of the negotiation situation, to determine who are the parties in the negotiation process (for women that would include who am I negotiating for?).

Wage parity comes when women understand the negotiation process. Unless students take a specific negotiations course, most will only have a cursory understanding of negotiations and the negotiating process. Negotiating is a skill that takes time for students to hone. Recommendations to help students improve their skills include having all students role-play negotiation exercises in class or inviting members of the business community to judge and provide feedback for students, specifically indicating how gender potentially entered into or affected the negotiation process. Through time, practising negotiation exercises and situations in class may help to increase female students' perception of competency in negotiating. Bringing community members into class to engage with students will also help female students begin to work on creating connections.

CONNECTIONS

Social capital is created when the relations among people facilitate instrumental action (Coleman, 1990), for instance, relationships with other people that foster job attainment and advancement (Siebert et al., 2001). Recruitment agencies, friends, acquaintances, and organizational employees who one can refer to for future employment, are positioned to foster social capital. In establishing social capital, both men and women have traditionally had a tendency to rely on same-sex contacts (Still and Guerin, 1986; Ehrich, 1994; Bussey, 2012). For women this is detrimental to their careers because they are not linking themselves to men who hold the majority of power positions in organizations (Travers et al., 1997; Bussey, 2012), thus women possess less social capital than men in the workforce. Since women have less access to people at the top, they need to be particularly focused on using networking and mentoring to further their career opportunities.

An integral part of what managers do is networking. It is 'the process of contacting and being contacted by people in our social network and maintaining these linkages and relationships' (Burke, 1993, p. 347). Networking plays a critical role in job attainment (Mavin and Bryans, 2002) as individuals who have a networking strategy are better positioned to find employment (Shantz et al., 2011). Networks also provide members with support, information, and lead to organizational advancement (Michael and Yukl, 1993).

According to Powell and Graves (2003), men and women's networks differ substantially. Women's networks are primarily kin-centred networks comprising warm relationships with peers, socio-cultural, and feminist-type organizations. Men use their networks more successfully, promoting self and business to a much greater extent (Chapman, 1986; Still and Guerin, 1986; Broadbridge, 2010). Men are more motivated to use their networking in a utilitarian or transactional fashion, with each contact being assessed in terms of pay-off (Van Emmerick et al., 2006).

Men favour male-oriented professional organizations, such as service, political, community-based and sporting organizations, to achieve career goals. They also tend to have a more geographically dispersed network. Women need to take advantage of the benefits of networking with men. Women who take advantage of opposite-sex networks have reduced intentions to leave an organization early, due to the necessary job ties created from networking (Ng and Chow, 2009). Networking also increases internal visibility (by accepting highly visible work assignments or by participating on taskforces or committees), provides the opportunity to prove one's capabilities, and is significantly related to career success for women. Furthermore, networking leads to an increased number of promotions, total compensation, and perceived career success (Forret and Dougherty, 2004).

The university environment provides a hotbed of networking opportunities, yet many students do not take advantage of these opportunities. Students should be encouraged to join professional and trade organizations related to their major course of study (Powell and Graves, 2003) and join campus groups and forums. Women in particular need to broaden their access to power by joining co-educational and mainstream networks (Ehrich, 1994). Students should be taught the importance of networks and immediately start to create networks once they begin their business studies. Educators can also engage students in networking simulations that provide concrete experiences, feedback and opportunities to reflect on their networking skills and how networking helps individuals find jobs (Sanyal and Neves, 1998; Friar and Eddleston, 2007). Practising networking skills in a mixed-gender environment is a start to allow women to build networks with their male counterparts and become more proficient at carrying out the behaviour in an organizational environment. Networking is not only important in and of itself, but most likely will lead to a successful mentor and/or sponsor relationship.

Mentoring is a powerful and critical resource used by organizations, to develop and enhance protégés' professional and personal development (Kram, 1983; Eisenberger et al., 2001). Mentoring relationships may develop informally or through formal organizational programmes. Mentoring may provide protégés with career guidance and/or psychosocial support (Kram, 1983). Career mentors act as coach, provide challenging assignments, protect and make the protégé visible within the organization in an attempt to advance the protégé's career (Allen et al., 2004). Psychosocial mentoring comes in the form of friendship, acceptance, counselling, emotional well-being, personal growth and self-worth, and career advancement (Tharenou, 2005).

Mentorships are critical for career progression (Sandberg, 2013) and are beneficial for women and minorities (Tharenou, 2005; Schipani et al., 2009). Mentoring relationships help women break through the glass ceiling and can lead to higher compensation, greater number of promotions, greater career and job satisfaction, greater loyalty, increased career commitment and decreased stress (Eisenberger et al., 2001; Allen et al., 2004; Tharenou, 2005; Schipani et al., 2009). Mentoring may also increase a protégé's confidence and help them navigate an organization's culture and politics (Lockwood, 2004).

The results are mixed when it comes to the gender of the mentor and protégé and the benefits of formal versus informal programmes. Career support from a female mentor to a female protégé is extremely important. Female mentors have dealt with similar constraints and have succeeded. However, as with networking, white male mentors are traditionally better positioned in organizations and are likely to be the most beneficial mentors for women (Powell and Graves, 2003). With male mentors, however, there is also a tendency to provide too much psychosocial mentoring versus career mentoring to female protégés. This needs to be carefully balanced, with more focus on career mentoring (Fowler et al., 2007).

The results are also mixed when it comes to finding a mentor through formal or informal means. Many studies demonstrate that, for women, formal mentoring programmes are more effective than informal mentoring (Washington, 2011). One study demonstrated that women who found mentors through formal programmes were 50 per cent more likely to be promoted than women who found mentors on their own (Ibarra et al., 2010). Powell and Graves (2003) argue that an effective mentoring relationship cannot be engineered and should grow organically to allow for a spontaneous mentor/protégé relationship to develop based on two people recognizing value in relating to one another. Unfortunately, women have a difficult time finding mentors (Ragins and Cotton, 1999; O'Brien et al., 2010), so creating a programme to provide some type of formal mentoring in the university setting is valuable.

Mentoring is clearly identified as a key to career development and is arguably indispensible for women's advancement to positions of power (Leck and Orser, 2013). Mentors select protégés based upon performance, potential, and trust. It is imperative that mentors trust protégés. Recent research demonstrates that male mentors trust their male protégés more than they trust female protégés, with trust being measured by a mentor's perception of the protégé's ability, benevolence, and integrity (Leck and Orser, 2013). Clearly, women are as benevolent and possess as much integrity as men so much of the trust issue may lie in the perception of ability. According to Sandberg (2013), 'Excel and you will get a mentor' (p. 68).

Much of what we discussed about education relative to networking applies to mentoring. Business members in the community are generally quite willing to extend their knowledge and encouragement to students. To increase mentorship possibilities, faculty or advisors should encourage students to meet at least one business leader that shares subject matter interests. A graded exercise where the student must conduct research on the industry and the individual and attend the meeting with well thought-out questions can be used to facilitate the establishment of a mentee/mentor relationship.

We have to add a caveat about mentoring that instructors should share with students. Clearly females need mentoring relationships for career advancement, yet many potential male mentors in the USA are reluctant to select a female protégé due to possible sexual innuendo. A majority of men in upper-level positions are hesitant to have a one-on-one meeting with a more junior female and about one-half of junior women avoid close contact with a senior man (Powell and Graves, 2003; Hewlett et al., 2010). Suggestions for establishing a more comfortable relationship for mentors/protégés of the opposite sex include focusing mentoring meetings in places where both parties can feel comfortable, meeting for a few minutes after a meeting, having breakfast and lunch meetings, and meeting at coffee shops.

COMPETENCY

According to Powell and Graves (2003), mentoring and networking are valuable pursuits; however, there are few substitutes for competency and self-efficacy, that is, the 'beliefs in one's capabilities to organize and execute the courses of action required to produce given attainments' (Bandura, 1997, p.3). Both men and women must work at building their competencies and increasing their self-efficacy. Beginning in early education through college, girls demonstrate far more competence and success in the classroom than boys. However, boys demand and get more classroom attention. These measures do not suggest that girls are smarter than boys, but that boys receive more attention based on their gender, and girls do not get the recognition that they deserve (Powell and Graves, 2003). Even in the light of grades, stereotypes extend to perceptions of cognitive abilities, with men perceived as being more analytical and precise, and better at abstractions, reasoning and problem-solving, while women are seen as being imaginative, intuitive, perceptive and creative (Carli and Eagly, 1999). Naturally, a great concern is that men do not see women as leaders. Of greater concern however, is the fact that women do not perceive or believe in themselves as leaders (Paris and Decker, 2012). The perception that women are stereotypically feminine and do not fit the image of the ideal leader is still pervasive and not only affects the evaluation and perception of women in a leadership role, but may also affect women's self-efficacy and perceptions of themselves as leaders (Paris and Decker, 2012; Coder and Spiller, 2013).

Self-efficacy, as a construct, has strong empirical support for its relationship to leadership. An individual's perception of their leadership capabilities may have more impact on their selection and acceptance of a leadership position than gender or gender roles (Coder and Spiller, 2013). The lack of self-efficacy may also make women want to check out of the leadership career path prematurely, because they do not believe that they can do it all. Many women do not believe that they have what it takes to be a leader and also worry prematurely that they may not be able to balance a family and a career, therefore take themselves out of the game before it starts (Widnall, 1988; Sandberg, 2013).

Many female students may have 'imposter syndrome', where due to pervasive sexism, women doubt their own abilities and achievements, feel inadequate and have a fear of eventually being found out. These feelings of inadequacy can lead to a decreased self-efficacy, which may result in female students having lower performance expectations, being less confident speaking in class, and having concerns that speaking in class may reveal inadequacies (Widnall, 1988). Even male communication patterns may negatively affect women, in that when men communicate in a competitive fashion, belittling the opponent in a 'take down' manner, they shake the confrontation off and walk away. Women have a tendency to internalize messages and hold on to negative messages for weeks or months, until it is internalized and damages the self-esteem (ibid.).

Male and female students need to be aware of the many accomplishments of female leaders and debunk the negative female stereotypes. For instance, the Fortune 500 organizations that have the highest number of females represented on the board of directors have a 46 per cent higher return on equity than those organizations with fewer women directors (Catalyst, 2011). To increase perceptions of successful female leaders faculty needs to discuss stereotypes and the implication for women's careers, and demonstrate how many women have limited their own career progression by placing unnecessary limitations on themselves (Chesterman and Ross-Smith, 2006).

Faculty and advisors need to believe in female students. Lower expectations on the part of faculty and advisors are quickly perceived by students and can lead to lower self-efficacy. Having an initial one-on-one consultation at the beginning of the term or having students fill out a bio-form will help faculty and advisors get to know their students and their career goals and interests.

Female faculty members need to lead the change to foster the career goals of female students. One exercise would be engaging female students in activities that stretch their experiences, knowledge and skills. To demonstrate that women have what it takes to be successful and competent leaders, educators should actively encourage them to take up a challenge or to even assign them challenging tasks. Challenging experiences have beneficial consequences such as learning and development (McCauley et al., 1994). Engagement with internships, service-learning courses, student consulting projects and alumni leadership organizations, help students to increase competencies and allow them to demonstrate these skills to others.

CONCLUSION

In this chapter, we have identified the knowledge, skills and abilities that benefit all students, but are of particular importance to female students. We addressed communication and the role it plays in perceived competency and negotiations, connections as in fostering networks and mentoring relationships, and the importance of increasing competency-based self-efficacy in our female business student population, as these are critical areas that women must understand and manage in order to 'Get In' and attain the job that they deserve. Most likely, communication, connections and competencies cause difficulties for many female students due to their lack of prominence in the curriculum of many business schools (Simpson and Ituma, 2007). Improved career planning services to provide better education and career information for women is essential (Perry and Gundersen, 2011). We cannot assume that our female students are working on these activities alone. Many, if not most, of our female students do not know what these skills entail let alone have knowledge of the hidden gender pitfalls. In this chapter, we have suggested strategies for educators in an attempt to provide our female students with career-managing tools and knowledge that they can utilize as they embark on successful and satisfying careers.

REFERENCES

Allen, T.D., L.T. Eby, M.L. Poteet, E. Lentz and L. Lima (2004), 'Career benefits associated with mentoring for protégés: a meta-analysis', *Journal of Applied Psychology*, **89**(1), 127–36.

Bandura, A. (1997), *Self-efficacy: The Exercise of Control*, New York: W.H. Freeman.

Barkacs, L. and S. Standifird (2008), 'Gender distinctions and empathy in negotiation', *Journal of Organizational Culture, Communications and Conflict*, **12**(1), 83–92.

Bass, B.M. (1990), *Bass and Stogdill's Handbook of Leadership*, 3rd edition, New York: Free Press.
Baumgardner, T.L., R.G. Lord and K.J. Maher (1991), 'Perceptions of women in management', in R.G. Lord and K.J. Maher (eds), *Leadership and Information Processing: Linking Perceptions and Performance*, Boston, MA: Unwin Hyman, pp. 95–113.
Becker, G.S., W.H.J. Hubbard and K.M. Murphy (2010), 'The market for college graduates and the worldwide boom in higher education for women', *American Economic Review: Papers and Proceedings*, **100**(2), 229–33.
Belliveau, M.A. (2005), 'Blind ambition: the effects of social networks and institutional sex composition on the job search outcomes of elite coeducational and women's college graduates', *Organization Science*, **16**(2), 134–50.
Bowles, H.R., L. Babcock and K.L. McGinn (2005), 'Constraints and triggers', *Journal of Personality and Social Psychology*, **89**(6), 951–65.
Brenner, O.C., J. Tomkiewicz and V.E. Schein (1989), 'The relationship between sex role stereotypes and requisite management characteristics revisited', *Academy of Management Journal*, **32**(3), 662–9.
Broadbridge, A. (2010), 'Social capital, gender and careers: evidence from retail senior managers', *Equality, Diversity and Inclusion*, **29**(8), 815–34.
Brownell, J. (1993), 'Communicating with credibility: the gender gap', *The Cornell Hotel and Restaurant Administration Quarterly*, **34**(2), 52–61.
Bryans, P. and S. Mavin (2003), 'Women learning to become managers: learning to fit in or to play a different game?', *Management and Learning*, **34**(1), 111–34.
Buckingham, M. (2012), 'Leadership development in the age of algorithm', *Harvard Business Review*, **90**(6), 86–94.
Burke, W.W. (1993), 'Networking', in N. Nicholson (ed.), *The Blackwell Encyclopedic Dictionary of Organizational Behavior*, Oxford: Blackwell Business, pp. 347–8.
Bussey, J. (2012), 'How women can get ahead: advice from female CEOs', accessed 4 June 2014 at http://online.wsj.com/articles/SB10001424052702303879604577410520511235252.
Carli, L.L. and A.H. Eagly (1999), 'Gender effects on social influence and emergent leadership', in G.N. Powell (ed.), *Handbook of Gender and Work*, Thousand Oaks, CA: Sage Publications, pp. 203–22.
Catalyst (2011), 'The bottom line: corporate performance and women's representation on boards (2004–2008)', accessed 16 December 2014 at www.catalyst.org/knowledge/bottom-line-corporate-performance-and-womens-representation-boards.
Catalyst (2012), 'Women CEOs of the Fortune 1000', *Knowledge Center*, accessed 1 July 2013 at www.catalyst.org/knowledge/women-ceos-fortune-1000.
Chapman, J. (1986), 'Improving the principal selection process to enhance the opportunities for women', *Unicorn*, **12**(1), 13–19.
Chesterman, C. and A. Ross-Smith (2006), 'Not tokens: reaching a "critical mass" of senior women managers', *Employee Relations*, **28**(6), 540–52.
Coder, L. and M.S. Spiller (2013), 'Leadership education and gender roles: think manager, think?', *Academy of Education Leadership Journal*, **17**(3), 21–51.
Coleman, J.S. (1990), *1990 Foundations of Social Theory*, Cambridge, MA: Harvard University Press.
Compton, M. (2007), 'The gender pay gap', *Women in Business*, **56**(6), 32–4.
Duehr, E.E. and J.E. Bono (2006), 'Men, women, and managers: are stereotypes finally changing?', *Personal Psychology*, **59**(4), 815–47.
Eagly, A.H. and B.T. Johnson (1990), 'Gender and leadership style: a meta-analysis', in R.M. Steers, L.W. Porter and G.A. Bigley (eds), *Motivation and Leadership at Work*, 6th edition, New York: McGraw-Hill, pp. 315–45.
Ehrich, L.C. (1994), 'Mentoring and networking for women educators', *Women in Management Review*, **9**(3), 4–10.
Eisenberger, R.M., S. Armeli, B. Rexwinkel, P.D. Lynch and L. Rhoades (2001), 'Reciprocation of perceived organizational support', *Journal of Applied Psychology*, **86**(1), 42–51.

Fisher, H. (1999), *The First Sex: The Natural Talents of Women and How They Are Changing the World*, New York: Ballantine Books.

Fiske, S.T. and S.E. Taylor (1991), *Social Cognition*, 2nd edition, New York: McGraw-Hill.

Forret, M.L. and T.W. Dougherty (2004), 'Networking behaviors and career outcomes: differences for men and women?', *Journal of Organizational Behavior*, **25**(3), 419–37.

Fowler, J.L., A.J. Gudmundsson and J.G. O'Gorman (2007), 'The relationship between mentee–mentor gender combination and the provision of distinct mentoring functions', *Women in Management*, **22**(8), 666–81.

Frankel, L.P. (2004), *Nice Girls Don't Get the Corner Office: 101 Unconscious Mistakes Women Make That Sabotage their Careers*, New York: Business Plus.

Friar, J.H. and K.A. Eddleston (2007), 'Making connections for success: a networking experience', *Journal of Management Education*, **31**(1), 104–27.

Gallois, C., V.J. Callan and J.A. Palmer (1992), 'The influence of applicant communication style and interviewer characteristics on hiring decisions', *Journal of Applied Social Psychology*, **22**(13), 1040–59.

Gentile, M. (1998), *Managerial Excellence Through Diversity*, Prospect Heights, IL: Waveland Press.

Gorman, E.H. (2005), 'Gender stereotypes, same-gender preferences, and organizational variation in the hiring of women: evidence from law firms', *American Sociological Review*, **70**(4), 702–28.

Halpern, J.J and J.M. Parks (1996), 'Vive la différence: differences between males and females in process and outcomes in a low-conflict negotiation', *International Journal of Conflict Management*, **7**(1), 45–70.

Heilman, M.E., A.S. Wallen, D. Fuchs and M.M. Tamkins (2004), 'Penalties for success: reactions to women who succeed at male gender typed tasks', *Journal of Applied Psychology*, **89**(3), 416–27.

Hewlett, S.A., K. Peraino, L. Sherbin and K. Sumberg (2010), *The Sponsor Effect: Breaking Through the Last Glass Ceiling*, Cambridge, MA: Harvard Business Review.

Ibarra, H., N.M. Carter and C. Silva (2010), 'Why men still get more promotions than women', *Harvard Business Review*, **88**(9), 80–85.

Jahnke, C.K. (2011), *The Well-Spoken Woman*, Amherst, NY: Prometheus Books.

Juodvalkis, J.L., B.A. Grefe, M. Hogue, D.J. Svyantek and W. DeLamarter (2003), 'The effects of job stereotype, applicant gender and communication style on ratings in screening interviews', *International Journal of Organization Analysis*, **11**(1), 67–84.

Kram, K.E. (1983), 'Phases of mentor relationships', *Academy of Management Journal*, **26**(4), 608–25.

Lagace, M. (2003), 'Negotiating challenges for women leaders', *Harvard Business School Working Knowledge*, accessed 1 July 2013 at http://hbswk.hbs.edu/item/3711.html.

Leck, J. and B. Orser (2013), 'Fostering trust in mentoring relationships: an exploratory study', *Equality, Diversity, and Inclusion: An International Journal*, **32**(4), 410–25.

Lewicki, R.J., B. Barry and D.M. Saunders (2007), *Essentials of Negotiation*, 5th edition, New York: McGraw-Hill.

Lockwood, N. (2004), 'Mentoring Series Part I: the value of mentoring', *Research Articles*, Society for Human Resource Management, accessed 28 June 2013 at http://www.shrm.org/Research/Articles.

Lord, R.G. and K.J. Maher (eds) (1991), *Leadership and Information Processing: Linking Perceptions and Performance*, Boston, MA: Unwin Hyman.

Mackie, D.M., S.T. Allison, L.T. Worth and A.G. Asuncion (1992), 'Social decision making processes: the generalization of outcome-biased stereotypic inferences', *Journal of Experimental Social Psychology*, **28**(1) 43–64.

Mavin, S. and P. Bryans (2002), 'Academic women in the UK: mainstreaming our experiences and networking for action', *Gender and Education*, **14**(3), 235–50.

McCauley, C.D., M.N. Ruderman, P.J. Ohlott and J.E. Morrow (1994), 'Assessing the developmental components of managerial jobs', *Journal of Applied Psychology*, **79**(4), 544–60.

Michael, J. and G. Yukl (1993), 'Managerial level and subunit function as determinants

of networking behavior in organizations', *Group and Organization Management*, **18**(3), 328–51.
Moore, T. and M. Yakhou (2006), 'Foreign language requirements for business students: an update', *Journal of College Teaching and Learning*, **3**(6), 65–8.
Ng, I. and I.H. Chow (2009), 'Cross-gender networking in the workplace: causes and consequences', *Gender in Management: An International Journal*, **24**(8), 562–76.
O'Brien, K.E., A. Biga, S.R. Kessler and T.D. Allen (2010), 'A meta-analytic investigation of gender differences in mentoring', *Journal of Management*, **36**(2), 537–54.
Paris, L.D. and D.L. Decker (2012), 'Sex role stereotypes: does business education make a difference?', *Gender in Management: An International Journal*, **27**(1), 36–50.
Perry, J. and D.E. Gunderson (2011), 'American women and the gender pay gap: a changing demographic or the same old song', *Advancing Women in Leadership*, **31**, 153–9.
Powell, G. (2012), 'Six ways of seeing the elephant: the intersection of sex, gender, and leadership', *Gender in Management*, **27**(2), 119–41.
Powell, G. and L.M. Graves (2003), *Women and Men in Management*, 3rd edition, Thousand Oaks, CA: Sage Publications.
Ragins, B.R. and J.L. Cotton (1999), 'Mentor functions and outcomes: a comparison of men and women in formal and informal mentoring relationships', *Journal of Applied Psychology*, **84**(4), 529–50.
Sandberg, S. (2013), *Lean In: Women, Work, and the Will to Lead*, New York: Alfred A. Knopf.
Sanyal, R.N. and J.S. Neves (1998), 'Networking: a simulation of job search behavior', *Simulation and Gaming*, **29**(2), 260–64.
Schein, V.E. (1973), 'The relationship between sex-role stereotypes and requisite management characteristics', *Journal of Applied Psychology*, **57**(2), 95–100.
Schein, V.E. (1975), 'Relationships between sex role stereotypes and requisite management characteristics among female managers', *Journal of Applied Psychology*, **60**(3), 340–44.
Schein, V.E. (1994), 'Managerial sex typing: a persistent and pervasive barrier to women's opportunities', in M.J. Davidson and J.E. Burke (eds), *Women in Management: Current Research Issues*, London: Paul Chapman, pp. 41–52.
Schein, V.E. and R. Mueller (1992), 'Sex role stereotyping and requisite management characteristics: a cross-cultural look', *Journal of Organizational Behavior*, **13**(5), 439–47.
Schein, V.E., R. Mueller and C. Jacobsen (1989), 'The relationship between sex role stereotypes and requisite management characteristics among college students', *Sex Roles*, **20**(1–2), 103–27.
Schipani, C.A., T.M. Dworkin, A. Kwolek-Folland and V.G. Mauer (2009), 'Pathways for women to obtain positions of organizational leadership: the significance of mentoring and networking', *Duke Journal of Gender Law & Policy*, **16**(89), 89–136.
Shantz, A., K. Wright and G. Latham (2011), 'Networking with boundary spanners: a quasi-case study on why women are less likely to be offered an engineering role', *Equity, Diversity and Inclusion: An International Journal*, **30**(3), 217–32.
Shuayto, N. (2013), 'Management skills desired by business school deans and employers: an empirical investigation', *Business Education & Accreditation*, **5**(2), 93–105.
Siebert, S.E., M.L. Kramer and R.C. Liden (2001), 'A social capital theory of career success', *Academy of Management Journal*, **44**(2), 219–37.
Silva, C. and N. Carter (2011), 'New research busts myths about the gender gap', *HRB Blog Network, Harvard Business Review*, 6 October 2011, accessed 1 July 2013 at http://blogs.hbr.org/cs/2011/10/new_research_busts_myths_about.html.
Simpson, R. (2006), 'Masculinity and management education: feminizing the MBA', *Academy of Management Learning and Education*, **5**(2), 182–93.
Simpson, R. and A. Ituma (2007), 'Transformation and feminization: the masculinity of the MBA and the "un-development" of men', *Journal of Management Development*, **28**(4), 301–16.
Small, D., L. Babcock and M. Gelfand (2003), 'Why women don't ask', unpublished manuscript, Pittsburgh, PA: Carnegie Mellon University.

Spence, J.T. (1984), 'Masculinity, femininity, and gender-related traits: a conceptual analysis and critique of current research', in B.A. Maher and W.B. Maher (eds), *Progress in Experimental Research, Vol. 13*, New York: Academic Press, pp. 2–66.

Still, L.V. and C. Guerin (1986), 'Gender aspects of career networking practices of men and women managers', *Women in Management Series*, Paper No. 5, Nepean College of Advanced Education, School of Business, University of Western Sydney.

Sullivan, S.E. and E.H. Buttner (1992), 'Changing more than the plumbing: integrating women and gender differences into management and organizational behavior courses', *Journal of Management Education*, **16**(1), 76–89.

Tharenou, P. (2005), 'Does mentor support increase women's career advancement more than men's? The differential effects of career and psychosocial support', *Australian Journal of Management*, **30**(1), 77–109.

Travers, C., S. Stevens and C. Pemberton (1997), 'Women's networking across boundaries: recognizing different cultural agendas', *Women in Management Review*, **12**(2), 61–7.

US Department of Education, National Center for Education Statistics (2012), 'The condition of education 2012', Indicator 47, accessed 24 November 2014 at http://nces.ed.gov/pubsearch/pubsinfo.asp?pubid=2012045.

Van Emmerick, I.J.H., M.C. Euwema, M. Geschiere and M.F.A.G. Schouten (2006), 'Networking your way through the organization: gender differences in the relationship between network participation and career satisfaction', *Women in Management Review*, **21**(1), 54–66.

Washington, C.E. (2011), 'Mentoring, organizational rank, and women's perceptions of advancement opportunities in the workplace', *International Journal of Business and Social Science*, **2**(9), 162–78.

Widnall, S. (1988), 'AAAS Presidential Lecture: voices from the pipeline', *Science*, **241**(4874), 1740–45.

Wood, J. (2003), *Gendered Lives: Communication, Gender, and Culture*, Belmont, CA: Thomson Wadsworth.

2. The internship class: subjectivity and inequalities – gender, race and class
Elaine Swan

This chapter will show how internships are increasingly the first step into a career, but a step structured by inequalities. The chapter argues that gender, race and class affect access to internships. Thus, many unpaid internships are in feminized professions, and the cultural performance of femininity inflects the subjectivity expected on many internships. The focus of this chapter is the category 'internship' but there are various terms for work-related experience. The names vary with the length of the experience, depending on whether they are school or university related and their timing in a degree course (Lawton and Potter, 2010; Perlin, 2011; Allen et al., 2013). Terms include: work experience, placement, practicum, industry experience, sandwich placements. Interns may be school students, undergraduates, graduates, postgraduates and even people mid-career looking to change careers (Perlin, 2011). Internships vary in length from a few days, a few weeks to a whole year. They may be paid, but some are unpaid because internships are constructed as an 'opportunity' not a 'job' with clear role description and conditions. This is the case in many countries including the USA, Germany, Australia and the UK. For example, a recent survey in the UK found that just under a fifth of internships did not pay a wage and just under a third paid less than the adult minimum wage (Lawton and Potter, 2010). Some argue that these figures are higher (Beckett, 2011; Perlin, 2011; Intern Aware, 2013).

Most industries organize internship programmes: advertising, engineering, finance, journalism, law, medicine, engineering, marketing and public relations; many non-government organizations too, from large international organizations such as Oxfam to small volunteer-run organizations. In the UK, in 2010 one in five employers intended to hire interns, offering over a quarter of a million places over the summer (Lawton and Potter, 2010). It is even possible to undertake an internship 'virtually' in order to gain 'international' experience (Franks and Oliver, 2012). At the end of the internship, there is no guarantee of employment (Allen et al., 2013; Frenette, 2013).

The chapter examines the proliferation and politics of internships in relation to universities, using the term for the different kinds of work experiences outlined above. Thus, for many undergraduates, internships are compulsory for the completion of their degrees. Furthermore, they constitute a major part of universities' 'employability' strategies and their claims to provide 'work-ready' teaching (Johnson, 2011; Allen et al., 2013). Through internships, capitalism and neoliberalism have reconfigured the nature of work, labour relations, the workforce and universities (Perlin, 2011; Ross, 2012). In its crudest sense, universities encourage often young and vulnerable students to work for free for workplaces that do not guarantee full working conditions and benefits or long-term offers of employment. Nowadays, undertaking an internship is tantamount to a mandatory requirement for entry into the labour market, often a necessity to complete a degree, and frequently unpaid internships are supposed to be like 'apprenticeships': on-job training for white collar and professional careers in feminized occupations such as PR, advertising and fashion, and 'masculine' areas such as engineering, law, medicine.

Interns, journalists and academics write across various media that internships in their various forms are structured by profound inequalities. Competition to gain certain internships is tough. As a result, even as they are exploited, interns have to be compliant, undertake menial work, display enthusiasm and gratitude and put up with the frequent lack of on-job training. This can be understood as the rise of a 'feminized' internship subjectivity, increasingly represented in films such as *The Devil Wears Prada* and TV programmes such as BBC's *The Apprentice*, Channel 4's *Jamie's Kitchen* and the more recent *Running in Heels*, which describes the young women working for a fashion magazine as 'eager to impress' (Schwarz, 2013).[1]

US labour theorist Andrew Ross suggests that internships are the 'fastest-growing job category' (2012, p. 23). US journalist and author of the book *Intern Nation* Ross Perlin (2011) provides some evidence. For example, of 9.5 million students in US higher education, about three-quarters have undertaken an internship at least once before graduating; much of this work is unpaid. Fifty per cent of interns in the USA are unpaid, in the UK 37 per cent and in Germany 51 per cent (ibid.). In the UK, Perlin suggests that there are 100 000 unpaid internships, with less than 1 per cent of interns working for Members of Parliament receiving the UK minimum wage. Ross Perlin argues: 'All of US – employers, parents, schools, government agencies, and interns themselves – are complicit in the devaluing of work, the exacerbation of social inequality, and the disillusionment of young people in the workplace that are emerging as a result of the intern boom' (ibid., p. 8).

A range of commentators discuss the inequalities and ethics of internships (Johnson, 2010; Lawton and Potter, 2010; Perlin, 2011; Allen et al.,

2013; Frenette, 2013). Thus, students, interns, journalists and trade unions agree that internships are exploitative on many counts: lack of pay or poor pay, unstable and insecure work, few tangible benefits, and poor quality of work experience offered (Lawton and Potter, 2010; Beckett, 2011; Perlin, 2011; Schwarz, 2013). As a result, critics argue that the nature of work itself is being restructured, as an internship has become a transaction in which experience and learning, and not money as in the past, are exchanged for work performed (Perlin, 2011; Ross, 2012; Allen et al., 2013).

Drawing on this emergent critical work, the focus of this chapter is on university-related internships, and it discusses types of work experiences, their espoused aims, growing critiques and the role of universities in supporting and challenging the internship industry. The aim is to foreground the perpetuation of raced, classed, and gendered inequalities of the internship economy, examining what the author refers to as 'internship subjectivity'.

INTERNSHIPS

In universities internships are deployed in different ways (Lawton and Potter, 2010; Johnson, 2011; Perlin, 2011; Allen et al., 2013). They can form a core part of a subject, comprise the subject itself, or sit outside of a subject but be linked to a course. They can be full-time or part-time, be undertaken as part of a semester/term, during the holidays or sandwiched between different years of a course. Internships are now being encouraged as part of extra-curricular activities. Internships may earn credit and be assessed.

The process for obtaining an internship varies across courses and universities. Some universities have 'placement administrators' who broker internships; in others, academics responsible for subjects mediate between students and organizations, and in many universities students have to find their own, applying along with many other students directly to employers. Some universities offer internship programmes designed with an industry 'partner': for example, Monash University in Australia and Oxfam. Many run internship fairs where students can meet organizations offering internships. What is noticeable now is that there are very few courses without internships and these affect graduates' chances of future paid employment (Allen et al., 2013).

In response to this proliferation, a whole international industry has sprung up offering vacancies, recruitment, advice, and international internship programmes. There is also a growing middle-class 'pay-to-work' economy as internships can be bought from companies that find and place students (Steffen, 2010). Desk research shows that agencies also run internships to countries like China, offering work and 'international' experience, providing accommodation, mentoring and training and recreation activities, but this comes at a considerable cost to the intern and/or their family (Steffen, 2010). A growing exclusionary mechanism is the auctioning of internships at private schools and colleges in the USA and the UK to raise money for charity and purchased by wealthy parents (Beckett, 2011). For example, *The Guardian* reported that at the UK Conservative Party annual Black and White Party, a selection of prestigious internships had been auctioned off to party donors. For between £2000 and £4000, wealthy Tory supporters were able to secure a week or a fortnight's work experience for their children, at employers ranging from City firms to *Tatler* magazine to the PR company Bell Pottinger (ibid.). There are also websites such as http://studentinternships.com.au, which present advice on how to package their CVs (résumés). Competition for well-known organizations and industries is intense.

The stated aims of internships across universities and industry are fairly consistent (Johnson, 2011; Frenette, 2013). Thus, it is claimed that students can gain experience in their ideal profession or occupation, or test organizations and sectors. Universities suggest that students can apply learning from a subject or course. Additional benefits are said to be creating contacts, developing specialist sector-specific skills, and becoming more employable. International internships are said to offer the distinctive advantage of the development of language and inter-cultural skills, giving students 'global advantage' (Webber, 2005). In essence, internships are overwhelmingly positioned in terms of the opportunity for 'learning' (Perlin, 2011).

This emphasis on the subjectivity of internships is also emphasized in an online article by British journalist Andy Beckett (2011). He suggests that 'the psyche of the middle-class worker' has become entrepreneurial so that young professionals see themselves as 'brands that require investment, such as unpaid work, to get established'. This is, for him, in line with the neoliberal ideology that executive salaries aside, labour costs should be ruthlessly minimized and things be given away or done for 'free'. He sums it up that 'these trends may make the internship the quintessential modern workplace experience'.

INTERNSHIP ACTIVISM

Journalists have been at the forefront of critiques of internships. For example, Perlin's (2011) influential book called *Intern Nation* has been well reviewed by journalists and academics. His overall argument is that because internships are unregulated, interns are exploited in coercive relations. He sees it as a 'new Wild West' in which full-time, permanent, unionized labour is being replaced by short-term, temporary, precarious work. In essence, he questions the educational value of internships on a number of counts. First, employers rarely train interns and therefore they end up in a cycle of going from one unpaid internship to another. Second, they are expected to do menial work and work long hours. Third, they rarely obtain employment. Internships promise career training and skills development but do not deliver this. He criticizes universities for the way many degrees depend on internships for their completion. Like Beckett and others (Lawton and Potter, 2010), he highlights that the income inequality of internships means internships reproduce privilege and social inequality because only people from wealthy backgrounds can afford to undertake unpaid internships in journalism, politics, media, television and the arts. This limits who we hear from in the media and who produce 'culture'. Meanwhile, internships exclude the young people who cannot afford them, or do not have the confidence, the contacts or the parental backing to take part (Lawton and Potter, 2010; Beckett, 2011; Allen et al., 2013). The growth of internships has contributed to the narrowing class composition of many professions (Beckett, 2011).

Unions and campaigning organizations have also been involved in trying to stop exploitation by employers. In the UK, the Trades Union Congress has lobbied for interns to receive the national minimum wage. They and Intern Aware, a national campaigning organization for 'fair, paid internships', argue that interns should be made aware of their employment rights including paid holidays. Importantly, Intern Aware has focused on the exclusionary nature of internships. Focusing more on class than race, they show how internships offer unfair advantage to wealthier young people first in accessing work experiences, and second, as a result of accessing internships, in entering the labour market. They argue that because many internships are unpaid they become unaffordable for many young people; in addition, they make the point that most internships are based in London where the cost of living is highest and rents are prohibitive, particularly if you are in debt from paying your degree fees, and are working for free. They write on their webpage: 'This means that too many young people are locked out of the opportunities they deserve by unpaid internships. While those who can afford to live for free are able to gain experience and get a foot on the career ladder, the vast majority are left behind. It is simply unfair.'

Their other argument is that, contrary to Perlin (2011), interns do complex work, being given duties, responsibilities, deadlines, performance measures and monitoring, and yet are often unpaid. Like others, they see NGOs, public sector bodies and charities as a major part of the unpaid internship problem. In the USA, activists for wages for internships are starting to run consciousness-raising groups. Intern Labor Rights, an outpost of the Arts & Labor Occupy group, describes how internships 'devalue the fundamental dignity of work' and that 'unpaid internships produce a culture of self-denigration in the workforce' (cited in Schwartz, 2013, p. 45).

Finally, interns themselves have challenged exploitation in a number of ways, from using social media to exposing their working conditions to using the law to sue. For example, there is a satirical US Twitter called N+interns started by interns at a New York literary magazine (Schwarz, 2013). A successful Kickstarter campaign raised enough crowd-sourced funding in the USA for an investigation into unpaid internships (ibid.). There have been over 20 lawsuits filed by interns over the past two years, some of which have resulted in interns being awarded back pay. Some of these have been for sexual harassment.

For example, Eric Glatt, a former intern on the film *Black Swan* who sued Fox Searchlight for unpaid wages and the judge ruled in his favour in 2011, has said in a recent interview: 'The decision I made to sue was because I recognized a real structural problem with the economy. No one would expect someone to go into a factory and work six months for free. People understand that automatically as labor' (ibid.). Glatt is critical of the role of universities:

> I think schools and universities have completely abrogated their responsibility to their students. They may make an argument in their own minds that the value of experiential learning is so high that it makes sense to confer credit for work done – experiential work done on a work site. But they're not paying attention to the labor law . . . They're educational institutions, they're not labor institutions. They're not paying attention to the fact that this is undermining the health of the labor market their students are graduating into. (Cited in Dougherty-Johnson, 2013)

As much of the activism emphasizes, one of the ironies is that internships meant to offer work experience are often not seen as 'work' per se but learning. Thus, interns are rarely referred to as employees or workers; even graduates refer to themselves as students (Allen et al., 2013).

THE ROLE OF UNIVERSITIES

Academics are beginning to debate the role of universities in legitimizing internships. For example, Jessica Johnson (2011) argues that internships on degree courses are the extension of the project of universities as serving the demands of business, and the means for 'producing graduates who are skilled and flexible workers for twenty-first-century industries' (p. 176). This raises the critical question: 'what happens to the role of the university to develop a capacity for the public good beyond market and employer considerations?' (ibid.). Neoliberalism values education for rendering people suitable for the market. University internships are central to producing entrepreneurial subjects for neoliberal workplaces. She writes that educational ideals and graduate attributes are made to be responsive to the needs of employers, through which students are seen as 'human capital'. In sum, this means that education is viewed as an investment not a means of individual and social emancipation or transformation.

She argues strongly that students have been 'interpellated' (or hailed) by neoliberalism. Thus, students are 'attracted by the promise of university qualifications improving both their labor market and consumer power potential' (ibid.). Students themselves see university education as offering 'a smooth transition into professional practice' (ibid.). She tried to teach the students with critical resources, but they were so inculcated into ideologies and practices of individualism that they continued to 'craft . . . biographies to be exploited for their future employment options within a competitive market economy' (Johnson, 2011, p. 180). In particular, she noticed that they reproduced a neoliberal, privatized ideal of 'choice'. Thus, they understood choice as the product of their own intrinsic desire or rational calculations. Choice was not understood as something inflected by race, class and gender. Increasingly she suggests that students increasingly found it difficult to imagine, and easily ignored, how choice was shaped by a social-cultural context and the product of the workings of power. Students reproduced the language of the market and did not learn to see the world through more critical or democratic ways. Universities then reproduce students with a sense of their own entitlement and privilege rather than political disquiet.

POSITIONAL ADVANTAGE

Kim Allen and colleagues put universities at the centre of the reproduction of inequalities, but their focus is on the processes that enable white middle-class students to gain 'positional advantage' (Allen et al., 2013). They insist that internships 'are not just about learning about the world of work, but a "filtering site" in which students are evaluated through classifying practices that privilege middle-class ways of being' (p. 433). This filtering classifies students as 'being (or failing to be) the "right" subjects demanded by neoliberalism' (p. 447). The inequality of internships is not then just about unpaid labour.

Allen et al. (2013) argue that universities and workplace organizations privilege resource-rich middle-class students. Internships need to be understood as sets of relations and practices that privilege an entrepreneurial 'disposition'. This means having the capacity to be enterprising, resourceful, individualistic and self-sufficient. At the core of this disposition is the capacity to accumulate value through gaining experiences and learning. This value is then exchanged in the labour market. They argue that this capacity is quite clearly gendered and classed. Citing Beverley Skeggs, they emphasize that working-class students: 'do not have access to the same starting point, the same approach to accrual, access to the knowledge of how to accrue effectively and access to the same sites for optimizing the[ir] cultural capital' (Skeggs, 2004, cited in Allen et al., p. 434). They go on to write:

> The capacity to produce oneself and be recognized as an 'employable' student and ideal future ... worker is dependent on having access to a range of unequally distributed resources – or economic, social and cultural capitals (Bourdieu, 1984) – and the knowledge of how to display these in ways that align with broader institutional and societal practices and relations. (Ibid., p. 434)

In sum, their point is that the ideal neoliberal self is not universal but exclusionary, being modelled on a middle-class, masculinized, rational subject able to accrue capitals and exchange them.

The gendering and classing of the internship disposition means that students find it difficult to access internships, and also once on them, to be seen as successful. As a consequence of negative work placement experiences, some students feel a sense of failure. Their experiences mean that they think that a particular sector is simply not for 'people like us' (Allen et al., 2013). This has an effect on their future employability and the resulting shaping of the sector.

The entry into internships – the starting point for a potential career trajectory – is unevenly distributed by gender and race, as well as class. Thus, recent research on the creative and media industries shows that work opportunities are distributed through an economy of contacts and networks (Blair, 2001; Gill, 2007; Frenette, 2013). Having contacts who can provide projects or work experiences is the 'key mechanism for securing work' (Blair, 2001, p. 154). Invisible informal networks distribute internship opportunities and involve the grapevine, family referrals and personal recommendations and are difficult for racially minoritized groups to access. The informality of these 'mechanisms of connections' raises questions about fairness, being difficult for racialized minorities and working-class people to access (Blair, 2001). Knowing the right people is key but 'informal practices tend to reinforce, rather than challenge, existing inequalities, and do not serve equal opportunities' (Gill, 2009, p. 172).

Family and friends can be very important in securing offers of jobs, recommending individuals and providing job information (Blair, 2001; Gill, 2007, 2009). Entry to internships and jobs, and subsequent progression within the media industry is 'contingent upon collegial ties, networking and individual reputation' (Ursell, 2006, p. 144). Familiarity, collegiality and reputation become the criteria for offering individuals future work or promotions. As media academic Gillian Ursell writes of the media industry:

> Familiarity and reputation as the criteria for selection for work mitigate against those who are unfamiliar and those yet without repute. Unfamiliarity extends to those from minority cultures, those who prefer not to be 'one of the lads' and those who cannot be available on demand because of family commitments – usually women. (Ibid.)

People choose people they know, and recruit in their own image people 'like them' (Gill, 2007, 2009). Helen Blair argues that those who assimilate the shared culture and values of a cultural industry are more likely to achieve success (2001, p. 157). This is reminiscent of Nirmal Puwar's (2004) excellent work on the way organizations recruit people who approximate their 'ideal worker' through a 'somatic norm' – a classed, raced and gendered way of looking, sounding, moving, and dressing. Thus, one way to characterize these practices on work placements is as the 'internship somatic norm'. But being an intern is more than how you look and sound, it involves a particular form of subjectivity.

INTERNSHIP SUBJECTIVITY

Having discussed the uneven access to internships, and introduced the idea of the internship somatic norm, the chapter now examines how internship can be understood as economically and culturally feminized. Allen et al. (2013) argue that accruing work experiences and learning as capital is middle class and masculine but the rest of the chapter argues that accumulating experiences and capital in enabled by performing a feminized subjectivity.

Scholarship suggests there are two different forms of labour feminization (Adkins, 2002; Swan, 2006). Economic feminization refers to the increasing participation of women in the labour market; women's entry into the vertical and hierarchical divisions of labour previously occupied by men; and the differential conditions of different jobs according to whether men or women occupy them. Thus, peripheral, part-time, lowly paid, flexible work with limited benefits has been associated historically with women. According to one study by Phil Gardner (2011) of Intern Bridge, a research and consulting firm, more than three in four unpaid interns were women. Many industries that rely on unpaid internships, such as fashion, PR, media, the arts and NGOs, are feminized. Thus, internships can be understood as economically feminized.

Cultural feminization of work is used to describe the way that work qualities traditionally associated with white middle-class women are now valued by organizations. These qualities may include emotional competences, communication skills, unique skills in empathy and intimacy, and aesthetic strategies (Clarke and Newman, 1997; Kerfoot, 2000, 2002; Leathwood, 2005; Newman, 2005; Swan, 2006, 2008). In this view, performances of white middle-class femininity have become important new workplace resources for both men and women in producing their jobs and identities. In this version of feminization, the cultural, rather than the economic, is foregrounded as the key determinant of gender (Adkins and Lury, 1996; Adkins, 2002).

We can see how internships are feminized culturally in representations in adverts. Thus, interns are expected to be 'flexible, passionate, dedicated, do all kinds of work with grace, be grateful ... and submissive', as Madeline Schwarz argues in her incisive critique (2013, p.41). Consequently, and somewhat provocatively, she refers to interns as the 'happy housewives of the working world' (ibid.). She makes this point to emphasize that interns are expected to act in traditionally feminine ways, and like housewives, to work for free because they love their work. She writes:

> Advice for interns usually stresses their need to be adaptable, as well as enthusiastic, submissive, and obedient ... Countless job descriptions repeat their demands: ... flexible, enthusiastic and highly motivated with a positive attitude; enthusiastic and flexible learners, capable of both taking direction and working independently. By requiring that workers at the beginning of their careers learn these behaviors, employers ... teach them how to be grateful for whatever work opportunities they may have, no matter how unfruitful. No task should be too unpleasant and no job too much of an imposition for someone just happy to have the chance to work. It's not enough to recognize one's gratefulness for actually having a job. The key is in showing it. (Schwarz, 2013, p.42)

In sum then, interns are expected to perform being an intern by inhabiting a feminine somatic norm and subjectivity. It is difficult, as the chapter has outlined, to opt out of participating in internships and thus, behaving in a deferential compliant manner, acting grateful for the opportunity, becomes a key way to access and survive an internship (Schwarz, 2013).

Yet, even access to this highly constrained and subservient way of working is not open to everyone due to class and race, as Allen et al. (2013) and others argue.

CONCLUSION

This chapter has argued that internships reproduce financial, social and cultural inequalities structured by class, gender and race. Internships are difficult to access without certain kinds of cultural, economic and social capital. Indeed, being seen as a success in an internship means inhabiting a feminized subjectivity, not open to all. At the same time, cashing in on their value in the labour market requires a more masculine, rational, middle-class subject focused on accrual strategies, exchanging experience and learning for an employment contract, all of which entails classed knowledge about how to accrue, exchange and being able to access the sites where such capital is valued (Skeggs, 2004, cited in Allen et al., 2013, p. 435). Internships are highly competitive, exploitative and many unpaid with little direct training and mentoring. And yet in spite of these inequalities, internships are vital for completing degrees and starting careers in many professions. So what needs to change? The chapter finishes by outlining a number of recommendations that could start to address the reproduction of exploitation and discrimination.

Reflexivity at University

For Johnson one way forward is for academics to encourage critical reflexivity in themselves and students. This means more than facilitating 'reflective practices that are . . . merely individualized, self-referential and therapeutic' (2011, p. 181). Practices of critical reflexivity must be more ambitious, involve teaching to develop graduates as 'engaged professionals committed to social justice', questioning, dissenting and challenging. The questioning of assumptions, particularly those that reflect relationships of power within social and political contexts, is the key difference between this type of critical reflection and other forms of self-reflection. Thus, she writes: 'In order to negotiate the tensions between the promise of the university as the critic and conscience of society operating within neoliberal economic realities, more research is needed to supply detailed, specific methods of teaching that contribute to a broader project of imagining a post-neoliberal future' (ibid.).

Value All Forms of Work

The definition of what constitutes work including unpaid, part-time, and insecure work is critical for Schwarz so that we see internships as work. She argues that legal recourse is crucial. She emphasizes that students and interns should be supported in understanding and asserting that their time and effort have value. This value is 'more than the remote idea of a "networking opportunity" or one step further up a mythical career ladder' (2013). Referencing the Wages for Housework movement, which provided a model for a new way to talk about work, she says that all workers need to see the value of their efforts and organize to be paid accordingly.

Speaking About Inequality

Allen et al. (2013) have produced a toolkit for staff and students in British universities. This provides practical recommendations for addressing inequalities, including greater transparency when advertising placements; clearer guidance for students on their rights, including national minimum wage legislation; collecting monitoring data to identify inequalities in work placements; and providing financial support for working-class students. An important part of their work was producing recommendations related to the 'unspeakability' of inequality. They found that inequalities in internships were often ignored and not recognized as 'legitimate resistance but as deficit weakness' (p. 249). The toolkit therefore provides suggestions for how universities can provide a space and discourse for students to share their experiences of inequalities, seeing them not as the outcome of individual failings but of wider systematic inequalities.

Employers

Perlin (2011) argues that employers can do a range of things. They must advertise positions in an open and transparent manner, provide a 'strong training and mentoring component' and seek advice on best practice and legal requirements from HR professionals, trade unions, employment lawyers and intern advocacy groups. Employers can support students from under-represented groups.

Interns

Perlin (2011) suggests that prospective interns must discriminate between internships that are offered openly and fairly, and those that are available to those with connections; between those that pay and those that do not. Finally, he adds that interns must know their rights.

Whilst these recommendations are complex and require widespread rethinking of the role of interns and internships, and indeed universities, higher education could play a vital catalytic role.

NOTE

1. *The Devil Wears Prada* is a 2006 film based on the novel of the same name on the trials and tribulations of an assistant working at a fashion magazine; the BBC's *The Apprentice* is a reality programme running since 2005 in which men and women compete for a position with British businessman Alan Sugar; UK Channel 4's reality programme *Jamie's Kitchen* showed chef Jamie Oliver working alongside 15 young, unemployed apprentices learning to cook mentored by himself and other chefs; and in UK Channel 4's *Running in Heels* three women work as interns at the US fashion magazine *Marie Claire*, competing for a position.

REFERENCES

Adkins, L. (2002), *Revisions: Gender and Sexuality in Late Modernity*, Buckingham, UK: Open University Press.
Adkins, L. and C. Lury (1996), 'The cultural, the sexual, and the gendering of the labour market', in L. Adkins and V. Merchant (eds), *Sexualising the Social: Power and the Organization of Sexuality*, Basingstoke, UK: Macmillan.
Allen, K., J. Quinn, S. Hollingworth and A. Rose (2013), 'Becoming employable students and "ideal" creative workers: exclusion and inequality in higher education work placements', *British Journal of Sociology of Education*, **34**(3), 431–52.
Beckett, A. (2011), 'Intern nation by Ross Perlin – review', accessed 14 March 2013 at www.theguardian.com/books/2011/may/08/intern-nation-ross-perlin-review.
Blair, H. (2001), '"You're only as good as your last job": the labour process and labour market in the British film industry', *Work, Employment and Society*, **15**(1), 149–69.
Clarke, J. and J. Newman (1997), *The Managerial State*, London: Sage.
Dougherty-Johnson, B. (2013), 'Q&A with Eric Glatt, former intern who sued Fox Searchlight', *Motiongrapher*, 18 July 2013, accessed 17 March 2014 at http://motionographer.com/2013/07/18/qa-with-eric-glatt-former-intern-who-sued-fox-searchlight-2/.
Franks, P.C. and G.C. Oliver (2012), 'Experiential learning and international collaboration opportunities: virtual internships', *Library Review*, **61**(4), 272–85.
Frenette, A. (2013), 'Making the intern economy: role and career challenges of the music industry intern', *Work and Occupations*, **40**(4), 364–97.
Gardner, P. (2011), *The Debate over Unpaid College Internships*, report, Austin, TX: Intern Bridge.
Gill, R. (2007), *Technobohemians or the New Cybertariat? New Media Work on Amsterdam a Decade After the Web*, Amsterdam: Institute of Network Cultures.
Gill, R. (2009), 'Creative biographies in new media: social innovation in web work', in A. Pratt and P. Jeffcutt (eds), *Creativity, Innovation and the Cultural Economy*, London: Routledge, pp. 161–78.
Intern Aware (2013), website accessed 14 March 2014 at www.internaware.org.

Johnson, J. (2011), 'Interrogating the goals of work-integrated learning: neoliberal agendas and critical pedagogy', *Asia-Pacific Journal of Cooperative Education*, **12**(3), 175–82.
Kerfoot, D. (2000), 'Body work: estrangement, disembodiment and the organizational "other"', in J. Hassard, R. Holliday and H. Wilmott (eds), *Body and Organization*, London: Sage.
Kerfoot, D. (2002), 'Managing the "professional man"', in M. Dent and S. Whitehead (eds), *Managing Professional Identities: Knowledge, Performativity and the 'New' Professional*, London: Routledge.
Lawton, K. and D. Potter (2010), *Why Interns Need a Fair Wage*, London: The Institute for Public Policy Research.
Leathwood, C. (2005),'"Treat me as a human being – don't look at me as a woman": femininities and professional identities in further education', *Gender and Education*, **17**(4), 387–409.
Newman, J. (2005), 'Enter the transformational leader: network governance and the micro-politics of modernization', *Sociology*, **39**(4), 717–34.
Perlin, R. (2011), *Intern Nation: How to Earn Nothing and Learn Little in the Brave New Economy*, London: Verso Books.
Puwar, N. (2004), *Space Invaders*, London: Berg Publishers.
Ross, A. (2012), 'In search of the lost paycheck', in T. Scholz (ed.), *Digital Labor: The Internet as Playground and Factory*, London: Routledge, pp. 13–32.
Schwartz, M. (2013), 'Opportunity costs: the true price of internships', *Dissent*, **60**(1), 41–5.
Skeggs, B. (2004), *Class, Self, Culture*, London: Routledge.
Swan, E. (2006), 'Therapeutic cultures at work', in D. McTavish and K. Miller (eds), *Women in Leadership and Management: A European Perspective*, Cheltenham, UK and Northampton, MA, USA: Edward Elgar Publishing, pp. 52–70.
Steffen, H. (2010), 'Student Internships and the Privilege to Work', in J.G. Ramsey (ed.), *Cultural Logic. Culture & Crisis*, accessed 6 July 2013 at http://clogic.eserver.org/2010/Steffen.pdf.
Swan, E. (2008), '"You make me feel like a woman": therapeutic cultures and the contagion of femininity', *Gender, Work & Organization*, **15**(1), 88–107.
Ursell, G. (2006), 'Working in the media', in D. Hesmondhalgh (ed.), *Media Production*, Maidenhead, UK: Open University Press.
Webber, R. (2005), 'Integrating work-based and academic learning in international and cross-cultural settings', *Journal of Education and Work*, **18**(4), 473–87.

3. Understanding and researching 'choice' in women's career trajectories
Patricia Lewis and Ruth Simpson

In a special issue on 'Meritocracy, Difference and Choice' published in *Gender in Management: An International Journal*, we highlighted how women presented their career trajectories as a matter of personal choice in that careers were seen by women to be 'in their own hands' (Simpson et al., 2010). Women claimed that opportunities were open and freely given, accepting in an uncritical manner contemporary discourse of equal opportunity and merit-based procedural fairness. This was despite the fact that observations and experiences of gender injustice in their organizations frequently fell short of the meritocratic ideal. Here, women referred to personal choice to justify their lower positions in the organization, as well as the slower career progress observed among female colleagues and peers. As we argued in the article, the uptake and internalization of the rhetoric of choice helped women negotiate the tensions between their belief in gender-neutral meritocracy as a driver of their careers and the reality of gender disadvantage encountered. Thus, if women are presented as having choice (for example, to prioritize family over career) and if unequal outcomes can be presented as the result of choices they have made, then the impact (in the eyes of women) of discrimination can be denied.

In this chapter, we take some of these ideas forward by considering some of the 'cultural conditions' that make choice appear so persuasive in accounts of career experiences. As our article above demonstrated, choice was presented by women as both voluntary and highly desirable. It was rendered an individualistic phenomenon divorced, unproblematically, from the social and cultural context in which it was supposedly undertaken and in which its consequences were subsequently 'played out'. In addressing this disassociation, we contextualize the emergence of choice around careers by connecting it to the cultural discourse of postfeminism. Reflecting a primacy placed on individualization (for example, Beck, 1992) and on the role of the individual, divorced from structures such as gender and class, in shaping his or her own biography, postfeminism is oriented towards an understanding of feminine agency and a new 'choosing femininity' that suggests women can 'have it all'. In connecting the phenomenon of choice to its social and cultural context, we highlight in particular the (hidden and hitherto unrecognized) influence of postfeminism in Hakim's (2000) account of preference theory – a theory that has been highly influential in both policy and academia and that proposes that labour market outcomes are largely the result of individual choices made. In surfacing these more hidden dimensions of her work, we argue for a consideration of the fundamental conditions that make choice appear desirable and voluntary in accounts of careers more generally.

OPTING OUT?

Writing at the beginning of the 1990s, McDowell (1991, p.417) argued that 'the feminization of the labour market is amongst the most far-reaching of the changes of the last two decades'. The associated identification of women as the 'bearers' of sought-after 'feminine' attributes perceived as necessary for the success of contemporary organizations has contributed to an influx of women into the public world of work. The increase in women's labour force participation rates is evident in statistics that record the amount and type of economic activity in various countries. A 2010 report from *The Economist* stated that nearly six million of the eight million new jobs created in the European Union since 2000 have been taken up by women. Within the American context, *The Economist* reported that women were on course to become the majority of the workforce in the USA while at the same time making up the bulk of university graduates in OECD countries and swelling the ranks of professional workers in a number of Western countries.

Nevertheless, despite this notable increase in women's labour force participation, a parallel phenomenon is women's apparent return to the domestic sphere to look after children. Dubbed the 'opt-out revolution', a well-known *New York Times Magazine* article written in 2003 by Lisa Belkin explored the factors prompting professional women to leave the workforce in order to stay at home with their children. Ten years later, Lisa Miller, in an article entitled 'The retro wife: feminists who say they're having it all by choosing to stay home', similarly considers the phenomenon of women choosing home and motherhood as an alternative to professional work. According to Miller (2013), in the US context the 'number of stay-at-home mothers rose incrementally between 2010 and 2011 [with] some of the biggest increases among young mothers aged 25 to 35'. Similarly, in the British context the proportion of women born between 1985 and 1994 currently in the workforce is lower than that for the cohort of women born ten years earlier. Continued increases in the numbers of women working appears to have stalled, with younger women working less than their slightly older counterparts. In the UK context the proportion of mothers working full-time peaked at around 30 per cent in 2008 and then fell to 29 per cent where it has remained (Cooper, 2013). Earlier research (Percheski, 2008) that specifically sought to test the claim that women are 'opting out' of professional employment found little evidence of American women withdrawing from the labour force. Nevertheless, Percheski did find that the employment levels of professional women have been fairly constant, signalling that the number of younger women entering the professional ranks has stalled. As Percheski (2008, p. 514) states:

> [W]hile it is more feasible for younger cohorts to simultaneously pursue a career and raise children than it was for older cohorts, professional women with children are still much less likely to work full-time or long hours than are their male colleagues with children or their female colleagues without children. Women's employment experiences still do not resemble those of men.

CHOICE FEMINISM

While much criticism has been levelled at Miller's article – labelled as irritating people like sandpaper on sunburn by Emily Matchar (2013) – one explanation for the co-existence of a return to domesticity with some of the highest levels of female labour force participation is the emergence of choice feminism. Connected to the cultural phenomenon of postfeminism, choice feminism is described by Kirkpatrick (2010) as an emergent disposition within contemporary feminism that places an emphasis on individual action and choice. According to choice feminism, a woman can work or opt out of the labour force to be a full-time mother, she can have a large family or a small family, she can marry, cohabit or stay single – these are all perceived as feminist choices, as long as they are chosen by individual women. Choice feminism is characterized by four principles. First, it privileges the individual woman, believing that she is in the best position to know what is 'right' for her. Second, the suggestion that a woman's choice might 'harm' her is rejected in favour of emphasizing the independence a woman has over her own life. From this position, an individual woman should only be constrained if her actions harm another. Third, feminism and the gains it has made are seen as progressive and irreversible, that is, victories achieved through feminist action are believed to be a permanent fixture of the present-day environment. Finally, feminist disapproval of women's individual choices is rejected based on the belief that the individual woman is the only person who knows her own personal situation. No one else is in a position to judge this (ibid.).

Choice feminism produces a type of feminism that presents itself as inclusive, tolerant and accepting, including an ever-widening array of activities within its ambit but rejecting criticism of any behaviours, decisions or actions. It is seeking to replace more militant feminist agendas that were critical of traditional femininity and the activities such as 'homemaking' associated with it. Those who are in favour of choice feminism believe that the emphasis on choice is reflective of a commitment to pluralism, self-determination and not being judgemental about others (Snyder-Hall, 2010). Feminist principles of female freedom and self-realization are drawn upon to justify the embracing of traditional gender roles such as wife and mother, while at the same time an attempt is made to escape from what are seen as feminism's more repressive elements to allow individuals to make their own personal choices.

PREFERENCE THEORY

A manifestation of choice feminism in the context of work and careers is Hakim's (2000) highly influential preference theory, which though widely cited has been heavily criticized. This states that labour market outcomes are determined by individual choice rather than societal or structural factors, giving rise to at least three types of career. In what follows, we review Hakim's preference theory, which valorizes choice, presenting it as the explanation for the continuing differential career outcomes between women and men. As discussed above, in completing this review we argue that the centrality of choice in Hakim's explanation of the career locations of men and women, but mainly women, needs to be connected to the cultural discourse of postfeminism, which has a significant influence on how choice is configured within the context of women's careers. We suggest that this connection allows us to contextualize the emergence of choice around careers, facilitating the identification of a research agenda that examines its origins, usage and consequences. This allows us to move away from seeing choice as simply an individual matter women face in their everyday lives as suggested by choice feminism to understanding it as a major problematic for the study of women's careers.

Preference theory, claimed by its proponent to be a 'historically informed, empirically based, multidisciplinary perspective' (Hakim, 2006, p. 286) has been developed over a number of publications (Hakim, 1998, 2000, 2003a, 2003b, 2004). It departs from sociological theory in the emphasis placed on individual choices rather than societal or structural factors in labour market outcomes as well as from traditional economics, which consigns preferences to the margins through the assumption they remain stable in economic decision-making. Instead, drawing on longitudinal data collected in the USA and the UK charting the lifestyle preferences of men and women and how they influence the employment decision, choices and the preferences on which they rest are placed at the centre of analysis. Hakim identifies three types of lifestyle preferences that lead individuals to respond in different ways to their social, economic and political environment. While the theory can be applied to men and women, it is concerned primarily with women's choices between family work and market work – seen by Hakim (2000) as a 'genuine choice' in modern affluent societies as the result, in particular, of two 'revolutions': contraception and equal opportunities. These have meant that women face options in the twenty-first century that were not previously available (and that are not currently available to men). The most important choice is between a life centred on private, family work and a life centred on market work or other activities in the public sphere – a choice that is open to women from all social classes. Preference theory is thus positioned as a 'universalistic' theory in that, as Hakim argues, in any society that has experienced these two revolutions (contraception, equal opportunity) 'the full heterogeneity of women's work-lifestyle will emerge and women's employment patterns will polarize as a consequence' (2000, p. 179). Positioned as the only theory to explain occupational segregation and the continuing pay gap (Hakim, 2006), it moves 'beyond sex and gender' (ibid., p. 280) to consider, as a unisex theory, how men and women can now make choices as to social roles and preferred lifestyles.

In her arguments, Hakim acknowledges the significance of 'reflexive modernity' (Giddens, 1991; Beck et al., 1994) and the influence of individualization whereby, freed from social structures such as those relating to class, family and nation, agency rather than structure becomes a determinant of behaviour. Men and women have not only gained the freedom to choose their own biography, values and lifestyles but are also forced to make their own decisions because of the loss of universal certainties and agreed conventions (Giddens, 1991, cited in Hakim, 2006; see also Beck et al., 1994). To take greater account of how gender frames the lives of men and women, Hakim (2000) developed preference theory, based on 'empirically based' statements of choices women and men make in late modernity, as independent of but 'consonant with' the reflexive project of the self. Here she draws on Bourdieu's (1977) concept of dispositions, which she frames as 'attitudes, values and preferences' to capture women's choices between alternative lifestyles. As Bourdieu (ibid.) argues, during economic stability, dispositions cease to be exclusively marks of social position and become more idiosyncratic 'personally chosen options' offered by local, national and global cultural environments. Preference theory accordingly reinstates (heterogeneous) preferences as an important determinant of women's behaviour and suggests that attitudes, values and preferences are becoming more important than constraints associated with social structure in the lifestyle choices of individuals in modern, affluent Western societies.

There are four main tenets to preference theory. First, choices and options available to women have increased since the 1960s due to various factors including widely available contraception giving women control over their fertility; the equal opportunities 'revolution' that ensures women's 'equal access to all positions, occupations and careers in the labour market' (Hakim, 2000, p.3); the expansion of white collar work and work that may be attractive to 'second earners' and the increasing importance of attitudes, values and preferences (what she sees as 'dispositions') in the lifestyle choices of 'prosperous liberal modern' societies. Second, women are heterogeneous in their preferences and priorities with regard to the 'conflict' between family life and employment. Here she highlights the emergence of three 'ideal type' preference groups (home centred, work centred and adaptive), which are discussed further below. Third, this heterogeneity of interests captured in these groups creates conflicting interests – which she contrasts with the comparatively common interests shared by the more homogeneous groups of men and which she sees as a key source of patriarchy's persistence and the success of men in institutionalizing social conventions and rules that support male dominance. Women therefore struggle to find a common voice and to organize around a single goal – something men have benefitted from as they further their own relatively homogeneous interests. In fact, as she argues, home-centred and work-centred women may have interests that coincide with those of men (the former supporting men's economic success and possible priority for jobs; the latter sharing men's concerns with the priorities of work and employment) – a commonality that feminists, from her perspective, have been slow to recognize. Finally, women's heterogeneity is seen as the main cause of women's variable response to social engineering policies in the form of public policy to support women at work and/or to support their role within the home.

This heterogeneity is based upon three work–life preferences and associated groups. As Hakim argues, these groups can be found in all Western countries – irrespective of different national policies – though through the twin revolutions of equal opportunities and contraception find particular purchase in the USA and the UK. However, as she points out, they comprise sociological 'ideal types' based on empirical research results. Few women have lives that conform exactly to the three. The first, 'home-centred women', who are seen to make up 20 per cent of the total, prioritize family life and children, accept the sexual division of labour in the home and prefer not to work. These 'homemakers' undertake family work: education and social development of children, creating a home, maintenance of family relationships, organizing leisure activities, household management and the management of consumption. This may also include personal development and body maintenance as a 'trophy wife'. While some home-centred women never work, others do so until marriage or children. For example, they may invest in a short-term career (for example, air hostess, secretary, receptionist) prior to marriage and/or return to work when caring responsibilities diminish as long as the hours and location are convenient. Such jobs are often treated as a 'hobby' or as an alternative to voluntary work. Many have a good education and qualifications. Education is seen as an 'intellectual dowry' brought to a marriage partnership – a form of cultural capital (Bourdieu, 1984) that shapes the family lifestyle (for example, through consumption and leisure activities) and helps define the family's position. Home-centred women treat university as an 'elite marriage market' and as a way of meeting men of equivalent or higher social status (work performs a similar function). As Hakim (2000) argues, the marriage career still offers more opportunities for upward mobility than through employment and suggests an increasing use of the marriage market to achieve upwards mobility (as she suggests, 'most women prefer to marry up the social ladder if they can', p.197). While acknowledging that conclusions are based on research undertaken up until the 1980s and therefore not fully incorporative of the effects of more recent equal opportunity policies, she sees the advantages of marital mobility for home-centred women as unchanged: 'The picture of consistent disadvantage for women produced by comparisons of the employment successes of men and women is replaced by a picture of equality when women's marital mobility is compared with men's employment career mobility' (Hakim, 2000, p.160). In other words, women can do 'as well from marriage careers as do men from employment careers' (ibid., p.161) and can trade advantages such as 'physical attractiveness, sexuality and erotic capital' (ibid., p.195) in addition to the more orthodox cultural capital for upwards mobility – 'power assets' that go unacknowledged, she suggests, in feminist research except in the context of male control. Moreover, women have a choice between the marriage market and the labour market as a means of achieving social status – and can switch from one (for example, career) to the other (for example, marriage) if the right opportunity, or man, comes along. Here, beauty and brains can therefore be equally effective paths to success, a fact that she suggests is increasingly recognized by women today.

At the other end of the spectrum and also making up 20 per cent, 'work-centred women' prioritize employment and the public sphere (politics, sport, art). These women are seen by Hakim to adopt the stereotypical history and attitudes of the male career. Childless women are concentrated into this group but are not exclusive to it. Some work-centred women have children but motherhood is not central to their identity or a 'principal activity' in their lives. They demonstrate a long-term commitment to employment and invest seriously in educational qualifications and other training. Family is fitted around career rather than vice versa.

The third category, 'adaptive women', forms the largest and most diverse category – comprising approximately 60 per cent of the total and includes women who want to combine work and family without either taking priority – for example, choosing to become school teachers because they can be at home during the summer months. As Hakim argues, previous research has tended to assume that because of its size, adaptive women account for and are representative of all women. These women are not totally committed to work careers and can, for example, have unplanned careers that unfold 'more by accident than design' (ibid., p. 166) or can be characterized as 'drifters', that is, women with no definite ideas about the life they want but who respond to opportunities as they arise and to changes in the social and economic environment as well as to whether and who they marry. In the latter respect, their plans depend very much on their husbands – they may engage in a 'two-person career' supporting a more successful partner; they may work following a divorce or to boost a moderate income; they may engage in part-time or work full-time throughout marriage and childrearing but, unlike work-centred women, with less commitment to their career from the start. In seeking to combine employment with a major role in the family, adaptive women are likely to choose a partner that can be both a provider and share status and tastes. In other words, they effectively use the marriage market and the labour market to achieve their goals. As a whole, the group is vocal and diverse with ambivalent attitudes and mixed objectives – highly responsive to government policies as well as to 'accidents and opportunities' in their social and economic environment (ibid., p. 167).

The heterogeneity captured in the three 'ideal type' groups forms the basis for conflicting interests. This is a phenomenon that Hakim sees as 'going beyond' the current emphasis on diversity in feminist theory based on ethnicity, sexuality, nationality, and class, and that, despite inherent differences, are not seen within this theory to 'break up' the assumed homogeneity among women as a whole. Instead, she highlights conflicting needs, attitudes and priorities and (sometimes shifting) lines of disagreement. For example, home-centred women are likely to 'resent public subsidies for childcare for "irresponsible" and "selfish" working mothers' (ibid., p. 176). Adaptive and work-centred women may share an interest in equal opportunity policies that give them fairer access to the labour market – but come into conflict with home-centred women who 'look to the male breadwinner for support' (ibid.) and who are 'ambivalent' about giving equal chances to women and men in the labour market. Home-centred women may also resent the devaluation of the homemaker role implied in these policies, while for some career women, full-time homemakers may represent everything they have rejected and left behind. In other words, Hakim highlights a diversity of lifestyle choices and hence different levels of responsiveness to public policy: adaptive women are responsive to all policies, those in the work-centred category respond to employment policies, while home-centred women respond to social and family policies.

As the above suggests, Hakim theorizes differences between men and women that lie in contrast to the liberal feminist orientation to sameness and the post-modern emphasis on diversity that is, as she argues, predicated nonetheless on an assumption of female homogeneity. Differences between men and women are, she states, 'relatively small' but they are 'cumulative and point to *qualitatively* different priorities for a large part of the workforce' (2000, p. 140; her emphasis). Men are more aggressive and competitive than women and chase money, power and status more systematically, forming the basis of a sexual division of labour. This is manifest in the fact that the growing number of women entering high-level management roles is balanced by 'substantial numbers' of women who still choose a life centred around home and family. These contrasting preferences cut across 'class, ethnic group, education and ability differences' (Hakim, 2000, p. 155). In addition, she maintains that even the most successful women reject role reversal 'in favour of a partner who is at least equal, preferably superior, in earnings, status or power' (ibid.) – as the previous discussion on the marriage market suggests.

Hakim's work has generated considerable and often 'acrimonious' debate (Crompton and Lyonette, 2005). Several arguments have been made against her conclusions regarding the significance of personal preferences and the subsequent polarization of women in the twenty-first century. Of significance are the critiques of her orientation to sexual difference above (for example, Crompton and Lyonette, 2005) and the feminist contention (for example, Ginn et al., 1996; McRae, 2003; Crompton and Lyonette, 2005; Crompton, 2007) that sexual discrimination and structural constraints rather than choice have led to women's weaker position in the labour market. Many of these authors position Hakim's theory as 'gender essentialist' in terms of the significance she attaches to sexual difference and draw on the argument that choices are socially constructed with social structures and societal norms remaining the dominant and primary determinants of behaviour. From this perspective, Hakim is seen to have overemphasized the significance of 'unfettered choice' that places women's career progress firmly in their own hands (Kumra, 2011) thereby downplaying the effects of discriminatory institutional and societal processes. Ginn et al. (1996), for example, highlight, in response to Hakim's (1991) paper entitled 'Grateful slaves', how her emphasis on women's attitudes and orientations as contributory factors to work-based inequality obscures the more fundamental factors that relate to government and employment policy and lack of 'family-friendly' working. Similarly, McRae (2003) draws attention to empirical evidence suggesting that choices for women are not 'free' but are constrained through normative and structural factors. The former captures attitudes towards family and paid employment as well as women's 'inner voices' that mean that they differ in their perceived abilities to act on the choices offered; the latter highlights job availability and the cost of childcare. Crompton and Harris (1998), while accepting the likely heterogeneity of women, cast doubt on the polarization thesis as being an outcome of individual preference and choice. Instead they draw attention to the increasing social division and polarization in the UK that forms part of post-industrialization and broader structural changes in the economy.

In response, Hakim draws on empirical ('solid') evidence to support her view that even after equal opportunities, men and women continue to differ in their work behaviour and labour market orientation (with men being characteristically more competitive and career focussed), which are then translated into differences in life goals (suggesting, in their supposed lack of attention to evidence, that feminists have become overly ideological and 'non-scientific'). Further, such evidence, she contends, points to the importance of women's attitudes and chosen identities that are often based on acknowledgement of men as primary breadwinners and which orient women themselves as homemakers and/or secondary earners (Hakim, 2000, 2003b, 2004). As such, societal norms such as sex-role attitudes and patriarchal values have only a 'weak link' (Hakim, 2007) with personal preferences. Therefore 'self-classification as a primary earner or a secondary earner is determined by chosen identities rather than imposed by external circumstances' (Hakim, 2000, p. 275). This means, for example, that 'Women will remain the minority in the very top echelons of any society because only a minority of women are work-centred in the way that most men are, and because competitiveness increases as one moves up the occupational ladder' (ibid., p. 277). In fact, as she points out, in modern societies sex and gender are 'redundant concepts' (Hakim, 2007) already replaced by lifestyle preferences as the crucial differentiating characteristic in labour supply (Hakim, 2000, 2007) as well as in social activities and social roles more generally (Hakim, 2004).

Hakim's work has been significant not only because of the level of academic debate that her ideas have engendered, as briefly reviewed above, but also because of the potential influence of her work on the policy agenda. Thus, in a recent report published by the UK Centre for Policy Studies (Hakim, 2011, p.44), she concludes that equal opportunity policies based on equality of outcomes are 'a fruitless goal and a waste of public funds' as women will choose what they think best suits them in the workplace. However, the wider cultural and historical context of this powerful choice agenda, given purchase in both public and private spheres, is overlooked – its uptake generally accepted as positive and 'good'. In the following section, we outline the fundamental principles of postfeminism and in so doing help locate choice discourse and Hakim's work in particular within its socio-cultural frame. This enables us to have a better understanding of contemporary attitudes towards gender disadvantage at work and why women adhere to choice agendas in their own explanations of career circumstances.

POSTFEMINISM – THE CULTURAL LOCATION OF CHOICE

Notwithstanding its ubiquitous usage, postfeminism remains a contested term, with analyses in academic, activist and populist arenas not leading to an agreed-upon understanding. However, despite disagreement, central to the various interpretations of postfeminism is the presence of the emboldened, confident, pleasure-seeking, 'have-it-all' woman of sexual and financial agency (Chen, 2013). While some commentators such as Faludi (1992) and Whelehan (2000) have defined the appearance of this female character as a manifestation of anti-feminism, retro-sexism or revived patriarchy, others, including Gill and Scharff (2011), have argued that 'a new femininity is being constructed . . . that addresses young women as autonomous, confident and desiring sexual subjects who actively and knowingly make choices in stark contrast to women's traditional image of passivity and subordination' (Chen, 2013, p.442). Thus, postfeminism is characterized by a prominence given to individualism, an emphasis on self-surveillance, the revival and reappearance of natural sexual difference and the resexualization of women's bodies and by the retreat to the home, discussed at the beginning of the chapter, as a matter of choice not obligation.

This new active 'choosing' femininity is connected to discourses that integrate the feminist aim of gender parity and women's freedom with the renaissance of traditional personas such as that of the mother connected to the emergence of a discourse of intensive mothering. According to Gill (2007, p. 163):

> [P]ost-feminism articulates a distinctively new sensibility ... because of its tendency to entangle feminist and anti-feminist discourses ... [making its] constructions of contemporary gender relations ... profoundly contradictory ... Yet these contradictions are not random, but contain the sediments of other discourses in a way that is patterned ... The patterned nature of the contradictions is what constitutes the sensibility, one in which notions of autonomy, choice and self-improvement sit side-by-side with surveillance, discipline and the vilification of those who make the 'wrong' choices.

Thus, central to the post-feminist sensibility Gill identifies is an increased importance being attached to the 'choosing' individual, with a particular emphasis placed on the role individual choice plays in the outcomes of people's lives. Here, there is a contemporary assumption that individuals shape their own destiny through the choices they make and as such are required to construct, perform and pull together their biographies themselves (Beck, 1992). From this perspective, inequalities connected to position in the social structure, such as whether an individual is male or female, are understood as individual problems. The experience of inequality and the consequences of an unequal situation in a woman's life are put down to the consequence of her own choices. The solution to the experience of inequality is located with the individual, with people being encouraged to believe that individual energy, improved competitiveness, effort and achievement are enough to surmount social constraints. This obscuring of underlying social structures by individualization translates into a pervasive belief, particularly among young women, that while gender inequalities may persist, they believe that they do not impact on them. Alternatively if they do ever face gender constraints they assert that they can overcome such restrictions through their own personal effort and determination.

From the above we can see that the cultural location of choice lies within a post-feminist discourse. Hakim's preference theory is accordingly a manifestation of this discourse – beginning with the assumption that gender injustice is now a thing of the past in the West. Preference theory asserts that women in Western countries now live beyond a world of sexism and that feminism is obsolete and irrelevant to women's lives as the battle for gender equality has been won. The achievement of 'equality' according to preference theory means that discriminating differences between men and women have decreased while differences connected to variations in gender characteristics have increased. The positive account of women's contemporary position, that is, that they can 'have it all' and therefore are beyond need of help is dependent on the notion of choice that connects women's position (or lack of) in the workforce to their personal tastes and preferences, detaching individual women from social structures and presenting their decisions as operating outside any system of constraints (Gill, 2007; McRobbie, 2009). Thus, in answer to the question 'What do women want?', preference theory and the cultural discourse of postfeminism from which it derives suggests that they want choice but according to Probyn (1990, p. 156): 'it is choice freed of the necessity of thinking about the political and social ramifications of the act of choosing'. In other words, choice is rendered highly individualistic, divorced from considerations of the social implications of choice or where the act of choosing sits within a broader social and cultural landscape of attitudes and practices.

Because preference theory produces a celebratory account of contemporary women's lives, as such it cannot adequately explain their reality in terms of ongoing experiences of inequality. The latter have certainly not disappeared – but the cultural discourse of postfeminism and theories such as preference theory reduce women's ability to name their experiences as discriminatory as many within a post-feminist gender regime do not want to describe themselves as disempowered. Instead, as our paper referred to in the introduction suggests (Simpson et al., 2010), contemporary women, particularly young women, prefer to emphasize their agency and ability to make choices, presenting what happens to them as solely in their own hands. While many critiques of Hakim (as seen above) focus on the constraints of choice, less attention has been directed at the conditions that make choice desirable and voluntary. This begs the question of how to account for the ways in which individuals willingly and actively make choices, perceiving those choices as positive and representative of their 'freedom'. In response, we argue that empirical research and subsequent theorizing need to consider the question of why contemporary individuals place so much value on choice, despite evidence of contradictory outcomes and continuing gender-based disadvantage (ibid.), and what are the specific conditions that support its privileged position. We begin this endeavour by suggesting a programme of research, summarized in Table 3.1, which can act as a starting point for a contextually based inquiry into the significance of choice for understanding women's careers.

From an epistemological standpoint, research needs to consolidate our current sources of understanding concerning the significance of choice in women's careers, charting how and when discourses of choice emerged. This may well involve a revisiting of gender and career literature to explore how knowledge and understanding of choice, both explicitly

Table 3.1 Researching 'choice' in women's careers

Research Focus	Key Questions
Epistemology	What do women know about the concept of choice?
	What do researchers know about the concept of choice?
	How does this knowledge about choice come about?
	How has the discourse of choice emerged?
Methodological	How should the concept of choice be studied?
Ontological	What is the nature of choice within women's career plans?
	How do women 'do' choice in their careers?
	How real are women's 'choices'?
Temporal & spatial	What is the relationship between early career experiences and recourse to choice in mid-to-late career decisions?
	Are there specific types of organizations that are more likely to promote 'choice' as a career issue for women?
	Are women more likely to draw on the discourse of choice in masculinized as opposed to feminized work spaces?
Political	What role has the notion of 'choice' played in concealing ongoing gender inequality in women's careers?
	How do work organizations use 'choice' in their human resource management practices?
	How is 'choice' represented within organizational contexts?
	Is 'choice' a de facto feminized organizational phenomenon?
Reflexive	How should Gender and Organization Studies (GOS) work with the belief in gender-neutral organization associated with use of the discourse of choice when interpreting career experience?
	Is it enough for GOS researchers to demonstrate the gendered nature of organizational phenomena as a counterpoint to its claimed 'neutrality'?
	What does the ubiquity of the notion of choice tell us about the contemporary world of work, careers and organizations?

Source: Adapted from Kavanagh (2013).

and implicitly, have developed over time. On an empirical level, research must also explore how choice 'plays out' in women's lives, the meanings attached to choice, the processes involved in its exercise and the perceived outcomes in terms of its manifestations. Here, attention must be paid to temporal and spatial dimensions such as the different meanings and values placed on choice in the context of changing experiences associated with particular life stages and career trajectories; the significance of organizational culture and organizational practices for how choices are constricted and perceived. For example, as suggested earlier, younger women are more likely to adhere to discourses of choice and to have faith in their own ability to manage their careers, while older women, who may well have encountered gender disadvantage, are more 'seasoned' in their views. In a similar vein, women seeking to progress in male-dominated organizations may distance themselves from what they see as damaging gender-based discourses and adhere to (gender-neutral) meritocracy and choice instead. Other work can usefully focus on the power dynamics of choice to consider how choice discourses foreclose the possibility for a collective, feminist voice and how (for example, human resource management) commitment to choice and opportunity conceal gender disadvantage beneath a rhetoric of individual responsibility (Lewis and Simpson, 2010). These agendas raise issues concerning the most appropriate methods for exploring the significance of choice in men's and women's working lives as well as how best as researchers to challenge claims of gender neutrality and to critically embed such challenges into our interpretations of career experiences.

CONCLUSION

In this chapter, we have moved away from current considerations of the significance of choice in women's careers to consider some of the cultural conditions that make choice appear so persuasive in accounts of career experiences. In other words, we have looked beneath the assumptions often expressed concerning the voluntary nature of choice and its inherent desirability – arguing for a need to locate choice within its particular cultural terrain. These more fundamental aspects of choice are rarely addressed in the literature on women's careers. Indeed, while our earlier paper (Simpson et al., 2010) highlighted the significance of choice in understanding women's attitudes and values, the underlying principles on which the primacy given to choice is based was not subject to specific scrutiny – a gap this chapter has sought to address. We have done this through an analysis of Hakim's (2000) preference theory, placing its principles and prescriptions within the context of postfeminism. This has allowed us to understand more fully the purchase her theory (and discourses of choice more generally) has had in contemporary accounts of women's careers and to highlight the need for contextually sensitive research into how and why choice frames career understandings and career experiences.

REFERENCES

Beck, R. (1992), *Risk Society: Towards a New Modernity*, London: Sage.
Beck, U., A. Giddens and S. Lash (1994), *Reflexive Modernization*, Cambridge, UK: Polity Press.
Belkin, L. (2003), 'The opt-out revolution', *New York Times Magazine*, 26 October, 42–47, 58, 85–86.
Bourdieu, P. (1977), *Outline of a Theory of Practice, Vol. 16*, Cambridge, UK: Cambridge University Press.
Bourdieu, P. (1984), *Distinction*, London: Routledge.
Chen, E. (2013), 'Neoliberalism and popular women's culture: rethinking choice, freedom and agency', *European Journal of Cultural Studies*, **16**(4), 440–52.
Cooper, K. (2013), 'Baby first, job later for young women', *The Sunday Times*, 28 July.
Crompton, R. (2007), 'Gender inequality and the gendered division of labour', in J. Browne (ed.), *The Future of Gender*, Cambridge, UK: Cambridge University Press.
Crompton, R. and F. Harris (1998), 'A reply to Hakim', *British Journal of Sociology*, **49**(1), 144–9.
Crompton, R. and C. Lyonette (2005), 'The new gender essentialism – domestic and family choices and their relation to attitudes', *British Journal of Sociology*, **56**(4), 601–20.
Economist, The (2010), 'Female power', *The Economist*, 2 January.
Faludi, S. (1992), *Backlash: The Undeclared War Against Women*, London: Chatto & Windus.
Giddens, A. (1991), *Modernity and Self-Identity: Self and Society in Later Modern Age*, Cambridge, UK: Polity Press.
Gill, R. (2007), 'Postfeminist media culture: elements of a sensibility', *European Journal of Cultural Studies*, **10**(2), 147–66.
Gill, R. and C. Scharff (eds) (2011), *New Femininities: Postfeminism, Neoliberalism and Subjectivity*, Basingstoke, UK: Palgrave Macmillan.
Ginn, J., S. Arber, J. Brannen, A. Dale, S. Dex, P. Elias, P. Moss, J. Pahl, C. Roberts and J. Rubery (1996), 'Feminist fallacies: a reply to Hakim on women's employment', *The British Journal of Sociology*, **47**(1), 167–74.
Hakim, C. (1991), 'Grateful slaves and self-made women: fact and fantasy in women's work orientations', *European Sociological Review*, **7**(2), 101–21.
Hakim, C. (1998), 'Developing a sociology for the twenty-first century: preference theory', *British Journal of Sociology*, **49**(1), 137–44.
Hakim, C. (2000), *Work Lifestyle Choices in the 21st Century: Preference Theory*, Oxford: Oxford University Press.
Hakim, C. (2003a), *Models of the Family in Modern Societies: Ideals and Realities*, Aldershot, UK: Ashgate.
Hakim, C. (2003b), 'Public morality versus personal choice', *British Journal of Sociology*, **53**(3), 339–46.
Hakim, C. (2004), *Key Issues in Women's Work: Female Diversity and the Polarization of Women's Employment*, London: Glass House Press.
Hakim, C. (2006), 'Women, careers and work–life preferences', *British Journal of Guidance and Counselling*, **34**(3), 279–94.
Hakim, C. (2007), 'Dancing with the devil? Essentialism and other feminist heresies', *British Journal of Sociology*, **58**(1), 123–32.
Hakim, C. (2011), *Feminist Myths and Magic Medicine*, Centre for Policy Studies, January, accessed 25 November 2014 at http://www.cps.org.uk/files/reports/original/111026184004-FeministMythsandMagicMedicine.pdf.
Kavanagh, D. (2013), 'Children: their place in organization studies', *Organization Studies*, **34**(10), 1487–503.
Kirkpatrick, J. (2010), 'Introduction: selling out? Solidarity and choice in the American feminist movement', *Perspectives on Politics*, **8**(1), 241–5.
Kumra, S. (2011), 'Exploring career "choices" of work-centred women in a professional service firm', *Gender in Management: An International Journal*, **25**(3), 227–43.

Lewis, P. and R. Simpson (eds) (2010), *Revealing and Concealing Gender: Issues of Invisibility in Organizations*, Basingstoke, UK: Palgrave Macmillan.
Matchar, E. (2013), 'The complex, often idealistic reasons feminists become housewives', *The Atlantic*, 20 March.
McDowell, L. (1991), 'Life without father and Ford: the new gender order of post-Fordism', *Transactions of the Institute of British Geographers*, **16**(4), 400–419.
McRae, S. (2003), 'Constraints and choices in mothers' employment careers: a consideration of Hakim's preference theory', *British Journal of Sociology*, **54**(3), 317–38.
McRobbie, A. (2009), *The Aftermath of Feminism*, London: Sage.
Miller, L. (2013), 'The retro wife: feminists who say they're having it all by choosing to stay home', *New York Magazine*, 17 March.
Percheski, C. (2008), 'Opting out? Cohort differences in professional women's employment rates from 1960 to 2005', *American Sociological Review*, **73**(3), 497–517.
Probyn, E. (1990), 'New traditionalism and post-feminism: TV does the home', *Screen*, **31**(2), 147–59.
Simpson, R., A. Ross-Smith and P. Lewis (2010), 'Merit, special contribution and choice: how women negotiate between sameness and difference in their organizational lives', *Gender in Management: An International Journal*, **25**(3), 198–208.
Snyder-Hall, R.C. (2010), 'Third wave feminism and the defence of "choice"', *Perspectives on Politics*, **8**(1), 255–61.
Whelehan, I. (2000), *Overloaded: Popular Culture and the Future of Feminism*, London: Women's Press.

4. Gender scripts as access codes to management positions
Edeltraud Hanappi-Egger

In Western societies gender is usually specified along two categories, 'men' and 'women', each associated with different sets of capabilities and aptitudes, and consequently with different fields of responsibility. This serves to perpetuate a dualistic ordering structure of our society in which a range of occupations and positions have come to be male or female dominated (see Lorber and Farell, 1991). Querying the assumption that identities are biologically determined, some academics have elaborated fresh approaches to the concept of gender, in particular sex categorization and gender roles. Undermining the older, strictly biological approach, the perspective of gender as a social construction has gained in prominence and has been applied to various areas of research.

Nevertheless, in daily life as well as in organizational practice, we can still find evidence of the strength and persistence of the dualistic gender concept based on a strict and exclusive division into the categories male/female. This hegemonic gender concept defining the 'norm' as either heterosexual and male, or heterosexual and female, with associated feminine or masculine characteristics, leads to a strong gender segregation of the societal world along these norms and to the marginalization of 'non-norm' groups (such as homosexuals). Butler (2006) calls this the 'heterosexual matrix', which defines socially accepted norm settings and thus reinforces given power structures.

Since organizations are generally considered to be open systems (see Scott, 1986) forming a 'recursive constitution' with their environments, they mirror these socially constructed gender relations, which are thus reproduced rather than invented at the organizational level. Clearly gender segregation and gender hierarchies are organizational phenomena – such as the gender-specific division of labour or gender-specific hierarchies resulting in a dearth of women in top management positions. In view of these facts, the topic of 'gender and management' has long been debated by feminist academics, in contrast to mainstream thinking that has always seen organizations as gender-neutral. For example, until relatively recently, gender topics were widely ignored in management literature (Clegg et al., 2006; Broadbridge and Hearn, 2008; Hanappi-Egger, 2011).

Today gender-specific segregation in the workplace is still a pressing problem at both the horizontal and vertical levels. Although a great deal of effort has been expended in past years to find a way of overcoming these gender segregations, it has proved difficult to implement lasting change. The latest statistics confirm the global persistence of the division of labour based on gender in a wide array of professions and working fields, as well as gender-related hierarchies, especially in management. For example, the *Global Gender Gap Report* (Hausmann et al., 2012) states that no country in the world has yet reached total gender equality. The top ten countries listed by the report include the four Nordic nations of Iceland, Finland, Norway and Sweden, where the labour force participation of women is the highest in the world, salary disparities are the lowest, and also the gender-specifics in leadership positions are less pronounced. These achievements are strongly linked to the transformation of given societal gender relations in terms of innovative work–life balance models for parents:

> [S]hared participation in childcare, more equitable distribution of labour at home, better work–life balance for both women and men. . . . Finally there has also been success with a top-down approach to promoting women's leadership. In Norway, since 2008, publicly listed companies have been required to have 40% of each sex on their boards. (Hausmann et al., 2012, p. 22)

Hanappi-Egger (2011) highlights the fact that gender phenomena in organizations are often not a result of direct discrimination, but more indirect and subtle forms of inclusion and exclusion. Organizations are gendered spaces where gender is an integral part of their structures and processes (Acker, 1990, 2006), but also where a system of gendered regimes is established and reproduced (Gherardi, 1995; Gherardi and Poggio, 2001; Conell, 2006). The particular focus of this chapter will be on the role of 'gender scripts', which, by impacting sense-making processes as well as the meaning of management, provide the structural framework for organizational practices. The concept of 'gender scripts' will be combined with the theory of institutional work in order to underline the contribution of agencies to the maintenance of certain habitus and structural frameworks.

GENDERED ORGANIZATIONS, GENDER SCRIPTS AND INSTITUTIONAL WORK

This chapter deals with the issue of gender in management from a sense-making perspective (Weick, 1985), and in particular will emphasize the role of 'gender scripts'. Since the processing of information in social interactions is time consuming and rather complex, people apply mental models (usually unconsciously) that they have learnt from their environment in order to evaluate and react to situations more efficiently. These mental models consist of schemata and scripts that serve to reduce the complexity of the real world (ibid.) by excluding non-relevant information and by interpreting the information flow by means of prior knowledge. The disadvantage of such cognitive structures consisting of schemata and scripts is that they are highly resistant to disconfirmation and change (Hanappi-Egger, 2012). The acquisition of schemata and scripts begins in childhood and can be described as the 'socialization' of the individual. Later on, schemata and scripts are validated and reconfirmed in daily life and business (see Schank and Abelson, 1977; Levy and Fivush, 1993; Hanappi-Egger and Kauer, 2010).

However, it is important to realize that it is not only *situations* that are classified and evaluated in this way; schemata and scripts also serve to categorize *individuals* in terms of a set of specific characteristics and often the first obvious (and visible) criterion used to classify an individual is their sex. This means that whenever people come together for any form of social intercourse, sex categorization is prevalent in terms of the gender assignment of each person, accompanied by stereotypical gender-role expectations: 'Men were typically seen as stronger and more active characterized by high needs for achievement, dominance, autonomy and aggression. Women, in contrast, were viewed as weaker and less active, more concerned with affiliation, nurturance and deference' (Deaux and Kite, 1989, p. 99). If asked to list stereotypical feminine or masculine attributes, people tend to produce much the same list, since these roles are to a large extent socially constructed (see also Hanappi-Egger, 2006). Although today the vast majority of people are aware of stereotypical notions of gender and gendered roles, very few are conscious of the fact that they themselves use such notions in their daily lives (see Heintz et al., 2007; Ridgeway, 2011).

What Does this Mean for Organization Studies and Management?

In the early days of management studies, publications in this field treated the 'gender topic', if at all, as referring strictly to women and their particular workplace needs and requirements, based on their supposed inferior physical capabilities (see Beneria, 1995; Beblo et al., 1999; Hanappi-Egger, 2011). Later this essentialist and difference-oriented view was discussed and challenged by feminist organization theorists (Oakely, 1972; Kanter, 1977; Acker, 1990; Mills, 1992; Gherardi, 1995), so that meanwhile the focus of research is on the meaning and social construction of gender. It is argued that organizations are gendered spaces, producing and reproducing gender hierarchies by processes and structures as well as by individual identity work to make sense of the organizational (gender) cultures (cf. Alvesson and Willmott, 2002).

Despite the general trend of research towards the construction of gender, many scholars in organization studies still prefer to investigate the issue of gender-*specifics* in management. In doing so, they automatically assume and refer to differences between men and women. In her study on the relationship between sex role stereotypes and requisite management characteristics, Schein revealed that successful middle managers 'are perceived to possess characteristics, attitudes, and temperaments more commonly ascribed to men in general than to women in general' (1973, p. 95). This relationship between sex stereotypes and perceived management characteristics was found in both the male and female sample (see Schein, 1973, 1975). Schein came to the conclusion that sex-role stereotyping in management leads to a widely held 'think male–think manager' phenomenon. Different studies in this field confirm that an automatic link is made in people's minds between an imagined manager and the male sex (Willemsen, 2002).

Regardless of whether the assumption of fundamental sex-related differences between men and women has its origins in biology or in the theory of socialization, gender stereotypes function to reproduce the notion of basic difference. Hence, gender stereotypes are used by men as well as women to categorize and frame themselves and others, based on social norms and expectations of how men and women are and should be (Eagly and Karau, 2002). They not only serve as descriptive features but also as prescriptive ones to produce an idea of how men and women must behave. As such they function as 'gender scripts' (see also Hanappi-Egger and Kauer, 2010; Hanappi-Egger, 2011; Eberherr and Hanappi-Egger, 2012). Of course, 'scripts' in the sense of guiding principles and behavioural orientation also exist with respect to professional roles such as those assigned to managers. Studies show that women who adopt masculine managerial styles are rated lower than men displaying the same style, for whom such behaviour is accepted and accredited (Kent and Moss, 1994; Kolb, 2002; Rhode, 2003). These findings show that stereotypic ascriptions of management undermine women in their professional lives (Rhode, 2003). Female-associated behaviour is seen as inappropriate to the demands of managerial identities: managers are generally required to be 'forceful', 'rational', 'competitive', 'strong' and 'independent', whereas stereotypical female characteristics are antithetical to this, namely 'kind', 'friendly' and 'selfless' (Fagenson, 1990, p. 268). Although there are in the meantime some new concepts in management (for example, transformational leadership), Hopkins (2000) argues that organizations are still dominated by masculine norms and values.

In addition, several studies have shown that leadership styles tend to be rather similar, sharing an array of features that little reflect the sex of managers (Wajcman and Martin, 2002; Hanappi-Egger, 2012). This can perhaps be attributed to common socialization processes within organizations that aim to produce homogeneous 'workers' or 'managers' and that, by serving as a form of gatekeeping, strongly dictate an individual's career path and chances of promotion (Meyerson and Ely, 2003; Hanappi-Egger, 2011, 2013). Furthermore, as Rose (2007) shows, female managers are quite well aware of female stereotypes, which they strive to subvert by adopting a male-attribute leadership style.

Doing Gender as Institutional Work

While there exists a broad scholarly discourse on gender in organizations, the role of gender scripts, in particular, masculinity constructions (Conell, 2000; Whitehead, 2002), as a form of 'institutional work' has received little attention. This represents a promising new approach since institutional work deals with the co-evolution and mutual influence of agency and structure, or as Lawrence et al. (2011, p. 54) describe it, the ability of agencies 'to transcend the totalizing cognitive influence of institutions' or 'to resist and often challenge the conforming pressures of institutions'.

As Lawrence et al. (2009) emphasize, organizational members take an active role in the shaping of organizational structures; they put a great deal of effort – consciously or unconsciously – into sustaining and disrupting institutions. Managers can be viewed as special actors in organizations, namely those who are explicitly responsible for the sustainability of organizations. In this management context, legitimation plays a crucial role in discursive institutional work (cf. Suddaby and Greenwood, 2005; Vaara and Tienari, 2008; Schildt et al., 2011). Taken-for-granted knowledge and the shared understanding of the role and function of managers are particular instances of legitimation, while the adoption by managers of a managerial identity has been described by Hwang and Colyvas (2011, p. 63) as a special form of institutional work: 'In this sense, actor identities are "scripts" that define roles and link actors with legitimate repertoire of actions, interests, and purposes in particular social domains.'

As already discussed, managerial scripts are gendered scripts that define the taken-for-granted knowledge and commonly shared understanding of the role and function of managers as well as their characteristics. Hanappi-Egger (2011) argues that, from a historical perspective, the managerial identity script has always been strongly interwoven with the particular living contexts of men (see also England and Folbre, 2005; for further details on the history of management see Hanappi-Egger, 2014).

Thus, men were deemed physically and mentally predisposed to the job of management, while conversely the belief gained currency that there exists an obvious and natural contradiction between women and the field of management – a stereotypical view that to some extent persists today.

These male-oriented management scripts have become well-established normalized forms. As taken-for-granted knowledge they are silently accepted and reproduced without question, ensuring their persistence. From this point of view, these (gendered) scripts can be considered mediatory tools of normalization and social control (Foucault, 1992), which create and confirm different notions of subjectivity by providing organizations with credible knowledge about gender patterns and relations (see Ely, 1995, 2003). This means that gender as sex in terms of biological classification was (and partially still is) fundamental to organizational thinking – leading once again to the reproduction of the dualistic gender concept of men and women. In fact, the mainstream debate in organization studies still focuses on traditional difference-oriented models in terms of male and female traits dictated by nature, so that academics themselves can be accused of contributing to the continuation of stereotypical gendered ways of thinking (Alvesson and Billing, 1997).

Nevertheless, some scholars of organization studies have in recent years become interested in investigating the social construction of gender codes in management. Thus, the previously ignored contradictions and ambiguities associated with gender topics in organizations have become the subject of much current research (see for example, Czarniawska, 2005; Calás and Smircich, 2009; Hanappi-Egger, 2011). As a result of this scientific work management identity scripts have been revised, replacing the strict biological assignment of managerial characteristics (being a man) by gender codes – more precisely, masculinity codes. This means that the norm for describing 'good management' is no longer men per se, but rather codes of masculinity.

Traditional management scripts have been rewritten by introducing gender patterns in terms of job descriptions, skills and particularly the characteristics necessary to be a manager, as well as by integrating gender patterns and codes of femininity and masculinity into organizational structures and processes. For example, Wajcman and Martin (2002) have used the narratives of female and male managers to demonstrate that their career stories are already 'non-gendered' in terms of reflecting similar norms, values and self-constructions concerning their own understanding of being a manager. This means that there is no significant difference between men and women describing their role as managers.

Hanappi-Egger (2011) has undertaken similar studies in the areas of science, engineering and technology (the so-called SET fields), which show that female engineering students have similar 'non-gendered' self-constructions with respect to their professional understandings and codes of conduct. Nevertheless, deconstruction of their narratives revealed underlying 'non-gendered' characteristics strongly couched in terms of masculinity. The same phenomenon was noted in a study of female IT experts who quit their jobs: their self-identities were largely defined by male-associated attributions, leading to a permanent feeling of 'not belonging' to their chosen field, which finally led the women to quit their profession (see Hanappi-Egger, 2012).

While gender scripts certainly still exist in the form of stereotypical beliefs and behaviour, public discussion on gender equality has encouraged organizations to make greater efforts to promote gender balance (see Styhre, 2013 for a discussion on how public discourse impacted gender equality in the Church of Sweden). Hence there is little doubt that the traditional and rigid sex-based form of gender script is slowly being abandoned in organizations and management in order to foster the inclusion of women. Nevertheless, the fundamental notion that management tasks demand a specific and unique array of characteristics and that there is an ideal form of organizational identity both persist, although now expressed by codes of masculinity than simply the fact of 'being a man' (Alvesson and Empson, 2006). Today the face of management is no longer 'male', but rather defined by codes of masculinity that individuals of both sexes are expected to adopt.

Institutions have been defined as 'those (more or less) enduring elements of social life that affect the behaviour and beliefs of individuals and collective actors by providing templates for action, cognition, and emotion, nonconformity with which is associated with some kind of costs' (Lawrence et al., 2011, p. 53). This definition follows the thinking of the traditional school of structuralism (Giddens, 1984, 1987) and the social theory of Bourdieu with its concept of habitus. In his analysis, Bourdieu pointed out that 'through the habitus, the structure of which it is the product governs practice, not along the paths of a mechanical determinism, but within the constraints and limits initially set on its inventions' (Bourdieu, 1990, p. 55). Hence, the habitus is seen to generate, co-determine and shape common-sense attitudes and behaviour within the limits of regulatory structures. And in a similar way Tsoukas and Chia (2002, p. 570) have defined the organization as 'an attempt to order the intrinsic flux of human action, to channel it toward certain ends, to give it a particular shape, through generalizing and institutionalizing particular meanings and rules'. In other words, habitus represents the expression of the given organizational scripts determining expected behaviour and identity, so that, with respect to management, habitus is related to gender.

Hanappi-Egger (2013) presents a case study showing how these organizational gender scripts function as gatekeepers, especially for management positions, to ensure the reproduction of intended behaviour and establish organizational codes that guide the sense-making processes of employees. Since managers' organizational scripts are often constructions of masculinity, women who are willing to share these self-understandings still face potential contradictions arising from their particular societal role and their assignment to tasks in the reproductive field, a situation called 'double-binding' (see also Powell and Butterfield, 2003; Ely, 2003; Muzio et al., 2013; Hanappi-Egger, 2014).

Institutional work can be understood as the effort to sustain existing (gendered) power structures by reproducing gender scripts that achieve 'projective agency' (Emirbayer and Johnson, 2007) in the sense of future-oriented intentionality (that is, the role of management). On the other hand much effort is expended on pushing the idea of a 'masculine' coding of management, that is, institutional work is performed as 'doing gender' (West and Zimmermann, 1987). This leads to the phenomenon that women tend to adapt to the male gender script of managers (Hanappi-Egger, 2013) or as Ozbilgin and Tatli (2005, p. 864) describe it: 'habitus at the organizational level is reproduced by the conscious, unconscious, conforming and deviant acts of organizational members who compete for hegemony over the terms used by organizational cultures'. Clearly this is exactly the point mentioned by Willmott (2011, p. 70) when referring to the 'collective process of institutional reproduction in which the so-called powerless are active participants, rather than passive or disregarded'. This results in the production and reproduction of a specific understanding of management incorporated into organizational practices and their structural frames, and which is actively maintained even by those who are oppressed and subordinated by it. In our case women contribute to gender regimes by actively participating in the reproduction of gender scripts assigned to management and by sharing the habitus as taken for granted.

SUMMARY AND RECOMMENDATIONS

This chapter has given an overview of the issue of gender scripts and their role in contributing to the production and reproduction of gender segregation in organizations. In particular, it has looked at several gender-specific phenomena related to managerial identity constructed as masculinity codes. While there has been a shift of understanding from the belief that management is a man's profession to an acceptance of the social construction of masculine norms, it is still easier and more straightforward for men

Gender scripts as access codes to management positions 69

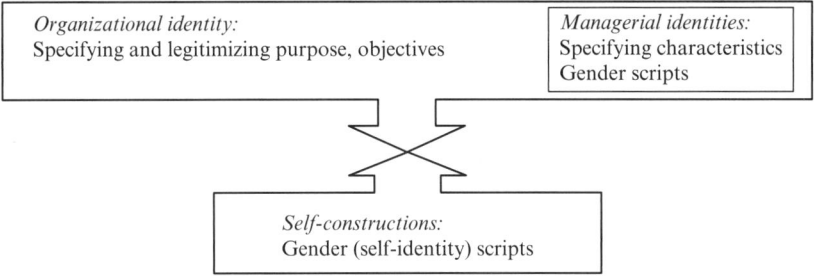

Source: Adapted from Hanappi-Egger (2011, p. 123).

Figure 4.1 Gender scripts and managerial identity

to match these masculinity gender scripts. This can lead to biased hiring and promotion policies for management positions that serve to perpetuate the so-called 'leaky pipeline' effect (see also Blickenstaff, 2005), that is, the higher the management position the fewer the number of women. Thus, gender hierarchies in management are maintained and reproduced.

These gender scripts are also part of individuals' internal mental models, so that when the gendered code of an organization is perceived, potential employees or managers might decide for self-exclusion in view of the expected gender role behaviour and its mismatch with their self-identity. The dynamics of the role of gender scripts and managerial identity can be sketched as shown in Figure 4.1.

One aspect of the (gendered) organization identity is the role expectation inherent in the managerial identity, specified as characteristics that are highly gendered in terms of masculinity constructions. Those gender scripts are signalled and perceived by people who, depending on their self-identity constructions, are more or less attracted by the organizational values. Thereby, exclusion as well as self-exclusion is established in a subtle way. In particular, the underlying gender scripts – expected gender role behaviour and gender attribution – play an indirect yet vital role.

In order to overcome those subtle gendered regimes and the gender-specific reproduction of managerial identities, more is required than simply increasing the proportion of women in higher positions: the underlying gender scripts have to be made visible (for an innovative methodological approach compare Hanappi-Egger and Warmuth, 2010; Hanappi-Egger, 2013). In other words, these gender scripts have to be critically examined and institutional work has to be changed. This can be done most efficiently by changing the institutional framework, specifically by tackling the three key elements that serve to constitute and maintain institutions, defined by

Scott (2001) as the regulative, normative and cultural-cognitive pillars. For our purposes this would involve adjusting the legal framework, that is, shaping the recruitment and promotion process by means of gender mainstreaming and quotas (regulative), introducing a monitoring and reporting system in terms of gender equality (normative), and finally questioning the common beliefs and taken-for-granted knowledge, specifically what it means to be a 'good' manager (cultural-cognitive). While measures on the first pillar can be initiated by (public) discourse and employment legislation, action on the second pillar requires organizational effort to monitor and evaluate innovatory programmes (which might, of course, lead also to pure lip service).

The third cognitive level is the most crucial since it affects organizational paradigms such as the values and norms of management. Thus, it is clear that a number of internal and external organizational changes have to be initiated. In general this is not an easy task: if their positions of power and authority are threatened by change, dominant groups are likely to be a source of stiff resistance. Nevertheless, if organizations wish to be less exclusive and discriminatory, and are interested in exploiting the innovative capacity of diversity, they must take a close look at the role of gender scripts in establishing barriers and maintaining the status quo. A wide range of competences, perspectives and characteristics are required to meet future challenges and succeed in the task of rewriting gender scripts, particularly in the field of management. In any case, there is little doubt that rigid and biased managerial identities and self-constructions inhibit two fundamental human resources: creativity and innovation (for concepts and tools to handle future management challenges see Danowitz et al., 2012). Hence, it could be stated that organizations – in order to fully use the innovation potential – have to be more inclusive. Not only women would benefit from such a development, but definitely also men – at least those with less traditional and dualistic gender identities.

REFERENCES

Acker, J. (1990), 'Hierarchies, jobs, bodies: a theory of gendered organizations', *Gender and Society*, **4**(2), 139–58.
Acker, J. (2006), 'Inequality regimes: gender, class, and race in organizations', *Gender Society*, **20**(4), 441–64.
Alvesson, M. and Y.D. Billing (1997), *Understanding Gender and Organizations*, London/Thousand Oaks, CA/New Delhi: Sage.
Alvesson, M. and L. Empson (2006), 'The construction of organizational identity', Lund Institute of Economic Research Working Paper Series No. 3, Lund University.
Alvesson, M. and H. Willmott (2002), 'Identity regulation as organizational control: producing the appropriate individual', *Journal of Management Studies*, **39**(5), 619–44.

Beblo, M., G. Krell, K. Schneider and B. Soete (eds) (1999), *Okonomie und Geschlecht* [Economy and Gender], Munich: Rainer Hampp Verlag.
Beneria, L. (1995), 'Toward a greater integration of gender in economics', *World Development*, **23**(11), 1839–50.
Blickenstaff, J.C. (2005), 'Women and science careers: leaky pipeline or gender filter?', *Gender and Education*, **17**(4), 369–86.
Bourdieu, P. (1990), *The Logic of Practice*, Stanford, CA: Stanford University Press.
Broadbridge, A. and J. Hearn (2008), 'Gender and management: new directions in research and continuing patterns in practice', *British Journal of Management*, **19**(S1), 38–49.
Butler, J. (2006), 'Imitation and gender insubordination', in J. Storey (ed.), *Cultural Theory and Popular Culture: A Reader*, 3rd edition, Harlow, UK: Pearson Education Limited, pp. 255–70.
Calás, M. and L. Smircich (2009), 'Feminist perspectives on gender in organization research: what is and is yet to be', in D.A. Buchanan and A. Bryman (eds), *The SAGE Handbook of Organizational Research Methods*, London: Sage, pp. 246–69.
Clegg, S., M. Kornberger, C. Carter and C. Rhodes (2006), 'For management?', *Management Learning*, **37**(1), 7–27.
Conell, R.W. (2000), *The Men and the Boys*, Sydney: Allen & Unwin.
Conell, R.W. (2006), 'Glass ceilings or gendered institutions? Mapping the gender regimes of public sector worksites', *Public Administration Review*, **66**(6), 837–49.
Czarniawska, B. (2005), 'Doing gender unto the other: fiction as a mode of studying gender discrimination in organizations', *Gender, Work & Organization*, **13**(3), 234–52.
Danowitz, M.A., E. Hanappi-Egger and H. Mensi-Klarbach (2012), *Diversity in Organizations: Concepts and Practices*, Basingstoke, UK: Palgrave Macmillan.
Deaux, K. and M.E. Kite (1989), 'Thinking about gender', in B.B. Hess and M.M. Ferree (eds), *Analyzing Gender: A Handbook of Social Science Research*, Newbury Park, CA: Sage, pp. 92–117.
Eagly, A.H. and S.J. Karau (2002), 'Role congruity theory of prejudice toward female leaders', *Psychological Review*, **109**(3), 573–98.
Eberherr, H. and E. Hanappi-Egger (2012), 'The power of implicit distinction practices: changing (gender) differences in organization', 28th EGOS Colloquium, Aalto University & Hanken School of Economics, Helsinki, 5–7 July 2012.
Ely, R. (1995), 'The power in demography: women's social constructions of gender identity at work', *Academy of Management*, **38**(3), 589–634.
Ely, R. (2003), 'Leadership: overview', in R. Ely, E.G. Foldy and M.A. Scully (eds), *Reader in Gender, Work, and Organization*, Malden, MA: Blackwell Publishing, pp. 153–8.
Emirbayer, M. and V. Johnson (2007), 'Bourdieu and organizational analysis', *Theory and Society*, **37**(1), 1–44.
England, P. and N. Folbre (2005), 'Gender and economic sociology', in N. Smelser and R. Swedberg (eds), *Handbook of Economic Sociology*, Princeton, NJ: Princeton University Press, pp. 627–49.
Fagenson, E. (1990), 'At the heart of women in management research: theoretical and methodological approaches and their biases', *Journal of Business Ethics*, **9**(4–5), 267–74.
Foucault, M. (1992), *Uberwachen und Strafen* [Discipline and Punish], 10th edition, Frankfurt: Suhrkamp.
Gherardi, S. (1995), *Gender Symbolism and Organizational Cultures*, London/Thousand Oaks, CA/New Delhi: Sage.
Gherardi, S. and B. Poggio (2001), 'Creating and recreating gender order in organizations', *Journal of World Business*, **36**(3), 245–58.
Giddens, A. (1984), *The Constitution of Society*, Cambridge, UK: Polity Press.
Giddens, A. (1987), 'Structuralism, post-structuralism and the production of culture', in A. Giddens and J. Turner (eds), *Social Theory Today*, Cambridge, UK: Polity Press, pp. 195–223.
Hanappi-Egger, E. (2006), 'Gender and diversity from a management perspective: synonyms

or complements?', *Journal of Organisational Transformation & Social Change*, **3**(2), 121–34.
Hanappi-Egger, E. (2011), *The Triple M of Organizations: Man, Management and Myth*, Vienna/New York: Springer.
Hanappi-Egger, E. (2012), 'Shall I stay or shall I go? On the role of diversity management for women's retention in SET professions', *Equality, Diversity and Inclusion: An International Journal*, **31**(2), 144–57.
Hanappi-Egger, E. (2013), 'Backstage: the organizational gendered agenda in science, engineering and technology professions', *European Journal of Women's Studies*, **20**(3), 279–94.
Hanappi-Egger, E. (2014), 'Homo oeconomicus and "his" impact on gendered societies', in M. Evans, C. Hemmings, M. Henry, S. Madhoc, A. Plomien and S. Wearing (eds), *The SAGE Handbook of Feminist Theory*, London: Sage.
Hanappi-Egger, E. and A. Kauer (2010), 'Gendered scripts: studying hidden assumptions in business contexts', *Gender in Management: An International Journal*, **25**(6), 497–508.
Hanappi-Egger, E. and G. Warmuth (2010), 'Gender-neutral or gender-blind? On the meaning of structural barriers in computer science and engineering', Joint International IGIP-SEFI Annual Conference, Trnava, Slovakia, 19–22 September 2010.
Hausmann, R., L. Tyson and S. Zahidi (2012), *The Global Gender Gap Report*, Geneva: World Economic Forum.
Heintz, B., M. Merz and C. Schumacher (2007), 'Die Macht des Offensichtlichen: Bedingungen geschlechtlicher Personalisierung in der Wissenschaft' [The power of evidence: conditions for a gendered individualization in science], *Zeitschrift für Soziologie*, **36**(4), 261–81.
Hopkins, J. (2000), 'Signs of masculinism in an "uneasy" place: advertising for "Big Brothers"', *Gender, Place and Culture*, **7**(1), 35–55.
Hwang, H. and J. Colyvas (2011), 'Problematizing actors and institutions in institutional work', *Journal of Management Inquiry*, **20**(1), 62–6.
Kanter, R.M. (1977), *Men and Women of the Corporation*, New York: Basic Books.
Kent, R.L. and S.E. Moss (1994), 'Effects of sex and gender role on leader emergence', *The Academy of Management Journal*, **37**(5), 1335–46.
Kolb, D.M. (2002), 'Negotiations through a gender lens', Working Paper No. 15, Center for Gender in Organizations, Simmons School of Management, Boston, MA.
Lawrence, T., R. Suddaby and B. Leca (2009), *Institutional Work: Actors and Agency in Institutional Studies of Organizations*, New York: Cambridge University Press.
Lawrence, T., R. Suddaby and B. Leca (2011), 'Institutional work: refocusing institutional studies of organization', *Journal of Management Inquiry*, **20**(1), 52–8.
Levy, G.D. and R. Fivush (1993), 'Scripts and gender: a new approach for examining gender-role development', *Developmental Review*, **13**(2), 126–46.
Lorber, J. and S. Farrell (eds) (1991), *The Social Construction of Gender*, Newbury Park, CA: Sage.
Meyerson, D.E. and R.J. Ely (2003), 'Using difference to make a difference', in D.L. Rhode (ed.), *The Difference 'Difference' Makes*, Stanford, CA: Stanford University Press, pp. 129–43.
Mills, A.J. (1992), 'Organization, gender and culture', in A.J. Mills and P. Trancred (eds), *Gendering Organizational Analysis*, Newbury Park, CA: Sage, pp. 93–111.
Muzio, D., D. Brock and R. Suddaby (2013), 'Professions and institutional change: towards an institutionalist sociology of the professions', *Journal of Management Studies*, **50**(5), 699–721.
Oakley, A. (1972), *Sex, Gender and Society*, San Francisco, CA: Harper and Row.
Ozbilgin, M. and A. Tatli (2005), 'Book review essay: understanding Bourdieu's contribution to organization and management studies', *Academy of Management Review*, **30**(4), 855–77.
Powell, G. and A. Butterfield (2003), 'Gender, gender identity, and aspirations to top management', *Women in Management Review*, **18**(1/2), 88–96.
Rhode, D.L. (ed.) (2003), *The Difference 'Difference' Makes: Women in Leadership*, Stanford, CA: Stanford University Press.

Ridgeway, C.L. (2011), *Framed by Gender. How Gender Inequality Persists in the Modern World*, Oxford: Oxford University Press.
Rose, C. (2007), 'Does female board representation influence firm performance? The Danish evidence', *Corporate Governance: An International Review*, **15**(2), 404–13.
Schank, R.C. and R.P. Abelson (1977), *Scripts, Plans, Goals and Understanding*, Hillsdale, NJ: Lawrence Erlbaum.
Schein, V.E. (1973), 'The relationship between sex role stereotypes and requisite management characteristics', *Journal of Applied Psychology*, **57**(2), 95–100.
Schein, V.E. (1975), 'Relationships between sex role stereotypes and requisite management characteristics among female managers', *Journal of Applied Psychology*, **60**(3), 340–44.
Schildt, H., S. Mantere and E. Vaara (2011), 'Reasonability and the linguistic division of labor in institutional work', *Journal of Management Inquiry*, **20**(1), 82–6.
Scott, R.W. (1986), *Grundlagen der Organisationstheorie* [Fundamentals of Organization Theory], Frankfurt: Suhrkamp.
Scott, R.W. (2001), *Institutions and Organizations*, Thousand Oaks, CA: Sage.
Styhre, A. (2013), 'Gender equality as institutional work: the case of the Church of Sweden', *Gender, Work & Organization*, **21**(2), 105–20.
Suddaby, R. and R. Greenwood (2005), 'Rhetorical strategies of legitimacy', *Administrative Science Quarterly*, **50**(1), 35–67.
Tsoukas, H. and R. Chia (2002), 'Organizational becoming: rethinking organizational change', *Organization Science*, **13**(5), 567–82.
Vaara, E. and J. Tienari (2008), 'A discursive perspective on legitimation strategies in multinational corporations', *Academy of Management Review*, **33**(4), 985–93.
Wajcman, J. and B. Martin (2002), 'Narratives of identity in modern management: the corrosion of gender difference?', *Sociology*, **36**(4), 985–1002.
Weick, K. (1985), *Der Prozess des Organisierens* [The Process of Organizing], Frankfurt: Suhrkamp.
West, C. and D. Zimmerman (1987), 'Doing gender', *Gender and Society*, **1**(2), 125–51.
Whitehead, S. (2002), *Men and Masculinities*, Cambridge, UK: Polity Press.
Willemsen, T.M. (2002), 'Gender typing of the successful manager – a stereotype reconsidered', *Sex Roles*, **46**(11/12), 385–91.
Willmott, H. (2011), '"Institutional work" for what? Problems and prospects of institutional theory', *Journal of Management Inquiry*, **20**(1), 67–72.

5. Gendered understanding of recruitment processes: applications and résumés
Ulla Hytti

'Think manager–think male' suggests a gender stereotype that explains why women may have it substantially more difficult in entering management positions. This stereotype suggests that being a man comes with characteristics and competences requested and valued by the recruiters (Kniveton, 2008) and, vice versa, when thinking about managers we may automatically associate them with men. On the other hand, gender discrimination in job recruitment is prohibited by law in most Western European countries. For example, in Finland it is against the law to inquire about the job applicants' plans for having a family. Yet, it would be naive to assume that gender does not also play a role in recruitment processes in a country like Finland.

Recruitment is a key human resource management (HRM) lever in building a diverse workforce (Evans, 2012). Although résumés (CVs) and their evaluation are the first step in most employment decisions, there is a lack of solid understanding of the résumé evaluation process when compared to, for example, employment interview research (Cole et al., 2007). HRM books as well as interviews with recruiters put forward an objective view of recruitment processes. However, extant research seems to suggest that the actual processes are based much more on intuition, emotions and tacit knowledge than the official story suggests (Proença and De Oliveira, 2009). Hence, one can assume that by investigating the job résumé evaluation process it is possible to look at these non-rational, intuitive processes from a gender perspective in a much more reliable and interesting way than, for example, by interviewing the recruiters.

This chapter focuses on how gender is 'done' when examining, reviewing and evaluating job applications and résumés, and analyses how gender is being produced and reproduced through gendering processes (West and Zimmerman, 1987). Since gender discrimination is constrained by law and by social standards, gender practices are complex, nuanced and multifaceted. The chapter explicitly shows how these subtle and nuanced gender practices are carried out in the context of recruitment. Methodologically, the chapter relies on the idea of scripts and scripting behaviour (Garfinkel, 1989), as, typically, job applications and résumés contain a lot of information that needs to be processed effectively. Hence, it is not possible to consider each and every detail but the reviewers will need to make some decisions with little or unconscious processing – for example, to judge if a person possesses or does not possess certain characteristics, abilities or skills (Cole et al., 2005). Consequently it is interesting to analyse the résumé evaluation discussion and the different automatic or non-automatic scripts therein.

RECRUITMENT DECISION-MAKING AND GENDER

Cole et al. (2007) draw our attention to the fact that although résumés and their evaluation are the first step in most employment decisions, there is a lack of solid understanding of the résumé evaluation process if compared to, for example, employment interview research. Hence, they suggest that more research into investigating pre-employment assessments is needed and a better understanding of how recruiters integrate applicants' résumé information is critical. Proença and De Oliveira (2009) conducted a study in Portugal to investigate decision-making processes with regard to CV analysis and selection. In the first phase of their study they interviewed participants and the results confirmed a rational step-by-step process based on explicit policy and evaluation of candidates' abilities to perform well in the position. In the second phase the participants were handed 20 CVs and asked to classify them into three categories – rejected, accepted or stand-by – and they were asked to state their reasoning. Based on the analysis the authors conclude that the actual process relies much more on intuition, emotions and tacit knowledge than was evident based on the interviews.

Some studies have already focused on gender in the context of recruitment. Kniveton (2008) found that recruiters consider men to have more male management characteristics, which were also seen as 'good' management skills. Holgersson (2013) studied homosociality in the context of top management recruitment in Sweden, where homosociality is applied to refer to men's preference for recruiting other men. She suggests that homosociality is done through two practices of redefining competences and doing hierarchy, which results in a preference for certain men and the exclusion of women. In redefining competences the acceptability and suitability criteria are matched with the preferred male candidate. Competences associated with men and masculinity are valued and competences that are valued also become male and masculine. Hierarchy is done 'when senior men identify, groom and select younger men that in return make themselves available and visible, conform to the management norm and at the same time contribute something new and valuable' (Holgersson, 2013, p. 463). She further concludes that this is an unreflexive practice where the adverse consequences upon women are not recognized.

Even if gender equality policies and practices are promoted, the findings demonstrate that they may lack 'teeth' or may even be counterproductive in actually influencing gender equality (Van den Brink et al., 2010; Evans, 2012). For example, initiatives to promote upward mobility of women in academia are being hijacked by gender practices. To suggest there is a need for such initiatives also indicates that women are being thought of as inferior since they are not measured against the male candidates (Van den Brink et al., 2010). Hence, this reflects the gender-neutral view that if only women are good enough, their advancement in academia, for example, is guaranteed.

Naturally we need to refrain from the idea that gender practices in recruitment refer simply to women. Hareli et al. (2008) investigated whether hiring decisions were influenced by perceived femininity and masculinity as inferred from the applicants' previous career history. The results suggest that when the applicants had previously occupied another gender-atypical position, both women and men were perceived more suitable for a new gender-atypical job. In addition, men with gender-atypical career histories were considered less suitable for a gender-typical position. Consequently, gender is associated with not only the applicant's gender and the associated competences but also with the type of work. To put it simply, a man doing a 'woman's job' becomes more of a woman than the men holding 'men's jobs'.

Individuals also include non-work-related experience in their résumés and applications – for example, about their hobbies to project certain values, or activities in different life domains in general. Recruiters will also apply this information in their decision-making (Wilkin and Connelly, 2012). Tanguay et al. (2012) analysed the impact of sports participation and gender on inferences drawn from résumés. Based on the study it was found that recruiters did infer a difference in the skills athletes possess. Hence, not only previous work history but also non-work-related experiences count in the recruitment evaluation. The results further specify that the type of sport (team/individual) further impacts the recruiters' evaluation. Finally, women athletes were perceived as having better team skills, as well as being more likeable and well rounded than male athletes. Consequently, it is the combination of gender and the type of non-work experience that is interesting.

ETHNOMETHODOLOGICAL PERSPECTIVE USING COGNITIVE SCRIPT THEORY

Methodologically, this chapter is based on Garfinkel's (1989) ethnomethodological perspective on how ordinary activities are produced (also see Ten Have, 2007; for other organization studies applying this approach, refer to, for example, Linstead, 2006; Fox, 2008; Llewellyn, 2008). According to this perspective, there is an expectation of a proper way of behaving – social order – governing social encounters such as the evaluation of the job applications and résumés. In this chapter the aim is to analyse what kind of gendered scripts are applied in the HRM context, and in particular as part of the recruitment process. We believe that by identifying the scripts and the scripting behaviours it is also possible to uncover the social order governing the processing of job applications.

Script is 'a schematic knowledge structure held in memory that specifies behaviour or event sequences that are appropriate for specific situations' (Gioia and Poole, 1984, p. 449). Scripts are considered important as they provide a unique approach to understanding how people understand social events. They are considered to have a dual function for individuals as they enable the understanding of events and they provide a guide to appropriate behaviour in that given contextual situation. Scripts can be acquired directly – through experience – but also indirectly by means of communication or media. Consequently, individuals do not need to be experienced recruiters to enact scripted behaviour of the résumé evaluation process. However, although it is wrong to assume that scripts are the basis of all automatic behaviour without processing, people do not devote equally intensive thought to all decisions. Familiar or stereotypical situations can be handled with little or unconscious processing (Gioia and Poole, 1984). Cole et al. (2007) demonstrate how the recruiters use résumé information to form causal judgements regarding whether or not applicants possess certain work-related skills or abilities. In a similar vein, cognitive schemas and specifically role schemas, that is, how the recruiter expects an individual occupying a certain role to behave, are used for evaluation and serve as a basis to predict future behaviour of the individual. Llewellyn and Spence (2009) argue that, during recruitment interviews, candidates act and are treated in ways that would not be considered normal or acceptable in other settings and that it is possible to identify these interviews as 'job interviews' if only by listening to just a short excerpt. In a similar vein, we may expect that résumé evaluation talk can be identified as this type of very distinguishable kind of discussion, which may be analysed.

DATA COLLECTION

The research materials were collected by organizing four focus groups: two made up of HR professionals and recruiters and two with 'individuals in transition' (unemployed professionals seeking a new job and updating their skills and knowledge base by participating in a further education training programme). Thus, the two types of groups are positioned differently to the job application process, which was believed to be interesting given the approach selected. If the gender scripts are culturally shared and 'highly scripted' then they can be identified in all of the group discussions irrespective of the participants' position or their individual experiences of recruiting.

The focus groups were assigned one job advertisement (for a CEO in a local affiliate of a multinational company in two of the focus groups and for a marketing manager in a similar company in the other two focus groups) and job applications and résumés of six applicants. The materials were developed by the researcher based on real-life materials. However, the details of the advertisements and applications were changed to create match cases of different kinds of career portfolios including different forms of paid, unpaid and voluntary work, and non-work (Clinton et al., 2006). The aim was to invite the focus groups to discuss openly and generally 'how different careers are evaluated in recruitment decision-making', and therefore the applicants have a broad variety of different types and durations of work experience (see Table 5.1). Hence, the stated aim was not focused on gender or any particular issue. In fact, the focus on gender only became interesting inductively based on the preliminary analysis. For this reason the mix of candidates is not balanced but consists of four men and two women. Methodologically, this is an important consideration as the discussion yielded rich information about how different types of work and non-work experiences were evaluated and hence it is possible to mirror these evaluations against each other.

DATA ANALYSIS

In this chapter the analysis is focused on what kind of scripts the participants draw upon when assessing the candidates and what kind of scripted processing can be identified in the discussion. All the focus group discussions, which lasted between 58 minutes and 1 hour 20 minutes, were transcribed verbatim. Next, the transcriptions were carefully read to identify different themes and issues, and to also identify recurring themes between the different interview sessions. This yielded several interesting themes but

Table 5.1 Background information of the applicants

Applicant	Age & Sex	Education	Work Experience	Other
Simo Saarinen	46 years, male	MSc (Bus. Adm.), 1989	5½ years as CEO/self-employed in a small importing firm 5½ years as CEO in a small manufacturing firm 6 years in sales and other business expert positions	No explanation given in the résumé for the business exit
Asta Laine	30 years, female	MSc (Bus. Adm.), 2008	2 years as CEO/director in a foundation 2 years as project coordinator in the business school Several short-term, for example, summer jobs, in different organizations	Hobbies: handicraft, poetry and folk dancing
Mikko Jokela	47 years, male	MSc (Eng.)	16 years in project and factory management in manufacturing firms (14 years with one employer)	Lists a lot of hobbies in the résumé (in particular different sports)
Matti Virtanen	28 years, male	MSc (Bus. Adm.)	2 years as sales manager in a sports organization Some short-term, for example, summer jobs	Former professional athlete Hobbies: football and dogs
Heikki Saarenpää	45 years, male	Has studied in a School of Business Adm. (no degree)	11 years as CEO/self-employed in an importing company 4 years as head of department in a sales company 11 years in sales and marketing 4 years in sales	Sold his business in 2010 Hobbies: sports, cooking and culture
Katja Kondratjeff	35 years, female	MSc (Bus. Adm.), 2003	2 years in an importing company (responsible for operations in Finland) Short-term project manager or trainee positions	Has taken parental leave twice, first for 3 years and then for 1.5 years Hobbies: cooking and family life, including baby swimming

for the purposes of this study it was decided to focus on two stereotypically gendered themes – that of parental leave and experience gained from being a professional athlete. Both these experiences – parenting and professional sports – can be conceptualized as gaps in the organizational career trajectory and they were also discussed along these lines. Gaps in working history are often presented as a challenge when seeking a new job as they may even imply mental health problems or stays in prison (Clarke, 1989), and hence they are both important to study further but also may provide important insight for further analysis. These gaps are also very different and distinguishable from each other – and carry with them strong gender connotations – providing a basis for interesting insights and parallels despite their very different nature. Finland is known for gender equality, which can be seen in the way men are increasingly assuming responsibilities in the family and household matters. The parental leave system allows parents to choose whether it is the mother or father who stays at home with the child when the child is under 12 months of age. Nevertheless, it is still primarily mothers who stay at home (Lammi-Taskula, 2008; Haas and Rostgaard, 2011). Hence, despite gender-neutral institutional arrangements the practice of parental leave continues to be highly gendered in Finland. In addition, while women play sports and are active as athletes it is also known that most female athletes – in particular, in team sports – cannot earn a living as professional athletes. It is only the male leagues that are able to attract sponsors and hire professional athletes and, depending on the sport, even they find it quite difficult. Hence, being a professional athlete in team sports carries a strong male connotation.

OUTCOMES

In this section we take two examples of possible gaps: maternity and parental leave of a female candidate and a gap resulting from being a professional soccer player of a male candidate. Since it is typical for the reviewers to discuss and mirror the applicants against one another, in the analysis this strategy is also applied. In addition to reflecting these two cases against one another, some examples from the discussion with regard to the other candidates are presented in the analysis.

Katja, a candidate with maternity and parental leave in her résumé, is discussed in one of the groups:

> She is not giving any clues why she is seeking a job here in this region [involving a move from Eastern to Western Finland]? And when you look at her working history, you'll find this maternity and parental leave, which means probably

that she has small children and if this work involves travelling to Sweden, so does she have any support networks?

Yes, absolutely [this needs to be explained]. Otherwise it raises a question why this [person] would come here . . .

Since she has this handicap due to certain issues it needs to be explained in the résumé somehow that this person despite this would be worth checking and there was really nothing in the résumé . . .

Contrary to what many women's magazines would like to suggest, the long maternity and parental leaves in the résumé do not evoke the 'mom as the master manager and organizer' script but the more traditionally placed 'handicap script'. In this script the candidate is expected to explain very clearly how she might be a good candidate despite the 'deficiencies' in her résumé. She would also need to explain how she could move from her current place of residence and accept a job with travelling requirements. As a woman she is assumed to occupy the role of the household or family manager and she needs to ensure that the children are cared for if she takes up a job that involves travelling. Her spouse is not suggested as a potential and capable person for this duty but a reference is made to other 'support networks', which is an expression used to refer to grandparents or other relatives.

In another discussion the group had first considered the other candidates before reviewing and evaluating Katja's application. After a long silence the weaknesses and strengths in her application are listed and finally the group decides it is time to make a decision on who will be invited for an interview. First, the group decides to see and interview two more experienced men but then decides the following:

[A]nd the third one would be this [Katja] yeah. Of these younger applicants I would choose this Katja.

I also thought of three, and one would get some contrast by asking this Mrs person [Katja] and then clearly two more experienced men.

Hence, this script can be seen to be influenced by considerations of gender neutrality and sensitivity. The long silence is indicative of the need to think and process what to say of this candidate. Her selection for the interview as one of three can be seen as a surprising turn in the overall discussion and one cannot help but understand this as a way of trying to accommodate the gender equality script and avoid any accusations of gender discrimination. However, mirroring Katja (as the 'Mrs person') against the two 'clearly more experienced men' leaves us with the impression that she is merely a token and this comparative setting makes the other two candidates (the experienced men) look even better.

In another group the choice of people to interview results in a selection of men. Due to gender sensitivity and legal issues involved in gender discrimination as part of the recruitment, in the other focus group discussions this stereotypical script is complemented with further processing:

> What would the gender equality council say when we have cold-heartedly left the women . . .?
> Isn't this exactly gender equality that we deal with the applications according to their merits?
> Yes, isn't it so. There were no good female candidates.

The gender equality script pushes the participants to aim to find one woman for the interview. Like in the previous script only the choice of men seems difficult. The excerpt seems to demonstrate that the participants understand this selection to be only ceremonial, and in this case, for example, Katja is not seriously considered but is invited only to fill the quota, and whether this is really worth the effort of Katja travelling several hours is questioned. The final comment visualizes her taking her baby into the baby swimming class, which she has listed as one of her hobbies in her résumé, and against that visual image it is definitely difficult to see how she could be able to fill in the requirements of the job:

> I would have liked to see one woman [Katja] at the interview . . .
> But she would need to come here all the way from Eastern Finland so that you want to see her.
> How does her current family situation enable such a demanding task . . . [She is] now taking her baby to baby swimming and so . . .

In the final excerpt from the discussion about Katja, the group recognizes the gender practice with regard to the résumés and applications in themselves. Women as the primary family caretakers need to say how the family is not a problem for them in terms of taking care of their work. Men as the primary breadwinners in the family do not need to take the family into account. The assumption is that there is a wife who assumes the main responsibility for the family and children:

> This [Katja] is the only one who discusses her family background more, it becomes evident from the résumé and also from this application.
> Is this typical for women? Do they have this family tie, do they experience that it is more important to make the family visible? Men are a bit more detached, that they can just be themselves. Women need to say somehow that this [family] is not a problem, is this it?

It is not simply family and parental leave that are gendered and produce gendered scripts. The other female candidate, Asta, is slightly more experienced than Katja. She has been in charge of the operations and acted

Gendered understanding of recruitment processes 83

as a CEO, but in a foundation, not in a 'real' firm. Despite this management experience this wrong type of organization also creates a handicap for Asta together with her other, non-work-related interests. Hence she becomes labelled and stereotyped as an artistic person, not suited for a managing an industrial firm:

> In my view [she is] fully clever but then there were these rock festivals, and I wrote here – excuse me but – I wrote 'artistic type' and a question mark.
> Artistic type [laughter] handicraft, poetry . . .
> Is she really up to managing a manufacturing firm, has she experience, I was not inviting her [for an interview] . . .

The above excerpt seems to suggest that here management experience is not enough. Asta's experience from running a foundation, possibly a gender-typical area for women, does not provide her with the capabilities and skills necessary for running a manufacturing firm.

One of the candidates, Matti, is a recent graduate from a business school and while his work experience is not extensive, his application is reviewed appreciatively:

> Here is one – if we are grooming someone here, here is one for whom this would fit like a nose into a head, if we think this from the individual's point of view.
> If we think that here is Matti Virtanen, MSc in business in 2008 and has held these types of sales positions already while studying so this would be a clear step up the ladder for him.

In all of the groups it is not his education or experience that interest them most but his experience from working as a professional athlete, as a soccer player at national level. Overall, this evokes a very positive assessment of his abilities for both of the two positions (marketing manager and CEO). His capabilities are considered strong due to the team-working skills, and ambitious and goal-oriented behaviour he has learned as an athlete. His lack of work-related experience and prolongation of his studies are excused because of sports. The two women candidates have a business degree and due to their relatively short work experience the position would be a good step up for them as well; however, they lack the experience from sports.

While in Katja's case the responsibility was assigned to her for making it explicit why she is a worthy candidate for the position, in Matti's case it is the group that starts providing the reasons:

> [T]hat [previous working experience] has been a little like peanuts compared to this job [he applies to].
> Yes, he has been a professional athlete.

> One needs to start somewhere [Matti has worked in marketing for the local soccer team after his professional athlete career], it is positive if you can keep the TPS (name of the local team in Turku) on the dry [that is, profitable], it is quite an achievement. [Laughter]
>
> He is clearly the candidate with the biggest potential because if you have made it as a professional in soccer, it says a lot about attitude and goal-orientation there . . .

While this script is automatic and hence could be interpreted as highly stereotypical, it is not fully accepted:

> I started wondering that what you said . . . [Matti's] working history, it has a long break. That he has not been in practice, how many summers did go by, four or five summers have gone by where he had not practically worked at all so what has he done?
>
> [Matti] has been a professional athlete . . . so in a way it could be forgivable that the studies have taken him a bit longer.
>
> [I]t doesn't have to be sports, some people work at the same time [while studying], and they can have a family. You cannot overemphasize the role of sports . . .

Another male candidate, Mikko, is also discussed for the positions. It is interesting to parallel the discussion about Mikko with Asta. Asta was labelled as the 'artistic type' and Mikko is the 'production type'. This conveys the résumé evaluation process and the need to quickly sort the individuals into different categories and piles, and to assign them quickly into artistic or production types helps in this process. Stereotyping is a tool for recruiters to make sense of candidates:

> But this Mikko for example, this production man, experienced engineer who is fluent in languages, he has a long work history of . . . but I would not invite him, long work history but production oriented, not for this job . . .
>
> I paid attention to the same thing, I wrote here that 'Production type' . . .

In another group, attention is paid to Mikko's non-work profile. The following excerpt leads us to think that when for a woman having family and small children in particular may be considered a liability, not having a family and children may also be a liability in the case of a man. Not having a family is unusual and may result in him not being domesticated but creating havoc at Christmas parties. At the same time it can also be advantageous as he may commit fully to the organization, but in Mikko's case this interpretation is suspect due to his many hobbies that may give the impression of being active but that this high level of activity may not always be beneficial for the company:

> Did I understand correctly that he [Mikko] did not have any family, no wife or children [are discussed] . . . Single . . . [laughter] Horror at [office] Christmas parties.

> His level of commitment to the organization is very high when he does not have [a family] ... No wonder he has so many hobbies, it gave an active impression at least.

SUMMARY AND CONCLUSIONS

This chapter has focused on investigating how gender is done when examining, reviewing and evaluating job applications and résumés. The contribution of the chapter explicitly shows the nuanced gendered practices in the context of recruitment, an area strongly influenced by gender equality laws and social norms. Methodologically the study has relied on the idea of scripts and scripting behaviour (Garfinkel, 1989) in that when reviewing job applications and résumés it is not possible to give equal thought to all details and therefore some decisions are made with little processing. Even though in this study the groups had only six applicants to consider they still resorted to stereotyping (artistic type, production type), and applied these stereotypes to make decisions as to who to select for an interview.

The research materials were gathered from four focus groups that were differently positioned to the job application process (two groups of experienced recruiters and HR managers and two groups of active job seekers). Based on the analysis there were no major differences between the discussions in the different groups, in terms of the job applicants' groups of being more forgiving to the gaps and deficiencies in the applications and in the applicants' capabilities and skills. All of the groups consisted of both women and men but no particular patterns were identified based on the participant gender. Women were no more or less favourable to the candidate with the parental leave in her résumé than men. The results therefore demonstrate that first, the résumé evaluation processes in general, and second, the way gender is done, are culturally shared and scripted. Therefore, recruiters and job seekers, as well as men and women, are resorting to and reproducing the similar scripts.

Gender discrimination is naturally a very sensitive issue when it comes to recruiting. Hence, the participants of the focus groups needed to be quite reflexive of what they said and how they evaluated Katja, an applicant with quite a few gaps in her résumé due to parental leave. Legally the parental leave does not provide reasons to reject a candidate but this, however, takes place in everyday life. They either took time in the group to reflect upon this – marked by the long silence in the middle of a very active discussion where one found it hard to be given an opportunity to speak – or they made it explicit that they would have liked to also have women in the interview but regretted that there were not any good female

86 *Handbook of gendered careers in management*

candidates. They also pondered upon how their decision to choose only men will look from the outside and hence the gender equality demands made it very difficult to choose only men and they needed to process this decision actively. Possibly due to this pressure, in one group the decision to invite a woman was taken despite the inferiority of the candidate in relation to the competition from two more experienced men. Hence, she could be understood as a token (Kanter, 1977; Poutanen and Kovalainen, 2013) invited for an interview without any serious consideration for her employment. Her inexperience will provide a good contrast for the experienced men and it is easy to choose between them. However, from the outside the gender equality laws and norms are fulfilled once a woman is included among the interviewees. Hence, it is possible to understand this as a process of tokenism that creates and reinforces the unequal gender positions in recruitment. The selection of these particular candidates provides visibility for the dominant group of men and emphasizes the differences between them and the female candidate through contrasting (Poutanen and Kovalainen, 2013).

On the other hand, Katja's 'handicap script' is produced in reference to her résumé with parental leave: the discussion pushes the responsibility towards the candidate. She should be able to convince the evaluators why she should be considered as a candidate despite her 'handicap'. It is also noted that she is sharing information about and explaining her family situation, and this is identified as a gender practice by the evaluators. Women need to accommodate and explain how they can manage work besides their family and small children, while men need not tell this story. This may be a double-edged sword for the female applicants: they need to explain how the family is not a problem for them in terms of taking care of their work but while doing this, they also project gender-typical behaviour of being family oriented, and hence are suspected of not being able to perform successfully in the demanding job of a manager, for example. On the other hand, the lack of family and children may be a handicap for men. For a man, having a wife and family may be a stabilizing factor and this may help them to project a reliable and stable image. A single man is suspected of causing turmoil at the firm's social events. This is a stereotypical expectation of male behaviour: single men will always be on the lookout for (sexual) partners, which may have unwelcome consequences at the organization.

The parental leave as a gap in the hierarchical organizational work history in this study is mirrored against the professional sports experience. It was impressive how the experiences of a professional male soccer player were highly valued for both positions in this study – a marketing manager and a CEO – even though the applicant's relevant work experience was not extensive. His competences developed in sports can be understood as masculine and male, which are valued for a position in management (Holgersson, 2013). The lack of relevant work experience was noted by some of the participants with the consequence that it was the other participants who started defending the candidate and explaining the merits and abilities gained as a professional athlete. This is possibly related to not only the sports per se but the fact that it is team sports, soccer, that are associated with ambition, goal-orientation and team-working abilities. The notable difference is that it was not the candidate (Matti) who is held responsible for making sense of this gap as with Katja. Nevertheless, appreciating certain types of non-work experiences (professional sports) over others (parental leave) is a highly gendered process. Women have fewer opportunities than men to play sports at a professional level, and they typically take more parental leave than men. In addition, having hobbies that could be seen as feminine and work experience from organizations that are labelled as feminine seem not to qualify as relevant experience or profile the candidate as a serious applicant for a job in the manufacturing company.

This research was not originally designed to study the role of gender, parental leave or professional sports experience in recruitment but more broadly to investigate different types of careers and how they are assessed in recruitment decision-making. The downside of this approach is that there were only two female candidates to be discussed. For the purposes of this research question it would have been interesting to have even more variation between the different candidates, for example, to mirror the evaluation of a male and female candidate with parental leave or of professional athletes representing different sports. However, this limitation is also the strength of this approach. The participants in the groups were not pushed into discussing gender, parental leave, sports experience or any particular issue with regard to the candidates but they could freely choose what issues to talk about, which makes the focus group discussions all the more pertinent.

To summarize, based on an inductive study of focus groups discussing potential candidates it became obvious how gender plays an important role in recruiters' evaluations. Overt gender discrimination is avoided but gendering is done in subtle and nuanced ways. First, the evaluators infer gendered expectations for the behaviour of mothers with children and of single men. Second, the applicants' work and non-work experiences become valued differently depending on the gendered labels assigned to them. More research is called for to investigate the job recruitment processes from a gender perspective. Future studies could apply a similar process to this research but include matches of the different cases (men and women with parental leave and with professional sports experience) as it would be highly interesting to know how men with parental leave, for example, are evaluated in recruitment.

REFERENCES

Clarke, J. (1989), *The Right Way to Write Your Own C.V.*, Kingswood, UK: Elliot Right Way Books.
Clinton, M., P. Totterdell and S. Wood (2006), 'A grounded theory of portfolio working experiencing the smallest of small businesses', *International Small Business Journal*, **24**(2), 179–203.
Cole, M.S., H.S. Field and J.O. Stafford (2005), 'Validity of résumé reviewers' inferences concerning applicant personality based on résumé evaluation', *International Journal of Selection and Assessment*, **13**(4), 321–4.
Cole, M.S., R.S. Rubin, H.S. Field and W.F. Giles (2007), 'Recruiters' perceptions and use of applicant résumé information: screening the recent graduate', *Applied Psychology: An International Review*, **56**(2), 319–43.
Evans, C. (2012), 'Recruitment initiatives aimed at increasing the gender diversity within ITEC employment. Not so "gender neutral"?', *Equality, Diversity and Inclusion: An International Journal*, **31**(8), 741–52.
Fox, S. (2008), '"That miracle of familiar organizational things": social and moral order in the MBA classroom', *Organization Studies*, **29**(5), 733–61.
Garfinkel, H. (1989), *Studies in Ethnomethodology*, Cambridge, UK, Polity Press.
Gioia, D.A. and P.P. Poole (1984), 'Scripts in organizational behavior', *Academy of Management Review*, **9**(3), 449–59.
Haas, L. and T. Rostgaard (2011), 'Fathers' rights to paid parental leave in the Nordic countries: consequences for the gendered division of leave', *Community, Work & Family*, **14**(2), 177–95.
Hareli, S., M. Klang and U. Hess (2008), 'The role of career history in gender based biases in job selection decisions', *Career Development International*, **13**(3), 252–69.
Holgersson, C. (2013), 'Recruiting managing directors: doing homosociality', *Gender, Work and Organization*, **20**(4), 454–66.
Kanter, R.M. (1977), *Men and Women of the Corporation*, New York: Basic Books.
Kniveton, B.M. (2008), 'Recruiters/selectors' perceptions of male and female trainee managers', *Journal of European Industrial Training*, **32**(6), 404–17.
Lammi-Taskula, J. (2008), 'Doing fatherhood: understanding the gendered use of parental leave in Finland', *Fathering: A Journal of Theory, Research, & Practice about Men as Fathers*, **6**(2), 133–48.
Linstead, S. (2006), 'Ethnomethodology and sociology: an introduction', *Sociological Review*, **54**(3), 399–404.
Llewellyn, N. (2008), 'Organization in actual episodes of work: Harvey Sacks and organization studies', *Organization Studies*, **29**(5), 763–91.
Llewellyn, N. and L. Spence (2009), 'Practice as a members' phenomenon', *Organization Studies*, **30**(12), 1419–39.
Poutanen, S. and A. Kovalainen (2013), 'Gendering innovation process in an industrial plant – revisiting tokenism, gender and innovation', *International Journal of Gender and Entrepreneurship*, **5**(3), 257–74.
Proença, M.T.V.C. and E.T.V.D de Oliveira (2009), 'From normative to tacit knowledge: CVs analysis in personnel selection', *Employee Relations*, **31**(4), 427–47.
Tanguay, D.M., R.R. Camp, M.L. Endres and E. Torres (2012), 'The impact of sports participation and gender on inferences drawn from résumés', *Journal of Managerial Issues*, **24**(2), 191–206.

Ten Have, P. (2007), 'Ethnomethodology', in C. Seale, G. Gobo, J.F. Gubrium and D. Silverman (eds), *Qualitative Research Practice*, London: Sage Publications, pp. 139–52.
Van den Brink, M., Y. Benschop and W. Jansen (2010), 'Transparency in academic recruitment: a problematic tool for gender equality?', *Organization Studies*, **31**(11), 1459–83.
West, C. and D. Zimmermann (1987), 'Doing gender', *Gender and Society*, **1**(2), 125–51.
Wilkin, C.L. and C.E. Connelly (2012), 'Do I look like someone who cares? Recruiters' ratings of applicants' paid and volunteer experience', *International Journal of Selection and Assessment*, **20**(3), 308–18.

6. Presumed incompetent: perceived lack of fit and gender bias in recruitment and selection
Madeline E. Heilman, Francesca Manzi and Susanne Braun

Despite women's advancement in the workplace, their representation in male-dominated fields and occupations remains distressingly low. Women now comprise about half of the workforce, but very few end up at the top levels of business organizations. In 2013, women held only 16.9 per cent of corporate board seats in the USA, and only 4.6 per cent of executive directors were women (Catalyst, 2014). Percentages are similar in the UK: 15 per cent of board directors were women, and they comprised less than 7 per cent of the executive positions in British companies (Catalyst, 2012).

What accounts for the scarcity of women in traditionally male roles? It is not a consequence of differential experience, education or skills. The overall percentage of undergraduate and graduate degrees (both Master's and doctoral) obtained by women in the USA and the UK now exceeds that of men (National Center for Education Statistics, 2010; Higher Education Statistics Agency, 2012). Moreover, in terms of cognitive skills and abilities, women and men tend to be more similar than different (Biernat and Deaux, 2012). Rather, we posit that women's participation in the workplace is hindered by gender bias in evaluation, and that this bias has its origin in gender stereotypes.

This chapter will focus on how gender bias affects the recruitment and selection of women in traditionally male occupations. We will describe the process by which gender stereotypes produce gender bias in hiring decisions, and illustrate how, despite evidence to the contrary, women can be judged as undeserving of jobs typically held by men. The 'lack of fit' model (Heilman, 1983, 2001) will be used as a framework for understanding the causes and consequences of gender bias in the recruitment and selection of women in organizations. It also will serve as a model for suggested remedial action.

GENDER STEREOTYPES

Stereotypes are a structured set of beliefs about the attributes of a group of people that are ascribed to individuals categorized as a member of that group. As one of the most salient human features, gender often serves as a cue for these types of generalizations (Blair and Banaji, 1996), and gender stereotypes commonly dominate inferences about the characteristics of men and women. These stereotypes, and the assumptions they carry about what men and women are like, are the basis of gender bias.

The Content of Gender Stereotypes

Research has demonstrated that stereotypes about women differ significantly from stereotypes about men. While men tend to be thought of as 'agentic', women tend to be thought of as 'communal' (for example, Diekman and Eagly, 2000). Agency comprises attributes such as achievement orientation (for example, able, successful), assertiveness (for example, dominant, forceful) and autonomy (for example, independent, self-reliant); while communality denotes consideration for others (for example, caring, helpful), affiliation with others (for example, sociable, likable) and emotional sensitivity (for example, tender, sensitive). Moreover, the content of gender stereotypes tends to be oppositional, such that women are seen not only as communal but also as lacking agency, and men are seen not only as agentic but also as lacking communality.

The Persistence of Gender Stereotypes

There is some indication that gender stereotypes have changed as women's roles in society have changed (for example, Duehr and Bono, 2006), but this finding is overshadowed by a large body of literature indicating that the characteristics ascribed to men and women have remained quite consistent over time (Auster and Ohm, 2000; Spence and Buckner, 2000). A recent survey of 529 men and women from different age groups and backgrounds found that men are still rated significantly more highly than women on assertiveness and capability, and women still are rated significantly more highly than men on communal traits (Hentschel et al., 2013).

Gender stereotypes are also pervasive. They have been shown to be consistent across cultures (Williams and Best, 1990), to exist in work as well as non-work settings (Heilman et al., 1989), and to be held by women as well as men (Parks-Stamm et al., 2008). In addition, there is evidence that gender stereotypes can be activated automatically without evaluators' awareness of their impact (Banaji and Hardin, 1996).

In the following section we will illustrate the impact of gender stereotypes on recruitment and selection processes. Specifically, we will consider how women can be disadvantaged when applying for a position not because of their characteristics or experience, but because of the attributes associated with their gender.

THE LACK OF FIT MODEL

Gender stereotypes have important implications for perceptions of how well women fit with different workplace positions. This is particularly the case when these positions are perceived to be male gender-typed.

The Gender Typing of Workplace Roles and Positions

Male gender-typed occupations are thought to require characteristics that are associated with men, not with women. These requirements are assumed in roles and positions that are disproportionally dominated by men simply because of the skewed gender representation. Research has indeed demonstrated high correlations between sex ratios of job incumbents and the ascribed gender type (Cejka and Eagly, 1999).

However, some roles are male gender-typed because of culturally shared inferences about the nature of the job's responsibilities. For upper-level positions in organizations (for example, top management), agentic behaviours are thought to be necessary for success (Gaucher et al., 2011). In fact, research repeatedly supports the idea that the attributes thought to be prototypical of successful managers are those that coincide with stereotypic conceptions of men (for example, Powell et al., 2002; see also Powell, 2011 for an overview). Moreover, inferences about job responsibilities are determined by the context in which the job exists. Occupational sector (military vs education), professional subfield (corporate law vs family law), and functional area (finance vs human relations) can have implications for inferences about job responsibilities, and therefore play a role in determining whether and to what degree a job is viewed as male gender-typed.

Lack of Fit Perceptions

Lack of fit perceptions are triggered by the perceived mismatch between what women are thought to be like and what people believe it takes to succeed in male gender-typed occupations (Heilman, 1983, 2001, 2012). Because of gender stereotypes, women are thought to lack the agentic characteristics necessary for successful performance in these jobs (Heilman et al., 1989; Schein, 2001). This incongruity between conceptions of women and beliefs about job requirements creates a perceived 'lack of fit' that has important consequences for women's entry into organizations. Specifically, it creates the expectation that a female applicant is ill equipped to perform the job and will not be competent if selected. These negative performance expectations form the basis of gender bias in employment decision-making.

Negative Performance Expectations and Information Processing

Negative performance expectations arising from lack of fit perceptions have major consequences for selection decisions because they promote cognitive distortion in the way evaluators process information about job candidates. Performance expectations are tenacious and have a way of perpetuating themselves (Heilman and Haynes, 2008). If potentially disconfirming information can be discounted or dismissed, then the performance expectation can be maintained and possibly even reinforced, making revision unnecessary. There are several ways in which negative performance expectations can affect information processing:

- *Attention.* Research shows that information consistent with expectations is readily attended to, but inconsistent information may not even be noticed (for example, Plaks et al., 2001). For example, information about excellence in a reference letter may be overlooked if this information is inconsistent with expectations. But noticing potentially disconfirming information is not sufficient to challenge expectations; it also has to be attended to. This does not happen if the perceiver discounts the information as irrelevant. If, for example, a female candidate's successful performance is attributed not to her skills and talents but rather to a lucky break or an easy task, this information is likely to be ignored, leaving the original expectation unchallenged. These ideas are consistent with the finding that evaluators spend less time attending to the work behaviours of individuals about whom there are stereotype-based expectations than about individuals for whom there are no such expectations (Favero and Ilgen, 1989).
- *Information interpretation.* Even if expectation-inconsistent information is attended to, its interpretation can nullify its effect. Evidence shows that the meaning attached to an action can be influenced by expectations (Kunda et al., 1997), and gender-based expectations have been shown to result in very different interpretations of the

same behaviour (Taylor et al., 1978). For example, being decisive and forceful may be viewed as an indication of leadership in a man, but of 'being bossy' in a woman (Sandberg, 2013). Consequently, rather than challenging negative performance expectations arising from lack of fit perceptions, the gendered interpretation of a potentially disconfirming behaviour can serve to reinforce them.

- *Recall of information.* Research has shown that people remember expectation-consistent information at a higher rate than expectation-inconsistent information (Fyock and Stangor, 1994; Pittinsky et al., 2000). For women undergoing screening and assessment as part of a selection process for male-typed jobs, this translates into lesser recall of stereotype-inconsistent information about past behaviours or accomplishments, even if such information is highly relevant to the position (Perry et al., 1994). Recall can even be distorted to the point that people 'remember' events that did not happen (for example, erroneously recalling an unpleasant interchange that did not actually occur), if these events are consistent with their beliefs (Higgins and Bargh, 1987; Lenton et al., 2001).

Thus, the negative performance expectations arising from lack of fit perceptions can lead to distortions in information processing that produce biased evaluations of women, no matter what their credentials are for the job. These biased evaluations then become the basis of selection decisions.

LACK OF FIT PERCEPTIONS AND SELECTION DECISIONS

The larger the perceived discrepancy between what women are thought to be like and what is thought to be required for job success in male-typed positions, the greater the perceived lack of fit and the more negative performance expectations will be. More negative performance expectations should, according to the lack of fit model, result in higher levels of gender bias in evaluations and selection decisions. Empirical evidence supports this proposition, suggesting that both components of the model – the activation of gender stereotypes when a woman is considered for a job and the gendered perception of the job itself – affect the occurrence of gender bias.

Gender Type of Position

Positions seen as male in gender type should produce more negative performance expectations of women than positions not seen as male gender-typed, leading to higher levels of gender bias and more negative selection outcomes. A meta-analysis of 49 studies in social and organizational psychology provides support for this idea (Davison and Burke, 2000). The results revealed a consistent bias against women in selection decisions when the position was male gender-typed, with women receiving lower selection ratings and lower compensation offers than men. Bias was not evident when the position was not male gender-typed, and in fact reversed when the position was female gender-typed. So, as lack of fit ideas would predict, whether a position is or is not male gender-typed has a profound effect on the incidence of gender bias.

There also are degrees of gender typing: a position is male gender-typed to the extent to which stereotypic male qualities are thought to be necessary for successful performance (Heilman, 2001; Eagly and Karau, 2002). This can vary as a function of the context. Thus, being a manager at a daycare centre may have different implications for gender typing than being a manager at a financial services firm. It also can vary as a function of the job itself – some jobs are inherently more male gender-typed because of the degree to which 'male' skills and abilities are thought to be required. Whatever its source, however, the result should be the same – the greater the degree of male gender-typing the more bias against women should be evident. This prediction has been tested repeatedly. For example, Lyness and Heilman (2006) demonstrated that women in a large financial services company received less favourable evaluations than men in line jobs (for example, business management, operations management, sales) but not in staff jobs (for example, human resources, administration, external affairs). Thus, even in the same company, negative evaluations were associated with the degree of male gender typing of the position.

Stereotype Activation

Lack of fit perceptions and subsequent negative performance expectations should be exacerbated when gender stereotypes are highly activated. This occurs when gender is salient. As we have mentioned, gender tends to be an inherently salient cue in our environment – readily seen and requiring little thought to discern. Nonetheless, there are conditions that can highlight a woman's gender that, according to the lack of fit model, should also heighten the activation of gender stereotypes and produce more negative evaluative outcomes for women applying to male-typed jobs.

Research bears this out. Investigations of the 'beauty is beastly' effect (Heilman and Stopeck, 1985a, 1985b; Johnson et al., 2010; Braun et al., 2012) demonstrated that physical attractiveness, which was shown to enhance femininity perceptions, led to more negative evaluations of women applying for and performing in male gender-typed positions. Research also has demonstrated that information about a woman being a mother, a societal role that unquestionably makes gender salient, aggravates gender bias in screening recommendations and selection decisions (Heilman and Okimoto, 2008).

Thus, personal attributes that make gender salient can fuel the occurrence of gender bias, but so can structural factors. In particular, there is evidence that token or near-token status, which no doubt makes gender stand out, leads to more stereotyped characterizations of women, and a lesser likelihood of being selected for a male gender-typed position (Heilman and Blader, 2001).

Even organizational practices such as affirmative action and diversity initiatives that are designed to foster gender equality in organizations can draw attention to gender and inadvertently activate stereotypes. Research has indeed shown how women who are thought to be beneficiaries of affirmative action or diversity initiatives are rated as less competent and recommended smaller salary increases than men and women who are not associated with these organizational practices (Heilman and Welle, 2006).

THE ROLE OF AMBIGUITY IN FACILITATING GENDER BIAS

While a perceived lack of fit leads to negative expectations about women's performance, ambiguity amplifies the impact of these expectations on selection decisions. High levels of ambiguity give decision-makers latitude, and performance expectations provide a convenient and efficient guide for making judgements in such situations (Heilman and Haynes, 2008). Ambiguity is high when the information about the job candidate is incomplete, inconsistent or not relevant, when the identification of criteria for consideration is lacking and the rules for comparing candidates are not fixed, and when there is lack of clarity about who is responsible for past accomplishments. It is in these situations that the greatest amount of gender bias would be anticipated.

The Amount and Type of Information Available

When evaluators are provided with incomplete information about applicants, they have to 'fill in the blanks'. Expectations provide a readily available framework for doing that. As a consequence, stereotype-based performance expectations have a stronger impact on subsequent evaluation and decision-making if evaluators receive limited information.

Whilst it has been shown that evaluations of women as compared to men are less favourable when evaluators receive little information about the target (Swim et al., 1989), providing a substantial amount of information about an applicant does not necessarily ensure less gender-biased evaluations. Rather, the information must be job relevant (Heilman, 1984) and unequivocal in its implications for performance (Heilman and Haynes, 2005) in order to avert negative evaluations.

Consistency of the information also is a factor (Chaiken and Maheswaran, 1994; Hodson et al., 2002). Most often, there are both strengths and weaknesses in a person's work history and background, and this mixture requires decision-makers to weigh one type of information against another in making a judgement. This leaves much to the decision-maker's discretion; it is a situation that allows for expectations to dominate in determining what information is given most weight. In such situations, the resolution has been shown to be detrimental to women (Uhlmann and Cohen, 2005). The disparity in competence impressions of women and men whose performance has shown improvement or decline is a case in point (Manzi et al., 2012).

The Specification of Evaluative Criteria and their Standardization

The more poorly defined the judgement criteria, the more expectations can be expected to play a role in evaluative decisions. There are many ways in which judgement criteria can be poorly defined. The evaluative focus can be vague. Impressions of personal characteristics, such as whether a person will be a 'good team player' or a 'forward thinker' are subjective, and more vulnerable to distortion than impressions that have their origins in concrete information about accomplishments and work history. Indeed, there is evidence that evaluators rate communication competence and interpersonal competence less reliably than they rate work quality (Viswesvara et al., 1996).

In addition, the evaluative criteria can be unspecified. Research has shown that when selection benchmarks are left unstated, evaluators tend to define the criteria for job success to be consistent with their preferred job candidate. Evaluators have in fact found people to overstate or understate the importance of the same performance criterion depending on whether it was attributed to a man or a woman (Uhlmann and Cohen, 2005).

The absence of a standardized evaluative structure also can increase the impact of expectations in the evaluation process (Bragger et al., 2002; Biernat et al., 2010). Without such a structure, evaluators are not constrained to consider particular types of information about a job candidate, or to treat all the information in the same way regardless of who the candidate is. This means that different criteria can be used and that the same criteria can be weighted differently when judging different people. Non-uniform standards promote the use of expectations in the processing of information and, not surprisingly, it has been shown that a structured procedure integrating specific observed behaviours rather than an overall judgement reduces gender bias in evaluations (Bauer and Baltes, 2002).

Clarity About the Source of Performance

Ambiguity that arises from lack of information about who is responsible for a joint performance outcome – attributional ambiguity – can also enhance the power of expectations to affect evaluations (Heilman and Haynes, 2005). Attributional ambiguity leaves an opening for negative expectations to provide easy answers about who actually deserves credit for a joint success or blame for a joint failure. Not only is this an issue in the review of past performance, but it is also increasingly an issue in the selection process itself. With the rise of group interviews and assessment centres as selection procedures, team-based evaluations have become increasingly important in hiring decisions. The source of performance is more ambiguous in team settings than in individual task-based work and, therefore, if used for selection, it can be problematic for the evaluation and selection of women, especially in male gender-typed domains.

Studies have demonstrated that when women and men work together on a male gender-typed task, women are given less credit for a successful joint outcome, and are viewed as having made a smaller contribution to it (ibid.). Moreover, women are blamed more than men for joint failures (Caleo and Heilman, 2010). There is little reason in any of these studies not to give equal credit for these outcomes; only predetermined ideas based on expectations can account for the discrepancies. Thus, ambiguity about the source of performance appears to promote the use of stereotype-based expectations, impeding women from getting the credit they deserve.

GOOD PRACTICE RECOMMENDATIONS

Lack of fit perceptions have potentially devastating consequences for women's access to positions that have traditionally been held by men. This is especially problematic given that these positions tend to hold the highest prestige and status, as well as monetary and social rewards (Cejka and Eagly, 1999). But gender bias not only affects the women who are its victims; organizations also suffer by losing highly educated, skilled and competent human capital. One of the most relevant concerns of any organization is attracting and hiring the most qualified employees, people who can add to productivity and become an asset to the company. Advocating recruitment and selection procedures that secure gender-fair outcomes is not only socially correct, but is also necessary to ensure that half of the population is not ignored in the search for the best person for a vacant position. In the face of skilled labour shortage and demographic change (Forbes, 2013), organizations increasingly rely on the selection of well-trained women and men. Furthermore, recent studies provide support for the idea that having women on corporate boards increases organizations' sustainability. Companies with more women tend to be more effective in dealing with acquisitions and mergers, as well as less prone to risky transactions (Levi et al., 2014).

As we have seen, the disparity in the selection of men and women for certain occupations is not always driven by actual differences in abilities or competences, but by negative performance expectations that are triggered by lack of fit beliefs. We suggest that organizations can mitigate the occurrence of gender bias by instituting procedures that (1) counteract the negative expectations that result from lack of fit perceptions, (2) reduce the ambiguity in evaluation processes that encourage the use of these expectations, and (3) weaken the effects of these expectations by increasing evaluators' motivation for accurate assessment of candidates.

Preventing Negative Expectations

If gender stereotypes are not activated, then the processes leading to lack of fit perceptions and negative performance expectations can be derailed. Good hiring practices seek to eliminate stereotype activation by promoting gender-blind résumé screenings that reduce the salience of gender and the negative expectations about performance it provokes. But this is not always possible – certainly not after the initial phases of the selection process unfold and personal contact is necessary. Though organizations should enforce these practices when possible, they also can utilize other methods to avoid stereotype activation.

One such method lies in the composition of the applicant pool. As we mentioned in this chapter, gender is made salient by numerical scarcity, and there is evidence that increased proportional representation of women in the applicant pool reduces the activation of stereotypes and favourably affects women's career opportunities (Heilman, 1980). Thus, ensuring that women are represented in the pool when applicants are initially being considered can potentially downplay the salience of gender in the subsequent evaluation of these applicants. By designing job advertisements to attract women and men the number of women in the application pool can be increased (Gaucher et al., 2011). Also, by sharing job advertisements with large external and internal audiences rather than in selected, often male-dominated networks (Ibarra, 1997), organizations can attract more women to apply. By decreasing the chances of gender stereotypes being activated, lack of fit perceptions can be weakened and negative performance expectations averted.

Furthermore, broadening conceptions of traditionally male occupations can help to mitigate negative performance expectations. This is likely to occur naturally as women are gradually being placed in traditionally male roles. However, organizations also can actively aid in this process by redefining how they characterize traditionally male gender-typed positions. For example, this may be accomplished by including relevant female-typed traits in job descriptions (for example, interpersonal skills) and using gender-fair language when advertising typically male-typed jobs (Gaucher et al., 2011). These actions decrease the likelihood that a position is perceived to be male gender-typed. As we have seen earlier in this chapter, this can alleviate lack of fit perceptions and the negative expectations of women that they induce.

Reducing Ambiguity in the Selection Process

Reducing ambiguity in selection procedures can deter gender bias in selection decisions. We have argued that the more concrete, consistent, and comprehensive the information given to evaluators, the clearer the criteria for evaluations, and the more well defined the method for combining different information types, the less latitude evaluators have to make inferences grounded in the gender-based expectations they hold.

An effective way to create less biased decision-making processes is the use of standardized structured interviews and forms when evaluating applicants. But any attempt at creating a fixed structure for evaluation – one that cannot be used differently for different job candidates – will be an aid in keeping expectations in tow when critical decisions are made.

Furthermore, as team-based evaluations become more important in selection processes and input sources are less clear, it is important to reduce attributional ambiguity by also obtaining individual performance information whenever possible. Collecting past information about individual performance (for example, via job references, CVs [résumés]) can and should always be used to supplement information obtained in group settings and provide a check on stereotype-based expectations in determining judgements about women.

Promoting Accuracy Goals

Another way to promote fair evaluations of women applying for male-typed jobs is to increase the motivation of evaluators to be accurate. Research has shown that when people have an accuracy goal, their automatic reliance on expectations as 'rules of thumb' is decreased. As social pressures for not being prejudiced or sexist have become the norm, evaluators are becoming more concerned with making fair and unbiased decisions. Encouraging this type of behaviour by highlighting potential biases in the decision-making process may in fact increase people's motivation to 'do the right thing'. Furthermore, advancing an explicit goal of fairness in candidate evaluations may promote more comprehensive and careful processing of relevant information, while actively encouraging the discarding of irrelevant factors.

However, stereotypes tend to be activated automatically, despite people's best intentions to be fair. Therefore, we also recommend that human resources departments make strides to hold evaluators accountable for their judgements. If evaluators are required to justify their decisions to fellow members of a selection team or to their superiors, they are likely to try to make a good impression. Accountability will thus encourage them to engage in a more impartial and reliable assessment of job candidates in the hope of appearing thorough and judicious (Mero et al., 2003).

Finally, in promoting accuracy goals it is important to create a sense of future interdependence between the evaluator and the potential employee. If the evaluator anticipates that an applicant's future performance may have implications for his or her own well-being in the organization, precision in identifying a candidate's strengths and weaknesses will be in the evaluator's best interest. Self-interest concerns are apt to promote a careful processing of information – one that avoids taking the easy route provided by performance expectations.

CONCLUSIONS

We have argued in this chapter that gender bias directed against women is a product of stereotype-based lack of fit perceptions and the negative performance expectations they promote. We also have outlined a set of remedial measures to minimize the effects of bias in selection decisions and ensure that the positions women attain will be commensurate with their education and skills. Understanding the processes that give rise to gender bias and the conditions that encourage its occurrence is necessary if we are to eliminate it from organizational decision-making. Only then, when every job candidate is considered solely on his or her own merits, will we realize the promise of equality for working women and the benefit of resource maximization for organizations.

REFERENCES

Auster, C.J. and S.C. Ohm (2000), 'Masculinity and femininity in contemporary American society: a re-evaluation using the Bem Sex-Role Inventory', *Sex Roles*, **43**(7), 499–528.
Banaji, M.R. and C.D. Hardin (1996), 'Automatic stereotyping', *Psychological Science*, **7**(3), 136–41.
Bauer, C.C. and B.B. Baltes (2002), 'Reducing the effects of gender stereotypes on performance evaluations', *Sex Roles*, **47**(9–10), 465–76.
Biernat, M. and K. Deaux (2012), 'A history of social psychological research on gender', in A.W. Kruglanski and W. Stroebe (eds), *Handbook of the History of Social Psychology*, New York: Psychology Press, pp. 475–98.
Biernat, M., K. Fuegen and D. Kobrynowicz (2010), 'Shifting standards and the inference of incompetence: effects of formal and informal evaluation tools', *Personality and Social Psychology Bulletin*, **36**(7), 855–68.
Blair, I.V. and M.R. Banaji (1996), 'Automatic and controlled processes in stereotype priming', *Journal of Personality and Social Psychology*, **70**(6), 1142–63.
Bragger, J.D., E. Kutcher, J. Morgan and P. Firth (2002), 'The effects of the structured interview on reducing biases against pregnant job applicants', *Sex Roles*, **46**(7–8), 215–26.
Braun, S., C. Peus and D. Frey (2012), 'Is beauty beastly? Gender-specific effects of leader attractiveness and leadership style on followers' trust and loyalty', *Zeitschrift für Psychologie*, **220**(2), 98–108.
Caleo, S. and M.E. Heilman (2010), 'Who gets the credit and who gets the blame? Differential reactions to men and women's joint work', paper presented at the annual meeting of the Society for Industrial and Organizational Psychology, Atlanta, GA.
Catalyst (2012), 'Women board directors and women executive directors in FTSE 100, 2008–2012', accessed 31 July 2013 at http://www.catalyst.org/knowledge/women-board-directors-and-women-executive-directors-ftse-100-2008-2012.
Catalyst (2014), 'Women CEOs of the Fortune 1000', accessed 26 November 2014 at http://www.catalyst.org/knowledge/women-ceos-fortune-1000.
Cejka, M.A. and A.H. Eagly (1999), 'Gender-stereotypic images of occupations correspond to the sex segregation of employment', *Personality and Social Psychology Bulletin*, **25**(4), 413–23.
Chaiken, S. and D. Maheswaran (1994), 'Heuristic processing can bias systematic processing: effects of source credibility, argument ambiguity, and task importance on attitude judgment', *Journal of Personality and Social Psychology*, **66**(3), 460–73.
Davison, H.K. and M.J. Burke (2000), 'Sex discrimination in simulated employment contexts: a meta-analytic investigation', *Journal of Vocational Behavior*, **56**(2), 225–48.
Diekman, A.B. and A.H. Eagly (2000), 'Stereotypes as dynamic constructs: women and men of the past, present, and future', *Personality and Social Psychology Bulletin*, **26**(10), 1171–88.
Duehr, E.E. and J.E. Bono (2006), 'Men, women, and managers: are stereotypes finally changing?', *Personnel Psychology*, **59**(4), 815–46.
Eagly, A.H. and S.J. Karau (2002), 'Role congruity theory of prejudice toward female leaders', *Psychological Review*, **109**(3), 573–98.
Favero, J.L. and D.R. Ilgen (1989), 'The effects of ratee prototypicality on rater observation and accuracy', *Journal of Applied Social Psychology*, **19**(11), 932–46.
Forbes (2013), 'America's skilled trades dilemma: shortages loom as most-in-demand group of workers ages', accessed 27 March 2014 at http://www.forbes.com/sites/emsi/2013/03/07/

americas-skilled-trades-dilemma-shortages-loom-as-most-in-demand-group-of-workers-ages/.

Fyock, J. and C. Stangor (1994), 'The role of memory biases in stereotype maintenance', *British Journal of Social Psychology*, **33**(3), 331–43.

Gaucher, D., J. Friesen and A.C. Kay (2011), 'Evidence that gendered wording in job advertisements exists and sustains gender inequality', *Journal of Personality and Social Psychology*, **101**(1), 109–28.

Heilman, M.E. (1980), 'The impact of situational factors on personnel decisions concerning women: varying the sex composition of the applicant pool', *Organizational Behavior and Human Performance*, **26**(3), 286–95.

Heilman, M.E. (1983), 'Sex bias in work settings: the lack of fit model', *Research in Organizational Behavior*, **5**, 269–98.

Heilman, M.E. (1984), 'Information as a deterrent against sex discrimination: the effects of applicant sex and information type on preliminary employment decisions', *Organizational Behavior and Human Performance*, **33**(2), 174–86.

Heilman, M.E. (2001), 'Description and prescription: how gender stereotypes prevent women's ascent up the organizational ladder', *Journal of Social Issues*, **57**(4), 657–74.

Heilman, M.E. (2012), 'Gender stereotypes and workplace bias', *Research in Organizational Behavior*, **32**, 113–35.

Heilman, M.E. and S.L. Blader (2001), 'Assuming preferential selection when the admissions policy is unknown: the effects of gender parity', *Journal of Applied Psychology*, **86**(2), 188–93.

Heilman, M.E. and M.C. Haynes (2005), 'No credit where credit is due: attributional rationalization of women's success in male-female teams', *Journal of Applied Psychology*, **90**(5), 905–16.

Heilman, M.E. and M.C. Haynes (2008), 'Subjectivity in the appraisal process: a facilitator of gender bias in work settings', in E. Borgida and S.T. Fiske (eds), *Psychological Science in Court: Beyond Common Knowledge*, Mahwah, NJ: Larry Erlbaum Associates, pp. 127–56.

Heilman, M.E. and T.G. Okimoto (2008), 'Motherhood: a potential source of bias in employment decisions', *Journal of Applied Psychology*, **93**(1), 189–98.

Heilman, M.E. and M.H. Stopeck (1985a), 'Attractiveness and corporate success: different causal attributions for males and females', *Journal of Applied Psychology*, **70**(2), 379–88.

Heilman, M.E. and M.H. Stopeck (1985b), 'Being attractive, advantage or disadvantage? Performance-based evaluations and recommended personnel actions as a function of appearance, sex, and job type', *Organizational Behavior and Human Decision Processes*, **35**(2), 202–15.

Heilman, M.E. and B. Welle (2006), 'Disadvantaged by diversity? The effects of diversity goals on competence perceptions', *Journal of Applied Social Psychology*, **36**(5), 1291–319.

Heilman, M.E., C.J. Block, R.F. Martell and M.C. Simon (1989), 'Has anything changed? Current characterizations of men, women, and managers', *Journal of Applied Psychology*, **74**(6), 935–42.

Hentschel, T., M.E. Heilman and C. Peus (2013), 'Have perceptions of women and men changed? Gender stereotypes and self-ratings of men and women', paper presented at the Society of Personality and Social Psychology Annual Conference, New Orleans.

Higgins, E.T. and J.A. Bargh (1987), 'Social cognition and social perception', *Annual Review of Psychology*, **38**(1), 369–425.

Higher Education Statistics Agency (2012), 'Student introduction 2011/12', accessed 31 July 2013 at http://www.hesa.ac.uk/index.php?option=com_content&task=view&id=2705&Itemid=278.

Hodson, G., J.F. Dovidio and S.L. Gaertner (2002), 'Processes in racial discrimination: differential weighting of conflicting information', *Personality and Social Psychology Bulletin*, **28**(4), 460–71.

Ibarra, H. (1997), 'Paving an alternative route: gender differences in managerial networks', *Social Psychology Quarterly*, **60**(1), 91–102.

Johnson, S.K., K.E. Podratz, R.L. Dipboye and E. Gibbons (2010), 'Physical attractiveness biases in ratings of employment suitability: tracking down the "beauty is beastly" effect', *The Journal of Social Psychology*, **150**(3), 301–18.

Kunda, Z., L. Sinclair and D. Griffin (1997), 'Equal ratings but separate meanings: stereotypes and the construal of traits', *Journal of Personality and Social Psychology*, **72**(4), 720–34.

Lenton, A.P., I.V. Blair and R. Hastie (2001), 'Illusions of gender: stereotypes evoke false memories', *Journal of Experimental Social Psychology*, **37**(1), 3–14.

Levi, M., K. Li and F. Zhang (2014), 'Director gender and mergers and acquisitions', *Journal of Corporate Finance*, **28**(C), 185–200.

Lyness, K.S. and M.E. Heilman (2006), 'When fit is fundamental: performance evaluation and promotions of upper-level female and male managers', *Journal of Applied Psychology*, **91**(4), 777–85.

Mero, N.P., S.J. Motowidlo and A.L. Anna (2003), 'Effects of accountability on rating behaviour and rater accuracy', *Journal of Applied Social Psychology*, **33**(12), 2493–514.

Manzi, M.F., S. Caleo and M.E. Heilman (2012), 'Improvement in performance but little change in evaluation: the tenacity of stereotype-based expectations about women', paper presented at the Annual Meeting of the Society for Personality and Social Psychology, San Diego, CA.

National Center for Education Statistics (2010), 'Degrees conferred by sex and race', accessed 31 July 2013 at http://nces.ed.gov/fastfacts/display.asp?id=72.

Parks-Stamm, E.J., M.E. Heilman and K.A. Hearns (2008), 'Motivated to penalize: women's strategic rejection of successful women', *Personality and Social Psychology Bulletin*, **34**(2), 237–47.

Perry, E.L., A. Davis-Blake and C.T. Kulik (1994), 'Explaining gender-based selection decisions: a synthesis of contextual and cognitive approaches', *Academy of Management Review*, **19**(4), 786–820.

Pittinsky, T.L., M. Shih and N. Ambady (2000), 'Will a category cue affect you? Category cues, positive stereotypes and reviewer recall for applicants', *Social Psychology of Education*, **4**(1), 53–65.

Plaks, J.E., S.J. Stroessner, C.S. Dweck and J.W. Sherman (2001), 'Person theories and attention allocation: preferences for stereotypic versus counterstereotypic information', *Journal of Personality and Social Psychology*, **80**(6), 876–93.

Powell, G.N. (2011), 'The gender and leadership wars', *Organizational Dynamics*, **40**(1), 1–9.

Powell, G.N., D.A. Butterfield and J.D. Parent (2002), 'Gender and managerial stereotypes: have the times changed?', *Journal of Management*, **28**(2), 177–93.

Sandberg, S. (2013), *Lean in: Women, Work, and the Will to Lead*, New York: Random House.

Schein, V.E. (2001), 'A global look at psychological barriers to women's progress in management', *Journal of Social Issues*, **57**(4), 675–88.

Spence, J.T. and C.E. Buckner (2000), 'Instrumental and expressive traits, trait stereotypes, and sexist attitudes: what do they signify?', *Psychology of Women Quarterly*, **24**(1), 44–53.

Swim, J., E. Borgida, G. Maruyama and D.G. Myers (1989), 'Joan McKay versus John McKay: do gender stereotypes bias evaluations?', *Psychological Bulletin*, **105**(3), 409–29.

Taylor, S.E., S.T. Fiske, N.L. Etcoff and A.J. Ruderman (1978), 'Categorical bases of person memory and stereotyping', *Journal of Personality and Social Psychology*, **36**(7), 778–93.

Uhlmann, E.L. and G.L. Cohen (2005), 'Constructed criteria: redefining merit to justify discrimination', *Psychological Science*, **16**(5), 474–80.

Viswesvaran, C., D.S. Ones and F.L. Schmidt (1996), 'Comparative analysis of the reliability of job performance ratings', *Journal of Applied Psychology*, **81**(5), 557–74.

Williams, J.E. and D.L. Best (1990), *Measuring Sex Stereotypes: A Multination Study*, revised edition, Thousand Oaks, CA: Sage Publications.

7. Talking yourself into work: insights from sociolinguistics about gender and the employment interview
Mary Barrett

This chapter gives a brief critical history of three phases of linguistic research into gender and language: an essentialist phase, a constructionist phase and a post-structuralist phase. It pays particular attention to the post-structuralist phase, which focuses on how meaning is actively constructed by both parties to a speech event such as a conversation, and the consequences of particular judgements by the more powerful participants, especially in 'gate-keeping' conversations such as job interviews. We pay particular attention to research into naturally occurring conversations, which employs conversation analysis (CA), an interactional sociolinguistics technique. Campbell and Roberts's (2007) CA-based study of intercultural employment interviews yielded complex, detailed understandings about how candidates' speech led to favourable or unfavourable assessments of them during the employment interview. In this chapter we re-analyse Campbell and Roberts's data from a gender perspective and find that some aspects of what is often stereotypically considered 'women's language' – aspects that conflict with the 'rules' of interview performance – are likely to lead to unfavourable assessments of women as potential employees. This strongly suggests that some types of interview interaction that are normative for women, for example, high levels of frankness, high levels of personal disclosure and narrativized speech, are likely to act to women's disadvantage when they attempt to 'get in' to organizations. The chapter concludes with a summary of the implications of the re-analysis for women's entry into the world of paid work, including suggestions about how interviewees and interviewers can overcome these unfavourable and unfounded judgements.

RESEARCH INTO GENDER AND LANGUAGE: THREE PHASES

The history of academic research into language and gender can be seen as forming three phases: an essentialist phase, a constructionist phase and a post-structuralist phase.

The Essentialist Paradigm

The early stages of academic linguistic interest in women's speech style in the 1970s and 1980s saw women's speech styles theorized in one of three ways: as inferior to that of men (for example, Lakoff, 1973), dominated by that of men (for example, Zimmerman and West, 1975; Spender, 1980) or as different from but equal to that of men (for example, Hirschman, 1973; Tannen, 1990, 1994, 1996, 1999; Coates, 1993; Holmes, 1995). Tannen, whose work bridges popular literature and academic research, exemplifies the 'difference' perspective. She argues that men and women use language in contrasting ways, which stems from their different conceptualizations of the world and their goals within it. For example, Tannen (1990) says that for men the world is a competitive place in which conversation and speech are used to build status and demonstrate independence, whereas for women the world is a network of connections, so they use language to seek and offer support and intimacy. Men seek solutions to problems, leading them to give advice, whereas women seek comfort and sympathy for their problems. These contrasts are echoed in men's preference for conversation oriented to obtaining information and women's orientation to conversation about feelings, men's preference for direct imperatives and women's preference for super-polite forms, men's greater ease with conflict and women's avoidance of conflict in favour of compromise.

Researchers within the essentialist perspective differ about whether women's speech styles should be changed to emulate the more powerful and authoritative speech styles of men. However, as Cameron (1995) points out, citing etiquette manuals from the fifteenth century, the view that women are naturally and properly quiet has a long history. So it is not surprising that essentialist theorists are united in regarding certain aspects of speech as the direct outcome of the speaker's gender, and seeing men's speech as reliably different from women's speech. Essentialist studies produced catalogues of gender-related speech differences, for example, gender-linked differences in vocabulary, interruption, talk time, topic initiation and topic maintenance. Despite criticisms of this research, for example that it reinforces gender dualism (Hollway, 1994), perpetuates gender stereotypes (Crawford, 1995), and produces a research culture that exaggerates sex differences (Hare-Mustin and Maracek, 1994), studies that search for and discuss evidence of gendered conversational styles continue to be published (for example, Mapstone, 1998; Conrick, 1999; Goddard and Patterson, 2000).

The Constructionist Paradigm

In the 1990s, research into language and gender shifted towards a constructionist viewpoint, theorizing gender as a complex and fluid social property located in the interaction between speakers (for example, Butler, 1990; Bohan, 1993; West and Fenstermaker, 1993; Crawford, 1995; Wodak, 1997; Bucholtz et al., 1999). This perspective draws attention to how gender is naturalized in common usage by analysing written and visual tests including radio broadcasts, advertisements, newspaper articles and CCTV footage, noting the similarities and differences between languages and speech communities in how they encode and express sexism. The feminist language reform movement (cf. Pauwels, 1998), which aims to change the biased representation of the sexes in language whereby men are portrayed as the norm, is part of this approach. However, since some constructionist research continues to treat gender as an independent variable, exploring how men 'do' masculinity and women 'do' femininity, but not the reverse (Cameron, 1998; Stokoe, 2000), it has been argued that it reinstates the essentialist frameworks it aimed to replace (for example, Cameron, 1998; Stokoe, 2000).

Post-structuralist Approaches to Language and Gender

Post-structuralist perspectives have also had an impact in gender and language research, particularly for analysing and interpreting discourses. Following Foucault (1972, p. 49), we define discourses here as 'practices that systematically form the objects of which they speak'. Discourses are 'forms of knowledge, sets of assumptions, expectations, values and ways of explaining the world that govern mainstream cultural practices' (Baxter, 2006, p. 156). Post-structuralist perspectives point to essentialist views that assume that the genders are different as a dominant discourse, that is, the essentialist viewpoint constitutes rather than reveals reality. The idea that women and men are different in how they communicate is a staple not only of recent bestsellers on the subject (for example, Tannen, 1990, 1994; Gray, 1992), but also of much language and gender research literature. Three other features of post-structuralist approaches are important in this context. First, post-structuralist approaches exemplify a stance of incredulity towards meta-narratives (Lyotard, 1984, p. xxiv), that is, they avoid sweeping theorizations about causes and effects in favour of locating, describing and analysing small-scale, localized and temporary settings. Second, post-structuralist perspectives exemplify a belief in the multiplicity of human identity. People's identity comprises a complex and sometimes contradictory mix of gender, age, class, ethnicity, education, language, personality, and so on. Finally, the idea of 'identity in process' is important. Within any single speech event, male and female speakers constantly negotiate their subject positions within interwoven and often competing or contradictory institutional discourses.

Interactional Sociolinguistics and Post-structural Approaches to Language and Gender

Interactional sociolinguistics, through the technique of CA, is allied to post-structural perspectives in foregrounding what Schegloff, one of CA's original practitioners and proponents, referred to as 'the problem of relevance' (Schegloff, 1991, p. 49). Even though gender linguistically permeates everything that is encoded, said and implied, post-structuralist perspectives show how other factors – a speaker's ethnicity, education, age, workplace role, the conversation's institutional context – are also encoded in a person's talk. Since we can characterize people and speech events in so many different ways, the question arises: which one is the right one, for analytical purposes? CA identifies how, in natural speech situations, speakers frame specific factors as relevant when they are talking to others.

The alliance between CA and post-structuralism has not been unproblematic. Some feminist researchers with a post-structuralist orientation for example, regard Schegloff's requirement that speakers in an interaction explicitly invoke gender as 'unbearably limiting' (for example, Kitzinger, 2000) for research with a political agenda such as feminism. More recently, however, Schegloff himself (for example, Schegloff, 1997) and some feminist researchers, for example, Stokoe (2000) and Speer (2005), have advocated widening CA techniques to allow analysts' perspectives on an issue to be included even when speakers do not explicitly make the issue relevant. This is particularly important when the topic being discussed is already problematized.

CHARACTERISTICS OF CONVERSATION ANALYSIS RESEARCH

Conversations range from the casual, 'socializing' event of two friends chatting on the phone to conversations we intuitively recognize as aimed

> Patient: This- chemotherapy (0.2) it won't have any effects on havin' kids, will it?
> Doctor: (2.2)
> Patient: It will?
> Doctor: I'm afraid so.
>
> *Notes for interpreting symbols in CA transcripts:*
>
> One or more colons indicate the expansion of the previous sound, for example, Tha::t.
>
> A '?' marks upward intonation characteristic of a question.
>
> Underlining indicates stress placed on a word or part of a word.
>
> { } indicates a change of body position or body movement.
>
> Extended brackets mark overlap between speakers [ ].
>
> Numbers in parentheses for example (0.2) indicate pauses in tenths of a second; (.) indicates a micropause.
>
> xxxxxx indicates a pause of several seconds.
>
> A double letter, for example, nno, indicates a repetition of the n sound, i.e., a stutter.
>
> A hyphen, for example, th-, indicates an incomplete word.
>
> An equals sign = indicates the absence of a discernible gap between the end of one speaker's utterance and the beginning of another speaker's utterance.
>
> C = Candidate; I = Interviewer.
>
> *Source:* Frankel (1984, p. 153), cited in ten Have (1999, p. 33).

at accomplishing other things, some of them serious: discussing a prognosis with a doctor, reporting an emergency, giving a witness statement, getting married. All entail myriad aspects of what Sacks (1984) refers to as 'the technology of conversation': pacing, silences, assessments, turn-taking systems, mechanisms for indicating what is salient in the conversation, and so on. CA determines how these technologies accomplish the 'actions' that differentiate types of conversation. An important insight of early CA practitioners is that the sequential location of an utterance (which can include pauses, intakes of breath, the extent and frequency of overlaps, and so on) is crucial to creating its practical meaning. This can be seen in the example from an analysis of a medical consultation below.

According to Frankel (1984), the much longer than normal pause (2.2 seconds) from the doctor, which follows a question framed as an optimistic statement, interrupts the 'preference for agreement' rule of conversations. So the location of the pause in the sequence of utterances allows the doctor to signal they are unable to endorse the patient's optimistic assessment. The patient's interpretation of the meaning of the interruption leads the patient to reverse their earlier statement into the more direct question format, 'It will?', which, in turn, allows the doctor to confirm the earlier negative assessment with: 'I'm afraid so' (ibid.). This small example shows the affinity between CA and the post-structuralist orientation towards analyses of local, ephemeral situations where meaning is constituted moment by moment as an artefact of interaction. The development of audio and visual recording technologies have enabled highly detailed analysis of naturally occurring data, and CA research typically shares information about such things as the direction of a speaker's gaze and facial expressions in relation to their utterances.

CA-BASED RESEARCH INTO JOB INTERVIEWS

CA has been used most frequently to analyse conversations recorded for legal or other purposes, such as police interviews, court proceedings, or gatherings of public interest. There is relatively little research on employment interviews using CA or CA-influenced techniques, however, perhaps because employment interviews usually take place in confidential settings. Exceptions include the empirical investigations of the roles and outcomes of same- and cross-sex applicant–recruiter dyads by Graves and Powell (1995, 1996), and Linell and Thunqvist's (2003) analysis of simulated job interviews with young unemployed people. Gumperz et al. (1979) used CA-oriented sociolinguistic techniques to analyse the features of communicative style that lead to negative or positive judgements of candidates for jobs. Roberts and Campbell (2005) and Campbell and Roberts (2007), in their research into job interviews with migrants to the UK, extend the work of Gumperz and his colleagues on these inferential processes by linking them to current organizational discourses around the job interview.

This relatively small body of previous research points up how little work has been done on naturally occurring data to explore how gender underlies the assumptions, structures and outcomes of employment interviewing. This is not to deny the wealth of research attention to employment interviews generally. There have been many research-based challenges to the employment interview's reliability, validity and usefulness in recruitment and selection for employment, as well as investigations of the role of the interview in applicants' decision-making about job offers. The popular literature is similarly replete with reviews, textbooks, popular books, articles and websites that describe and discuss roles and sequences in interview scripts, tell interviewers how to construct good-quality questions, and interviewees how to construct good-quality answers, and create favourable impressions via their attire, demeanour, and the documents associated with seeking employment: résumés, curricula vitae and cover letters.

Employment interviews are pivotal points in most individuals' lives: they give entry to paid work and, potentially, employment security, advancement opportunities, dignity as productive members of society and specific standards of living. From an employer's perspective too, skills shortages have increased the difficulty of finding 'the right candidate for the job'. Employment interviews themselves are taking longer as candidates are interviewed intensively and often several times after the initial résumé check indicates acceptable knowledge, skills and abilities (Arthur et al., 1999; Cheney et al., 2004). Finally, in an era when legislation in many countries prohibits sex-based and other forms of discrimination, it is important to investigate how aspects of talk-in-interaction in the employment interview conversation may combine to discriminate unfairly, albeit unwittingly, against specific groups.

REVISITING A PREVIOUS STUDY: CAMPBELL AND ROBERTS (2007)

This section shows how the CA analysis of Campbell and Roberts (2007), who focused on intercultural issues leading to unfairness in their study of job interviews, also reveals gender issues in the interactions between interviewers and interviewees. Campbell and Roberts analysed 40 hours of recorded job interviews of 21 white British candidates, 21 British minority ethnic candidates, and 19 candidates who were born outside the UK and for whom English was not an expert language. The authors also held brief interviews with several candidates and gave video feedback to interviewers. They found the most common reasons for rejecting candidates related either to aspects of personality, for example, 'untrustworthiness', or general assessments of skill deficiencies, for example, 'poor communication skills'. Less frequently the interviewers referred to cultural stereotypes (Campbell and Roberts, 2007, p. 244) as a basis for not offering a candidate a position. The authors argue that these judgements, which adversely affected a significant proportion of the candidates born abroad, were an artefact of candidates' talk. Specifically, unfavourable judgements arose from interviewers' perceptions that candidates produced 'jarring' juxtapositions of personal and institutional modes of speaking and identities, and that their talk showed an inadequate synthesis of personal and institutional discourses. Candidates could be judged unfavourably by producing rote-learned 'textbook' answers that used buzzwords but did not employ the candidates' own voice. However, candidates who were judged overly personal or informal in how they presented themselves were also seen as 'unprofessional' (ibid.). The authors conclude that to be successful, interviewees must synthesize their talk at the micro level of lexical, grammatical, rhetorical and interactional features with their talk at the macro level of the underlying organizational ideologies – dedication to work, flexibility to meet the employer demands, customer service, and so on. This is a linguistic feat that the life-worlds of non-native English speakers born outside the UK are less likely to have equipped them to master.

Campbell and Roberts's study did not indicate that more women than men were unsuccessful in securing a job, and they gave examples of successful conversation strategies – those that successfully married institutional and personal discourses – that emanated from female candidates. Nevertheless, their analysis of candidates' job interview talk and how interviewers judge it also recalls the findings about language and gender derived from feminist linguistics research, and feminist findings about women's experience of work. We demonstrate this in the next few sections, where we summarize and present a short re-analysis of Campbell and Roberts's (2007) data under three headings that pertain equally to gender: the competence of impersonality, the competence of personal disclosure, and the claim to belong.

The Competence of Impersonality

Part of being competent at job interview talk means using institutional language rather than 'the here and now biographical talk of personal stories about the self' (Campbell and Roberts, 2007, p. 248). Institutional language, according to Bourdieu (1991), is characterized by 'impartiality, symmetry, balance, propriety, decency and discretion', and by the creation of a certain professional distance between the people using it. Auer (1998) and Morales-López et al. (2005) point out commonly occurring linguistic features of impartiality, including more analytic framing of talk (for example, giving lists of characteristics and argumentative modes of structuring speech); more employment of technical vocabulary and abstract formulations (for example, nominalizations and grammatical metaphors); reduced use of the personal pronoun particularly as a grammatical subject; and the use of certain types of modality, in which candidates evaluate their experience in terms of what they should believe and do, for example: 'It's important to be flexible', 'Your work is more important than your social life'.

In the interviews analysed by Campbell and Roberts, candidates born outside the UK were assessed by the interviewer/s as having poorly synthesized personal and institutional discourses. An example is candidate Yohannes.

In analysing the following extract, Campbell and Roberts point out

Yohannes, Ethiopian, unsuccessful

1. I: an example where you been working as part of a team=
2. C: = mhm
3. I: to achieve something=
4. (20 seconds of talk deleted)
5. C: and we were friendly we were not er:m bothering to argue this is your
6. your job is my job we are all together we had togetherness (.) they are very
7. helpful (.) they are a lot of integration each other e:r if something happen
8. we have to sort it out ourselves (.) instead of complaining to each other we
9. have to (.) know (.) the first thing whoever comes first mm say for example if
10. you have a job today interview and then he offer the job in that place we tell
11. that person if he doesn't understand he asks he can ask us five to six times
12. doesn't matter =
13. I: = mhm
14. C: er:m because he is new at least for one month he might get confused he
15. might
16. I: what to do- has to do- okay ho- how many of you in th- in that team
17. C: e:r we were (.) me Mohammed about five people (3) that was in valet
18. service [and that was in
19. I: right okay]
20. C: was in public [area
21. I: how] many rooms would you be covering on a- any given date
22. C: er:m (.) one room we had we had guests' laundry to bring it from the
23. floors
24. I: okay
25. C: then we have to wash them in e:r machine or if not we send them to l- er
26. dry cleaning (1) and we have to do go and get that erm but th:e how much it
27. costs (5) and then we have to give them back to the customers (6)

Source: This and all subsequent natural language extracts are from Campbell and Roberts (2007).

how Yohannes employs a personal style in lines 5–15 but fails to recognize the need to discuss teamworking in terms of its benefit to the organization rather than his personal enjoyment. At line 17 he abandons this personal discourse in favour of an impersonal listing of tasks required of him. However, the interviewers considered this insufficiently personalized and evidence that Yohannes was unwilling to take responsibility. But Yohannes's switch to a depersonalized style was not something he did unprompted; it was in response to a cue from the interviewer at line 16, who returned the conversation to a formal register and a low, almost banal, level of questioning. In following this cue from the interviewer, Yohannes obeyed the 'rules' of the job interview, but the consequence was to make his responses appear rather dull and lacking in initiative.

Similarly, candidate Alison, who was being interviewed for a hospital receptionist's position, was criticized by the interviewers for framing her response to a question about security of medical records in a personalized, non-technical way:

> C: ... they're coming in here and hoping that their medical records ... are as safe as they possibly could be.

She spoke in terms of empathy with patients' affectivity and vulnerability, rather than explicitly using the language and categories of customer service and data protection legislation to frame her response. This was seen as 'unprofessional' (Campbell and Roberts, 2007, p. 252).

These features of Yohannes's and Alison's speech that cost them the job are also consistent with so-called 'women's language'. The linguistic features of impartiality required in the two job interviews just discussed are at odds with the language of 'women's linguistic culture' as discussed in 'difference' perspectives of feminist research. Analytical, abstract and argumentative talk go against female linguistic culture, which stresses empathy and comfort rather than analytical approaches to problems (Tannen, 1996). Difference perspectives on language and gender suggest that for women to demonstrate the institutional competence of impersonality, discretion and distance means they are required to bridge a greater cultural gap than men. A post-structuralist perspective reveals the same problem. The interviewer's power means they can use the 'rules' of the job interview to 'cue' female candidates – who recognize and obey the rules – into responding in ways the interviewer has already judged to be unprofessional.

The Competence of Personal Disclosure

As well as demonstrating the competence of impersonality, Campbell and Roberts (2007) found that candidates need to show its apparent opposite: a competence of personal disclosure that reveals them to be well-rounded individuals who are aligned at a personal level with the values and preferred behaviours of the organization. The competence of personal disclosure includes being able to create specific narratives concerning the self. For example, describing interpersonal interactions with difficult workmates can be set up to show that the candidate is not bothered by this and regards it simply as a 'challenge'. The euphemism 'challenge' reframes something that is normally unpleasant and frustrating as interesting and even enjoyable. Personal disclosure also requires candidates to give vivid accounts of their motivations and values in a way that shows them to be oriented to the organization's needs. In successful candidates these

Talking yourself into work 115

> Pippa, White British, successful
> 1. C: erm well it is I think t-m-majority of the jobs that I have worked in I
> 2. have been erm customer focussed and <u>deadlines</u> and under pressure (.)
> 3. hhh erm <u>catering</u> I've m-you know
> 4. I1: mmm
> 5. C: my family own a business and I've worked in that since the age of nine (.)
> 6. you know helping them out (.) erm but that's I suppose that's a
> 7. different field altogether from=
> 8. I1: =yeah
> 9. C: customer focus but (1) I've sort of gone off on a tangent now. hhh (3)
> 10. I1: nno it's (1) I mean the range of experience just [shows you
> 11. C: mmm]
> 12. I1: in many ways that you're used to=
> 13. C: =yeah I'm quite
> 14. I1: having new things thrown at you so (.) no I-I don't see anything (.) (to
> 15. I2) anything you need to add to that (xxxxxxx)?
> 16. I2: no I'm comfortable with that

features would be delivered in a 'high-involvement' conversational style: using colloquial vocabulary and idiosyncratic language, popular sayings and direct speech quotations. The interviewer indicates approval of the candidate's personal disclosure by echoing the candidate's micro-level behaviours, rather than ignoring, correcting, or translating them. This is shown in the above extract.

In lines 1–9 Pippa discusses her personal history in her family business to inject the required element of personalization and demonstrate her understanding of organizational demands. The interviewers respond here and elsewhere with a high level of back channelling, overlap and positive appraisal, giving the interaction a conversational mood (Campbell and Roberts, 2007, p. 255). They allow additions, digressions and questions about their personal views, thereby establishing affiliative alliances rather than cutting the interviewee off, as they did with Yohannes. Instead of switching into formal language and low-level questioning as they did in Yohannes's interview, the interviewer completes Pippa's sentence at line 14 using Pippa's colloquial language. This helps her – the interviewers summarize and endorse what she says about the value of her previous experience.

Pippa, a woman, was successful. However, feminist research, and specifically constructionist approaches to gender and language, indicate a gender aspect in the 'work as identity-forming' competence of personal disclosure. Just as candidates born outside the UK doing low-paid work typically do not use their work to form their identity (Campbell and

Roberts, 2007), women whose jobs are often subject to day-to-day and even year-by-year interruptions for domestic, childcare and eldercare reasons are unlikely to speak about their work as identity forming. For both groups – people from outside the country in which they are seeking a job, and women with family responsibilities – there is a wider gulf between the discourses they generally use to talk about themselves, and those they can readily use to indicate the value of their experience to the organization.

THE CLAIM TO BELONG

Demonstrating mastery of the impersonal and personal discourses of the job interview reinforces a candidate's implicit claim to 'belong' to the organizational world of the interviewer. The copious literature on 'organizational fit' (including this volume) suggests that the demonstration of belonging is also an independent competence. The personalization discourse typically requires a confessional approach, where the candidate admits to weaknesses. The strong attention devoted to the 'tell me about your weaknesses' question in the popular job interview advice literature shows the question's importance in the personal disclosure competence of job interview language. The skill required is difficult and delicate: to use personal language to demonstrate awareness of one's deficiencies or foibles and how they are likely to be viewed in the organization, and yet to manage this to one's advantage. It is easy to get it wrong, particularly if the 'weakness' is a fundamental aspect of the person or their identity. Sara is a case in point.

Campbell and Roberts (2007, p. 263) point out that Sara described a *genuine* individual foible, her 'Maltese' tendency to 'talk with her hands' (line 5). While Campbell and Roberts do not make this point, it is worth noting that this was a more honest response to the 'weakness' question than invoking homogenized personal characteristics such as 'time-management issues', which may be easier to reframe as correctible or even strengths in disguise. Sara's highly personal, narrativized and satirical acting out of her 'Maltese' behaviour and the possible reaction of her colleagues to it shows her reflexive awareness of self, which ought to be an advantage in a job interview. However, it breaks the rules of the job interview game, which are imposed by the interviewer. The interviewer disqualifies it as an appropriate example (line 28), viewing it as 'indiscreet', and explicitly linking it to Sara's ethnic identity: 'I know she's Maltese, but . . .' (Campbell and Roberts, 2007, p. 263). The effect of the interviewer's judgement is to construct Sara as an outsider to both the organizational and the national culture.

Talking yourself into work 117

Sara, Maltese, unsuccessful

1. I: {[looking down] how- how do you ensure (.) you know wh- when you're a
2. manager that you (.) you learn from} {[I looks at C] experience and you pick
3. up particular lessons from past mistakes} {[I looks down, begins writing]} (1)
4. (25 seconds of talk deleted)
5. C: I mean I'm Maltese {[C moves arms] I <u>tend</u> to <u>talk</u> with my <u>hands}</u> and one
6. thing that's really brought up quite often when I'm talking in a meeting you
7. know I'm sitting there with my]} {[C gesticulates with hands, I looks up and
8. nods] hands flailing away like this} {[I looks down] which puts everybody off
9. because they're looking at you know {[I looks up, C moves arms] what on
10. earth is she doing} {[I looks down] doing this [business
11. I: right]
12. C: so I've made a conscious effort to keep my hands in my lap [I mean
13. I: i-]
14. C: that that is one [thing that somebody told me
15. I: how do you er:m]} {[I looks up] (.) how do you ensure though if you
16. (choose) somebody in your team that maybe they they maybe don't want to be
17. too critical you know they're only really sort of being positive or being nice
18. for the sake of it really is that not a danger some times
19. C: that is a danger but-
20. I: they might not want to say that actually you was pretty- you were just
21. mumbling it was pretty awful but I daren't say that because she's the boss}
22. (15 seconds of talk deleted)
23. I: so can you give me some examples of things you've picked up then from
24. using that
25. C: well I just did that that was the one that comes [to mind
26. I: the one about] are there any other sort of things that
27. C: er:m-
28. I: apart from you know your own sort of body language and things which (.)
29. you know I think from presentations we always there's always things to pick
30. up there
31. C: mm
32. I: sort of ex- examples maybe s- substan- in terms of-

It is possible to analyse the same incident from a gender perspective. Both essentialist and constructionist perspectives on gender and language point to highly personalized, intimate, narrativized talk that incorporates emphatic body language as characteristic of female speech (for example, Hirschman, 1973). So referring to this personal foible overtly is likely to draw attention to the speaker's gender as well as her ethnicity. Moreover, for women, who more typically seek and offer empathy rather than strategize solutions to problems, the need in the job interview to strategize personal weaknesses imposes a male institutional norm. Gender, as well as ethnicity, can operate in institutional discourses to discriminate between organizational members and non-members, as 'language serves to confirm and consolidate the organizations which shape it' (Fowler et al., 1979, p. 190). Institutional discourses are used more frequently, interviewer language becomes more depersonalized, and requirements for relevancy and 'appropriate' discourse use (as defined by the interviewer) become stricter when rejecting those who are constructed as not belonging (Bourdieu, 1991; Roberts and Campbell, 2005, 2006).

IMPLICATIONS

So far, naturally occurring employment interviews seem to have remained relatively inaccessible – or at least infrequently accessed – as sites for empirical research into gender and language. Nevertheless, this brief re-examination of data from a study of employment interviews in intercultural settings has implications for future interviewees and interviewers. First, CA analysis of interviews heightens our recognition of the interview as a performance. This is in many ways already obvious from the wealth of advice to candidates, especially women, about clothing, demeanour, hair, make-up, and so on. The need to adjust one's costume to fit the show foreshadows the insights from CA that the art of the interview is to predict and then artfully match one's linguistic self-presentation at micro- and macro-levels to the discourses of the organization one expects to join. Candidates may consider challenging interview norms, but the speed and subtlety of interview interactions and the inequality of the interviewer–candidate power relationship make this risky and difficult.

Second, our gender-oriented re-analysis of Campbell and Roberts (2007) suggests that the competences involved in managing job interview languages are likely to present specific hazards for women, first because the required linguistic strategies conflict with elements of women's linguistic culture and, second, because the dominant discourse that work is more important than one's outside commitments is more sustainable for men than for women. These results signal that interviewees and interviewers alike need to continue to maintain and improve their awareness of the discourses that predominate at work, and continue to question them.

Finally, the re-analysis reinforces Eckert and McConnell-Ginet's observation (2003, p. 304) that 'the claims people make with language . . . are claims about who they are'. But, contrary to appearances, the interviewer is not purely a passive audience or recipient of the interviewee's claims. CA shows how interviewers impose their own judgements and claims, however unwittingly, about who the interviewee is in their moment-by-moment co-creation of the interview conversation. Interviewers, however, are alone in assessing interviewees' success at the interview, despite their contribution to constructing the performance.

WAYS FORWARD

Exposing how the linguistic norms of interviews tend to create unfair outcomes prompts questions about what should be done to rectify the situation. The options for interviewees to do this are limited because of their less powerful position in the job interview context. Regular interview practice appears to be a good option, especially if candidates are informed about the framing of responses that goes on in interviews. Doing this kind of practice is not easy, however, especially if one is inexperienced with interviews, as young people and women who have been outside the paid workforce for a long time are likely to be. Linell and Thunqvist (2003) found it was difficult for young people to maintain the framing needed to practise employment interviews. Buzzanell (2000) advocates a new, 'power-sharing' approach to employment interviewing but this is not yet mainstream practice.

The fact that the power balance in job interviews lies with the interviewer suggests that changing interviewer awareness and practice has much to offer. Training in interview techniques, particularly from an equal opportunities perspective, is now common in large organizations. However, some current training in interviewer questioning techniques, such as how to 'drill down' to the 'truth' of what a candidate is saying using deductive questioning techniques (see Roberts, 2013, for a description) actually contributes to the problem. Interviewers are also often constrained by the need to be accountable for interview results, which often requires them to write notes during the interview (see Roberts and Campbell, 2005). This tends to make interviewers keen to ensure interviews are easily processable – and leads them to push candidates into modes of talking that are easy for interviewers to take notes about. They are likely to punish candidates who cannot produce these modes by changing the line of questioning, hyper-clarifying, removing eye contact and so on during the interview, or by assessing them as poor communicators afterwards. Interviewer training should be changed and expanded to make interviewers aware of how the interview as a whole, and their linguistic behaviours in particular, can help – but also actively disadvantage – specific candidate groups, including women. Alternative behaviours are possible, such as allowing candidates to tell their stories in their own way and in their own time. If interviewers are aware of how they may unfairly construct specific ways of speaking as indicative of organizational 'belonging' or otherwise, they are more likely to suspend such judgements. This is not a radical shift, but rather an extension of good practice in ensuring interview questions are relevant to the job.

CONCLUSION

In *Verbal Hygiene*, Deborah Cameron voices her concern about how 'ideas about language are recruited to non-linguistic concerns' and the importance of 'exposing . . . unspoken assumptions [about language] to critical scrutiny' (Cameron, 1995, p. 11). The aim is to 'challenge verbal hygiene practices we find objectionable, defend those we find value in, and know which is which' (ibid., p. 10). In our re-analysis of Campbell and Roberts's (2007) data, we mobilized these authors' use of linguistic interactional analysis to challenge gender-based assumptions about the unspoken elements of job interview language. This language context is crucial because job interviews are still the primary way that women and men get in to organizations. We also pointed to some practical ways these unspoken assumptions can be made explicit, revealing their dubious foundations. Much more work of the same kind is possible and necessary; we invite other researchers to join in to the benefit of organizations and their would-be members.

REFERENCES

Arthur, M.B., K. Inkson and J.K. Pringle (1999), *The New Careers: Individual Action and Economic Change*, London: Sage.
Auer, P. (1998), 'Learning how to play the game: an investigation of role-played job interviews in East Germany', *Text*, **18**(1), 17–38.
Baxter, J. (2006), 'Putting gender in its place: a case study on constructing speaker identities in a management meeting', in M. Barrett and M. Davidson (eds), *Gender and Communication at Work*, Aldershot, UK: Ashgate, pp. 154–65.
Bohan, J.S. (1993), 'Regarding gender: essentialism, constructionism and feminist psychology', *Psychology of Women Quarterly*, **17**(1), 5–21.
Bourdieu, P. (1991), *Outline of a Theory of Practice* (trans. R. Nice), Cambridge, UK: CUP.
Bucholtz, M., A.C. Liang and L.A. Sutton (eds) (1999), *Reinventing Identities: The Gendered Self in Discourse*, Oxford: OUP.
Butler, J. (1990), 'Performative acts and gender constitution: an essay in phenomenology and feminist theory', in S.-E. Case (ed.), *Performing Feminisms*, Baltimore, MD: Johns Hopkins University Press.
Buzzanell, P.M. (2000), 'The promise and practice of the new career and social contract: illusions exposed and suggestions for reform', in P.M. Buzzanell (ed.), *Rethinking Organizational and Managerial Communication from Feminist Perspectives*, Thousand Oaks, CA: Sage, pp. 209–35.
Cameron, D. (1995), *Verbal Hygiene*, London: Routledge.
Cameron, D. (1998), 'Gender, language and discourse: a review essay', *Signs*, **23**(4), 945–73.

Campbell, S. and C. Roberts (2007), 'Migration, ethnicity and competing discourses in the job interview: synthesizing the institutional and the personal', *Discourse & Society*, **18**(3), 243–71.

Cheney, G., L.T. Christensen, T.E. Zorn and S. Ganesh (2004), *Organizational Communication in an Age of Globalization: Issues, Reflections, Practices*, Prospect Heights, IL: Waveland.

Coates, J. (1993), *Women, Men and Language*, Harlow, UK: Longman.

Conrick, M. (1999), *Womanspeak*, Dublin: Marino Books.

Crawford, M. (1995), *Talking Difference: On Gender and Language*, London: Sage.

Eckert, P. and S. McConnell-Ginet (2003), *Language and Gender*, Cambridge: CUP.

Foucault, M. (1972), *The Archaeology of Knowledge*, London: Routledge.

Fowler, R., B. Hodge, G. Kress and T. Trew (1979), *Language and Control*, London: Routledge.

Frankel, R.M. (1984), 'From sentence to sequence: understanding the medical encounter through microinteractional analysis', *Discourse Process*, **7**(2), 135–70.

Goddard, A. and L.M. Patterson (2000), *Language and Gender*, London: Routledge.

Graves, L.M. and G.N. Powell (1995), 'The effect of sex similarity on recruiters' evaluations of actual applicants: a test of the similarity–attraction paradigm', *Personnel Psychology*, **48**(1), 85–98.

Graves, L.M. and G.N. Powell (1996), 'Sex similarity, quality of the employment interview and recruiters' evaluation of actual applicants', *Journal of Occupational and Organizational Psychology*, **69**(3), 243–61.

Gray, J. (1992), *Men are from Mars, Women are from Venus: How to Get What You Want in Your Relationships*, London: Harper Collins.

Gumperz, J.J., T.C. Jupp and C. Roberts (1979), *Cross-talk: A Study of Cross-cultural Communication* [film and notes], London: BBC/National Centre for Industrial Language Training.

Hare-Mustin, R.T. and J. Maracek (1994), *Making a Difference: Psychology and the Construction of Gender*, New Haven, CT: Yale University Press.

Have, P. ten (1999), *Doing Conversation Analysis: A Practical Guide*, London: Sage.

Hirschman, L. (1973), 'Female–male differences in conversational interaction', paper presented at Linguistic Society of America, San Diego.

Hollway, W. (1994), 'Beyond sex difference: a project for feminist psychology', *Feminism & Psychology*, **4**(4), 538–46.

Holmes, J. (1995), *Women, Men and Politeness*, Harlow, UK: Longman.

Kitzinger, C. (2000), 'Doing feminist conversation analysis', *Feminism & Psychology*, **10**(2), 163–93.

Lakoff, R. (1973), 'Language and woman's place', *Language in Society*, **2**(1), 45–79.

Linell, P. and D. Thunqvist (2003), 'Moving in and out of framings: activity contexts in talks with young unemployed people within a training project', *Journal of Pragmatics*, **35**(3), 409–34.

Lyotard, J.-F. (1984), *The Postmodern Condition: A Report on Knowledge*, Minneapolis, MN: University of Minnesota Press.

Mapstone, E. (1998), *War of Words: Women and Men Arguing*, London: Chatto and Windus.

Morales-López, E., G. Prego-Vásquez and L. Domínguez-Seco (2005), 'Interviews between employees and customers during a company restructuring process', *Discourse & Society*, **16**(2), 225–68.

Pauwels, A. (1998), *Women Changing Language*, New York: Addison Wesley Longman.

Roberts, C. (2013), 'The gate-keeping of Babel: job interviews and the linguistic penalty', in A. Duchêne, M. Moyer and C. Roberts (eds), *Language, Migration and Social Inequalities: A Critical Sociolinguistic Perspective on Institutions and Work*, Bristol, UK: Multilingual Matters, pp. 82–94.

Roberts, C. and S. Campbell (2005), 'Fitting stories into boxes: rhetorical and textual constraints on candidates' performances in British job interviews', *Journal of Applied Linguistics*, **2**(1), 45–73.

Roberts, C. and S. Campbell (2006), *Talk on Trial: Job Interviews, Language and Ethnicity*, Report No. 344, London: Department for Work and Pensions.

Sacks, H. (1984), 'Notes on methodology', in J.M. Atkinson and J. Heritage (eds), *Structures of Social Action: Studies in Conversation Analysis*, Cambridge, UK: Cambridge University Press, pp. 21–7.

Schegloff, E.A. (1991), 'Reflections on talk and social structure', in D. Boden and D.H. Zimmerman (eds), *Talk & Social Structure*, Berkeley, CA: University of California Press, pp. 44–70.

Schegloff, E.A. (1997), 'Whose text, whose context?', *Discourse & Society*, **8**(2), 165–87.

Speer, S. (2005), *Gender Talk: Feminism, Discourse and Conversation Analysis*, London: Routledge.

Spender, D. (1980), *Man Made Language*, Boston, MA: Routledge and Kegan Paul.

Stokoe, E.H. (2000), 'Towards a conversation analytic approach to gender and discourse', *Feminism & Psychology*, **10**(4), 590–601.

Tannen, D. (1990), *You Just Don't Understand: Women and Men in Conversation*, New York: William Morrow.

Tannen, D. (1994), *Talking from 9 to 5: Women and Men at Work*, New York: Avon.

Tannen, D. (1996), *Gender and Discourse*, New York: OUP.

Tannen, D. (1999), 'The display of (gendered) identities in talk at work', in M. Bucholtz, A.C. Liang and L.A. Sutton (eds), *Reinventing Identities: The Gendered Self in Discourse*, Oxford: OUP, pp. 221–40.

West, C. and S. Fenstermaker (1993), 'Power, inequality and the accomplishment of gender: an ethnomethodological view', in P. England (ed.), *Theory on Gender/Feminism on Theory*, New York: Aldine de Gruyter, pp. 151–74.

Wodak, R. (ed.) (1997), *Gender and Discourse*, London: Sage.

Zimmerman, D.H. and C. West (1975), 'Sex roles, interruptions and silences in conversation', in B. Thorne and N. Henley (eds), *Language and Sex: Difference and Dominance*, Rowley, MA: Newbury House.

8. 'This is just the way it is': executive search and gendered careers
Charlotte Holgersson and Janne Tienari

In this chapter, we explore gendered careers in management with a particular focus on executive search. We highlight the ways in which executive search consultants – or headhunters, as they are commonly known – describe the search process and make sense of the persistent lack of women in top business positions. As professional service providers, executive search consultants are influential in the contemporary global economy. Recruitment of key individuals in companies, as well as public sector and not-for-profit organizations, is increasingly carried out with the confidential help of external experts. Executive search consultants assist decision-makers in identifying, evaluating, and recruiting competent and suitable people for their top positions (Coverdill and Finlay, 1998). In so doing, they act as gatekeepers in elite labour markets (Faulconbridge et al., 2009). On a general level it is well established that executive search sustains the powerful position of white men in business life (Dreher et al., 2011; Doldor et al., 2012).

We suggest that executive search practice is crucial for understanding gendered careers in management and for shedding new light on how and why women are excluded from the upper echelons of contemporary organizations. The reproduction of gender relations and inequality in search processes may take idiosyncratic forms across societies, but the outcome in different conditions is remarkably similar: men prevail over women (Tienari et al., 2013). While executive search serves to deny women access to top jobs, extant research also suggests that it excludes most men, as it defines in an increasingly narrow way the necessary qualities of the 'ideal' executive (Meriläinen et al., 2015).

We argue that the exclusion of women in practices of executive search is primarily about the active inclusion of a particular type of man rather than overt discrimination of women. Search processes reproduce meanings about necessary qualities in top management and support the selection of men fitting into the mould. We suggest that these subtle reproductive dynamics deserve more attention in the study of gendered careers in management (Holgersson, 2013). In this chapter, we elaborate on how the active inclusion of men is done, often inadvertently, and suggest different ways to understand it theoretically. The empirical location of our study is Sweden, a North European society that is widely known for being gender egalitarian. Based on our analysis of interviews with Swedish headhunters, we seek to disrupt this image.

The chapter is structured as follows. First, we introduce Sweden as a socio-cultural context for making sense of executive search and gendered careers. On the basis of our empirical study, we then present a narrative of executive search, and finally offer three different theoretical perspectives on it.

WELCOME TO SWEDEN, THE LAND OF EQUALITY!

Sweden is a wealthy industrialized Western democracy. While being a relatively poor country in the nineteenth century, by the 1930s Sweden became one of the most prosperous societies in the world through the development of a welfare state model based on state-coordinated capitalism (Esping-Andersen, 1990). This was coined as the 'people's home' where all Swedes regardless of economic and class background were entitled to social welfare and well-being. Solidified during the era of the people's home, with national-level agreements between employers and trade unions (Isaksson, 2008), the management tradition in Sweden is employee-oriented and democratic (Jönsson, 1995). It is argued that the distinctive characteristics of management in Sweden are fairness, cooperation, conflict avoidance and consensus as well as rationality and pragmatism (Zander, 2000; Sandberg, 2013).

However, since the 1990s, Sweden has been influenced by transnational economic processes of a neoliberal market ideology in the form of deregulation, privatization, and emphasis on shareholder value. This is reflected in Swedish organizations and the ways in which they are managed. Swedish management is subject to an 'ideological Americanization' through the influence of consultancy firms and a widespread adoption of management models and practices originating in the USA (Docherty and Huzzard, 2003).

At the same time, striving for gender equality remains a distinct feature of Swedish policy-making. In the *Global Gender Gap* reports offered by the World Economic Forum, for example, Sweden regularly scores in the top five (Hausmann et al., 2012). General awareness of the importance of gender issues is high, and since the 1970s in particular, the state and governments in Sweden have been influenced by women's movements (Bergqvist et al., 2007). This is reflected in the rhetoric of governmental policy documents. The aim of the current Swedish government's gender equality policy, for example, is 'on the one hand, to combat and change systems that preserve the gender-based distribution of power and resources at societal level, and on the other, to create the conditions for women and men to enjoy the same power and opportunities to influence their own lives' (Swedish Government, 2013).

Drawing explicit attention to societal power structures and means of influencing these structures is distinctive of the Swedish approach to gender equality: 'When women and men share power and influence in all aspects of community life, we will have a fairer and more democratic society' (ibid.). At the same time, a more instrumentalist understanding of equality is also apparent: 'gender equality also contributes to economic growth by promoting people's skills and creativity' (ibid.). In brief, the discourse on gender and diversity in Sweden is a mix of arguments based on moral rights and the utilitarian business case (Omanović, 2006).

There is a relatively long tradition of women's participation in working life in Sweden. The 1970s were a particularly active time for legislative changes enabling the participation of both sexes in the labour market. In 1974, parental benefit was introduced, allowing both parents to share the parental leave. Today each parent is entitled to parental benefit for 240 days, of which 60 days are reserved for each parent separately. In 1979, the Gender Equality Act was enacted. The present legislation not only forbids gender-based discrimination in the workplace, but also demands that employers take proactive measures in order to provide equal opportunities. A new comprehensive Discrimination Act came into force in 2009, highlighting issues of ethnicity, religion and sexuality alongside gender. Thus far, however, this legislation has had little effect in terms of the composition of top management in Swedish organizations (Holgersson, 2013).

Overall, and similarly to the other Nordic countries, Sweden is characterized by a paradox that is the simultaneous presence of gender equality and inequality. Although women and men in Sweden are equally represented in Parliament, and the welfare state model even in its revised form enables women and men to combine paid work with having a family, they continue to face different opportunities in the labour market and in the workplace. Women currently make up approximately 50 per cent of the labour force in Sweden. The majority of women, 68 per cent, work full-time, while 32 per cent work part-time – this can be compared to 90 per cent of employed men who work full-time and 10 per cent part-time (Statistics Sweden, 2012). Also, the labour market is markedly differentiated into distinct male- and female-dominated sectors. Women are in the majority in several key areas in the public sector (for example, healthcare and education), while many industries remain clearly male dominated. Vertical gender segregation is also prevalent: women are under-represented in management positions in the private sector, comprising some 25 per cent of all managers (ibid.). At the top, segregation is even clearer. When writing this text, 12 out of 254 (4.7 per cent) publicly listed companies in Sweden had a female CEO (*Affärsvärlden*, 2013).

EXECUTIVE SEARCH IN SWEDEN

Approximately 100 consultancy firms in Sweden specialize in recruitment, and most of these firms offer some kind of executive search service. Large global consultancies have carved out a strong position in the Swedish market, but local firms and one-person enterprises are also active. The market has grown considerably. In 2000, executive search firms employed approximately 800 people, but by 2011 the figure had risen to some 1400 (Konsultguiden, 2013). Executive search consultants have become a powerful player in Swedish society and business.

The following narrative offers insights from within, through the eyes of the search consultant, to make sense of the role that gender plays in processes of executive search. The narrative is based on interviews with seven Swedish executive search consultants, five men and two women, who are involved in recruiting top managers and who have shown an interest in diversity issues. While the age (between 35 and 70) and affiliation (Swedish and multinational search firms) of the consultants varied, their descriptions of the significant features of the search process were notably similar. We noticed that the interviewees not only depicted the process in similar ways, but their descriptions of how gender plays a role therein were also notably consistent.

Our interviews were originally carried out for the purposes of a cross-cultural comparative study of executive search (Tienari et al., 2013). For this chapter, we revisited the interview transcripts. We crafted a common Swedish headhunter narrative, written in the form of an 'I', that incorporates the key themes and storylines found in the individual interviews. This does not imply that the headhunter's talk does not contain ambiguities and contradictions. On the contrary, it is these recurring ambiguities and contradictions that render the narrative interesting from the point of view of gendered careers.

The Headhunter's Narrative

I am an executive search consultant based in Sweden, and I would like to tell you about my work and the people I work with. The search process comprises a number of phases, which structure my interactions with clients and candidates. I call these phases profiling, listing, and involving the client.

Profiling
In the beginning, I need to establish the relationship and secure the contract with the client. I mingle with chairs and board members, CEOs, and heads of divisions. I've been around the block a few times, and decision-makers in companies and other organizations know me. They also know and trust the executive search firm where I'm employed. Before I started to work in executive search I worked as a director in several companies. I have a credible track record in business – and I know what it is like to be a top manager and have responsibility for profits and losses and personnel. I nurture trusting relationships. Taking care of my network is the foundation of my work.

After I've secured an assignment, I must find ways to make the client specify his [sic] needs. What is the job about and what is expected of the person who is to do the job? Once I have a good understanding of the job, I try to pinpoint the particular qualities and competencies that are expected of a suitable candidate. This means that I must tread lightly. I lead my clients to articulate their expectations and preferences, but avoid pushing them too far. It is crucial to find out what the client is really looking for. That's what I call profiling – one of the key activities in the search process – in a nutshell. My job is an ongoing juxtapositioning of what the client expects and values on the one hand, and screening what relevant candidates there are on offer on the other. Profiling is a precarious task. When I start to look around for possible candidates, I need to tease out more information about those qualities and skills that the client has put forth as relevant. When I start evaluating potential candidates, I must carefully consider their suitability for the client organization. In other words, I must be sensitive to how the candidates would fit into its particular culture.

I'm committed to professional excellence. I'm aware of the fact that we need more women in top positions in companies. This makes sense from the point of view of talent. I want to make sure that the best candidate is always selected, irrespective of gender. That is my responsibility and prerogative, as I'm confident that clients are not interested in the gender of the candidates, but their skills. Having said that, it is interesting to note that many of my clients say that they are interested in recruiting more women in top positions, although this is seldom expressed as a specific requirement. It is self-evident that we should be looking for women candidates. Then you have some clients, mainly from the public sector, that are very outspoken about their expectations. A lack of women in the initial stage of the search process requires a thorough explanation; you are told off if you don't come up with any female candidates.

At other times, it is not clear whether the client prefers a man or a woman, or whether it makes a difference to them in the first place. With my experience, I'm able to find this out although it is not clearly articulated up front. This is where my cultural knowledge plays a role; I know what you can and can't say out loud in Sweden. I know what is considered embarrassing, and this can vary across companies and industries, too. The cultural codes are there for me to interpret and work on.

I haven't really given much thought to race or ethnicity. The issue does not come up in the discussions with clients, although I guess many clients would appreciate more international management teams. After all, foreign trade is the heart of Swedish business. The integration of second-generation immigrants into Swedish society is a particularly important question in general, but unfortunately it does not come to the fore in my job, where I deal with top and middle management positions specifically. Also, good international candidates are few and far between. Attracting competent non-Swedish executives to take up a top position here in Sweden is notoriously difficult. The financial compensation is still low in comparison to North America and the UK, and the taxes are high. The climate is not exactly appealing either. Then again, foreigners wouldn't be able to speak Swedish, which is still a prerequisite for most top jobs here. I guess this is the case pretty much everywhere. It would be impossible to manage a firm based in France without being able to speak French.

All in all, more heterogeneity in top management would probably be a good thing. However, diversity is not a selling point vis-à-vis Swedish companies. Some are very conscious about it, others are just ignorant. Many say that they value diversity in general but when it comes to diversity at top management levels, clients are not really interested. In the end, you sort of assume that they expect a white heterosexual Swede.

As I mentioned earlier, in principle this includes women, but it is often difficult to find female candidates with the right work experience. I'm searching for people for top positions so I must live with the tip of the iceberg, so to speak. The problem lies much deeper than in top management. More women and minorities ought to be promoted to relevant positions down the line where they would become visible and where they could get the skills and experience needed to climb into top positions. That would make my job easier. Now I need to wrestle with the existing management culture that is rather conservative. And I can't recruit someone that will not be accepted by the management team or the employees anyway. We need to present candidates that we know can do the job – and the client can then choose the one they like best. It's important that they like the candidate because, as we say, you base your recruitment on competence but you fire people because of personality.

Listing
Next, I come up with a wide pool of potential candidates for the position at hand. I compile what we call a 'long list'. I usually look for someone who has done well in a similar position and management challenge elsewhere. I come up with names from my network or probe it for tips for candidates who match the client's preferred profile. Like so many of my colleagues I specialize in particular industries, and draw on my personal experience in these industries in choosing which candidates to include on the list. The role of my in-house research assistants – or analysts as we call them – can also be significant in, for example, performing searches online.

A colleague of mine says that she tries to contact both men and women for tips since men are so much better at recommending other men. This might be a good way to expand the pool of candidates. However, many of our competitors are very male dominated. All the consultants are men and they just have female personal assistants. The industry is male dominated, but I'm glad to say that our firm is a little different, we have a woman consultant and a couple of analysts that are women. I firmly believe that our structured approach helps us to find more female candidates.

When I have decided on my long list I begin to narrow it down. I talk to candidates on the phone, take references, and evaluate the candidates' appropriateness and willingness to take up the position. Once I have a reasonable number of candidates who are interested in being involved in the process, I'll discuss them informally with the client, just to check that we have understood each other correctly and that I haven't missed out on some important criteria.

We're talking about top positions here. The ways in which clients define the position and the profile of the ideal candidate contribute to the challenge of finding suitable female candidates. The client typically comes up with loads of criteria that they think are hugely relevant. Finding someone to match all the criteria is very difficult, of course. Relevant management experience is usually the most important criterion. The client may say that 'I definitely want a woman' and then it turns out that it's just impossible to find a woman who matches all their expectations. For example, I've been asked to find a woman who has been in the management team of an industrial company. I screened the relevant industries and realized that there were very few women in the managerial ranks of these companies in the first place. And if you find them, they often occupy positions such as human resources or communications, and those posts do not lead to CEO positions. This is just the way it is. In the end, you realize that finding female candidates remains a wish rather than a demand from the client's side.

In other words, it is not always possible to present candidates of both sexes to the client even if one would like to and the client would, in principle, appreciate that. In my company the goal is to present at least two candidates of each gender to the client. However, particular management positions are so clearly male or female dominated that you often need to compromise on this principle. You end up with men in male-dominated positions such as CEOs and COOs, and you tend to end up with women for communications or human resources positions.

Today, the client is likely to hint that they want to set age limits for the search. It depends on the position at hand, of course, but it seems to me that the preferred candidates are getting younger. I have a case that I'm working on where my client is looking for a Chief Financial Officer. They say they are seeking someone who is between 35 and 40 years old, and who has been in charge of a business unit, preferably in a couple of different companies. Well, it is difficult to find a woman with a family who has had the time to do all that. I've decided to extend my search to slightly older women, too, maybe up to 45 or so, just in case. From my experience, I know that I'm going to have to convince the client to be more open about potential candidates that are a little older. I can modify the criteria slightly to find a woman and hopefully, once the client is presented with a great woman candidate, age is no longer a key concern. In general, clients today seem to be looking for some kind of superperson. That is often an elusive ideal that no candidate is able to fulfil, man or woman.

I select a handful of top candidates for more in-depth screening. This is my 'short list'. I interview the top candidates, and on this basis I choose which candidates I will eventually present to the client. In fact, we call these discussions rather than interviews. I have discussions with potential candidates where I disclose the identity of my client. I tell the candidate what I know about the organization, and check if the candidate is still interested. I will also ask questions about the candidate's career and life in general. I want to find a person whose life story is comprehensible and coherent and somehow sticks together. I get anxious if there is some kind of jag in the story, something that does not make sense and that the candidate is not able to account for. Executive search is a delicate process vis-à-vis candidates too, not just clients. I'm dealing with highly competent people with big egos, and they need to be treated with respect.

I talk to the really promising candidates several times and get to know them better. The screening gets more personal as I make sure that the client will not encounter any surprises. Some of my colleagues use these elaborate psychological personality tests, but I've learned to rely on my own expertise and gut feeling and my detective work. It's always relevant to ask around and get to talk to people who are, or have been, close to the candidate in question. If you are good at using references you don't need personality tests. I'm constantly on the lookout for personal information regarding my top candidates, something that interviews and personality tests do not reveal. If I'm lucky, I'll come across some crucial information. The slightest hint of misbehaviour or problems with alcohol, for example, and that person is out.

Not that there is much room for drinking nowadays. Corporate managers need to be in excellent physical condition. A healthy lifestyle is important, and I get suspicious if someone is overweight. It tells me that this person might not be taking good care of himself. The same goes for clothes and personal hygiene. You don't give a good impression if you are not neat and tidy. Recruiting someone at this level is a great investment and you don't want to leave your business in the hands of someone who is not capable of self-control. Also, the candidate's appearance must be in line with the traditions and norms in the industry in question. It is important for the candidate to fit into the company culture.

We talk less about the candidate's family situation. We do make notes about the candidate's marital status and children, but there is actually little value in that kind of information unless the job requires a major change in lifestyle, like relocating abroad. I've seen some male candidates who have accepted an offer to move abroad without consulting their wife and have had to come back a couple of days later and decline. Female candidates, in contrast, seldom accept an offer without discussing it with the family. They bring up family issues with me and sometimes with the client, making sure that they understand that she has family obligations. But then again, I've had male candidates that have declined offers due to family reasons. For top jobs such as a CEO I want to meet the spouse, which of course is almost always a woman. These jobs are not quite like other top management positions; you literally don't have any personal life.

Involving the client

Finally, I involve the client in talking to the top candidates. I present a small number of candidates to key decision-makers in the client firm, often the CEO and members of the board of directors that form the search committee. I try to 'coach' both sides to create the best possible conditions for them to get to know each other. However, the selection always lies with the client. I find candidates for them to choose from, and help them to make an informed decision.

Time and again you realize how conservative clients are. They don't want to take risks with the people they recruit to their top posts. Come to think of it, most search consultants are conservative, too. They are not keen on taking the risk of disappointing their clients. At the same time, female candidates tend to question their own ability to fulfil the task even though they are often more competent than their male competitors. They can sometimes even sound surprised when I have identified them as a potential candidate.

Of course, I do a lot of follow-up work with clients and candidates. I keep in touch with candidates, both the ones I have helped to find new positions and those who were not chosen, since they might be relevant for other positions in the future. I spend a lot of time on the phone just touching base with my network; the foundation of my work. I'll say this again: it is unfortunate that it is so difficult to get more women into top positions in business. But this is just the way it is. Maybe we should challenge our clients more? Maybe we should encourage women candidates more? Maybe women themselves should become more active?

THEORETICAL READINGS

'This is just the way it is' is something that we heard frequently in our interviews with Swedish executive search consultants. It serves as an emblem for this chapter as it signifies the continuity – and the active maintenance of stability – in executive management. It highlights the reflective consultant's helplessness in bringing about change. It also brings to the fore the ambiguities and contradictions that characterize executive search. How to make sense of the executive search consultant's narrative then? At least three theoretical perspectives and readings suggest themselves.

A first possible reading of the headhunter's narrative seeks to make sense of the specific practices of executive search that are gendered and have gendered consequences. These practices consist of recurring activities organized around shared understandings between the various parties involved (Schatzki, 2001). Particular practices such as profiling, listing, and involving the client have developed over time and they carry expectations of how the service should be carried out professionally, as well as what constitutes a successful outcome. Executive search is independent and confidential external advice informed by specific norms of professionalism (Beaverstock et al., 2010). It is a form of consultancy service that is produced together with the client. However, the relationship between the consultant and the client is an asymmetrical one as the client always makes the final decision regarding recruitment. The consultant's sphere of influence is thus determined by their ability to act as an intermediary; to match the client's expectations and preferences with their network and pool of available candidates (Coverdill and Finlay, 1998).

Successful matching entails an understanding of the client's needs and their specific culture, and this calls for developing rapport with the client. Avoiding the risk of mismatch or 'cultural clash' can be seen as a necessary element of the asymmetry in the relationship. Calling the client's preferences and wishes into question can be perceived as a breach of professional norms. The asymmetrical relationship is, however, moderated by the status of the consultant and the prestige of the firm they represent. The higher the status of the consultant and prestige of the firm, the more room there may be for the consultant to challenge established norms and practices.

Khurana (2002) offers an alternative perspective on the normative aspects of executive search. He suggests that there are three primary elements of intermediation by headhunters, which he calls coordinating, mediating, and legitimatizing. Headhunters coordinate the activities of the client firm's key decision-makers. They mediate confidentially between people with fragile egos, career concerns, and an interest in maintaining their personal reputation. Crucially, headhunters also legitimate the search by signalling to constituents that the process is conducted professionally and with the best interests of the participants in mind. Khurana (2002) captures this intermediation with a metaphor, suggesting that executive search is a theatrical process: its outcome is that people are hired 'in the image of the corporate chieftains whom search firms seek to serve' (p. 131). In other words, the executive search process is theatrical in a specific way; it is marked by hidden expectations and norms affecting how executives should look and how executive management should be performed. Our narrative reveals that age, for example, is embedded in the client's expectations and preferences and that this has consequences in terms of gender (cf. Faulconbridge et al., 2009; Dreher et al., 2011).

Our second theoretical reading of the headhunter's narrative is based on considering the impact of gendered structures and relations in society on the search process, thus contextualizing the studied phenomenon (Tienari et al., 2002), rather than on focusing on the specific features of the search process. Executive search does not take place in a vacuum. It is sensitive to the socio-cultural and societal conditions where it is performed or 'done' by consultants, clients, and candidates (Tienari et al., 2013). Search practices in which representations of the ideal candidate are reproduced only take on meaning when the parties involved recognize them as legitimate and 'normal'. While the outcomes of search processes in terms of male dominance may be similar across societies, the discourses on the reasons behind it are likely to vary. For example, women's family responsibilities and their impact on performing executive management are framed differently in different societal contexts (ibid.).

As a context for executive search, Sweden is illuminative of these societal specificities. The paradox of simultaneous equality and inequality looms large. Executive search consultants' assumption that their clients appreciate female candidates in the search process reflects the overarching principle of gender equality in Swedish society. The relative downplaying of women's family responsibilities as a career hindrance is a specific example of this. In fact, headhunters put some of the blame on women's own lack of proactivity in relation to their careers. This is again typical of a society where the assumption is that gender equality has, to a significant extent, been achieved. At the same time, there is a basic awareness among the consultants we interviewed that conditions for managing a managerial career differ for women and men. However, such awareness does not necessarily mean that the consultants are aware of how their own actions reproduce inequalities. This is an example of what Mathieu (2009) describes as a gap between discursive and practical consciousness in Swedish organizations: search consultants are able to articulate the problem in principle, but these articulations seldom translate into concrete actions for change (cf. Giddens, 1979).

Holgersson (2013) argues that, among men in top positions in Swedish organizations, the lack of reflexivity concerning the privileges that they enjoy throughout their careers may explain why it is possible for male homosocial practices to prevail in a societal context with a gender-egalitarian ideology. This is amplified by the persistent gender-based segregation in the Swedish labour market. Horizontal segregation contributes to vertical segregation: female-dominated managerial positions such as human resources and communications turn out to be dead-end jobs in terms of advancement to top executive posts. Age, too, seems to work differently for women and men in Sweden. Specific assumptions about age (and the characteristics of a person of a certain age) prevail, and the ideal top management candidate is middle-aged with a long and successful track record (ibid.). Considering that women in Sweden continue to take the largest share of parental leave, the pool of middle-aged female candidates with the 'right' track record is inevitably limited.

However, some Swedish consultants seek to translate awareness into action, albeit in subtle ways, by looking for female candidates that are somewhat older than the client has originally specified, for example. A propitious interpretation of such interventions would suggest tempered radicalism, that is, a strategy for change in which open confrontation is avoided in favour of smaller more muted actions (Meyerson and Scully, 1995). Overall, the 'tip of the iceberg' argument in the headhunter's narrative above is noteworthy. It suggests that the main problem does not lie with the executive search consultants, but with the clients who have not promoted women to those positions in their organizations from where the step to top management is typically taken. Executive search consultants are in this way forced to inherit a more general problem. At the same time, they are active in reproducing the very same management culture that may in practice discriminate against women. Nevertheless, they have the opportunity to impact upon the pool of potential candidates and, in this way, they are perhaps able to modify the client's preferred profile of a successful candidate.

Finally, our third theoretical reading of the headhunter's narrative suggests that established practices of executive search can be conceived of as an inherent part of a wider system of stratification and reproduction of elites in society, thus taking the socio-cultural and societal perspective further to problematize questions of ethnicity and class in relation to gender. According to the most recent comprehensive study of Swedish elites (Göransson, 2007), the business elite is argued to be the most homogeneous in terms of ethnicity compared to other elite groups within, for example, politics. Only 2 per cent of all CEOs and chairs of the board, irrespective of gender, were born outside Sweden and only 5 per cent had a foreign background (that is, at least one parent born outside Sweden). The Swedish business elite is also homogeneous in terms of class background. A majority of CEOs and chairs, both women and men, follow in the footsteps of their fathers who also had management positions, and a vast majority had a higher education degree in business administration or engineering, mostly from prestigious universities. Incidentally, not only is the business elite the most wealthy of all elite groups in Swedish society, it is also the group that reports having the most conservative political opinions.

Moreover, the business elite in Sweden comes across as closed, since a major part of their networks are mainly confined to the business elite – both national and international – that have developed during their careers (ibid.). Interestingly, men and women in the business elite claim that the most important success factors for a business career are education and personal contacts. In fact, women in the Swedish business elite assert that an important reason behind the low number of women in top management positions in business is that the recruitment is based on informal networks (ibid.). Extant literature has outlined executive search consultants' role in reproduction of transnational elites in the global economy (Faulconbridge et al., 2009). However, there is a lack of accounts of their influence locally, which means that we are unable to explore how practices of executive search contribute to the reproduction of such homogeneous and closed elites as the one found in Sweden.

We suggest that elite formation and reproduction in particular societal conditions such as Sweden can be viewed from two complementary perspectives. On the one hand, while the question of promoting more women into top management continues to be on the agenda in Sweden, and there is a general agreement that diversity is something positive, the issue of ethnicity and race is seldom discussed in relation to management. Although there appears to be general interest in including people of different nationalities (or Swedes with international experience) in management teams in multinational corporations in particular, inclusion of people with a migrant background does not seem to be a topic for discussion. Executive search consultants are typically not asked to take this into account in their assignments. Perceptions of what is suitable and necessary for a management career continue to be modelled according to a specific bourgeois lifestyle that presupposes a person with a prestigious university degree and a specific track record. And, once again, the problem of exclusion is distanced – placed somewhere else, on the clients, or on society as a whole.

This can be linked to the critique of the Swedish gender equality model that argues that the model builds on women's common interests, but has in fact neglected and marginalized the interests of immigrant women (De los Reyes et al., 2003). It is well established that the career opportunities for young people of immigrant origin – men and women – differ radically from their indigenous Swedish counterparts (Knocke, 2000; Göransson, 2007). As long as management cultures are not questioned from a more radical intersectional perspective, increasing the number of women in management positions is synonymous to increasing the number of white, most probably heterosexual, women who conform to a bourgeois lifestyle. The outcome is a narrow conception of what management competencies in terms of skills and experience are necessary and what kind of lifestyle is required to be able to gain such competencies and to become a successful executive.

On the other hand, something that is hidden between the lines in our narrative pertains to the fact that bodies of candidates play a crucial role in the executive search process. Particular understandings of the 'ideal' executive body (cf. Acker, 1990) are reproduced in, and through, search practices that disadvantage not only women but also many (if not most) men (Meriläinen et al., 2014). What concerns both men and women is that perceptions of bodily normality are becoming increasingly narrow (Longhurst, 2001; Kenny and Bell, 2011). 'I get a bit suspicious if someone is overweight', as the headhunter in our narrative put it. Extant literature has argued that the normality of executive bodies is increasingly determined by reference to top athletes (Sinclair, 2011). Executives are expected to display healthy, active, energetic, mobile, and durable bodies that signal determination and competitiveness (Meriläinen et al., 2014). We suggest that nurturing a specific form of athletic body – and incorporating this as a criterion in executive search – can be interpreted as contributing to class distinctions. A specific lifestyle is necessary in order to produce and keep up healthy, active, and energetic bodies fit for management (Holgersson, 2003). In Sweden, sports that are popular among corporate executives such as marathon running, cross-country skiing, and cycling require not only time for exercise but also financial resources for personal trainers, quality gear, training camps, and competitions (Johansson, 2012). Such a lifestyle is mainly available to people with a certain income – white ethnic Swedes – who use sports as a forum to develop their elite networks.

CONCLUSION

In this chapter, we have argued that the exclusion of women in practices of executive search is primarily not about overt discrimination of women, but the active inclusion of a particular type of man with the right track record at the right time (age) and with the right bodily characteristics and lifestyle. We have specified how executive search practices serve to reproduce norms and expectations regarding candidates who correspond to a specific gendered management ideal. We have also shown how established practices in the client–consultant relationship circumscribe the consultants' opportunities to challenge this ideal. We have considered the impact of socio-cultural and societal conditions on executive search, and looked at search processes from the perspective of the (re)production of elites.

These insights have implications for studying gendered careers in management. Our study is carried out in the particular socio-cultural context of Sweden where a considerable number of the population, 20 per cent, is of immigrant origin. Unemployment is today higher for this group and many are over-represented in low-skilled and low-paid jobs (Schierup, 2006), which Neergaard (2006) calls subordinate inclusion. This state of affairs is reproduced by the crucial role that social networks continue to play in recruitment (Knocke et al., 2003; Behtoui, 2006; Tovatt, 2011). In relation to such observations and our findings, we suggest that it is particularly important to further explore how class interacts with gender and ethnicity in the process of recruitment to different hierarchical levels in organizations, in order to deepen our understanding of the reproduction of inequalities in gendered and ethnicized organizations in the global economy. Exclusion of women from top management is merely the tip of the iceberg, and it is not only a question of men and women, but race, ethnicity, and class, too.

REFERENCES

Acker, J. (1990), 'Hierarchies, jobs, bodies: a theory of gendered organizations', *Gender and Society*, **4**(2), 139–58.
Affärsvärlden (2013), 'Trendbrott – färre kvinnliga börs-vd:ar' [Fewer women CEOs in listed companies], *Affärsvärlden*, accessed 14 April 2014 at www.affarsvarlden.se/hem/nyheter/article3785188.ece.
Beaverstock, J.V., J.R. Faulconbridge and S.J.E. Hall (2010), 'Professionalization, legitimization and the creation of executive search markets in Europe', *Journal of Economic Geography*, **10**(6), 825–43.
Bergqvist, C., T. Olsson Blandy and D. Sainsbury (2007), 'Swedish state feminism: continuity and change', in J. Outshoorn and J. Kantola (eds), *Changing State Feminism*, Basingstoke, UK: Palgrave Macmillan, pp. 224–45.
Behtoui, A. (2008), 'Informal recruitment methods and disadvantages of immigrants in the Swedish labour market', *Journal of Ethnic and Migration Studies*, **34**(3), 411–30.
Coverdill, J.E. and W. Finlay (1998), 'Fit and skill in employee selection: insights from a study of headhunters', *Qualitative Sociology*, **21**(2), 105–27.
De los Reyes, P., I. Molina and D. Mulinari (2003), *Maktens (o)lika förklädnader. Kön, klass och etnicitet i det post-koloniala Sverige* [The Many Disguises of Power. Gender, Class and Ethnicity in Postcolonial Sweden], Stockholm: Atlas.
Docherty, P. and T. Huzzard (2003), 'Marknads-, management- och medarbetartrender 1985–2005' [Market, management and co-workership trends 1985–2005], in C. von Otter (ed.), *Ute och inne i svenskt arbetsliv*, Stockholm: Arbetslivsinstitutet, pp. 135–57.
Doldor, E., S. Vinnicombe, M. Gaughan and R. Sealy (2012), *Gender Diversity on Boards: The Appointment Process and the Role of Executive Search Firms*, Equality and Human Rights Commission, Research Report No. 85, Manchester, UK: Equality and Human Rights Commission.
Dreher, G.F., J.L. Lee and T.A. Clerkin (2011), 'Mobility and cash compensation: the moderating effects of gender, race, and executive search firms', *Journal of Management*, **37**(3), 651–81.
Esping-Andersen, G. (1990), *The Three Worlds of Welfare Capitalism*, Cambridge, UK: Polity Press.
Faulconbridge, J.R., J.V. Beaverstock, S.J.E. Hall and A. Hewitson (2009), 'The "war for talent": the gatekeeper role of executive search firms in elite labour markets', *Geoforum*, **40**(5), 800–808.
Giddens, A. (1979), *Central Problems in Social Theory*, London: Macmillan.
Göransson, A. (ed.) (2007), *Maktens kön: kvinnor och män i den svenska makteliten på 2000-talet* [The Gender of Power: Women and Men in the Swedish Elite in the 00-ties], Nora: Nya Doxa.
Hausmann, R., L.D. Tyson and S. Zahidi (2012), *The Global Gender Gap Report 2012*, Geneva: World Economic Forum.
Holgersson, C. (2003), *Rekrytering av företagsledare: en studie i homosocialitet* [Recruitment of Managing Directors. A Study of Homosociality], Stockholm: Stockholm School of Economics.
Holgersson, C. (2013), 'Recruiting managing directors: doing homosociality', *Gender, Work & Organization*, **20**(4), 454–66.
Isaksson, P. (2008), *Leading Companies in a Global Age – Managing the Swedish Way*, VINNOVA Report VR 2008:14, Stockholm: VINNOVA.
Johansson, J. (2012), 'Becoming healthy organization leaders', unpublished manuscript, Stockholm: Stockholm University School of Business.
Jönsson, S. (1995), *Goda utsikter – svenskt management i perspektiv* [Good Prospects – Swedish Management in Perspective], Stockholm: Nerenius and Santérus.
Kenny, K. and E. Bell (2011), 'Representing the successful managerial body', in E.L. Jeanes, D. Knights and P. Yancey Martin (eds), *Handbook of Gender, Work and Organization*, Chichester, UK: John Wiley and Sons, pp. 163–76.

Khurana, R. (2002), *Searching for a Corporate Savior. The Irrational Quest for Charismatic CEOs*, Princeton, NJ: Princeton University Press.
Knocke, W. (2000), 'Integration or segregation? Immigrant populations facing the labour market in Sweden', *Economic and Industrial Democracy*, **21**(3), 361–80.
Knocke, W., I.-B. Drejhammar, L. Gonäs and I. Kerstin (2003), *Retorik och praktik i rekryteringsprocessen* [Rhetoric and Practice in the Recruitment Process], Stockholm: Arbetslivsintitutet.
Konsultguiden (2013), 'Rankinglistor' [Ranking lists], accessed 16 August 2013 at www.konsultguiden.se/rankinglistor.
Longhurst, R. (2001), *Bodies: Exploring Fluid Boundaries*, London: Routledge.
Mathieu, C. (2009), 'Practicing gender in organizations: the critical gap between practical and discursive consciousness', *Management Learning*, **40**(2), 177–93.
Meriläinen, S., J. Tienari and A. Valtonen (2015), 'Headhunters and the "ideal" executive body', *Organization*, **22**(1), 3–22.
Meyerson, D.E. and M.A. Scully (1995), 'Tempered radicalism and the politics of ambivalence and change', *Organization Science*, **6**(5), 585–600.
Neergaard, A. (2006), *På tröskeln till lönearbete: diskriminering, exkludering och underordning av personer med utländsk bakgrund* [On the Threshold to Paid Work: Discrimination, Exclusion and Subordination of People with a Foreign Background], Stockholm: Norstedts Juridik.
Omanović, V. (2006), *A Production of Diversity: Appearances, Ideas, Interests, Actions, Contradictions and Praxis*, Gothenburg: BAS Publishing.
Sandberg, A. (ed.) (2013), *Nordic Lights. Work, Management and Welfare in Scandinavia*, Stockholm: SNS.
Schatzki, T.R. (2001), 'Introduction: practice theory', in T.R. Schatzki, K. Knorr Cetina and E. von Savigny (eds), *The Practice Turn in Contemporary Theory*, New York: Routledge, pp. 10–23.
Schierup, C.-U. (2006), 'Migration, arbetsmarknad och välfärdsstat i förändring' [Migration, labour market and welfare state in transition], in P. de los Reyes (ed.), *Arbetslivets (o) synliga murar, SOU 2006:59*, Stockholm: Norstedts Juridik.
Sinclair, A. (2011), 'Leading with body', in E.L. Jeanes, D. Knights and P. Yancey Martin (eds), *Handbook of Gender, Work and Organization*, Chichester, UK: John Wiley and Sons, pp. 117–30.
Statistics Sweden (2012), 'På tal om kvinnor och män. Lathund om jämställdhet' [Talking of Women and Men – A Quick Guide to Gender Equality), accessed 16 August 2013 at www.scb.se/statistik/_publikationer/LE0201_2012A01_BR_X10BR1201.pdf.
Swedish Government (2013), 'Gender equality', accessed 16 August 2014 at www.government.se/sb/d/4096.
Tienari, J., S. Quack and H. Theobald (2002), 'Organizational reforms, "ideal workers" and gender orders: a cross-societal comparison', *Organization Studies*, **23**(2), 249–79.
Tienari, J., S. Meriläinen, C. Holgersson and R. Bendl (2013), 'And then there are none: on the exclusion of women in processes of executive search', *Gender in Management: An International Journal*, **28**(1), 43–62.
Tovatt, C. (2011), 'Young people's entry into the labour market – opportunities, strategies and gatekeepers', *Themes No. 37/11, Themes on Migration and Ethnic Studies*, Linköping: Linköping University, ISV-REMESO.
Zander, L. (2000), 'Management in Sweden', in M. Warner (ed.), *Management in Europe*, London: Thomson Learning Business Press, pp. 345–53.

9. Inclusion and exclusion processes in the executive search business: an intersectional approach
Regine Bendl, Helga Eberherr and Angelika Schmidt

Executive search consultants, also called 'headhunters', play a crucial role in the filling of leadership positions (for example, Finlay and Coverdill, 1999; Faulconbridge et al., 2009). They support corporate decision-makers in identifying, evaluating and recruiting competent and suitable people for their top jobs. Thus, executive search consultants can also be considered as gatekeepers in elite labour markets (Faulconbridge et al., 2009; Dreher et al., 2011). In their four-stage relationship (profiling, long-listing, short-listing, decision-making; Taylor and Bergmann, 1987), the executive consultants and the clients must make a lot of explicit but also implicit far-reaching decisions in order to select the 'best-fitting'[1] candidate for the job. Their task is to deal with consistent, contradictory as well as paradoxical elements in this process of selection. Decisions with regard to the qualification, skills, ability, knowledge and experience of the applicants are taken at the different stages of the whole selection process, but diversity dimensions – also considered as social categories,[2] such as the gender of the applicant, his or her ethnicity, age, (dis)abilities, sexual orientation, as well as his or her religious beliefs – also seem to influence the decisions taken in the executive search process.

Research is scarce on the role of social categories in this special recruitment process, which is based on the contract between the client and the executive research consultant. In a recent cross-cultural study carried out across Finland, Sweden and Austria, Tienari et al. (2013) explored how executive search consultants propagate male dominance in and through their practices (for example, by buying in the client's expectations to hire a male applicant). With a focus on the increase of women in leadership positions, Doldor and colleagues (2012) reveal novel practices adopted by some of the UK's leading executive search firms: (1) challenging clients when defining a brief for a board opening, (2) reaching out to female candidates and (3) supporting/mentoring them through the board appointment process (see Atewologun and Doldor, 2013). Furthermore, Bendl et al. (2011) also shed light on the (re)production of ethnicity in executive search consultants' practices. Despite the fact that ethnicity is constructed differently in the countries compared in their study, and that different white ethnicities are dominant, their data show that executive search consultants' practices are similar across national boundaries, and tend to either silence issues of ethnicity or reproduce ethnic constructions of 'us' and 'them', which affects the decision-making process when selecting a candidate.

These three studies, however, refer mainly to one dimension of diversity, and do not highlight an intersectional perspective or the impact that such a perspective may have on the decisions taken in the executives' search process and selection. Thus, based on the recruitment literature focussing on gender, ethnicity, age, (dis)abilities, sexual orientation, and religion – also called the Big 6 (see for example, Hardmeier and Vinz, 2007) – this chapter examines the following question: besides gender, what roles do the diversity dimensions of ethnicity, age, sexual orientation, religion and (dis)ability play in the executive search process, and how can their roles be specified or characterized? By exploring and cross-examining the relevance, dynamics and impacts of these diversity dimensions in the recruitment literature, we intend to highlight their intersectional qualities for the executive search selection processes. By characterizing and specifying these intersectional perspectives we contribute to a more differentiated understanding of inclusion and exclusion processes in executive search and, thus, we provide additional insight into the reproduction of women as a minority in top management positions.

Next, we will introduce the modalities of the executive search process. Then, we will present the theoretical conceptual aspects of intersectionality that guide our text. Afterwards, based on a literature review of the recruitment literature, we will describe the impact that each of the different diversity dimensions has on the recruitment process. We then discuss these results in the context of modalities of inclusion and exclusion in the executive search process and, finally, end our text with implications for the executive search process.

MODALITIES OF INCLUSION AND EXCLUSION IN THE EXECUTIVE SEARCH PROCESS

Executive search consultants specialize in filling corporate vacancies by searching for adequate candidates or headhunting an individual from other organizations. In the form of a consultancy service, executive search consultants are bridging gaps, or structural holes (Burt, 1995), between people who would otherwise remain disconnected. They represent a third party that benefits from establishing, guiding and manipulating the relationship of two others – the employer and the employee (Finlay and Coverdill, 2000).

It is an agreement between the executive search consultant and the client that states that the search consultant will provide candidates for a position that the employer is seeking to fill. The way in which a job order is generated is enormously significant because it offers answers to the question of what constitutes the relationship between the clients and the executive searcher (ibid.). Most of the executive search consultants consider their business as 'relationship driven' (ibid.): for them the building of relationships with the clients represents a key for successful searching and, consequently, for their whole business. However, this relationship does also imply a power of the clients over the executive search consultants. Formerly prevalent portraits of clients as victims, marionettes or passive consumers of consulting have been extensively revised (Höner and Mohe, 2009). Nowadays, numerous images of the client are evident: they represent sceptical purchasers or partners in the co-production of decisions such as the selection of executives (Sturdy and Wright, 2011). In this decision process executive search consultants are assuming power in defining selection criteria and in assessing the (un)suitability of candidates against these criteria (Tienari et al., 2013). Relevant decisions are necessary at different stages: first the job profile has to be specified; next, long- and short-lists are drawn up where inclusion and exclusion is practised; and the last step is the decision on the most favourable candidate, which is taken by the client. In this process, headhunters are searching for a good fit between the client and the applicant, for which not only the client's subjective evaluation of quality but also the executive search consultant's evaluations play a pivotal role (Coverdill and Finlay, 1998).

In an executive search process, headhunters are dealing with a variety of expectations and tensions (Tienari et al., 2013), and contradictions and paradoxes (Whittle, 2006), based on the necessity to establish and cultivate a good working relationship with the client. Both the client's and the executive search consultant's assumptions of personal skills, and how these fit with the requirements of the client and their organization, are thus likely to influence the search process and its outcome. In other words, the denotation of a 'good fit' depends on the client's and the executive search consultant's 'interpretative schemes', meaning their value system and their professional understanding on the one hand, and their knowledge of the sector and the job market on the other. In line with Giddens (1984), the term 'interpretative schemes' is specified as a kind of mental framework that guides actions; thus, executive search consultants actualize sets of

Inclusion and exclusion processes in the executive search 143

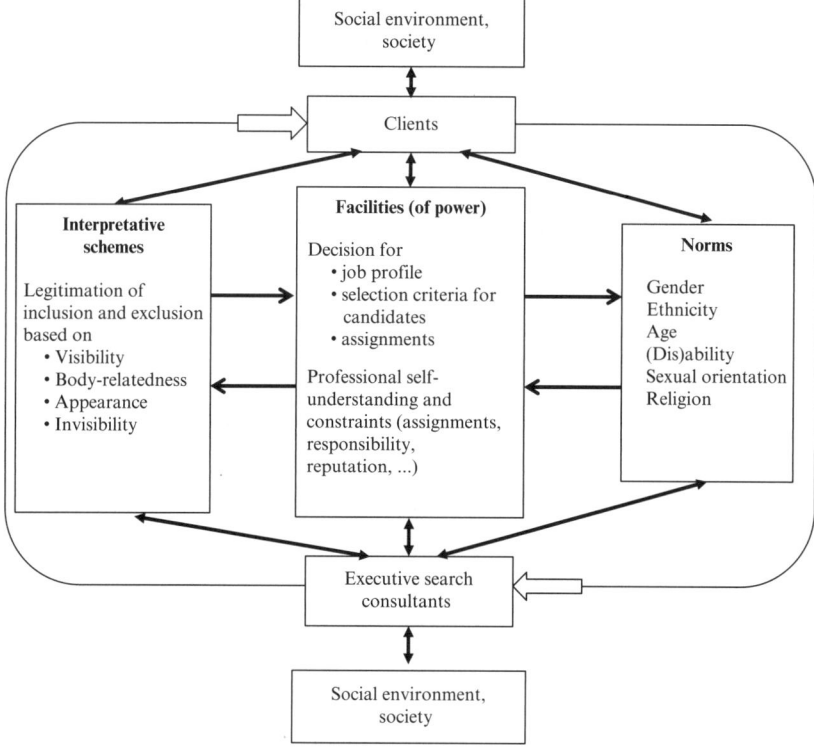

Source: Bendl (2013).

Figure 9.1 Modalities of inclusion and exclusion in the executive search process

rules in terms of signification and legitimation in their daily searching and selecting routines. According to Giddens's dimensions of the duality of structure, interpretative schemes, as well as facilities (of power) and norms, play a crucial role, because they provide the framework within which the executive search consultants' and clients' practices and actions become legitimate, which allows them flexibility in defining the selection and decision criteria (cf. Wilz, 2001). Based on Giddens's (1984) 'structuration theory', Figure 9.1 illustrates the relationship between clients and executive search consultants by modelling these search processes.

Figure 9.1 conceptualizes the executive search process as a duality of structure by modelling the relationship between the clients and the executive search consultant, as driven by interpretative schemes, facilities of power and norms (level of modalities, according to Giddens). In this two-way process, the interpretative schemes influence the decision for job profiles, selection criteria and job assignments, as well as the client's and executive search consultant's professional self-understanding – all notions that also have an impact on the norms ascribed to the different diversity dimensions. On the other hand, these (stereotypical) norms affect choices regarding job profiles, selection criteria and assignments, as well as professional self-understanding and, as a consequence, the discourse of legitimation between clients and executive search consultants. As such, the executive search process represents a process in which legitimation, power and stereotypes interact based on the mutual relationship (contract) of the clients and the executive search consultant.

INTERSECTIONALITY

Over the last decade, the concept of intersectionality has gained increasing importance in gender studies (Collins, 1999; Brah and Phoenix, 2004; Davis et al., 2006; Phoenix and Pattynama, 2006; Verloo, 2006; Yuval-Davis, 2006; Klinger et al., 2007; Davis, 2008a, 2008b) as well as in organization and diversity studies (McCall, 2001, 2005; Munro, 2001; Acker, 2006; Calás and Smircich, 2006; Styhre and Eriksson-Zetterquist, 2008; Ferree, 2009; Zanoni et al., 2010). Generally, intersectionality perspectives aim to examine 'how predominant classification systems such as class, gender, sexuality, and ethnicity/race co-exist and are simultaneously mutually constitutive and thus constantly influence how social life is structured and organized' (Styhre and Eriksson-Zetterquist, 2008, p. 568). In other words, intersectional analysis also aims to develop an analytical understanding of the singularities and specificities of different diversity dimensions, while at the same time examining categorical interferences and connections (Bendl et al., 2012, p. 80). For this chapter we consider intersectionality as a theoretical, analytical and empirical agenda, used to study the emergence of multiple social differentiation processes in relation to specific domains of knowledge and power in organizations (see Figure 9.1). It allows us to focus on the simultaneous and dynamic interaction of various diversity dimensions in the executive search process. Gender and other diversity dimensions cannot be seen as permanently salient in organizational practices. Therefore, it is crucial to understand how age, disability, ethnicity, gender, religion and sexual orientation are enacted and become relevant in the executive search process.

DIVERSITY DIMENSIONS IN THE RECRUITMENT LITERATURE

Our review of the recruitment literature shows that, for the last three decades, sex and gender[3] represent the most researched of all the diversity dimensions (for example, Powell, 1987; Hardin et al., 2002; Van den Brink et al., 2006). Independent of sector and regional location, most of these studies show that the gender of both the applicant and the recruiter affect the recruitment process. In most cases it has been found that male and female recruiters evaluate male and female applicants differently. For example, Powell (1987) was among the first to identify effects of recruiters' sex on recruiters' responses and the effect of applicants' sex on applicants' responses on the one hand, and effects of applicants' gender on recruiters' responses and effects of recruiters' gender on applicants' responses on the other. Hardin et al. (2002) found that female recruiters rate male recruits somewhat higher than female recruits, and, furthermore, that they offer significantly higher salaries to male recruits. Cole et al. (2004) demonstrated that male and female recruiters differ in their ratings of male and female applicants' reports of work experience and extracurricular activity information on their résumés: female recruiters perceive male applicants' résumés to report more on work experiences than those of female applicants, while male recruiters perceive female applicants as having more extracurricular interests than male applicants. Furthermore, female recruiters rate both male and female applicants as detailing similar amounts of extracurricular activity on their résumés. In addition to this, Gorman's (2005) findings show that when selection criteria include a greater number of stereotypically masculine characteristics, women constitute a smaller proportion of new recruits, and that, equally, when criteria include more stereotypically feminine traits, women are better represented among new recruits. Women decision-makers also fill more vacancies with women than do men decision-makers. Additionally, Van den Brink et al. (2006, p. 535) showed that a predominantly male selection committee for professorial appointments can have negative consequences for female applicants due to the 'similar-to-me' effect. Moreover, Pinar and colleagues (2009, p. 306) reveal that regardless of the gender of a recruit, female recruiters are more likely to target females. Their findings illustrate that female recruiters seem to be more optimistic and confident than male recruiters with regard to the recruits' ability in selling to female buyers. Finally, with regard to the executive search process, Tienari et al. (2013) suggest that the core practices of the executive search process constrain consultants in their efforts to introduce female candidates to the process, and to increase the number of women in corporate top management.

Bendl et al. (2013) show that male clients prefer male applicants, that women self-select (take themselves out) from the application process more often than men, and that male and female bodily ascriptions operate as a filter in the selection process.

All these research results suggest that individuals wish to preserve their contextual gender norms, and that they are prejudiced against those who violate the norms (see also Frable, 1989). As a consequence, we derive from the existing literature that gender ascriptions and stereotypes play an important role in the (re)production of facilities of power and the interpretative schemes that are applied in the executive search process.

Studies on the role of ethnicity[4] within the recruitment process are very scarce and their focus is quite widespread. They focus either on the disadvantages of different ethnicities in the recruitment process (for example, Pearson, 2012) or demonstrate how ethnicity is addressed within the recruitment process in different sectors (athletics, police, healthcare, information technology, for example, Jain, 1998; Sheffield et al., 1999; Cashmore, 2001; Waters et al., 2007; McMurray et al., 2010; Paule, 2011). Pearson (2012) highlights the recruitment of indigenous Australians with linguistic and numeric disadvantages within the mining industry. In order to work against social dislocation of marginalized indigenous groups, she proposes the substitution of discriminatory recruitment practices with alternative methods aimed at identifying human work-related potential. In the field of sport (intercollegiate recruitment process), Paule (2011) identified that the failure to consider white as a race during the recruitment process meant that the Caucasian coaches who were interviewed in the study only focussed on issues regarding the black athletes. The results of this study demonstrated that the lack of consideration for white as a race is in line with the view of sport as a 'raceless' space on the one hand, yet, on the other hand, decisions are being taken based on racial stereotypes. On the subject of the Australian Police, McMurray et al. (2010) found differing perspectives between the police and ethnic communities in terms of the recruitment of culturally and linguistically diverse staff. While the police experience difficulties with regard to language skills and educational background when recruiting applicants, ethnic communities perceive a lack of sincerity on the part of the police when recruiting culturally and linguistically diverse staff. Similar ethnicity-related exclusion processes can be found in the National Health Service (NHS) in Great Britain. Based on other studies Sheffield et al. (1999) note that black nurses were not even interviewed for jobs, that doctors from ethnic minority backgrounds with foreign names were less likely to be short-listed by consultants, and that ethnic minority doctors were being forced into less popular specialities. Furthermore, a comparison of Austria, Finland and Sweden by Bendl and colleagues (2011) on the role of ethnicity in the executive search process showed that ethnicities are constructed as binaries (also dual and hierarchical) within the executive search process: as ethnicities representing 'the norm' and those representing 'the other', depending on the context. Bendl et al. (2012) also reveal discrimination processes based on different perceptions of ethnic minorities between the clients and executive search consultants, as well as a reported lack of consciousness regarding whiteness as race. Additionally, they found that whiteness is reproduced between the clients and the executive search consultants – by the agreement on the necessity to have a homogeneous staff and to have a new employee who should fit into the organization/team.

As the existing recruitment literature shows, ethnicity, like gender, plays a role within the recruitment process; ethnic norms also influence the facilities of power and the interpretative schemes applied in the executive search process. In contrast to gender, the effect of ethnicity seems to be highly context dependent, but, like gender, hierarchical dualities between perceived norms and the exceptions to these are found to exist within the recruitment process.

Research on age,[5] ageing and age discrimination has increased considerably in organizational and human resource literature in the last decade (see for example, Duncan and Loretto, 2004; Eberherr et al., 2008; Moulaert and Biggs, 2013; Ollier-Malaterre et al., 2013). However, for recruiting processes research on age is rather rare (see Riach, 2007). Riach (2007) identifies discursive strategies regarding how the social construction of age, for example the 'older worker', contributes towards age inequalities in recruitment processes. Riach (2007, p. 1719) specifically highlights a discursive strategy 'where the older worker is validated through essentializing characteristics as derived from age'. Therefore, older workers are essentialized in recruitment practices by the consideration of the chronological age of applicants as an important personal characteristic. Chronological age limits are used as especially important criteria in selection processes (Weuster, 2012a, 2012b). With regard to executive search consultancy, Bendl and colleagues (2013) show similar results: that is, age in combination with experience counts as one of the most important decision criteria for top management positions. According to the interviewed executive search consultants, age limits do exist in the executive search process, depending on the position advertised (for example, junior managers 25–35, managers 40–45) generally the age group 50+ counts as a critical limit when hiring a new recruit. Furthermore, Bendl et al. (2013) found that age seems to be the second most important diversity dimension after gender, influencing the modalities of inclusion and exclusion in the executive search process.

Legal regulations such as the ADA (Americans with Disabilities Act) in the USA or the European Anti-Discrimination Legislation in Europe are currently changing the way in which employers screen and hire applicants with disabilities. However, almost no literature exists on the influence of disabilities on the recruitment process. As one of the few examples, Gouvier et al. (2003) showed that an applicant with a physical disability (for example, a back injury) was rated more favourably overall when compared with job applicants with other forms of disabilities. Furthermore, according to Bruyère et al. (2004), employers admit that attitudes and stereotypes are significant barriers to employing people with disabilities. Other more general texts on workplace and disability report on experiences of workplace discrimination among disabled employees (for example, Baldwin and Johnson, 1994; Stevens 2002; Chan et al., 2005; Kennedy and Harris, 2005) or demonstrate perceived barriers to employment, for example, attitudes of employers, transportation and discrimination in hiring (Ren et al., 2008).

With regard to the executive search process, Bendl and colleagues (2013) found that clients refer to disability mainly in terms of problems with the employees' protection against dismissal, and prefer to pay fines resulting from the non-employment of persons with disability. However, the executive search consultants refer to two aspects of self-selection regarding disabled recruits: either they do not tend to apply at all, or, if disabled candidates apply who do not fit the job specification, the executive search consultants do not reject the applicant directly but make the applicant aware that he or she does not fit with the job profile. The executive search consultants hope that these applicants self-select and abstain from the application (ibid.).

Together, these findings indicate that the actors involved in recruitment processes are aware of the sensitivity surrounding the matter of disability. But as the scarce literature in the field of recruitment and disability shows, the issue of disability does not feature at the forefront of recruitment processes. Furthermore, different forms of disabilities demand different considerations in the recruitment process – a matter that is not discussed in the literature. However, like gender, age and ethnicity, disability seems to influence the executive search process. As an unmarked norm, 'ableism' represents the standard norm in the executive process, otherwise more managers with disabilities would be in management and CEO positions.

The European Commission report on sexual orientation (European Commission, 2008) states that '27% of citizens were not in favour of measures to improve equality in the workplace on the grounds of sexual orientation'. This percentage represents the most unfavourable response (for sexual orientation) when compared with other discrimination grounds such as gender, ethnic origin, religion or beliefs, age and disability. In fact, on the basis of gender norms, heterosexuality serves 'as the established and accepted norm to which all other sexual orientations are compared. Other sexual orientations thus challenge traditional conceptions of gender and sexuality and are subsequently deemed abnormal and subordinate' (Cunningham et al., 2010, pp. 401f; see also Wright and Clarke, 1999; Jackson, 2006; Sartore and Cunningham, 2009). In organizational research, sexual orientation seems to be one of the lesser-researched diversity dimensions (see for example, Tonks, 2006), although in recent years research on sexual orientation in the workplace has increased (for example, Frohn, 2007; Losert, 2007; Pringle, 2008; Köllen, 2010; Colgan, 2011; Gregory, 2011; Roberts, 2011; Wright, 2011; Beckett, 2012; Bendl et al., 2012; Brower, 2013; Caven et al., 2013). With regard to the recruitment literature, texts on sexual orientation are scarce. One of the rare studies is situated in the context of the sport industry (Cunningham et al., 2010), addressing fitness clubs and the hiring of personal trainers. Additionally, Hebl and colleagues (2002) demonstrated that sexual minority applicants experienced subtle forms of discrimination during the interview process. They found that interviewers engaged in shorter conversations and made less eye contact with homosexual (gay and lesbian) applicants than with heterosexual applicants. Such differential treatment has meaningful implications, as without equal opportunities legislation during the interview process, homosexual (lesbian and gay) candidates lose out on opportunities to be hired (see also Cunningham et al., 2010). Bendl et al. (2013) demonstrate that, most of the time, sexual orientation is treated as a private or lifestyle choice with no relevance in the executive search selection process, by both the client and the executive search consultant. The invisibility of sexual orientation is stated by search consultants as being crucial for its assumed irrelevance. However, the executive search consultants who were interviewed also indicated that, in the *profiling stages*, the clients mention sexual orientation as selection criteria in the context of 'fitting to the culture of the organization'. Even though sexual orientation is a greatly neglected diversity dimension in the recruitment literature – or more precisely, a diversity dimension that is negotiated in the closet – ascribed LGBTQIA[6] stereotypes seem to influence how heteronormativity is reproduced via norms, interpretative schemes and facilities of power in the executive search process.

While in political contexts religion[7] plays a profound role, research results at the intersection of religion and organizations in general (level of the institution; ideas, beliefs and attitudes; individual level), as well as for recruitment in particular, are scarce (Dickson and Hargie, 2006; Tracey, 2012). One of the rare examples of the examination of religiosity on a structural level is Pratt (2000), who examined how a direct-selling organization (Amway) was infused with Christian religious values and beliefs. With a wider focus on spirituality, King and Holmes (2012) explore the intersection of spirituality and work and its impacts on organizational recruitment. They distinguish between spirituality of work, seen as a set of organizational values and culture, and spirituality at work (or faith at work). Their differentiation shows manifold connotations of spirituality and refers to the ongoing debate of the distinction between spirituality and religion in the workplace (Mitroff and Denton, 1999; Polley et al., 2005; Schaeffer and Mattis, 2012; Gebert et al., 2014), which may also be a criterion in the selection process.

The absence of systematic analysis regarding the role of religion in recruiting is particularly interesting, as in most countries the exercise of religion is protected by the law; the USA, for example, is home to more than 40 major religious and spiritual traditions, each with their own nuanced set of beliefs, values, practices and cultural traditions (Schaeffer and Mattis, 2012). The recent findings of Bendl et al. (2013) on the executive search process in a Catholic-dominated European country are in line with this evidence: most of the clients do not mention religion at all in the whole process, therefore many executive search consultants claim to have no experience with their clients in terms of religion. A smaller group of clients and executive search consultants shows two reactions to religion: first, they present religion as a problem if it is practised too intensively. For example, Islam is seen as a source of irritation, and some recruiters consider prayer time and women's headscarves to be problematic. Second, clients do not want to have female candidates with veils or scarves. Altogether, the study shows that with regard to religion, it is Islam that brings about the most discussion and that is presented as 'the other', whereas in this context Catholicism is seen as the unmarked norm.

In summary, this review of the recruitment literature unveils the differing relevance of the diversity dimensions: gender, ethnicity and age seem to be discussed more thoroughly in the recruitment literature than disability, religion and sexual orientation. The research results show that binary (dual and hierarchical) constructions are (re)produced within the different diversity dimensions. The context-dependent 'norm' determines the 'other' (for example, young–old; abled–disabled; male–female). However, the norm remains unaddressed in the recruiting process, especially with regard to sexual orientation and religion, whereas in terms of gender, ethnicity and age, the norms influencing the decision process are addressed.

CONCLUSION

By referring to our model of modalities of inclusion and exclusion in the executive search process (see Figure 9.1) and our literature review results, we are able to identify/generate the following three interpretative schemes that influence the intersection of the selected diversity dimensions in the executive search process.

First, visible characteristics play a more important role than invisible ones in both general recruiting processes and the executive search process. Usually, visible diversity dimensions include gender, race, age, ethnicity, or physical appearance. Because of their visibility, these social categories are well suited to the signification and ascription processes of the (re)production of meaning. Along these visible diversity dimensions, collectively shared patterns of valuation are enacted and stereotypes are actualized (see also Neckel, 2000, p.43).

Body relatedness seems to be a second axis from which diversity dimensions can be reflected upon or tied together. Closely linked to the interpretative scheme of visibility, body relatedness stands for specific aspects of visibility, namely those visibilities attached to body appearances like abled or disabled bodies, young or old bodies, fat or thin bodies and so on.

Third, and as a consequence of the first and the second interpretative schemes or frameworks for legitimation and rationalization of inclusion and exclusion, invisible characteristics are framed as irrelevant and insignificant. As Morrish and O'Mara (2011) point out, invisible diversity dimensions tend not to be managed. Usually these dimensions include religion, national origin, or illness.[8] Sexual orientation also seems to be a good example of an invisible social category in the workplace, which is valued as irrelevant in the executive search context because of the ascribed invisibility. Clair et al. (2005) also emphasize that most of the organizational research on diversity in the workplace has focused on visible diversity dimensions, but has left the invisible ones relatively unexplored. Because of the far-reaching importance of these diversity dimensions in the search processes, we discuss an immanent discursive hierarchical order that is determined by the valuing system of relevance to the search consultants. Further, we assume that there is a strong interplay between the position in this hierarchical order and the visibility of the diversity dimensions, which means that the diversity dimensions with high visibility have more importance or a higher impact – implicit or explicit – in the executive search process. Further research could shed light on these questions of (re)enhancements. In order to bring more women, more disabled people, more immigrants, and more people who define themselves as LGBTQIA into management positions, more awareness by clients and consultants is needed in terms of their norms and interpretative schemes in relation to the different diversity dimensions. More reflexivity of the clients and consultants in terms of how their interplay and the relevance that they ascribe to the diversity dimensions constitutes the 'ideal male manager' (for example, Holgersson, 2013) may alter their rules of signification and legitimation in their daily searching and selecting routines.

As a concluding remark we would like to emphasize the importance of routinized knowledge as a guiding knowledge in the executive selection process. In order to direct executive search agencies towards a more differentiated and inclusive process, we recommend the introduction of diversity management as an organizational practice in executive management search firms. Such organizational practices could open up dialogues between the executive search consultants and their clients in order to lay open the underlying impacts of diversity dimensions as categories of difference and exclusion and thus to redefine the modalities of inclusion and exclusion in the executive search process.

NOTES

1. For the notion of person–organization fit as an important legitimation strategy in selection processes see, for example, Bowen et al. (1991) and Bozionelos (2005).
2. To our knowledge, diversity dimensions or social categories do not mean personal characteristics in the sense of individual characteristics. Rather, diversity dimensions as social categories are defined as practices of ascription, understood as processes of categorizations or differentiations following hierarchical orders and value systems.
3. Gender refers to cultural and social differences between the sexes, whereas sex refers to biological differences.
4. We understand ethnicity as a product of self- and group identity that is formed in extrinsic as well as intrinsic contexts and social interaction. Further, as a symbolic representation it is produced, reproduced and transformed over time (cf. Baumann, 2004). Ethnicity is characterized by its dichotomy of 'Us' and 'Them', meaning that only the majority is viewed as non-ethnic.
5. Age has a multitude of associated meanings and interpretations (European Commission, 2008). The biological definition of age refers to the biological processes of a living organism, chronological ageing refers to how old a person is and finally, social ageing refers to society's expectations and norms of how people should act as they grow older respective to how people are expected to be in different chronological age stages.
6. Lesbian, Gay, Bisexual, Transgender, Queer, Intersex, Asex.
7. Religion encompasses 'the feelings, thoughts, experiences, and behaviors that arise from a search for the sacred and the means and methods (for example rituals or prescribed behaviors) of the search that receive validation and support from within an identifiable group of people' (Hill et al., 2000, p. 66).
8. For further research on the influence of invisible social identities on workplace interactions see, for example, Clair et al. (2005) and Simpson and Lewis (2005).

REFERENCES

Acker, J. (2006), 'Inequality regimes: gender, class, and race in organizations', *Gender Society*, **20**(4), 441–64.
Atewologun, D. and E. Doldor (2013), 'Women at the top: where now, and what next with women at the top? Reflections on the "Women at the Top" 2012 Conference', *Equality, Diversity and Inclusion – An International Journal*, **32**(2), 223–9.
Baldwin, M. and W.G. Johnson (1994), 'Labour market discrimination against men with disabilities', *The Journal of Human Resources*, **29**(1), 1–19.
Baumann, T. (2004), 'Defining ethnicity', *The SAA Archaeological Record*, **4**(4), 12–14.
Beckett, C. (2012), 'Silence in the sexual agenda of a UK probation service', *Equality, Diversity and Inclusion: An International Journal*, **31**(8), 753–67.
Bendl, R. (2013), 'Diskursive Praktiken von Executive Search Consultants beim Auswahlprozess von Führungskräften. Eine intersektionale Analyse' [Discursive practices of executive search consultants in the selection process of managers. An intersectional analysis], paper presentation, 25 March 2013, Munich.
Bendl, R., H. Eberherr and H. Mensi-Klarbach (2012), 'Vertiefende Betrachtungen zu ausgewählten Diversitätsdimensionen' [In-depth analyses of selected dimensions of diversity], in R. Bendl, E. Hanappi-Egger and R. Hofmann (eds), *Diversität und Diversitätsmanagement*, Vienna: Facultas Wuv, pp. 79–136.
Bendl, R., H. Eberherr and A. Schmidt (2013), 'Intersecting diversity dimensions in the executive search process and the (re-)production of professional identities', paper presentation, 4–7 July 2013, at the 29th EGOS Colloquium, Montreal.
Bendl, R., C. Holgersson, S. Meriläinen and J. Tienari (2011), 'No issue: executive search consultants reproducing white male dominance in management', paper presentation, 7–9 July 2011, at the 27th EGOS Colloquium, Gothenburg.
Bowen, D.E., G.E. Ledford and B.R. Nathan (1991), 'Hiring for the organization, not the job', *Academy of Management Executive*, **5**(4), 35–51.
Bozionelos, N. (2005), 'When the inferior candidate is offered the job: the selection interview as a political and power game', *Human Relations*, **58**(12), 1605–31.
Brah, A. and A. Phoenix (2004), 'Ain't I a woman? Revisiting intersectionality', *Journal of International Women's Studies*, **5**(3), 75–86.
Brower, T. (2013), 'What's in the closet: dress and appearance codes and lessons from sexual orientation', *Equality, Diversity and Inclusion: An International Journal*, **32**(5), 491–502.
Bruyère, S.M., W.A. Erickson and S. VanLooy (2004), 'Comparative study of workplace policy and practices contributing to disability non-discrimination', *Rehabilitation Psychology*, **49**(1), 28–38.
Burt, R.S. (1995), *Structural Holes. The Social Structure of Competition*, Cambridge, MA: Harvard University Press.
Calás, M.B. and L. Smircich (2006), '"From the woman's point of view" ten years later: towards a feminist organization studies', in S. Clegg, C. Hardy and W.E. Nord (eds), *Handbook of Organization Studies*, London: Sage, pp. 284–346.
Cashmore, E. (2001), 'The experiences of ethnic minority police officers in Britain: under-recruitment and racial profiling in a performance culture', *Ethnic and Racial Studies*, **24**(4), 642–59.
Caven, V., S. Lawley and J. Baker (2013), 'Performance, gender and sexualised work: beyond management control, beyond legislation? A case study of work in a recruitment company', *Equality, Diversity and Inclusion: An International Journal*, **32**(5), 475–90.
Chan, F., B.T. McMahon, G. Cheing, D.A. Rosenthal and J. Bezyak (2005), 'Drivers of workplace discrimination against people with disabilities: the utility of attribution theory', *Work*, **25**(1), 77–88.
Clair, J.A., J.E. Beatty and T.L. MacLean (2005), 'Out of sight but not out of mind: managing invisible social identities in the workplace', *Academy of Management Review*, **30**(1), 78–95.
Cole, M., H. Field and W. Giles (2004), 'Interaction of recruiter and applicant gender in résumé evaluation: a field study', *Sex Roles*, **51**(9/10), 597–8.

Colgan, F. (2011), 'Equality, diversity and corporate responsibility: sexual orientation and diversity management in the UK private sector', *Equality, Diversity and Inclusion: An International Journal*, **30**(8), 719–34.
Coverdill, J.E. and W. Finlay (1998), 'Fit and skill in employee selection: insights from a study of headhunters', *Qualitative Sociology*, **21**(2), 105–27.
Cunningham, G.B., M.L. Sartore-Baldwin and B.P. McCullough (2010), 'The influence of applicant sexual orientation, applicant gender, and rater gender on ascribed attributions and hiring recommendations of personal trainers', *Journal of Sport Management*, **24**(4), 400–15.
Davis, K. (2008a), 'Intersectionality as buzzword: a sociology of science perspective on what makes a feminist theory successful', *Feminist Theory*, **9**(1), 67–85.
Davis, K. (2008b), 'Intersectionality in transatlantic perspective', in G.-A. Knapp and C. Klinger (eds), *UberKreuzungen. Fremdheit, Ungleichheit, Differenz* [Crossovers. Alienation, Inequality, Difference], Münster: Westfälisches Dampfboot, pp. 19–35.
Davis, K., M. Evans and J. Lorber (2006), *Handbook of Gender and Women's Studies*, London: Sage Publications Ltd.
Dickson, D. and O. Hargie (2006), 'Sectarianism in the Northern Ireland workplace', *International Journal of Conflict Management*, **17**(1), 45–65.
Doldor, E., S. Vinnicombe, M. Gaughan and R. Sealy (2012), *Gender Diversity on Boards: The Appointment Process and the Role of Executive Search Firms*, Equality and Human Rights Commission, UK.
Dreher, G.F., J.-Y. Lee and T.A. Clerkin (2011), 'Mobility and cash compensation: the moderating effects of gender, race, and executive search firms', *Journal of Management*, **37**(3), 651–81.
Duncan, C. and W. Loretto (2004), 'Never the right age? Gender and age-based discrimination in employment', *Gender, Work & Organization*, **11**(1), 95–115.
Eberherr, H., A. Fleischmann and R. Hofmann (2008), 'Labour market and organisational perspectives on age(ing) – bringing gender, diversity, and intersectionality into focus', in M. Beisheim, F. Maier, L. Kreil and B. Gusenbauer (eds), *Constructions of Women's Age at the Workplace*, Frankfurt am Main: Peter Lang, pp. 15–30.
European Commission (2008), *The 2007 European Year of Equal Opportunities for All. Thematic Reports*, December 2008, accessed 30 December 2013 at ec.europa.eu/social/main.jsp?catId=89&langId=en&newsId=483&moreDocuments=yes&tableName=news.
Faulconbridge, J.R., J.V. Beaverstock, S. Hall and A. Hewitson (2009), 'The "war for talent": the gatekeeper role of executive search firms in elite labour markets', *Geoforum*, **40**(5), 800–808.
Ferree, M.M. (2009), 'Inequality, intersectionality and the politics of discourse: framing feminist alliances', in E. Lombardo, P. Meier and M. Verloo (eds), *The Discursive Politics of Gender Equality: Stretching, Bending and Policymaking*, New York/London: Routledge, pp. 86–104.
Finlay, W. and J.E. Coverdill (1999), 'The search game: organizational conflicts and the use of headhunters', *The Sociological Quarterly*, **40**(1), 11–30.
Finlay, W. and J.E. Coverdill (2002), *Headhunters: Matching in the Labor Market*, Ithaca, NY: Cornell University Press.
Frable, D.E.S. (1989), 'Sex typing and gender ideology: two facets of the individual's gender psychology that go together', *Journal of Personality and Social Psychology*, **56**(1), 95–108.
Frohn, D. (2007), *'Out im Office?' Sexuelle Identität, (Anti-)Diskriminierung und Diversity am Arbeitsplatz* [Out in the Office? Sexual Identity, (Anti-)Discrimination and Diversity in the Workplace], Cologne: Schwules Netzwerk.
Gebert, D., S. Boerner, E. Kearney, J.E. King, K. Zhang and L.J. Song (2014), 'Expressing religious identities in the workplace: analyzing a neglected diversity dimension', *Human Relations*, **67**(5), 543–63.
Giddens, A. (1984), *The Constitution of Society. Outline of the Theory of Structuration*, Cambridge, UK: Polity Press.
Gorman, E.H. (2005), 'Gender stereotypes, same-gender preferences, and organizational

variation in the hiring of women: evidence from law firms', *American Sociological Review*, **70**(4), 702–28.
Gouvier, W.D., S. Sytsma-Jordan and S. Mayville (2003), 'Patterns of discrimination in hiring job applicants with disabilities: the role of disability type, job complexity and public contact', *Rehabilitation Psychology*, **48**(1), 175–81.
Gregory, M.R. (2011), '"The faggot clause": the embodiment of homophobia in the corporate locker room', *Equality, Diversity and Inclusion: An International Journal*, **30**(8), 651–67.
Hardin, J.R., K.F. Reding and M.H. Stocks (2002), 'The effect of gender on the recruitment of entry-level accountants', *Journal of Managerial Issues*, **14**(2), 251–66.
Hardmeier, S. and D. Vinz (2007), 'Diversity und Intersectionality – Eine kritische Würdigung der Ansätze für die Politikwissenschaft' [Intersectionality – a critical assessment of approaches to political science], *Femina Politica*, **16**(1), 23–33.
Hebl, M.R., J.B. Foster, L.M. Mannix and J.F. Dovidio (2002), 'Formal and interpersonal discrimination: a field study of bias toward homosexual applicants', *Personality and Social Psychology Bulletin*, **28**(6), 815–25.
Collins, P.H. (1999), 'Moving beyond gender: intersectionality and scientific knowledge', in M.M. Ferree, J. Lorber and B.B. Hess (eds), *Revisioning Gender*, London: Sage, pp. 261–84.
Hill, P.C., K.I. Pargament, R.W. Hood, M.E. McCullough, J.P. Swyers, D.B. Larson and B.J. Zinnbauer (2000), 'Conceptualizing religion and spirituality: points of commonality, points of departure', *Journal for the Theory of Social Behavior*, **30**(1), 51–77.
Höner, D. and M. Mohe (2009), 'Behind clients' doors: what hinders client firms from "professionally" dealing with consultancy?', *Scandinavian Journal of Management*, **25**(3), 299–312.
Jackson, S. (2006), 'Interchanges: gender, sexuality and heterosexuality: the complexity (and limits) of heteronormativity', *Feminist Theory*, **7**(1), 105–21.
Jain, H.C. (1998), 'The recruitment and selection of visible minorities in Canadian police organizations, 1985–1987', *Canadian Public Administration*, **31**(4), 463–82.
Kennedy, R.B. and N.K. Harris (2005), 'Employing persons with severe disabilities: much work remains to be done', *Journal of Employment Counseling*, **42**(3), 133–9.
King, J.E. and O. Holmes (2012), 'Spirituality, recruiting, and total wellness: overcoming challenges to organizational attraction', *Journal of Management, Spirituality & Religion*, **9**(3), 237–53.
Klinger, C., G.-A. Knapp and B. Sauer (2007), *Achsen der Ungleichheit. Zum Verhältnis von Klasse, Geschlecht und Ethnizität* [Axes of Inequality. On the Relationship Between Class, Gender and Ethnicity], Frankfurt am Main: Campus.
Köllen, T. (2010), *Bemerkenswerte Vielfalt: Homosexualität und Diversity Management – Betriebswirtschaftliche und sozialpsychologische Aspekte der Diversity – Dimension 'sexuelle Orientierung'* [Remarkable Diversity: Homosexuality and Diversity Management – Business and Social-psychological Aspects of Diversity – Dimension 'Sexual Orientation'], Mering: Hampp.
Losert, A. (2007), 'Die Diversity-Dimension "sexuelle Orientierung" in Theorie und Praxis – eine Bestandsaufnahme mit Ausblick' [The diversity dimension "sexual orientation" in theory and practice – a survey with a view], in I. Koall, V. Bruchhagen and F. Höher (eds), *Diversity Outlooks, Managing Diversity zwischen Ethik, Profit und Antidiskriminierung*, Hamburg: Lit. Verlag, pp. 320–36.
McCall, L. (2001), *Complex Inequality: Gender, Class, and Race in the New Economy*, New York: Routledge.
McCall, L. (2005), 'The complexity of intersectionality', *Signs: Journal of Women in Culture & Society*, **30**(3), 1771–800.
McMurray, A., A. Karim and G. Fisher (2010), 'Perspectives on the recruitment and retention of culturally and linguistically diverse police', *Cross Cultural Management: An International Journal*, **17**(2), 193–210.
Mitroff, I. and E. Denton (1999), *A Spiritual Audit of Corporate America: A Hard Look at Spirituality, Religion, and Values in the Workplace*, New York: Jossey-Bass.

Morrish, L. and K. O'Mara (2011), 'Queering the discourse of diversity', *Journal of Homosexuality*, **58**(6–7), 974–91.
Moulaert, T. and S. Biggs (2013), 'International and European policy on work and retirement: reinventing critical perspectives on active ageing and mature subjectivity', *Human Relations*, **66**(1), 23–43.
Munro, A. (2001), 'A feminist trade union agenda? The continued significance of class, gender and race', *Gender, Work & Organization*, **8**(4), 454–71.
Neckel, S. (2000), *Die Macht der Unterscheidung. Essays zur Kultursoziologie der modernen Gesellschaft* [The Power of Discrimination. Essays on the Sociology of Culture in Modern Society], Frankfurt/New York: Campus.
Ollier-Malaterre, A., T. McNamara, C. Matz-Costa, M. Pitt-Catsouphes and M. Valcour (2013), 'Looking up to regulations, out at peers or down at the bottom line: how institutional logics affect the prevalence of age-related HR practices', *Human Relations*, **66**(10), 1373–95.
Paule, A. (2011), 'Judging a book by its cover: examining the role of race in the intercollegiate athletic recruitment process', *International Journal of Business and Social Science*, **2**(5), 23–31.
Pearson, C. (2012), 'Recruitment of indigenious Australians with linguistic and numeric disadvantages', *Research and Practice in Human Resource Management*, **20**(1), 66–80.
Phoenix, A. and P. Pattynama (2006), 'Intersectionality', *European Journal of Women's Studies*, **13**(3), 187–92.
Pinar, M., M. McCuddy and P. Trapp (2009), 'Do recruiter gender, applicant gender, and target market gender impact the recruiting outcome? Perceptions of Turkish recruiters', *The Business Review*, **12**(1), 301–7.
Polley, D., J. Vora and P.N. SubbaNarasimha (2005), 'Paying the devil his due: limits and liabilities of workplace spirituality', *International Journal of Organizational Analysis*, **13**(1), 50–63.
Powell, G. (1987), 'The effects of sex and gender on recruitment', *Academy of Management Review*, **12**(4), 731–43.
Pratt, M.G. (2000), 'Building an ideological fortress: the role of spirituality, encapsulation and sensemaking', *Studies in Cultures, Organizations & Societies*, **6**(1), 35–69.
Pringle, J.K. (2008), 'Gender in management: theorizing gender as heterogender', *British Journal of Management*, **19**(1), 110–19.
Ren, L.R., R.L. Paetzold and A. Colella (2008), 'A meta-analysis of experimental studies on the effects of disability on human resource judgements', *Human Resource Management Review*, **18**(3), 191–203.
Riach, K. (2007), '"Othering" older worker identity in recruitment', *Human Relations*, **60**(11), 1701–26.
Roberts, S. (2011), 'Exploring how gay men manage their social identities in the workplace: the internal/external dimensions of identity', *Equality, Diversity and Inclusion: An International Journal*, **30**(8), 668–85.
Sartore, M.L. and G.B. Cunningham (2009), 'Sexual prejudice, participatory decisions, and panoptic control: implications for sexual minorities in sport', *Sex Roles*, **60**, 100–13.
Schaeffer, C.B. and J.S. Mattis (2012), 'Diversity, religiosity, and spirituality in the workplace', *Journal of Management, Spirituality & Religion*, **9**(4), 317–33.
Sheffield, J., A. Hussain and P. Coleshill (1999), 'Organizational barriers and ethnicity in the Scottish NHS', *Journal of Management in Medicine*, **13**(4), 263–85.
Simpson, R. and P. Lewis (2005), 'An investigation of silence and a scrutiny of transparency: re-examining gender in organization literature through the concepts of voice and visibility', *Human Relations*, **58**(10), 1253–75.
Stevens, G.R. (2002), 'Employers' perceptions and practice in the employability of disabled people: a survey of companies in South East UK', *Disability & Society*, **17**(7), 779–96.
Sturdy, A. and C. Wright (2011), 'The active client: the boundary-spanning roles of internal consultants as gatekeepers, brokers and partners of their external counterparts', *Management Learning*, **42**(5), 485–503.

Styhre, A. and U. Eriksson-Zetterquist (2008), 'Thinking the multiple in gender and diversity studies: examining the concept of intersectionality', *Gender in Management: An International Journal*, **23**(8), 567–82.

Taylor, S. and T.J. Bergmann (1987), 'Organizational recruitment activities and applicants' reactions at different stages of the recruitment process', *Personnel Psychology*, **40**(2), 261–85.

Tienari, J., C. Holgersson, S. Merilainen and R. Bendl (2013), 'And then there are none: on the exclusion of women in processes of executive search', *Gender in Management – An International Journal*, **28**(1), 43–62.

Tonks, G. (2006), 'Sexual identity: HRM's invisible dimension of workplace diversity', *International Journal of Diversity in Organizations, Communities and Nations*, **6**(1), 35–48.

Tracey, P. (2012), 'Religion and organization: a critical review of current trends and future directions', *The Academy of Management Annals*, **6**(1), 87–134.

Van den Brink, M., M. Brouns and S. Waslander (2006), 'Does excellence have a gender? A national research study on the recruitment and selection procedures for professional appointments in the Netherlands', *Employee Relations*, **28**(6), 523–39.

Verloo, M. (2006), 'Multiple inequalities, intersectionality and the European Union', *European Journal of Women's Studies*, **13**(3), 211–28.

Waters, I., N. Hardy, D. Delgado and S. Dahlmann (2007), 'Ethnic minorities and the challenge of police recruitment', *The Police Journal*, **80**(2), 191–216.

Weuster, A. (2012a), *Personalauswahl I. Internationale Forschungsergebnisse zu Anforderungsprofil, Bewerbersuche, Vorauswahl, Vorstellungsgespräch und Referenzen* [Personnel Selection I. International Research Results on Requirements, Candidate Search, Pre-selection Interview and References], Wiesbaden: Gabler Verlag.

Weuster, A. (2012b), *Personalauswahl II. Internationale Forschungsergebnisse zum Verhalten und zu Merkmalen von Interviewern und Bewerbern I* [Personnel Selection II. International Research Results on the Behaviour and Characteristics of Interviewer and Applicants], Wiesbaden: Gabler Verlag.

Whittle, A. (2006), 'The paradoxical repertoires of management consultancy', *Journal of Organizational Change Management*, **19**(4), 424–36.

Wilz, S.M. (2001), 'Rethinking gender, work and organization – thinking about organization', paper presentation, 27–29 June 2001, at the Gender, Work and Organization Conference, Keele University, UK.

Wright, J. and G. Clarke (1999), 'Sport, the media and the construction of compulsory heterosexuality: a case study of women's rugby union', *International Review for the Sociology of Sport*, **34**(2), 227–43.

Wright, T. (2011), 'A "lesbian advantage"? Analysing the intersections of gender, sexuality and class in male-dominated work', *Equality, Diversity and Inclusion: An International Journal*, **30**(8), 686–701.

Yuval-Davis, N. (2006), 'Intersectionality and feminist politics', *European Journal of Women's Studies*, **13**(3), 193–209.

Zanoni, P., M. Janssens, Y. Benschop and S. Nkomo (2010), 'Guest editorial: unpacking diversity, grasping inequality: rethinking difference through critical perspectives', *Organization*, **17**(1), 9–29.

10. Breaking down barriers
Susan M. Adams

Career barriers faced by women are discussed in other chapters of this book and elsewhere. This chapter focuses on *how* to break down gender-related barriers from a change management perspective. In a meta-analytic study of predictors of career success, Ng et al. (2005) found different predictors for objective and subjective measures of success. Attention here is on objective career success (for example, career advancement such as promotions or pay raises) rather than on subjective career success (for example, job satisfaction or work engagement). Specifically, being female is negatively related to the objective career success measures of higher salaries and promotions (ibid.).

Bentley University's Center for Women and Business provides specific action steps that companies and their CEOs, women and public policy officials can take to advance women in business (Adams and Idea Exchange Writing Collaborative, 2012). The notable conclusion of this study is that a *concerted* effort is necessary by multiple parties to make substantive change (see the Appendix at the end of the chapter). The study proposes action steps for women, corporate leaders, managers and public policy officials that are needed to better retain, support and promote women in business. Some of the recommendations are simple to implement and already established practice in many companies. Others are more complex to implement because they will likely meet resistance for reasons presented in this chapter.

The next section provides examples of additional recommended actions for advancing women, noting key elements and highlighting potential stumbling blocks.

ADDRESSING THE BARRIERS TO WOMEN'S ADVANCEMENT

There are some effective and less impactful efforts underway by companies and women themselves to support, retain and promote women. Some countries have mandated quotas for corporate boards of directors resulting in dramatic increases in the number of women directors (for example, see Barsh et al., 2012; Deloitte, 2013) but those efforts do not address the barriers faced by those below the top level where resistance hides (Rivers and Barnett, 2013).

Women's groups called networks, affinity groups or employee resource groups (ERGs) are prevalent in offering support and training. However, these women's organizations can serve to reproduce patriarchal cultures rather than improving recruitment, retention and advancement of women if there is not a level of gender consciousness involved (Annis, 2003; Bierema, 2005; Rivers and Barnett, 2013). When women are just talking to women and seeking support from women, they are not integrating into the fabric of the organization as equals where men are the decision-makers. Many of the barriers women face are structural, based on male notions of work, and must be addressed by male managers who are in charge (Acker, 1990, 1992; Barsh and Yee, 2012). For example, women may miss out on international and operational assignments that lead to promotions because male managers, or women adopting the male-culture mind-set, assume that women will not want to take the positions if they have children (Metz, 2005); or in another example, that male-biased specified paths are the only ways to higher pay or promotions (cf. Adams, 1995; Judiesch and Lyness, 1999; Lyness and Schrader, 2006; Eagly and Carli, 2007; Stone, 2007; Rivers and Barnett, 2013; Sandberg, 2013).

Along the same lines, women's leadership and diversity training programmes abound. Most of the leadership programmes have a 'fix the woman' approach (reinforcing the male leader mind-set) rather than helping women develop their own identities as leaders (Ely et al., 2009). McKinsey reported that 63 per cent of the 235 European companies surveyed for a 2012 report had at least 20 different initiatives underway as part of the gender diversity efforts yet little progress is seen (Devillard et al., 2012). Their findings suggest that company programmes that are more successful include three elements: (1) a CEO and executive team that champion gender diversity with targets, (2) women's development programmes *and* (3) a set of enablers that identify and address policy and practice barriers for women. They suggest that all three elements are needed. Since women deal with a wide range of barriers from multiple sources (cf. Eagly and Carli, 2007; Indvik, 2009; Rivers and Barnett, 2013; Sandberg, 2013), comprehensive programmes involving multiple stakeholders with aligned values are better positioned to address barriers (Burnes and Jackson, 2011; Devillard et al., 2012; Rivers and Barnett, 2013).

Another issue to consider in designing effective diversity programmes is that businesses are dynamic systems with people maturing and facing new challenges as their responsibilities change and the people they interact with change. Comprehensive programmes need to be adaptive yet stable and pervasive: stable and pervasive with the mandated message for gender diversity and adaptive to the needs of those involved over time. Moreover, change programmes cannot be linear given these dynamic aspects of organizational life. People may adjust differently over time based on messaging signals from new managers and situations that threaten the favourability of their identities in the organization (Bisel and Barge, 2011).

A less comprehensive but clearly popular way companies are addressing barriers to the advancement of women is through flexible work programmes. WorldatWork (2013) finds that companies are dedicated to providing flexible work options, with 98 per cent continuing to offer programmes offered three years earlier. Flexible work options are designed to support working women with children but are desired equally by men (US Department of Commerce Economics and Statistics Administration, 2011a). With more dual career couples in the workforce, men are helping more at home (Pew Research Center, 2010) but are more reluctant to use such options, due to traditional gender roles and loss of income (Goux and Adams, 2012). This leads companies to see flexible work as a women's issue while there may be underlying systemic causes of work and organizational discontent being masked by using such work–family accommodations as a social defence (Padavic and Ely, 2013).

Two of McKinsey's studies (Barsh and Yee, 2011, 2012) in particular offer actionable suggestions. In the first study, Barsh and Yee (2011) describe three ways companies can address organizational barriers for women: change the conversation to focus more on progress rather than efforts, use data to create transparency of inequities by challenging entrenched mind-sets with the data, and rethink sponsorship so that managers take responsibility for opening doors to talented women. They drill deeper into these themes and expand their recommendations in the second study (Barsh and Yee, 2012), offering observations about women who have advanced to senior positions and steps companies can take to be leaders in promoting women to the top. They identified four kinds of barriers: structural barriers, lifestyle issues, institutional mind-sets and individual mind-sets. They recommend that leadership make the business case for change and model behaviour for the entire organization to follow, that organizational processes for accountability be revised to encourage desired practices, and that capabilities are built to facilitate change (for example, training sponsors for women's advancement). While these recommendations identify issues buried deep in organizations such as male-biased structures and mind-sets, they do not go far enough in establishing a sustainable, pervasive culture of gender equality that can outlive leadership changes unless ongoing systems are established to ensure that gender-biased mind-sets and structures do not emerge again. As noted above, a one-time fix will not work.

A Bain and Company report (Sanders et al., 2011) shares nine effective initiatives for overcoming career barriers that focus on two schools of thought that surfaced in their study. Assumptions and realities related to competing priorities (work and family) are problematic, particularly important to younger women with children. Differences in style, however, is the primary problem holding women back according to the study. Visible and committed leadership for gender diversity and support for men and women with family responsibilities are rated as the most effective in helping women to advance. Other effective recommendations focus on helping both men and women understand gender-based perceptions and learning to work in a diverse environment. Focusing on programmes to understand gender-based perceptions is the most effective first step toward eliminating gender-biased mind-sets and toward more sustainable change (Annis, 2003) because readiness for change is essential (Lewin, 1947; Burnes, 2009; Choi and Ruona, 2013).

CHANGE MODELS

With these many ideas in hand, the next steps to take in breaking down barriers for women are not complex or expensive but that does not seem to be happening. In this section, theoretical change models are discussed to better identify where resistance may be found. Three basic types of approaches are discussed: planned change, emergent (or continuous) change, and appreciative inquiry (AI). These approaches account for the bulk of intentional change conducted in organizations (Burnes, 2009).

Planned Change

Despite its age, Kurt Lewin's (1947) classic model of change is still the underlying framework of most intentional, planned change models used today. Lewin's model is a three-stage change process involving unfreezing (initiation to prepare people for change), change (adoption and adaptation of the change) and refreezing (acceptance, use and incorporation to sustain change). Examining the barriers women face, it is easy to conclude that the collective movement to advance more women in business has not yet reached the third stage since so many institutional barriers are still intact (Rivers and Barnett, 2013). Intolerance for gender-based differences along with interpersonal and societal barriers (see Lyness and Thompson, 1997; Catalyst, 2005; O'Neil and Bilimoria, 2005; Hakim, 2006; Eagly and Carli, 2007; Webber and Williams, 2008; Ibarra and Obodaru, 2009; Want, 2009; Adams et al., 2010; Banaji and Greenwald, 2013) also point to a lack of awareness of the need to change, indicating that we are at least partly still in stage one of unfreezing. However, it is reasonable to conclude that the glimpses of progress with more legislative attention (Barsh et al., 2012; Deloitte, 2013), the explosion of diversity training in companies,[1] and awards for annual progress in lavish media events such as those hosted by Catalyst and Working Mother Media means that the women's career equity movement is in or approaching stage two where actual change is taking place in a growing number of companies. The diversity change facilitation industry seems to be institutionalized because there is a big enough need for more change assistance in the business world. This indicates that the corporate world has not reached stage three with established systems to ensure and sustain gender equality in the workplace.

Following Lewin, others interested in planned change approaches have promoted more specific steps within Lewin's approach. Kotter's (1996) eight-step model tells change agents and leaders what to do to unfreeze, change and refreeze behaviour. According to Kotter, managing the change process for results involves:

1. Establishing a sense of urgency.
2. Creating the guiding coalition.
3. Developing a vision and strategy.
4. Communicating the change vision.
5. Empowering employees for broad-based action.
6. Generating short-term wins.
7. Consolidating gains and producing more change.
8. Anchoring new approaches in the culture.

Using Kotter's model for the topic of this discussion, the sticking point may be in the first step. Organizational growth or risk management or other issues may be seen as more urgent than women's advancement in a company (see PWC, 2013, for examples of CEO priorities). Also, with the rapid pace of today's business world, constant change can create cynicism so that urgency to work on the 'women's issue' is seen as just another pet project, especially if the company is doing fine without addressing the issue. Stumbling at the first step means very little will happen since inertia has a stranglehold on change. Even if an organization with good intentions were to follow Kotter's process through the first seven steps, the eighth step of anchoring the change in the culture could be problematic since gender presents sub-cultures and unconscious biases (Barsh and Yee, 2011; Banaji and Greenwald, 2013).

Rice (2012) says that diversity efforts fail for four reasons: (1) responsibility for efforts is distributed across the organization rather than having a person or group responsible so that an integrated strategy is used; (2) activities rather than outcomes are measured; (3) efforts are focused on fixing the culture, which takes a long time, ignoring immediate needs; and (4) minority candidates for diversity roles are prioritized rather than seeking recognized high-performing line managers (whether minority or non-minority) who are in better positions to advocate for bold new approaches. These are tactical faux pas that ignore the realities of organizational power and politics as typical sources of organizational change resistance.

Cox's (2001) change model for work on diversity offers a comprehensive approach to organizational change to address the issues raised by Rice (2012). The circular model that acknowledges a continuous, incremental nature of change has five components with associated activities:

- *leadership* – management philosophy, vision, organizational design, personal involvement, communication strategy and strategic integration;
- *research and measurement* – preliminary diagnostics, comprehensive culture assessment, baseline data, benchmarking, measurement plan;
- *education* – managing change education, development of in-house expertise, modification of existing training, addressing all three phases of the learning process;
- *alignment of management systems* – work schedules and physical environment, orientation, recruitment, performance appraisal, compensation and benefits, training and development, promotion;
- *follow-up* – accountability, continuous improvement, reporting process for performance results, knowledge management programme.

Cox's planned change approach is only as good as the leadership is strong and committed to get the initiative started and genuine. Unconscious biases and other agendas can easily creep into this process in a similar way as noted above. Oversight is needed to constantly check that measures and new systems used are not biased, which is often difficult when conducted by the very people who may be biased.

Organization development (OD) began as a process for planned organizational improvement, primarily at the group level, that takes into account the human side of organizations (French and Bell, 1999; Burnes, 2009). Over time, as the process was extended to organization-wide transformations, some argue that practices have become less tied to the original justice and democratic values that guided earlier OD work (Worley and

Feyerhern, 2003; Bradford and Burke, 2004; Greiner and Cummings, 2004; Burnes, 2009).

Bartunek et al. (2011) discuss the contemporary OD-based Whole-Scale™ Change[2] method as moving from the current condition forward. It is guided by an adaptation of David Gleicher's formula and highlights the role of resistance (Bunker and Alban, 1997; James and Tolchinsky, 2007). The formula, $D \times V \times F > R = \Delta$, means that change will occur when dissatisfaction with the status quo (D) times a clear and compelling vision (V) times first steps to get change going (F) is greater than the level of resistance (R) (Beckhard and Harris, 1987). Notice that the formula is multiplicative. If any of the three variables, D, V, or F, is missing the entire left side of the formula becomes zero and resistance prevails. This OD model draws on both planned and continuous approaches in that there are planned targets as described by the formula but the process may be more organic to utilize pockets of momentum and energy wherever they are in the organization. Once again, those who are resisting due to unconscious biases are unlikely to notice that they are resisting change. For example, not offering a travel assignment to a woman so she can take care of her children may be done with good intentions from a manager's point of view but is a career killer from a woman's point of view (Metz, 2005; Eagly and Carli, 2007; Rivers and Barnett, 2013).

Furthermore, the Whole-Scale™ method takes time working with participants to collect data, understand the meaning of data about the situation, develop change goals and commit to specific action and timing to hold each other accountable (James and Tolchinsky, 2007). The collaborative process assumes that positive emotions will result from the process (Bartunek et al., 2011) so that hearts and minds are engaged in the direction the organization is heading. The Cox (2001) and Kotter (1996) planned change process models also take steps that address the factors in Gleicher's formula but in a more imposed rather than collaborative, elicited manner. Managers may resist using the Whole-Scale™ or other OD approaches because of the time commitment needed that takes so many employees away from daily duties.

Emergent (or Continuous) Change

The emergent change approach with numerous variations has become the most widely used method of change (Burnes, 2009). Burnes (2009, p. 372) summarizes that the 'approach starts with the assumption that change is not a linear process or a one-off isolated event but is a continuous, open-ended, cumulative and unpredictable process of aligning and re-aligning an organization to its changing environment'.

It could be argued that Cox's circular diversity model could be seen as an emergent change approach despite its ordered, designated steps because it continuously cycles, adjusting along the way. Weick and Quinn's (1999) notion of continuous change (in contrast to planned change models) may explain, in part, what is happening in the movement to break down barriers so more women can reach senior leadership positions. According to Weick and Quinn, when change is adaptive, meaning reactive, rather than intentionally planned, discrete events, Lewin's process is flipped. Thus, the recommended process is to first examine the current situation by freezing it to identify what needs to change, then make desired changes, and finally, unfreeze to allow the system to continue. While many organizations are intentionally addressing barriers to advancing women by creating women's support groups (for example, women's affinity and employee resource groups) and flexible work arrangements, savvy women themselves have adapted their ways to the male environment by mimicking successful men's leadership styles and career paths (Catalyst, 2005; Eagly and Carli, 2007). For example, Sandberg (2013) is advocating that women should lean in and be proud of 'bossy' behaviour that is similar to men's behaviour. If women continue to act like men to get ahead, this adaptation may be serving to further institutionalize career barriers at the organizational level by providing evidence that no change is needed since some women are successful (Rivers and Barnett, 2013). This adaptation by successful women business leaders is evidence of the complexity of dealing with change at the individual, interpersonal, group, organizational and societal levels in a dynamic environment. To Sandberg's credit, she is also promoting societal change to dispel the negative connotations associated with being a 'bossy' woman (Sandberg and Chávez, 2014).

Appreciative Inquiry (AI)

The appreciative inquiry approach could rightfully be labelled an emergent approach but it is discussed separately here because of its popularity. AI focuses on identifying strengths to envision and create a possible future (Cooperrider and Whitney, 2005). The four Ds of the Cooperrider and Whitney model are discovery, dream, design and destiny. Other appreciative inquiry authors and consultants have used different terms but the process of appreciating and leveraging assets to envision and create a new future is the same.

Applying this approach hypothetically, a 'discovery' happens with the realization that the pool for talent is increasingly women since they constitute more than half the college-educated candidates for employment (US Department of Commerce Economics and Statistics

Administration, 2011a, 2011b). Also, women's collaborative leadership style and risk management thinking are some of the advantages (Eagly and Carli, 2007) that should appeal to the business world (Rosener, 1990) given the history of poor decision-making that precipitated the last three economic crises. Following the recent financial crisis, the question, 'Where would we be if Lehman Brothers had been Lehman Sisters?' was shared in the media with the implication of a less negative outcome. This envisioning of a business world with increased female presence to take advantage of diverse perspectives and talents can be a dream element. The planning and implementation to bring the vision to fruition follow. Glass cliff studies demonstrate how chasing a dream of more women in leadership positions can go awry or have seemingly no effect (Ryan and Haslam, 2005; Adams et al., 2009). Ryan and Haslam (2005) found that women directors were more likely to be placed in precarious companies in the United Kingdom (UK) than men. Reasons include many of the blinded actions discussed before in this chapter such as implicit leadership expectations, in-group bias and group dynamics as well as sexism. Adams et al. (2009) found different results with CEO appointments in the United States. There, women had a slight advantage in appointments as CEOs in more financially healthy companies, where no heroes were needed to save the companies. A relevant lesson can be derived from these studies – namely, that quantitative data may not provide a full picture of potentially gendered paths to leadership where women had to prove themselves worthy in more risk-laden ways than men (Adams et al., 2009; Ryan and Haslam, 2009).

Reliance on quantitative measures of progress or achievement of a dream is a downfall of all the change management approaches discussed: checking a box when enough women are on corporate boards or in executive suites does not address the process-related inequalities. In the next section, ways to address change resistance that may be hampering progress are explored.

ADDRESSING CHANGE RESISTANCE

Kottke and Agars (2005) argue that the underlying processes of social cognitions, justice, threat and utility must be considered and managed for women's initiatives to be successful. Appealing to these matters is found in successful influence tactics. For example, Cialdini (1993, 2009) finds that there are six principles of influence to obtain behavioural compliance: authority, consensus, consistency, liking, reciprocation and scarcity. These principles are applicable to change efforts for advancing women in business because they address individual-level cognitive and emotional connections to the issue. Appealing to the need for diversity at the top applies the scarcity principle; exposing more senior leaders and managers to high-potential women provides opportunities for the liking principle to work; the authority principle is used when change leaders and senior managers provide direction; consensus and consistency are fundamental to the Whole-Scale™ process and for promoting gender fairness in challenging assignments, fair pay and promotions; and women invoke the reciprocation principle when they help managers with problems. The principles of influence can be used to break down resistance and intervene in multiple layers of the organization where barriers exist.

Howard Gardner (2004) describes seven levers that can be used to change minds: reason, research, resonance, representational re-descriptions, resources and rewards, real-world events and resistances. The levers can be tapped in a variety of ways such as storytelling, modelling behaviour, experience or celebrating small wins to engage one's thinking or feelings. Reaching men and women or business leaders and public officials may necessitate the use of different levers and methods (Annis, 2003; Gardner, 2004). Men with wives and daughters facing career barriers have experiences that will likely make them resonate with dissatisfaction with the status quo arguments and be more ready for change.

A simplistic view of the Cox and Kotter models suggests reliance on logic and experience to encourage decisions to change behaviour and organizational systems. However, Kotter and Cohen (2002) conclude that change is more effective when changing 'hearts' is also included with efforts to change minds. They say that there are many ways to engage feelings through experiences and even with data during the change process. Addressing feelings can help break down social and psychological resistance (Kottke and Agars, 2005).

Applying Gleicher's formula once again to the advancement of women in business organizations, change requires dissatisfaction with the number or percentage of women senior leaders, a view of what organizational life and results would look like with more women in senior ranks and instructions on what to do first to start the change. With high enough levels of the three factors, resistance will be overwhelmed but only if a large enough coalition is convinced. Thus, organizational change of this nature is the culmination of individual change of hearts and minds to produce changes in behaviour.

INDIVIDUAL- AND ORGANIZATIONAL-LEVEL LEARNING

The notion of single- (how to follow rules), double- (how to change rules) and triple-loop learning (learning how to learn) also offers a framework toward solutions (Argyris and Schön, 1974; Flood and Romm, 1996; Snell and Man-Kuen Chak, 1998). Single-loop solutions assist women in adapting to the male business environment. Companies offer women's affinity groups and traditional management training programmes as examples of single-loop learning solutions to the problem of advancing women. These types of programmes have not been fruitful in breaking down systemic barriers (Bierema, 2005).

Double-loop solutions address changes in the business environment and society to be more inclusive and supportive to eliminate gender-based biases for women. Company cultures that value a variety of leadership styles, offer flexible work options and eliminate biased evaluation, pay and promotion processes, are practising double-loop learning. These efforts to address systemic barriers are a step in the right direction but not likely to produce sustainable change.

Triple-loop solutions focus on creating new ways of working together for a current and a sustainable future that benefits all involved. At the societal level, public debate and new policies could result in equitable access (for example, affordable childcare options). Whole-Scale™ method change and AI change initiatives are good ways to encourage triple-loop learning in companies if done repetitively. An example of a triple-loop learning outcome from a diversity initiative might be utilization of flex options for both men and women without negative career implications. This outcome confronts inequities and assumptions. At the individual level, people need to understand and act on their personal resistance and anxieties to achieve personal triple-loop learning. For example, competing commitments may be the source of restrained change for individuals (Kegan and Lahey, 2001). These may include issues such as work–life conflict or the desire to maintain current workplace relationships for individual employees.

Summarizing the ways to break down resistance to change efforts, a key factor is acknowledgement of the need for multiple stakeholders to get involved. Women need assistance from those in power in companies and society. Assumptions made by all parties need to be acknowledged and revised through dialogue. Finally, different approaches will be necessary to engage the hearts and minds of multiple stakeholders. See Figure 10.1.

We have examined ways to change the current status of women in

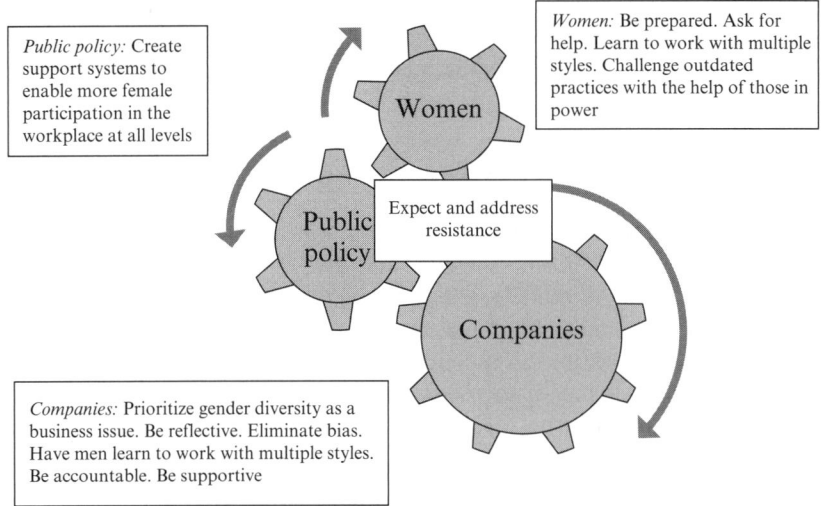

Figure 10.1 Working in concert to break down women's career barriers

business, and ways to deal with resistance to change approaches that may be complicit in perpetuating the status quo. The final part of this chapter now turns to conclusions and the future.

CONCLUSION

Women constitute 51 per cent of the US population; women receive more degrees than men at all academic levels; college-educated women are marrying later, having fewer and waiting later to have children; and nearly 40 per cent of working mothers are single or the primary breadwinner for their families (US Department of Commerce Economics and Statistics Administration, 2011a, 2011b; Wang et al., 2013). Even though there are more highly educated women in the workforce than ever before, male-designed institutions have not changed. Business structures and practices and societal expectations still cater to men's ways of working. Recent figures show that women own 30 per cent of all US businesses (National Women's Business Council, 2012). Key factors influencing women to leave companies to start their own businesses include not seeing advancement opportunities and disillusionment with their organizations. Work–life balance is not seen as a major reason (Buttner and Moore, 1997; Mallon and Cohen, 2001). Hence, the root of much of the lost talent in the corporate world is of their own making but there is work to be done by all stakeholders.

We have known the problems women face from decades of research but change is easier said than done. As this review of change processes and ways to meet resistance suggest, there are numerous approaches and tools to use. What we seem to be lacking are individuals, organizations and societies to pick up the tools and get to work in a concerted fashion. Constant media attention to the topic, government initiatives around the world, the voices of high-profile business leaders and time on the agenda in Davos at the annual meeting of the World Economic Forum are beating the drums for change but doing little. These attention-grabbing events employ the engagement of emotions in reporting sensationally, but unfortunately the full story is often lost as is the need for personal action (Fox and Renas, 1977; Rivers and Barnett, 2013). We have not reached the tipping point that Malcolm Gladwell (2000) says comes from the little things nor will we reach that point without more action from multiple stakeholders in dealing with the little things mentioned in this chapter and by women around the world.

An underlying theme of all that has been mentioned in this chapter is caring enough to do something about it. Each woman (and man) that makes it to the top and pulls up more women breaks down barriers. They need to care enough to do it. The demands of the Millennial generation of workers with an interest in social equality will break down more barriers if they stick to their family values through their child-rearing years *and* if companies care enough to offer family-friendly, non-career-killing work arrangements for both men and women. Governments can care enough to step in with legislation if companies continue to neglect gender inequities. Companies, social institutions (for example, universities) and governments can care enough to encourage others to care through vendor requirements such as not doing business with companies who are not addressing gender biases in pay and advancement. Investors can use their influence as Calvert Investments is doing by not investing in companies that do not have corporate board diversity. Societies can care enough to acknowledge the needs of women in the workplace and implement solutions using the examples of Sweden and Norway. Once enough people in each stakeholder group care enough to use their resources and political clout to solve the problem of gender-based career barriers, the tipping point is possible from the little things that each stakeholder group contributes. This *concerted* effort with everyone doing their part can break down barriers for women so that companies can tap the talents of all in the workforce.

NOTES

1. Diversity training in the workplace has become so large that there are now organizations that provide ranked lists of diversity trainers to help companies sift through the options. See, for example, http://finddiversitytrainers.com/.
2. See http://www.wholescalechange.com/methodology.html, last accessed 10 December 2014.

REFERENCES

Acker, J. (1990), 'Hierarchies, jobs, bodies: a theory of gendered organizations', *Gender and Society*, **4**(2), 139–58.

Acker, J. (1992), 'Gendering organizational theory', in A. Mills and P. Tancred (eds), *Gendering Organizational Analysis*, Newbury Park, CA: Sage, pp. 248–60.

Adams, S.M. (1995), 'Part-time work: models that work', *Women in Management Review*, **10**(7), 21–31.

Adams, S.M. and Idea Exchange Writing Collaborative (2012), *Advancing Women in the Workplace Idea Exchange*, Bentley University Center for Women and Business, accessed 21 June 2013 at http://www.bentley.edu/centers/sites/www.bentley.edu.centers/files/centers/VIVA%20CWB%20Report_Final_print_0.pdf.

Adams, S.M., A. Gupta and J.D. Leeth (2009), 'Are female executives over-represented in precarious leadership positions?', *British Journal of Management*, **20**(1), 1–20.

Adams, S.M., A. Gupta and J.D. Leeth (2010), 'Maximizing compensation: organizational level and industry gender composition effects', *Gender in Management: An International Journal*, **25**(5), 366–85.

Annis, B. (2003), *Same Words, Different Language*, London: Piatkus.

Argyris, C. and D.A. Schön (1974), *Theory in Practice: Increasing Professional Effectiveness*, San Francisco, CA: John Wiley and Sons.

Banaji, M.R. and A.G. Greenwald (2013), *Blindspot: Hidden Biases of Good People*, New York: Delacorte Press.

Barsh, J. and L. Yee (2011), 'Changing companies' minds about women', *McKinsey Quarterly*, September, accessed 18 June 2013 at http://www.mckinsey.com/insights/organization/changing_companies_minds_about_women.

Barsh, J. and L. Yee (2012), 'Unlocking the full potential of women at work', McKinsey and Company, accessed 28 November 2014 at http://www.mckinsey.com/careers/women/~/media/Reports/Women/2012%20WSJ%20Women%20in%20the%20Economy%20white%20paper%20FINAL.ashx.

Barsh, J., S. Devillard and J. Wang (2012), 'The global agenda', *McKinsey Quarterly*, November, accessed 18 June 2013 at http://www.mckinsey.com/insights/organization/the_global_gender_agenda.

Bartunek, J.M., J. Balogun and B. Do (2011), 'Considering planned change anew: stretching large group interventions strategically, emotionally, and meaningfully', *Academy of Management Annals*, **5**(1), 1–52.

Beckhard, R. and R. Harris (1987), *Organizational Transitions*, 2nd edition, Reading, MA: Addison-Wesley.

Bierema, L.L. (2005), 'Women's networks: a career development intervention or impediment', *Human Resource Development International*, **8**(2), 207–24.

Bisel, R.S and J.K. Barge (2011), 'Discursive positioning and planned change in organizations', *Human Relations*, **64**(2), 257–83.

Bradford, D.L. and W.W. Burke (2004), 'Introduction: is OD in crisis?', *Journal of Applied Behavioral Science*, **40**(4), 369–73.

Bunker, B. and B. Alban (1997), *Large Group Interventions: Engaging the Whole System for Rapid Change*, San Francisco, CA: Jossey-Bass.

Burnes, B. (2009), 'Reflections: ethics and organizational change – time for a return to Lewinian values', *Journal of Change Management*, **9**(4), 359–81.
Burnes, B. and P. Jackson (2011), 'Success and failure in organizational change: an exploration of the role of values', *Journal of Change Management*, **11**(2), 133–62.
Buttner, E.H. and D.P. Moore (1997), 'Women's organizational exodus to entrepreneurship: self-reported motivations and correlates of success', *Journal of Small Business Management*, **35**(1), 34–46.
Catalyst (2005), *Women 'Take Care', Men 'Take Charge': Stereotyping of U.S. Business Leaders Exposed*, New York: Catalyst.
Choi, M. and W.E.A. Ruona (2013), 'Individual readiness for organizational change', in H.S. Leonard, R. Lewis, A.M. Freedman and J. Passmore (eds), *The Wiley-Blackwell Handbook of the Psychology of Leadership, Change and Organizational Development*, Oxford: John Wiley and Sons, pp. 331–46.
Cialdini, R.B. (1993), *Influence: The Psychology of Persuasion*, New York: HarperBusiness.
Cialdini, R.B. (2009), *Influence: Science and Practice*, 5th edition, Upper Saddle River, NJ: Pearson.
Cooperrider, D.L. and D. Whitney (2005), *Appreciative Inquiry: A Positive Revolution in Change*, San Francisco, CA: Berrett-Koehler.
Cox, T. (2001), *Creating the Multicultural Organization: A Strategy for Capturing the Power of Diversity*, San Francisco, CA: Jossey-Bass.
Deloitte (2013), *Women in the Boardroom: A Global Perspective*, 3rd edition, accessed 21 June 2013 at http://www.deloitte.com/assets/Dcom-Tanzania/Local%20Assets/Documents/Deloitte%20Article_Women%20in%20the%20boardroom.pdf.
Devillard, S., W. Graven, E. Lawson, R. Paradise and S. Sancier-Sultan (2012), 'Women matter: making the breakthrough', McKinsey and Company, accessed 18 June 2013 at http://www.mckinsey.com/client_service/organization/latest_thinking/women_matter.
Eagly, A.H. and L.L. Carli (2007), *Through the Labyrinth*, Boston, MA: Harvard Business School Press.
Ely, R.J., H. Ibarra and D.M. Kolb (2009), 'Taking gender into account: theory and design for women's leadership development programmes', *Academy of Management Education and Learning*, **10**(3), 474–93.
Fox, H.W. and S.R. Renas (1977), 'Stereotypes of women in the media and their impact on women's careers', *Human Resource Management*, **16**(1), 28–31.
Flood, R.L. and N.R.A. Romm (1996), *Critical Systems Thinking: Current Research and Practice*, New York: Plenum Press.
French, W.L. and C.H. Bell (1999), *Organization Development*, 6th edition, Upper Saddle River, NJ: Prentice Hall.
Gardner, H. (2004), *Changing Minds: The Art and Science of Changing Our Own Minds and Other People's Minds*, Boston, MA: Harvard Business School Press.
Gladwell, M. (2000), *The Tipping Point: How Little Things Can Make a Big Difference*, New York: Little, Brown and Company.
Goux, D. and S.M. Adams (2012), 'Millennials in the workplace', Bentley University Center for Women and Business, accessed 28 March 2014 at http://www.bentley.edu/centers/center-for-women-and-business/millennials-workplace.
Greiner, L.E. and T.G. Cummings (2004), 'Wanted: OD more alive than dead!', *Journal of Applied Behavioral Science*, **40**(4), 374–91.
Hakim, C. (2006), 'Women, careers, and work–life preferences', *British Journal of Guidance and Counselling*, **34**(3), 279–94.
Ibarra, H. and O. Obodaru (2009), 'Women and the vision thing', *Harvard Business Review*, **86**(1), 62–70.
Indvik, J. (2009), 'Women and leadership', in P.G. Northouse (ed.), *Leadership Theory and Practice*, 5th edition, Los Angeles, CA: Sage, pp. 265–99.
James, S. and P. Tolchinsky (2007), 'Whole-scale change', in P. Holman, T. Devane and S. Cady (eds), *The Change Handbook: The Definitive Resource on Today's Best Methods for Engaging Whole Systems*, San Francisco, CA: Berrett-Koehler, pp. 162–78.

Judiesch, M.K. and K.S. Lyness (1999), 'Left behind? The impact of leaves of absence on managers' career success', *Academy of Management Journal*, **42**(6), 641–51.
Kegan, R. and L.L. Lahey (2001), 'The real reason people won't change', *Harvard Business Review*, **79**(10), 84–92.
Kotter, J.P. (1996), *Leading Change*, Boston, MA: Harvard Business School Press.
Kotter, J.P. and D.S. Cohen (2002), *The Heart of Change*, Boston, MA: Harvard Business School Press.
Kottke, J.L. and M.D. Agars (2005), 'Understanding the processes that facilitate and hinder efforts to advance women in organizations', *Career Development International*, **10**(3), 190–202.
Lewin, K. (1947), 'Frontiers in group dynamics', in D. Cartwright (ed.), *Field Theory in Social Science*, London: Social Science Paperbacks.
Lyness, K.S. and C.A. Schrader (2006), 'Moving ahead or just moving? An examination of gender differences in senior corporate management appointments', *Gender and Organization Management*, **31**(6), 651–76.
Lyness, K.S. and D.E. Thompson (1997), 'Above the glass ceiling? A comparison of matched samples of female and male executives', *Journal of Applied Psychology*, **82**(3), 359–75.
Mallon, M. and L. Cohen (2001), 'Time for a change? Women's accounts of the move from organizational careers to self-employment', *British Journal of Management*, **12**(3), 217–30.
Metz, I. (2005), 'Advancing the careers of women with children', *Career Development International*, **10**(3), 228–45.
National Women's Business Council (2012), *Annual Report*, accessed 8 June 2013 at http://nawbo.org/pdfs/NWBC_2012AnnualReport_FINAL.pdf.
Ng, T.W.H., L.T. Eby, K.L. Sorensen and D.C. Feldman (2005), 'Predictors of objective and subjective career success: a meta-analysis', *Personnel Psychology*, **58**(2), 367–408.
O'Neil, D.A. and D. Bilimoria (2005), 'Women's career development phases: idealism, endurance, and reinvention', *Career Development International*, **10**(3), 168–89.
Padavic, I. and R.J. Ely (2013), 'The work–family narrative as a social defense', Gender and Work: Challenging Conventional Wisdom Research Symposium, Harvard Business School, 1 March 2013.
Pew Research Center (2010), *Millennials: A Portrait of Generation Next. Confident. Connected. Open to Change*, Pew Research Center, accessed 28 March 2014 at http://www.pewsocialtrends.org/files/2010/10/millennials-confident-connected-open-to-change.pdf.
PWC (2013), *16th Annual Global CEO Survey US Executive Summary*, accessed 23 June 2013 at http://www.pwc.com/gx/en/ceo-survey/2013/pdf/us-ceo-survey-2013.pdf.
Rice, J. (2012), 'Why make diversity so hard to achieve?', *Harvard Business Review*, **90**(6), 40.
Rivers, C. and R.C. Barnett (2013), *The New Soft War on Women: How the Myth of Female Ascendance is Hurting Women, Men and Our Economy*, New York: Jeremy P. Tarcher/Penguin.
Rosener, J.B. (1990), 'Ways the women lead', *Harvard Business Review*, **68**(6), 119–25.
Ryan, M.K. and S.A. Haslam (2005), 'The glass cliff: evidence that women are over-represented in precarious leadership positions', *British Journal of Management*, **16**(2), 81–90.
Ryan, M.K and S.A. Haslam (2009), 'Glass cliffs are not so easily scaled: on the precariousness of female CEOs' positions', *British Journal of Management*, **20**(1), 13–16.
Sandberg, S. (2013), *Lean In: Women, Work, and the Will to Lead*, New York: Alfred A. Knopf.
Sandberg, S. and A.M. Chávez (2014), 'Sheryl Sandberg and Anna Maria Chávez on "Bossy," the other B-word', *Wall Street Journal*, 8 March 2014, accessed 28 March 2014 at http://online.wsj.com/news/articles/SB10001424052702304360704579419150649284412.
Sanders, M., J. Hrdlicka, M. Hellicar, D. Cottrell and J. Knox (2011), 'What stops women from reaching the top? Confronting the tough issues', accessed 23 June 2013 at http://www.bain.com/offices/australia/en_us/Images/BAIN_BRIEF_What_stops_women_from_reaching_the_top.pdf.

Snell, R. and A. Man-Kuen Chak (1998), 'The learning organization: learning and empowerment for whom?', *Management Learning*, **29**(3), 337–64.

Stone, P. (2007), *Opting Out? Why Women Really Quit Careers and Head Home*, Berkeley, MA: University of California Press.

US Department of Commerce Economics and Statistics Administration (2011a), *Women in America*, accessed 19 June 2013 at http://www.whitehouse.gov/sites/default/files/rss_viewer/Women_in_America.pdf.

US Department of Commerce Economics and Statistics Administration (2011b), *Women in STEM: A Gender Gap to Innovation*, accessed 18 June 2013 at http://www.esa.doc.gov/Reports/women-stem-gender-gap-innovation.

Wang, W., K. Parker and P. Taylor (2013), 'Breadwinner moms', Pew Foundation, accessed 18 June 2013 at http://www.pewsocialtrends.org/files/2013/05/Breadwinner_moms_final.pdf.

Want, S.C. (2009), 'Meta-analytic moderators of experimental exposure to media portrayals of women on female appearance satisfaction: social comparisons as automatic processes', *Body Image*, **6**(4), 257–69.

Webber, G.R. and C.L. Williams (2008), 'Mother in "good" and "bad" part-time jobs: different problems, same results', *Gender and Society*, **22**(6), 752–77.

Weick, K.E. and R.E. Quinn (1999), 'Organizational change and development', *Annual Review of Psychology*, **50**(1), 361–86.

WorldatWork (2013), *Survey on Workplace Flexibility 2013*, accessed 7 June 2013 at http://www.worldatwork.org/waw/adimLink?id=73898.

Worley, G.C. and A.E. Feyerhern (2003), 'Reflections on the future of organization development', *Journal of Applied Behavioral Science*, **39**(1), 97–115.

APPENDIX: IDEA EXCHANGE RECOMMENDATIONS

The full report lists the 78 action steps associated with the recommendations for companies and all the items for CEOs and women. It is available at: http://www.bentley.edu/centers/sites/www.bentley.edu.centers/files/centers/VIVA%20CWB%20Report_Final_print_0.pdf (last accessed 28 November 2014).

Recommendations for Companies (Sample Items)

1. Invert the traditional approval process by making managers get approval to deny an employee's request for a flexible/alternative schedule.
2. Set a corporate policy that says your company will not sell products with advertising that sexualizes girls or is sexist in nature.
3. Embed gender diversity initiatives into strategic conversations and strategic planning.
4. Require existing board members to sponsor a female leader.

24-hour CEO Challenge: 16 Ways to Make a Difference for Women (Sample Items)

1. Task your Chief Administrative Officer or the head of Human Resources with assessing your strategic framework documents with a defined deadline for reporting back. If a gap exists in addressing diversity, set a goal of amending the documents.
2. Are you fully committed to gender diversity? Show that you are willing to 'walk the talk' by issuing an all-employee email or memo emphasizing your personal commitment and intent to institute substantive change.
3. Host a 'coffee chat' with a select group of influential leaders in your organization. Share your personal story. How have you or the women in your life (mother, wife, sister, daughter, etc.) successfully addressed the challenges working women face? Or share what actions you've taken to overcome these challenges. Then listen while the leaders tell you why they have (or have not) furthered the company's goal of increasing female representation at the highest levels.

Advice for Working Women: 22 Ways Women Can Help Themselves (Sample Items)

1. Find out who is involved in the strategic planning process in your organization. If there are no women, approach your CEO to discuss the best way to ensure greater diversity in the process.
2. Confront and replace your own self-limiting, embedded mind-sets.
3. Realize that you too have a lot to give others. Network with other women and provide support. Become a mentor or, if you are in a position to help, be an active sponsor for other women.

PART 2

GETTING ON

11. Theories of vertical segregation in feminized occupations: rethinking dominant perspectives and making use of Bourdieu
Kate Huppatz

Feminized occupations such as nursing, teaching, social work and librarianship are gendered because they are numerically dominated by women and aligned with femininity. They are also gendered because men have long secured a disproportionate number of the senior and powerful positions within the upper echelons of these fields. This chapter is concerned with this second process – vertical segregation. Vertical segregation is a widespread social problem that exists in all economies and across diverse occupations and is a particularly vexing feature of feminized occupations. As Anker (1997, p. 136) identifies, occupational segregation is problematic because excluding parts of the population from workforce positions is a waste of human resources and it indicates that the labour market is inflexible and so unable to adapt efficiently to change. Sectorial segmentation is also obviously disadvantageous to women: it impacts women's income and statuses as well as the ways they are viewed by others and the ways women view themselves. What is more, this is a longstanding issue; occupational segregation is a problem that has plagued the workforce since women first entered the labour market and it is an issue that still demands research and theorizing because we do not yet understand exactly how it is perpetuated or how it might be resolved.

This chapter reviews dominant approaches to gendered patterns in career trajectories and the attainment of senior and management positions in feminized careers. It suggests that the gendering of feminized jobs might be better understood using Pierre Bourdieu's triad of concepts: habitus, capital and field. While Bourdieu is not often utilized for this type of research, his theory is perhaps gaining momentum within the sociology of work, management, and organizational studies, and several authors have put forward a case for the appropriation of his conceptual approach. For example, in their review of four of Bourdieu's key works, Ozbilgin and Tatli (2005, p. 855) argue that management and organization studies may benefit from a stronger engagement with his theory, suggesting that it offers a means with which to carry out 'multilevel' research, a framework for attending to reflexivity in this process, and a methodological and epistemological solution to the agency/structure and subjectivism/objectivism dichotomies. Everett (2002, p. 56) offers an overview of Bourdieu's key concepts, suggesting they should be appropriated more frequently in organizational studies because 'Bourdieu's research ladder offers a fine critical yet reflexive vista from which to better view the organization'. Similarly, Emirbayer and Johnson (2008, p. 36) emphasize the use value of Bourdieu's habitus and capital concepts (they point out that many organizational researchers operationalize the field concept but neglect habitus and capital) and write that Bourdieu enables researchers to understand the relationship between organizations and society either by conceptualizing organizations-as-fields or organizations-in-fields: 'Bourdieu's framework provides a powerful new set of tools with which to analyze precisely how organizations structure, and are structured by, the larger social configurations in which they are embedded.'

This chapter speaks to this literature and makes the case for a number of the arguments put forward by the above authors. However, it does emphasize (as the author does elsewhere; see for example, Huppatz, 2009, 2012; Huppatz and Ross-Smith, 2010; Huppatz and Goodwin, 2013) that Bourdieu's approach also allows for the analysis of gender relations and suggests how a Bourdieusian analysis overcomes limitations in extant literature on vertical segregation and, unlike many other papers that advocate for Bourdieu (Vaughan, 2008 is an exception), gives specific examples of how this appropriation might take place for the study of gendered relations and their intersections in feminized work. The chapter first reviews two patterns of vertical segregation in feminized occupations, then introduces several of the dominant approaches to vertical segregation as well as their shortcomings and, in the final section, puts forward a proposal for making use of Bourdieu.

PATTERNS OF VERTICAL SEGREGATION IN FEMALE-CONCENTRATED WORK

While it cannot be assumed that vertical segregation necessarily exists in all feminized occupational hierarchies (Snyder and Green, 2008, find little evidence for vertical segregation in nursing in America, for example), this type of occupational segmentation is an assiduous inequality in many countries. For example, in Australia men only comprised 19 per cent of the primary teachers and 43 per cent of secondary teachers in 2010. However, at the same time, they held 43 per cent of the leadership positions

(Principal, Deputy/Vice Principal positions and their equivalents) in primary schools and 61 per cent of the leadership positions in secondary schools. Men also maintained the majority of the Principal posts across the sector whereas women held a higher proportion of Deputy Principal positions (McKenzie et al., p.xiii). This pattern is less pronounced in nursing in Australia but a gender imbalance is still noticeable. In 2011 men made up 10 per cent of the nursing workforce (Australian Bureau of Statistics, 2013) yet they also held 14 per cent of the non-clinical areas and management posts and occupied 11 per cent of the nursing education positions (Health Workforce Australia, 2013).

These patterns have not gone unnoticed by social scientists; many researchers have identified certain commonalities in men's career pathways in feminized jobs. In the next section this chapter provides an overview of the theoretical perspectives on, or that can be applied to, vertical segregation in feminized occupations. Broadly, the literature identifies labour supply and labour demand factors (Anker, 1997) that contribute to this social problem. Explanations that focus on supply factors concentrate on what employees 'prefer' in terms of work arrangements, and career goals and supply explanations concentrate on the type of employee that employers and organizations 'prefer' (although researchers do not see these preferences as individual – they are impacted by wider gendered social processes; ibid.). Some of the most influential theoretical approaches, reviewed in this next section, include human capital theory, preference theory, token theory and the gendered institutions approaches (including the 'glass escalator' perspective). All of these understandings overlap in some way but nevertheless offer unique explanations.

THE DOMINANT PERSPECTIVES ON VERTICAL SEGREGATION

Human Capital Theory

Developed by Mincer (1958) and Becker (1962), human capital theory suggests that employers use 'human capital' measures of productivity including qualifications, experience and geographical mobility (cited in Brown and Jones, 2004). This approach proposes that women spend less time in the workforce due to family responsibilities and so they accumulate less human capital. As a consequence employers are more likely to promote men to senior positions because men are better qualified. Human capital theory therefore assumes that women are more dedicated to their families than to their jobs, and men, on the other hand, are career oriented; it rests on functionalist assumptions about the specializations and interests of men and women (Poggio, 2010).

Brown and Jones (2004) tested out the applicability of human capital theory for understanding vertical segregation in feminized work using a survey of 484 registered nurses in New South Wales, Australia. Brown and Jones found that while human capital theory may be able to explain why women (who often take up part-time work) do not achieve full-time management roles, it cannot explain why full-time careers are the norm within management. Human capital theory also cannot explain why men are still advantaged in promotion when women are similarly qualified or why men might receive promotion when they have limited experience. The theory therefore cannot account for why the same capital is valued differently depending on whether it is held by a man or woman or why women are paid less than men. However, Brown and Jones's data did indicate that men are more likely to have higher qualifications and less likely to have career breaks than women; they conclude that career breaks and part-time work are incompatible with senior positions, whether an organization is ordained as 'family friendly' or not.

Preference Theory

Preference theory, developed by Catherine Hakim (2002), is a derivative of human capital theory (Poggio, 2010). A cornerstone of Hakim's argument is the idea that women are now liberated in that they are free to make decisions and choose their lifestyles. A consequence of this liberation is heterogeneous work trajectories for women. Hakim bases her analysis on three questions on women's lifestyle preferences and work commitment from a 1999 national British survey and finds that there are three types of women: women who have home-centred, work-centred, or adaptive lifestyle preferences. Hakim contends that women tend to be less invested in their careers than men and this explains why men advance to senior positions and women do not. She also suggests (2002, p. 22) that her approach explicates why women are concentrated in feminized occupations that allow for flexibility and work–family balance, such as teaching. This theory cannot, however, explain why men claim to be 'pushed' into management (see Williams, 1992) or why women encounter discrimination in promotion and management (as is evident elsewhere, for example, Broadbridge, 2010; Huppatz, 2012). Hakim fails to adequately consider structural or cultural constraints. This is because, like human capital theory, this approach is built upon functionalist assumptions of male and female preferences, but also because she overemphasizes women's freedom. As McRae (2003) writes, preferences are only part of women's stories, women also experience a whole range of constraints inside and outside of institutions. Yet in preference theory 'No mention is made of teenage pregnancy, inadequate housing, differential access to higher education, unequal returns to education. According to Hakim, *accidents of time and place* shape people's lives, not social structure (2002, p. 275)' (McRae, 2003, p. 334; original emphasis). Finally, Hakim's typological conceptualization cannot consider how preferences might change over time. Preference theory therefore cannot fully account for women's 'choices' and work trajectories.

Tokenism

An alternative to human capital approaches is Kanter's (1977) well-known token theory. Token theory focuses on organizational constraints to explain vertical segregation and was developed as a result of observations of male–female interaction in a study of an industrial sales force dominated by men. Kanter (1977, p. 968) defines tokens as 'people identified by ascribed characteristics (master statuses such as sex, race, religion, ethnic group, age, etc.) or other characteristics that carry with them a set of assumptions about culture, status, and behaviour highly salient for majority category members'. Drawing on Simmel's argument that group structure qualitatively impacts group interaction, Kanter (ibid., p. 965) finds that female tokens and male–female interactions are dramatically affected by a work environment dominated by men. For Kanter, there are three important factors that impact interaction in this environment: visibility, polarization and assimilation. First, as they are a numerical minority, tokens are highly visible so that 'they capture a larger awareness share' (ibid., p. 971). Second, tokens are polarized in that there is a heightened sensitivity to their uniqueness to the majority. Third, tokens are assimilated so that they fit the stereotype for their group whether it is suited to them or not. These three factors are associated with particular 'interaction dynamics' that evoke a typical response from tokens, and negative consequences (ibid., p. 972). Kanter outlines three of these interaction dynamics: (1) visibility pressures women to perform, (2) polarization leads to the affirmation of group boundaries and token isolation, and (3) assimilation leads to role entrapment for tokens.

While Kanter did not research a feminized organization, she claims that her theory is 'gender-neutral' and pertains to other token experiences, including work environments where men are a numerical minority. Kanter suggests that in cases where a token is actually from a dominant group the content of token and dominant interaction may change but the dynamics would remain the same. For example, male tokens may be trapped in a role that bears favourably on views of their competence rather than negatively.

Yet, Kanter's approach cannot sufficiently explain how tokenism works differently for men and women; it cannot explain why white men experience limited disadvantage as tokens (Zimmer, 1988; Acker, 1990). Acker (1990, p. 143) argues that, 'In posing the argument as structure or gender, Kanter also implicitly posits gender as standing outside of structure, and she fails to follow up her own observations about masculinity and organizations (1977, 22).' Similarly, Zimmer (1988) contends that inequality in gendered workplaces is less about numerical under-representation and more about a culture of sexism that blankets society more generally. This is why there is little evidence to suggest that raising the quantity of tokens will produce equality in employment.

Gendered Institutions

Acker (1990, 1992) departs from this type of perspective in that she provides a structural approach to occupational segregation that is thoroughly gendered. Acker argues that gender is evident in institutions and proposes that there are even 'gendered institutions'. Acker (1992, p. 568) states that 'the term "gendered institutions" means that gender is present in the processes, practices, images and ideologies, and distributions of power in the various sectors of social life'. The economy is one of the institutions that are organized along gendered lines but so are smaller organizations like hospitals, libraries and schools. Acker is most concerned with organizational logic. She argues that organizational logic appears to be gender-neutral but there is a gendered substructure that informs work activities and also the theorizing of organizational academics. Acker claims that jobs and hierarchies are constructed as genderless in organizational logic; the workers that fill them are seen as disembodied and exist only to labour. Acker claims that the closest thing that actually exists to a disembodied worker is the full-time, life-long, male worker who can rely on a wife to take care of his family and personal needs. The caring obligations of female workers make them least likely to fit this ideal and they are ranked low on hierarchies as a consequence. There is little place for women's bodies in organizations: 'While women's bodies are ruled out of order, or sexualized and objectified, in work organizations, men's bodies are not. Indeed, male sexual imagery pervades organizational metaphors and language, helping to give form to work activities' (Acker, 1990, p. 152). Therefore, despite being presented as gender-neutral, jobs are implicitly gendered and incorporate the gendered division of labour and the public–private divide.

Acker's understanding of gendered organizational logic applies to a diversity of organizations and offers a structural explanation for why vertical segregation exists in feminized work. The connections that she makes between wider gendered cultural processes and institutions mean that she overcomes some of the shortcomings of the human capital and token theories. However, as Acker sees organizations as inherently gendered, within her earlier analysis change is not possible unless organizations themselves are abolished. This prevents an imagining of how current organizations could be improved and any understanding of how some organizations might be more gendered than others (Britton, 2000). More recently, Acker (2006, p.455) has proposed that strategies for change might focus on 'inequality-reducing mechanisms' but she maintains that change would still be very difficult.

The Glass Escalator

A variant of the gendered institutions approach is Williams's (1992) 'glass escalator' perspective (Budig, 2002). Like Acker, Williams sees organizations as producing gender inequality but highlights that a glass escalator fast-tracks men to senior positions and management careers in feminized occupations. Williams's glass escalator concept was formulated from a US study involving 99 in-depth interviews with men and women in four types of feminized work including nursing, elementary school teaching, librarianship and social work. Williams's data reveal that while tracking sometimes limits men from specialities that are deemed as feminine within these occupations, tracking also results in men advancing to positions that are not only considered gender appropriate, but are also more prestigious and better paid. While women frequently hit a 'glass ceiling' when moving through organizational hierarchies, men encounter a 'glass escalator': 'Often, despite their intentions, they face invisible pressures to move up in their professions, as if on a moving escalator, they must work to stay in place' (Williams, 1992, p.256). Williams therefore found that tokenism is experienced differently by men and women and that the glass escalator is a useful metaphor for capturing the specificity of male workers' experience, overcoming the gender-neutrality of other approaches.

Williams's metaphor has had a profound resonance for occupational segregation theorists and has become an 'everyday' terminology, but, as her approach builds on Acker's, it features the same limitations. In addition, Williams (2013) has recently turned a critical lens to her concept and claims that it is historically specific (in its focus on 'traditional' models of work organization rather than more recent 'neoliberal' models of work organization where job security, career ladders, loyal service rewards and full-time work are not guaranteed), workplace specific (it only pertains to middle-class jobs that feature a hierarchy), as well as incapable of considering the impact of race, class and sexuality on career experience and trajectory. Williams (2013, p. 16) therefore argues that 'We need new concepts and metaphors to explain gender inequality in neoliberal times'. In the next section this chapter argues for an old set of concepts to be applied in new ways – for the applicability of Bourdieu's theory to the analysis of vertical segregation in feminized work.

PRESENTATION OF THE THEORY: THE CASE FOR BOURDIEU'S CONCEPTS

Why is Bourdieu's theory an alternative to these approaches? Although Bourdieu was mostly concerned with social class relations and does not present a theory of organizations per se, his conceptual triad is also very adaptable to the analysis of contexts beyond his own research interests. Below is an account of how his concepts can be applied to understand vertical segregation in a study on feminized work (Huppatz, 2009, 2012; Huppatz and Goodwin, 2013) that explains how his theory addresses the shortfalls in other perspectives on vertical segregation. For this research interviews were carried out with 53 male and female nurses, social workers, exotic dancers and hairdressers (48 women and five men, 25 nurses and 20 social workers). However, for the purpose of this chapter, the findings will focus on the data pertaining to nursing and social work, two occupations that operate within a 'paid caring field'.

Habitus

The habitus concept is the key to Bourdieu's dialectic approach to structure and agency. The habitus both generates and unifies practices that are informed by durable dispositions that are internalized histories and structures. The habitus therefore provides a link between wider social processes and individual actions. The habitus frames bodily conduct and so the concept also enables researchers to focus on workers' bodily realities (walking, talking, modes of dress) within workplaces. As the habitus is informed by histories and environments, groups that share histories and environments exhibit 'homogeneity of the habitus' (Bourdieu, 1990, p. 80). This means that gender groups share similarly structured habitus and this may result in 'masculine' and 'feminine' dispositions that inform homologous practices, competencies and ambitions. The habitus concept therefore helps explain why women might pursue nursing and social work in greater numbers than men without resorting to gender essentialism. The female nurses and social workers interviewed described a sense of 'fit' between their occupations and their identities that male nurses and social workers did not – this can be understood as a fit between feminine habitus and the feminized occupational environment (nursing and social work cultures have long been associated with caring, which is aligned with mothering and femininity – there is a more detailed historical account of this alignment in Huppatz, 2012) and continuity was found between their 'choices' and the choices of their mothers, in that their mothers also pursued feminized work. This concept is therefore useful for understanding horizontal segregation. It also explains why many of the women interviewed expressed little interest in promotions that take them away from hands-on 'caring' activities. The interviews with male workers revealed that the lack of fit between masculine habitus and the environment made them more visible (just as Kanter's theory of tokens suggests) and this had positive effects in relation to career progression. The habitus concept therefore allows the researcher to connect individuals with institutional divisions and workplace processes as well as gender culture outside of the workplace.

Capital

Capital is economic and symbolic wealth and so the presence or absence of capital plays a role in the creation of inequality. Bourdieu mostly refers to three types of capital: economic, social and cultural capital. Economic capital is goods that can be converted into money or property rights, social capital is beneficial social relations that distribute advantage, and cultural capital is cultural knowledge that is objectified, institutionalized or embodied. The latter type of capital was found to be evident and gendered in feminized occupational spaces. This has led the author to argue with other Bourdieusian feminists that the embodied capital concept can be reworked in order to understand gendered advantage (see, for example, Skeggs, 1997). In *Gender Capital at Work* (2012) the author argues that feminine, female, masculine, and male-embodied capitals operate in gendered occupations and that this type of wealth might be termed 'gender capital'. For example, women workers spoke of how caring demeanours and female bodies assisted them in accessing these occupations but had limited use in the domain of management, whereas the male workers interviewed suggested that pushiness and aggressiveness are masculine embodiments that advance men in the occupations. One male participant pointed out that his body was an asset in accessing senior positions in that it is not aligned with mothering and therefore career interruption. Male workers also talked about how they embody (what they see to be) feminine qualities (for example, compassion) and these qualities appeared to act as gender capital in that the men reported that they made them better at their jobs. Women, on the other hand, were mostly devoted to stereotypically feminine dispositions and so, because feminine dispositions are subordinated to masculine dispositions, were less likely to profit from gender capital. Gendered embodiments therefore play a role in position taking and movement through occupational space and this concept is unlike human capital in that it is thoroughly gendered and it helps to explain the connections between work trajectories and gender power relations.

Field

For Bourdieu a field is a social network of objective relations. Society is made up of many fields that overlap in different ways but each field is also governed by its own particular logic – by a set of rules and norms. Individuals who operate within a field take up positions that are determined by the structure and volume of their assets (capital) and although fields are mostly stable, they are also characterized by struggle as agents attempt to accumulate further capital. The analysis did not focus on an institution and so did not conceptualize an organization-as-field. Rather it looked more broadly at occupations, focusing on occupations-in-fields (as opposed to organizations-in-fields, as Emirbayer and Johnson, 2008 suggest). Bourdieu did not conceptualize occupations as fields; they are not characterized by common stakes and struggles that are unique to their spaces (Atkinson, 2009). However, occupations are impacted by fields and the activities within them, and clouds of individuals are also associated with types of occupations (for example, women are grouped in clouds in feminized occupations). Occupations can also have a field-like impact on the habitus even though they are not fields in themselves; they have particular cultures and operate in specific environments and this structures workers' embodiments. Occupations are therefore significant spaces or subspaces of social action. In this study the occupations appeared to be characterized by struggles over the gendered meanings that are assigned value in these spaces. So, for example, female nurses formed an informal social network, a 'necessary sisterhood', and within this network 'femaleness' became a social capital that sometimes helped in job acquisition and promotion. This was an attempt to change the state of play in the occupations and elevate the symbolic meaning of femaleness in relation to maleness. In this way, individual nurses worked together to impact the structure of occupational spaces and because (along with similar capitals) these struggles characterized nursing and social work, it was concluded that the occupations are located within a 'paid caring field'.

The notion of social space and the field concept therefore assists in relational thinking, which Bourdieu argues is necessary for understanding social problems. Gender is more than biology or a position, it can only be understood as a relationship, and so he asserts that it must be understood 'as it establishes itself *in the whole set of social spaces and subspaces*' (Bourdieu, 2001, p. 102; original emphasis). Furthermore, gender identities and inequalities can only be grasped by examining how a field or social space has developed (so, for example, nursing has been imagined as 'mothering' at many points in its history; see Huppatz, 2012 for a more detailed discussion), and its relationship to other fields and subspaces (for example, in the cases of nursing and social work there are connections to the family, including family hierarchies).

Doxic Order and Symbolic Violence

The final concepts that may be of use to researchers who seek to understand vertical segregation are doxic order, symbolic violence and reflexivity. The doxic order is a classificatory system of understandings (such as binary stereotypes of masculinity and femininity) that impact social fields and social action. Individuals embody this order via the habitus and this directs their classifications of each other but also their classifications of themselves so that the women interviewed largely naturalized their caring capacities and women's place in social work and nursing. This same logic naturalizes men's prevalence in leadership positions. In one of the few passages where he did consider the gendering of occupations, Bourdieu (2001, p. 95) wrote that this symbolic system is pivotal for understanding gendered occupational segregation: 'The constancy of habitus that results from this is thus one of the most important factors in the relative constancy in the structure of the division of labour.' In this way, old structures of gender and the family live on and are objectified in paid work.

For Bourdieu, power often operates below direct institutional discrimination, unconsciously and without calculated organization by oppressors, as if by 'magic'. Power is activated through the symbolic or doxic order and maintained by 'symbolic violence', through acts that reinstate the position of the dominant. Symbolic violence gives power to everyday acts of 'injunctions, suggestions, seduction, threats, reproaches, orders or calls to order' (ibid., p. 42). This type of violence was evident in the narratives of the female nurse and social work manager interviewees, in the often subtle and unspoken discrimination they experienced.

A final consideration in relation to these concepts is that although Bourdieu does emphasize the reproduction of social practice and the strength of the doxic system, he also highlights the significance of reflexivity. For Bourdieu, where there is dominance there is always the possibility for resistance. The dominated do not always see this system as self-evident and so reflexivity is often a particular characteristic of the marginalized; women can have the unique perspective of outsiders. Resistance to the gender order was clear in women's participation in a 'necessary sisterhood', in the distance that some female workers created between their own identities and caring, in women's descriptions of caring performances, and in their problematization of male dominance of management and senior positions. Vertical segregation is challenged in these ways and these practices may result in its discontinuity.

WHAT ABOUT SOCIAL CLASS?

Bourdieu's theoretical formulation was designed to understand class relations and so is also perfectly suited to the analysis of socioeconomic inequality. This is important in researching work practices and processes because, as Acker (1990, p. 154) comments, social class and gender are interrelated in organizations – job classification and evaluation systems organize and reinforce class relations. Williams (2013, p. 18) also argues for the inclusion of class in the analysis of gendered work, suggesting that her concept of the glass escalator is inadequate because it 'analyzes male privilege without critiquing capitalist exploitation'. In addition, Lupton (2006) finds survey evidence that class intersects with gendered patterns in feminized work: working-class men are disproportionately represented in these areas and may be seeking out social mobility. This means that heightened masculine motivation for promotion may also be heightened class motivation. For Bourdieu the habitus embodies class histories and structures that inform common practices and the capitals that individuals bear are impacted by class experience. Making use of this framework, it was found that working-class women were more likely to see nursing and social work as a means of upward mobility and therefore use femininity tactically in this process. It was also discovered that working-class women workers were much less likely to reach management positions even though they more readily claimed to have an economic interest in the occupations. This suggests that they are less likely to have a feel for management 'games' while middle-class women profit from a class advantage that sometimes (but not often) neutralizes gender disadvantage. Class processes therefore add to and complicate the production of vertical segregation.

SUMMARY AND RECOMMENDATIONS

Vertical segregation is a persistent feature of feminized work. This chapter has reviewed the dominant theoretical perspectives that have attempted to explain this phenomenon and highlighted their strengths and weaknesses. It has been argued that while these prominent understandings have played an important role in unpacking many of the key elements of this phenomenon, they have fallen short in significant ways. This chapter has proposed that a Bourdieusian analysis enables researchers to move beyond the structure/agency dichotomy to consider how occupational divisions are the result of a combination of free will, constraint and supply and demand factors. The human capital and token theories lack a multilevel analysis that can link workplace or institutional practices to everyday interactions and wider cultural forces. The chapter has drawn on the author's own research to show how the triad of habitus, capital and field along with doxic order, reflexivity and symbolic violence overcome these shortcomings. In addition, a reworking of embodied cultural capital enables an understanding of gender that moves beyond the functionalist presumptions of human capital theories and facilitates an analysis of gender as both a cultural asset and a detriment. It has been argued that a Bourdieusian analysis allows for a consideration of the ways in which social class complicates vertical segregation, and so redresses the absence of intersectionality that is found throughout much organizational and management research.

What is still missing here is an analysis of how ethnicity intersects with class and gender in vertical segregation processes. A number of writers highlight the significance of ethnicity for organizational analysis. For example, Acker (2006) suggests that the abstract worker may be white as well as male and that gender, class and ethnicity may be described as operating relationally within 'inequality regimes' in organizations. Williams (2013) reminds gender researchers that attention to ethnicity is necessary so that white, middle-class women's experiences are not universalized. Wingfield (2009) and Duffy (2007) write that race is an important aspect of gender segregation – racial minority men are disproportionately represented in most feminized work, just as working-class men may be. Wingfield (2009) also suggests that racial minority men do not profit from vertical segregation. My own research does not explore the intersection of ethnicity with gender and class but this is indeed another element of vertical segregation that needs to be examined in more detail. Although ethnicity, like gender, was not always prominent in Bourdieu's theorizing, his concepts could allow for an intersectional analysis that incorporates this form of marginalization. Just as they have for gender, theorists have reworked his concept of cultural capital to account for the 'specific effect of ethnicity on the organization, distribution and transmission of cultural capital relative to other variables' (Bennett et al., 2009, p. 235). Any analysis of vertical segregation that includes ethnicity would need to consider and perhaps apply this reworking to understand how ethnicity may influence position taking, the nature of struggle and the operation of power in an occupational or institutional space.

Further research is therefore needed to understand the full scope of this framework for analysing vertical segregation. Although it has been explained here how this theory is an improvement on dominant perspectives and has been operationalized in the author's own research on two occupations, in order to understand its full potential for researching vertical segregation it must be widely appropriated to examine occupations and organizations (as-fields and in-fields) as well as relations of gender, class *and* ethnicity within those spaces.

REFERENCES

Acker, J. (1990), 'Hierarchies, jobs, bodies: a theory of gendered organizations', *Gender & Society*, **4**(2), 139–58.
Acker, J. (1992), 'From sex roles to gendered institutions', *Contemporary Sociology*, **21**(5), 565–9.
Acker, J. (2006), 'Inequality regimes: gender, class and race within organizations', *Gender & Society*, **20**(4), 441–64.
Anker, R. (1997), 'Theories of occupational segregation by sex: an overview', *International Labour Review*, **136**(3), 315–39.
Atkinson, W. (2009), 'Rethinking the work–class nexus: theoretical foundations for recent trends', *Sociology*, **43**(5), 896–912.
Australian Bureau of Statistics (2013), *Doctors and Nurses 4102.0 – Australian Social Trends*, April 2013, accessed 28 November 2014 at http://www.abs.gov.au/AUSSTATS/abs@.nsf/Lookup/4102.0Main+Features20April+2013.
Becker, G.S. (1962), 'Investment in human beings', *Journal of Political Economy*, **70**(5), 9–49.
Bennett, T., M. Savage, E. Silva, A. Warde, M. Gayo-Cal and D. Wright (2009), *Culture, Class, Distinction*, Oxon: Routledge.
Bourdieu, P. (1990), *Outline of a Theory of Practice*, Cambridge, UK: Cambridge University Press.
Bourdieu, P. (2001), *Langage et pouvoir symbolique* [Language and Symbolic Power], Paris: Seuil.
Britton, D. (2000), 'The epistemology of the gendered organization', *Gender & Society*, **14**(3), 418–34.
Broadbridge, A. (2010), 'Choice or constraint? Tensions in female retail executives career narratives', *Gender in Management: An International Journal*, **25**(3), 244–60.
Brown, C. and L. Jones (2004), 'The gender structure of the nursing hierarchy: the role of human capital', *Gender, Work & Organization*, **11**(1), 1–25.
Budig, M. (2002), 'Male advantage and the gender composition of jobs: who rides the glass escalator?', *Social Problems*, **49**(2), 258–77.
Duffy, M. (2007), 'Doing the dirty work: gender, race and reproductive labour in historical perspective', *Gender & Society*, **21**(3), 313–36.

Emirbayer, M. and V. Johnson (2008), 'Bourdieu and organizational analysis', *Theory and Society*, **37**(1), 1–44.
Everett, J. (2002), 'Organizational research and praxeology of Pierre Bourdieu', *Organizational Research Methods*, **5**(1), 56–80.
Hakim, C. (2002), 'Lifestyle preferences as determinants of women's differentiated labour market careers', *Work and Occupations*, **29**(4), 428–59.
Health Workforce Australia (2013), *Australia's Health Workforce Series – Nurses in Focus*, Health Workforce Australia: Adelaide.
Huppatz, K. (2009), 'Reworking Bourdieu's "capital": feminine and female capitals in the field of paid caring work', *Sociology*, **43**(1), 45–66.
Huppatz, K. (2012), *Gender Capital at Work: Intersections of Femininity, Masculinity, Class and Occupation*, Basingstoke, UK: Palgrave Macmillan.
Huppatz, K. and S. Goodwin (2013), 'Masculinised jobs, feminised jobs and men's "gender capital" experiences: understanding occupational segregation in Australia', *Journal of Sociology*, **49**(2–3), 291–308.
Huppatz, K. and A. Ross-Smith (2010), 'Management, women and gender capital', *Gender, Work & Organization*, **17**(5), 547–66.
Kanter, R. (1977), 'Some effects of proportions on group life: skewed sex ratios and responses to token women', *American Journal of Sociology*, **82**(5), 965–90.
Lupton, B. (2006), 'Explaining men's entry into female concentrated occupations: issues of masculinity and social class', *Gender, Work & Organization*, **13**(2), 103–28.
McKenzie, P., G. Rowley, P. Weldon and M. Murphy (2011), *Staff in Australia's Schools 2010: Main Report on the Survey*, Australian Council for Education Research, November 2011, accessed 28 November 2014 at http://research.acer.edu.au/cgi/viewcontent.cgi?article=1013&context=tll_misc.
McRae, S. (2003), 'Constraints and choices in mothers' employment careers: a consideration of Hakim's preference theory', *British Journal of Sociology*, **54**(3), 317–38.
Mincer, J. (1958), Investment in human capital and personal income distribution', *The Journal of Political Economy*, **4**(LXVI), 281–302.
Ozbilgin, M. and A. Tatli (2005), 'Book review essay: understanding Bourdieu's contribution to organization and management studies', *Academy of Management Review*, **30**(4), 855–77.
Poggio, B. (2010), 'Vertical segregation and gender practices. Perspectives of analysis and action', *Gender in Management: An International Journal*, **25**(6), 428–37.
Skeggs, B. (1997), *Formations of Class and Gender*, London: Sage.
Snyder, K. and A. Green (2008), 'Revisiting the glass escalator: the case of gender segregation in a female dominated occupation', *Social Problems*, **55**(2), 271–99.
Vaughan, D. (2008), 'Bourdieu and organizations: the empirical challenge', *Theory and Society*, **37**(1), 65–81.
Williams, C. (1992), 'The glass escalator: hidden advantages for men in the "female" professions', *Social Problems*, **39**(3), 253–67.
Williams, C. (2013), 'The glass escalator revisited: gender inequality in neoliberal times', *Gender & Society*, **27**(5), 609–29.
Wingfield, A. (2009), 'Racializing the glass escalator: reconsidering men's experiences with women's work', *Gender & Society*, **23**(1), 5–26.
Zimmer, L. (1988), 'Tokenism and women in the workplace: the limits of gender-neutral theory', *Social Problems*, **35**(1), 64–77.

12. Women's beliefs about breaking glass ceilings
Paul Smith

There is clear evidence that men maintain a far higher proportion of leadership and upper management positions than women in many countries such as Australia (Equal Opportunity for Women in the Workplace Agency, 2010), Canada (Catalyst, 2012), China (Forsythe and Zhao, 2011), Malaysia (Ahmad-Zaluki, 2012), South Africa (Booysen and Nkomo, 2010), UK (Thomson et al., 2008) and USA (Powell, 2012). However, when speaking at corporate workshops for managers I make an impact with two trivia questions, each with a big message. I often begin a training session on breaking glass ceilings with the following question: 'How many men and women have walked on the moon?' A trivia buff might call out the generally accepted answer: '12.' Actually, it should be a two-part answer. For men, the answer is 12. For women, the answer is zero. Twelve to zero is not a rational distribution because in many ways women are better suited to space travel than men (Weitekamp, 2004). The message? Gender-based inequality not only exists on earth, we have spread this phenomenon to the moon. Obstacles created by men have been placed in front of women for a long time. For example, there are 3218 names in the Bible but only 181, that is less than 6 per cent, are female (Caroselli, 1998). Gender inequality has indeed been around for millennia.

The above observations reinforce that researchers have to keep asking, why do glass ceilings exist and why do they persist? Valuable insights can be found in Eagly and Karau's (2002) role congruity theory of prejudice toward women leaders. Women can receive a double dose of discrimination courtesy of widely accepted beliefs about gender differences. Cultures around the world typically view women as communal and men as agentic. Communal characteristics include being nurturant, helpful and kind. On the other hand, agentic attributes include being assertive, ambitious, independent and self-confident (Heilman and Okimoto, 2007; Phelan et al., 2008). Women aspiring to be leaders can miss out because leaders are most often seen as being agentic (Duehr and Bono, 2006; Eagly and Carli, 2007; Weyer, 2007). Then, if women leaders do show agentic behaviour they can be seen in a negative light, because that contradicts the stereotype of women being communal (Okimoto and Brescoll, 2010; Mavin and

Grandy, 2012). To paraphrase Winston Churchill, it is a Catch-22 inside a double standard.

Eagly and Karau (2002) propose that these stereotypes and beliefs are at the foundation of the problem of glass ceilings. Their theory was the catalyst for research into gender stereotypes by Smith et al. (2012b) who sought to develop a questionnaire that assessed the levels of support women had for attitudes towards women's career advancement and therefore, their thoughts about glass ceilings.

Clearly, both men and women may support stereotypes about women's potential and ability to be successful in organizations (Elsaid and Elsaid, 2012). Furthermore, a literature review showed there was a strong need for a new measure of women's attitudes toward glass ceilings. Only six instruments were found: Women As Managers Scale (WAMS; Terborg et al., 1977), Managerial Attitudes Toward Women Executives Scale (MATWES; Dubno et al., 1979), Women Workplace Culture Questionnaire (WWC; Bergman, 2003) and three unnamed instruments used by Jackson (2001), Wood and Lindorff (2001) and Elacqua et al. (2009). It should be noted that belief, attitude and opinion are used interchangeably in accordance with a popular dictionary of psychology (Reber, 1985).

Whilst the WAMS is probably the most popular of these measures as it has been used extensively (Elsaid and Elsaid, 2012), it only assesses a single factor and has been linked to concerns about levels of reliability and validity (Crino et al., 1981; Cordano et al., 2003). Likewise, the MATWES is unifactorial. In contrast, the WWC gives feedback on four factors but Bergman (2003) has identified a limitation as this scale was largely tested on well-educated women working at the same university. Three unnamed instruments have been used in glass ceiling research. First, Jackson's (2001) questionnaire was developed with 47 women managers in California; Wood and Lindorff (2001) sampled a bigger group in an Australian study, but still achieved low reliabilities for the resultant scale. Last, Elaqua et al. (2009) reported the development of a measure that resulted from an investigation of the glass ceiling in a giant American insurance company. Like some of the other measures, factor analysis details are missing.

Reviewing the handful of glass-ceiling-related questionnaires identified the need for a multifactorial measure of women's beliefs about glass ceilings with good psychometric properties. Consequently, the Career Pathways Survey (CPS; Smith et al., 2012b) was constructed. Its theoretical foundations are developed from Eagly and Karau's (2002) role congruity theory of prejudice against women leaders, which identifies the negative consequences of stereotypes for women. CPS items give coverage to diverse variables related to women's career progress such as work–family balance, sexist barriers in organizations, role models, sexual harassment, benefits of higher education, lack of promotion opportunities, jealousy from female colleagues, successful organizations wanting to retain talented female leaders, networking and guidance by mentors.

Smith (2012) sought a way to group women's beliefs about glass ceilings. This goal got a big boost with the discovery of a qualitative research paper by Wrigley (2002). After carrying out in-depth interviews with 27 women managers Wrigley proposed a new theoretical concept. She called it 'negotiated resignation' and describes it as being linked with denial. She thought she heard some half-hearted denials about glass ceilings. This leads to resignation as it allows women to avoid showing commitment to advancing their careers. However, Wrigley did not mention that women might have valid reasons for not wishing to seek promotions, such as discrimination and harassment if they seek leadership roles. Smith (2012) described these beliefs as examples of resignation. Also missing in Wrigley's analysis was any mention of beliefs from women who are happy not rising the corporate ladder because they did not wish to have unhealthy lifestyles often associated with achieving promotions, such as working long hours. Smith (2012) labelled these beliefs as examples of acceptance.

Consequently, Wrigley's theory was used as a springboard by Smith (2012) to build a four-factor model (see Figure 12.1). This shows the

High	*Acceptance* 'We don't want what men want'	*Denial* 'There's a level playing field'
Satisfaction with career level		
	Resignation 'We give up, it's too painful'	*Resilience* 'Let's break through the glass ceiling'
Low		
	Low Desire to pursue career promotion **High**	

Figure 12.1   Women's beliefs about glass ceilings: a four-factor model

relationships between four different sets of beliefs women might have about glass ceilings: resilience, denial, acceptance and resignation. These four groups were identified after a review of the literature on women's career advancement and in particular the extensive research undertaken by Eagly and Carli (2007). Furthermore, some items were also based on hundreds of comments shared by women who attended corporate workshops in my 15-year career as a corporate trainer. The model shows links to women's desire to pursue promotions and satisfaction with career level. It proposes that glass ceiling beliefs can lift or diminish women's desires to be promoted in organizations.

STRUCTURE OF THE CAREER PATHWAYS SURVEY

The CPS is a 38-item four-factor measure that allows researchers to examine opinions about glass ceilings from women at all stages of career advancement, as well as all levels and types of organizations. Women rate their level of agreement with each statement on a seven-point Likert scale, with anchors of strongly agree (1) and strongly disagree (7). The 40 items that underwent factor analysis are shown in the box below.

Item 17, 'Unfair preferential treatment is given to both women and men' (which was expected to measure denial) and Item 29, 'Women with high goals are not likely to achieve their work ambitions' (designed to measure resignation) were both eliminated after failing to load on the four-factor structure of the CPS, thus leaving 38 items.

The four dimensions of the CPS were supported by exploratory factor analysis of data collected from two samples of women ($N = 243$ and $N = 307$) working in a range of Australian organizations. Each factor achieved satisfactory internal consistency with Cronbach alphas ranging from 0.70 to 0.81. The CPS has the following structure: resilience (11 items, $\alpha = 0.70$), denial (ten items, $\alpha = 0.81$), resignation (ten items, $\alpha = 0.71$), acceptance (seven items, $\alpha = 0.72$):

- *Resignation* is defined as the belief that women suffer more negative consequences than men when pursuing career advancement and thus there are many reasons for women not attempting to break glass ceilings. Examples of this factor are: 'Women in senior management positions face frequent putdowns of being too soft or too hard'; 'Women are seldom given full credit for their successes'.
- *Acceptance* is defined as the belief that women prefer not seeking promotions to high-level positions. Instead, they give greater value to life goals such as family involvement. Examples of CPS items

CPS Items

1. Women face no barriers to promotions in most organizations.
2. Women prefer a balanced life more than gaining highly paid careers.
3. Networking is a smart way for women to increase the chances of career success.
4. Talented women are able to overcome sexist discrimination.
5. Smart women avoid careers that involve intense competition with colleagues.
6. Women are capable of making critical leadership decisions.
7. Women who have a strong commitment to their careers can go right to the top.
8. Jealousy from co-workers prevents women from seeking promotions.
9. Women and men have to overcome the same problems at the workplace.
10. Even women with many skills and qualifications fail to be recognized for promotions.
11. Women leaders are seldom given full credit for their successes.
12. Women have the same desire for power as men do.
13. Women have reached the top in all areas of business and politics.
14. Women commonly reject career advancement as they are keener to maintain a role raising children.
15. Women in senior positions face frequent put downs of being too soft or too hard.
16. The support of a mentor greatly increases the success of a woman in any organization.
17. Unfair preferential treatment is given to both women and men.
18. If women achieve promotions they might be accused of offering sexual favours.
19. Women are just as ambitious in their careers as men.
20. Women are more likely to be hurt than men when they take the big risks necessary for corporate success.
21. A supportive spouse/partner or close friend makes it easier for a woman to achieve success in her career.
22. Women are less concerned about promotions than men are.
23. Motherhood is more important to most women than career advancement.
24. Daughters of successful mothers are inspired to overcome sexist hurdles.
25. Women's nurturing skills help them to be successful leaders.
26. Women leaders suffer more emotional pain than men when there is a crisis within their teams.
27. Women have the strength to overcome discrimination.
28. Women reject the need to work incredibly long hours.
29. Women with high goals are not likely to achieve their work ambitions.
30. Women starting careers today will face sexist barriers.
31. Women believe they have to make too many compromises to gain highly paid positions.
32. Successful organizations seek and want to retain talented female staff.
33. Higher education qualifications will help women overcome discrimination.
34. Even very successful women can quickly lose their confidence.
35. Women know that work does not provide the best source of happiness in life.

36. Women executives are very uncomfortable when they have to criticize members of their teams.
37. Being in the limelight creates many problems for women.
38. The more women seek senior positions, the easier it will be for those who follow.
39. It will take decades for women to reach equality with men in high-level management positions.
40. When women are given opportunities to lead they do effective jobs.

  assessing acceptance are: 'Motherhood is more important to most women than career development'; 'Women reject the need to work incredibly long hours'.
- *Denial* of glass ceilings is based on statements that show why some women believe glass ceilings are now myths and non-existent. Two CPS items measuring this factor are: 'Women starting careers today will face sexist barriers' (reverse scored); 'Women and men have to overcome the same problems at the workplace'.
- *Resilience* is the belief that women can be promoted to the highest levels of organizations and therefore are capable of breaking through glass ceilings. Examples include: 'When women are given opportunities to lead they do effective jobs'; 'The more women seek senior positions, the easier it will be for those who follow'.

The theoretical background of the CPS was further developed in the study reported by Smith et al. (2012a). The empirical research outline is shown in Figure 12.2. This study tested the concurrent criterion validity of the CPS by exploring the relationships between the four factors identified by the CPS and five major subjective career success constructs: career satisfaction, happiness, emotional well-being, physical health and work engagement. Work engagement is a composite of three important variables (vigour, dedication, absorption) that have been associated with success and well-being in organizations (Bakker et al., 2008). It has been summed up as being the opposite of burnout, and consequently, it has become a major goal of human resources managers to seek engaged employees (Chughtai and Buckley, 2011). The study used the popular nine-item version of the Utrecht Work Engagement Scale (UWES-9; Schaufeli et al., 2006).

The hypotheses tested by Smith et al. (2012a) were based on two theories of optimism/pessimism: dispositional optimism (which focuses on beliefs about the future) and explanatory-style optimism (which emphasizes the habitual ways we explain events in the present or past). The former theoretical approach was proposed by Scheier and Carver (1985) and the latter

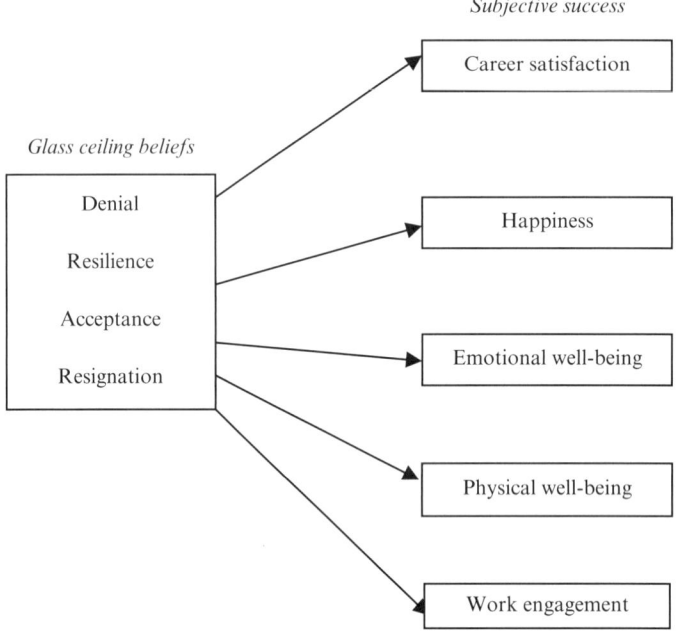

Figure 12.2 Relationships between women's glass ceiling beliefs and subjective success

by Seligman (1991). Both approaches have extensive research profiles in the literature but neither has been connected to women's beliefs about their career progress. A search of the literature on women's careers and their subjective career success found no theoretical models that included beliefs about glass ceilings. Therefore, we considered resilience, denial, acceptance, and resignation as expressions of optimism or pessimism.

In this cognitive conceptualization of glass ceiling attitudes, there is the following dichotomy. Resilience and denial involve optimism as they that assert women can be promoted to the top levels of organizations. On the other hand, resignation and acceptance are pessimistic sets of beliefs as they assert that the gender imbalance in leadership will remain as most women have no leadership goals. Following cognitive therapy's premises about the influence of beliefs (Beck, 1976; Hawton et al., 1989), it follows that the optimistic attitudes of resilience and denial should lead to positive emotions and behaviours such as career satisfaction, happiness, work engagement, physical and emotional well-being. Furthermore, the pessimism associated with resignation and acceptance should negatively influence the subjective career success variables.

The hypotheses were largely supported in research carried out by Smith et al. (2012a). Regression analyses found that denial was the strongest predictor of career satisfaction and work engagement. Resilience was positively associated with happiness and work engagement, but not with career satisfaction. In contrast, and as predicted, resignation was negatively related to happiness and both emotional and physical health. Acceptance showed a predicted negative association with work engagement. In sum, findings from the regression analyses suggest that denial has the strongest positive association with subjective success and resignation has the most negative relationship. The results from this study support the view that resilience and denial are both optimistic sets of attitudes towards women's chances of becoming leaders, while acceptance and resignation are pessimistic attitudes towards women achieving promotion to leadership positions. Thus, the findings supported the hypotheses and the concurrent validity of the CPS. It is also noteworthy that in each of the five regression analyses glass ceiling beliefs accounted for much more variance than the combined effect of the control variables age, education, marital status, number of children and management level.

The results of the above validation study could have implications for women 'getting on', that is, advancing in their careers. An outlook toward glass ceilings that largely consists of denial and resilience beliefs may increase career satisfaction, work engagement and happiness, and consequently, increase the chance of breaking through the glass ceiling. Conversely, a woman who has strong resignation and acceptance attitudes toward glass ceilings may be less likely to climb the corporate ladder due to associated lower levels of work engagement and happiness.

PRACTICAL IMPLICATIONS OF THE CPS

The CPS could be used by organizations wanting to boost the leadership qualities of their employees, both managers and staff. It would be worthwhile for organizations to consider providing training programmes to analyse glass ceiling beliefs after testing with the CPS. This may help women at all levels of the organization to understand reasons for their career goals with respect to either keenness or reticence to seeking promotions. The CPS could play a role with the assessment of new recruits: women who score high on resignation might benefit from training and mentoring that help them examine the validity of their negative thoughts about women seeking promotions. Testing of women workers within an organization might help confirm that the culture is likely to lead to high levels of resignation among the women working for that organization.

These empirical findings could then act as a catalyst for the CEO and high-level executives to initiate major changes to reduce and hopefully reduce gender discrimination.

The CPS was originally designed only to be used to assess beliefs of women. However, the CPS could play a role identifying other contexts, such as sexist cultures in an organization by testing both female and male employees (especially managers). If negative stereotypes towards women leaders are shown to be common, a corporate culture change would be recommended. This organizational restructuring could begin with changes in policies and strategies used in the hiring of job applicants, promoting those already with the organization and 'headhunting' (searching and recruiting) of those with impressive track records of success. The CPS might be used in each of these selection processes.

The development and validation of the CPS is in agreement with the argument proposed by Powell (2012) that the dismantling of glass ceilings will be accelerated when researchers and organizations find new ways to investigate leadership. A second unifying theme in this research is the important role cognitive training may play in developing leadership skills. History over millennia shows that it is extremely difficult to carry out large-scale social changes, or even organizational changes, to reduce discrimination and prejudice against women as leaders (Lerner, 1986). Therefore, women might improve chances of career advancement by assessing and modifying personal thoughts, such as glass ceiling beliefs. It should be emphasized that by suggesting such personal change approaches, it is not another attempt to blame women for the gender imbalance in leadership.

If women learn skills to have more optimistic beliefs about glass ceilings (that is, resilience and denial), this may translate into increased career satisfaction, better psychological and physical well-being, as well as higher levels of work engagement. These positive outcomes have been found to be related to work performance and therefore could be an advantage when women are seeking promotions (Mills et al., 2013). Women wishing to become leaders may also benefit from identifying their workplace optimism using the Workplace Explanations Survey (WES; Smith et al., 2013) to assess their explanatory styles for negative and positive events that occur in organizations. Cognitive training can then be used to help develop (even) more optimistic explanations, which in turn have been shown to increase resilient behaviour and produce greater success due to higher self-confidence and commitment to achieving big goals (Proudfoot et al., 2009; Reivich et al., 2011; Seligman, 2011). Hopefully, one of the successes will include being promoted. Assessments using the CPS could facilitate greater awareness for women and their employers of possible causes of the range of important variables that make up subjective career success.

SUGGESTIONS FOR FUTURE RESEARCH

There is the considerable support given for the existence of four groups of stereotypic thinking about glass ceilings (Smith et al., 2012a, 2012b). It follows that the CPS can be recommended for future quantitative research into the causes and consequences of glass ceilings. However, there is no empirical evidence to show that glass ceiling beliefs are stable state-like psychological constructs. If longitudinal studies provide evidence of the long-term stability of glass ceiling beliefs, they might be considered as relevant as personality traits, an area that has been extensively examined for its role in subjective career success (Judge and Hurst, 2008). Research into the relationships between personality traits and glass ceiling attitudes would be a valuable addition to career success literature.

Longitudinal studies will not only assess the stability of glass ceiling beliefs over time, but also when women change organizations and careers. Therefore, it is recommended that future research investigates the role of career category. Future research should investigate whether glass ceiling beliefs are affected by changes in employers. Furthermore, the CPS could be used to determine if there are differences in women's glass ceiling beliefs across employment sectors, especially where women dominate (for example, public relations and social services) and in male-dominated careers (for example, finance, heavy industry and trades).

The findings with the CPS (Smith et al., 2012a, 2012b) are an important contribution to the literature on optimism, both dispositional and explanatory style, as they provide evidence about relationships between optimism and success constructs not previously investigated. Importantly, women working in organizations should consider the multiple connections between their well-being and their attitudes toward glass ceilings. More research is needed to clarify the relationships between glass ceiling beliefs and optimism/pessimism away from the workplace. Commonly used measures of optimism such as the Life Orientation Test (LOT-R; Scheier et al., 1994) and Attributional Style Questionnaire (Peterson et al., 1982) could be included in further research into attitudes to glass ceilings. In addition, the CPS could be used in conjunction with the WES (Smith et al., 2013), which has been developed specifically to measure optimism for subjects working in any type of organization. These three optimism questionnaires can help test the concurrent validity of the CPS.

The significant relationships found by Smith et al. (2012a) provide hints for lifting the subjective success of women working in organizations. Importantly, many studies have shown that the five subjective career success constructs that were measured in this study, that is, career satisfaction and happiness (Fisher, 2010), emotional well-being (Wright et al., 2007), physical health (Judge and Hurst, 2008) and work engagement (Bakker et al., 2008) are antecedents for career success. Clearly, this could lead to major benefits for organizations such as higher productivity and lower absenteeism.

It must be emphasized that the range of significant relationships reported thus far in research using the CPS are based on cross-sectional studies. Therefore, inferences about causal directives remain as speculations until supported from longitudinal and experimental studies. Research across organizations and cultures will help to answer important questions left unanswered by the present research. Importantly, it is recommended that future studies attempt to confirm whether glass ceiling beliefs show stability, especially before and after women are promoted to top levels of organizations. Do these women have higher levels of the optimistic beliefs toward glass ceilings (resilience and denial) and lower levels of pessimistic attitudes (resignation and acceptance) than those women who are not promoted? If women's glass ceiling beliefs have a long-term stability, possibly over many decades as has been shown with an optimistic explanatory style (Burns and Seligman, 1989), it will emphasize the value of testing with the CPS. Other relevant research questions could include:

- What are the causes of women having different beliefs about glass ceilings? This would necessitate studies of variables such as parental, educational and religious influences.
- Do women change their views about glass ceilings after becoming married or having children?
- If an organization is led by a woman, do the women and men working in that organization have positive (optimistic) attitudes about women being promoted?

It is recommended that participants in future research provide organizational details such as the number of women at senior levels and the success of diversity policies. Further research will need to extend the concurrent and convergent validity of the CPS. Positive psychology principles are increasingly more prevalent in workplace research due to the ability of these variables to boost organizational success, effective leadership and flourishing in difficult situations (Mills et al., 2013). Therefore, it is appropriate that the CPS be tested in combination with other measures of positive psychology constructs besides optimism. These include hope

(Snyder, 2002), character strengths (Peterson and Park, 2006), psychological capital (Luthans et al., 2007), leadership efficacy (Hannah et al., 2008), zest (Peterson et al., 2009), thriving (Porath et al., 2012) and mental toughness (Marchant et al., 2009).

REFERENCES

Ahmad-Zaluki, N.A. (2012), 'The pre- and post-IPOs gender composition of board of directors in Malaysia', *Gender in Management: An International Journal*, **27**(7), 449–62.
Bakker, A.B., W.B. Schaufeli, M.P. Leiter and T.W. Taris (2008), 'Work engagement: an emerging concept in occupational health psychology', *Work & Stress*, **22**(3), 187–200.
Beck, A.T. (1976), *Cognitive Therapy and the Emotional Disorders*, New York: Penguin Books.
Bergman, B. (2003), 'The validation of the Women Workplace Culture Questionnaire: gender-related stress and health for Swedish working women', *Sex Roles*, **49**(5/6), 287–97.
Booysen, L.A.E. and S.M. Nkomo (2010), 'Gender role stereotypes and requisite management characteristics: the case of South Africa', *Gender in Management: An International Journal*, **25**(4), 285–300.
Burns, M.O. and M.E.P. Seligman (1989), 'Explanatory style across life span: evidence for stability over 52 years', *Journal of Personality and Social Psychology*, **56**(3), 471–7.
Caroselli, M. (1998), *Great Session Openers, Closers, and Energizers*, New York: McGraw-Hill.
Catalyst (2012), *2011 Catalyst Census: Financial Post 500 Women Board Directors*, accessed 29 November 2014 at http://www.catalyst.org/knowledge/2011-catalyst-census-financial-post-500-women-board-directors.
Chughtai, A.A. and F. Buckley (2011), 'Work engagement: antecedents, the mediating role of learning goal orientation and job performance', *Career Development International*, **16**(7), 684–705.
Cordano, M., R.F. Scherer and C.L. Owen (2003), 'Dimensionality of the Women As Managers Scale: factor congruency among three samples', *The Journal of Social Psychology*, **143**(1), 141–3.
Crino, M.D., M.C. White and G.L. DeSanctis (1981), 'A comment on the dimensionality and reliability of the Women As Managers Scale', *Academy of Management Journal*, **24**(4), 866–76.
Dubno, P., J. Costas, H. Cannon, C. Wankel and H. Emin (1979), 'An empirically keyed scale for measuring managerial attitudes toward female executives', *Psychology of Women Quarterly*, **3**(4), 357–64.
Duehr, E.E. and J.E. Bono (2006), 'Men, women, and managers: are stereotypes finally changing?', *Personnel Psychology*, **59**(4), 815–46.
Eagly, A.H. and L.L. Carli (2007), *Through the Labyrinth: The Truth About How Women Become Leaders*, Boston, MA: Harvard Business School.
Eagly, A.H. and S.J. Karau (2002), 'Role congruity theory of prejudice toward female leaders', *Psychological Review*, **109**(3), 573–98.
Elacqua, T.C., T.A. Beehr, C.P. Hansen and J. Webster (2009), 'Managers' beliefs about the glass ceiling: interpersonal and organizational factors', *Psychology of Women Quarterly*, **33**(3), 285–94.
Elsaid, A.M. and E. Elsaid (2012), 'Sex stereotyping managerial positions: a cross-cultural comparison between Egypt and the USA', *Gender in Management: An International Journal*, **27**(2), 81–99.
Equal Opportunity for Women in the Workplace Agency (2010), *EOWA 2010 Australian Census of Women in Leadership*, accessed 29 November 2014 at https://www.wgea.gov.au/sites/default/files/2010_census_tag.pdf.
Fisher, C.D. (2010), 'Happiness at work', *International Journal of Management Reviews*, **12**(4), 384–412.

Forsythe, M. and Y. Zhao (2011), 'It's still a man's world for Chinese women', *Sydney Morning Herald*, 25 June 2011, 23.
Hannah, S.T., B.J. Avolio, F. Luthans and P.D. Harms (2008), 'Leadership efficacy: review and future directions', *The Leadership Quarterly*, **19**(6), 669–92.
Hawton, K., P.M. Salkovskis, J. Kirk and D.M. Clark (eds) (1989), *Cognitive Behaviour Therapy for Psychiatric Problems: A Practical Guide*, Oxford: Oxford University Press.
Heilman, M.E. and T.G. Okimoto (2007), 'Why are women penalized for success at male tasks? The implied communality deficit', *Journal of Applied Psychology*, **92**(2), 81–92.
Jackson, J.C. (2001), 'Women middle managers' perception of the glass ceiling', *Women in Management Review*, **16**(1), 30–41.
Judge, T.A. and C. Hurst (2008), 'How the rich (and happy) get richer (and happier): relationship of core self-evaluations to trajectories in attaining work success', *Journal of Applied Psychology*, **93**(4), 849–63.
Lerner, G. (1986), *The Creation of Patriarchy*, New York: Oxford University Press.
Luthans, F., B.J. Avolio, J.B. Avey and S.M. Norman (2007), 'Positive psychological capital: measurement and relationship with performance and satisfaction', *Personnel Psychology*, **60**(3), 541–72.
Marchant, D.C., R.C.J. Polman, P.J. Clough, J.G. Jackson, A.R. Levy and A.R. Nicholls (2009), 'Mental toughness: managerial and age differences', *Journal of Managerial Psychology*, **24**(5), 428–37.
Mavin, S. and G. Grandy (2012), 'Doing gender well and differently in management', *Gender in Management: An International Journal*, **27**(4), 218–31.
Mills, M.J., C.R. Fleck and A. Kozikowski (2013), 'Positive psychology at work: a conceptual review, state-of-practice assessment, and a look ahead', *The Journal of Positive Psychology*, **8**(2), 153–64.
Okimoto, T.G. and V.L. Brescoll (2010), 'The price of power: power seeking and backlash against female politicians', *Personality and Social Psychology Bulletin*, **36**(7), 923–36.
Peterson, C. and N. Park (2006), 'Character strengths in organizations', *Journal of Organizational Behavior*, **27**(8), 1149–54.
Peterson, C., N. Park, N. Hall and M.E.P. Seligman (2009), 'Zest and work', *Journal of Organizational Behavior*, **30**(2), 161–72.
Peterson, C., A. Semmel, C. von Baeyer, L.Y. Abramson, G.I. Metalsky and M.E.P. Seligman (1982), 'The Attributional Style Questionnaire', *Cognitive Therapy and Research*, **6**(3), 287–99.
Phelan, J.E., C.A. Moss-Racusin and L.A. Rudman (2008), 'Competent yet out in the cold: shifting criteria for hiring reflect backlash toward agentic women', *Psychology of Women Quarterly*, **32**(4), 406–13.
Porath, C., G. Spreitzer, C. Gibson and F.G. Garnett (2012), 'Thriving at work: toward its measurement, construct validation, and theoretical refinement', *Journal of Organizational Behavior*, **33**(2), 250–75.
Powell, G.N. (2012), 'Six ways of seeing the elephant: the intersection of sex, gender, and leadership', *Gender in Management: An International Journal*, **27**(2), 119–41.
Proudfoot, J.G., P.J. Corr, D.E. Guest and G. Dunn (2009), 'Cognitive-behavioural training to change attributional style improves employee well-being, job satisfaction, productivity, and turnover', *Personality and Individual Differences*, **46**(2), 147–53.
Reber, A.S. (1985), *The Penguin Dictionary of Psychology*, London: Penguin Books.
Reivich, K.J., M.E.P. Seligman and S. McBride (2011), 'Master resilience training in the U.S. army', *American Psychologist*, **66**(1), 25–34.
Schaufeli, W.B., A.B. Bakker and M. Salanova (2006), 'The measurement of work engagement with a short questionnaire', *Educational and Psychological Measurement*, **66**(4), 701–16.
Scheier, M.F. and C.S. Carver (1985), 'Optimism, coping, and health: assessment and implications of generalized outcome expectancies', *Health Psychology*, **4**(3), 219–47.
Scheier, M.F., C.S. Carver and M.W. Bridges (1994), 'Distinguishing optimism from neuroticism (and trait anxiety, self-mastery, and self-esteem); a reevaluation of the Life Orientation Test', *Journal of Personality and Social Psychology*, **67**(6), 1063–78.

Seligman, M.E.P. (1991), *Learned Optimism*, New York: Knopf.
Seligman, M.E.P. (2011), 'Building resilience', *Harvard Business Review*, **89**(4), 100–106.
Smith, P. (2012), 'Connections between women's glass ceiling beliefs, explanatory style, self-efficacy, career levels and subjective success', PhD thesis, University of Wollongong, Australia.
Smith, P., P. Caputi and N. Crittenden (2012a), 'How are women's glass ceiling beliefs related to career success?', *Career Development International*, **17**(5), 458–74.
Smith, P., N. Crittenden and P. Caputi (2012b), 'Measuring women's beliefs about glass ceilings: development of the Career Pathways Survey', *Gender in Management: An International Journal*, **27**(2), 68–80.
Smith, P., P. Caputi and N. Crittenden (2013), 'Measuring optimism in organizations: development of a workplace explanatory style questionnaire', *Journal of Happiness Studies*, **14**(2), 415–32.
Snyder, C.R. (2002), 'Hope theory: rainbows in the mind', *Psychological Inquiry*, **13**(4), 249–75.
Terborg, J.T., L.H. Peters, D.R. Ilgen and F. Smith (1977), 'Organizational and personal correlates of attitudes toward women as managers', *Academy of Management Journal*, **20**(1), 89–100.
Thomson, P., J. Graham and T. Lloyd (2008), *A Woman's Place is in the Boardroom: The Roadmap*, Basingstoke, UK: Palgrave Macmillan.
Weitekamp, M.A. (2004), *Right Stuff, Wrong Sex: America's First Women in Space Program*, Baltimore, MD: Johns Hopkins Press.
Weyer, B. (2007), 'Twenty years later: explaining the persistence of the glass ceiling for women leaders', *Women in Management Review*, **22**(6), 482–96.
Wood, G.J. and M. Lindorff (2001), 'Sex differences in explanations for career progress', *Women in Management Review*, **16**(4), 152–62.
Wright, T.A., R. Cropanzano and D.G. Bonett (2007), 'The moderating role of employee positive well being on the relation between job satisfaction and job performance', *Journal of Occupational Health Psychology*, **12**(2), 93–104.
Wrigley, B.J. (2002), 'Glass ceiling? What glass ceiling? A qualitative study of how women view the glass ceiling in public relations and communication management', *Journal of Public Relations Research*, **14**(1), 27–55.

13. Risk aversion among women: reality or simply 'doing gender'?
Mary Shapiro, Susan Hass, Sylvia Maxfield and Vipin Gupta

Conventional wisdom maintains that men are risk-takers and women are risk-averse. Additionally, empirical studies that measure risk through financial resource allocation experiments (Powell and Ansic, 1998; Eckel and Grossman, 2003) and in studies of health and safety precautions, such as seat-belt use and recreational drug use (Harrant and Valiant, 2008) support that gendered division in risk-taking. However, through our survey of over 650 managerial American women and interviews with ten women professionals, women spoke about risks they had taken, the factors that influenced their decisions, and the outcomes of those decisions. Our research indicates that women do take risks; their risk decision-making is sensitive to many gender-neutral factors; and that risk-taking has been critical to moving ahead in their careers. So why the persistence of the risk-aversion moniker for women?

In this chapter, we will explore women's risk-taking, the possible gendered dynamics that may explain why women's risk-taking is often invisible in organizations even as they do take risks, and the factors that influence their decisions to take on those risks. We will draw on our research and interviews to give 'real life' examples of our findings. Finally, we will offer suggestions about how you and your career can benefit from your own pursuit of risk-taking activities.

PRESENTATION OF THEORY AND CONCEPTS

To understand the interwoven nature of risk-taking and masculinity, you only need to look at the language the media used to report on the 2008 global financial meltdown. Wall Street brokers were 'credit default swap cowboys' and the entire Street was 'the Wild West' (Morgenson, 2008) with 'too much testosterone' (Syed, 2008). At the same time, numerous financial sector CEOs speculated whether the financial crisis could have been averted had more women been the decision-makers, both domestically, in each country and globally (De Vita, 2008). In October 2008, Iceland, after declaring bankruptcy, turned to two women to rebuild its financial system 'after the banking empire built by its young male business-schooled elite collapsed'. A government official noted, 'Now, the women are taking over ... to clean it up' (O'Connor, 2008). Both the gendered language used to describe the 2008 risk-induced financial chaos and the claims that a greater presence of women would have prevented the crisis reveal the pervasive and enduring conflation between risk-taking and masculinity: men take risks and women do not.

Are Women Risk-averse?

Scholars have long explored gender and risk-taking by examining how men and women make decisions in three primary areas: health and physical safety; finance; and strategy in a professional work context. What have they found? In some contexts, women may be risk-averse, or they may approach risk in different ways than men; in other contexts they may be just as risk-taking.

Women are consistently found to be less risky in decisions made about physical health and safety, specifically questions about drinking, smoking, seat-belt usage, and/or unprotected sex (Harrant and Valliant, 2008). Turning to the economic world, scholars have looked at gender and risk in three different types of financial decisions. In gambling scenarios, women tend to take fewer risks, possibly due to being more conservative about the likelihood of positive outcomes (Fehr-Duda et al., 2006). In scenarios of insurance against loss, men and women's decision-making was found to be similar (Schubert et al., 2000). In investment scenarios, while there is more evidence of gender differences (Beckman and Menkhoff, 2008), there were smaller gaps found in European studies (Badunenko et al., 2009) than in US studies (Hibbert et al., 2008), suggesting a cultural influence. Finally, research in specific managerial contexts such as decision-making in entrepreneurial and intrapreneurial ventures finds much less, if any, evidence of gender bias (Castillo and Cross, 2008).

Given these mixed findings in the research, why does the label of risk aversion persist for women compared to men, and how does that moniker impact women's careers? Are there gendered dynamics that obfuscate or mislabel women's risk-taking? What might cause organizations to overlook the risks their women are taking, and the beneficial results those women may be producing? Conversely, what may women be doing differently in taking up risks that result in their risk-taking remaining invisible?

By being labelled risk-averse, women may have less opportunity to take up the risky assignments that are important precedents to significant achievement. Kouzes and Posner (2002) link risk-taking and leadership.

In their study of thousands of professionals, they identified 30 behaviours essential in the exercise of leadership, including taking risks, encouraging others to take risks, and learning from failed risks. Indeed, Johnson and Powell (1994) propose that taking fewer risks may be a major cause of 'glass ceilings' in corporate promotion ladders.

Why is Women's Risk-taking Invisible?

Applying the literature on gender offers possible explanations for the reasons women's risk-taking continues to be largely invisible.

Unrecognized risk-taking

Most societies may not *see* women taking risks because most cultures do not *expect* them to take risks. As humans, we tend to see what we look for as a means of confirming our beliefs (Hitt et al., 2009) and, conversely, we miss what we do not look for, through unintentional blindness (Simons and Chabris, 1999). Risk-taking may even be invisible to the woman risk-taker herself (Moreschi, 2005).

Additionally, two role-congruent behaviors around claiming risk success may render risk-taking invisible. First, women do not seek the conventionally visible measures of successful risk-taking found in most organizations, namely promotions to high-status positions (Shapiro et al., 2009). Second, a lack of self-promotion due to women's gendered socialization 'not to brag' about themselves may further hide their successful risk-taking (Tannen, 1994). Even when a woman does talk about the risks she has taken she may do so using the word 'we' to refer to her own accomplishments, thus redirecting attribution for the risk-taking elsewhere (Tannen, 1995).

Cost mitigation

Women may undertake strategies to keep their risks hidden in an effort to not get penalized for acting outside society's expectations for women. Since risk-taking is linked with masculinity, women are left with the classic 'double bind': act like a woman, and be called risk-averse, or act like a man, and have one's character and motives called into question. Carly Fiorina, in her role as CEO of Hewlett-Packard, is a case in point: she was accused of being 'cocky' as she took the risk of acquiring Compaq (Lashinsky, 2002). In an effort to keep a low profile as a risk-taker, women may use the following three strategies, either intentionally or unconsciously due to gendered socialization: not seek visible rewards for their risk-taking, not self-promote themselves as risk-takers, and/or deflect their successes to others.

Women may not seek out the conventional and most visible measure of successful risk-taking found in most organizations, namely promotions to high-status positions. A 2006 study of 600 professional American women found that 'advancing to a prestigious position' ranked fifteenth out of 16 possible career goals (Shapiro et al., 2007). Without that tangible marker of success, women's risk-taking may be less visible and less recognized even when it occurs. Women may also not talk about their successes to other people. This lack of self-promotion, due to women's gendered socialization 'not to brag' (Tannen, 1995) about themselves, may further hide their successes. If they do not call attention to the accomplishments produced by the risks they have undertaken, the risk-taking may go unnoticed. Even when women are receiving recognition for their achievements, they tend to deflect that praise to the contributions of others. Tannen (1995) states that women often attribute their successes externally, acknowledging the efforts of the team or the help given by others. This deflection downplays their ownership of the risk that the project represents and is even more damaging, given that others are socialized to attribute women's successes to luck, task ease, or a significant effort on her part (Valian, 1999).

Role congruency
Women may engage in another role-congruent behavior that leads to the perception that they are risk-averse: they include others in their risk decision-making. Trait theory identifies characteristics that are socially attractive for men and women. For women, traits include being collaborative, yielding, and sensitive to the needs of others (Bem, 1974; Prentice and Carranza, 2002), all contributing to the expectation that women will be collaborative and inclusive in their decision-making. Observers, looking at women's collaboration through a gendered lens, may see the inclusion of others as revealing uncertainty or indecisiveness; it may make women appear incapable of making decisions unilaterally (Tannen, 1994). While a woman may be collecting ideas, testing her own, or building consensual commitment by asking, 'What would you do?' some listeners may see the question as a literal invitation to make the decision for her. She is not a collaborator, she is risk-averse.

OUR RESEARCH

Given the connection between risk-taking and an individual's ability to build a track record of success, be recognized as an organizational contributor, and move along a career path towards significant leadership, we chose to explore the extent of women's risk-taking and the factors they considered in the risk decision. We created the Simmons (2008)

Gender and Risk database by surveying 660 managerial women attending Simmons' Women's Leadership Conference (Gupta et al., 2009). It is important to acknowledge that this is a US sample and predominantly Caucasian (80 per cent). However, because these women had significant work experience, both in tenure (41 per cent had more than 20 years in the workforce) and in level of responsibility (44 per cent were in middle management and 14 per cent in senior management), they also represent well-seasoned professionals deep into their careers. The women were asked to reflect on one 'business/professional opportunity [they had taken], whose success is not assured, that required learning by doing, and where [you] had to take personal responsibility for failures on the way'. These opportunities included taking on a new job, leading a major change initiative, and taking on a major business development opportunity. We intentionally did not label these opportunities 'risky'.

The survey's first question was a version of the traditional financial portfolio allocation question: what percentage of a fixed sum of dollars would you invest in a new project with unlimited potential reward but high outcome uncertainty? Approximately 1 per cent chose to re-allocate the entire budget, and two-thirds re-allocated less than 50 per cent of the dollars available, earning the moniker of 'risk-averse'.

However, when asked to reflect on how frequently they had actually taken on certain business/professional opportunities, women in the survey embraced risk: 80 per cent reported 'sometimes' or 'often' pursuing a major change initiative, 79 per cent reported 'sometimes' or 'often' pursuing a major new programme, 77 per cent reported 'sometimes' or 'often' pursuing a new job, and 56 per cent reported 'sometimes' or 'often' pursuing a major business development opportunity. These frequencies reveal that women do take risks, both smaller ones, which society may expect of them, but also large, transformative (and socially unexpected) ones (ibid.). Women take risks frequently, even while they may not label their actions as risky. We also found that in their risk decision-making, women considered many gender-neutral factors. Their risk equation included such considerations as: 'Would the risk enable them to make an impact?' 'How would it impact their financial status?' 'Did they have the ability to be successful?' 'What did others say about taking on the risk?'

To better understand women's thinking about and strategies for taking on risk, we interviewed ten women with long careers marked with risk-taking. They came from seven different industries (non-profit, financial services, government, technology, consulting, retail and consumer goods) and were in a wide range of functions, including information technology, talent management, finance, owner/CEO, and marketing. We asked each to select from the same list of business/professional opportunities as was on the survey, and then reflect on that risk-taking as we asked a series of questions, including what was the impact they were hoping to achieve, what were the factors that went into the decision equation, from whom did they seek advice, and what was the outcome.

For the rest of the chapter we will explore six of these women's risk-taking equations, specifically delving into how power, self-efficacy, and their networks factored into those decisions. We will share their best practices and conclude with recommendations for women.

POWER

Many scholars agree that the need for power inside organizations arises from three dynamics: first, there is a limited or fixed amount of resources available. Resources could be financial, numbers of people, and on a more micro-level, the time and energy a person has available to expend on work. Second, there are numerous demands competing for those resources. People often have to choose between those demands. Finally, many organizational structures make people interdependent on each other: for me to get my work objectives accomplished, I must rely on you (Bolman and Deal, 2003). While power is neutrally defined as 'a desire to make an impact' (McClelland and Burnham, 2003, p. 120) historically it has been interlinked with masculinity. Groshev (2002) conducted an extensive multidisciplinary, cross-cultural literature review on the definition of power and concluded, 'the discourse that produced the various definitions of power . . . has clearly been masculinized, so the terms are more relevant to men' (p. 6). For the last 30 years, feminist scholars have sought to examine power from a woman's experience. Rejecting the classic male definition of 'power *over*', feminists' conceptions include 'power *to*', which is about empowerment (Kitzinger, 1991) and 'power *with*' (Guinier, 1998; Fletcher, 2004).

In our research, we defined power as 'the power to make an impact' and found that it strongly motivates women to take risks. The stronger the desire for power, the more likely a woman will take on the risky opportunities. Our findings are consistent with sex-blind studies where the desire for power correlates with risk-taking (Anderson and Galinsky, 2006; Gaubatz, 2008).

The stories of our interviewees enunciated how power to make an impact spurred their risk-taking. Often being able to turn around a decline in the organization was appealing. And in many cases, the risk of trying to improve declining situations was compounded by the additional risks of changing career paths or industries.

214   *Handbook of gendered careers in management*

Clean Slate

Two women pursued risky opportunities to make significant impact because the appeal to start with a 'clean slate' and build from the ground up was irresistible. Donna became the Executive Director of a century-old zoo in Northeast America. In doing so she accepted two challenges: first, running a large capital campaign to pay for the total renovation of the zoo; and second, managing the renovation itself. For the past 70 years, previous executive directors had been unsuccessful in inspiring the zoo's Board of Directors to do the truly hard work of raising funds. As a result, there had been no major capital improvements to the zoo for that period of time; the exhibits were still primarily animals in small cages; the infrastructure was crumbling; and the zoo was in danger of losing its professional accreditation. Upon seeing the zoo, 'the charming classic architecture and the great canopy of mature trees', Donna knew she could transform the zoo into a significant attraction for the city. The ability to make a sweeping impact was attractive to her. She would 'have control over what would happen. I could be transformative here. I could start with a "clean slate". There were no brand-new exhibits that I wouldn't be allowed to change, even if I hated them. I could create an entirely new holistic story for the zoo.'

Colleen wanted to continue making a difference in healthcare reform, so when she sold the information technology company she had led for ten years to a Fortune 500 company, she did not accept their offer to lead the company as a division of the acquirer. She was excited by the upcoming healthcare reforms and believed she could influence the conversation about and implementation of the new US law requiring health insurance for all. The acquiring company wanted her to focus on its core business, so Colleen made her choice. Her board supported the decision, especially since all the employees would be retained by the acquirer. Colleen helped effect the transition to the new company for several months and then left the company, as agreed. She went on to have a voice in the implementation of the healthcare reforms and started a new company within 18 months of selling her prior company.

Deep Change

The excitement of leading deep change as a 'call to action' by key people at the top of their organizations spurred some women to take up risky assignments. MacKenzie was attracted to a job at a non-profit organization that assists low-income people and communities. During the interview process, the Executive Director spelled out the significant impact he expected her to make: to completely change the way they approached the consulting side of their business, to 'challenge the status quo of "backward-looking financial analyses"'. MacKenzie found the possibility of making a big impact 'seductive. I wanted to be in a position where I had leverage.' Additionally, she would have the full support of the Executive Director, who told her, 'I am hiring you to stir the pot ... I expect you to be a trouble-maker. We'll make change together.'

After leading Marketing and Development at a private liberal arts college, Lisa pursued an opportunity that involved changing both her career path (from fundraising to human resources) and industries (from academia to financial services). Seeking a new job that would offer the ability to stretch, learn intellectually, and 'validate risk-taking', Lisa was hired to lead Talent Management at a large financial services organization. Her position was newly created, signalling her mandate to make deep changes in 'the way the entire leadership operated to get the right talent in the right position for business growth'. With support from the CEO and direction from her boss, Lisa was prompted to 'rip off the Band-Aid', even while recognizing that building a completely new approach to talent management had significant implications for top leadership in the company and the business.

Career Impact

Charlotte and Ellen took risks to positively impact their careers. Charlotte recognized that to make an impact on her organization she needed to move into the job position that would enable her to do so. As a senior manager in a large publicly held financial services organization she was in a 'junior' level of influence. In order to 'be included in the big decisions of the bank' she needed to get to a higher tier of executives. When she was offered almost double the number of bank branches to manage, she accepted the position. This would enable her to showcase her ability to 'lead and manage in three key areas: operations, sales, and customer retention'. By turning failing branches around, she could both make an impact on the organization's bottom line, and secure her position at the table when critical strategic decisions were being made.

Ellen was educated in art, had held a series of jobs as an art director, but knew she wanted a more financially rewarding job that would give her more status. She was a 'people person' and accepted the Manager of Professional Development position at a top global consulting firm, a position that would utilize her skills of conflict resolution, negotiation, team leadership, and relational skills. Though she was not a typical hire and she had no direct experience in human capital, Ellen had confidence in the management skills she brought to the job. She would be managing staff, interacting daily with demanding partners, assessing situations and making decisions with little time for long-term assessment. This was all new for her, and while her prior jobs provided some skills needed for this new job, they were not sufficient. She did not initially understand the complexity of the job, but soon realized that either one can think on one's feet and problem-solve, or one could not. She could.

SELF-EFFICACY

Self-efficacy, a person's belief in his or her ability to succeed, is a concept integral to risk-taking (Bandura, 1997). If people believe that they have the capabilities to perform the actions required to achieve a goal, they are more likely to take a risk because they believe they can succeed. Research on mixed-sex populations shows that self-efficacy predicts career goals (Ballout, 2009). Studies designed to explore gender differences in the impact of self-efficacy on individual choices and performance find little evidence of gender difference (Mueller and Conway, 2008).

Our survey found that self-efficacy strongly predicts risk-taking by women. The stronger her feelings of efficacy, the more likely her efforts would be successful, and the more likely she would take on risky activities. This finding is consistent with sex-blind studies showing the strong impact of self-efficacy on risk-taking (Llewellyn et al., 2008).

All the women we interviewed knew they could do the job and be a success. They never questioned their abilities. For some, the risky opportunity relied on skills they had already developed earlier in their careers. For others, particularly those that changed careers and industries, they were confident that their broad skills would allow them to be successful. For example, Ellen changed jobs from one industry that she was trained for (art) to one that she had no background in (consulting). But she believed the new job would rely on her innate ability to negotiate and support people, and that her management skills, and her ability to think on her feet and problem-solve, would serve her well.

Themes emerged regarding to what they attributed their high self-efficacy:

- *Ability to recover*. Charlotte attributed her confidence to 'how I'm built: failure is not an option'. She also believed that her relative youth (mid-40s) made any risk-taking less risky: 'If I failed I could always do it again sometime.' MacKenzie believed that with her skills, particularly as a 'project doer', she could do something else

if her new job at the non-profit financial organization did not work out. Donna recognized that since she had financial security in the form of savings and a working spouse, she 'wouldn't find myself on the street' if she failed and lost her job.
- *Family upbringing.* Donna also gives credit to her family for her confidence. 'My mother used to quote her maternal grandmother, who grew up on a farm in Ireland. That farmer mentality is: "Don't look at the entire field. Focus on plowing one row at a time."' With that mentality Donna knew she could make a positive difference at the zoo. 'I could tear the zoo down in phases; I knew I just had to raise enough funding for one new exhibit; make that exhibit fabulous to show people what "fabulous" looked like; and then I could get future donors for the next exhibit and the next.'
- *Good alternatives.* Lisa was content to continue working at her liberal arts college. While she knew that would mean her career would advance more slowly, she was successful there and could continue to lead a large team and produce results. Just as in negotiations, having a strong BATNA (Best Alternative to a Negotiated Agreement) created confidence (Fisher and Uri, 1981).

NETWORKS

The usefulness of networks in career advancement is well documented. The people in your network can be a source of information about job opportunities; they can advance your name as a candidate into areas where you personally do not have contacts; and they can be a source of emotional support, feedback, and advice (Trefalt et al., 2011). While research indicates that networking improves career success for women (Seiger and Wiese, 2009), it has also been found that women do not generally engage with professional networks as much as men (Rothstein and Davey, 1995).

In contemplating risk-taking, we speculated that women would turn to their personal/family networks more than their professional networks. Because most working women retain the primary responsibility for family care (Degroot and Armando, 2005), we expected to find that women would consult with their family sphere, seeking to identify how possible risk-taking would affect home as well as work, essentially attempting to pre-empt work–family conflict (Cabrera, 2007). This was not the case for the women in our survey: while women sought the advice of both family and professional networks in their decision-making about smaller ongoing risks, for bolder, larger risks they turned to their professional networks.

All the women we interviewed used their professional networks for discussion and information about the actual opportunity. MacKenzie did 'a lot of due diligence inside the organization'. She spoke to the CEO to see if she could articulate the organization's mission and vision 'in a way I could believe in'. Colleen had signed a confidentiality agreement so she relied exclusively on her personal attorney. Women also tapped into their personal network, usually their spouse or other family members, to see if they would get the support they needed from them. Charlotte spoke to her family 'to confirm that my husband and small children could step up and become more independent' since she would not be around as much.

Two others relied on their networks in unique ways. Ellen spoke to several relatives who worked in consulting. Since she was making a dramatic career change, her prior professional network was not valuable in advising her. She had 14 interviews before she was hired and doubted that anyone outside the industry would be able to coach her during the process. Lisa, in moving from academia to finance, spoke to her husband, professionals in the industry, and her career coach. It was with her coach that she had an 'ah ha moment'. He asked her to review her career and identify the moments where she had had the most growth: 'It was when my personal aspirations and the company's direction came together, when I was being challenged . . . and when I was most uncomfortable.' She knew she had to move.

RISK OUTCOMES

Were the women we surveyed and interviewed successful in their risk-taking? Of the 660 women in our survey, 60 per cent reported that the risks they have taken have moved their careers forward; 23 per cent reported that the risks have pulled their careers backward. The women we interviewed were uniformly cognizant of the positive impact their risk-taking had on their careers. Many of their successes were in how they managed the risky opportunity. MacKenzie was successful in transforming how a major line of work was conducted at her non-profit, and has had five promotions in six years. Part of her success was due to attrition: people who were unwilling to step up to more consulting left the organization. Part of it was also due to following her hiring manager's advice and 'fight like a guy' with male legacy resisters. Finally, she persistently nudged people to change. 'If I know we are going to do something differently, I work hard on getting the right buy-in. I ask them, "What are you uncomfortable with? How can I help you get your head around this?"'

Charlotte successfully managed the risk in her new position through strategic communication. She anticipated that some of the branches she took on would 'fail' the new standards and that people would leave because they did not like the changes. She prepared the senior advocates who she needed to guide and support her, in advance for those inevitable negative outcomes. Donna spread the 'pain' over time, breaking the fundraising into three phases. With each new exhibit momentum built for the next round of fundraising.

CONCLUSION

Embedded in the stories of our risk-taking women are many recommendations regarding how to think about risk as a career strategy, how to actually do the cost–benefit risk assessment decision, and then how to make the risk-taking visible to the organization.

Risk as a Career Strategy

Every woman spoke about risk as a key to growth and career advancement. No one said accepting the risk was easy, and several spoke passionately about facing their fears. Lisa, in her move from academia into Talent Management, said, 'I had 25 years of professional experience, but (in my new job) I couldn't ground myself in anything – I was new to the company, new to the role, new to the industry. I had been successful in the job I was leaving but now I was scared to death.' What prompted to her to push through that fear? 'I didn't want to fail to grow because I was afraid to fail.' Ellen echoes those sentiments.

Taking on significant organizational problems and driving organizational change represented high risk–reward opportunities for all our women. In doing so, Lisa counselled that you have to 'be confident when you don't have the skills/knowledge. Growth is about what you don't know.'

This call for courage, confidence, and the willingness to grow could be advice to men or women looking to advance their careers. Indeed, only one woman talked about the added importance of women taking on risks. Being on the 'radar screen of Talent Planning' Charlotte was offered a promotion. She believed she could not say no. To do so, all kinds of 'red flags would have gone up for me, one, as a woman, two, as a woman of color, and three, as a mother. All kinds of questions would be raised: Do I have the intelligence? Am I committed? Do I have the business acumen?' Indeed, in the face of socialized gendered expectations of women as risk-averse, actively seeking out risks may be even more essential for women.

Factors in the Risk Equation

Many of our women had an extensive list of factors to consider in assessing the risky opportunity. Moving beyond assessing their readiness (having the skills, expertise, and knowledge), their confidence, and the support of their personal relationships, our women considered the risk itself and the context in which the risk would occur.

Regarding the risk itself:

- Who was in the position before me . . . and why are they gone? Why was that person not able to be successful in the position? What has changed in the organization, and what barriers/challenges may still remain?
- Who will I report to? Does this change initiative have their full support? Do I have their support? How public will they make that support to other key people?
- How can the risk be mitigated? What coalitions can I build, particularly with more senior-level leaders who are willing to publicly support the risk?
- How can the risk be spread over time? Are there ways to test the change and then reconsider? Are there 'small wins' that can be generated to build momentum?
- What resources will be available for this assignment? Is the organization willing to 'get what they pay for?'

Regarding the organizational context:

- What is the organization's culture on risk-taking? Who takes risks and who does not? In what ways is risk-taking supported or not? How quickly are new and risky initiatives shut down . . . or given the chance to grow?
- What is the impact on your career/reputation of saying 'no' to a risky opportunity that is offered to you? What happens to risk-takers who are unsuccessful (are they sidelined forever or are they rewarded for taking calculated risks)?

Making Risk Visible

The challenge for women is not *how* to take risks, as they already do so. Instead, to overcome the risk-aversion label, the challenge for women may be making the risks they take visible and capturing the credit for risk-taking in ways that signal their success to those around them:

- *Use the language of risk.* When speaking about their work or taking on a task, women should name the risk and articulate their cost–benefit calculation. For those charged with big changes, such as MacKenzie whose Executive Director hired her to 'stir the pot', this would not be necessary. But for others, naming the risk they are taking is critical.
- *Promote their accomplishments.* Women need to let senior decision-makers know about their work. Charlotte was very deliberate in her communication plan. 'I was very good at communicating to lots of people about our successes. I'd let them know "this branch passed an audit". I was very intentional about sending that news to people who I knew would forward my emails to people, like the CEO, who was out of my direct line of communication.' When Donna talks about the transformation at the zoo, she gives all the credit to the team. While this can backfire for women, she still feels she gets a lot of industry/professional visibility for her accomplishments.
- *Develop an internal sponsor.* In many organizations, because of the risk-averse label, women may not even be put on the shortlist when risky projects are being discussed and doled out. The assumption is: she will not want to take the risk. To counter this, women must develop a relationship with someone who will put her name on the list of candidates. If she cannot be in those meetings, her sponsor can represent her. For many of our women, including MacKenzie, that sponsor was their hiring manager.

In this chapter, we explored the gendered dynamics that may obfuscate women's risk-taking, and offered best practices from women who have successfully managed risk to the benefit of their careers and their organizations. To conclude we offer two points of caution. One, it is important to recognize that our samples, both of our survey and of our interviews, are largely composed of white, middle- and upper-middle-class, professional American women. Both the reader here, and the career scholar, would do well to consider how the risk-taking of women at lower social-economic levels, who are racially diverse, or are in non-managerial jobs, may have different experiences and different advice. Cross-cultural studies would also help identify how gender-neutral factors might potentially interact with the contextual factors, such as societal and organizational culture dimensions identified in the GLOBE programme (House et al., 2004) to influence women's risk-taking.

Second, while we explored what women may do to manage and make their risk visible, organizations must also take up responsibility for avoiding over-gendered or under-gendered stereotypes. By acting on conventional stereotypes, organizations may unwittingly divert risky (and career-enhancing) opportunities from their female employees and fail to tap women who want to take risks, do take risks, and can do so successfully. Conversely, organizations must guard against assuming all men are risk-lovers and, as a result, tap the wrong person to take risks to achieve organizational goals.

With measured, thoughtful risk-taking, on both the parts of women and their organizations, women, their careers, and their organizations will benefit.

REFERENCES

Anderson, C. and A.D. Galinsky (2006), 'Power, optimism and risk-taking', *European Journal of Psychology*, **36**(4), 511–36.
Badunenko, O., N. Barasinska and D. Schafer (2009), 'Risk attitude and investment decisions across European countries – are women more risk-averse investors than men?', Working Paper No. D.6.2, DIW Berlin.
Ballout, H.I. (2009), 'Career commitment and career success: moderating role of self-efficacy', *Career Development International*, **14**(7), 655–70.
Bandura, A. (1997), *Self-efficacy: The Exercise of Control*, New York: W.H. Freeman.
Beckman, D. and L. Menkhoff (2008), 'Will women be women? Analyzing the gender difference among financial experts', Discussion Paper No. 391, Economics Department, Leibniz Universität, Hanover.
Bem, S. (1974), 'The measurement of psychological androgyny', *Journal of Clinical and Counseling Psychology*, **42**(2), 155–62.
Bolman, L. and T. Deal (2003), *Reframing Organizations: Artistry, Choice, and Leadership*, San Francisco, CA: Jossey-Bass.
Cabrera, E.F. (2007), 'Opting out and opting in: understanding the complexities of women's career transitions', *Career Development International*, **12**(3), 218–37.
Castillo, M.E. and P.J. Cross (2008), 'Of mice and men: within gender variation in strategic behavior', *Games and Economic Behavior*, **64**(2), 421–32.
Degroot, J. and T. Armando (2005), 'Historical perspective on social change', accessed 22 May 2007 at http://wfnetwork.bc.edu/encyclopedia_entry.php?id=1690andarea=All.
De Vita, E. (2008), 'Let women tame the macho excess', *Management Today*, accessed 29 November 2014 at http://www.managementtoday.co.uk/news/865053/.
Eckel, C.C. and P.J. Grossman (2003), 'Men, women and risk aversion: experimental evidence', in C. Plott and V. Smith (eds), *Handbook of Experimental Economic Results*, New York: Elsevier.
Fehr-Duda, H., M. de Gennaro and R. Shubert (2006), 'Gender, financial risk, and probability weights', *Theory and Decision*, **60**(2–3), 283–313.
Fisher, R. and W. Uri (1981), *Getting to Yes*, New York: Houghton Mifflin.
Fletcher, J. (2004), 'The paradox of post heroic leadership: an essay on gender, power and transformational change', *Leadership Quarterly*, **15**(5), 647–61.
Gaubatz, K.T. (2008), 'Maastricht and motivations: an empirical lever for understanding European integration', paper presented at the Annual Meeting of the International Studies Association's 49th Annual Convention, 'Bridging Multiple Divides', San Francisco, CA, accessed 4 March 2009 at www.allacademic.com/meta/p253146_index.html.
Groshev, I.V. (2002), 'Gender perceptions of power', *Sociological Research*, **41**(1), 5–20.
Guinier, L. (1998), *Lessons and Challenges of Becoming Gentlemen*, New York: New York University Press.

Gupta, V., S. Maxfield, M. Shapiro and S. Hass (2009), 'Gender and risk: busting the myth of women as risk-averse', *CGO Insights No. 28*, Center for Gender in Organizations, Simmons School of Management, Boston, MA.

Gupta, V., M. Shapiro, S. Maxfield and S. Hass (2013), 'Risk seeking career strategies and women's career success', *Journal of Contemporary Issues in Business Research*, **2**(6), 189–204.

Harrant, V. and N.G. Vaillant (2008), 'Are women less risk-averse than men?', *Evolution and Human Behavior*, **29**(6), 396–401.

Hibbert, A.M., E. Lawrence and A. Prakash (2008), 'Are women more risk-averse than men?', working paper, Florida International University, Miami, FL.

Hitt, M., C. Miller and A. Colella (2009), *Organizational Behavior: A Strategic Approach*, Hoboken, NJ: Wiley.

House, R., P. Hanges, M. Javidan, P. Dorfman and V. Gupta (eds) (2004), *Culture, Leadership, and Organizations: The GLOBE Study of 62 Cultures*, Thousand Oaks, CA: Sage Publications.

Kitzinger, C. (1991), 'Feminism, psychology and the paradox of power', *Feminism and Psychology*, **1**(1), 111–29.

Kouzes, J. and B. Posner (2002), *The Leadership Challenge*, San Francisco, CA: Jossey-Bass.

Johnson, J.E.V. and P.I. Powell (1994), 'Decision making, risk and gender: are managers different?', *British Journal of Management*, **5**(2), 123–38.

Lashinsky, A. (2002), 'Now for the hard part', *Fortune*, **146**(10), 94–102.

Llewellyn, D.J., X. Sanchez, A. Asghar and G. Jones (2008), 'Self-efficacy, risk-taking and performance in rock climbing', *Personality and Individual Differences*, **45**(1), 75–81.

McClelland, D.C. and D.H. Burnham (2003), 'Power is the great motivator', *Harvard Business Review*, **81**(1), 117–26.

Moreschi, R. (2005), 'An analysis of the ability of individuals to predict their own risk tolerance', *Journal of Business and Economics Research*, **3**(2), 39–48.

Morgenson, G. (2008), 'Naked came the speculators', *The New York Times*, 9 August 2008, accessed 29 November 2014 at http://www.nytimes.com/2008/08/10/business/10gret.html?pagewanted=all&_r=0.

Mueller, S.L. and M. Conway (2008), 'Gender-role orientation as a determinant of entrepreneurial self-efficacy', *Journal of Developmental Entrepreneurship*, **13**(1), 3–20.

O'Conner, S. (2008), 'Iceland calls in women bankers to clean up "young men's mess"', *Financial Times*, accessed 29 November 2014 at http://www.ft.com/cms/s/0/6107e59c-9988-11dd-9d48-000077b07658.html#axzz3KTGtqWUg.

Powell, M. and D. Ansic (1998), 'Gender differences in risk behavior in financial decision-making: an experimental analysis', *Journal of Economic Psychology*, **18**(6), 605–28.

Prentice, D.A. and E. Carranza (2002), 'What women and men should be, shouldn't be, are allowed to be, and don't have to be', *Psychology of Women Quarterly*, **26**(4), 269–81.

Rothstein, M.G. and L.M. Davey (1995), 'Gender differences in network relationships in academia', *Women in Management Review*, **10**(6), 20–26.

Schubert, R., M. Gysler, M. Brown and H.W. Brachinger (2000), 'Gender specific attitudes towards risk and ambiguity: an experimental investigation', working paper, Center for Economic Research, Swiss Federal Institute of Technology, Zurich.

Seiger, C.P. and B.S. Wiese (2009), 'Social support from work and family domains as an antecedent or moderator of work–family conflicts?', *Journal of Vocational Behavior*, **75**(1), 26–37.

Shapiro, M., C. Ingols and S. Blake-Beard (2007), 'Optioning in versus opting out: women using flexible work arrangements for career success', *CGO Insights No. 25*, Center for Gender in Organizations, Simmons School of Management, Boston, MA.

Shapiro, M., C. Ingols, R. O'Neill and S. Blake-Beard (2009), 'Making sense of women as career self-agents: implications for human resource development', *Human Resource Development Quarterly*, **20**(4), 477–501.

Simons, D.J. and C.F. Chabris (1999), 'Gorillas in our midst: sustained inattentional blindness for dynamic events', *Perception*, **28**(9), 1059–74.

Syed, M. (2008), 'What caused the crunch? Men and testosterone', *The Times*, 30 September 2008, accessed 29 November 2014 at http://www.thetimes.co.uk/tto/life/article1855274.ece.

Tannen, D. (1994), *Talking From 9 to 5: How Women's and Men's Conversational Styles Affect Who Gets Heard, Who Gets Credit, and What Gets Done at Work*, New York: William Morrow.

Tannen, D. (1995), 'The power of talk: who gets heard and why', *Harvard Business Review*, **73**(5), 138–48.

Trefalt, S., D. Merrill-Sands and D. Kolb (2011), 'Closing the women's leadership gap: who can help?', *CGO Insights No. 32*, Center for Gender in Organizations, Simmons School of Management, Boston, MA.

Valin, V. (1999), *Why So Slow? The Advancement of Women*, Cambridge, MA: MIT Press.

14. Pursuing, doing and reviewing mentoring relationships
Jane L. Fowler

Kram's (1980) seminal research on mentoring relationships has been the impetus for the past 35 years of research on definitions, functions, roles, outcomes, barriers, developmental stages and phases, impact of race and gender, diversity, formality versus informality, and the effectiveness of structured programmes, to name just a few issues. Kram commented to me over lunch in 2000 that at the time she was conducting her original research she 'never imagined that interest in mentoring would take off in such a big way'. If Kram was surprised after 20 years, imagine the astonishment of Homer – who created the character of Mentor in his ancient Greek poem *The Odyssey*, believed to have been composed near the end of the eighth century BC – if he were to discover that Hargreaves and Fullan in 2000 wrote an article titled 'Mentoring in the new millennium'. The concept of mentoring has indeed stood the test of time.

One area of research that has received particular attention is the impact of gender on mentoring (for example, Wanberg et al., 2003; Ragins, 2007; Ensher and Murphy, 2011; Blood et al., 2012). It has been well documented that mentoring, as an overall phenomenon, is an effective tool for helping women advance within organizations (for example, Schein et al., 1996; Ragins, 1999; De Vries et al., 2006; Hersby et al., 2009). This assertion, however, should not imply that mentoring is less effective for men: indeed, there is no shortage of literature espousing that mentoring is extremely beneficial for both genders (for example, Lunding et al., 1978; Allen et al., 2004; Schunk and Mullen, 2013). However, despite the overall effectiveness of mentoring, women remain under-represented in higher levels of organizations (Oakley, 2000; Dworkin et al., 2012). Facts such as this are the reason that Broadbridge and Simpson (2011) advocated for researchers not to get caught up in the 'gender issues have been solved movement', but to engage in deeper critical investigation of the underlying roots – the practices and processes – that result in gender differences. For example, if men and women have unequal access to mentors, what are the structural barriers that cause this? If male mentees receive more career development than female mentees, what are the processes and practices that contribute to this? And so on. Some of these gender issues will be revisited throughout the chapter.

Despite the abundant literature on mentoring, and the multitude of anecdotal reports by actors, artists, writers, athletes, business people and politicians who have been positively influenced by their 'mentor', little has been written about the logistics of establishing, developing and maintaining a mentoring relationship. This will be a focus in the current chapter. After outlining a simple conceptual framework that shows three facets to mentoring – pursuing, doing, and reviewing – the main points for consideration by those potentially or currently involved in a mentoring relationship will be discussed.

This chapter has several contextual factors within which the material should be read. First, mentoring as discussed here is the relationship between a person with advanced experience and knowledge, and a less experienced person who seeks assistance, guidance, and support for their career, personal and/or professional development (Fowler and O'Gorman, 2005). Second, the type of mentoring relationship assumed here is one that is in a work and organizational context. Third, the premise of this chapter is that thinking about and acting on the processes described here will lead to a more effective mentoring relationship. Fourth, several key concepts have been presented in summary form with the intent that readers will explore further as desired. Fifth, the ideas presented do not necessarily follow a linear process but often occur concurrently with each other. Sixth, although the material is aimed primarily at mentees, it is equally relevant (with minor adjustments) to mentors. Seventh, some of the ideas presented will take on more or less significance and priority depending on your particular situation, needs and relationship. Finally, the material is intended to encourage you to ask questions of yourself and your mentoring partner, rather than prescribing the answers.

PRESENTATION OF THE CONCEPTUAL FRAMEWORK

The conceptual framework that underpins the ideas presented in this chapter is depicted in Figure 14.1. It shows three main facets to mentoring: pursue, do and review. For each of these three parts, equal consideration and attention should be given to the content (*what* you are pursuing, doing and reviewing) and the process (*how* you are pursuing, doing and reviewing). Let us consider that in more detail.

Pursuing a mentoring relationship incorporates determining your levels of desire, willingness and readiness to be in a mentoring relationship;

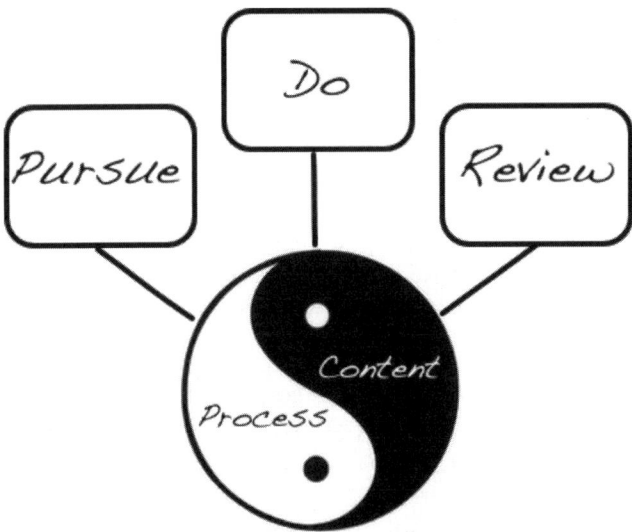

Figure 14.1 A conceptual framework for mentoring: pursue, do, and review

approaching a potential mentee or mentor; negotiating the relationship; setting goals; and making plans. *Doing* mentoring occurs when the mentor and mentee engage and work together; perform a number of functions and roles; and follow the plans they have set to achieve their goals. An effective mentoring partnership will prioritize maintaining a healthy relationship as it works toward goals. *Reviewing* takes place throughout the mentoring process as the partners reflect on and discuss their progress toward goals; consider adjustments and changes to plans; evaluate their ways of working together; and consider the overall effectiveness of the mentoring relationship. If a mentoring relationship terminates, whether it be spontaneously, planned, or because it has simply run its course, it is wise to mutually and individually reflect on and review the overall relationship so that learning might inform and improve future mentoring.

These three facets neatly align with the subtitle of this book: 'Getting In' or *pursuing* and beginning a mentoring relationship; 'Getting On' or *doing* what is done in a mentoring relationship; and 'Getting Out' what you can get out of a mentoring relationship by regularly *reviewing* the effectiveness of what and how you are doing. We now turn our attention to what and how.

The importance of giving equal consideration and attention to both the *content* (what) and *process* (how) of mentoring corresponds with the yin–yang principle of Chinese philosophy. The yin–yang principle guides a holistic understanding of a phenomenon, with neither the yin nor yang claiming priority over the other; they are equal in status (Mou, 2008). The conceptual framework presented here illustrates that neither the content (for example, *what* goals have been set) nor the process (for example, *how* the relationship is negotiated) has priority or more importance over the other. Indeed, as the yin–yang philosophy suggests (Fung, 1948), if one part dominates – for example, negotiating a healthy relationship – the other part will be affected – for example, achievement of goals. As with the yin and yang, the content and process of mentoring should be balanced, interactive, complementary and co-exist in harmony (ibid.). And so should the relationship between mentor and mentee!

PURSUING AND ESTABLISHING A MENTORING RELATIONSHIP

There are some key content (for example, goals and outcomes) and process (for example, working together) questions to ask when considering whether to pursue a mentoring relationship.

Mentoring Benefits

First, what am I likely to get out of mentoring? A vast amount of research has identified benefits for those involved. For example, mentees have reported job and career satisfaction and career commitment as a result of having a mentor (Colarelli and Bishop, 1990; Burke and McKeen, 1997; Young and Perrewé, 2000; Allen et al., 2004), and mentors have identified career enhancement, recognition and reward by peers and superiors, building support networks, and a sense of meaningfulness and fulfilment as a result of being a mentor (Allen et al., 1997; Fowler et al., 2001; De Janasz et al., 2003; Ghosh and Reio, 2013). Both mentees and mentors have identified positive interpersonal relationships as one of the most significant outcomes of mentoring (Fowler et al., 2001).

The benefits of mentoring extend beyond the individuals involved, to the organizations in which they work (Young and Perrewé, 2000; Noe et al., 2002; Allen and Eby, 2003; De Janasz et al., 2003; O'Neill, 2005; Payne and Huffman, 2005; Henriques and Curado, 2009; Ghosh and Reio, 2013). In response, organizations are increasingly implementing formal mentoring programmes for their employees and in doing so are increasing levels of support, satisfaction, commitment, skill development and networking (De Vries et al., 2006; Fowler et al., 2006; Weinberg and Lankau, 2011). Thus, it is not surprising that employees are choosing to participate in mentoring programmes that are offered or individually seeking out and pursuing mentoring relationships.

The notion that men and women may differentially benefit from mentoring relationships has, in general, not received empirical support (for example, Fagenson, 1988, 1989; Dreher and Ash, 1990; Corzine et al., 1994; Mobley et al., 1994; Ragins and Scandura, 1994; Baugh et al., 1996; Kirchmeyer, 1998). These studies, however, have tended to use typically measured outcome variables (for example, promotion, salary, job satisfaction) that may not be those most affected by a mentoring relationship. Indeed, a number of studies have found a gender difference when exploring less typical outcome variables. For example, Collins (1983) found that female mentees received support and encouragement and viewed their mentors as instrumental in increasing their self-confidence, providing growth opportunities, and increasing their visibility within the organization. However, there was no male comparison group. Although not tested statistically, Reich (1985, 1986) observed that female mentees were more likely than male mentees to report benefits related to gains in self-confidence, enhanced awareness of their strengths, stimulation of their thinking, feedback about their weaknesses, job goal-setting, and identifying and utilizing their talents. Fowler (2002) explored a range of benefits that had been identified by mentees and mentors themselves, rather than being researcher determined, and found that mentees reported an enhanced interpersonal relationship as an outcome of having a female mentor (regardless of gender of mentee), that mentors reported an enhanced interpersonal relationship if they were in a cross-gender relationship (regardless of the composition), and that productivity is increased for male mentors (regardless of gender of mentee). It may be that moving beyond typically measured outcome variables will uncover gender differences in regard to more meaningful mentoring benefits (for example, confidence, awareness, talents, enhanced relationships). Broadbridge and Simpson (2011) also pointed out that research needs to not only identify gender differences but to 'reveal hidden, gendered practices' that are the reasons for such differences. For example, why is productivity increased for male mentors to a greater extent than female mentors?

Goal Setting and Action Planning

While it is encouraging to know that so many mentees and mentors benefit from their relationships, it is more useful and practical to think about what *you* wish to get from *your* mentoring relationship. This is the first step in identifying your goals and making plans to achieve those goals. The importance of goal setting is not new to mentoring research and practice.

Kram's (1985) early research noted the importance of setting and pursuing personal and professional goals as part of mentoring. More recently, Godshalk and Sosik (2003) described mentoring as a learning and competence goal-driven process. Indeed, they went so far as to suggest that different learning goal orientations between mentor and mentee might be one cause of an unsuccessful mentoring relationship.

The benefits of goal setting are well documented (for example, Latham, 2004; Latham and Locke, 2007). In short, goal setting improves performance in organizational settings, particularly if the goal is specific, challenging, attainable, and fosters learning (Dweck, 1986; Locke, 1996). Indeed, Armstrong (2006) argued that a SMART goal – specific, measurable, achievable, relevant, and time-bound – provides a better target for success. Further, goal setting and achievement are most effective when feedback is provided on progress (Locke, 1996), and a major mentoring role is to provide feedback on mentees' progress toward their goals (Douglas, 1997). Documenting goals and action plans lays out an agenda for both mentoring performance and evaluation.

Self- and Other-assessment

When you are thinking about your reasons for wanting to establish a mentoring relationship (content focus), it may be timely to assess whether you are ready and willing to be involved in mentoring (process focus) and who you may want to be your mentoring partner. This preparation strengthens the prospect of mentoring success (Lee et al., 2006). There is no firm evidence about *who* would make the 'best' mentor or mentee, although most researchers and practitioners argue that mentoring relationships are affected by the extent to which the mentor and mentee can identify with and relate to each other (for example, Ragins, 1989); the extent to which they perceive they are interpersonally similar. This makes sense. Perceived similarity between mentor and mentee is positively related to interpersonal attraction (Turban et al., 2002). In turn, interpersonal attraction enhances communication and builds trust and reciprocity (Kanter, 1977; Lincoln and Miller, 1979), relationship elements that are central to effective mentoring.

Taking Ayman and her colleagues' (Ayman, 1993; Korabik and Ayman, 2007; Ayman and Korabik, 2010) interpretation of the interpersonal interaction perspective on leadership, and drawing a parallel with mentoring, it could be argued that gender composition of the relationship makes a difference because male and female mentors would have different types of social interactions with their mentees and these interactions will influence mentoring outcomes. Indeed, several researchers have directly addressed the issue of gender in the choosing and matching of mentoring partners.

Allen and her colleagues (2004) suggested that mentoring is most effective for women when their mentor is female because of a shared understanding of challenges facing women. Burke and Collins (2001) found that female mentors are more likely than males to report that they are positive role models, effective communicators, and spend more time developing and coaching. From the mentees' perspectives, women reported greater interpersonal comfort when they had female mentors (Maccoby, 1990; Allen et al., 2005) and more developmental opportunities regardless of gender of mentor (Burke and Collins, 2001). Female mentees, compared to males, also reported experiencing fewer challenges in 'measuring up to a mentor's standards' but more relational challenges from male mentors (Ensher and Murphy, 2011). Conversely, Fletcher and Ragins (2007) argued that women might be valued less than men as potential mentors – possibly because female mentors have limited access to, or experience exclusion from, informal interaction networks (Mor Barak et al., 1998). This may potentially limit what they can do for their mentee.

Despite these proposed and evidenced gender differences, recent research has found that men and women are equally likely to experience being a mentee (Wanberg et al., 2003; Kammeyer-Mueller and Judge, 2008; O'Brien et al., 2010) but men are more likely to report undertaking the mentor role (O'Brien et al., 2010). These self-reports of involvement in mentoring raise an interesting question. It is assumed in most definitions and descriptions of mentoring that it is a dyadic relationship (Welsh et al., 2012); that both the mentor and mentee recognize that such a relationship exists. However, this might not be the case. For example, Burke and Collins (2001) provide evidence that self-ratings of leadership behaviour tend to be inflated; that there are differences between self-reported behaviour and actual leadership behaviour as reported by colleagues. Indeed, Welsh and her colleagues (2012) found little agreement between mentoring partners as to whether a mentoring relationship actually exists. Specifically, they found that many 'mentees' and 'mentors' perceived the presence of a mentoring relationship when the other person did not agree. Given that mentoring research typically asks participants if they have had an experience as a mentee or as a mentor, the findings of Welsh and her colleagues (2012) have significant implications for a great deal of mentoring research. For example, when finding that female mentors provide more psychosocial functions than male mentors, it may be reasonable to question whether the participants are actually mentees or mentors. In practice, a mentee who is wondering why more career development support is not forthcoming from their 'mentor' may do well to consider whether their 'mentor' views the relationship similarly.

The quandary posed above, as to whether a mentoring relationship actually exists, can be overcome quite effectively by taking on board the practical recommendations made throughout this chapter. Indeed, it would be difficult to go through the process of approaching a potential mentee or mentor, negotiating the relationship, sharing expectations, and setting goals and making plans without having a clear understanding that you are indeed involved in a mentoring relationship. As advised by Ensher and Murphy (2011) and recommended here, mentees and mentors would do well to convert implicit assumptions into explicit discussions before entering the relationship and to continue to revisit and review as the relationship progresses.

Negotiating the Relationship and Sharing Expectations

The final aspect of pursuing mentoring to be discussed here is negotiating the relationship. Huskins and his colleagues (2011) identified that negotiating expectations between mentees and mentors is regarded as an important and essential element of effective mentoring. In this author's experience, such a finding is an understatement. Negotiating, particularly sharing expectations, is emphatically the single most important element when pursuing, doing and reviewing mentoring. Indeed, when not done well, it is the single most common factor for discontinuing a mentoring relationship.

Negotiating and sharing expectations helps to ensure both parties receive what they need from the relationship, provides clear operating and organizing principles for doing mentoring, and sets up guidelines and criteria for reviewing mentoring (particularly in the case when expectations are not being met). Having an upfront discussion about, for example, recognizing you might differ in your perspectives, agreeing that you will raise concerns as they arise, and strategizing for conflict management makes it easier to revisit those expectations as the relationship progresses (Bickel and Rosenthal, 2011; Huskins et al., 2011). Undertaking this process also strengthens the interpersonal relationship, facilitates mutual trust and respect, and builds professionalism (Elliot et al., 2006; Huskins et al., 2011).

Some mentoring partnerships choose to develop formal written contracts or agreements, which Huskins and colleagues (2011) argued facilitates the process of negotiation. Others choose to discuss their expectations and make less formal notes about the outcomes of those discussions. However, because power differences between mentor and mentee may arise throughout the relationship, resulting in the mentee feeling vulnerable and hesitant to raise 'difficult' issues, expectations should be shared upfront in a safe space created by the mentor (Bickel and Rosenthal, 2011). Some researchers have found gender differences in approaches to negotiation. For example, men are more likely than women to negotiate task assignments, advancement, higher payment, and 'other issues at work' (Small et al., 2007). Bowles and her colleagues (2007) explained that this gender difference was because of nervousness by women when negotiating with men. It may be that male mentors have different expectations and styles of interacting when it comes to negotiating expectations with their mentees (Ensher and Murphy, 2011).

A final word on gender difference in pursuing and negotiating a mentoring relationship. According to Dworkin and her colleagues (2012) women tend to have shorter mentoring relationships than do men. This may affect long-term benefits because, as reported by Dreher and Ash (1990), extensive mentoring relationships are more likely to result in promotions, higher incomes, and satisfaction with pay and benefits. Given that negotiating and sharing expectations is a crucial element in the longevity of mentoring, it may be even more significant for women to put considerable thought and effort into 'pursuing' their mentoring relationship.

DOING MENTORING – DEVELOPING AND MAINTAINING A MENTORING RELATIONSHIP

Effort is required in the establishment stage of a mentoring relationship. This author's experience has repeatedly shown that the mentoring partners who invest time and effort into setting goals, making plans, and negotiating working agreements have the most successful partnerships. The adage 'you get out what you put in' is never truer than in mentoring. However, this is not only pertinent at the pursuing stage – but throughout the course of the relationship. Doing mentoring is not simply about the mentor being an active giver and the mentee being a passive receiver. Doing mentoring is about the mentor and mentee engaging and working together; following the plans they have set to achieve their goals; and maintaining a healthy and effective relationship. In doing so, the mentor performs a range of functions under the auspice of mentoring.

Mentoring Functions

The functions or roles that a mentor performs during the course of a relationship have been the most commonly investigated aspect of mentoring over the past 35 years. Kram (1980, 1985) identified two broad categories of mentoring functions – career and psychosocial functions. Career functions were those that assisted mentees in gaining corporate exposure, learning the ropes of organizational life and obtaining promotions. Psychosocial functions resulted in an increased sense of competence, effectiveness and self-worth. Numerous researchers have subsequently assessed the two categories of functions identified by Kram (for example, Burke, 1984; Schockett and Haring-Hidore, 1985; Noe, 1988; Scandura and Katerberg, 1988; Dreher and Ash, 1990; Scandura, 1992; Turban and Dougherty, 1994; Tepper et al., 1996; Wang et al., 2009; Hu et al., 2011; Zhuang et al., 2013), usually identifying one, two or three broad categories of functions. However, Fowler and O'Gorman (2005), in a large sample of mentees and mentors representing all four possible gender combinations, identified eight distinct functions of mentoring. Knowing that eight separate functions occur in mentoring is useful for several practical and theoretical reasons. First, it breaks down the sometimes nebulous concept of 'mentoring' into clearer, focused and 'doable' components. Second, it assists with choosing a mentor and the subsequent discussion around expectations in the contracting and negotiating phase of the relationship: what functions do I need from my mentor to meet my goals? Third, discussion around the functions can be used diagnostically when reviewing and evaluating the relationship: am I receiving the mentoring that I need? Fourth, researchers can investigate the prevalence, antecedent and consequences of distinct mentoring functions rather than rely on broader generalizations about 'psychosocial' or 'career' functions. For example, is it career mentoring in general that leads to increased opportunities for mentees, or the specific 'advocacy' aspect of career mentoring?

Research findings on gender differences in the provision and receipt of mentoring functions has been inconsistent (Wanberg et al., 2003; O'Neill, 2005; O'Brien et al., 2010). In the main, females are found to be stronger on relational aspects (for example, intimacy, self-disclosure, personal and emotional support, and friendship) and providing and receiving psychosocial functions (Gabriel and Gardner, 1999; Ickes et al., 2000; Burke and Collins, 2001; Fowler et al., 2007; Joseph and Newman, 2010; O'Brien et al., 2010). These findings are not surprising given that, as argued by Fletcher and Ragins (2007), women are relational carriers and responsible for developing and using enhanced communication skills when interacting with others.

The inconsistent findings and broad statements that are made to interpret those findings (for example, O'Brien and her colleagues (2010) had to explain that 'intimacy building behaviours' are represented in 'psychosocial support') are precisely the reasons that researchers must investigate distinct mentoring functions rather than simply 'psychosocial' and 'career' functions. According to Fowler and O'Gorman (2005) the eight functions provided by mentors are as depicted in Table 14.1.

Table 14.1 Mentoring functions performed by mentors to assist their mentees with personal, professional and career development

Function	Description
Personal and emotional guidance	Encourages the mentee to discuss personal issues, insecurities and aspirations and helps with decisions about balancing professional and personal issues and commitments
Learning facilitation	Facilitates the mentee in thinking things through for themselves and shares their wealth of experience to strengthen the mentee's understanding or learning
Coaching	Provides assistance in developing job-related skills and knowledge and provides professional or technical advice
Advocacy	Promotes, recommends or advocates the mentee to 'people that count' and uses their influence to 'go into bat' for the mentee
Career development facilitation	Provides general career advice and guidance, specific practical assistance (for example, gives feedback on CVs [résumés], discusses selection processes), and introduces the mentee to networks of people who can assist with her or his career
Role modelling	Models approaches, attitudes and values the mentee admires and would like to develop and displays skills and behaviours that the mentee would like to learn
Strategies and systems advice	Provides knowledge about the system or strategies for working within the system and discusses and provides advice on how to handle internal politics
Friendship	Develops a friendship with the mentee, possibly resulting in social activities outside the work setting

Some considerations about this range of functions

First, a mentee may not require their mentor to provide all functions – it will depend on their needs and goals. Second, different skills and behaviours are needed to perform different functions – while some skills and behaviours may not be current areas of strength, becoming a mentor may become the vehicle for developing in those areas. Third, it may be equally as effective to steer a mentee toward other appropriate sources – for example, a colleague, a training course, reading in a particular area – when a mentor cannot meet a particular need or desire. Finally and most importantly, although the mentor provides these mentoring functions, the mentee is responsible for engaging with the mentor to facilitate the provision of functions. Remember, mentoring is not about the mentee being a passive receiver – it is an exchange of behaviours between mentor and mentee (Young and Perrewé, 2000). For example, if a mentor is a learning facilitator, sharing their experience to strengthen the mentee's understanding or learning, then the mentee needs to listen, reflect and engage in discussion with the mentor about that experience.

Meeting Agendas

It has been established that inadequate negotiation of the mentoring relationship, including shared expectations, is the foremost factor for discontinuing a mentoring relationship. The second factor is having inadequately planned meetings – either about the content to be discussed or scheduling. Even partnerships that start with a great deal of enthusiasm and best intentions fall short of a satisfactory finish if those involved are not sure what to talk about when they meet. Although this may seem simple and obvious, it is not uncommon to hear a mentee or mentor say, 'When it came down to it, we ran out of things to talk about' or 'After our initial meetings, we struggled to move forward'. Typically this is followed, some time later, by the mentee saying, 'I know Marula is a really busy person and I didn't want to take up her time.'

The importance of setting goals, making plans and negotiating working agreements at the *establishment* stage of a mentoring relationship has been explained. However, this process needs to continue beyond establishment to the rest of the relationship. For example, while some are able and comfortable with taking a laissez-faire approach – and are quite successful in doing so – others benefit from preparing a brief agenda to keep their meetings planned, on track and focused. It really depends on the mentoring relationship you have. The agenda may be as simple as a few points that cover past, present and future issues. Whether or not you prepare an agenda does not determine the degree of informality and casualness with which you engage in your meetings. Indeed, other topics and tracks are likely to unfold as you meet together. Nevertheless, the agenda is a safety net to fall back on, a useful way of jotting down thoughts, events and reflections between meetings, and a means of recording the progress of your mentoring relationship.

Maintaining the Relationship

Of course, being respectful in your interactions, following agreements you have made, prioritizing the relationship, and maintaining trust and confidentiality about your interactions are necessary ingredients for an effective mentoring partnership (Elliot et al., 2006; Huskins et al., 2011). These aspects of your mentoring process, together with revision of your expectations, will benefit from review from time to time. Indeed, Huskins and his colleagues (2011) recommend revising expectations on an ongoing basis, at least once a year and perhaps more frequently.

REVIEWING PROCESS AND PROGRESS

Reviewing involves open discussion, reflection, and evaluation of progress on goals and action plans, outcomes, agreements negotiated, and effectiveness of the way the mentor and mentee are working together – all of the aspects included in the pursuing and doing phases. The discussion may reveal changes and adjustments that need to be made, while the plans and agreements made when establishing the relationship provide a benchmark for your review process. The effectiveness of the mentoring relationship is generally reviewed at a micro-level, although it is beneficial periodically to undertake a broader review (Ensher and Murphy, 2011).

The time and effort put into establishing the relationship will reap benefits when it comes to reviewing (Bickel and Rosenthal, 2011; Huskins et al., 2011). There may be times when difficult issues need to be raised. Bickel and Rosenthal (2011) suggested 'making the undiscussable, discussable' by reflecting on 'What would I most like to communicate?', 'How do I want the other person to feel after the conversation?', and 'How emotionally charged is this likely to be?'

It is possible that women might find this process of reflection and review easier to engage in than men. Women are more likely to reflect on their own traits and behaviour and have substantial experience in discussing, thinking about and explaining their inner thoughts and feelings (Belenky et al., 1986; Csank and Conway, 2004); they actively seek understanding with self-reflection and self-analysis (Belenky et al., 1986). While women are more likely to be open to both others and their own experience, men are less likely to be self-reflective on traits and characteristics and less self- and other-reflective about emotions (Conway, 2000).

Finally when a mentoring relationship terminates – whether spontaneously or planned – it is useful to mutually and/or individually reflect on and review the overall relationship. As Bickel and Rosenthal (2011) pointed out, 'not all mentoring relationships are going to bear fruit; some will die a natural death' (p. 1232). Regardless of how the relationship ends, it can achieve a respectful closure. Mentoring is an intergenerational process with successful experiences as a mentee or mentor influencing willingness and ability to undertake the role of mentor in the future (Ragins and Cotton, 1993; Ragins and Scandura, 1999; Young and Perrewé, 2000). Thus, experiencing and learning from mentoring partnerships will inform and improve future mentoring, including making the transition from mentee to mentor.

SUMMARY

This chapter has outlined some of the key aspects to consider when pursuing, doing and reviewing mentoring – and emphasized the value in attending to both the content and process as you do so. Practical suggestions in the form of guidelines and processes have been provided to assist mentees and mentors as they work together. The chapter has assumed that mentoring is career and professionally focused; that each mentoring dyad will determine the value, significance and usefulness of the suggestions and recommendations made; and that asking questions of your mentoring partner is a more effective way of pursing, doing and reviewing mentoring than having expert answers prescribed.

The chapter has also reported on literature about the impact of gender on many aspects of mentoring. Although results have been inconsistent, for example, whether females or males make the best mentoring partner, provide more or less mentoring functions, or accrue different benefits from mentoring, there is little doubt that mentoring is a beneficial tool for helping women advance in organizations. It is time for researchers to move beyond identifying gender differences and investigate the underlying practices and processes that cause those differences (Broadbridge and Simpson, 2011) – and for practitioners and organizations to take up the challenge of changing those practices and processes.

REFERENCES

Allen, T.D. and L.T. Eby (2003), 'Relationship effectiveness for mentors: factors associated with learning and quality', *Journal of Management*, **29**(4), 469–86.
Allen, T.D., R. Day and E. Lentz (2005), 'The role of interpersonal comfort in mentoring relationships', *Journal of Career Development*, **31**(3), 155–69.
Allen, T.D., M.L. Poteet and S.M. Burroughs (1997), 'The mentor's perspective: a qualitative inquiry and future research agenda', *Journal of Vocational Behavior*, **51**(1), 70–89.
Allen, T.D., L.T. Eby, M.L. Poteet, E. Lentz and L. Lima (2004), 'Career benefits associated with mentoring for protégés: a meta-analysis', *Journal of Applied Psychology*, **89**(1), 127–36.
Armstrong, M. (2006), *Performance Management: Key Strategies and Practical Guidelines*, 3rd edition, London: Kogan Page.
Ayman, R. (1993), 'Leadership perception: the role of gender and culture', in M.M. Chemers and R. Ayman (eds), *Leadership Theory and Research: Perspectives and Directions*, New York: Academic Press, pp. 137–66.

Ayman, R. and K. Korabik (2010), 'Leadership: why gender and culture matter', *American Psychologist*, **65**(3), 157–70.
Baugh, S.G., M.J. Lankau and T.A. Scandura (1996), 'An investigation of the effects of protégé gender on responses to mentoring', *Journal of Vocational Behavior*, **49**(3), 309–23.
Belenky, M.F., B.M. Clinchy, N.R. Goldberger and J.M. Tarule (1986), *Women's Ways of Knowing: The Development of Self, Voice, and Mind*, New York: Basic Books.
Bickel, J. and S.L. Rosenthal (2011), 'Difficult issues in mentoring: recommendations on making the "undiscussable" discussable', *Academic Medicine*, **86**(10), 1229–34.
Blood, E.A., N.J. Ullrich, D.R. Hirshfeld-Becker, E.W. Seely, M.T. Connelly, C.A. Warfield and S.J. Emans (2012), 'Academic women faculty: are they finding the mentoring they need?', *Journal of Women's Health*, **21**(11), 1201–8.
Bowles, H.R., L. Babcock and L. Lai (2007), 'Social incentives for gender differences in the propensity to initiate negotiations: sometimes it does hurt to ask', *Organizational Behavior and Human Decision Processes*, **103**(1), 84–103.
Broadbridge, A. and R. Simpson (2011), '25 years on: reflecting on the past and looking to the future in gender and management research', *British Journal of Management*, **22**(3), 470–83.
Burke, R.J. (1984), 'Mentors in organizations', *Group and Organization Management*, **9**(3), 353–72.
Burke, R.J. and C.A. McKeen (1997), 'Benefits of mentoring relationships among managerial and professional women: a cautionary tale', *Journal of Vocational Behavior*, **51**(1), 43–57.
Burke, S. and K.M. Collins (2001), 'Gender differences in leadership styles and management skills', *Women in Management Review*, **16**(5/6), 244–56.
Colarelli, S.M. and R.C. Bishop (1990), 'Career commitment: functions, correlates, and management', *Group and Organization Management*, **15**(2), 158–76.
Collins, N.W. (1983), *Professional Women and their Mentors: A Practical Guide to Mentoring for the Woman Who Wants to Get Ahead*, Englewood Cliffs, NJ: Prentice Hall.
Conway, M. (2000), 'On sex roles and representations of emotional experience: masculinity, femininity, and emotional awareness', *Sex Roles*, **43**(9), 687–98.
Corzine, J., G. Buntzman and E. Busch (1994), 'Mentoring, downsizing, gender and career outcomes', *Journal of Social Behavior and Personality*, **9**(3), 517–28.
Csank, P.A.R. and M. Conway (2004), 'Engaging in self-reflection changes self-concept clarity: on differences between women and men, and low- and high-clarity individuals', *Sex Roles*, **50**(7/8), 469–80.
De Janasz, S.C., S.E. Sullivan and V. Whiting (2003), 'Mentoring networks and career success: lessons for turbulent times', *Academy of Management Executive*, **17**(4), 78–93.
De Vries, J., C. Webb and J. Eveline (2006), 'Mentoring for gender equality and organizational change', *Employee Relations*, **28**(6), 573–87.
Douglas, C.A. (1997), *Formal Mentoring Programs in Organizations*, Greensboro, NC: Center for Creative Leadership.
Dreher, G.F. and R.A. Ash (1990), 'A comparative study of mentoring among men and women in managerial, professional, and technical positions', *Journal of Applied Psychology*, **75**(5), 539–46.
Dweck, C.S. (1986), 'Motivational processes affecting learning', *American Psychologist*, **41**(10), 1040–48.
Dworkin, T.M., V. Maurer and C.A. Schipani (2012), 'Career mentoring for women: new horizons/expanded methods', *Business Horizons*, **55**(4), 363–72.
Elliot, C., J.D. Leck, B. Orser and C. Mossop (2006), 'An exploration of gender and trust in mentoring relationships', *Journal of Diversity Management*, **1**(1), 1–11.
Ensher, E.A. and S.E. Murphy (2011), 'The mentoring relationship challenges scale: the impact of mentoring stage, type, and gender', *Journal of Vocational Behavior*, **79**(1), 253–66.
Fagenson, E.A. (1988), 'The power of a mentor: protégés' and nonprotégés' perceptions of their own power in organizations', *Group and Organization Studies*, **13**(2), 182–94.

Fagenson, E.A. (1989), 'The mentor advantage: perceived career/job experiences of protégés versus non-protégés', *Journal of Organizational Behavior*, **10**(4), 309–20.

Fletcher, J.K. and B.R. Ragins (2007), 'Stone Center relational cultural theory: a window on relational mentoring', in B.R. Ragins and K. Kram (eds), *The Handbook of Mentoring at Work: Theory, Research and Practice*, Thousand Oaks, CA: Sage.

Fowler, J.L. (2002), 'Mentoring relationships at work: an investigation of mentoring functions, benefits and gender', doctoral dissertation, Griffith University, Queensland, Australia.

Fowler, J.L. and J.G. O'Gorman (2005), 'Mentoring functions: a contemporary view of the perceptions of mentees and mentors', *British Journal of Management*, **16**(1), 51–7.

Fowler, J.L., A.J. Gudmundsson and J.G. O'Gorman (2007), 'The relationships between mentee–mentor gender combination and the provision of distinct mentoring functions', *Women in Management Review*, **22**(8), 666–81.

Fowler, J.L., A.J. Gudmundsson and L.M. Whicker (2006), 'The design, implementation and outcomes of a mentoring program', in R. Thorpe, M. McHugh and C. Leitch (eds), *Conference Proceedings 2006: British Academy of Management: 'Building International Communities Through Collaboration'*, Belfast: British Academy of Management, pp. 1–14.

Fowler, J.L., A.J. Gudmundsson, L.M. Whicker and S.E. Branch (2001), 'Mentoring functions: an instrument designed to measure the perceptions of mentors and mentees', in C. Strong (ed.), *Conference Proceedings 2001: British Academy of Management*, Cardiff: British Academy of Management.

Fung, Y. (1948), *A Short History of Chinese Philosophy*, New York: The Free Press: Macmillan.

Gabriel, S. and W.L. Gardner (1999), 'Are there "his" and "hers" types of interdependence? The implications of gender differences in collective versus relational interdependence for affect, behavior, and cognition', *Journal of Personality and Social Psychology*, **77**(3), 642–55.

Ghosh, R. and T.G. Reio (2013), 'Career benefits associated with mentoring for mentors: a meta-analysis', *Journal of Vocational Behavior*, **83**(1), 106–16.

Godshalk, V.M. and J.J. Sosik (2003), 'Aiming for career success: the role of learning goal orientation in mentoring relationships', *Journal of Vocational Behavior*, **63**(3), 417–37.

Hargreaves, A. and M. Fullan (2000), 'Mentoring in the new millennium', *Theory into Practice*, **39**(1), 50–56.

Henriques, P.L. and C. Curado (2009), 'Pushing the boundaries on mentoring: can mentoring be a knowledge tool?', *Journal of Business Economics and Management*, **10**(1), 85–97.

Hersby, M.D., M.K. Ryan and J. Jetten (2009), 'Getting together to get ahead: the impact of social structure on women's networking', *British Journal of Management*, **20**(4), 415–30.

Hu, C., E.K. Pellegrini and T.A. Scandura (2011), 'Measurement invariance in mentoring research: a cross-cultural examination across Taiwan and the U.S', *Journal of Vocational Behavior*, **78**(2), 274–82.

Huskins, W.C., K. Silet, A.M. Weber-Main, M.D. Begg, V.G. Fowler, J. Hamilton and M. Fleming (2011), 'Identifying and aligning expectations in a mentoring relationship', *Clinical and Translational Science*, **4**(6), 439–47.

Ickes, W., P.R. Gesn and T. Graham (2000), 'Gender differences in empathic accuracy: differential ability or differential motivation?', *Personal Relationships*, **7**(1), 95–109.

Joseph, D.L. and D.A. Newman (2010), 'Emotional intelligence: an integrative meta-analysis and cascading model', *Journal of Applied Psychology*, **95**(1), 54–78.

Kammeyer-Mueller, J.D. and T.A. Judge (2008), 'A quantitative review of mentoring research: test of a model', *Journal of Vocational Behavior*, **72**(3), 269–83.

Kanter, R.M. (1977), *Men and Women of the Corporation*, New York: Basic Books.

Kirchmeyer, C. (1998), 'Determinants of managerial career success: evidence and explanation of male/female differences', *Journal of Management*, **24**(6), 673–92.

Korabik, K. and R. Ayman (2007), 'Gender and leadership in the corporate world: a multi-perspective model', in J.L. Chin, B. Lott, J.K. Rice and J. Sanchez–Hucles (eds), *Women*

and Leadership: Transforming Visions and Diverse Voices, Malden, MA: Blackwell, pp. 106–24.
Kram, K.E. (1980), 'Mentoring processes at work: developmental relationships in managerial careers', Dissertation Abstracts International, 41(05B).
Kram, K.E. (1985), Mentoring at Work: Developmental Relationships in Organizational Life, Glenview, IL: Scott Foresman.
Latham, G.P. (2004), 'The motivational benefits of goal setting', Academy of Management Executive, 18(4), 126–9.
Latham, G.P. and E.A. Locke (2007), 'New developments in and directions for goal-setting research', European Psychologist, 12(4), 290–300.
Lee, S., R. Theoharis, M. Fitzpatrick, K. Kim, J.M. Liss, T. Nix-Williams, D. Griswold and C. Walther-Thomas (2006), 'Create effective mentoring relationships: strategies for mentor and mentee success', Intervention in School and Clinic, 41(4), 233–40.
Lincoln, J.R. and J. Miller (1979), 'Work and friendship ties in organizations: a comparative analysis of relational networks', Administrative Science Quarterly, 24(2), 181–99.
Locke, E.A. (1996), 'Motivation through conscious goal setting', Applied and Preventive Psychology, 5(2), 117–24.
Lunding, F.J., G.L. Clements and D.S. Perkins (1978), 'Everyone who makes it has a mentor', Harvard Business Review, 56(3), 89–101.
Maccoby, E. (1990), 'Gender and relationships: a developmental account', American Psychologist, 45(4), 513–20.
Mobley, G.M., C. Jaret, K. Marsh and Y.Y. Lim (1994), 'Mentoring, job satisfaction, gender, and the legal profession', Sex Roles, 31(1–2), 79–98.
Mor Barak, M.E., D.A. Cherin and S. Berkman (1998), 'Organizational and personal dimensions in diversity climate', The Journal of Applied Behavioral Science, 34(1), 82–104.
Mou, B. (2008), Chinese Philosophy A–Z, Edinburgh: Edinburgh University Press.
Noe, R.A. (1988), 'An investigation of the determinants of successful assigned mentoring relationships', Personnel Psychology, 41(3), 457–79.
Noe, R.A., D.B. Greenberger and S. Wang (2002), 'Mentoring: what we know and where we might go', in J. Martocchio and G.R. Ferris (eds), Research in Personnel and Human Resources Management, Vol. 21, Bingley, UK: Emerald Group Publishing, pp. 129–73.
Oakley, J.G. (2000), 'Gender-based barriers to senior management positions: understanding the scarcity of female CEOs', Journal of Business Ethics, 27(4), 321–34.
O'Brien, K.E., A. Biga, S.R. Kessler and T.D. Allen (2010), 'A meta-analytic investigation of gender differences in mentoring', Journal of Management, 36(2), 537–54.
O'Neill, R.M. (2005), 'An examination of organizational predictors of mentoring functions', Journal of Managerial Issues, 17(4), 439–60.
Payne, S.C. and A.H. Huffman (2005), 'A longitudinal examination of the influence of mentoring on organizational commitment and turnover', Academy of Management Journal, 48(1), 158–68.
Ragins, B.R. (1989), 'Barriers to mentoring: the female manager's dilemma', Human Relations, 42(1), 1–22.
Ragins, B.R. (1999), 'Gender and mentoring relationships: a review and research agenda for the next decade', in G.N. Powell (ed.), Handbook of Gender and Work, Thousand Oaks, CA: Sage, pp. 347–70.
Ragins, B.R. (2007), 'Diversity and workplace mentoring relationships: a review and positive social capital approach', in T. Allen and L. Eby (eds), The Blackwell Handbook of Mentoring: A Multiple Perspectives Approach, Oxford: Blackwell Publishing, pp. 281–300.
Ragins, B.R. and J.L. Cotton (1993), 'Gender and willingness to mentor in organizations', Journal of Management, 19(1), 97–111.
Ragins, B.R. and T.A. Scandura (1994), 'Gender differences in expected outcomes of mentoring relationships', Academy of Management Journal, 37(4), 957–71.
Ragins, B.R. and T.A. Scandura (1999), 'Burden or blessing? Expected costs and benefits of being a mentor', Journal of Organizational Behavior, 20(4), 493–509.
Reich, M.H. (1985), 'Executive views from both sides of mentoring', Personnel, 62(2), 42–6.

Reich, M.H. (1986), 'The mentor connection', *Personnel*, **63**(2), 50–56.
Scandura, T.A. (1992), 'Mentorship and career mobility: an empirical investigation', *Journal of Organizational Behavior*, **13**(2), 169–74.
Scandura, T.A. and R.J. Katerberg (1988), 'Much ado about mentors and little about measurement: development of an instrument', paper presented at the meeting of the Academy of Management, Annaheim, CA.
Schein, V.E., R. Mueller, T. Lituchy and J. Liu (1996), 'Think manager–think male: a global phenomenon?', *Journal of Organizational Behavior*, **17**(1), 33–41.
Schockett, M.R. and M. Haring-Hidore (1985), 'Factor analytic support for psychosocial and vocational mentoring functions', *Psychological Reports*, **57**, 627–30.
Schunk, D.H. and C.A. Mullen (2013), 'Toward a conceptual model of mentoring research: integration with self-regulated learning', *Educational Psychology Review*, **25**(3), 361–89.
Small, D., M. Gelfand, L. Babcock and H. Gettman (2007), 'Who goes to the bargaining table? The influence of gender and framing on the initiation of negotiation', *Journal of Personality and Social Psychology*, **93**(4), 600–613.
Tepper, K., B.C. Shaffer and B.J. Tepper (1996), 'Latent structure of mentoring function scales', *Educational and Psychological Measurement*, **56**(5), 848–57.
Turban, D.B. and T.W. Dougherty (1994), 'Role of protégé personality in receipt of mentoring and career success', *Academy of Management Journal*, **37**(3), 688–702.
Turban, D.B., T.W. Dougherty and F.K. Lee (2002), 'Gender, race, and perceived similarity effects in developmental relationships: the moderating role of relationship duration', *Journal of Vocational Behavior*, **61**(2), 240–62.
Wanberg, C.R., E.T. Welsh and S.A. Hezlett (2003), 'Mentoring research: a review and dynamic process model', in J. Martocchio and J. Ferris (eds), *Research in Personnel and Human Resources Management, Vol. 22*, Bingley, UK: Emerald Group Publishing, pp. 39–124.
Wang, S., R.A. Noe, Z. Wang and D.B. Greenberger (2009), 'What affects willingness to mentor in the future? An investigation of attachment styles and mentoring experiences', *Journal of Vocational Behavior*, **74**(3), 245–56.
Weinberg, F.J. and M.J. Lankau (2011), 'Formal mentoring programs: a mentor-centric and longitudinal analysis', *Journal of Management*, **37**(6), 1527–57.
Welsh, E.T., D. Bhave and Y.K. Kyoung (2012), 'Are you my mentor? Informal mentoring mutual identification', *Career Development International*, **17**(2), 137–48.
Young, A.M. and L.P. Perrewé (2000), 'The exchange relationship between mentors and protégés: the development of a framework', *Human Resource Management Review*, **10**(2), 177–209.
Zhuang, W., M. Wu and S. Wen (2013), 'Relationship of mentoring functions to expatriate adjustments: comparing home country mentorship and host country mentorship', *The International Journal of Human Resource Management*, **24**(1), 35–49.

15. Women managers, careers and organizations
Viki Holton

The following quotes illustrate the current situation for women managers and are taken from recent research at Ashridge Business School, UK, into women's careers (Holton and Dent, 2012a, 2012b):

> I've never experienced any discrimination in my career.

> Even in this organization – with excellent support and help – I have seen so many women who have slipped through the cracks and left.

> Until we designed and launched the women's leadership programme there was nothing provided in development terms to help women develop their leadership style and appreciate the gender dimensions.

The first, from a female board member of an IT multinational, highlights the 'ideal' situation. There are some outstandingly good organizations where women are provided with exactly the same opportunities as their male colleagues but these remain the minority. The other quotes indicate some of the problems that women encounter (all the quotes in this chapter are anonymous). For every organization that provides a good environment for women managers there are many others that do not offer such a good place to work.

Since the 1980s the number of women entering the labour market as graduates and at professional and junior management levels has been increasing (Hammond and Holton, 1993; Rubery et al., 1999; Perrons, 2009). However, in the UK as in most other countries, there are still relatively few women at (or beyond) middle management level (Davidson and Burke, 2004; Broadbridge, 2007; *Economist*, 2011; Vinnicombe, 2011; International Labour Organization, 2012). Organizations with significant numbers of female senior managers remain unusual despite the best efforts of some good company initiatives. Although a national campaign called 'Opportunity Now' was launched in the UK, with research support from Ashridge Business School, the pace of change remains slow.

Recent press attention has focused on the lack of women at board level (Fontanella-Khan, 2012; Tranor, 2012; Costello, 2013; Medland, 2013) and, while this is an interesting and relevant debate, it is important that organizations look at ways to increase the numbers of women middle and senior managers. Only when the number of women increases at these levels will there be a 'next generation' ready to step up to board-level appointments. Although Sealy et al. (2008) identify an increasing number of women capable of taking such roles other evidence indicates that this is a comparatively small group. This can be illustrated in a typical annual company report (from a major UK employer) where, although numbers have increased in recent years, women hold only 21 per cent of senior leadership appointments (Barclays, 2013). Data from the European Commission also reveal a similarly small pool of potential applicants, as only 11 per cent of individuals appointed to the governing bodies of European listed companies are women (Desvaux et al., 2007).

This chapter looks at the issues found in Holton and Dent's (2012a, 2012b) research at Ashridge Business School. The study found a number of key factors that make a difference for women's careers, so it is perhaps as well to start with a key question – do women's careers differ significantly from those of their male colleagues?

There are a number of differences, not least the fact that women are often less likely than men to apply for promotion (Shellenbarger, 2012). It might be assumed that this should be changing – with a younger, more confident generation – but the Ashridge study and other evidence indicates that this does not seem to be the case (Holton and Dent, 2012a; Paris and Decker, 2012). Women are also less likely to be offered those early key assignments that are important on a CV (résumé), yet women highlight the importance of such opportunities and the value of sponsorship (Dent and Holton, 2012; Holton and Dent, 2012a, 2012b). A number of women mentioned that early on in their career a manager believed in their abilities, gave them a lot of encouragement and the necessary 'push' to go off and try something new. That is not to say that some men would not benefit from encouragement – but it is clearly something that holds women back. There are also negative stereotypes about working mothers and careers (Armstrong, 2013), as well as sex role stereotypes (Schein, 2001) and sexist attitudes (Dey and Shah, 2013). A man may be described in a positive way as 'aggressive' or 'tough' but these may become more negative terms if used about women managers (for example, Fels, 2004; Duehr and Bono, 2006; Mavin, 2008). Eagly and Carli (2007) refer to this as the conscious and unconscious bias that contributes to a resistance to women's leadership.

REVIEWING THE RESEARCH EVIDENCE

Survey data, with over 1400 women managers responding, as well as in-depth interviews with 20 women at senior or director level, identified a number of key issues in the Ashridge study, for example, the conflict that many women experience in trying to balance a career with the demands of raising a young family (Holton and Dent, 2012a, 2012b). The key years for building the experience and breadth of knowledge essential for senior management careers are usually the mid-twenties to late thirties and this often clashes with the time when many women are having children and looking after a young family.

The aim of the research was to better understand what helps women drive their careers and identify the challenges. The career experiences of women managers and what helps them in 'getting on' in careers highlight a number of ways that organizations might provide more help. One aspect identified was support from the boss; another was the chance to take on early, challenging projects that gave women opportunities that otherwise might not have happened. Our survey sample group consisted of women who were most likely to be working in large organizations and this is reflected in much of what is discussed below. The experience of women in smaller organizations may be similar in certain aspects, not least the importance of support from other people. Among the barriers women face were a number of practical issues including five themes, which are briefly outlined below.

Combining Work and Family Commitments

One of the continuing issues here is the negative impact part-time working (as well as family responsibilities) can have on women's careers. This is highlighted by Warren (2010) in 'Penalties of part-time work across Europe' and Mattis's (2001) article identifying the 'leaky' pipeline. The 'leaky' pipeline creates an image of what happens when women are more likely than men to leave at every career stage, for example, at the first management appointment or international assignment, or in mid-career.

One reason why women's progress in business has taken so long is because much has focussed on the role of the individual and too little has been about the role of the organization, for example, in offering regular career advice, development centres, leadership development and mentoring. A particular shortcoming in some companies has been a lack of willingness to resolve the clash women experience between traditional career paths and those 'young family' years. An exception to this is illustrated below by one senior manager, given the chance of job shadowing. Such support roles are not always seen as positive in career building but this one, with full membership of the group, and regarded as an equal by both the boss and the team members, did provide an excellent opportunity to build the key skills necessary to operate at director level in a multinational. As she explains:

I didn't want an international career at one time a couple of years back. I know it's critical for career success here but I had a young child and was keen to stay close to home and limit the amount of travelling that I previously had. The company found for me instead a senior support role to one of the most senior women in the business and so I worked with her and her team. It was an amazing learning experience for me and great as this was likely to be the next type of job I would apply for. I gained a huge amount of knowledge about operating at that next level and I was also fortunate in the fact that they included me as a full partner/team member.

Career Support and Signposting

Career support is important and needs to be practical. This may happen through regular career development reviews where an adviser is a 'career coach' with a broader view across different departments, sites, as well as across regions. This type of overview is particularly important in larger organizations and multinationals where career paths may be less clearly delineated.

Some women highlighted a lack of feedback from the organization, both in terms of their own skills as well as in respect of the 'big picture' careers advice. Too much seems to be left to ad hoc and/or informal processes such as whether a boss is likely to offer career support and coaching. A key issue is the importance of an early 'stretch' assignment: the chance to lead a project at the beginning of a career or be involved with a task identified as important to the organization. Not only is it about gaining new skills, it is also these opportunities that women said helped to build their confidence.

Most good career support structures take account of the fact that people learn best when they are challenged (in a good way) as it means moving out of their comfort zone. A story from the Ashridge research illustrates what happened in South Africa; it was an amazing opportunity for someone who had recently joined the company:

My very first job was project managing the roll-out of a new business venture from one part of the country into a national operation. The pilot scheme had effectively proved successful and they needed somebody to roll it out but it was highly operational in that it was a subsidiary servicing small companies under a different brand, so it was everything from setting up IT systems to buying trucks, to training drivers, to establishing scheduling routes for deliveries. So starting out from university not knowing the front end from the back end of a truck it was a brilliant opportunity for me . . . Just being thrown into the deep end doing transport economic modelling, none of the stuff that I studied, meant it was a real transition moment because I was project managing, as a real green novice, really seasoned specialists in each of the disciplines and having to work out how to mediate those personalities who were all male and probably 20 to

30 years my senior, was quite a challenge, but a very good one. So that was a welcome to the 'world of work' kind of moment and it was a very successful project so that helped!

Gaining Experience

An important building block in any career is the tricky area of gaining the right experience that will help women gain new skills, and increase the depth (or breadth) of their knowledge. The following examples illustrate different ways that women have gained experience and improved their management and leadership skills. Using a variety of sources is helpful. For example, being given responsibility for a new project; encouragement, support and mentoring to help individuals 'step up' for a leadership role (some organizations use the ambiguous term 'acting up' for this process); having the opportunity to move into an operational/international role; moving from a technical to a management role, or from support to operational:

> I stopped being group leader for material science and became group leader for devised physics. So, I bought the equipment, I hired the people, set up a method, and trained the people to use the method. I was the specialist, the absolute in-house specialist who knew everything. And then I moved to a larger group, which was much more of a managerial role rather than just being the 'priestess' of material science really. So, it was much more about theoretic people making their decision and using your judgement to decide if it's the right decision or not rather than necessarily knowing what to do and telling them.

Turning around projects, that is, leading a failing project and returning it to success, is a type of rescue mission, and 'troubleshooter' qualities are often highly valued in organizations. For this responsibility, as well as those noted above, many women said their boss encouraged them to take on such new responsibilities and provided positive support and coaching when they took on the new role or assignment:

> I was suddenly dumped with a project that was failing. And it was supposed to be, well, it was called the 'Breakthrough Project'. It was a project that was very much around material development and about inventing completely new materials, thinking outside the box. It was a project with team members from Japan and from the UK but was really producing nothing. Everybody had such unrealistic high expectations from this project, and was being very disappointed, and so they asked me to lead it. And although I wasn't particularly pleased to start with, because nobody likes to pick up a failing project, actually I learned an awful lot from it, and in the end we did some really useful stuff. But most importantly, it forced me to think about how the Japanese think differently, how – even though their mind doesn't necessarily work differently – the way they express their thinking is so very different.

248   *Handbook of gendered careers in management*

Observing other managers in order to review the key qualities of an outstanding manager can help and this often works well with the help of an experienced coach. It is not always appreciated but a good deal can also be learned from a bad manager. Some women interviewed said this was a very powerful lesson as it illustrates precisely what a manager should not do:

> I was basically tasked to start up a new group – the company was a start-up anyhow then – with new equipment, a new scope and new people. And I started and hired a technician and then I went on maternity leave. When I came back I reported to this technician who had been promoted to group leader. And the guy was a complete disaster; he couldn't cope and was a good example of what not to do as he made mistake after mistake. However, it was a useful experience, as I had time to think about what would I do if I was in that position – and what would I not do? Frankly, if I had gone straight in and led from the start I wouldn't have the time to consider so I would have just done it. So, that made me stronger in some unexpected ways.

And reflecting on the Japan project mentioned earlier:

> Sometimes it is easy to jump to conclusions without really listening to people properly; it really forced me to listen to them, and we included a couple of special trips to really try to understand where they were coming from. Obviously we were all scientists, so the same rules prevailed, but well, there were big differences about how we expressed ideas or convictions. The European or American way is generally to come up with a hypothesis and say, 'Oh, this is our hypothesis, this is why we want to do it' and appear very structured and very confident. And then sometimes it doesn't work, and so, 'Well, that's science!' While the Japanese were much more reticent to come up with a hypothesis and they seem to trust a lot more the gut feeling or be a bit shy of formulating a hypothesis, but they still wanted to do the work, because they still believed it was something that was worthwhile. And so it was a lot about giving them the space and the time to do what they believed was right, even if they could not clearly explain it to you in a hypothesis right there and then.

Her determination and willingness to look differently at the project issues helped achieve success; appreciating the value of patience was also good learning and helped her develop a management style that could accommodate those from different cultures. Managing change, as noted with 'troubleshooting', is an important business area. While many individuals may be able to deliver on finance, IT or marketing projects, far fewer excel with regard to leading change initiatives. It is also important to make sure there is support, maybe from a boss or a mentor, and all organizations need to provide a good support structure. Executive development is particularly helpful; a number of the women interviewed in the Ashridge study had decided to take an MBA qualification. A number of these were company sponsored; one woman was the first person in their organization given the opportunity to take a full-time MBA in North America, and another was from Scotland who was the first person within Social Services to receive sponsorship for an MBA (at Heriot-Watt University).

Support From Others: The People Around You

Support from others also makes a difference and the survey data below illustrate the key role that the boss and colleagues play in career development. Some organizations formalize such support with mentoring or executive education programmes or with projects such as 'the manager as coach'. This type of support is particularly important in early career and when women are in the minority in their workplace or profession; for example, at a technology conference only seven women attended among some 300 delegates (Sanders, 2012). The boss, colleagues and co-workers in the workplace and those at home, family and friends, can all help provide career support and advice, although it is the boss who is most important in this research (Table 15.1).

One (Chinese) woman interviewed in China spoke about learning from her boss who had a more relaxed managing style. It was really helpful to her – learning to be slightly more relaxed in her leadership style while still maintaining the seriousness and discipline that is more usual among Chinese managers.

Many of the women in the research mention the value of networking, which helped them stay in touch with colleagues they had known at different stages of their career. Mentors were also often mentioned and for some

Table 15.1   Career development support received

Response	%*	Count
Boss	86.8	1220
Colleagues	77.1	1084
Family	69.4	976
Friends	54.9	772
External coach	32.9	462
Internal mentor (a relationship with a more experienced role model)	29.4	413
External mentor	19.7	277
Internal coach (a relationship based on developing skills)	11.3	159

Note: *Respondents could select as many options as appropriate, so each item could equal 100 per cent.

a variety of mentors had helped provide them with different perspectives – for example, someone from an earlier organization as well as a past boss who had moved to a different business area. Mentors and coaches are sometimes thought of as being valuable only at early career stages but they are also useful at senior levels, not least by challenging assumptions, as shown below:

> I was about to apply for a senior role – a job which I'd already held plus my existing role for a number of months. Although I certainly did not think of the interview as a mere formality, and there were other serious contenders for the appointment, I felt very comfortable writing a formal presentation for the panel interview. It had been an interesting process, I knew all the panel members as well as knowing the job inside out and what I'd like to change about it! Fortunately I tried out the presentation with my coach and my husband who independently came back with similar comments . . . it wasn't a very interesting presentation – more worthy than exciting and was very unlikely to win me that promotion! I was surprised and shocked at the feedback. However, once I understood their criticisms I set about creating a better presentation.

The point about this story is that advice can help highlight weaknesses that an individual may miss either in terms of content, style or both, so it is really helpful to have a colleague, coach or family member who will honestly say what they think. And she did in fact win the promotion!

Virginia Rometty, Chief Executive of IBM, talks about her good fortune throughout her career being surrounded in IBM by people who wanted to mentor her (Miller, 2011). It is hugely important in helping people develop their potential and it is a pity that it is often left to chance or not seen as a valuable approach in executive development; too few organizations emphasize coaching and mentoring as key skills for all managers and leaders.

Some people feel uncomfortable asking for such help but as one woman said, 'the worst that can happen is that they say "no" but in my experience people are often flattered to be asked and are very generous with their time'. Another woman who now holds one of the most senior jobs in her organization described how she still keeps in touch with someone she first approached as a new, junior trainee when he was at Oxford, and one of the most respected experts in a specialist area: 'He kindly agreed to meet me and I remember that at our first meeting he was happy to spend a lot of time discussing the areas I was interested in, and offered me lots of advice and ideas that could help me develop my research.'

When Ashridge provided career support and advice for senior women in the National Health Service many of those involved gained key promotions (James and Wark, 1995). The individual feedback and coaching helped sharpen their skills, making them more focussed about their interview 'image' and how they presented themselves, which are key aspects of senior recruitment. There were also a number of skills-based workshops offered and the programme created a supportive network that had not existed before. Formal mentoring programmes can also be powerful. For example, established in 2009 a mentoring programme in a multinational was intended to drive competitive advantage, secure a strong pipeline of talent for the future and to help develop and accelerate the readiness of high-potential men and women for senior leadership positions (Dinolfo and Nugent, 2010). Mentoring provided ongoing feedback and advice on career progression, and personal development plans played a key role in helping individuals achieve their full potential. Just over 100 senior women took part between 2009 and 2011, with 26 per cent achieving promotion to a Vice President or to a Senior Vice President role. Initially the programme was run only for senior women but in 2013 the programme was rolled out locally for middle- and junior-level positions in individual business units. Local programmes are based on a global framework and tailored to meet the needs of individual countries and regions.

Working Mothers: Juggling Career and Family

Women in China or India, the UK, in various parts of Continental Europe, North America and elsewhere all highlighted similar issues in the Ashridge research when it came to juggling career and family issues. These difficulties are highlighted by Sheryl Sandberg (Sandberg, with Scovell, 2013) who was COO at Facebook but still went to great lengths to disguise the fact that she left the office early to go home to her baby son. When she later 'confessed' to this at a staff meeting it became a big story, which indicates perhaps the scale of the problem, and the fact she said that, 'we have a long way to go before flexitime is accepted in most workplaces'.

One obvious gap (between what would help individuals compared to what organizations currently offer) is the dearth of part-time roles at senior levels. This may partly explain the reluctance some feel about taking maternity leave, though not all take the approach of Marissa Mayer, Yahoo's Chief Executive. She returned to full-time work only two weeks after the birth of her son and has since created a public debate over her decision to cancel all 'working at home' options that had existed for many staff in the company (Warrell, 2013).

It might be reasonable to expect that the situation has improved for younger women but our research does not seem to indicate this is always the case and we came across a number of negative stereotypes about young working mothers. As one woman said: 'If colleagues in the rest of my organization realized I have a young family they will assume that I don't want a career.' One person, working for an international hotel, said that support from her family had been a key factor in helping her career: 'Without their support I would never have been able to work at senior level. Without the support of your family – whether it is time, availability and psychological support – it would not be possible to succeed.'

And as she points out this is not simply a gender issue: 'In my mind it doesn't matter whether you are a man or a woman, you need your family support if you want to grow in your career.' It is true, and these pressures may apply to men as well as to working women. This is also supported by UK research that identified a number of issues for women returning to work after maternity leave. The survey looked at the experience of new mothers returning to work and found that 14.8 per cent of mothers did not have a job to return to after taking maternity leave, and 11 per cent of women said they had been replaced by the person who had been in their role temporarily as maternity leave cover (Slater and Gordon Lawyers, 2013).

A recent development is the small but increasing number of long-distance commuting couples – sometimes from one part of the country to another, or perhaps with a family based in the UK and a commute to Germany, or commuting between Austria and the UK (Clegg, 2013).

Flexibility on the part of organizations would make a big difference – one woman at a senior operational level has the flexibility to distribute her five days of work across seven days according to what suits her best. One organization imposed a rule for all women returning from maternity leave – they could work whatever hours they wished. (Previously, managers had been reluctant to accept anything less than return to full-time work.) The change made a significant difference to the number of women returning, making it easier for them to work part-time if they wished to.

CONCLUSION AND RECOMMENDATIONS

There are a number of reasons why large organizations struggle with diversity issues and getting more women at senior and board level, not least because it is a complex issue, as highlighted by Eagly and Carli (2007). There is sometimes a mistaken belief that it is the type of project that only needs a single injection of energy and attention. Think instead of any other change project where success is important – a consistent, continuing approach is required with clear measures of success so that progress (or lack of progress!) can be regularly reviewed.

Another option that makes a difference is when diversity is dealt with in the same way as other business topics. A plan, measures of success and a supportive environment that will help change the organizational culture as necessary are not always evident when it comes to diversity issues. The role of the organization is critical and there are many practical approaches that will improve the situation for women. Career support is important, access to coaching and mentoring also helps and an awareness of potential gender differences such as Judith Baxter's work (2011) about how women business leaders use language. Some women get trapped in support roles – such as marketing, PR and HR – and may lack key financial knowledge, an essential for most senior executive roles. Anne Mulcahy, who was appointed as Chief Executive at Rank Xerox in 2000, talks about this dilemma (George, 2008). Outstanding in terms of marketing and sales success, she had been with the company for many years. However, Anne's knowledge base did not include corporate finance and she describes how in those early days her reliance on the financial expertise of colleagues helped with key meetings with shareholders and analysts. A mentoring or coaching programme that aimed to provide key finance, logistics, operational and international experience would be an easy way for many organizations to help women at middle management levels to acquire such key knowledge.

Organizations sometimes believe that if equality issues have been reviewed once then that is all that is required. In fact, the opposite approach is necessary – it is important to maintain a constant focus on equality (as well as measuring success). One organization has a simple traffic light system to assess each department on equality issues – something that interestingly created some healthy competition between different business areas. One multinational, Cisco, has identified a number of 'enablers' (Hewlett, 2009) including:

- accountability – clear targets and global diversity leaders for all regions;
- mentoring – global as well as local schemes for key people;
- the organizational culture – embedding the importance of diversity and inclusion into every level of the organizational chart.

There are a number of ways organizations can make a difference, not least by including women's career development as an agenda item in key business meetings. Others include:

- Looking at different ways to create a women-friendly working environment and consider work/life balance issues (Watson, 2013).
- Looking at ways to sponsor initiatives that will help create more opportunities for women. For example, L'Oréal has sponsored the

UNESCO Awards and fellowship scheme 'Science needs Women' for 15 years – www.facebook.com/forwomeninscience.
- Helping senior managers to understand more about women's careers is important. Cisco Chief Executive John Chambers sent copies of Sheryl Sandberg's book *Lean In* to his senior team as 'background reading'.
- Measuring progress, such as asking employees regularly in staff surveys whether their manager supports their efforts to balance work and life – the results are positive in one organization that uses this question and 89 per cent say that this does happen.
- Improving career development support and signposting for women.
- Offering leadership development also makes a difference. A number of employers such as Johnson & Johnson, Cisco, BT and Ernst & Young offer women's leadership programmes and an initiative introduced by diversity director Fleur Bothwick at Ernst & Young is regular career review discussions for women (Devi, 2013).

An interesting follow-up support structure after attending a leadership programme is used by Geeta Sheker and Beatrix Dart (Stupavsky, 2013). A programme for senior women at Rotman Business School includes support groups – described as Personal Advisory Boards – that operate after the programme is finished. Each group connects five or perhaps seven individuals and offers them a strong support structure to help with professional and leadership issues such as the following:

- Helping women to build a profile or personal 'brand', which helps them to be seen as 'can do' achievers; offering a range of developmental opportunities, temporary leadership appointments and job shadowing (Ibarra et al., 2013). Setting up a women's leadership programme is helpful. Apart from the skills offered it provides individuals with a strong network of others who are at similar career stages so that they can support each other.
- Providing mentoring and coaching opportunities for women at different levels of the business; this is particularly important to help women make that move from senior up to the next director-level appointment. As one woman commented in our research: 'When I went into my first board meeting I'd had no help or advice – I was the only woman and it was tough to find out just how I should behave.' There are still few role models – Carly Fiorina's biography published back in 2006 about her time as Chief Executive at Hewlett Packard is one example and the football director Karren Brady's biography (2013) is another. Others include Karen Linder's book

in 2012 about the women working with Warren Buffet at Berkshire Hathaway. Sheryl Sandberg's book *Lean In* is candid in revealing her experiences in a senior role at Facebook and some of the issues that block women's careers. She highlights the value of setting out an 18-month career plan as well as a long-term plan – and organizations that encourage this type of approach, and those that mix coaching with career development, invariably find that more change occurs.

- Identifying places, roles, and different management levels in the business where there is a lack of women. Finding out why and setting out to resolve the issue using a mix of short-term three-month plans as well as longer 18-month plans. Practical plans, along with senior-level support, will make a difference. All Nestlé businesses have annually reviewed local action plans to improve gender balance.
- Ensuring pay and bonus awards are not gender biased. Mika Brzezinski's book (2012) highlights continuing inequality in the USA and this also exists in many other countries. Often there may be a gender bias in promotions, as noted by Ibarra et al. (2010).

Of course, individual women have a part to play in all of this but it is organizations prepared to take action that will make the difference. What often goes wrong is that too much emphasis is placed on women to simply be more ambitious, organize their own career plan and also to 'fit in' to what often is a demanding all-hours requirement of many jobs. The long-hours working culture affects many professions including law (Oxford Insight, 2010). The pressures of moving around for career opportunities can be considerable and there also are the additional demands of jobs with a lot of travel or the expectation that travel can happen at 'a moment's notice'.

If more organizations raised their sights higher and aim to be 'best in class' in terms of creating a working culture that is more women friendly then a good deal more change will happen. There is no mystery about diversity issues and why so many organizations find it far more difficult than expected. The more organizations understand that diversity issues and women's career development are a business issue and treat them that way – rather than setting up a few ad hoc support groups or imposing HR projects – the more likely they are to create significant change.

The need to treat diversity as a mainstream business issue remains a significant challenge. Organizations that do not understand the business value simply create a few policy documents rather than making substantive changes in their organizational culture, working hours, career development or talent management programmes.

REFERENCES

Armstrong, C. (2013), 'The power mums', *Management Today*, April, 34–8.
Barclays (2013), *Barclays Bank PLC Annual Report 2013*, accessed March 2014 at http://reports.barclays.com/ar13/servicepages/downloads/files/barclays_bank_annual_report_2013.pdf.
Baxter, J. (2011), 'Survival or success? A critical exploration of the use of "double-voiced discourse" by women business leaders in the UK', *Discourse & Communication*, 5(3), 231–45.
Brady, K. (2013), *Strong Woman: The Truth About Getting to the Top*, London: Harper Collins.
Broadbridge, A. (2007), 'Dominated by women: managed by men? The career development process of retail managers', *International Journal of Retail & Distribution Management*, 35(12), 956–74.
Brzezinski, M. (2011), *Knowing Your Value: Women, Money and Getting What You're Worth*, New York: Weinstein Publishing.
Clegg, A. (2013), 'The trials of long-distance lives', *The Financial Times*, 7 February.
Costello, M. (2013), 'The glass ceiling proves to be tough', *The Times*, 6 March.
Davidson, M.J. and R.J. Burke (eds) (2004), *Women in Management Worldwide: Facts, Figures, and Analysis*, Aldershot, UK and Burlington, MA: Ashgate.
Dent, F. and V. Holton (2012), 'How women can navigate to become global leaders', *Global Focus: The EFMD Business Magazine*, 6(2), 40–43.
Desvaux, G., S. Devillard-Hoellinger and P. Baumgarten (2007), *Women Matter: Gender Diversity, a Corporate Performance Driver*, New York: McKinsey & Company.
Devi, S. (2013), 'Working for progress across a firm with global reach', *The Financial Times*, 20 February.
Dey, I. and O. Shah (2013), 'Sexism stalks Square Mile. An everyday story of the City's bias against women', *The Sunday Times*, 24 March.
Dinolfo, S. and J.S. Nugent (2010), 'Making mentoring work', New York: Catalyst, accessed May 2014 at http://www.catalyst.org./knowledge/making-mentoring-work-0.
Duehr, E.E. and J.E. Bono (2006), 'Men, women, and managers: are stereotypes finally changing?', *Personnel Psychology*, 59(4), 815–46.
Eagly, A.H. and L.L. Carli (2007), *Through the Labyrinth: The Truth About How Women Become Leaders*, Boston, MA: Harvard Business School Press.
Economist, The (2011), 'Still lonely at the top', *The Economist*, 399(8743), 61–3.
Fels, A. (2004), 'Do women lack ambition?', *Harvard Business Review*, 82(4), 50–60.
Fiorina, C. (2006), *Tough Choices: A Memoir*, London and Boston, MA: Nicholas Brealey.
Fontanella-Khan, J. (2012), 'Brussels drops women board quota plans', *The Financial Times*, 23 October.
George, B. (2008), 'America's best leaders: Anne Mulcahy, Xerox CEO', *US News*, 19 November, accessed March 2014 at http://www.usnews.com/news/best-leaders/articles/2008/11/19/americas-best-leaders-anne-mulcahy-xerox-ceo.
Hammond, V. and V. Holton (1993), 'The scenario for women managers in Britain in the 1990s', *International Studies of Management & Organization*, 23(2), 71–91.
Hewlett, S.A. (2009), 'Creating a sustainable inclusion and diversity strategy: build on your company's goals and strengths', accessed November 2014 at http://www.cisco.com/web/about/ac49/ac55/resource/archive_strategy.html.
Holton, V. and F.E. Dent (2012a), 'Women in business: a blueprint for individuals and organisations', *360 The Ashridge Journal*, Autumn, 30–37.
Holton, V. and F.E. Dent (2012b), *Women in Business: Navigating Career Success*, Basingstoke, UK and New York: Palgrave Macmillan.
Ibarra, H., N.M. Carter and C. Silva (2010), 'Why men still get more promotions than women', *Harvard Business Review*, 88(9), 80–85.
Ibarra, H., R. Ely and D. Kolb (2013), 'Women rising: the unseen barriers', *Harvard Business Review*, 91(9), 60–67.

International Labour Organization (2012), *Global Employment Trends for Women*, Geneva: ILO.
James, P. and V. Wark (1995), 'Replacing the ladders', *People Management*, **1**(11), 28–32.
Linder, K. (2012), *The Women of Berkshire Hathaway: Lessons from Warren Buffett's Female CEOs and Directors*, Hoboken, NJ: Wiley.
Mattis, M.C. (2001), 'Advancing women in business organizations: key leadership roles and behaviors of senior leaders and middle managers', *Journal of Management Development*, **20**(4), 371–88.
Mavin, S. (2008), 'Queen bees, wannabees, and afraid to bees: no more "best enemies" for women in management?', *British Journal of Management*, **19**(1), S75–S84.
Medland, D. (2013), 'Fundamental change could take "at least a generation"', *The Financial Times, Women and the Workplace Special Supplement*, 21 February.
Miller, C.C. (2011), 'For incoming IBM chief, self-confidence rewarded', *New York Times*, 27 October, 1–1.
Opportunity Now Campaign, see http://opportunitynow.bitc.org.uk for more information.
Oxford Insight (2010), *Obstacles and Barriers to the Career Development of Women Solicitors*, London: The Law Society.
Paris, L.D. and D.L. Decker (2012), 'Sex role stereotypes: does business education make a difference?', *Gender in Management*, **27**(1), 36–50.
Perrons, D. (2009), 'Women and gender equity in employment: patterns, progress and challenges', *IES Working Papers*, No. WP23, Brighton: Institute for Employment Studies.
Rubery, J., M. Smith and C. Fagan (1999), *Women's Employment in Europe: Trends and Prospects*, London and New York: Routledge.
Sandberg, S. and N. Scovell (2013), *Lean In: Women, Work and the Will to Lead*, London/ New York: W.H. Allen and Alfred A. Knopf.
Sanders, I. (2012), 'Technology's gender barrier', *The Financial Times*, 27 October.
Schein, V.E. (2001), 'A global look at psychological barriers to women's progress in management', *Journal of Social Issues*, **57**(4), 675–88.
Scott, J.L., R. Crompton and C. Lyonette (eds) (2010), *Gender Inequalities in the 21st Century: New Barriers and Continuing Constraints*, Cheltenham, UK and Northampton, MA, USA: Edward Elgar Publishing.
Sealy, R., S. Vinnicombe and V. Singh (2008), 'The pipeline to the board finally opens: women's progress in FTSE 100 boards in the UK', in S. Vinnicombe, V. Singh, R.J. Burke, D. Bilimoria and M. Huse (eds), *Women on Corporate Boards of Directors: International Research and Practice*, Cheltenham, UK and Northampton, MA, USA: Edward Elgar Publishing.
Shellenbarger, S. (2012), 'The XX factor: what's holding women back?', *Wall Street Journal*, 7 May.
Slater and Gordon Lawyers (2013), *No Mother's Day Celebration for Women Returning from Maternity Leave*, accessed March 2014 at www.slatergordon.co.uk/media-centre/press-releases/2013/03/no-mothers-day-celebration-for-women-returning-from-maternity-leave/.
Stupavsky, A. (2013), 'Making boardroom equality a reality', *University of Toronto Magazine*, Autumn.
Tranor, J. (2012), 'Women in the boardroom: Vince Cable urges top firms to diversify boards', *The Guardian*, 30 November.
Vinnicombe, S. (2011), 'Reflections on "locks and keys to the boardroom"', *Gender in Management: An International Journal*, **26**(3), 196–9.
Warrell, M. (2013), 'Back into the office! 3 reasons Marissa Mayer has made a smart move', *Forbes Magazine*, 27 February.
Warren, T. (2010), 'Penalties of part-time work across Europe', in J. Scott, R. Crompton and C. Lyonette (eds), *Gender Inequalities in the 21st Century: New Barriers and Continuing Constraints*, Cheltenham, UK and Northampton, MA, USA: Edward Elgar Publishing, pp. 102–22.
Watson, S. (2013), 'Tough at the top', *The Sunday Times Style Magazine*, 24 March.

16. How some women achieve success
Adelina M. Broadbridge

Over the last five decades research has been conducted on women in the labour force and management and various legislation has been passed, yet it remains the case that women have difficulty in advancing their careers (Barreto et al., 2009; Davidson and Burke, 2011) and are under-represented in managerial positions across most of the countries in the world (Berry and Bell, 2012; Office for National Statistics, 2013). Although some progress has indeed been made since the 1970s, some would argue this is relatively slow. In 1974 just 2 per cent of women occupied management positions in the UK (Equal Opportunities Commission, 2006), by 1988 this was around 12 per cent (Davidson, 1991), and now it is around a third (34.8 per cent) of managers (Office for National Statistics, 2013). This is against an employment rate for women of over two-thirds (67.2 per cent) in the UK, an increase from 53 per cent in 1971 (Office for National Statistics, 2014). The gender pay gap also remains high in Europe (Eurostat, 2014). Women continue to be under-represented in top executive positions (Eagly and Sczesny, 2009; Deloitte, 2012; Sharma, 2014) and where women do hold board positions they are much more likely to be non-executive posts rather than the more powerful executive positions (Vinnicombe et al., 2014, p.4). Bruckmuller and Branscombe (2010) comment that there is clear evidence that gender discrimination still exists in higher management, albeit operating somewhat more subtly.

Much of the literature on women's career development has justifiably concentrated on the barriers women encounter when attempting to advance their careers, many of which are discussed throughout the chapters in this handbook. However, as women aspire to more senior positions, they do have to consider how their own behaviours and perceptions fit with those associated with successful careers in their organizations (Davidson and Cooper, 1992; Vinnicombe and Singh, 2002), which are most often deemed to be characteristically male. Tienari et al. (2013) showed that executive search consultants and their clients contribute to the reproduction of male dominance in top management, and Holgersson (2013) pointed to the homosociality in recruiting managing directors and the preference for certain men and the exclusion of women. As Hanappi-Egger (see Chapter 4 of this handbook) argues, women tend to accept the social construction of masculine norms and adapt to the male gender script of managers and so gender hierarchies in management are maintained and reproduced.

The position taken in this chapter is to examine the position of women who have seemingly overcome such barriers, broken through the glass ceiling and are managing and leading at the top of their organizations. The purpose is to hear from successful women on what they perceive has helped them in their careers to date to see if lessons can be learnt regarding the advice to pass on to other women in their career development. The data come from a series of interviews with women at executive and operating board level in UK retail companies. Retailing as a sector was selected as it is an important employer of women and evidence exists to suggest that women are more likely to be employed in retail management positions than in other occupational sectors (Singh and Vinnicombe, 2004; Broadbridge, 2008, 2010; Corporate Women Directors International, 2013).

The 1990s saw the growth of the protean career (Hall and Mirvis, 1996), which involves independence and self-directed career behaviour (Hall, 1976) where employees take responsibly for, influence and adapt their own career management (Brousseau et al., 1996; Sullivan, 1999; Baruch, 2004; Sturges et al., 2010). Career self-management behaviour includes boundary management, networking, visibility, positioning, influencing, validating and building human capital, as well as being mobility oriented. It is influenced by an individual's career goals, the stage of their career and whether they want to stay in the same organization or move elsewhere. Organizations can encourage career self-management by providing developmental opportunities and career management interventions. Individual career management antecedents include personality traits (for example, self-esteem, extraversion and proactivity), work attitudes and gender (Sturges et al., 2010). Moreover, the protean career addresses whole life concerns and is not based *solely* on advancement (Hall and Mirvis, 1996) as traditional career models tend to be. Being engaged in work that makes a contribution to society and achieving work–life balance are two values that drive protean careers (Sargent and Domberger, 2007). As such, it is more useful for understanding women's careers (Cabrera, 2009).

However, there remain some problems concerning the protean model and gender issues. It regards the person (as opposed to the organization) as managing their career without challenging the underlying structure and culture of organizations, thus men's position is likely to continue to be privileged, enabling them to 'manage' their careers more efficiently and effectively than women. Although a protean career relates closely to an individual's accumulation of human capital, something that within the working environment is typically lower for women than men, it ignores the relative power of the management structures against the individual person to decide on who in the organization gets the experiences and opportunities necessary to develop one's career. It has received further criticism as being only relevant to elite professionals who have the power to be mobile or change their careers at will (Briscoe and Hall, 2006). Nevertheless, the notion of career self-management is one that is useful to understand the position of many high-achieving women.

SUCCESSFUL WOMEN

Of course, against adversity, some women have been successful in achieving senior positions in management and we need to explore the facilitators they encountered. Previous work has proposed that creating networks and mentoring programmes and having more diversity on committees are good organizational strategies for increasing women's leadership (Kalev et al., 2006). Baruch and Reis (Chapter 21 in this handbook) allude to the fact that acquiring social capital drives job promotion and job searches. As well as networking, Shapiro et al. (Chapter 13 in this handbook) discuss a person's belief in their own ability to succeed and the degree of risk-taking they are prepared to get involved with as facilitators in their careers. In a quantitative study, Broadbridge (2008) found that both women and men retail managers attributed their success to individual factors (for example, their own determination and attitude to work, attitude of mind, their performance, interpersonal skills and breadth of experience). Attracting support from those above them was also regarded as important, as was acquisition of relevant skills and being accepted by the organization. As stated at the beginning of the chapter, it is not all doom and gloom and some progress has been made over the previous five decades. As Vinnicombe et al. (2014, p. 4) note when considering the number of women on the FTSE 100 companies:

> This year we have seen three major breakthroughs on FTSE 100 boards: the percentage of women on them has broken the 20% level (20.7%), the number of women on them has exceeded the 200 mark (205) and the number of all male boards has dropped to two. (Vinnicombe et al., 2014, p. 4)

What is more, seven retail companies feature within the top 20 companies, totalling 21 women directors (five of whom hold executive as opposed to non-executive directorships). This certainly looks promising for the retail sector versus other sectors in the FTSE 100 listed companies. So is it possible to learn some lessons from them?

METHODOLOGY

Using the FTSE 350 list of retail directors, the population of women executive and non-executive retail board directors were contacted to participate in an in-depth interview. This population is small – for example, in 2014 this comprised only 33 women. Some of these initial contacts led to referrals to directors and senior executives (operating at board level) in large multiple non-listed companies. In total, 12 men and 13 women main board directors and senior executives were interviewed. The present analysis in this chapter draws on the 13 women respondents' narratives. The sample of women comprised nine senior executive directors and four main board directors; eight specialists and five general managers. Ten of the women were university graduates, while seven had other professional qualifications. Their ages ranged from 39 to 56 and 12 of the women were married or cohabiting. Two of the 13 were voluntarily childless, while the remaining 11 women with children all combined career and child rearing (note: nine had more than one child). The interviews were structured around broad themes (for example, perceived facilitators, barriers, influences, sacrifices, future ambitions, non-working lives), which were used as a base to develop the conversations, rather than superimpose a series of rigid questions that might introduce an interviewer bias to the process. Respondents were free and encouraged to talk about these themes in as much or little depth as they felt necessary; the intention was for the respondents to express their own accounts in their own terms.

Interviews were recorded and full transcriptions produced as a basis for data analysis. They were analysed through a process of 'immersion' (Marshall, 1981) and the content was analysed for their themes at various levels. The approach to the material involved trying to appreciate the inherent patterns from the data rather than impose preconceived ideas on the data. This chapter concentrates on the factors that these women attributed to advancing their careers, which may provide useful advice to others who want to progress theirs.

FACILITATORS IN CAREERS

Following the theme of this part of the book – 'Getting On' – the analysis in this chapter concentrates on what the women directors perceived to be the main facilitators in their careers, to see if a pattern emerged that could be translated to others starting their careers. Analysis of the transcripts surfaced various factors the women perceived to have facilitated their careers. The women did not all share the same experiences in their career development to date, demonstrating that career paths can be difficult to negotiate and understand (Oakley, 2000; Eagly and Carli, 2007). Nonetheless, what the analysis did reveal was the relative importance of the emergence of some key themes that have helped in the women's career development. These may prove to be potential keys to those wanting to get on in the future. They can be categorized into three broad categories: 'self-efficacy', 'education, training and experience' and 'the influence of others'. We discuss these in turn, although in reality their influences overlap and for many women it has been a combination of factors that have led to the success in their careers.

Self-efficacy – Own Characteristics, Abilities and Personalities

When asked the question, 'What did they consider to be the main facilitators in their careers to date?', the majority of the respondents mentioned their own natural ability and the importance of self-belief and being in control of their career development. They acknowledged that they themselves had played an active part in their success stories, drawing on their own individual factors. From all their stories the issue of confidence was at the fore.

Several had an inner confidence instilled from an early stage in their career: 'I was so determined because I felt confident in my own ability' (Julie), and, 'It was those sort of formative days [early in career] I think that have kind of given me the courage and the confidence to know I can do it' (Lyn). Sandra explained that being given responsibility early in your career and getting an early promotion builds up your confidence and with that, success: 'I believe confidence is incredibly important in terms of success.' Lisa recommended that women accept praise in order to build confidence:

> If someone tells you something good about yourself, believe them because so often we [women] don't believe, and if you don't believe why should anyone else? So if you can kind of master that one, that goes a long way to just inner self-confidence, which goes a long way to making decisions that are more about what you can do and less about what you can't do. It makes a big difference.

For others their confidence had been boosted (again, early on) from their upbringing and education. Much of this confidence has been imbued in them from significant others and/or their education (see below). In addition to confidence, there was some agreement over the type of person you are (which, of course, is potentially linked to confidence) that helped in progressing your career. Lyn attributed part of her success to her bubbly personality and her appetite for life. Frances wanted to 'prove her worth', while Hazel said, 'I just get on and do it'. Tracey believed, 'you have to learn fairly quickly to have a voice and to have an opinion and to be prepared to voice that opinion'. Later in her interview she explained, 'what I work out in organizations is who do I need to know, how can I help them'. Margaret explained, 'one of the reasons I think I got on is I never over-promised and always delivered what they needed but part of that involves working all the hours God sends and not whinging about it'. Many others (especially those with children) explained how time was paramount in their success stories, so Hazel stated, 'I'm very disciplined about how I use my time' and Sandra managed by 'planning and thinking'.

Alongside their self-belief and personality was their attitude to the job and a strong sense of work engagement, business acumen and drive to succeed. The majority of the women explained how their own hard work and energy, and at times their competitiveness, had helped in their careers. For example, Frances attributed her success to: 'I'd say a lot of bloody work, sheer hard work and force of will', while Jenny asserted, 'You do have to have a high degree of energy and a desire to want to succeed . . . a bit of determination in order to be successful . . . and a bit of passion and a bit of desire to want to do better than other people.' Janet attributed part of her success to 'your whole attitude to it so I think, you know, a desire to succeed . . . I am incredibly passionate about the business . . . having a proactive attitude', while Lyn declared:

> It's down to me having sheer determination and a massive drive for results, always looking to overachieve, to deliver, to get on at a lot of pace, which I think probably even more so when I have three children to juggle; it makes me even more focused . . . I'll always be pushing – pushing, pushing, pushing.

Volunteering and seeking out opportunities to enrich what you have were also seen to build self-confidence and help increase visibility. Many focused on a strategic outlook in their attitude to work. As Mel revealed:

> I think you have to by nature be quite driven and want to succeed . . . Although my specialism may be HR I always approached the job as running a business first . . . so I've a very commercial view rather than, you know we're just about the people side of it – that's very much secondary really; it's delivering a business strategy through people.

Alongside Mel's strategic outlook, various stories from the women demonstrated how they had put their head above the parapet and made an impact somehow. Lisa explained how at 18, 'I persuaded the owners of the business to let me run the store for six weeks and give me a trial at being the manager'. Tracey also said 'you know [boss] at [company] never came along and said "Tracey will you run Europe for me?" I went to him and said "no-one's looking after this and if we're going to make it work someone does – I'll do it because there's no-one else".' Hazel explained, 'I've almost got this antenna on the top of my head that spots issues before they happen, and can kind of can nip them in the bud and work with the line managers to kind of resolve them'.

Human Capital – Education, Skills and Experiences

Various literature has attributed the importance of human capital acquisition (people's education, qualifications, knowledge, skills, training, and experience) to the development of careers (for example, Becker, 1975; Tharenou et al., 1994; Igbaria and Chidambaram, 1997; Sheridan et al., 1997), and this was echoed by the senior women. Linked to self-belief was an acknowledgement that education was important in building skills. On being asked why she had been noticed by senior management, Fiona explained: 'I stood out from the crowd in the way that I can articulate myself and the way I can think things through and understand what they were saying, pick it up really quickly and add to that conversation which I think is your education.' Lyn talked about how a private education provided a standard of etiquette and decorum in communicating with people. Hazel, when talking about the benefits of her Master's in Business Administration (MBA) programme said: 'I can just talk a different language and understand a different language . . . I ended up a different person.' Mel also acknowledged the extent of appreciation a degree may obtain. She had learnt this from a former male boss who in the early stage of her career had told her to get a degree on the basis that 'not having a degree might hold you back'. Jenny also stated: 'having a degree definitely helps at the start of your career . . . there tends to be a reasonable correlation between somebody with a degree and how smart they are. It's unusual that somebody who's really smart hasn't gone to university.' The importance of education was reinforced later in the interview when she admitted regretting not having gone to 'a better university'. Mel later said, 'I think it's fair to say when you're looking at somebody's CV you do look at both the experience and the skills if you like, the qualifications that they've got so yeah, I think it [a degree] does make a difference'.

With regard to on the job training, there was clear recognition that certain blue chip companies provided a good training ground for a future career. Having these (from any sector) on your CV (résumé) could only be positive. In talking about one of these companies (joined at the beginning of her career) Frances explained: 'the training side of things was very, very strong and the opportunities that I had to go on personal development courses outside the technical ones has stood me in fantastic stead for the rest of my career really ... It gave me the opportunity to move and get other experiences.' Mel also stated: 'I was surprised at how marketable I was and I think when you're inside an organization like M&S [Marks and Spencer PLC] you don't appreciate that other people will look at it and think "that's a good business to cut your teeth in".' Frances also stated, 'you'd do six-month secondments to different departments and it was absolutely invaluable and I had that at such an early stage – it was just sort of imprinted in my DNA then'.

The literature highlighted how lack of breadth of experience could hold women back. Various women talked about their adaptability that brought broad experience. For example, Hilary spoke about how a move to consulting had spurred on her retail career as it had provided her with a much broader experience base, and this had given her exposure to many more kinds of people and companies. Others were proactive in developing their experiences for longer-term career gain even if it involved taking risks. For example, Lyn explained:

> I then thought well actually what I really would like to do to expand my skills is move into sort of core marketing and so I joined the export division. Now to do that I took a bit of a risk because they didn't have a vacancy at the grade I was at – the vacancy was at a lower level, well two grades down actually as a brand manager, and I decided that actually I so wanted to do this that I was prepared to take a risk on myself.

Social Capital – The Influence of Other People

Along with human capital, the acquisition of social capital has received recent research attention in the development of people's careers (for example, Adler and Kwon, 2002). One of the discernible facilitators in the women's careers had been the influence and support of other people. Some of this came from families, and in particular, fathers and husbands. Some spoke about how their father's influence had built their self-confidence and work ethic. Many more attributed the support of their husbands or partners. Interestingly, in certain instances there was a clear reversal of the traditional roles played by the couples. Of the 11 women with partners (all of whom were men), five of their partners did not work, while another worked just four days a week. Moreover, all the women talked about how encouraging and supportive their partners were of their careers. Several women also spoke about the additional domestic help they had in the form of nannies, cleaners and child minders (often mothers or sisters).

Within the work context it was significant from the interviews that almost every woman attributed the influence that other people had made to their careers. This took the form of others providing positive feedback; noticing them in some way, of building their confidence and opening doors for their career development. For the most part every respondent mentioned a few key people who had helped their career development. Although some women did have formal mentors, the majority of these relationships were built on a more informal basis. Several rested on the woman being noticed in some way: 'they decided I had the potential' (Fiona). Lyn told of how individuals had noticed and taken a risk on her. She had one boss who had pushed her into other industry things and enabled her to network with other industry contacts. She summarized this relationship as: 'he's just had this sort of lovely stamp on me I guess over the years but he's still able to help sort of nudge me in the right direction without really knowing it I suppose'. Lyn also spoke of another younger man as a big influence:

> I got a new boss at the time who was a young guy from [major blue chip company], he was also another influence because he had a completely different skill-set, very aggressive, very hard, very cut-throat negotiator but very supportive and he in fact gave me a massive break because he promoted me like about three steps in one go, which was unheard of at the time so I was the youngest senior manager . . . He took a risk on me.

Trust and belief were qualities talked about in several of the interviews and respondents spoke of building bonds with certain others: 'you build up a relationship, they trust you, they know your capabilities' (Margaret); 'I like to be in a position where I can really earn someone's trust and really prove my worth' (Frances); and 'I've also had pretty good sort of mentors and I think you seek out your own mentors typically and they're quite good at sounding boards . . . he was about my dad's age but it was good and I knew that he would always give me honest feedback' (Julie).

Janet said the tangible facilitator for her was 'the people that I've worked with so I've worked with some people who have had absolute faith in me and encouraged me and pushed me on to the next level'. Julie explained, 'usually what happens is you'll have a very good boss . . . She was one of my best early bosses because she believed in me and she gave me structure but enough freedom to get on with it really.' Lisa also claimed, 'facilitators have definitely been to work for a new fledgling company, to work for a female entrepreneur who was formidable . . . she was alpha male . . . but was also so inclusive in her style'.

The impact that confidence building from these women's bosses and mentors came through very strongly in all the interviews. Julie recounted a time earlier in her career when she had been put forward for a new job:

> I was quite hesitant when she proposed me for this level I went 'Oh no, I don't think I'm ready' and so she said 'No, I absolutely believe in you, I think you are'

and I think it takes people to say they believe in you and put you forward and put a support network round you and I'm conscious that I try and do that with my team now because that gave me a real step up.

Hilary explained how an earlier boss had let her do what she wanted, which was a great confidence booster, while Margaret said, 'It's their belief in you isn't it? They help you have self-belief because they believe in you and I think that's probably more important for a woman than it is for a man.' Sandra also felt that other people built up her confidence and Tracey also stated, 'what he did really well was put me in touch with the reality of what work was and made me stand up for myself and get some confidence pretty quickly'.

Summing up the influence of her mentors Lyn stated, 'they gave me the wings to go on and do it'. Tracey's account of the driving forces in her career summarizes many of the women's stories about their mentors:

I'd say one of the big facilitators in my career is I have worked for some fantastic people, people who challenge the way I've thought, who listen and who have given me room to work. They've given me the freedom to go and do stuff in my way. We'll have great debates about what, how, when, why, and they'll be very, lots of different sorts of challenging people.

DISCUSSION

This chapter has revealed the factors that women retail senior managers and directors attributed to their own successful career journeys. The combination of self, human capital and social capital work together to be a powerful force in the careers of senior women. As Cook and Glass (2014, pp. 91–2) assert: 'While barriers exist, they are penetrable under certain conditions.' In some respects the career facilitators reported by these women are not dissimilar to previous literature on career development issues, nor do they vary strongly from the men interviewed. So what experiences have made these women stand out from other women and enable them to reach the high positions in their organizations?

One is that one's own self-belief and confidence is a major asset to secure, and, arguably, success cannot be achieved without it. In fact, self-belief and confidence may be 'the' underlying facilitator in these women's careers. Lack of self-confidence has been debated as a common problem for many women in their careers (Simpson et al., 2004; Broughton and Miller, 2009; Cancer Research, 2014; Silvera, 2014) although Sandberg (2013) stresses that women need confidence to reach for opportunities. This is owing to socialization processes and the ways organizations have been constructed along masculine norms so that the ideal worker is strongly associated with the masculine; women in comparison are 'othered', seen as different or devalued or 'outsiders within' (Davies, 1996; Hanappi-Egger, 2012; Bleijenbergh et al., 2013; Wilson, 2014). No wonder under such circumstances many women might be seen to lack confidence. All the women in this research exhibited a lot of self-confidence acquired via their own capabilities, their families, education and support of others. The provision of education had bestowed on them a heightened sense of self-confidence. These are important factors for the future of women's career development.

It is clear that confidence and career success are interrelated, and the earlier this is built the better. Ideally, confidence should be instilled in childhood and reinforced through educational systems. As women have traditionally lacked confidence it is even more important that they develop this before getting to the work environment. In the work environment, education, training and experience can no doubt boost confidence even further and help to place women on more equitable terms with men. Even the choice of companies to apply to may make a difference to how a person's career is managed. For example, early on in people's careers blue chip companies are perceived as clear facilitators: they open up opportunities for individuals as well as potentially setting them up in the rest of their career.

For many of the women their success stories began at an early age. Right from the outset of their careers they had performed well, shown initiative, taken control and become noticed; with that came support, sponsorship and mentoring from bosses and significant others in (and outside) the organization. In turn, this augmented confidence and self-belief. They were very motivated by and engaged in their work, and self-belief had enabled them to become very driven in their careers and strive for exceptional performance. They put themselves forward, were not afraid to put their heads above the parapet and as a result became noticeable to important others who realized their potential and achievements. Their self-esteem, extraversion and proactive behaviours were all linked to their career self-management (Sturges et al., 2010).

While mentoring is said to be good for career development (Bozionelos et al., 2011; Woolnough and Fielden, 2014), none of the women talked about these relationships in a formal sense. However, the power of informal mentors where the relationship developed naturally was paramount. Thinking of this it might be because of the ease with which these mentors (many of whom were men) assisted the women's careers: in a formal relationship this might be less apparent. It was particularly noticeable that the influence of various men in their lives had in the main helped rather than hindered their careers and opposes ideas of homosociality (Holgersson, 2013). This was either through the confidence bestowed on the women by their fathers at an early age; their partners who had celebrated and championed their careers; and notably the support of a male boss or mentor. So while many organizational cultures, and the men within them, can act as a deterrent to women's careers, there are some men in senior positions who recognize the potential women have at an early age and encourage and nurture their development. Several of the women talked about these men being like father figures in their lives. There is no doubt that the support of these men had been a massive driver and it would be interesting to interview these men and find out what it is about them that supports and enables women to get on in the workplace. Perhaps they are senior enough to not feel threatened by the young talent entering the organization? Their behaviour may be drawing on social exchange theory (Blau, 1964), which suggests that the support they provide encourages reciprocal behaviour from the employee in the form of job performance and organizational citizenship. Nevertheless, they are *not* using homosocial behaviour and appointing in their own image (Kanter, 1977) when championing these women and many lessons can be learned from their behaviours.

The women in this study were not necessarily 'superwomen' juggling their career with their non-work arena. For the most part these women were not primarily responsible for household and family obligations, and so their approach to work enabled them to demonstrate complete commitment and loyalty (see Ford and Collinson, 2011). As over half of the women in a relationship had partners that were not in work, this enabled the women to focus and forge ahead with their careers and not have to consider the career of their partner when making decisions about their own. A couple of women said they would recommend that other women have their children early on in their career, explaining that it is easier to return to a fairly junior job after having children than a more senior position at a later stage.

CONCLUSION

This chapter has concentrated on the factors that have enabled senior women to get on in their careers. While it might be criticized for concentrating on a small number of women directors from one sector, retailing, it has uncovered some findings that are worthy of further investigation. From the findings it can be deduced that the personal characteristics an individual has, together with their education, training, experience and influence from significant others, can have considerable impact on their career development. A key to this was benefitting from all of these factors early in their careers and using this to build their confidence and networks. In summary, it may be concluded that the key issues for women regarding their career development is how their careers are integral with their confidence and own self-beliefs. In the main these women began developing and accelerating their careers early on: they had an ability to think out of the box and have the confidence to express their ideas and beliefs. This essential need for a confident approach was often nurtured by their education, families and also through the impact of having a natural mentor or sponsor early in their careers. Future research would be useful to gain a more complete understanding of how these women gained so much self-belief and confidence at an early age. The factors that have assisted in this no doubt will hold an important key to understanding their career success and progression. Talking to those in the positions of control and decision-making in companies is also valuable, especially those senior men who take women under their wings and develop their talents.

These women were also driven; they were prepared to do what it took to move forward, even if this meant mobility, long working hours and various sacrifices. They also had an ability to be transformational and transactional as the task demanded and an ability to be adaptable and flexible in their application of management styles. Various findings do reflect an unquestioning acceptance of the dominance of a male cultural norm, for example, driven and competitive behaviour, thrusting to push their career on no matter what, demonstrating total commitment and loyalty to the organization, which usually requires long hours, and being single-minded in their career rather than achieving a balanced lifestyle, getting childbearing out of the way so as to focus on career advancement. Nevertheless, alongside this, these women were very strong minded and had additionally attracted the support of senior men in the organization who could recognize their worth and were prepared to help push their career.

Moreover, adopting a self-management (Sturges et al., 2010) or protean approach (Hall and Mirvis, 1996) to your own career and taking a strategic vision as to where you want to be in the future is a clear career development facilitator. Quoting from Lewis Carroll (1865): 'Alice came to a fork in the road and saw a Cheshire cat in a tree. "Which road do I take?" she asked. "Where do you want to go?" was his response. "I don't know," Alice answered. "Then," said the Cat, "it doesn't matter."' By adapting a proactive and strategic approach to one's career it can help the individual to focus on where they truly want to go.

At the beginning of the chapter it was argued that women aspiring to senior positions need to consider how their own behaviours and perceptions fit with those of the company. The influence of prior training and the help of mentors obviously might entail learning from a male model of working. While this was not explicitly explored in the interviews, the extent to which these women, through their narratives, had embraced a male model of working is interesting to reflect upon. As Hazel commented '[Major FTSE 100 retail company] promoted people who fitted, looked right, and said the right things', while Lisa stated: 'If I was a youngster looking today at retail for a career and what does that mean I still would be thinking "I've got to be pretty alpha female to get on."' One might argue that their drive to succeed, sense of business acumen and competitiveness reveals a latent masculine behaviour. Lyn had learned much from the behaviour and skill set of a boss with a very masculine persona. Long hours of work were accepted as routine and work often spilled over in the home arena, leaving them little time for themselves. Risk-taking was also shown to pay off in the long run. These patterns of working do uphold a masculine way of working where commitment, length of the working week and loyalty are supported and reinforced. Moreover, while some women like Fiona recognized some issues of women getting on in organizations, others such as Lyn denied that gender was an issue either to them or in their organization. They did not believe that women face constraints in their careers and speculated that it was all associated with the choices women make. This denial perhaps demonstrates how these women have (unconsciously) accepted the male norms of the business and taken on these characteristics in their thinking. These two issues require further development and will be taken up in future research.

REFERENCES

Adler, P.S. and S.W. Kwon (2002), 'Social capital: prospects for a new concept', *Academy of Management Review*, **27**(1), 17–40.
Barreto, M., M.K. Ryan and M.T. Schmitt (2009), *The Glass Ceiling in the 21st Century: Understanding Barriers to Gender Equality*, Washington DC: American Psychological Association.
Baruch, Y. (2004), *Managing Careers: Theory and Practice*, London: FT Prentice Hall.
Becker, G.S. (1975), *Human Capital*, Chicago, IL: University of Chicago Press.
Berry, D. and M.P. Bell (2012), 'Inequality in organizations: stereotyping, discrimination, and labor law exclusions', *Equality, Diversity and Inclusion: An International Journal*, **31**(3), 236–48.
Blau, P.M. (1961), *Exchange and Power in Social Life*, Edison, NJ: Transaction Publishers.
Bleijenbergh, I.L., M.L. van Engen and C.J. Vinkenburg (2013), 'Othering women: fluid images of the ideal academic', *Equality, Diversity and Inclusion: An International Journal*, **32**(1), 22–35.
Bozionelos, N., G. Bozionelos, K. Kostopoulos and P. Polychroniou (2011), 'How providing mentoring relates to career success and organizational commitment: a study in the general managerial population', *Career Development International*, **16**(5), 446–68.

Briscoe, J.P. and D.H. Hall (2006), 'Special section on boundaryless and protean careers: next steps in conceptualizing and measuring boundaryless and protean careers', *Journal of Vocational Behavior*, **69**(1), 1–3.

Broadbridge, A. (2008), 'Senior careers in retailing: an exploration of male and female executives' career facilitators and barriers', *Gender in Management: An International Journal*, **23**(1), 11–35.

Broadbridge, A. (2010), 'Women at the top in British retailing: plus ça change?', *The Service Industries Journal*, **30**(9), 1–25.

Broughton, A. and L. Miller (2009), *Encouraging Women into Senior Management Positions: How Coaching Can Help*, Research Report No. 462, Brighton: Institute for Employment Studies.

Brousseau, K.R., M.J. Driver, K. Eneroth and R. Larsson (1996), 'Career pandemonium: realigning organizations and individuals', *Academy of Management Executive*, **10**(4), 52–66.

Bruckmuller, S. and N.R. Branscombe (2010), 'The glass cliff: when and why women are selected as leaders in crisis contexts', *British Journal of Social Psychology*, **49**(3), 433–51.

Cabrera, E.F. (2009), 'Protean organizations: reshaping work and careers to retain female talent', *Career Development International*, **14**(2), 186–200.

Cancer Research (2014), *Women Say Lack of Confidence Stops Them Getting to the Top*, accessed 16 July 2014 at http://www.cancerresearchuk.org/about-us/cancer-news/press-release/women-say-lack-of-confidence-stops-them-getting-to-the-top.

Carroll, L. (1865), *Alice's Adventures in Wonderland and Through the Looking Glass*, London: Macmillan.

Cook, A. and C. Glass (2014), 'Women and top leadership positions: towards an institutional analysis', *Gender, Work & Organization*, **21**(1), 91–103.

Corporate Women Directors International (2013), *CWDI Report on Women Directors of Top Retail and Consumer Product Companies Globally*, Washington, DC: CWDI.

Davidson, M.J. (1991), 'Women managers in Britain – issues for the 1990s', *Women in Management Review & Abstracts*, **6**(1), 5–10.

Davidson, M.J. and R.J Burke (2011), *Women in Management Worldwide, Progress and Prospects*, Aldershot, UK: Gower.

Davidson, M.J. and C.L. Cooper (1992), *Shattering the Glass Ceiling: The Woman Manager*, London: Paul Chapman Publishing Ltd.

Davies, C. (1996), 'The sociology of professions and the profession of gender', *Sociology*, **30**(4), 661–78.

Deloitte (2012), *2012 Board Practice Report: Providing Insight into the Shape of Things to Come*, Society of Corporate Secretaries and Governance Professionals and Deloitte Development LLC, accessed 29 May 2014 at http://www.corpgov.deloitte.com/binary/com.epicentric.contentmanagement.servlet.ContentDeliveryServlet/USEng/Documents/Board%20Governance/Deloitte%20Board%20Practices%20Report%202012.pdf.

Eagly, A. and L.L. Carli (2007), *Through the Labyrinth: The Truth About How Women Become Leaders*, Boston, MA: Harvard Business School Press.

Eagly, A. and S. Sczesny (2009), 'Stereotypes about women, men and leaders: have times changed?', in M. Barreto, M.K. Ryan and M.T. Schmitt (eds), *The Glass Ceiling in the 21st Century: Understanding Barriers to Gender Equality*, Washington, DC: American Psychological Association, pp. 21–47.

Equal Opportunities Commission (2006), *Sex and Power: Who Runs Britain? 2006*, Manchester, UK: EOC.

Eurostat (2014), *Gender Pay Gap Statistics*, European Commission, accessed 8 April 2014 at http://epp.eurostat.ec.europa.eu/statistics_explained/index.php/Gender_pay_gap_statistics.

Ford, J.M. and D. Collinson (2011), 'In search of the perfect manager? Work–life balance and managerial work', *Work, Employment and Society*, **25**(2), 257–73.

Hall, D.T. (1976), *Careers in Organizations*, Santa Monica, CA: Goodyear Publishing Company.

Hall, D.T. and P.H. Mirvis (1996), 'The new protean career: psychological success and the path with a heart', in D.T. Hall (ed.), *The Career Is Dead – Long Live the Career*, San Francisco, CA: Jossey-Bass, pp. 15–45.

Hanappi-Egger, E. (2012), '"Shall I stay or shall I go?" On the role of diversity management for women's retention on SET professions', *Equality, Diversity and Inclusion: An International Journal*, **31**(2), 144–77.

Holgersson, C. (2013), 'Recruiting managing directors: doing homosociality', *Gender, Work & Organization*, **20**(4), 454–66.

Igbaria, M. and L. Chidambaram (1997), 'The impact of gender on career success of information systems professionals: a human-capital perspective', *Information Technology & People*, **10**(1), 63–86.

Kalev, A., F. Dobbin and E. Kelly (2006), 'Best practices or best guesses? Assessing the efficacy of corporate affirmative action and diversity policies', *American Sociological Review*, **71**(4), 589–617.

Kanter, R.M. (1977), *Men and Women of the Corporation*, New York: Basic Books.

Marshall, J. (1981), 'Making sense as a personal process', in P. Reason and J. Rowan (eds), *Human Inquiry*, London: Wiley.

Oakley, J.G. (2000), 'Gender-based barriers to senior management positions: understanding the scarcity of female CEOs', *Journal of Business Ethics*, **27**(4), 321–34.

Office for National Statistics (2013), *Women in the Labour Market*, accessed 27 May 2014 at http://www.ons.gov.uk/ons/dcp171776_328352.pdf.

Office for National Statistics (2014), *Labour Market Statistics, March 2014*, accessed 11 April 2014 at http://www.ons.gov.uk/ons/dcp171778_354442.pdf.

Sandberg, S. (2013), *Lean In, Work, and the Will to Lead*, London: W.H. Allen.

Sargent, L.D. and S.R. Domberger (2007), 'Exploring the development of a protean career orientation: values and image violations', *Career Development International*, **12**(6), 545–64.

Sharma, S. (2014), 'Gender diversity on corporate boards – a study of NSE listed companies', *International Journal of Applied Research and Studies*, **3**(2), 1–8.

Sheridan, J.E., J.W. Slocum and R. Buda (1997), 'Factors influencing the probability of employee promotions: a comparative analysis of human capital, organization screening and gender/race discrimination theories', *Journal of Business and Psychology*, **11**(3), 373–80.

Silvera, I. (2014), 'YouGov poll: 44% of women blame themselves for lack of career progression', *International Business Times*, accessed 16 July 2014 at http://www.ibtimes.co.uk/yougov-poll-44-women-blame-themselves-lack-career-progression-1448762.

Simpson, R., J. Sturges, A. Woods and Y. Altman (2004), 'Career progress and career barriers: women MBA graduates in Canada and the UK', *Career Development International*, **9**(5), 459–77.

Singh, V. and S. Vinnicombe (2004), *Women Pass a Milestone: 101 Directorships on the FTSE 100 Boards. The Female FTSE Report 2003*, Cranfield, UK: Cranfield University School of Management.

Sturges, J., N. Conway and A. Liefooghe (2010), 'Organizational support, individual attributes, and the practice of career self-management behavior', *Group & Organization Management: An International Journal*, **35**(1), 108–41.

Sullivan, S.E. (1999), 'The changing nature of careers: a review and research agenda', *Journal of Management*, **25**(3), 457–84.

Tharenou, P., S. Latimer and D. Conroy (1994), 'How do you make it to the top? An examination of influences on women's and men's managerial advancement', *Academy of Management Journal*, **37**(4), 899–931.

Tienari, J., S. Meriläinen, C. Holgersson and R. Bendl (2013), 'And then there are none: on the exclusion of women in processes of executive search', *Gender in Management: An International Journal*, **28**(1), 43–62.

Vinnicombe, S. and V. Singh (2002), 'Sex role stereotyping and requisites of successful top managers', *Women in Management Review*, **17**(3/4), 120–30.

Vinnicombe, S., E. Dolder and C. Turner (2014), *The Female FTSE Board Report 2014*,

Cranfield, UK: Cranfield International Centre for Women Leaders, Cranfield University, School of Management.
Wilson, F. (2014), *Organizational Behaviour and Work: A Critical Introduction*, Oxford: Oxford University Press.
Woolnough, H.M. and S.L. Fielden (2014), 'The impact of a career development and mentoring programme on female mental health nurses: a longitudinal, qualitative study', *Gender in Management: An International Journal*, **29**(2), 108–22.

17. Creating and sustaining positive careers for women: a closer look at organizational context
Janet L. Kottke and Mark D. Agars

In this chapter, we explore the 'getting on' aspect of career advancement for women, with a specific focus on the importance of organizational context. In doing so, we first define contemporary conceptualizations of career success and then discuss briefly the ways in which career success may be perceived differently by women and men. We note that such gender differences in how career success is defined raises questions about the appropriateness of existing organizational efforts to foster employee careers. Despite these differences, we acknowledge that traditional measures of success remain valued; consequently, we review some of the most common barriers to women's success as defined traditionally, to which we make recommendations for organizations to break those barriers. Finally, we address the non-linear career with its attendant solutions and challenges.

WHAT CONSTITUTES CAREER SUCCESS?

At the outset, we need first to clarify that different definitions of career success are in use by researchers and employees. Objective indicators of success include salary, salary growth, number of promotions, as well as placement within the hierarchy of the organization. Alternatively, subjective markers of success refer to the individual's appraisal of his or her success, and include myriad measures such as job and career satisfaction, sense of identity, purpose, and work–life balance (Heslin, 2005). Longstanding approaches to defining career success have focused predominantly on employee attainment of successive promotions into positions with greater and more complex responsibilities and commensurate compensation (ibid.). Indeed, researchers often turn to objective indicators, discounting subjective factors as contaminated with life satisfaction or unrealistic optimism (cf., Ng et al., 2005; Hogan et al., 2013). Typically, the research on objective career success relies on the human capital model (Becker, 1975) as it coincides nicely with the idea that employees are rewarded according to their worth to the organization. Assets an individual brings to the organization (for example, education, previous work experiences) constitute value to the organization, and in turn are used to define success of an individual's career. This emphasis on objective indicators that largely represents financial and status-based accomplishments has increasingly been identified as insufficient, particularly in light of the greater recognition of protean career paths that fundamentally redefine career goals and expectations (Valcour and Ladge, 2008).

Although subjective approaches to assessing career success recognize that individual differences in the perceived value of career-related activities are likely and relevant, the bulk of research on subjective success has emphasized perceptions of career attainments via self-report measures of career and job satisfaction (Ng et al., 2005). Thus, this work has largely failed to consider the extent to which non-work factors may be considered when employees define success. In fact, alternative career models have sprung up to account for the non-linear, protean pathways that some have taken. Some of these models include adaptive preferences (Hakim, 2000), the kaleidoscope career (Mainero and Sullivan, 2006), and the boundaryless career (Arthur et al., 2005). The kaleidoscope career exemplifies changes in how careers may evolve; in this theory, as they age, individuals shift their attention to those aspects of their lives that best match their values and needs. The three key components of the theory are authenticity (alignment of roles with values), balance (equilibrium between work and non-work), and challenge (need for stimulating work). Recent research suggests that those born after the Baby Boomers desire more balance than their predecessors (Sullivan et al., 2009). Considering the generational shifts as well as the changes in how individuals are evaluating their career trajectories, a broader conceptualization may be needed to understand the nature of career success. The need to redefine career success already exists when we examine career differences between men and women.

GENDER DIFFERENCES IN DEFINING CAREER SUCCESS

The 'ideal' of defining career success in terms of ever-increasing compensation and perceived status is less of an ideal for women than it is for men. Many women who intend to become mothers view family and work as either/or propositions, whereas for men, both family and work are conceived as jointly feasible outcomes (Bianchi and Milkie, 2010). Indeed, there are substantial differences in how men and women define their career successes. In a qualitative study of 40 professionals (20 men and

20 women), Dyke and Murphy (2006) found differing themes, in that the greatest percentage of men most highly valued material success, whereas women identified work–life balance and relationships as the most critical indicators of success. Gender differences in career outcomes, however, are not limited to gender-based preferences. Fundamental to the differential career experiences of women and men are social and organizational expectations of men and women as tied to gender roles (Acker, 2012). To begin, while the female gender role has expanded to include work responsibilities, the domain of family, home, and child-rearing responsibilities still falls disproportionately on the shoulders of women (Bianchi and Milkie, 2010), as a commensurate expansion of the male gender role has not occurred (Hook, 2010; Geist and Cohen, 2011). Consequently, it is difficult for women to think about career issues without examining the implications for family.

The sex typing of jobs leading to segregation into lower-status positions for women (International Labour Office, 2010; Crompton and Lyonette, 2011) also demonstrates how organizations remain gendered in ways that affect career outcomes (cf., Kelly et al., 2010). While Crompton and Lyonette reported that women perceived choices about life balance to be the primary explanation for sex segregation (that is, substantially more so than discrimination), certainly the possibility remains that gender differences in career success indicators reflect women's acceptance of these gender-based structural limitations. Qualitative data, for example, suggest that at least for some professional women who made compromises to accommodate non-work demands and circumstances, they would have preferred a more traditional linear career (Schilling, 2012).

Nevertheless, there is mounting sentiment that even for men, the ideal focus of working 40 (or more) hours per week to climb the corporate ladder is less appealing than in eras past (Mainero and Sullivan, 2006). Research on the Millennial generation, for example, suggests that while traditional career-related goals remain important, greater emphasis is also placed on the importance of non-work activities (Ng et al., 2010). Although the limited research on this new population is far from clear (Deal et al., 2010) and some have found that generational differences may be exaggerated (Kowske et al., 2010), an increased consideration of personal life factors among Millennial generation members regularly emerges. Regardless of the pace at which non-work life balance factors become important to a broader segment of the work community, their importance to career outcomes for women is clear. What is also clear is that due to the gendered nature of work and occupations, as well as gender norm disparities in family responsibilities that continue to require most women to be the primary champion of family causes, the objective and subjective indicators of career success are, for the majority of women, inextricably linked. Consequently, for women, 'getting on' in organizations requires a broader consideration of both objective and subjective markers of career success.

BARRIERS TO WOMEN'S ADVANCEMENT

Traditionally Defined Career Pathways

From occupational segregation to gender role typing, a number of authors have summarized barriers to women's career advancement (cf., Kottke and Pelletier, 2013). One framework (Yukl, 2010) that succinctly outlines barriers to women's success suggests the following as primary:

- Women are more likely than men to be placed into dead-end jobs at organizational entry.
- Women are less likely to be sponsored or mentored.
- Women are less likely than men to acquire 'push' assignments that are instrumental to career development.
- Women are more likely to be evaluated harshly for engaging in non-typical roles (that is, leadership and management are perceived to be better done by men, for example, Eagly and Karau, 2002) with women in traditionally female roles not likely to be perceived as having the necessary prerequisites for advancement.
- Limited access to the organizational networks vital to visibility and knowledge of career opportunities.
- Exposure to harassment or other counterproductive behaviours from co-workers.

These barriers are not independent of each other, with several likely to be operating simultaneously. Without qualified mentorship for example, women are less likely to be made aware of the networks and the information from those networks that aid in acquiring challenging work assignments. Comparably, without a strong network or sponsor, a woman is less likely to be visible to decision-makers who select employees for 'push' assignments.

Mentorship, Sponsorship, Networking, or Vital Social Capital

Abundant research indicates that mentors and sponsors help in the orientation to the organization and in identifying career opportunities (Ragins and Cotton, 1999). The quality of the mentor–protégé relationship seems to be especially important to career outcomes, both objective and subjective (Ragins et al., 2000; Wanberg et al., 2003). Networking with peers as well as others at different levels of the hierarchy also has benefits for employees (Hezlett and Gibson, 2007). Research indicates that men and women have comparable numbers of contacts in their networks, but that men's contacts tend to be more influential, given that their contacts are more likely to be men, and of these, men who are more likely to hold positions of power in the organization. Furthermore, men are more likely than women to receive help from their male contacts (McGuire, 2002). Finally, it appears that men use their networks more strategically and instrumentally relative to women who tend to use their networks for social support and to survive in strongly masculine organizational cultures (Broadbridge, 2010). Thus, it should come as little surprise that social capital flows more so to men and that men are more likely to be advanced within organizations using that social capital.

Exposure to Harassment, Incivility, and Bullying

After the US Supreme Court decision that found for Goodyear, Lilly Ledbetter authored a book in which she detailed the pervasive harassment she experienced as (an often) sole female manager at Goodyear (Ledbetter and Lanier, 2013). Sadly, her experience is not unique. Women are more likely to be exposed to harassment (Fitzgerald, 1993; O'Leary-Kelly et al., 2009), incivility, which includes efforts to undermine perceptions of women's competence (Cortina, 2008), and bullying (Salin and Hoel, 2013) in the workplace. Some researchers (Fitzgerald, 1993) have estimated that 40 per cent of working women have been subjected to sexual harassment. Comparably, women are more likely to be bullied than men, although the occupations in which men are more likely to be bullied are instructive; that is, men are more likely to be bullied in occupations generally considered the domain of women (childcare, nursing) (Salin and Hoel, 2013). Similarly, incivility, which is conceived of as ambiguously aimed harm and not specifically gender related, is more often directed at women (Cortina et al., 2013). That women are more often the targets of these workplace behaviours strongly suggests that these behaviours are gendered in nature (Acker, 2012). Prevailing notions about the roots of these harmful behaviours suggest that all stem from the same basis: women are perceived of as interlopers in the workplace and do not fit well within the social strata of organizations, which serve as reproductions of their societies (cf., Glick et al., 2000; Glick and Fiske, 2001; Salin and Hoel, 2013). To be sure, women are not, in all cases, passive victims of these behaviours, and there are actions organizations can take to prevent and mitigate such hostile behaviours that impede women's career advancement.

Lack of Challenging Work Assignments that Lead to Advancement

Challenging work assignments are a critical aspect of advancing professionally. These 'stretch' or 'push' assignments provide individuals with the opportunities to develop new skills and knowledge, and to demonstrate competence that may be applied to other, more complex jobs (McCauley et al., 1995). The research on gender in this area is somewhat equivocal, with outcome differentials probably related to the definition of the challenging work assignment (that is, being asked to turn around a failing company (Ryan and Haslam, 2005) versus tackling a finite task not previously encountered). Most qualitative research suggests that women are simply offered less push assignments, with the corollary that the type of work that women often do has less challenge to begin with (Ohlott et al., 1994; Woodall et al., 1997). Other research suggests that men and women are offered comparable assignments, but that women are less likely to accept them (De Pater et al., 2009b). Two recent studies suggest, however, that women are equally accepting of challenging assignments (De Pater et al., 2009a; King et al., 2012), and other factors that have been suggested above prevent women from being offered these critical developmental opportunities.

'TRADITIONAL' PATHWAYS: BREAKING BARRIERS AND MOVING UP

As can be seen from the foregoing, many authors and researchers have identified key barriers in traditional pathways to women's achievement in the workplace. Here, we identify those that are most salient at the organizational level. Women typically have comparable or greater educational backgrounds relative to men (Lips, 2003, 2013) with the primary individual differential, that of work experience, which is often related to the organizational issue of work requirements (that is, women are more likely to take time off work to care for children or parents than men; International Labour Office, 2010). The following strategies are aimed primarily at the objective measures of career success, but research reveals that career satisfaction also results from these initiatives.

Creating a Culture of Inclusion for Women

Creating a culture of inclusion is the foremost step that organizations can take to provide sufficient support for women. Reward systems, mission statements and ceremonies all communicate to organizational members what is important (Schein, 2004). Furthermore, given the sometimes hostile reception that women receive in non-traditional jobs, it is critical that women-inclusive cultural expectations are clearly conveyed though practices and norms (Bilimori et al., 2008; Hanappi-Egger, 2012). For example, a zero tolerance for bullying and harassment would communicate that all employees are to be respected.

Supportive Leadership

Creating an inclusive culture begins at the top with leadership attuned to the needs of the diverse workforce and willing to fashion a culture that values diversity. Agars and Kottke (2004) and others (Rynes and Rosen, 1995; Thomas, 2006) note that the support of top leadership is key to the development of a satisfying workplace for women and minorities, and for the effective implementation of gender- and diversity-based activities.

Providing Mentoring and Networking Programmes

Research is reasonably clear that men and women have different networks, with men having access to more powerful networks than women. To address this incomparability, formal mentoring programmes (Chao et al., 1992; Blake-Beard, 2001) in which powerful advocates are matched with promising employees could go a long way toward relieving this inequality. Further, making mentors accountable for their protégés' success can also provide an incentive for allies to help women achieve. This has been found to be particularly true for women in male-dominated occupations (Ramaswami et al., 2010). In addition, providing realistic expectations about mentoring and network opportunities may also help all parties to the mentor–protégé relationship: protégés, top management and the organization (cf. O'Neil et al., 2011).

Assessing the Procedures for Performance for Gender Discrimination and Unfair Differentiation

Subtle biases may creep into performance assessment procedures, based on gender role expectations (Lyness and Heilman, 2006). For example, we might expect that women will display more organizational citizenship or leadership consideration behaviours (Kidder, 2002; Loughlin et al., 2011) and when they do not they are penalized in their annual reviews relative to men (cf., Kottke and Agars, 2005). Accordingly, regular monitoring of the processes that are used to evaluate employees and occasional audits of the resulting evaluation documents for differing standards can help alleviate this potential source of inequity.

'NOT SO TRADITIONAL' PATHWAYS: EXPLICITLY BLENDING WORK AND FAMILY OBLIGATIONS

Clearly, there are several organizational approaches that have been demonstrated to enhance career success for women, and we encourage organizations to continue to develop and explore possibilities. It is important to recognize, however, that these solutions have typically targeted objective measures of career success, primarily salary and advancement. As we explore career success beyond traditional objective and subjective measures tied closest to salary and advancement, less guidance is available. Related literature, however, may provide some direction.

Several authors have suggested (Dyke and Murphy, 2006; Smith et al., 2012), and we agree, that researchers should pay more attention to life and family issues when they theorize about and measure career success. Consequently, research on work and family may offer some insight into how to facilitate career success so defined. Indeed, as Bianchi and Milkie (2010) note, the distribution of formal work and family responsibilities is highly gendered, and women shoulder the great majority of family responsibilities. It is not surprising, therefore, that although family responsibilities have been found to have negative effects on subjective and objective measures of career success for all, those effects are significantly stronger for women than for men (Mayrhofer et al., 2008). Similarly, married women work fewer hours than unmarried women, but married men work more hours than unmarried men (Snir and Harpaz, 2006), reflecting the differential value of family factors on career outcomes as a function of gender. Consequently, career-based solutions for women are likely to necessarily include policies and practices that address work and family. That said, this does not mean that organizational work and family practices will lead to more positive perceptions of traditional forms of career success. Indeed, one recent study found that although women value the presence of organization-based work and family programmes, and were more committed to organizations in which they were offered, they did not perceive that such programmes led to opportunities for career advancement (Agars et al., 2011). Consistent with this disconnect, recently there has been a lament about the very limited impact work and family research has had on organizations and their employees (Kossek et al., 2011). Possibly, however, that disconnect is a function of the populations typically studied (cf., Agars and French, 2011), such as an insufficient consideration of gender, in conjunction with a tendency to apply traditional standards of success. Indeed, if career success as defined by non-traditional models of career paths is reconsidered, we likely find great value in the application of work and family programmes and alternative work arrangements for career success.

What is needed to make work–life balance possible? Managing competing work and family issues and alternative work arrangements.

Supportive Leadership

As before, leaders, especially direct supervisors, are in a critical position to influence employee work–life balance because they serve as a bridge between organizational policy and employee activity (Major and Lauzun, 2010). Supportive leader relationships have consistently been tied to reduced work–family conflict (Thomas and Ganster, 1995; Anderson et al., 2002; Frye and Breaugh, 2004; Ford et al., 2007), and employees are less likely to experience work and family conflict if their supervisors are supportive of their need to balance both (Thomas and Ganster, 1995). Leaders also enhance perceptions of balance through the creation of supportive culture around family (Major et al., 2008). Also noteworthy is that work–family culture and informal leader support appear to be more important in improved subjective outcomes (that is, reduced conflict) than formal organizational policies (Premeaux et al., 2007); these leader effects appear to be more important for women than for men (Agars and Tortez, 2013).

Alternative Work Arrangements

Alternative work arrangements refer to employment options such as telecommuting (Kossek et al., 2006), flexible work schedules (Galinski et al., 2004; Kelly and Moen, 2007), reduced workload (Hall et al., 2012), and job sharing (Boeri et al., 2008), which all have the potential to provide employees with greater capacity to manage boundaries and increase control over schedules and competing demands. In presenting a model of work–life balance, Voydanoff (2005) argues for and explicates the importance of boundary management and control to positive work and life outcomes, and the value of control at work has been related to both subjective and objective measures of career success (Moen et al., 2008). Indeed, effective implementation of alternative programmes and policies have the capacity to address non-traditional career factors including reducing work–life conflict (Thomas and Ganster, 1995; Golden et al., 2006), improving health and well-being (Raghuram and Wiesenfeld, 2004; Kossek et al., 2006) and enhancing work attitudes (Golden and Veiga, 2006).

Caveats
Despite their growing use (Bond et al., 2005), there is substantial evidence that alternative work arrangements are not often implemented effectively, and that little guidance is available to organizations or leaders looking to provide such solutions (Kelly and Kalev, 2006). Consequently, despite their potential benefit to health, well-being and effectiveness, managers are often unwilling to offer wide access to such programmes (Kelly and Moen, 2007). As noted earlier, supervisory support is vital to the implementation of these programmes. Lirio et al. (2008) found that not only are managerial behaviours important, but so too are managerial dispositions. For example, in their qualitative study of 83 cases, managers who were supportive of reduced load professionals not only helped to develop part-time options for employees, but also believed that doing so would result in a payoff for the company.

Finally, there is also the danger that alternative work arrangements actually result in more work and less balance (MacDermid et al., 2001; Siha and Monroe, 2006; Lewis and Humbert, 2010; Tomlinson and Durbin, 2010). Whether these consequences result from individual motives, societal expectations, and/or organizational failures, the result is that without thoughtful management, unintended consequences may obviate the possible benefits of these attempts at job restructuring. In turn, career success may be undermined.

CONCLUSION

We return to the opening question of 'What constitutes a successful career?' The answer to that question appears to be as varied and unique as the people who work: women, men, Baby Boomers, Generation X, Generation Y or Millennials. Our primary attention was that of women's careers, defined with both objective and subjective indicators. As we explored the landscape of the organization, we identified the realities that confront women in sustaining successful careers, however defined. We have offered suggestions that attempt to provide the needed space for women (and ultimately, men) to achieve the success that they seek, and to consider new career approaches, with special attention to work and life balance. It is our sincere hope that organizational initiatives will promote the ideal career model that includes a balance between life and work for all workers.

REFERENCES

Acker, J. (2012), 'Gendered organizations and intersectionality: problems and possibilities', *Equality, Diversity and Inclusion: An International Journal*, **31**(3), 214–24.

Agars, M.D. and K.A. French (2011), 'What if work and family research actually considered workers and their families?', *Industrial and Organizational Psychology*, **4**(3), 375–8.

Agars, M.D. and J.L. Kottke (2004), 'Models and practice of diversity management: a historical review and presentation of a new integration theory', in M.S. Stockdale and F.J. Cosby (eds), *The Psychology and Management of Workplace Diversity*, Oxford: Blackwood Press, pp. 55–77.

Agars, M.D. and L.M. Tortez (2013), 'LMX and work and family outcomes: the importance of follower gender', paper presented at the 26th Annual Conference of the Society for Industrial and Organizational Psychology, Houston, TX.

Agars, M.D., M. Balisi and C.R. Leier (2011), 'Work family practices and the advancement perceptions of women', paper presented at the 2011 Annual Meeting of the American Psychological Association, Washington, DC.

Anderson, S.E., B.S. Coffey and R.T. Byerly (2002), 'Formal organizational initiatives and informal workplace practices: links to work–family conflict and job-related outcomes', *Journal of Management*, **28**(6), 787–810.

Arthur, M.B., S.N. Khapova and C.P.M. Wilderom (2005), 'Career success in a boundaryless career world', *Journal of Organizational Behavior*, **26**(2), 177–202.

Becker, G.S. (1975), *Human Capital*, Chicago, IL: University of Chicago Press.

Bianchi, S.M. and M.A. Milkie (2010), 'Work and family research in the first decade of the 21st century', *Journal of Marriage and Family*, **72**(3), 705–25.

Bilimoria, D., S. Joy and X. Liang (2008), 'Breaking barriers and creating inclusiveness: lessons of organizational transformation to advance women faculty in academic science and engineering', *Human Resource Management*, **47**(3), 423–41.

Blake-Beard, S.D. (2001), 'Taking a hard look at formal mentoring programs: a consideration of potential challenges facing women', *Journal of Management Development*, **20**(4), 331–45.

Boeri, T., M.C. Burda and F. Kramarz (2008), *Working Hours and Job Sharing in the EU and USA: Are Europeans Lazy? Or Americans Crazy?*, Oxford: Oxford University Press.

Bond, J.T., E. Galinsky, S.S. Kim and E. Brownfield (2005), *2005 National Study of Employers*, New York: Families and Work Institute, accessed 2 December 2014 at http://familiesandwork.org/site/research/reports/2005nse.pdf.

Broadbridge, A. (2010), 'Social capital, gender and careers: evidence from retail senior managers', *Equality, Diversity and Inclusion: An International Journal*, **29**(8), 815–34.

Chao, G.T., P. Walz and P.D. Gardner (1992), 'Formal and informal mentorships: a comparison on mentoring functions and contrast with nonmentored counterparts', *Personnel Psychology*, **45**(3), 619–36.

Cortina, L.M. (2008), 'Unseen injustice: incivility as modern discrimination in organizations', *Academy of Management Review*, **33**(1), 55–75.

Cortina, L.M., D. Kabat-Farr, E.A. Leskinen, M. Huerta and V.J. Magley (2013), 'Selective incivility as modern discrimination in organizations: evidence and impact', *Journal of Management*, **39**(6), 1579–605.

Crompton, R. and C. Lyonette (2011), 'Women's career success and work–life adaptations in the accountancy and medical professions in Britain', *Gender, Work & Organization*, **18**(2), 231–54.

Deal, J.J., D.G. Altman and S.G. Rogelberg (2010), 'Millennials at work: what we know and what we need to do (if anything)', *Journal of Business and Psychology*, **25**(2), 191–9.
De Pater, I.E., A.E. van Vianen, A.H. Fischer and W.P. van Ginkel (2009a), 'Challenging experiences: gender differences in task choice', *Journal of Managerial Psychology*, **24**(1), 4–28.
De Pater, I.E., A.E. van Vianen, R.H. Humphrey, R.G. Sleeth, N.S. Hartman and A.H. Fischer (2009b), 'Individual task choice and the division of challenging tasks between men and women', *Group & Organization Management*, **34**(5), 563–89.
Dyke, L.S. and S.A. Murphy (2006), 'How we define success: a qualitative study of what matters most to women and men', *Sex Roles*, **55**(5–6), 357–71.
Eagly, A.H. and S.J. Karau (2002), 'Role congruity theory of prejudice toward female leaders', *Psychological Review*, **109**(3), 573–98.
Fitzgerald, L. (1993), 'Sexual harassment: violence against women in the workplace', *American Psychologist*, **48**(10), 1070–76.
Ford, M.T., B.A. Heinen and K.L. Langkamer (2007), 'Work and family satisfaction and conflict: a meta-analysis of cross-domain relations', *Journal of Applied Psychology*, **92**(1), 57–80.
Frye, N.K. and J.A. Breaugh (2004), 'Family-friendly policies, supervisor support, work–family conflict, family–work conflict, and satisfaction: a test of a conceptual model', *Journal of Business and Psychology*, **19**(2), 197–220.
Galinsky, E., J.T. Bond and E.J. Hill (2004), *When Work Works: A Status Report on Workplace Flexibility: Who Has It? Who Wants It? What Difference Does it Make?*, New York: Families and Work Institute.
Geist, C. and P.N. Cohen (2011), 'Headed toward equality? Housework change in comparative perspective', *Journal of Marriage and Family*, **73**(4), 832–44.
Glick, P. and S.T. Fiske (2001), 'An ambivalent alliance: hostile and benevolent sexism as complementary justifications for gender inequality', *American Psychologist*, **56**(2), 109–18.
Glick, P., S.T. Fiske, A. Mladinic, J.L. Saiz, D. Abrams and W.L. Lopez (2000), 'Beyond prejudice as simple antipathy: hostile and benevolent sexism across cultures', *Journal of Personality and Social Psychology*, **79**(5), 763–75.
Golden, T.D. and J.F. Veiga (2006), 'The impact of extent of telecommuting on job satisfaction: resolving inconsistent findings', *Journal of Management*, **31**(2), 301–18.
Golden, T.D., J.F. Veiga and Z. Simsek (2006), 'Telecommuting's differential impact on work–family conflict: is there no place like home?', *Journal of Applied Psychology*, **91**(6), 1340–50.
Hakim, C. (2002), 'Lifestyle preferences as determinants of women's differentiated labor market careers', *Work and Occupations*, **29**(4), 428–59.
Hall, D.T., M.D. Lee, E.E. Kossek and M. Las Heras (2012), 'Pursuing career success while sustaining personal and family well-being: a study of reduced-load professionals over time', *Journal of Social Issues*, **68**(4), 742–66.
Hanappi-Egger, E. (2012), '"Shall I stay or shall I go?" On the role of diversity management for women's retention in SET professions', *Equality, Diversity and Inclusion: An International Journal*, **31**(2), 144–57.
Heslin, P.A. (2005), 'Conceptualizing and evaluating career success', *Journal of Organizational Behavior*, **26**(2), 113–36.
Hezlett, S.A. and S.K. Gibson (2007), 'Linking mentoring and social capital: implications for career and organizational development', *Advances in Developing Human Resources and Organization Development*, **9**(3), 384–412.
Hogan, R., T. Chamorro-Premuzic and R.B. Kaiser (2013), 'Employability and career success: bridging the gap between theory and reality', *Industrial and Organizational Psychology*, **6**(1), 3–16.
Hook, J.L. (2010), 'Gender inequality in the welfare state: sex segregation in housework, 1965–2003', *American Journal of Sociology*, **115**(5), 1480–523.
International Labour Office (2010), *Women in Labour Markets: Measuring Progress and Identifying Challenges*, Geneva: ILO.

Kelly, E.L. and A. Kalev (2006), 'Managing flexible work arrangements in US organizations: formalized discretion or "a right to ask"', *Socio-Economic Review*, **4**(3), 379–416.
Kelly, E.L. and P. Moen (2007), 'Rethinking the clockwork of work: why schedule control may pay off at work and at home', *Advances in Developing Human Resources*, **9**(4), 487–506.
Kelly, E.L., S.K. Ammons, K. Chermack and P. Moen (2010), 'Gendered challenge, gendered response: confronting the ideal worker norm in a white-collar organization', *Gender and Society*, **24**(3), 281–303.
Kidder, D.L. (2002), 'The influence of gender on the performance of organizational citizenship behaviors', *Journal of Management*, **28**(5), 629–48.
King, E.B., W. Botsford, M.R. Hebl, S. Kazama, J.F. Dawson and A. Perkins (2012), 'Benevolent sexism at work: gender differences in the distribution of challenging developmental experiences', *Journal of Management*, **38**(6), 1835–66.
Kossek, E.E., B.B. Baltes and R.A. Matthews (2011), 'How work–family research can finally have an impact in organizations', *Industrial and Organizational Psychology*, **4**(3), 352–69.
Kossek, E.E., B.A. Lautsch and S.C. Eaton (2006), 'Telecommuting, control, and boundary management: correlates of policy use and practice, job control, and work–family effectiveness', *Journal of Vocational Behavior*, **68**(2), 347–67.
Kottke, J.L. and M.D. Agars (2005), 'Understanding the processes that facilitate and hinder efforts to advance women in organizations', *Career Development International*, **10**(3), 190–202.
Kottke, J.L. and K.L. Pelletier (2013), 'Advancing women into leadership: a global perspective on overcoming barriers', in M. Paludi (ed.), *Women and Management Worldwide: Global Issues and Promising Solutions*, Westport, CT: Praeger, pp. 55–85.
Kowske, B.J., R. Rasch and J. Wiley (2010), 'Millennials' (lack of) attitude problem: an empirical examination of generational effects on work attitudes', *Journal of Business and Psychology*, **25**(2), 265–79.
Ledbetter, L. and S.I. Lanier (2013), *Grace and Grit: My Fight for Equal Pay and Fairness at Goodyear and Beyond*, New York: Three Rivers Press.
Lewis, S. and L. Humbert (2010), 'Discourse or reality? "Work–life balance", flexible working policies and the gendered organization', *Equality, Diversity and Inclusion: An International Journal*, **29**(3), 239–54.
Lips, H.M. (2003), 'The gender pay gap: concrete indicator of women's progress toward equality', *Analyses of Social Issues and Public Policy*, **3**(1), 87–109.
Lips, H.M. (2013), 'The gender pay gap: challenging the rationalizations. Perceived equity, discrimination, and the limits of human capital models', *Sex Roles*, **68**(3–4), 169–85.
Lirio, P., M.D. Lee, M.L. Williams, L.K. Haugen and E.E. Kossek (2008), 'The inclusion challenge with reduced-load professionals: the role of the manager', *Human Resource Management*, **47**(3), 443–61.
Loughlin, C., K. Arnold and J.B. Crawford (2011), 'Lost opportunity: is transformational leadership accurately recognized and rewarded in all managers?', *Equality, Diversity and Inclusion: An International Journal*, **31**(1), 43–64.
Lyness, K.S. and M.E. Heilman (2006), 'When fit is fundamental: performance evaluations and promotions of upper-level female and male managers', *Journal of Applied Psychology*, **91**(4), 777–85.
MacDermid, S.M., M.D. Lee, M. Buck and M.L. Williams (2001), 'Alternative work arrangements among professionals and managers', *Journal of Management Development*, **20**(4), 305–17.
Mainero, L.A. and S.E. Sullivan (2006), *The Opt-out Revolt: Why People are Leaving Companies to Create Kaleidoscope Careers*, Mountain View, CA: Davies-Black.
Major, D.A. and H.M. Lauzun (2010), 'Equipping managers to assist employees in addressing work–family conflict: applying the research literature toward innovative practice', *The Psychologist-Manager Journal*, **13**(2), 69–85.
Major, D.A., T.D. Fletcher, D.D. Davis and L.M. Germano (2008), 'The influence of work–family culture and workplace relationships on work interference with family: a multilevel model', *Journal of Organizational Behavior*, **29**(7), 881–97.

Mayrhofer, W., M. Meyer, M. Schiffinger and A. Schmidt (2008), 'The influence of family responsibilities, career fields and gender on career success: an empirical study', *Journal of Managerial Psychology*, **23**(3), 292–323.

McCauley, C.D., L.J. Eastman and P.J. Ohlott (1995), 'Linking management selection and development through stretch assignments', *Human Resource Management*, **34**(1), 93–115.

McGuire, G. (2002), 'Gender, race and the shadow structure: a study of informal network and inequality in work organizations', *Gender and Society*, **16**(3), 303–22.

Moen, P., E. Kelly and Q. Huang (2008), 'Work, family, and life-course fit: does control over work time matter?', *Journal of Vocational Behavior*, **73**(3), 414–25.

Ng, E.S., L. Schweitzer and S.T. Lyons (2010), 'New generation, great expectations: a field study of the millennial generation', *Journal of Business and Psychology*, **25**(2), 281–92.

Ng, T.W., L.T. Eby, K.L. Sorensen and D.C. Feldman (2005), 'Predictors of objective and subjective career success: a meta-analysis', *Personnel Psychology*, **58**(2), 367–408.

Ohlott, P.J., M.N. Ruderman and C.D. McCauley (1994), 'Gender differences in managers' developmental job experiences', *Academy of Management Journal*, **37**(1), 46–67.

O'Leary-Kelly, A.M., L. Bowes-Sperry, C.A. Bates and E.R. Lean (2009), 'Sexual harassment at work: a decade (plus) of progress', *Journal of Management*, **35**(3), 503–36.

O'Neil, D.A., M.M. Hopkins and S.E. Sullivan (2011), 'Do women's networks help advance women's careers? Differences in perceptions of female workers and top leadership', *Career Development International*, **16**(7), 733–54.

Premeaux, S.F., C.L. Adkins and K.W. Mossholder (2007), 'Balancing work and family: a field study of multi-dimensional, multi-role work–family conflict', *Journal of Organizational Behavior*, **28**(6), 705–27.

Ragins, B.R. and J.L. Cotton (1999), 'Mentor functions and outcomes: a comparison of men and women in formal and informal mentoring relationships', *Journal of Applied Psychology*, **84**(4), 529–50.

Ragins, B.R., J.L. Cotton and J.S. Miller (2000), 'Marginal mentoring: the effects of type of mentor, quality of relationship, and program design on work and career attitudes', *Academy of Management Journal*, **43**(6), 1177–94.

Raghuram, S. and B. Wiesenfeld (2004), 'Work–nonwork conflict and job stress among virtual workers', *Human Resource Management*, **43**(2–3), 259–77.

Ramaswami, A., G.F. Dreher, R. Bretz and C. Wiethoff (2010), 'Gender, mentoring, and career success: the importance of organizational context', *Personnel Psychology*, **63**(2), 385–405.

Ryan, M.K. and S.A. Haslam (2005), 'The glass cliff: evidence that women are over-represented in precarious leadership positions', *British Journal of Management*, **16**(2), 81–90.

Rynes, S. and B. Rosen (1995), 'A field survey of factors affecting the adoption and perceived success of diversity training', *Personnel Psychology*, **48**(2), 247–70.

Salin, D. and H. Hoel (2013), 'Workplace bullying as a gendered phenomenon', *Journal of Managerial Psychology*, **28**(3), 235–51.

Schein, E.H. (2004), *Organizational Culture and Leadership*, 3rd edition, San Francisco, CA: Jossey-Bass.

Schilling, E.H. (2012), 'Non-linear careers: desirability and coping', *Equality, Diversity and Inclusion: An International Journal*, **31**(8), 725–40.

Siha, S.M. and R.W. Monroe (2006), 'Telecommuting's past and future: a literature review and research agenda', *Business Process Management Journal*, **12**(4), 455–82.

Smith, P., P. Caputi and N. Crittenden (2012), 'How are women's glass ceiling beliefs related to career success?', *Career Development International*, **17**(5), 458–74.

Snir, R. and I. Harpaz (2006), 'The workaholism phenomenon: a cross-national perspective', *Career Development International*, **11**(5), 374–93.

Sullivan, S.E., M.L. Forret, S.M. Carraher and L.A. Mainiero (2009), 'Using the kaleidoscope career model to examine generational differences in work attitudes', *Career Development International*, **14**(3), 284–302.

Thomas, R.R. (2006), 'Diversity management: an essential craft of future leaders', in

F. Hesselbein and M. Goldsmith (eds), *The Leader of the Future 2: Visions, Strategies, and Practices for the New Era*, San Francisco, CA: Jossey-Bass, pp. 47–54.

Thomas, L.T. and D.C. Ganster (1995), 'Impact of family-supportive work variables on work–family conflict and strain: a control perspective', *Journal of Applied Psychology*, **80**(1), 6–15.

Tomlinson, J. and S. Durbin (2010), 'Female part-time managers: work–life balance, aspirations and career mobility', *Equality, Diversity and Inclusion: An International Journal*, **29**(3), 255–70.

Valcour, M. and J.J. Ladge (2008), 'Family and career path characteristics as predictors of women's objective and subjective career success: integrating traditional and protean career explanations', *Journal of Vocational Behavior*, **73**(2), 300–309.

Voydanoff, P. (2005), 'Social integration, work–family conflict and facilitation, and job and marital quality', *Journal of Marriage and Family*, **67**(3), 666–79.

Wanberg, C.R., E.T. Welsh and S.A. Hezlett (2003), 'Mentoring research: a review and dynamic process model', in J. Martocchio and G. Ferris (eds), *Research in Personnel and Human Resources Management, Vol. 22*, Bingley, UK: Emerald Group Publishing, pp. 39–124.

Woodall, J., C. Edwards and R. Welchman (1997), 'Organizational restructuring and the achievement of an equal opportunity culture', *Gender, Work & Organization*, **4**(1), 2–12.

Yukl, G. (2010), *Leadership in Organizations*, 7th edition, Upper Saddle River, NJ: Prentice Hall.

18. Women and leadership
Linda L. Carli

How does gender affect opportunities for leadership? This chapter examines the current status of women as leaders and explores factors that contribute to gender differences in attainment of leadership positions, including balancing work and family, the styles and performance of male and female leaders, gender stereotyping and discrimination, and the structure and culture of modern organizations.

Women today hold more leadership positions than at any time in the past. Currently, in the United States, 27 per cent of CEOs (US Bureau of Labor Statistics, 2013a, Table 11) and 52 per cent of all professional and managerial employees over all levels are women (ibid.). Women's representation in government leadership has also improved; women now hold 20 per cent of US Senate seats and 18 per cent of seats in the House of Representatives (Center for American Women and Politics, 2013). Similar increases in women's leadership have been found internationally. For example, of the 137 women who have served as presidents or prime ministers of nations, 75 first came into office since 2000, and most of them – 42 – in the last five years (Christensen, 2013). Yet, in spite of these advances, women clearly remain a small minority of political and government leaders, and continue to be under-represented in corporate leadership. Across all corporations in the United States, only 27 per cent of CEOs are women (US Bureau of Labor Statistics, 2013a, Table 11). The percentage of women leaders is even lower in the largest firms: in the Fortune 500, women make up 17 per cent of corporate boards, 14 per cent of executive officers (Catalyst, 2013a) and 4 per cent of CEOs (Catalyst, 2013b). Thus, the percentage of women drops at higher levels of management and in larger corporations. Similar findings have been reported in other countries (Catalyst, 2013c, 2013d), except for the relatively high percentage of women on corporate boards in Norway, where quotas mandate that women hold 40 per cent of board seats. Clearly, although women have advanced, they continue to experience challenges as leaders. These obstacles are not as impenetrable and obvious as those faced by women in the past, yet they remain a complex and subtle 'labyrinth' of challenges that slow or obstruct women's access to leadership (see Eagly and Carli, 2007).

THE COMPETING DEMANDS OF CAREER AND FAMILY

Human capital theory has historically linked women's lower pay and promotion to women's inadequate education, lower job commitment, and greater domestic responsibilities (Becker, 1975). However, women have outpaced men in educational attainment in the United States for over 40 years, earning more Bachelor's degrees than men since the early 1980s (US National Center for Education Statistics, 2010). Nor do women appear less interested than men in jobs that provide opportunities for authority and advancement. In a meta-analytic review examining gender differences in job preferences, when comparing women and men in similar occupations, results revealed no gender difference in the desire for leadership or promotions and women actually expressed a greater desire for influence, recognition, challenge and accomplishment than men (Konrad et al., 2000). National samples in the United States and other nations reveal that women have just as much interest in obtaining responsibility and advancement as men (Corrigall and Konrad, 2006; Galinsky et al., 2008). Similarly, a meta-analysis revealed that men and women report equal commitment to their work organizations (Aven et al., 1993). Women's commitment to their jobs is also evident in research on the rate at which men and women quit their jobs. Studies of managers and executives generally indicate that women quit slightly less often than men (for example, Lyness and Judiesch, 2001; McKay et al., 2007), although one large study of professional and managerial employees of varying rank revealed slightly higher quit rates among women (Hom et al., 2008).

Clearly, evidence does not support the contention that the paucity of female leaders is due to women's lack of education, interest in leadership and challenging work, or commitment to their jobs. However, women do differ from men in their commitment to family roles. According to a recent Gallup poll, most men and women prefer paid employment to a homemaker role, but a much lower percentage of men than women would choose homemaking (Saad, 2012). Although more women have jobs than in the past, women continue to spend more time than men on housework and childcare (US Bureau of Labor Statistics, 2013b, Table 1). In spite of the fact that families are smaller, men and women in the United States and Europe now spend more time caring for children than ever, with both employed and non-employed mothers spending more time than fathers (Gauthier et al., 2004; Bianchi, 2011). Thus, even as more women have entered the paid workforce, women have also simultaneously increased their time spent in childcare.

Women's commitment to family tends to increase the gender gap in leadership. Becoming a spouse or parent is associated with a reduction in paid work hours for women, but not for men (Corrigall and Konrad, 2006; Craig and Mullan, 2010). This is true even in high-status professions, where women remain more likely than their male counterparts to reduce their work hours to accommodate family responsibilities (for example, Boulis, 2004; Noonan and Corcoran, 2004). Taking breaks from employment or reducing work hours by working part-time result in long-term cumulative losses in income (Rose and Hartmann, 2004) and career breaks taken for motherhood are more costly than breaks taken for other reasons (Arun et al., 2004). Consequently, having children confers a 'motherhood penalty' in wages, such that women with children earn less than childless women (Budig and Hodges, 2010). Moreover, although family-friendly policies – such as the right to part-time employment and parental leave – do increase women's rate of employment, the increase is primarily in part-time work (Mandel and Semyonov, 2005; Blau and Kahn, 2013), which is less likely to lead to advancement than full-time employment (Blau et al., 2010). When long paid parental leaves and part-time work are available to parents, it is women who take these benefits, not men, and women as a consequence attain relatively fewer managerial positions; when such policies are not available, the women are less likely to take breaks in employment or to work part-time (Blau and Kahn, 2013). Thus, such policies strengthen the traditional gender division of labour in the family and do not increase women's leadership representation.

GENDER DISCRIMINATION AND STEREOTYPES

A presumption of the human capital explanation for gender differences in pay and promotion is that the gaps are mediated by gender differences in human capital. If so, statistically controlling for human capital variables such as job experience, part-time or full-time status, and number of breaks in employment should eliminate the gaps in pay and advancement, but this is not the case. Research in the United States, Australia and European nations has revealed that human capital accounts for only a portion of the gender gaps in pay and advancement, suggesting that the remaining unexplained gaps may be due to discrimination (for example, Elliot and Smith, 2004; Blau and Kahn, 2006; O'Dorchai, 2008). More direct evidence of gender discrimination comes from experiments comparing the evaluation of male and female job applicants who have identical records or résumés (CVs). In a meta-analysis of such studies, men were preferred over identically qualified women for male-dominated jobs and gender-neutral jobs, whereas women were preferred only for traditionally female-dominated positions, such as childcare worker (Davison and Burke, 2000).

Gender discrimination derives from the stereotypes that people hold about women, men, and leaders. According to role incongruity theory (Eagly and Karau, 2002), gender stereotypes take two forms: 'descriptive stereotypes' are shared beliefs about what men and women are like, and 'prescriptive stereotypes' are shared beliefs about what men and women ought be like. Prejudice and discrimination against women leaders results when people perceive incongruity between the descriptive and prescriptive characteristics associated with women and those associated with effective leaders.

Research in the United States and other nations reveals consensus about what men and women are thought to be like. People perceive men to be agentic – for example, competent, assertive, and authoritative, and women to be communal – warm, helpful, and nurturing (Williams and Best, 1990; Rudman and Glick, 2008). And what are leaders thought to be like? Research exploring this question includes studies using Schien's (1973) 'think manager–think male' paradigm, which assesses whether the stereotypes about leaders correlate more with stereotypes about men than with stereotypes about women, and Powell and Butterfield's (1979) 'agency–communion' paradigm, which assesses whether leaders are perceived as more agentic or more communal. A meta-analysis of 69 of these studies indicates that there is more similarity between the traits of leaders and men than between the traits of leaders and women (Koenig et al., 2011). Although this review revealed that the association of leadership with masculine traits has weakened somewhat with time and is less pronounced in less male-dominated settings or contexts, even now effective leadership remains strongly associated with agency.

Gender stereotypes obstruct women's leadership in several ways. Priming female stereotypes can elicit stereotype threat in women contemplating leadership (Davies et al., 2005). Studies have shown that women's leadership self-efficacy is especially undermined by the presence of subtle threats (Hoyt et al., 2010). Gender stereotypes also hinder women's leadership because they paint women as lacking agentic competence and lead to discrimination against women as leaders. Because of the doubts about women's agency, people generally hold women to a higher standard of competence than men. A meta-analysis revealed that women leaders receive lower evaluations than men for comparable levels of performance (Eagly et al., 1992). This male advantage in evaluation, controlling for performance, has also been found in a variety of contexts: with the perceptions of undergraduates (Foschi, 2000; Biernat, 2003; Carli, 2006), military cadets (Boldry et al., 2001), and managers (Heilman et al., 2004;

Heilman and Okimoto, 2007). One study found that when mixed-gender dyads were described as performing poorly at a management task, participants attributed the failure to the woman more than to the man (Haynes and Lawrence, 2012). Similarly, when a mixed-gender dyad was described as performing well at an investment task, participants credited the man with the success unless given strong evidence of the woman's contribution. Another study demonstrated that people have more difficulty recognizing expertise in a woman than in a man (Thomas-Hunt and Phillips, 2004).

These results suggest that women could overcome resistance to their leadership by performing exceptionally well and manifesting a highly agentic style of behaviour. However, this is not the case. On the contrary, highly agentic women are often penalized. People dislike women, but not men, who criticize others (Sinclair and Kunda, 2000; Atwater et al., 2001; Rudman et al., 2012), disagree with others (Carli, 2014), achieve success in masculine careers (Heilman et al., 2004; Heilman and Wallen, 2010), or even just behave highly competently (Heilman and Okimoto, 2007; Rudman et al., 2012). Furthermore, experiments have demonstrated that whereas men receive rewards for promoting themselves, women receive rewards for more modest and self-effacing behaviour (Wosinska et al., 1996; Rudman, 1998; Neal et al., 2012; Carli, 2014).

Why are agentic women penalized? In addition to descriptive stereotypes about women, prescriptive gender stereotypes also impede women's leadership opportunities by placing different demands on male and female leaders. In particular, studies have demonstrated that people believe that women should be more communal than men and that men should be more agentic than women (Prentice and Carranza, 2002; Seem and Clark, 2006). Therefore, the male prescriptions are compatible with stereotypes about effective leaders, but the female prescriptions are not. The combination of descriptive and prescriptive gender stereotypes create a unique challenge for women leaders: to be seen as an effective leader, women must overcome doubts about their agency, but to be seen as appropriate women, they must also be highly communal. This need to balance both demands creates a double bind.

Because people expect more communal behaviour in women than men, men receive more rewards than women do for helpful supportive behaviour. For example, one organizational study found that men who were helpful to their work colleagues had a higher promotion rate than less helpful men, but helpfulness had no effect on women's advancement (Allen, 2006). An experiment examining reactions to helpful and unhelpful co-workers found that helpfulness was rewarded in men but not women, and unhelpfulness was punished in women but not men (Heilman and Chen, 2005). Similarly, in another organizational study, subordinates responded favourably to considerate behaviour by their male leaders, but not by their female leaders (Mohr and Wolfram, 2008).

The resistance to female agency and demand for female communion has been found in both men and women. Yet, past research has generally revealed that men resisted female agency more than women do. A meta-analysis of studies examining differences in the evaluation of male and female leaders found that men were harsher in their evaluation of female leaders than women were (Eagly et al., 1992). Similarly, past studies have also revealed that women responded more favourably to female competence than men did (for example, Carli, 1990; Foschi et al., 1994; Carli et al., 1995; Matschiner and Murnen, 1999). In contrast, and more recently, some scholars have claimed that senior women are sometimes more resistant to female agency than men, a phenomenon known as the 'queen bee syndrome' (for example, Derks et al., 2011). Yet, empirical evidence for queen bees is lacking. Current research continues to show that men more than women associate leadership with masculine rather than feminine traits (Koenig et al., 2011) and men continue to show greater resistance to female authority than women do (for example, Uhlmann and Cohen, 2005; Reid et al., 2009). Additionally, the concept of the queen bee is an intrinsically sexist label that is applied only to women whereby women are uniquely penalized for not manifesting solidarity with other women (see Mavin, 2008). In essence, labelling women as queen bees reflects the double bind, requiring senior-level women who have established themselves as highly agentic to also maintain high levels of communal behaviour.

Because of the double bind, women's ability to influence others depends on a constricted range of behaviour (Carli, 1999) and women exert less influence overall than men do (Propp, 1995; Thomas-Hunt and Phillips, 2004; Carli, in press). In particular, people's evaluations of women are more contingent on perceived communion than are their evaluations of men (Johnson et al., 2008; Biernat et al., 2012). The results of pressure on women to convey both exceptional agency and exceptional warmth likely leads to gender differences in the way men and women lead.

GENDER AND LEADERSHIP STYLE

Unsurprisingly, given the greater demands on women leaders, research has revealed gender differences in leadership style. A meta-analysis of laboratory and organizational studies showed that female leaders manifest a more democratic style of leadership, allowing subordinates to participate in decision-making, whereas male leaders manifest a more autocratic and directive style (Eagly and Johnson, 1990; Van Engen and Willemsen, 2004). A large international study of over 12 000 leaders in 32 countries revealed greater consideration and support by female leaders and greater directiveness by male leaders (Van Emmerik et al., 2010). Another meta-analysis found that, compared with male leaders, female leaders employed a somewhat higher amount of transformational leadership, which involves developing, inspiring, and motivating subordinates, and a lower amount of laissez-faire or uninvolved leadership (Eagly et al., 2003). The meta-analysis also examined gender differences in transactional leadership, a style that involves focusing on subordinates' successes and failures. Female leaders relied more on one component of transactional leadership – rewarding subordinates for effective performance, and male leaders relied more on two components – avoiding problems until they became serious and punishing subordinates' failures. These patterns of differences in women's and men's leadership style are consistent with the demands of the double bind. Transformational leadership comprises a mix of feminine and masculine components and democratic leadership is clearly relatively communal (Eagly and Carli, 2007). Thus, women exhibit leadership that resolves some of the challenges created by the double bind.

In addition to examining gender effects on style, research has also examined the effectiveness of different styles of leadership. Although the benefits of democratic versus autocratic leadership depend on the particular leadership context (Gastil, 1994; Foels et al., 2000), a meta-analysis on transformational, transactional and laissez-faire leadership revealed strong evidence of the effectiveness of transformational leadership across a wide variety of contexts (Judge and Piccolo, 2004). The use of transformational leadership is associated with leader effectiveness, leader performance, organizational or team performance, follower satisfaction, and follower motivation. The effects of transactional leadership were mixed. One component of transactional leadership – the use of rewards – yielded favourable outcomes, but the other two components were much less effective: punishment weakly enhanced effectiveness and delaying action until problems become serious reduced effectiveness. Laissez-faire leadership also reduced effectiveness. These findings demonstrate that the leadership styles more commonly employed by women are considerably more effective than those employed by men, whereas the styles more commonly employed by men are relatively ineffective. Thus, the gender gap in advancement cannot be attributed to women's ineffective leadership style. But does that mean that women are just as effective as men?

Women's use of a relatively effective leadership style does not guarantee that women make better leaders than men. Effective leadership requires the support of followers who yield to the influence of their leaders. Female leaders, because of gender stereotyping and discrimination, have greater difficulty than male leaders in exerting influence. Nevertheless, in spite of this bias, a meta-analysis found no overall gender difference in effectiveness where effectiveness was based on either objective ratings of leaders' behaviours or on subjective ratings of co-workers, subordinates and others (Eagly et al., 1995). Another test for gender differences in effectiveness can be found in studies examining whether the financial success of organizations is associated with the percentage of female leaders. Studies using this approach have also included statistical controls to address concerns about reverse causality – that is, that any relation between organizational performance and female leadership may be due to the tendency of better-performing organizations to employ more female leaders. Studies using these controls have revealed mixed results. For example, one study found no benefit of gender diversity on firm performance, and some evidence of reduced performance (Adams and Ferriera, 2009). However, when the firms had poor governance, gender diversity enhanced firm performance, primarily because boards with a high percentage of women had tougher monitoring. A second study examining a sample of Fortune 1500 corporations found that gender diversity in top management teams was associated overall with improved firm performance, but only in firms whose strategies focused on innovation (Dezső and Ross, 2012).

Studies such as these have limitations. First, most 'diverse' firms included in research on the effects of gender diversity have only one woman on their top management teams or boards of directors. Given that the presence of tokens increases gender stereotyping and undermines women's influence (see Eagly and Carli, 2007), a higher percentage of women leaders would be needed to have true diversity and to obtain potential benefits of women's leadership (Torchia et al., 2011). Second, studies examining firm performance generally rely on changes in firms' stock value to reflect performance, but in one study of large US firms, stock prices fell in response to increased gender diversity, independent of any actual changes in firm profits (Dobbin and Jung, 2011). These results suggest that institutional investors, who control most shares of American companies, are affected by gender bias against female leaders and sell stocks of firms that increase female leadership.

ORGANIZATIONAL BARRIERS TO WOMEN'S LEADERSHIP

Modern organizational culture often presents impediments to women's advancement. Managerial positions usually demand longer than average work hours (Brett and Stroh, 2003; Jacobs and Gerson, 2004). Moreover, the model of the ideal employee is one who is totally devoted to the organization (Eagly and Carli, 2007). Men have less difficulty fulfilling this ideal because they have fewer domestic duties and more leisure time than women do. Even at high levels of leadership, compared with their male counterparts, female executives are less likely to hand over domestic responsibilities to their spouses and more likely to sacrifice personal interests to manage domestic duties (Catalyst, 2004).

Another organizational challenge to female leadership is women's lack of social capital. Access to professional networks and supportive mentors predicts increased salary and promotions (Ng et al., 2005), but women have less access to networks and mentors and less support from them than men do (Dreher and Cox, 1996; Forret and Dougherty, 2004; Timberlake, 2005). Networks and social connections typically are gender-segregated because people tend to affiliate with others who are similar to themselves (McPherson et al., 2001). In general, most powerful networks and mentors are male dominated and benefit men more than women (Eagly and Carli, 2007).

Finally, women also have more difficulty obtaining desirable developmental work assignments. One recent study, for example, revealed that men's assignments were more visible, had bigger budgets, had better staffing, involved more international experience, and were more critical to the organizational mission than were women's assignments (Silva et al., 2012). On the other hand, people prefer to assign women rather than men to leadership when the role involves great risk and failure is likely; such assignments are known as the glass cliff positions (Ryan et al., 2008). Research indicates that women are preferred in times of crisis because they are thought to possess the nurturing skills to help others cope and to be willing to accept blame for failure (for example, Ryan et al., 2011).

CONCLUSION

Clearly, women's under-representation as leaders is not a function of their lack of leadership ability or general interest in leading. Instead, women are obstructed in their leadership attainment due to gender inequalities in domestic responsibilities, stereotyping and discrimination, and organizational cultures that favour male employees.

What strategies are likely to help overcome the obstacles to women's leadership? One approach is for women to evince a leadership style that overcomes the double bind, the requirement that female leaders show warmth and communion while also conveying competence and agency.

One way to do this is to behave in ways that reflect a balance of communal and agentic qualities. Women are already doing this, to some extent, as is evident in their somewhat greater use of transformational leadership. In addition, women would benefit from greater sharing of domestic responsibilities with their romantic partners or other parties, and from improved social capital at work, particularly in the form of greater access to powerful networks and mentors. Although women who aspire to leadership could be more judicious in their choice of romantic partners and increase their networking efforts, they cannot overcome these barriers entirely on their own, but require organizational support. In particular, research on the efficacy of diversity programmes has found two effective organizational strategies for increasing women's leadership: creating networking and mentoring programmes for women and assigning responsibility for increasing diversity to particular committees, departments, task forces, or officers within the organization (Kalev et al., 2006). In addition, given that exposure to successful and similar female leaders enhances women's identification and interest in leadership (see Asgari et al., 2012), as does working with supportive female role models (Asgari et al., 2010), organizations could increase the visibility of female leaders and women's opportunities to work with them, thereby enhancing the likelihood of women's leadership aspirations.

In addition to the efforts of individuals and organizations, women's advancement is likely to be facilitated by changes in attitudes about leadership. In particular, there is increased recognition of the value of communal behaviour and a transformational style to effective leadership, a recognition that strengthens the association of leadership with feminine qualities. This and the increased numbers of visible female leaders should continue to topple old stereotypes equating masculinity with leadership and continue the tread of greater female representation in powerful positions.

REFERENCES

Adams, R.B. and D. Ferreira (2009), 'Women in the boardroom and their impact on governance and performance', *Journal of Financial Economics*, **94**(2), 291–309.

Allen, T.D. (2006), 'Rewarding good citizens: the relationship between citizenship behavior, gender, and organizational rewards', *Journal of Applied Psychology*, **36**(1), 120–43.

Arun, S.V., T.G. Arun and V.K. Borooah (2004), 'The effect of career breaks on the working lives of women', *Feminist Economics*, **10**(1), 65–84.

Asgari, S., N. Dasgupta and N. Cote (2010), 'When does contact with successful ingroup members change self-stereotypes? A longitudinal study comparing the effect of quantity vs. quality of contact with successful individuals', *Social Psychology*, **41**(3), 203–11.

Asgari, S., N. Dasgupta and J.G. Stout (2012), 'When do counterstereotypic ingroup members inspire versus deflate? The effect of successful professional women on young women's leadership self-concept', *Personality and Social Psychology Bulletin*, **38**(3), 370–83.

Atwater, L.E., J.A. Carey and D.A. Waldman (2001), 'Gender and discipline in the workplace: wait until your father gets home', *Journal of Management*, **27**(5), 537–61.

Aven, F.F., B. Parker and G.M. McEvoy (1993), 'Gender and attitudinal commitment to organizations: a meta-analysis', *Journal of Business Research*, **26**(1), 63–73.

Becker, G.S. (1975), *Human Capital*, 2nd edition, Chicago, IL: University of Chicago Press.

Bianchi, S.M. (2011), 'Family change and time allocation in American families', *Annals of the American Academy of Political and Social Science*, **638**(1), 21–44.

Biernat, M. (2003), 'Toward a broader view of social stereotyping', *American Psychologist*, **58**(12), 1019–27.

Biernat, M., M.J. Tocci and J.C. Williams (2012), 'The language of performance evaluations: gender-based shifts in content and consistency of judgment', *Social Psychology and Personality Science*, **3**(2), 186–92.

Blau, F.D. and L.M. Kahn (2006), 'The U.S. gender pay gap in the 1990s: slow convergence', *Industrial and Labor Relations Review*, **60**(1), 45–66.

Blau, F.D. and L.M. Kahn (2013), 'Female labor supply: why is the United States falling behind?', *American Economic Review*, **103**(3), 251–6.

Blau, F.D., M.A. Ferber and A.E. Winkler (2010), *The Economics of Women, Men, and Work*, 6th edition, Upper Saddle River, NJ: Prentice Hall.

Boldry, J., W. Wood and D.A. Kashy (2001), 'Gender stereotypes and the evaluation of men and women in military training', *Journal of Social Issues*, **57**(4), 689–705.

Boulis, A. (2004), 'The evolution of gender and motherhood in contemporary medicine', *Annals of the American Academy of Political and Social Science*, **596**(1), 172–206.

Brett, J.M. and L.K. Stroh (2003), 'Working 61 plus hours a week: why do managers do it?', *Journal of Applied Psychology*, **88**(1), 67–78.

Budig, M.J. and M.J. Hodges (2010), 'Differences in disadvantage: variation in the motherhood penalty across white women's earnings distribution', *American Sociological Review*, **75**(5), 705–28.

Carli, L.L. (1990), 'Gender, language, and influence', *Journal of Personality and Social Psychology*, **59**(5), 941–51.

Carli, L.L. (1999), 'Gender, interpersonal power, and social influence', *Journal of Social Issues*, **55**(1), 81–99.

Carli, L.L. (2006), 'Gender and social influence: women confront the double bind', paper presented at the 26th International Conference of Applied Psychology, Athens.

Carli, L.L. (2014), 'The labyrinth of leadership', annual meeting of the National Association of Graduate and Professional Students, Tufts University, Medford, MA.

Carli, L.L. (in press), 'Gender and social influence', in J. Burger (ed.), *Oxford Handbook of Social Influence*, Oxford: Oxford University Press.

Carli, L.L., S.J. LaFleur and C.C. Loeber (1995), 'Nonverbal behavior, gender, and influence', *Journal of Personality and Social Psychology*, **68**(6), 1030–41.

Catalyst (2004), 'Women and men in U.S. corporate leadership: same workplace, different realities?', accessed 2 December 2014 at http://www.catalyst.org/knowledge/women-and-men-us-corporate-leadership-same-workplace-different-realities.

Catalyst (2013a), 'Quick take: women in U.S. management and labor force', accessed 2 December 2014 at http://www.catalyst.org/knowledge/women-us-management-and-labor-force.

Catalyst (2013b), 'List: women CEOs of the Fortune 1000', accessed 2 December 2014 at http://www.catalyst.org/knowledge/women-ceos-fortune-1000.

Catalyst (2013c), 'Board seats held by women, by country', accessed 2 December at http://www.catalyst.org/knowledge/board-seats-held-women-country.

Catalyst (2013d), 'Women board chairs, by country', accessed 2 December 2014 at http://www.catalyst.org/knowledge/women-board-chairs-country.

Center for American Women and Politics (2013), 'Women in the U.S. Congress 2013', accessed 2 December 2014 at http://www.cawp.rutgers.edu/fast_facts/levels_of_office/documents/cong.pdf.
Christensen, M.K.I. (2013), *Worldwide Guide to Women in Leadership*, accessed 2 December 2014 at http://www.guide2womenleaders.com/index.html.
Corrigall, E.A. and A.M. Konrad (2006), 'The relationship of job attribute preferences to employment, hours of paid work, and family responsibilities: an analysis comparing women and men', *Sex Roles*, **54**(1–2), 95–111.
Craig, L. and K. Mullan (2010), 'Parenthood, gender and work–family time in the United States, Australia, Italy, France, and Denmark', *Journal of Marriage and Family*, **72**(5), 1344–61.
Davies, P.G., S.J. Spencer and C.M. Steele (2005), 'Clearing the air: identity safety moderates the effects of stereotype threat on women's leadership aspirations', *Journal of Personality and Social Psychology*, **88**(2), 276–87.
Davison, H.K. and M.J. Burke (2000), 'Sex discrimination in simulated employment contexts: a meta-analytic investigation', *Journal of Vocational Behavior*, **56**(2), 225–48.
Derks, B., N. Ellemers, C. van Laar and K. de Groot (2011), 'Do sexist organizational cultures create the queen bee?', *British Journal of Social Psychology*, **50**(3), 519–35.
Dezső, C.L. and D.G. Ross (2012), 'Does female representation in top management improve firm performance? A panel data investigation', *Strategic Management Journal*, **33**(9), 1072–89.
Dobbin, F. and J. Jung (2011), 'Corporate board gender diversity and stock performance: the competence gap or institutional investor bias?', *North Carolina Law Review*, **89**(3), 809–38.
Dreher, G.F. and T.H. Cox (1996), 'Race, gender, and opportunity: a study of compensation attainment and establishment of mentoring relationships', *Journal of Applied Psychology*, **81**(3), 297–308.
Eagly, A.H. and L.L. Carli (2007), *Through the Labyrinth: The Truth About How Women Become Leaders*, Cambridge, MA: Harvard Business School Press.
Eagly, A.H. and B.T. Johnson (1990), 'Gender and leadership style: a meta-analysis', *Psychological Bulletin*, **108**(2), 233–56.
Eagly, A.H. and S.J. Karau (2002), 'Role congruity theory of prejudice toward female leaders', *Psychological Review*, **109**(3), 573–98.
Eagly, A.H., M.C. Johannesen-Schmidt and M. van Engen (2003), 'Transformational, transactional, and laissez-faire leadership styles: a meta-analysis comparing women and men', *Psychological Bulletin*, **129**(4), 569–91.
Eagly, A.H., S.J. Karau and M.G. Makhijani (1995), 'Gender and the effectiveness of leaders: a meta-analysis', *Psychological Bulletin*, **117**(1), 125–45.
Eagly, A.H., M.G. Makhijani and B.G. Klonsky (1992), 'Gender and the evaluation of leaders: a meta-analysis', *Psychological Bulletin*, **111**(1), 3–22.
Elliott, J.R. and R.A. Smith (2004), 'Race, gender, and workplace power', *American Sociological Review*, **69**(3), 365–86.
Foels, R., J.E. Driskell, B. Mullen and E. Salas (2000), 'The effects of democratic leadership on group member satisfaction: an integration', *Small Group Research*, **31**(6), 676–701.
Forret, M. and T. Dougherty (2004), 'Networking behaviors and career outcomes: differences for men and women?', *Journal of Organizational Behavior*, **25**(3), 419–37.
Foschi, M. (2000), 'Double standards for competence', *Annual Review of Sociology*, **26**(2), 21–42.
Foschi, M., L. Lai and K. Sigerson (1994), 'Gender and double standards in the assessment of job applicants', *Social Psychology Quarterly*, **57**(4), 326–39.
Galinsky, E., K. Aumann and J.T. Bond (2008), *Times Are Changing: Gender and Generation at Work and at Home*, New York: Families and Work Institute, accessed 2 December 2014 at http://familiesandwork.org/site/research/reports/Times_Are_Changing.pdf.
Gastil, J. (1994), 'A meta-analytic review of the productivity and satisfaction of democratic and autocratic leadership', *Small Group Research*, **25**(3), 384–410.

Gauthier, A.H., T.M. Smeeding and F.F. Furstenberg (2004), 'Are parents investing less time in children? Trends in selected industrialized countries', *Population and Development Review*, **30**(4), 647–71.

Haynes, M.C. and J.S. Lawrence (2012), 'Who's to blame? Attributions of blame in unsuccessful mixed-sex work teams', *Basic and Applied Social Psychology*, **34**(6), 558–64.

Heilman, M.E. and J.J. Chen (2005), 'Same behavior, different consequences: reactions to men's and women's altruistic citizenship behavior', *Journal of Applied Psychology*, **90**(3), 431–41.

Heilman, M.E. and T.G. Okimoto (2007), 'Why are women penalized for success at male tasks? The implied communality deficit', *Journal of Applied Psychology*, **92**(1), 81–92.

Heilman, M.E. and A.S. Wallen (2010), 'Wimpy and undeserving of respect: penalties for men's gender-inconsistent success', *Journal of Experimental Social Psychology*, **46**(4), 664–7.

Heilman, M.E., A.S. Wallen, D. Fuchs and M.M. Tamkins (2004), 'Penalties for success: reactions to women who succeed at male gender-typed tasks', *Journal of Applied Psychology*, **89**(3), 416–27.

Hom, P.W., L. Roberson and A.D. Ellis (2008), 'Challenging conventional wisdom about who quits: revelations from corporate America', *Journal of Applied Psychology*, **93**(1), 1–34.

Hoyt, C.L., S.K. Johnson, S. Murphy and K. Skinnell (2010), 'The impact of blatant stereotype activation and group sex-composition on female leaders', *The Leadership Quarterly*, **21**(5), 716–32.

Jacobs, J.A. and G. Gerson (2004), *The Time Divide: Work, Family, and Gender Inequality*, Cambridge, MA: Harvard University Press.

Johnson, S., S. Murphy, S. Zewdie and R. Reichard (2008), 'The strong, sensitive type: effects of gender stereotypes and leadership prototypes on the evaluation of male and female leaders', *Organizational Behavior and Human Decision Processes*, **106**(1), 39–60.

Judge, T.A. and R.F. Piccolo (2004), 'Transformational and transactional leadership: a meta-analytic test of their relative validity', *Journal of Applied Psychology*, **89**(5), 901–10.

Kalev, A., F. Dobbin and E. Kelly (2006), 'Best practices or best guesses? Assessing the efficacy of corporate affirmative action and diversity policies', *American Sociological Review*, **71**(4), 589–617.

Koenig, A.M., A.H. Eagly, A.A. Mitchell and T. Ristikari (2011), 'Are leader stereotypes masculine? A meta-analysis of three research paradigms', *Psychological Bulletin*, **137**(4), 616–42.

Konrad, A.M., J.E. Ritchie, P. Lieb and E. Corrigall (2000), 'Sex differences and similarities in job attribute preferences: a meta-analysis', *Psychological Bulletin*, **126**(4), 593–641.

Lyness, K.S. and M.K. Judiesch (2001), 'Are female managers quitters? The relationships of gender, promotions, and family leaves of absence to voluntary turnover', *Journal of Applied Psychology*, **86**(6), 1167–78.

Mandel, H. and M. Semyonov (2005), 'Family policies, wage structures, and gender gaps: sources of earnings inequality in 20 countries', *American Sociological Review*, **70**(6), 949–67.

Matschiner, M. and S.K. Murnen (1999), 'Hyperfemininity and influence', *Psychology of Women Quarterly*, **23**(3), 631–42.

Mavin, S. (2008), 'Queen bees, wannabees, and afraid to bees: no more "best enemies" for women in management?', *British Journal of Management*, **19**(Suppl. 1), S75–S84.

McKay, P., D. Avery, S. Tonidandel, M. Morris, M. Hernandez and M. Hebl (2007), 'Racial differences in employee retention: are diversity climate perceptions the key?', *Personnel Psychology*, **60**(1), 35–62.

McPherson, M., L. Smith-Lovin and J.M. Cook (2001), 'Birds of a feather: homophily in social networks', *Annual Review of Sociology*, **27**(1), 415–44.

Mohr, G. and H. Wolfram (2008), 'Leadership and effectiveness in the context of gender: the role of leaders' verbal behaviour', *British Journal of Management*, **19**(1), 4–16.

Neal, T.M.S., R.E. Guadagno, C.A. Eno and S.L. Brodsky (2012), 'Warmth and competence on the witness stand: implications for the credibility of male and female expert witnesses', *Journal of the American Academy of Psychiatry and the Law*, **40**(4), 488–97.

Ng, T.W.H., L.T. Eby, K.L. Sorensen and D.C. Feldman (2005), 'Predictors of objective and subjective career success: a meta-analysis', *Personnel Psychology*, **58**(2), 367–408.

Noonan, M.C. and M.E. Corcoran (2004), 'The mommy track and partnership: temporary delay or dead end?', *Annals of the American Academy of Political and Social Science*, **596**(1), 130–50.

O'Dorchai, S. (2008), 'Do women gain or lose from becoming mothers? A comparative wage analysis in 25 European countries', *Brussels Economic Review*, **51**(2/3), 243–67.

Powell, G.N. and D.A. Butterfield (1979), 'The "good manager": masculine or androgynous?', *Academy of Management Journal*, **22**(2), 395–403.

Prentice, D.A. and E. Carranza (2002), 'What women and men should be, shouldn't be, are allowed to be, and don't have to be: the contents of prescriptive gender stereotypes', *Psychology of Women Quarterly*, **26**(4), 269–81.

Propp, K.M. (1995), 'An experimental examination of biological sex as a status cue in decision-making groups and its influence on information use', *Small Group Research*, **26**(4), 451–74.

Reid, S.A., N.A. Palomares, G.L. Anderson and B. Bondad-Brown (2009), 'Gender language and social influence: a test of expectation states, role congruity, and self-categorization theories', *Human Communication Research*, **35**(4), 465–90.

Rose, S.J. and H.I. Hartmann (2004), *Still a Man's Labor Market: The Long-term Earnings Gap*, Washington, DC: Institute for Women's Policy Research, accessed 2 December 2014 at http://www.iwpr.org/publications/pubs/still-a-mans-labor-market-the-long-term-earnings-gap.

Rudman, L.A. (1998), 'Self-promotion as a risk factor for women: the costs and benefits of counterstereotypical impression management', *Journal of Personality and Social Psychology*, **74**(3), 629–45.

Rudman, L.A. and P. Glick (2008), *The Social Psychology of Gender: How Power and Intimacy Shape Gender Relations*, New York: Guilford Press.

Rudman, L.A., C.A. Moss-Racusin, J.E. Phelan and S. Nauts (2012), 'Status incongruity and backlash effects: defending the gender hierarchy motivates prejudice against female leaders', *Journal of Experimental Social Psychology*, **48**(1), 165–79.

Ryan, M.K., A.S. Haslam, M.D. Hersby and R. Bongiorno (2011), 'Think crisis–think female: the glass cliff and contextual variation in the think manager–think male stereotype', *Journal of Applied Psychology*, **96**(6), 470–84.

Ryan, M.K., S. Haslam, M.D. Hersby, C. Kulich and C. Atkins (2008), 'Opting out or pushed off the edge? The glass cliff and the precariousness of women's leadership positions', *Social and Personality Psychology Compass*, **1**(1), 266–79.

Saad, L. (2012), *In U.S., Half of Women Prefer a Job Outside the Home*, accessed 2 December 2014 at http://www.gallup.com/poll/157313/half-women-prefer-job-outside-home.aspx.

Schein, V.E. (1973), 'The relationship between sex role stereotypes and requisite management characteristics', *Journal of Applied Psychology*, **57**(2), 95–100.

Seem, S. and M. Clark (2006), 'Healthy women, healthy men, and healthy adults: an evaluation of gender role stereotypes in the twenty-first century', *Sex Roles*, **55**(3–4), 247–58.

Silva C., N.M. Carter and A. Beninger (2012), 'Good intentions, imperfect execution? Women get fewer of the "hot jobs" needed to advance', New York: Catalyst, accessed 3 December 2014 at http://www.catalyst.org/system/files/Good_Intentions_Imperfect_Execution_Women_Get_Fewer_of_the_Hot_Jobs_Needed_to_Advance.pdf.

Sinclair, L. and Z. Kunda (2000), 'Motivated stereotyping of women: she's fine if she praised me but incompetent if she criticized me', *Personality and Social Psychology Bulletin*, **26**(11), 1329–42.

Thomas-Hunt, M.C. and K.W. Phillips (2004), 'When what you know is not enough: expertise and gender dynamics in task groups', *Personality and Social Psychology Bulletin*, **30**(12), 1585–98.

Timberlake, S. (2005), 'Social capital and gender in the workplace', *Journal of Management Development*, **24**(1), 34–44.

Torchia, M., A. Calabrò and M. Huse (2011), 'Women directors on corporate boards: from tokenism to critical mass', *Journal of Business Ethics*, **102**(2), 299–317.

Uhlmann, E.L. and G.L. Cohen (2005), 'Constructed criteria: redefining merit to justify discrimination', *Psychological Science*, **16**(6), 474–80.
US Bureau of Labor Statistics (2013a), 'Labor force statistics from the current population survey', accessed 2 December at http://www.bls.gov/cps/.
US Bureau of Labor Statistics (2013b), 'News release: American time-use survey – 2012 results', accessed 2 December 2014 at http://www.bls.gov/news.release/pdf/atus.pdf.
US National Center for Education Statistics (2010), 'Digest of education statistics, 2010', accessed 2 December 2014 at http://nces.ed.gov/programs/digest/d10/tables_3.asp#Ch3aSub4.
Van Emmerik, H., H. Wendt and M.C. Euwema (2010), 'Gender ratio, societal culture, and male and female leadership', *Journal of Occupational and Organizational Psychology*, **83**(4), 895–914.
Van Engen, M.L. and T.M. Willemsen (2004), 'Sex and leadership styles: a meta-analysis of research published in the 1990s', *Psychological Reports*, **94**, 3–18.
Williams, J.E. and D.L. Best (1990), *Measuring Sex Stereotypes: A Multination Study*, Newbury Park, CA: Sage.
Wosinska, W., A.J. Dabul, R. Whetstone-Dion and R.B. Cialdini (1996), 'Self-presentational responses to success in the organization: the costs and benefits of modesty', *Basic and Applied Social Psychology*, **18**(2), 229–42.

19. 'Woman as a project': key issues for women who want to get on
Sharon Mavin, Jannine Williams, Patricia Bryans and Nicola Patterson*

The following chapter explores senior women's key issues for women who want to get on as managers and leaders. We present analysis drawn from a wider qualitative study of 81 senior women who hold UK FTSE 100/250 executive/non-executive director and/or influential leader positions, set against a background assumption that 'male-defined constructions of work and career success continue to dominate organizational research and practice' (O'Neill et al., 2008, p. 727). The senior women participants have achieved a traditionally 'masculine strategic situation' (Tyler, 2005, p. 569) in breaking through the gendered glass ceiling (Morrison et al., 1987) and in doing so may be viewed as no longer 'the organizational second sex' or 'others of management' (Tyler, 2005, p. 572). The study, following Ellemers et al. (2012) and Chesterman et al. (2005), therefore explores experiences of women in high places who have overcome gendered barriers to achieve senior leader positions, and advances Terjesen et al.'s call for 'truly innovative research into the female directors' experiences' currently lacking in the literature (Terjesen et al., 2009, p. 332).

Our analysis, subsequent themes and conceptualization result from 81 senior women's responses to the interview question: what are the key issues women need to be aware of as they progress into senior positions? We recognize that women share experiences of oppression and marginalization as 'elite' women leaders in patriarchal organizations, however, at the same time we also acknowledge that the women participants are not a homogeneous group and also have different experiences (Griffin, 1995; Bryans and Mavin, 2003).

We are aware that our analysis of key issues for women who want to get on is influenced by the participants' biographies, career histories, bio-data, life stages and their societal and organizational contexts. Our assumptions are that 'women's careers are complex and multidimensional, yet work practices appear to exist in a single dimension – the male defined organizational dimension' (O'Neill et al., 2008, p. 735) and that after decades of women working, the predominant attitude is still 'think manager–think male' (Schein, 2007). These contextual factors provide a gendered background to, but are not the focus of, our research. We offer six themes that encapsulate senior women's key issues for women who want to get on as managers and leaders and draw upon doing gender well and differently against sex category (Mavin and Grandy, 2011, 2012) to conceptualize our contribution of 'woman as a project'; an architecture for instrumental personal organizing of holistic (personal and career) lives.

UNDERSTANDINGS OF GENDER

Gender is a social construction, a socially produced binary division and distinctions between women and men, and masculinities and femininities (Acker, 1992). This position reflects recent developments in gender studies that have moved the debate from essentialized concepts that located masculine behaviours or traits associated with men and feminine behaviours or traits associated with women as a consequence of biology. Gender can now be understood as an achievement; we 'do gender' through ongoing negotiations, through a 'complex of socially guided perceptual and interactional and micropolitical activities that cast particular pursuits as expressions of masculine and feminine "natures"' (West and Zimmerman, 1987, p.126). Constructing this argument, West and Zimmerman distinguish between sex, sex categorization and gender. This is a feminist tactic of separating physiological differences (sex) and social behaviours (gender) to unpack gender and open up the binary to scrutiny and disruption. However, there remains some debate over the connections between sex and gender, as it is suggested that when doing gender, people are already categorized by sex, as the body cannot be said to be neutral (Kelan, 2010). The fruitfulness of the gender binary continues to occupy gender researchers, as the potential to destabilize the binary has implications for the values, behaviours and meanings available to, and acceptable for, both women and men (Mavin and Grandy, 2011, 2012). Rather than undoing gender (Butler, 1990, 2004), it is suggested that gender undergoes processes of being re-done or done differently (Mavin and Grandy, 2011) as women move into spaces and ways of organizing previously considered a male/masculine enclave and also when they perform masculinities.

This chapter is based upon this position; that gender can be done well and differently against sex category through simultaneous, multiple enactments of femininity and masculinity (Mavin and Grandy, 2011, 2012). Women can do gender well if they do so in congruence with the female sex category whilst simultaneously doing gender differently by engaging in behaviours associated with masculinity (Mavin and Grandy, 2011). We continue to incorporate sex category into doing gender, as we recognize that gender is done from a body that is not neutral, but already positioned via sex category (Kelan, 2010). This position recognizes that the gender binary – femininities and masculinities – and management can begin to become decoupled (Billing, 2011) as women reduce negative backlash when they manoeuvre between the behaviours expected of women and those expected of men in becoming leaders (O'Neill and O'Reilly, 2010). This process of doing gender well and differently is dynamic; however, we recognize that through ongoing gender stereotyping in society and organizations, women and men continue to evaluate themselves and are evaluated by others against the femininity–masculinity binary divide (Mavin and Grandy, 2011, 2012).

THE CONTEXT FOR UK SENIOR WOMEN LEADERS

The UK context in terms of seniority remains largely male. The recent female FTSE report by Sealy and Vinnicombe (2013), which outlines the numbers and location of women in top UK companies, highlights that only 17.3 per cent of women hold directorships in the FTSE 100 and as low as 13.3 per cent in the FTSE 250. In real terms FTSE 100 women hold only 18 executive directorships versus 292 men and the FTSE 250 has only 32 women with executive directorships versus 558 men. Of the FTSE 100 appointments in the past six months, 74 per cent have been to men. The *Sex and Power Report, Who Runs Britain?* (Counting Women In, 2013) outlines how Britain is ranked only sixtieth out of 190 states for the number of women legislators and in a population of 51 per cent women, only 36.4 per cent of public appointments are women: 22.5 per cent of women are Members of Parliament; 14.2 per cent are university Vice Chancellors; and 15.6 per cent are High Court Judges. This picture presents the societal context for women and the saliency of ongoing research into women's experiences of management and leadership and in particular, individual senior women's experiences.

These stark figures reflect organizational contexts and structures that we contend remain gendered in ways that detrimentally shape women's experiences (Connell, 1987; Gherardi, 1994) as they move towards and take up management and leadership positions. Understanding the perpetuation of gendered organizing contexts requires an appreciation of the role of patriarchy and hegemonic masculinity. Patriarchy as socio-structural practices (Walby, 1989) provides the backcloth to gendered relations as it operates at macro (societal), meso (organizational) and micro (everyday interactions) levels (Connell, 1987; Billing, 2011). Patriarchy is expressed through hegemonic masculinity that maintains assumptions of masculine superiority (Knights and Kerfoot, 2004) and perpetuates the association of men/masculinities with management and leadership (Connell, 1987; Gherardi, 1994). Women who want to get on experience a double bind whereby they are expected to perform femininities associated with being a 'woman' whilst also demonstrating behaviours expected of managers/leaders (associated with masculinity) (Gherardi, 1994). In order to manoeuvre between these expectations and the gendered contexts they construct, senior women may opt to perform femininities and masculinities simultaneously and so do gender well and differently (Mavin and Grandy, 2011, 2012). Yet, women may also engage in or ventriloquize patriarchal attitudes (Brown, 1998). Engaging with patriarchy has consequences for the behaviours and relationships women can develop and sustain, and limits the femininities deemed to be appropriate for women to gendered stereotypes (for example, caring, empathic, compliant), which Connell (1987) suggests can be called emphasized femininities. Women may challenge hegemonic masculinities' construction of 'accepted' femininities by doing gender well (for example, engaging in such stereotypical femininities) and simultaneously doing gender differently (for example, by engaging in competition and ambition) (Mavin and Grandy, 2011, 2012).

An embedded resistor to women's doing gender well and differently is the masculine form of management associated with senior positions, argued to be 'imbued with conceptions of rationality and instrumental control, taken for granted and which render gender largely unproblematic' (Ross-Smith and Kornberger, 2004, p.296). Such masculine rationality is centred on control, 'an extreme version of competitive masculinity' (Ross-Smith and Chesterman, 2009, p.6) where senior leadership is understood as a 'masculine strategic situation' (Tyler, 2005, p.569) that shapes senior positions through embedded patriarchy and hegemonic masculinity reproducing masculine discourses and practices (Ross-Smith and Chesterman, 2009). Such contexts offer interesting and potentially informing sites through which senior women's experiences can be explored. Further, while women are now associating themselves with management and leadership (Billing, 2011), women may still need to manage negative responses if they jolt other organizational members' gendered expectations (Mavin, 2009), in particular those who do not associate management and leadership with women. We recognize that women may not have awareness of the extent to which these gendered contexts shape experiences, therefore these debates ground our research question: what are the key issues women need to be aware of as they progress into senior positions?

RESEARCH APPROACH

The data were derived from semi-structured interviews with 81 senior women working in UK-based organizations: 36 women directors/non-executive directors in UK FTSE 100/250 companies and 45 elite leaders identified as 'influential' in an annual regional newspaper supplement about the 'top 250/500 influential leaders' in a UK region (*The Journal*, 2008). Participant ages range from 33 to 67 years. Seventy-three women self-declared as white British/Irish/Other white backgrounds; two as black/mixed backgrounds, with six non-declared. Sixty-two women worked full-time, 14 part-time, with five non-declared. Face-to-face (56) and telephone (25) interviews took place, averaging approximately one-and-a-half hours. Interviews were recorded and transcribed by a professional transcribing service. We did not ask senior women what they perceived as career success or career barriers; rather, we explored women's reflections on their journeys to date. A flexible interview guide was used that began with life/career history, asked participants about their experiences of being a woman moving into senior positions and progressed to areas of friendship, competition, cooperation and ambition. Questions prompting reflections and learning were also included at the end of the interview.

Building upon Elliott and Stead (2008, p. 168) 'in order to get to the heart of women leaders' experiences' we focus here upon analysis of data that emerged in response to the question 'What are the key issues women need to be aware of as they progress into senior positions?', answered by all 81 participants. Analysis of these responses and cross-transcript analysis was highly iterative, moving between 'phases of coding, literature review, and conceptualization of the data' (Ladge et al., 2012, p. 1456). While the first author completed the initial coding inductively by creating thematic categories, through discussion all authors agreed on the final themes presented here. We now discuss each of the emergent themes to explore the key issues for women who want to get on as managers and leaders.

SENIOR WOMEN'S KEY ISSUES FOR WOMEN WHO WANT TO GET ON

We are conscious reflexively of the interview questions being grounded in aspects of gender and of the research specifically publicized as focussing upon senior women's relationships with other women at work. Therefore, the interviews provided a unique opportunity to ask senior women what they viewed as the key issues for women who want to progress to senior positions. We recognize that the senior women and researchers were

310 *Handbook of gendered careers in management*

co-constructing learning from the participants' career journeys and experiences to date during the interview as a site for reflective learning. The following six themes emerged from analysis of senior women's accounts and provide a broad overview of the key issues identified.

To Be or Not to Be a Woman . . .

This theme reflects the senior women's positioning of themselves as women leaders or as gender-neutral leaders against the gender binary. Those who positioned themselves as gender-neutral leaders did not want being a woman to be relevant to their positions and were clear that it was business that counted; there was almost nothing that was a problem unique to women and if individuals want to achieve, they could do so regardless of gender. This gender-neutral positioning was reflected in comments that women should not ask for nor expect special treatment or to be treated any differently from men. Senior women recommend that women do not use their femininity, their appearance or being a woman as an excuse, thus eliminating gender and constraining women's opportunities to do gender well.

Those women who positioned themselves as women leaders felt that women should stop worrying about being women, value themselves as women and stop apologizing for being women. They did not want women to become men, to adopt male traits or to become one of the boys. There was an overall awareness from the participants of the gendered nature of organizations and of the discrimination women still face, and advice was for women to be realistic about the possibility of being the only woman in the room as they rise hierarchically – by doing your homework, picking the right company (women-readiness) and being aware of having to confront masculine heroic leader expectations. Their advice was to be aware of assuming and deploying authority while at the same time not be too aggressive and testosterone driven and 'frighten the horses', which could limit the appointment of other women. Thus, women are able to do gender differently but not too differently against the binary that they render themselves and other women vulnerable.

Senior women make comparisons to men in identifying their key issues for women who want to get on. They recommend that women reflect on the way men go for the 'quick wins' (influencing key people) when they get promotion and have already got a plan for 'everybody to say how brilliant they are', whereas women get 'too stuck into the job' rather than the relationships around them. Senior women repeatedly point out that women must work harder than men, be on top of their game and not make mistakes, which are less tolerated than when men make them. Again, senior women recommend that women lose or tone down their femininity in the leader role, in that women should ensure their focus is not on their clothes and children (femininity) but on their competence (masculinity) when appearing in the press/media because this is the case for men.

Family Matters

Further contradictions surface in the theme of 'family matters' where, dependent upon the women's positioning of themselves against the gender binary, family matters should not be a barrier to women who want to get on, or family matters should not be an issue for an organization, that is, women should not expect special treatment, even though in general they recognized that the weight of family responsibilities falls to women. This was also influenced by the senior women's age and life stage in that younger senior women (birth year from 1965) were more adamant that the organization had a responsibility to support women in successfully managing family matters and a senior career. However, women at later life stages (birth year before 1965) did recommend that women should not be afraid of having a family, a personal life and a career and to remember 'you cannot go home and cuddle a career'. Regardless, senior women agree that women should plan and organize their family matters in ways that work with their overall life and career ambitions, including choosing the right partner carefully. Some of the senior women who had children told us of how their partners work at home, work part-time or have retired to take the lead in family responsibilities, so that personal relationships were grounded in equality. This type of life planning requires early self-awareness and decision-making for women and an integration of personal life choices and career.

Again senior women compared themselves to men in terms of family matters, where it was perceived that men in organizations did not understand the impact of maternity and returning to work for women leaders. Senior women recommend that women talk more and act positively about these issues as a means of 'normalizing' women's experiences. An example of this is a senior woman discussing that she did not accept any resignations from women on maternity leave or upon return 'until the hormones had reduced'.

Becoming More Authentic and Building Self-efficacy

Being 'true' to yourself, being yourself, being genuine, becoming authentic, knowing oneself, what you stand for, knowing your values and having a moral compass were highlighted as incredibly important enablers of success.

This 'becoming more authentic' was discussed in terms of how women should work hard on knowing who they really are, reflect on management and leadership styles and on the way they develop relationships. Integrated with becoming more authentic is advice for women to develop and demonstrate self-efficacy as a leader – believing in one's capabilities to organize and take action to succeed (Bandura, 1977). There were numerous comparisons between men and women's levels of self-efficacy and self-belief in their abilities in delivering the top jobs in organizations, with women recommended to develop their self-belief, resilience and to value their abilities. This leadership self-efficacy is not grounded in a general concept of confidence or competence (Vinnicombe, 2013). These women are highly competent and knowledgeable. Rather, this self-efficacy reflects women committing effort to achieving their own specific outcomes, attributing failure to things within their control and recovering quickly from setbacks (Bandura, 1977). This includes imagining/visualizing yourself in a position, to reduce insecurity and build self-efficacy; ignoring any 'little voices' of self-criticism or self-doubt; developing leadership self-efficacy through organizing all aspects of life to enable women to perform to the best of their abilities; developing self-belief, resilience, confidence in own abilities and valuing themselves in ways that reduce insecurity. Women are recommended to work at reducing personal over-sensitivity and investing in development techniques to manage over-worrying and anxiety, seen as debilitating, energy sapping and a barrier to women's self-efficacy in senior roles.

Investing in Your Development

The theme of 'investing in your development' has a functional 'do this and that' feel but at its core the process of women committing to personal learning and development was a key issue that provides the scaffolding for women 'becoming more authentic and developing self-efficacy'. Senior women recommended that women who want to get on are prepared to learn, change, adapt and be flexible; are prepared to rehearse and practice 'being' a leader; are prepared to commit to coaching for job interviews; to engage in networking, join professional organizations and get onto organizational talent programmes. Spending time observing senior leaders, in terms of what to do and not to do, learning to operate in contingent ways and identifying strong role models were also key issues, as well as developing relationships with other external senior women to discuss challenges. Senior women emphasize women not being afraid to commit to coaching and mentoring early in their careers to support personal development and to develop emotional intelligence and self-awareness, critical to becoming more authentic and supporting the achievement of other key issues.

There was no doubt that long-term career planning, being overt about which role is next for you; swapping careers, sectors, moving sideways; planning and making career moves along the lines of a game of chess, were key issues for women who want to get on – utilizing agency in manoeuvring towards their life goals. Investing in their own development for the future to support career planning and thus making themselves the project, was reiterated as critical.

Outstanding Credibility but Not the Solid Lieutenant

In demonstrating competence as a key issue for women who want to get on, senior women advised women to be on top of their game, the expert, with internal (self-belief and self-efficacy) and external (enacted/reputational) credibility, demonstrated through competence and delivery and high professional standards. Women who want to get on should be trusted as an expert advisor; be loyal; be seen to take responsibility; know everything there is to know about an organization's purpose whilst developing their own personal brand. Senior women had no doubt that women have to work harder than men to get on and have to make sacrifices but their counter-advice was for women to balance this exceptional credibility without working too hard, to prevent exhaustion. Women should not take on too much and underperform. Women must be able to have a vision of the wider world and with their own brand make an impact on the organization. However, again this is a balancing act for women and should be enacted without getting stuck in middle management positions or becoming too much of a specialist, in that if women focus on the specifics of the job, they risk being overlooked in terms of leadership potential. Therefore, women should learn to balance their exceptional credibility without being 'the solid lieutenant', developing their potential; moving from 'doer to thinker creator'.

Functionally senior women identified profit and loss and line management experience as critical issues for women who want to get on. Women should take a strategic role in developing excellent relationships with stakeholders and shareholders and demonstrate understanding of the bottom line; to get the profit and loss responsibility and move sideways to access it like a game of chess (doing gender differently and seizing the masculine strategic prerogative), as well as simultaneously demonstrating how they can nurture and act corporately within the organization and have line management experience (doing gender well by meeting more feminine stereotypes).

The notion of women organizing themselves is reflected again in this theme. Senior women used a metaphor of juggling balls to reflect what was necessary in women's home and professional life. This is a common theme in women in management research, the juggling of multiple roles and family concerns, evidencing the proposal that women's career choices are about more than just paid work (O'Neill et al., 2008). Therefore, women need to be good organizers, multi-taskers, good delegators and be able to 'steal with pride' rather than re-invent the wheel to demonstrate exceptional credibility. The critical message is that women are advised to organize their work and personal lives to provide an architecture that enables their progression.

Bravery Counts

The final theme of 'bravery counts' reflects the realities of putting the key issues into action and relates to organizational politics and women's personal behaviours and performance. Women in management are often reluctant to engage in and often disassociate themselves from organizational politics as distasteful, viewed as a boy's game related to the masculine strategic objective (Tyler, 2005). However, in a similar way to understanding themselves and becoming more authentic, senior women advise women to invest in fully understanding the organizational context, relationships and organizational politics; to know their audiences and be instrumental in how they communicate and perform when engaging with them. Here senior women advise women to do gender differently in that political behaviour is normally the domain of men but this can also be perceived as recommending women to conform to masculine norms.

In understanding how the social organization works, women are recommended to act as the de facto leader before formal appointment. In their career planning women should work out who is influential and/or what organizations will be critical to progress, thus emphasizing the instrumentality of career planning. Women are recommended to identify who is a good sponsor in order to politically align themselves, influence people and develop appropriate allies and to recognize the need for, and develop their own, 'political and organizational savvy' if they want to get on, so that they learn the invisible rules of the game or 'combat' and understand 'sub-agendas' and 'political currents that run beneath' the organization. Understanding organizational politics and social relations enables women to fully engage and influence and also to know where their allies and enemies are located and how to manage them.

Senior women also recommend that women who want to get on are brave and take risks and are prepared to 'seize the moment' in their behaviours and actions as a manager or leader – feeling the fear and doing it anyway. Women should go for 'quick wins' influencing significant others, move out of their comfort zone to gain experience and be prepared to stand alone when necessary. In practice this means speaking out, asking the 'pertinent questions', asking 'one good question in every meeting', therefore being assertive, confident, having an opinion and pushing yourself forward and doing gender differently. Senior women advise that women should not be afraid to challenge (and do gender differently) but they need to be prepared 'for the fact that people will not like it', as masculine behaviour from women jolts gender stereotypes (Mavin, 2009), provoking backlash responses. Senior women recommend that knowing and understanding your audiences helps mediate this backlash. In terms of challenging gendered stereotypes, senior women advise that women are prepared to 'sing their own praises', 'cultivate the art of gentle boasting', being able to express ambition and competition confidently, being 'very overt about the next job they want' and continually reviewing aspirations so that they can articulate these when appropriate. 'Bravery counts' reflects senior women's recognition of how risky the performance of masculinities is for individual women and the need to find a balance between behaviours needed to challenge the stereotypes and not 'frightening the horses'.

WOMAN AS A PROJECT

Women's experiences take place within gendered contexts and structures at the macro-meso-micro level that constrain and enable women's agency. We recognize that studies into women in management at the individual micro level face the danger of falling into the 'blame the woman' trap, so that women are treated as deficit against male norms, with suggested strategies at risk of being perceived as 'fixing the women' (Mavin, 2008). This is illustrated by Sheryl Sandberg's (2013) recent argument that women can have it all but they subconsciously sabotage their own careers through fear, guilt and willingness to conform to stereotypes, versus the debates that highlight that change is required at the macro level, in society (for example, Counting Women In, 2013) and at the meso level, in organizations to change masculine cultures and adapt to the needs of women in the workplace (for example, Mavin, 2001; Bryans and Mavin, 2003; Maddock, 2005). We recognize the need for change at each level, along with a commitment to gender politics for women managers and leaders, where women are more aware of, and better prepared to learn, 'the rules of the game' at each of the levels in order to be able to challenge, disrupt and orchestrate change through various strategies appropriate to individual women. One way forward for women who want to get on within gendered contexts is to view themselves as their own project.

The themes presented are interlinked, complex, fluid, simultaneous, at times contradictory and take place within gendered contexts against a masculine norm of management and leadership. The themes are relational, socially constructed and reflect how women do gender well and differently, simultaneously against the gender binary (Mavin and Grandy, 2011, 2012). In analysing senior women's experiences as a means of further understanding key issues for women who want to get on we offer a conceptualization of 'woman as a project'. Woman as a project is grounded within gendered contexts and integrates two features: conscious awareness of doing gender well and differently simultaneously and instrumental personal organizing (Figure 19.1).

This conceptualization draws upon a project as a conceptual, processual plan (evolving, adapting and co-constructed with others), for women's awareness, outlook, preparation and decision-making, which enables women to engage in contingency planning in their life course and to prepare for actions and alternative actions. As a concept, 'woman as a project' is supported by an architecture for design, structure and behaviour in navigating women's whole life course, enabling consciousness to the gendered contexts and possibilities for women's decision-making and agency within their personal and work lives. 'Woman as a project' requires a commitment to self-awareness, understanding oneself, one's values, ambitions and aspirations, across and at key points in their lives. In approaching their lives as a project, women commit time, effort and planning, over time and space, in processes of holistic, instrumental, personal 'organizing' that requires commitment to the significant organizing of women's lives, aspirations, ambitions across their life and not just work history. In this way we respond differently to the call by Jackson and Hirsh (1990) that careers should be accommodated around the reality of women's lives, allowing them to make a meaningful investment in both occupational and family roles, proposing a holistic integration to enable women's instrumentality and agency.

'Woman as a project' provides an architecture to integrate women's lives that incorporates two significant features: conscious awareness of doing gender well and differently against sex category, including gender-aware positioning self as a woman leader or as a leader, and instrumental personal organizing. Through these features the project architecture integrates as interlocking processes, the key issues that senior women identified for women who want to get on as managers or leaders. 'Woman as a project' enables women to view their life course from a holistic perspective rather than one that is compartmentalized and in this way takes account of the complex and interwoven choices and constraints in women's career and life development (Powell and Mainiero, 1992) as well

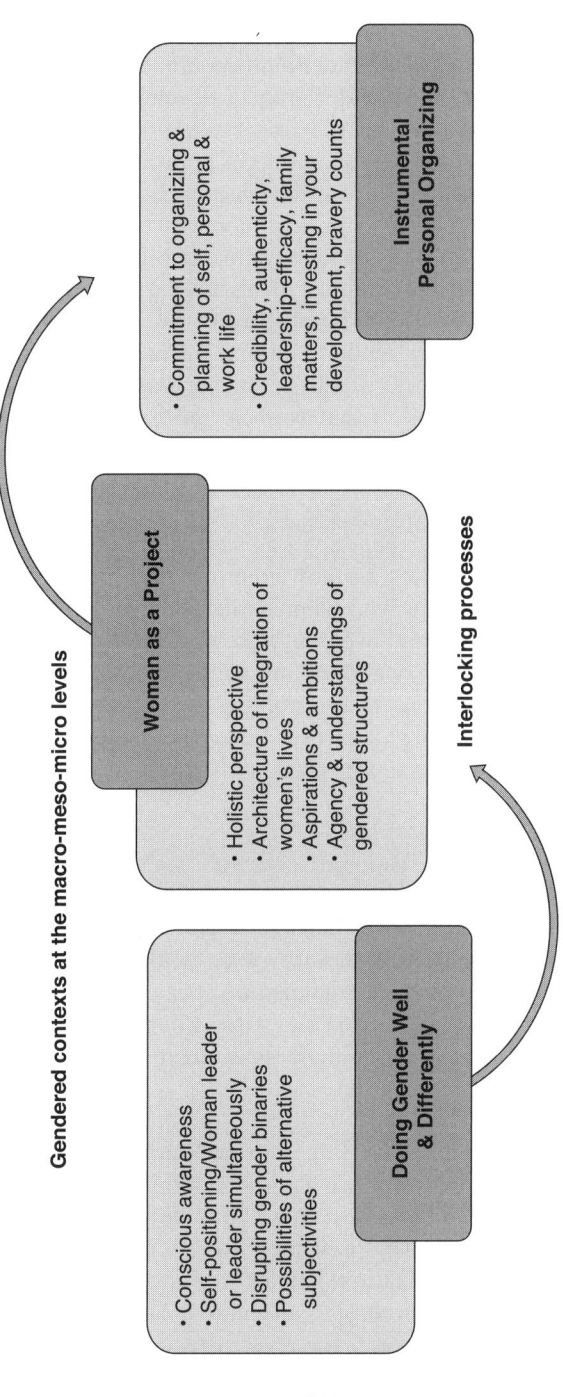

Figure 19.1 Woman as a project: key issues for women who want to get on

as acknowledging how women's career and life responsibilities ebb and flow against life stages (O'Neill and Bilimoria, 2005). This commitment to 'woman as a project' is grounded, not in developing women against a deficit model of male norm at the macro-meso-micro levels but as a guiding architecture for how a woman might approach and/or construct themselves in organizing their life's ambitions and aspirations.

A feature of the 'woman as a project' concept is a micro-level individual consciousness of doing gender well and differently against sex category, which opens up possibilities of disrupting male norm assumptions and gendered expectations. Raising awareness amongst women of their performances of doing gender well and differently simultaneously may enable alternative subjectivities to be further embedded and accepted in society and organizations so that women and men are more able to demonstrate a range of subjectivities. We contend that what is unique about this study is the senior women's awareness of the continuing gender binary for managers and leaders and their advice for other women to be conscious of positioning themselves as women leaders or as gender-neutral leaders. These choices are not either/or; they can be contingent and can operate simultaneously as women 'do' manager and leader roles. Contradictions surfaced from women who position as gender-neutral leaders but who expect society and organizations to be changing to adapt to women's family and caring responsibilities. We contend that it is the conscious *awareness* of these contradictions that empowers women's agency and that the 'woman as a project' architecture has the potential to enable this awareness.

Becoming more authentic with self-efficacy is a theme within the project architecture. In advancing Mainiero and Sullivan's (2005) claims that authenticity and being true to oneself will be prevalent late career, as the theme held resonance across over half the senior women involved in the research and was evident across senior women who share similar hierarchical positions (the top of their organization) but different career stages (that is, they are mid- to late career) and who also spanned the age range of the research population, becoming more authentic has risen in priority and is no longer apparent just at late career.

Through the themes of 'family matters', 'outstanding credibility but not solid lieutenant' and 'investing in development', senior women emphasize that women who want to get on should instrumentally organize and plan their lives. This is not a new finding in the field of careers for women in management where women are often thwarted in this by gendered society and organizational structures and expectations, sometimes resulting in women developing alternative career patterns against a hierarchical male norm career. However, this current research offers a 'holistic' way of viewing life course beyond career planning. Senior women tell us that rather than focussing solely on the job they are doing, women could make themselves the 'organizing project' in terms of their 'whole' life rather than just work. In not being the 'solid lieutenant' or 'stuck in middle management', the concept of 'woman as a project' highlights how women could 'stop doing the doing' and stop fully committing to their current role, to step back and focus upon themselves as their lifetime project. Women who want to get on are encouraged to see *themselves* as something to be more instrumentally organized, planned, evaluated and implemented successfully. We contend that the 'woman as a project' concept takes place within multiple gendered relationships and contexts, where becoming consciously gender aware of doing gender well and differently and instrumental personal organizing are key enablers and where an architecture integrates through instrumental organizing, chess-like career planning, development of key competences, personal and family matters, strategic life planning and engaging in learning and development.

CONCLUSION

We are aware that this research may be limited by the nature of the sample, senior women in UK organizations, and that this could open up criticism from those who argue that limiting studies of women's careers in management to samples of elite/successful women represents only a small proportion of the population of women in management, so that generalizations may not be relevant for the majority of women (O'Neill et al., 2008). The chapter is underpinned by an assumption that the learning offered is for those women who are motivated to progress. We contend that as the 'woman as project' concept integrates women's personal and career lives, it has transferability to women at all levels and life stages in management and leadership.

To summarize the chapter, we have outlined the emergent themes resulting from our analysis of senior women's responses to the question 'What are the key issues women need to be aware of as they progress into senior positions' and theorized six emergent themes drawing upon doing gender well and differently simultaneously against sex category to offer a concept of 'woman as a project' and its associated architecture as an enabler to supporting women who want to get on as managers and leaders in organizations.

NOTE

* Our thanks go to the senior women who engaged in the research and to the research assistants on the wider 'Senior Women at Work' project, Edita Petrylaite and Dr Stephanie Haeussler, Northumbria University.

REFERENCES

Acker, J. (1992), 'Gendering organizational theory', in A. Mills and P. Tancred (eds), *Gendering Organizational Analysis*, Newbury Park, CA: Sage Publications, pp. 248–60.
Bandura, A. (1977), 'Self-efficacy: toward a unifying theory of behavioural change', *Psychological Review*, **84**(2), 191–215.
Billing, Y.D. (2011), 'Are women in management victims of the phantom of the male norm?', *Gender, Work & Organization*, **3**(18), 298–317.
Brown, B. (1998), *Unlearning Discrimination in the Early Years*, Stoke-on-Trent: Trentham Books.
Bryans, P. and S. Mavin (2003), 'Women learning to become managers: learning to fit in or to play a different game?', *Management Learning*, **34**(1), 111–34.
Butler, J. (1990), *Gender Trouble: Feminism and the Subversion of Identity*, London: Routledge.
Butler, J. (2004), *Undoing Gender*, New York: Routledge.
Chesterman, C., A. Ross-Smith and M. Peters (2005), 'The gendered impact on organisations of a critical mass of women in senior management', *Policy and Society*, **24**(4), 69–91.
Connell, R.W. (1987), *Gender and Power*, Sydney: Allen and Unwin.
Counting Women In (2013), *Sex and Power 2013, Who Runs Britain?*, accessed 3 December 2014 at http://www.fawcettsociety.org.uk/latest/press-releases/sex-and-power-2013-who-runs-britain/.
Ellemers, N., F. Rink, B. Derks and M.K. Ryan (2012), 'Women in high places: when and why promoting women into top positions can harm them individually or as a group (and how to prevent this)', *Research in Organizational Behavior*, **32**(5), 163–87.
Elliott, C. and V. Stead (2008), 'Learning from leading women's experience: towards a sociological understanding', *Leadership*, **4**(2), 159–80.
Gherardi, S. (1994), 'The gender we think, the gender we do in our everyday organizational lives', *Human Relations*, **47**(6), 591–610.
Griffin, C. (1995), 'Feminism, social psychology and qualitative research', *The Psychologist*, **8**(3), 119–21.
Jackson, C. and W. Hirsh (1991), 'Women managers and career progression: the British experience', *Women in Management Review*, **6**(2), 10–16.
Kelan, E.K. (2010), 'Gender logic and undoing gender at work', *Gender, Work & Organization*, **2**(17), 174–94.
Knights, D. and D. Kerfoot (2004), 'Between representations and subjectivity: gender binaries and the politics of organizational transformation', *Gender, Work & Organization*, **11**(4), 430–54.
Ladge, J., J. Clair and D. Greenberg (2012), 'Cross-domain identity transition during liminal periods: constructing multiple selves as professional and mother during pregnancy', *Academy of Management Journal*, **55**(6), 1449–71.
Maddock, S. (2005), 'The leadership role of women in social regeneration in the UK', *International Journal of Public Sector Management*, **18**(2), 128–38.
Mainiero, L.A. and S.E. Sullivan (2005), 'Kaleidoscope careers: an alternate explanation for the "opt-out" revolution', *The Academy of Management Executive*, **19**(1), 106–23.
Mavin, S. (2001), 'Women's career in theory and practice: time for change?', *Women in Management Review*, **16**(4), 183–92.

Mavin, S. (2008), 'Queen bees, wannabees and afraid to bees: no more best enemies for women in management', *British Journal of Management*, **19**(1), 575–84.
Mavin, S. (2009), 'Navigating the labyrinth: senior women managing emotion', *International Journal of Work, Organisation & Emotion*, **3**(1), 81–7.
Mavin, S. and G. Grandy (2011), 'Doing gender well and differently in dirty work', *Gender, Work & Organization*, **20**(3), 232–51.
Mavin, S. and G. Grandy (2012), 'Doing gender well and differently in management', *Gender in Management: An International Journal*, **27**(4), 218–31.
Morrison, A.M., R.P. White and E. van Velsor (1987), *Breaking the Glass Ceiling*, Reading, MA: Addison-Wesley.
O'Neill, D.A. and D. Bilimoria (2005), 'Women's career development phases: idealism, endurance, and reinvention', *Career Development International*, **10**(3), 168–89.
O'Neill, O.A. and C.A. O'Reilly (2010), 'Careers as tournaments: the impact of sex and gendered organizational culture preferences on MBAs' income attainment', *Journal of Organizational Behavior*, **31**(6), 856–76.
O'Neill, D.A., M.M. Hopkins and D. Bilimoria (2008), 'Women's careers at the start of the 21st century: patterns and paradoxes', *Journal of Business Ethics*, **80**(4), 727–43.
Powell, G.N. and L.A. Mainiero (1992), 'Cross-currents in the river of time: conceptualizing the complexities of women's careers', *Journal of Management*, **18**(2), 215–37.
Ross-Smith, A. and C. Chesterman (2009), '"Girl disease": women managers' reticence and ambivalence towards organizational advancement', *Journal of Management and Organization*, **15**(5), 582–95.
Ross-Smith, A. and M. Kornberger (2004), 'Gendered rationality? A genealogical exploration of the philosophical and sociological conceptions of rationality, masculinity and organization', *Gender, Work & Organization*, **11**(3), 280–305.
Sandberg, S. (2013), *Lean In: Women, Work, and the Will to Lead*, New York: Random House.
Schein, V.E. (2007), 'Women in management: reflections and projections', *Women in Management Review*, **22**(1), 6–18.
Sealy, R. and S. Vinnicombe (2013), *The Female FTSE Report, False Dawn of Progress for Women on Boards*, Cranfield, UK: Cranfield International Centre for Women Leaders, Cranfield University.
Terjesen, S., R. Sealy and V. Singh (2009), 'Women directors on corporate boards: a review and research agenda', *Corporate Governance: An International Review*, **17**(3), 320–37.
The Journal (2008), '500 of the most influential people in the North East', NCJ Media, 6 June, accessed 8 December 2014 at http://thejournal.newspaperdirect.com/epaper/viewer.aspx.
Tyler, M. (2005), 'Women in change management: Simone de Beauvoir and the co-optation of women's otherness', *Journal of Organizational Change Management*, **18**(6), 561–77.
Vinnicombe, S. (2013), 'Gender, professions and society forum workshop', Newcastle University Business School, Newcastle University, 28 June.
Walby, S. (1989), 'Theorising patriarchy', *Sociology*, **23**(2), 213–34.
West, C. and D.H. Zimmerman (1987), 'Doing gender', *Gender and Society*, **2**(1), 125–51.

20. Women on boards in Australia: achieving real change or more of the same?
Alison Sheridan, Anne Ross-Smith and Linley Lord

Board roles are often framed as the ultimate career achievement for 'successful' corporate leaders (Stern and Westphal, 2010). Women's limited access to the most senior levels of organizations, including the board level, is well recognized internationally (Davies et al., 2011; Deloitte, 2011) and responses to women's under-representation differ across countries. The governments of Iceland, Israel, Norway and Spain have opted to legislate for women's representation on boards, to varying degrees and with varying timelines for compliance (Catalyst, 2012; GovernanceMetrics International, 2013). Other countries, such as Sweden, Finland, the UK and the USA, have elected to take a more 'hands off' approach, with efforts to increase women's access to boards focusing more on self-regulation than government intervention. Following a surge in calls for quotas to be applied in Australian boardrooms in 2009 (Broderick, 2009; Fox, 2013), it is this more self-regulatory approach that has been followed in Australia.

In what was widely seen as a turning point in the corporate regulatory environment in late 2010, the Australian Securities Exchange (the ASX), revised its Corporate Governance Principles. From 1 January 2011, Principle 3 of the ASX Corporate Governance Principles required sharemarket-listed companies to provide details in their annual reports of the number of women on their boards, in senior management roles and across the organization, to introduce gender targets and report on their effectiveness. As we note in more detail later in the chapter, until that point most of corporate Australia was steadfastly against any form of government-imposed quota or regulation for women on boards.

There has been what some would term a significant increase in the number of women appointed to the ASX-listed boards since this Principle was enacted (Australian Institute of Company Directors, 2013a; KPMG, 2013). In the period 2008 to December 2010 the percentage of female directors in the ASX200 moved from 8.30 per cent to 10.70 per cent (a 2.4 per cent increase). In the period since Principle 3 was enacted, the percentage of women has increased to 17.60 per cent (December 2013) (6.6 per cent increase). Whilst the numbers are still below 20 per cent, the rate of increase has doubled (Australian Institute of Company Directors, 2014a). It is also worth noting that the Australian approach has been promoted as a model for other countries to follow (Sealy et al., 2011). The question we address in this chapter is whether the increasing representation of women on corporate boards as we have seen in Australia since 2011 will lead to greater leadership opportunities for women more generally and more diversity on boards, or is it just a case of 'more of the same'? We critically appraise the actions that have been taken by key institutions within Australia to increase women's access to corporate boards, for the purposes of opening the debate further to questions around women 'getting on'.

WOMEN ON CORPORATE BOARDS

As the issue of women's under-representation on boards has gained more attention internationally, the number of sites monitoring and comparing the relative proportions of women has grown (Catalyst, 2012; Workplace Gender Equality Agency, 2012; GovernanceMetrics International, 2013; Sealy and Vinnicombe, 2013). As can be seen in Table 20.1, the board seats held by women vary across countries, with Norway representing the highest proportion (at 36.3 per cent) and Saudi Arabia the lowest (at 0.1 per cent) reported. The range for board chairs is far less, from 10.7 per cent of boards in Norway with women as chairs, to ten of the 23 countries having no women as board chairs of their listed companies.

In terms of the number of women on boards, Norway's 'leading' position reflects the government-imposed regulatory approach implemented through the amendment passed to its Public Limited Companies Act in 2003, which required firms to have at least 33–50 per cent of each gender depending on the size of the board. Non-compliance with the amendment results in dissolution of the company, which is the same sanction as for non-compliance with any of the Public Limited Companies Act's requirements. In 2002, women made up a mere 6.8 per cent of board members in Norway, and 470 of the 611 public limited companies did not have a single woman on the board (Davies et al., 2011). By 2012, they made up 36.3 per cent. Norway now has the highest proportion of women directors internationally (Nielsen and Huse, 2010a, 2010b; Seierstad, 2012).

THE AUSTRALIAN CONTEXT

Since 2002, the representation of women on boards in Australia has been monitored by the Equal Opportunity for Women in the Workplace

324 *Handbook of gendered careers in management*

Table 20.1   *Representation of women board directors (WBD)*

Country	% Board Seats Held by Women[a]	% Women Board Chairs[a,b]	Nature of Monitoring[b,c]	Sanctions[b,c]
Saudi Arabia	0.1	0	Nil	Nil
Qatar	0.3	0	Nil	Nil
United Arab Emirates	0.8	0	N/A	N/A
Australia	8.4	3	Comply or explain (1 January 2011)	Nil
China	8.5	3.7	N/A	N/A
Switzerland	9.1	1.8	N/A	N/A
New Zealand	9.3	0	Nil	Nil
Belgium	9.4	4.2	Quotas – requires 33% of each gender (2011 for state-owned enterprises and 2017–18 for publicly traded companies)	If board comprises fewer than the minimum number of each gender, any new appointment or reappointment of the majority gender will be deemed void
Spain	10.2	0	Quotas – requires 40% of each gender by 2015	Nil
United Kingdom	10.7	2.5	Target of 25% WBD for FTSE 100 companies by 2015	Nil
Poland	10.8	12.5	Corporate governance code recommends gender balance on boards	Nil, but companies attaining quota will get priority for government contracts
Austria	10.8	0	Companies must publish all gender diversity initiatives to promote women onto management board	N/A
Israel	12.6	0	Quotas of at least one woman director for publicly traded companies (1999)	Nil
Germany	12.9	1.2	Comply or explain (2010)	Nil
Netherlands	13.1	0	Target determined by company (compliance by 2016)	Non-compliance will require formal explanation

Table 20.1 (continued)

Country	% Board Seats Held by Women[a]	% Women Board Chairs[a,b]	Nature of Monitoring[b,c]	Sanctions[b,c]
Canada	13.1	2.2	Nil	Nil
Denmark	15.6	0	Comply or explain	Nil
South Africa	15.8	3.6	Comply or explain (1 September 2009)	Nil
United States	16.1	2	Catalyst annual reports and disclosure to Securities and Exchange Commission	Nil
France	16.6	2	Quotas (compliance by 2015)	Nominations void and fees suspended for all board members if non-compliance
Sweden	26.4	2.4	Comply or explain	Nil
Finland	26.4	0	Comply or explain (1 January 2010)	Nil
Norway	36.3	10.7	Quotas 40% WBD (compliance by 2009)	Fines/dissolution

Sources:
a. GovernanceMetrics International (2013).
b. 30 Per Cent Club (2011).
c. Deloitte (2011).

Agency (EOWA) (renamed the Workplace Gender Equality Agency in 2012) through its Census of Women Board Directors (EOWA, 2002, 2003), subsequently the bi-annual Census of Women in Leadership (EOWA and Catalyst, 2004; EOWA, 2006, 2008, 2010). The purpose of such monitoring was to 'measure women's participation in corporate leadership' (EOWA, 2006, p.4) and, until recently, the cumulative picture was not bright. In 2002, women's representation on boards was 8.2 per cent and by 2010 it was 8.4 per cent (EOWA, 2010, p.4).

Prompted by such dispiriting progress, in 2009 there were a number of calls to action (Baird and Wilkinson, 2010). Katy Lahey, then Chief Executive of the Business Council of Australia, argued for gender quotas as did other influential and high-profile business women, including Margaret Jackson, the former Chair of Qantas, one of Australia's iconic companies

(ABC News, 2009) and the Federal Human Rights and Equal Opportunity Commissioner, Elizabeth Broderick (Broderick, 2009; Braund, 2010). Norway's success in increasing women's representation through quotas was often raised by proponents of gender quotas. In 2009 a national conference on boardroom diversity in Australia heard a keynote speech by Arni Hole, the Norwegian Director General Ministry of Children and Equality. Her presentation citing the benefits of quotas (Hole, 2009) attracted significant media attention across Australia. Not all of this was positive, as there was also vocal resistance to the prospect of quotas, both by individuals and industry bodies. For example, the Australian Institute of Company Directors (AICD), the peak professional body for company directors in Australia, strongly resisted any calls for quotas (Korporaal, 2009) as did David Gonksi, then chair of the ASX (Braund, 2010). A number of high-profile women also came out against such affirmative action and vocalized their strong preference for 'meritocracy' (Marriott, 2009; UWA Business School, 2010).

With the prospect of government intervention being mooted in public debate (Baird and Wilkinson, 2010), a committee was established to advise the Federal Minister of Superannuation and Corporation Law on diversity on boards. In its final report, the Committee took a conservative stance and argued against imposing gender or other quotas on private sector companies and recommended encouraging 'boards and shareholders, in their own interest, to give full consideration to issues of diversity in board composition' (Corporations and Markets Advisory Committee, 2009, p. 48). The Committee maintained that in the private sector the accountability of directors to shareholders was paramount and to impose quotas would undermine effective governance. Instead, they argued for 'convincing leaders and shareholders of the benefits of a more open approach to the identification and selection of directors' (ibid.).

This same theme is evident in the public documents of the Equal Opportunity for Women in the Workplace Agency. In its 2010 Census, EOWA acknowledged 'that nothing significant has occurred in Australian business culture in the past eight years to address the systemic inequity that continues to prevent talented and capable women from contributing at this high level' (EOWA, 2010, p. 4). Nevertheless, it did not agitate for government intervention and instead promoted the role of champions within the organizations and mentoring programmes as offering the most scope for change.

As part of its charter, the ASX oversees compliance with its operating rules and promotes standards of corporate governance among Australia's listed companies (Australian Securities Exchange, 2010). In response to the increasing public disquiet expressed around women's poor representation on the boards of publicly listed companies (Broderick, 2009), the ASX Corporate Governance Council revised its Corporate Governance Principles. In what has proved to be something of a 'game changer', from 1 January 2011, Principle 3 of the ASX Corporate Governance Principles requires share-market-listed companies to provide details in their annual reports of the number of women on their boards, in senior management roles and across the organization. The Principle requires listed companies to implement gender diversity policies and targets, report on how effective these have been and to make public the 'skills and diversity' criteria employed for board appointments. Under Listing Rule 4.10.3, ASX-listed companies have to report their corporate governance practices against the Principles, and where their practices are not consistent with the Principles, they must disclose this and the reasons why. This self-regulation is based on an 'if not why not' approach to reporting (Fels, 2010), and holds for all of the Corporate Governance Principles.

The ASX Corporate Governance Council (2010) contextualized the decision to include a diversity principle very firmly in the foundations of the 'business case' for diversity (Robinson and Dechant, 1997), which focuses on the benefits for the company of embracing the spirit of the changes to the ASX Principles. This argument is reinforced by the supporting principles provided by the AICD, where it notes that 'increased gender diversity on boards is associated with better financial performance, and that improved female workforce participation at all levels positively impacts the economy' (AICD, 2010c, p. 6). How the changes would open up more career opportunities for women, while not a primary focus for the ASX Principles, is identified as a matter to consider in the diversity checklist prepared by the AICD for companies to help get them started; for example, 'developing and overseeing the introduction of programs and initiatives aimed at developing a pipeline of female talent, including mentoring and coaching programs' (AICD, 2010c, p. 9).

ENACTING THE PRINCIPLES

An analysis of the first year's set of disclosures under the new Principle was carried out by KPMG, funded by the ASX's Education and Research Program (KPMG, 2013, p. 2) and was based on a quantitative analysis of a sample of 2188 companies listed on the ASX as at 30 September 2012. Distinguishing by market capitalization, the sample comprised 198 of the top 200 companies (ASX200), 200 of the next largest 300 companies (ASX201-500) and 200 of the remaining 1688 companies (ASX501+) listed on the ASX. Two of the top 200 companies were not included as one

Table 20.2 Compliance with reporting (%)

	ASX200	ASX201-500	ASX501+
Diversity policy and reporting			
Established diversity policy	93	85	58
Explanation of why not	6	12	34
No explanation	1	3	8
Measurable objectives			
Established objectives	82	59	61
Explanation of why not	16	37	28
No explanation	2	4	11
Disclosure of proportion of women			
Whole organization	93	79	67
Senior executive	90	71	56
Board	84	73	59

Source: KPMG (2013).

was suspended from trading at the time of the report and the other was an exempt foreign entity. Compliance with the disclosures required under Principle 3, namely that entities should have a diversity policy and disclose this; their annual reports should contain measurable objectives for achieving gender diversity and their progress towards achieving these; and the annual reports should detail the proportions of women employees across the whole organization, in senior executive positions and at the board level, was collated and analysed.

While the overall compliance rates were high for setting diversity policies, as can be seen in Table 20.2, the compliance varied according to the size of the organization (KPMG, 2013). The smaller the organization, the less likely it was to report, and if it did report, the more likely it was to explain why it was not complying. Similarly, with respect to the setting of measurable objectives for gender diversity, it was the ASX200 companies where compliance was highest, while for smaller companies there was a greater likelihood to not have reported at all, or when they did report, to explain why they had not set the objectives. With respect to disclosing the proportion of women across the whole organization, at senior executive level and at board level, once again the disclosures varied by size. For the ASX200 companies, 93 per cent reported for the whole organization while this fell to only 58 per cent of the ASX501+ companies reporting.

In terms of reporting women's representation across the organization (Table 20.3), the two most common reasons for not disclosing this

Table 20.3 Women's representation across different levels of organization (%)

Gender Diversity Metrics	ASX200	ASX201-500	ASX501+
Women in organization	35	34	25
Senior executive	20	34	15
Board	15	10	8

Source: KPMG (2013).

concerned the size of the organization and that the monitoring was in developmental stages.

INSTITUTIONAL SUPPORT FOR INCREASING WOMEN'S REPRESENTATION ON BOARDS

As the self-regulation model for increasing women's representation on boards was pursued in Australia, the role of key institutions in scaffolding the changes in the Corporate Governance Principles should be recognized (Sheridan et al., 2012). The AICD has been active in promoting its commitment to increasing women's representation on boards without resorting to quotas. For example, it now monitors women's appointments to ASX200 board positions, works with both federal and state governments to deliver scholarships for its training programmes to prepare women for board roles and provides resources on its website to support organizations' efforts to increase gender diversity. The Human Rights and Equal Opportunity Commission has promoted gender diversity through its 'male champions of change' initiative (Male Champions of Change, 2011) and the Workplace Gender Equality Agency continues to monitor women's representation in leadership (Workplace Gender Equality Agency, 2012).

MONITORING OF ASX200 BOARD POSITIONS

As noted earlier, when the debates about gender quotas were mooted in 2009, the AICD was resistant to quotas. For instance, the AICD's CEO is quoted as saying that '(t)he idea of mandated quotas for female representation on boards is wrong in principle, has difficulties in practice, is tokenistic and is counterproductive to the end goal of increasing board diversity' (AICD, 2011b, p.1). As the Principle related to diversity was taken on by the ASX, the AICD has provided a regular public space for the monitoring of this to occur through its website.

Focusing on the ASX200 companies, quarterly reports are now provided on the AICD website detailing the new appointments to ASX200 company boards. These are reproduced in Figure 20.1.

The focus on the ASX200 companies, the progress they are making with the number of new board appointments that are women, and the ensuing impact on the proportion of women holding board positions, does point to some 'success' from a body-counting perspective. Considering these results in the context of the KPMG report on all ASX-listed companies, it is clear that the ASX200 grouping reflects the area where the most engagement with the changes to the Governance Principles has occurred. The number of women on ASX200 boards increased from 8.3 per cent in 2009 to 17.3 per cent in December 2013. The limitation of the body-counting approach by the AICD is that it simply reports the number of women appointed; there is no unpacking of whether current women board members are taking on more roles because they are a 'known brand' (Sheridan and Milgate, 2005), or whether the changes have really opened up the board positions to a wider pool of women.

To examine this, we have drawn on publicly available information to explore the profiles of female board appointments. From Table 20.4, we can see in 2010 that there were 23 women holding 47 board roles in the ASX200. By 2012, another 16 women were appointed, to add a further 28 board roles held by women. The backgrounds, qualifications and previous board experiences of these 16 women are captured in Table 20.5. In terms of whether one can discern an opening up of board positions to a wider pool of women, a few trends are worth noting. The first of these is that 40 per cent (6/15) of the net new appointments have overseas senior-level management or board experience. While this differs from the 2010 profiles of women board members, where less than 1 per cent (1/26) had overseas experience, a similar phenomenon was noted in the UK in the 2009 Female FTSE report (Sealy et al., 2009). The next feature is that the new overseas recruits have considerably less 'small' board and not-for-profit experience than local recruits.

In addition, new recruits are less likely to have been CEOs of large publicly listed companies and tend to have some form of association with the AICD. It is well established that there is a paucity of women in CEO roles in listed companies (a traditional pathway to the boardroom) in Australia (Workplace Gender Equality Agency, 2012), and the KPMG report reinforced this. Unsurprisingly, then, there were no CEOs of ASX-listed companies among the new women appointees in 2012. Our analysis of the background of the women reveals, without exception, they all have

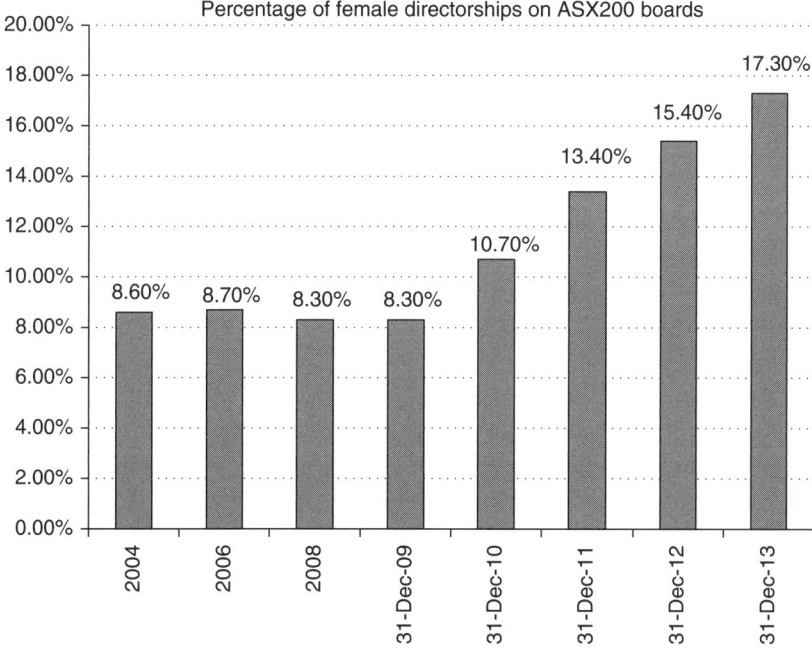

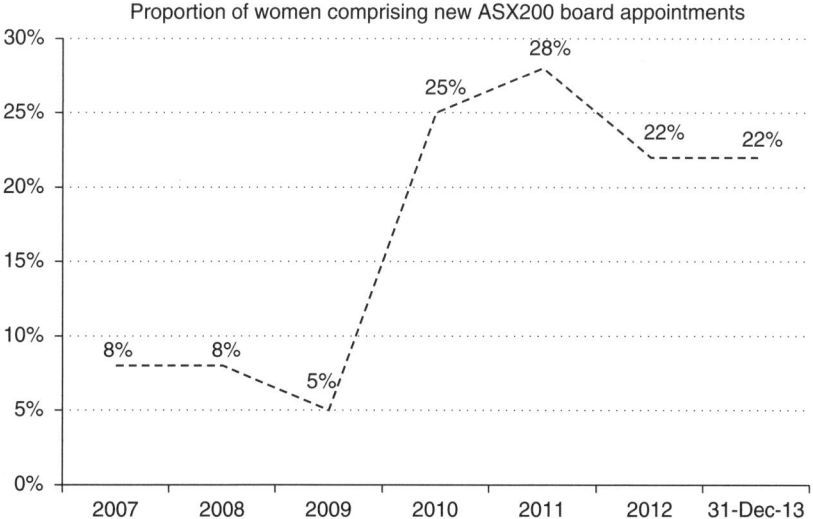

Source: AICD Statistics, at http://www.companydirectors.com.au/
Director-Resource-Centre/Governance-and-Director-Issues/Board-Diversity/Statistics.

Figure 20.1   AICD monitoring of women's representation on boards

Table 20.4 Female ASX200 board appointments 2010, 2012

Number of Board Appointments	Number of Women Sitting on Top 200 ASX-listed Boards in 2010	Number of Women Appointed to Top 200 ASX-listed Boards in 2012 (Net New)
1	11	8
2	5	6
3	3	2
4	3	0
5	1	0
Total	23	16

Table 20.5 Female pathways to ASX200 board appointments 2010, 2012

Criteria	2010	%	2012 (Net New)	%
CEO ASX listed	1	4.35	0	0
Executive ASX listed	3	13.04	2	12.50
CEO other	1	4.35	7	43.75
Executive other	18	78.26	14	87.50
UG qualifications	At least 15	65.21	At least 13	81.25
PG qualifications	At least 11	47.82	At least 5	31.25
Professional qualifications (e.g., CPA)	At least 4	17.39	At least 1	6.25
AICD Fellow	At least 7	30	At least 2	12.5
Professional services	At least 10	43.48	At least 4	25
Industry experience related to boards	At least 11	47.82	At least 14	87.50
Previous board experience				
– ASX listed	0	0	0	0
– Other corporation	2	8.69	8	50
– Overseas	At least 1	4.35	At least 5	31.25
– Government	5	21.74	6	37.50
– Not-for-profit	At least 11	47.82	At least 7	43.75
– University	At least 2	8.69	0 known	
– Industry body	At least 2	8.69	At least 2	12.50

extensive 'technical skills' or expertise in, as Dunn (2010, p. 567) describes, 'critical skill knowledge-based areas' that would be valuable to the organization. Seven have professional experience in a niche their organization serves; for example, a retail store founder and food scientist was appointed to a retail board, a supply chain specialist to the board of a procurement company, a geophysicist to a resources board, and a publishing background/digital transition specialist to a telecommunications company. In the remaining nine the women have backgrounds in finance, investment, accounting, law, or as a lobbyist. This appears to be a somewhat different pattern to that observed in the most recent UK census of women on boards (Sealy and Vinnicombe, 2013), which found little evidence to suggest that new female board appointments came from outside the corporate mainstream. The obvious explanation for this is that the pool of male directors is much greater than the pool of female directors. Several of the women with more generalist management experience founded and/or owned their own companies before working in a larger organization. Many of them serve on boards in these industries, and their technical skills in these areas would be an asset to almost any organization. It can be argued that the appointment of these 16 new women provides some evidence of a widening of the pool of talent from which board members are chosen.

For recently appointed women, as has been noted in other international contexts (Branson, 2012), access to one top-listed board is a pathway to getting on another. In the Australian context we note that 50 per cent of the new women recruits have more than one board membership. Those with more than one appointment achieved the additional appointments within one year. From their wider analysis of board appointments, the AICD reinforce this message where they note 'the proportion of female directors who hold more than one ASX200 directorship is significantly higher than male directors (27.9 per cent compared to 12.4 per cent)' (AICD, 2012, p.4). It is difficult to draw any conclusions in relation to the lack of small board experiences, however, our analysis of local recruits suggests that experience on not-for-profit boards, especially the more prestigious ones associated with the arts and high-profile charities, would seem to be a pathway to the ASX200.

FIXING THE WOMEN

A number of key institutions have developed training and mentoring programmes for women to better prepare them for board roles. This resonates with an approach common in the 1990s for training programmes designed to 'fix the women' (Sheridan, 1998). As Table 20.5 suggests, there is no doubt that the most recent new appointees are extremely well qualified for their board appointments. Notable, here, is the role the AICD appears to play in influencing the agenda around the appointment of women to ASX200 boards. Consistent with its checklist of matters to consider for companies complying with the ASX Principle 3 in terms of providing mentoring or coaching programmes for women, in 2010 the AICD implemented a high-profile mentoring programme with the stated aim of increasing the number of women at board and senior executive level (AICD, 2010a). The mentoring programme was designed to pair 'leading chairmen and directors . . . and qualified women in a 12-month mentoring relationship'. Not surprisingly, all but one of 95 mentors listed on the ASX website are Fellows of the AICD.

Candidates for mentoring are 'qualified' if they are deemed to be 'ASX200 board ready'. The AICD criteria for 'board ready' in 2010 included 'women who already have experience on the boards of ASX200 and other listed companies, unlisted public companies, large private companies, government bodies and not-for-profits, as well as senior executive women within ASX-listed companies and other appropriately qualified women from professional and other backgrounds' (ibid.). The Principles essentially remained the same for 2013. The question that has to be asked here is, if these women are 'board ready', why would they need more mentoring? It would appear that the main value of the AICD mentoring programme for women in this situation is their proximity to the high-profile male and female board members and chairs who make up the list of mentees (AICD, 2014b). One could suggest therefore that the development of networks associated with this further enhances 'board-ready' women's opportunities to obtain more board appointments.

In another very subtle step towards controlling the board appointment agenda, the AICD offers its 'Board Ready' program' via the diversity link on its web page suggesting 'organisations use "Board Ready" to enhance the leadership, communication and board skills of female executives' (AICD, 2013a). Actions such as these do appear to be a matter of different standards applying to women and men in their access to board positions. It seems women have to demonstrate their 'readiness' through being trained and mentored, while men are judged on their potential (Kolb et al., 2010). These sorts of approaches continue to reinforce the 'naturalness' of men being in such positions, while women's access requires them to prove their worth. The ASX is a compliance body. It is not within its charter to provide opportunities for women to obtain board positions. Nonetheless, one could argue that the ASX and the AICD are 'joined at the hip'. The AICD is part of the powerful ASX Governing Council. Both male and female ASX200 board members publicly endorse the mentoring programme (Sheridan et al., 2012).

The Business Council of Australia (BCA), a national body providing a forum for Australian business leaders to contribute to public policy debates, also established a mentoring programme known as the C-Suite

Project in 2010. Its focus was on increasing the number of female CEOs and CFOs in ASX200 companies. Like the AICD programme, its aim was to 'identify talented women and open up pathways for them to rise to the top of the corporate ladder' (Business Council of Australia, 2010). These mentoring programmes represent a potent narrative reinforcing the rhetoric of the need for change – or do they? Our concern with this approach is that the process of screening and selection for the programme, combined with the guidance by existing chairs, is likely to promote more of the same. There is a risk that the tendency to limit entry into the corporate elite 'to demographically similar individuals who share certain elite social and educational credentials' (Westphal and Stern, 2006, p. 170) will be reinforced through these processes. This in turn leads to a reinforcement of appointing in your own image, a phenomenon that is frequently referred to as the similarity–attraction paradigm (Berscheid and Walster, 1969).

Another strategy employed provides for scholarships for 'board-ready' women to complete the AICD's Corporate Directors Course, a key site for governance training. Federally, the Office for Women provided funds for 70 women to access AICD scholarship in 2010 (worth A$200 000), and in 2011 and 2013, the State of Victoria Government provided scholarships for another 68 women (AICD, 2011a, 2013b). When announcing the federal scholarship programme in 2010, the AICD noted 'the program is intended to be a practical way to help achieve greater diversity on boards by providing talented women with the knowledge they need to help them secure private sector and public sector directorships' (AICD, 2010b). The description of the Victorian scheme stated that 'the program is aimed at increasing the knowledge, skills and confidence of Victorian women to enable them to join private, public and community sector boards and to effectively contribute as a Director'. Given that these women have to demonstrate 'board readiness' to attain the scholarships, their need for additional training is questionable.

The Australian Human Rights Commission (AHRC) has also played a role in fostering the wider discourse that is normalizing an expectation of women taking on more leadership roles in corporate Australia. In 2011, the AHRC released a public letter from 13 business leaders, self-labelled as the 'Male Champions of Change' (MCC), to other business leaders in which they reflect on their experiences in elevating the representation of women in leadership. The intention of the letter was to promote a conversation among business leaders. The potency of this action lies in it being 'from male leaders to other male leaders, rather than an anonymous research report' (AHRC, 2011). As key actors in the corporate sector, these 'Male Champions of Change' views hold more sway than, for instance, academics or representatives from EOWA, who had raised similar points for many years (EOWA, 2010). When the CEOs of some of Australia's leading firms are prepared to be associated with increasing women's representation in leadership, there are normative pressures on others to be seen to be involved.

CONCLUSION

From our brief review of women's representation on boards in Australia between 2010 and 2013, it is clear there has been some (limited) opening of board roles to women. We do, however, have a concern with the 'fix the women' (Ely and Meyerson, 2000) approach that seems implicit in many of the actions taken and the use of body counting as the metric for measuring the 'success' of such actions. Simply adding women (and often the same women) without addressing the underlying 'gendering' of board practices fails to challenge the masculine norms that are well recognized within the corporate sector (Acker, 2006). While it could be argued that new members with different backgrounds and experiences to those existing board members will 'bring different interpretive frameworks and social definitions of behaviour to the organization' (Oliver, 1992, p. 575), we are cautious in making this claim. As Meyerson and Tompkins (2007) point out, there are many cases demonstrating how 'outsiders' are socialized to insider ways of thinking. We argue that the processes such as those enacted by the AICD and ASX – mentoring and scholarships to undertake the AICD training for already 'board-ready' women – may in fact moderate the likelihood of outsiders, in this case women board members, retaining their critical consciousness (Freire, 1970) and thus feeling comfortable about bringing in their own interpretative frameworks and social definitions of behaviour to the board. Freire's (1970) concept of critical consciousness is aligned with Meyerson's (2001, p. xi) notion of 'tempered radicals' who 'are people who want to succeed in their organizations yet want to live by their values or identities, even if they are somehow at odds with the dominant culture of their organizations'. On balance it would seem that a set of actions were put in place that appear set to reproduce the existing board director archetype.

Dunn (2010) suggests that women should develop specialized knowledge and skills especially in banking and law as a career pathway. Our research confirms this as a pathway and also suggests that specialist knowledge in a particular industry sector leads to women's board appointments. We agree that the pool is widening and it could be argued that a new archetype for 'board-ready' women is emerging. However, we are concerned that this archetype is narrowly defined and potentially restrictive in its application and may not lead to a challenging of 'like promoting like' (Kanter, 1977). As a result gender regimes in relation to board appointments will remain unchallenged. What may lead to more fundamental change is to open up programmes such as those described in this chapter to women who are not considered 'board ready', and to couple the mentoring by the ASX chairs and directors with mentoring by key leaders who are not on boards. The interrogation of the way 'we do things' through such a coupling may prompt more fundamental change and openness to diversity, and open pathways to boards for more women.

The initial indicators of the success of this self-regulation approach to gender diversity on boards are promising. Following a decade of little change to women's low representation on ASX200 boards, their representation has doubled. Ongoing monitoring of the statistics by the AICD ensures these numbers remain visible, but body counting alone is not enough. While the numbers may be increasing, the processes by which 'board-ready' women gain access to board positions appears to require more than is expected for their male counterparts. A deeper understanding of the board appointment processes and how they reinforce who 'fits' these existing structures, rather than examining how they continue to collude to exclude many 'board-ready' women, is warranted if we are to see more women 'getting on'.

REFERENCES

30 Per Cent Club (2011), 'International comparison', accessed 8 December at http://web.archive.org/web/20130108123832/http://www.30percentclub.org.uk/research/international-comparison/.
ABC News (2009), 'Quotas needed to boost women on boards: Jackson', *ABC News*, accessed 3 December 2014 at http://www.abc.net.au/news/2009-10-22/quotas-needed-to-boost-women-on-boards-jackson/1113196.
Acker, J. (2006), 'Inequality regimes: gender, class and race in organizations', *Gender and Society*, **20**(4), 441–4.
ASX Corporate Governance Council (2010), *Corporate Governance Principles and Recommendations*, 2nd edition, Sydney: Australian Securities Exchange.
Australian Human Rights Commission (AHRC) (2011), 'Male champions of change: our experiences in elevating the representation of women in leadership – a letter from business leaders', accessed 3 December 2014 at https://www.humanrights.gov.au/publications/dear-colleague-our-experiences-elevating-representation-women-leadership-letter.
Australian Institute of Company Directors (AICD) (2010a), 'Directors take the lead in helping put women on boards', accessed 14 October 2014 at http://www.companydirectors.com.au/General/Header/Media/Media-Releases/2010/Directors-take-the-lead-in-helping-put-women-on-boards.
Australian Institute of Company Directors (AICD) (2010b), 'New scholarships to increase diversity on boards', accessed 19 December 2011 at http://www.companydirectors.com.au/General/Header/Media/Media-Releases/2010/New-scholarships-to-increase-diversity-on-boards.

Australian Institute of Company Directors (AICD) (2010c), 'New corporate governance recommendations on diversity: tips for getting started', accessed 3 December 2014 at http://www.companydirectors.com.au/~/media/74D2D5583872433FB9FBB71672576E87.ashx.
Australian Institute of Company Directors (AICD) (2011a), 'Victorian women's governance scholarship program 2012', accessed 19 December 2011 at http://www.companydirectors.com.au/Director-Resource-Centre/Governance-and-Director-Issues/Board-Diversity/Scholarship-Program.
Australian Institute of Company Directors (AICD) (2011b), 'Opinion: quotas are not the answer', accessed 19 December 2011 at http://www.companydirectors.com.au/Director-Resource-Centre/Publications/Company-Director-magazine/2011-back-editions/September/Opinion-Quotas-are-not-the-answer.
Australian Institute of Company Directors (AICD) (2012), 'ASX200 snapshot report November 2012', Sydney: AICD, accessed 3 December 2014 at http://www.companydirectors.com.au/~/media/CA1C2E8B5D9E4703AC02740624756287.ashx.
Australian Institute of Company Directors (AICD) (2013a), 'Board Ready program', accessed 22 August 2013, at http://www.companydirectors.com.au/Director-Resource-Centre/Governance-and-Director-Issues/Board-Diversity/Board-Ready-Program.
Australian Institute of Company Directors (AICD) (2013b), 'Victorian women's governance scholarship program 2013', accessed 8 December at http://www.companydirectors.com.au/Director-Resource-Centre/Governance-and-Director-Issues/Board-Diversity/Diversity-Scholarship-Program/Victorian-Womens-Governance-Scholarship-program-2015/Scholarship-Recipients-2013.
Australian Institute of Company Directors (AICD) (2014a), 'Appointments to S&P/ASX200 boards', accessed 14 March 2014 at www.companydirectors.com.au/Director-Resource-Centre/Governance-and-Director-Issues/Board-Diversity/Statistics.
Australian Institute of Company Directors (AICD) (2014b), 'Chairmen's mentoring program', accessed 3 December 2014 at http://www.companydirectors.com.au/Director-Resource-Centre/Governance-and-Director-Issues/Board-Diversity/Mentoring-Programs.
Australian Securities Exchange (2010), 'The ASX Group', accessed 12 January 2011 at http://www.asxgroup.com.au/the-asx-group.htm.
Baird, M. and W. Wilkinson (2010), 'Women, work and industrial relations in 2009', *Journal of Industrial Relations*, **52**(3), 355–69.
Berscheid, E. and E.H. Walster (1969), *Interpersonal Attraction*, New York: Addison-Wesley Publishing Co.
Branson, D. (2012), 'Intitiatives to place women on corporate boards of directors – a global snapshot', *The Journal of Corporation Law*, **37**(4), 793–814.
Braund, C. (2010), 'Where to in 2011?', *WomenOnBoards*, accessed 3 December 2014 at http://www.womenonboards.org.au/pubs/articles/cb1012-summary.htm.
Broderick, E. (2009), 'Make room at the table for women', *The Australian Financial Review*, accessed 3 December 2014 at http://www.humanrights.gov.au/about/media/media_releases/op_ed/20091029_make_room.html.
Business Council of Australia (2010), 'CEOs step up to take direct action on women in top jobs', accessed 3 December 2014 at http://www.bca.com.au/Content/101669.aspx.
Catalyst (2012), 'Women on boards: quick takes', accessed 30 March 2013 at http://www.catalyst.org/publication/433/women-on-boards.
Corporations and Markets Advisory Committee (CAMAC) (2009), 'Diversity on boards of directors', Sydney: CAMAC, accessed 3 December 2014 at http://www.camac.gov.au/camac/camac.nsf/byHeadline/PDFFinal+Reports+2009/$file/Board_Diversity_B5.pdf.
Davies, M., A. Ducas, A. Mackenzie, J. Parker, D. Casserly and W. Vinnicombe (2011), *Women on Boards*, London: UK Government.
Deloitte (2011), 'Women in the boardroom: a global perspective', accessed 3 December 2014 at http://www2.deloitte.com/content/dam/Deloitte/tz/Documents/Deloitte%20Article_Women%20in%20the%20boardroom.pdf.

Dunn, P. (2010), 'Breaking the boardroom gender barrier: the human capital of female corporate directors', *Journal of Management and Governance*, **16**(4), 557–70.
Ely, R. and D. Meyerson (2000), 'Theories of gender in organizations: a new approach to organizational analysis and change', *Research in Organizational Behavior*, **22**, 105–53.
Equal Opportunity for Women in the Workplace Agency (EOWA) (2002), *Australian Census of Women Board Directors*, Sydney: EOWA.
Equal Opportunity for Women in the Workplace Agency (EOWA) (2003), *Australian Census of Women Board Directors*, Sydney: EOWA.
Equal Opportunity for Women in the Workplace Agency (EOWA) (2006), *Australian Census of Women in Leadership*, Sydney: EOWA.
Equal Opportunity for Women in the Workplace Agency (EOWA) (2008), *Australian Census of Women in Leadership*, Sydney: EOWA.
Equal Opportunity for Women in the Workplace Agency (EOWA) (2010), *Australian Census of Women in Leadership*, Sydney: EOWA.
Equal Opportunity for Women in the Workplace Agency and Catalyst (2004), *Australian Census of Women Executive Managers and Women Board Directors*, Sydney: EOWA.
Fels, A. (2010), 'Executive remuneration in Australia', *Australian Accounting Review*, **20**(1), 76–82.
Freire, P. (1970), *Pedagogy of the Oppressed*, New York: Continuum.
Fox, C. (2013), 'The higher you go, the wider the gap', in CEDA (ed.), *Women in Leadership: Understanding the Gender Gap*, Melbourne: CEDA, pp. 21–32.
GovernanceMetrics International (2013), 'GMI ratings' 2013 women on boards survey', accessed 3 December 2014 at http://www3.gmiratings.com/home/2013/05/gmi-ratings-2013-women-on-boards-survey/.
Hole, A. (2009), 'Diversity deployed: is there merit in quotas?', paper presented at the 2nd Diversity on Boards Conference, Sydney.
Kanter, R. (1977), *Men and Women of the Corporation*, New York: Basic Books.
Kolb, D., J. Williams and C. Frohlinger (2010), *Her Place at the Table: A Woman's Guide to Negotiating Five Key Challenges to Leadership Success*, San Francisco, CA: Jossey-Bass.
Korporaal, G. (2009), 'AICD moves to boost number of women directors', *The Australian*, accessed 3 December 2014 at http://www.theaustralian.com.au/business/aicd-moves-to-boost-number-of-women-directors/story-e6frg8zx-1225802765048.
KPMG (2013), 'ASX corporate governance council principles and recommendations on diversity', accessed 3 December 2014 at https://www.kpmg.com/AU/en/IssuesAndInsights/ArticlesPublications/Documents/asx-corporate-governance-council-principles-diversity.pdf.
Male Champions of Change (2011), 'Our experiences in elevating the representation of women in leadership: a letter from business leaders', Canberra: Australian Human Rights and Equal Opportunity Commission, accessed 3 December at https://www.humanrights.gov.au/sites/default/files/document/publication/mcc2011.pdf.
Marriott, A. (2009), 'Breaking the glass ceiling: are gender quotas a good idea?', *The Vecci Blog*, accessed 8 December 2014 at http://www.vecci.org.au/policy-and-advocacy/news/blog/2009/12/16/breaking-glass-ceiling-are-gender-quotas-good-idea.
Meyerson, D. (2001), *Temper Radicals*, Boston, MA: Harvard Business School Publishing.
Meyerson, D. and M. Tompkins (2007), 'Tempered radicals as institutional change agents: the case of advancing gender equity at the University of Michigan', *Harvard Journal of Law and Gender*, **30**(2), 303–22.
Nielsen, S. and M. Huse (2010a), 'Women directors' contribution to board decision-making and strategic involvement: the role of equality perception', *European Management Review*, **7**(1), 16–29.
Nielsen, S. and M. Huse (2010b), 'The contribution of women on boards of directors: going beyond the surface', *Corporate Governance: An International Review*, **18**(2), 136–48.
Oliver, C. (1992), 'Sustainable competitive advantage: combining institutional and resource-based views', *Strategic Management Journal*, **18**(9), 697–713.

Robinson, G. and K. Dechant (1997), 'Building a business case for diversity', *Academy of Management Executive*, **11**(3), 21–31.
Sealy, R. and S. Vinnicombe (2013), *The Female FTSE Board Report 2013: False Dawn of Progress for Women on Boards*, Cranfield, UK: Cranfield International Centre for Women Leaders, Cranfield University.
Sealy, R., S. Vinnicombe and E.B. Doldor (2009), *The Female FTSE Board Report 2009*, Cranfield, UK: Cranfield School of Management, Cranfield University.
Sealy, R., E. Doldor, V. Singh and S. Vinnicombe (2011), 'Women on boards: 6 month monitoring report', Cranfield University for the UK Government, accessed 3 December 2014 at https://www.gov.uk/government/uploads/system/uploads/attachment_data/file/363077/bis-14-1121-women-on-boards-6-months-monitoring-report-october-2014.pdf.
Seierstad, C. (2012), 'Can quotas challenge gender inequality regimes? The effects of quotas on corporate boards in Norway', paper presented at the Academy of Management Conference, Boston, MA.
Sheridan, A. (1998), 'Patterns in the policies: affirmative action in Australia', *Women in Management Review*, **13**(7), 243–52.
Sheridan, A. and G. Milgate (2005), 'Accessing board positions: a comparison of female and male board members' views', *Corporate Governance: An International Review*, **13**(6), 847–55.
Sheridan, A., A. Ross-Smith and L. Lord (2012), 'Institutional influences on changing gender ratios on corporate boards: an Australian case study', paper presented at the Academy of Management Conference, Boston, MA.
Stern, I. and J. Westphal (2010), 'Stealthy footsteps to the boardroom: executives' backgrounds, sophisticated interpersonal influence behaviour, and board appointments', *Administrative Science Quarterly*, **55**(2), 278–319.
UWA Business School (2010), 'To quota or not to quota: women in leadership', *UWA News*, accessed 3 December 2014 at http://www.news.uwa.edu.au/201007092652/quota-or-not-quota-women-leadership.
Westphal, J.D. and I. Stern (2006), 'The other pathway to the boardroom: how interpersonal influence behavior can substitute for elite credentials and demographic majority status in gaining access to board appointments', *Administrative Science Quarterly*, **51**(2), 169–204.
Workplace Gender Equality Agency (2012), '2012 Australian census of women in leadership', Sydney: WGEA, accessed 3 December 2014 at https://www.wgea.gov.au/sites/default/files/2012_CENSUS%20REPORT.pdf.

21. Global career challenges for women crossing international borders
Yehuda Baruch and Cristina Reis

Any type of work involving a global move is challenging, and in many cases such challenges are more significant, and even severe, for women. Global careers are careers that span across more than a single country and may take a number of forms (Baruch et al., 2013). Traditional corporate expatriation is just one of them, and one that does not always offer common competitive ground for men and women. Other types of global careers may be a better fit for women in their quest to develop fulfilling careers.

Barriers to women's global careers appear on three levels. At the individual level, this can range from how women manage their own ideological structural barriers as well as their emotional attachments and putting into practice their creative ideas (for example, Apter, 1993; Sullivan et al., 2009). At the organizational level, companies may hesitate or even refrain from sending women abroad (for example, Adler, 1994). This could be due to indirect discrimination, but also because of (over-)protection of those considered vulnerable. National-level barriers may be structural and cultural. For example, in certain cultures, women face stronger barriers and are even blocked from certain global career moves (for example, Omair, 2009).

In this chapter we introduce three theoretical models: the push–pull model, the kaleidoscope career model and the intelligent career capital model. In the light of these models we analyse examples of global career challenges for women at the three levels described above. We decided to use all three models since most research on women and global careers concentrates on only one perspective or mostly on women expatriates engaging in corporate executive careers (Altman and Shortland, 2008).

Shortland and Altman (2011) have noted a continuation of the discussion about a shortage of women engaging in international assignments and recommend a development of the traditional linear career with the use of flexible arrangements to accommodate a balance between home and work responsibilities. While family–work (or life–work) balance is a major issue for many women (Kossek et al., 2010), work interference with other spheres of life can be more significant and salient when global work is involved. Women's careers tend to be non-linear, disjointed, interrupted and different from men's, who tend to have linear career paths (Cabrera, 2006; see also Levinson, 1978, 2011, who also distinguished between men's and women's career development and stages). Because global work is still the exception and as women are exceptions in global career moves, the tendency of women to have non-linear career paths may suggest that going global would better fit women executives, yet the evidence is that women are not appointed to global roles as much as men (Altman and Shortland, 2008). In general, for women, either on their own or accompanied by their spouse, the global career does not seem favourable, in particular when deciding whether to expatriate. As we will demonstrate below, women tend to face greater hurdles compared with men.

A number of authors have tried to pin down and explain the reasons for the barriers to women in making a global expatriate career (for example, Stroh et al., 2000; McKenna and Richardson, 2007; Altman and Shortland, 2008). Global assignments might be seen as a 'trap', thus women may have to avoid global career options. This often seems to be the case for women executives. According to the *Fortune 500* magazine (Catalyst, 2013) women as executive officers in leadership positions accounted for only 14.3 per cent in 2012 but this did not necessarily take into consideration women undertaking global tasks as immigrants. In our analysis, we also consider women immigrants who undertake global moves.

In addition to the glass ceiling while trying to climb the corporate ladder, women are typically offered high-risk leadership roles in the shape of an additional hurdle called the 'glass cliff' (Ryan and Haslam, 2007; Haslam and Ryan, 2008). The findings from Haslam and Ryan (2008) show a self-fulfilling prophesy of failure (Merton, 1968) since women 'are more likely than men to be appointed to leadership positions associated with increased risk of failure and criticism because these positions are more likely to involve management of organizational units that are in crisis' (Haslam and Ryan, 2008, p. 530). Women not only fall into taking this self-defeating route – there are also other hurdles. Women being divided in terms of their relationships with other high-potential women, sometimes possibly seeing them as a threat, instead of trying to serve as a role model, has generated many conflicts (Hakim, 2000). Hakim (2000, 2006, 2010) distinguishes between different types of women (for example, family-orientated, career-orientated and adaptive women) to propose the preference theory, which predicts patterns of women labour market participation. It is worth noting that she argues that in the past small elites of women from wealthy families, or prosperous families with liberal ideas, did sometimes have real choices, just as their brothers did. For Hakim, in much of contemporary society genuine choices are open to the vast majority of women and not just the few, yet there are signs that many women choose to opt out of the organizational system in search of a balanced life (for example, see Mainiero and Sullivan's 2005 kaleidoscope career model, which presents work and non-work aspects of life) as well as out of their original national cultures in search of work (for example, see Markus, 2013, for Brazilian women who engaged in a global move in search of better working conditions).

A global career-related and family-focused factor is the need for a partner who would be ready and willing to take on the role of 'trailing spouse', a decision not easily taken (Konopaske et al., 2005), and is more significant when the expatriate employee is a woman (Harvey and Wiese, 1998). As international assignments require the spouse, usually a woman, to forfeit the accustomed structure and continuity for the expatriate life, and with males typically being the higher earner in dual-career couples, this exacerbates the challenges that expatriate women along with male partners experience (Linehan, 2002; Mayrhofer and Scullion, 2002).

THE PUSH-PULL MODEL

First we look at the push-pull model for global moves (Figure 21.1), which should also be instrumental in pointing out solutions (or lack of them).

The push versus pull factors model leads us to ask the following question: 'How do values, beliefs, and needs influence a decision to move or

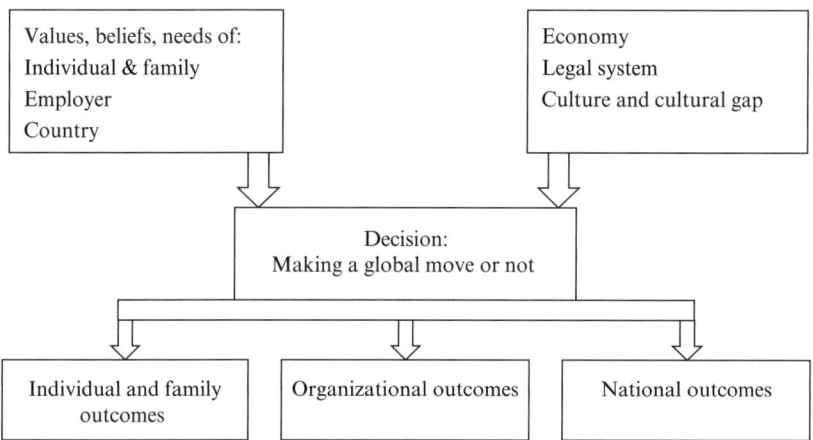

Source: Adapted and expanded from Baruch (1995).

Figure 21.1 The push-pull model for expatriation – women's perspective

stay for women?' We provide examples at the individual, organizational, and national levels. All these examples manifest that, in a perfect world, there could or should be a playground for everyone, but in reality, women face greater hurdles, and sometimes obvious barriers:

- *At the individual level.* Traditional expatriation can be a great opportunity for career progress, but it might also be a dead-end route. Other global move options exist, such as self-initiated expatriation, flexpatriation,[1] inpatriation,[2] short assignments, globetrotting, to name a few (see Baruch et al., 2013 for a variety of options for global moves).
- *At the organizational level.* The organizational past experience, culture, and certainly its strategic view about expatriation can be instrumental for the relevance, if any, of gender discrimination in decision-making for expatriation (Baruch and Altman, 2002).
- *At the national level.* There are national differences in the levels of support and awareness for work–life balance practices and other cultural practices in people management (Ollier-Malaterre, 2009). In principle, economic forces act as both push and pull factors, when people choose to move due to better economic conditions in their target destination compared with their home country. Theoretically, it should work the same for men and women, yet, because men remain the main 'breadwinner' in most families, the economical/financial considerations will be more salient for men. While in typical Organisation for Economic Co-operation and Development (OECD) countries there are non-discriminatory measures, the legal system varies within nations. It would require legal considerations, such as a certain amount of money an entrepreneur needs to bring into the targeted country in order to open business, or greater hurdles to gain work permits. Cultural gaps exist where in some countries women will not be easily accepted as managers (for example, in the Middle East or some Far Eastern countries) and the cultural issue of family class background seems to prevail in some patriarchal cultures (for example, South America).

THE KALEIDOSCOPE CAREER MODEL (KCM)

Although we have discussed in relation to the push-pull model why women tend to opt out of global assignments, we now question why they face difficult challenges when they cross borders and how they manage to survive with a good or less optimistic outcome for their careers and lives.

We add the kaleidoscope career model (KCM) to the push-pull model as a valid and eye-opening framework. According to Mainiero and Sullivan (2005) the kaleidoscope career model, used initially for workers' concerns and demands, fits how women (and men) run both work and non-work aspects of life. They suggested that women can benefit from this new career landscape by making different arrangements that fit their roles and relationships in new ways. The KCM perspective offers three mirrors or an analysis in three parameters: authenticity, balance and challenge:

1. Whether individual internal values are aligned with their external behaviours and the type of work and careers undertaken.
2. Whether they have work–non-work demands and interests.
3. Whether the motives for women to engage in 'global careers' (our adaptation) are more than just searching for better-paid jobs or positions. Are they looking for career advancement, more autonomy, knowledge, higher responsibility, and so on?

While the first and third points would apparently work the same way for men and for women, the second point is significantly different between men and women – including within the organizational realm. Work–life balance issues are typically more salient for women than for men, and the importance may vary across life stages as well as social class background.

THE KCM AND THE INTELLIGENT CAREER CAPITAL FRAMEWORK

We now add another individual perspective model to the KCM: the intelligent career capital framework. There are three important dimensions of the individual intelligent career capital framework, which can be summarized in terms of 'knowing why', 'knowing how' and 'knowing whom' (DeFillippi and Arthur, 1994; Inkson and Arthur, 2001; Eby et al., 2003). The 'knowing why' career capital dimension concentrates mainly on the identification with self-purpose through work. Relating this idea to global careers is the *intention* to pursue a global career (Gregersen et al., 1998; Caligiuri and DiSanto, 2001). This dimension observes individual identity detachment from employers and opens a new outlet for individual career experiences (Arthur et al., 1999; Eby et al., 2003). Issues such as motivation and personal sense of worth are connected with self-confidence in leading to a desired career (Jones and Lichtenstein, 2000; Inkson and Arthur, 2001). In this sense, engaging in a foreign assignment usually consists of opportunities to gain new experiences, career progression and financial benefits (Miller and Cheng, 1978; Tung, 1998; Stahl et al., 2002). Other authors (for example, Bossard and Peterson, 2005) argue that individual involvement in international assignments is focused on the search for interesting work and is not necessarily linked to company career promotion. The search for self-fulfilment of the 'knowing why' dimension of career capital is also in line with the concept of internal career issues of the protean career (Hall, 1976).

The second point of the KCM model, work–non-work demands and interests, can be aligned to the 'knowing why' career capital dimension but this dimension is particularly problematic for global women expatriates, as for them the conflict between work and family may be stronger (for example, Harris, 2004; Hakim, 2006). According to Mainiero and Sullivan (2005), while both men and women posit 'challenge' as the leading factor in their early careers, in mid-career women emphasize 'balance' and later 'authenticity', whereas mid-career men emphasize the 'authenticity' mirror and later 'balance'. Following the KCM model, this implies that for mid-career women expatriation would be less desirable than for men.

Another career capital dimension is 'knowing how', which focuses mainly on individual skills and knowledge required to perform up to organizational standards (Defillippi and Arthur, 1994). It differs from the concept of human capital in the emphasis on training and development and on the acquisition of transferable skills that can be used across organizations (Eby et al., 2003). In general, it has been recognized that during international assignments across contexts, individuals learn cross-cultural management global business skills (Roberts et al., 1998; Antal, 2000; Carpenter et al., 2000; Caligiuri and Di Santo, 2001; Stahl et al., 2002; Suutari, 2003). This dimension is manifested in the third point of the KCM model above and in the growing trend of self-initiated expatriation (Dickmann and Harris, 2005; Altman and Baruch, 2012).

The third dimension of career capital is not discussed in the KCM model but is of great importance for women who opted in to global assignments. The 'knowing whom' career capital dimension refers to all professional and personal career-relevant networks and contacts (DeFillippi and Arthur, 1994; Parker and Arthur, 2000; Borgatti and Cross, 2003). It is related to the literature on social capital (Raider and Burt, 1996), referring to assets that can be developed through a network of relationships useful to individual career development (Jones and DeFillippi, 1996; Nahapiet and Ghoshal, 1998; Adler and Kwon, 2002). Research shows that personal and professional contacts give individuals an advantage in information and career opportunities (for example, Granovetter, 1973; Burt, 1992) and these advantages consist of accessing unique information in advance, and a way of getting supportive referrals by attracting connections and prestige (Burt, 1992). It is by knowing 'who knows what' that the individual obtains unique information (Borgatti and Cross, 2003). Research suggests that expatriates significantly expand their business networks during their foreign assignments as well as with senior management at headquarters (Antal, 2000). More effort is required to keep in contact with former colleagues at headquarters, and a lot of energy and investment is required to generate new social capital in the host country.

In the light of these two models we continue our discussion at the individual level and include challenges for women who are undertaking global work and assignments.

WOMEN EXPATRIATES – CHALLENGES AT THE INDIVIDUAL LEVEL

Hypothetically, women expatriates have the same challenges as have been described for men in the literature, particularly related to the three career capital dimensions. Yet, as we described above, women tend to face greater and more complex hurdles. This may be the reason that some authors continue to observe a shortage of women engaging in international assignments and recommend breaking through the traditional linear career by using flexible arrangements to accommodate a balance between home and work responsibilities (Shortland and Altman, 2011).

The work–non-work demands and interests dimension of the KCM model and 'knowing why' career capital dimension have been critical for men expatriates but never to the extent they can be for women. Men's major concerns have been to get their wives' involvement in their international assignments to support them personally and professionally; however, male spouses/partners accompanying women expatriates in their international assignments may experience this as a challenge to their masculinity, particularly if men have their identities attached to their work locally. Nevertheless, some women have been able to engage their male partners in their expatriate assignments since there is great variety in men's typologies. In the 1980s and the 1990s, studies on masculinities have specifically developed men's typologies (for example, Hearn and Morgan, 1990; Seidler, 1994). It is possible that certain types of men are willing to accompany their partner/wife expatriates and even engage themselves in some sort of international assignments and, at the same type, support women expatriates personally at home if they have dependants, and professionally in the same way that wives help men expatriates.

Another critical factor, at least for married women, is having the 'right husband', as Sheryl Sandberg, Facebook COO, claimed (Groth, 2011).

She envisions the future of women in leadership positions with a husband that shares 50 per cent of the household tasks (or outsourcing these tasks) and who also has a successful career. She reflects on her own life and her own husband who is a successful entrepreneur. However, Sheryl has also been criticized for telling other women how to commit to such choices since these do not seem available to all women. We consider that these opportunities are accessible to a certain type of women of a certain social class background, in the same way, as we mentioned above, that Hakim (2000, 2006) noticed that in the past, elite women in wealthy and/or liberal families sometimes had similar opportunities to their brothers.

In truly global firms, expatriation at some stage is inevitable, or at least should be anticipated (Baruch and Altman, 2002). It *is* possible for an employee to signal to a firm that she would be reluctant to move globally since it implies engaging in different structures and cultures and is therefore more challenging. However, refusing to move globally would practically mean the end of future career prospects for those aspiring to become executives (Reis, 2004). Women should find a way to signal to their managers and to HR what would be the best timing for them to embark on a global assignment.

Other groups often featured in the literature are single women and gay couples who undertake these international assignments. In this regard, and as Reis (2004) pointed out for future research, we still know very little about their global careers.

WOMEN ACADEMICS WITH GLOBAL CAREERS

Academic institutions are becoming global and so are the careers of academics. Although some researchers might think that international collaborations, research and journal articles facilitate a global standing academically, this is not always so in the context of day-to-day lives. Richardson and Zikic (2007) examined the challenges of engaging in an international academic career and found that a global academic career can be complex, with transience and risk as two important dimensions of the challenge, in addition to bringing positive opportunities for fulfilment. Another important finding from these authors is that engaging in an academic global career requires support that extends beyond cross-cultural training.

Women with academic careers face similar challenges to corporate women but with less recognition of the hurdles they have to overcome. There is a lot less money involved in the process of moving countries and lower salaries, but no less responsibility and extreme challenges that take their free time away (for example, the obligation to deliver a certain amount of refereed publications). Both the KCM model and the capital career dimensions fit the analysis of their careers, including the less explored 'know whom' dimension. Academic women move globally because of their own international connections and professional credibility, and few make these global moves alone without spouses or partners – spouses or partners who are usually academics themselves.

The sabbatical is a long-term institutional practice in established research universities. Sabbaticals are considered a professional and personal benefit (Sima, 2000), typically leading to improved innovations and revitalization of staff, helping academics to avoid skills obsolescence and gain significant learning experiences. A sabbatical term may be given to academics and is dependent on the policies of the institutions they work for. It may mean they have to present a detailed plan of a temporary international assignment. In this situation academic women have the same hurdles as women in corporations as expatriates (usually with a lot less money and without family support).

WOMEN WITH VIRTUAL GLOBAL CAREERS

There are several ways women can engage in a global career through virtual means of communication. For example, Sandberg (2013) suggested ways of doing virtual work for women who stay at home. But would a virtual global career be a possibility for women who live with strong economic, legal and cultural barriers?

Women in difficult contexts can surpass these barriers if they engage in a global career but only if they are knowledgeable of other business cultures and have certain conditions of freedom and time on their own. In the United Arab Emirates, women's career development is connected to social status and family connections, with strong barriers to their own individual initiatives (Omair, 2009). Analysing women in these situations in the light of the KCM model challenges women's identities since their individual values they have lived with all their lives may not be aligned with what is demanded 'virtually' of their external behaviours. Much has been written regarding virtual work and non-work demands in terms of flexible work and remote work that permit women to manage their own time in a way that is more personally effective but not necessarily less demanding. Regarding the third point of the KCM model, virtual work may provide autonomy, knowledge, career advancement and development.

In the light of the capital career framework, it is worth discussing the career capital dimension 'knowing whom'. If women have similar issues to the women in the United Arab Emirates (ibid.) and their career development is connected to social status and family connections, they may have difficulties in motivating themselves and in engaging in reliable business social networks that provide them an outlet for the development of their global careers. Although there are global initiatives to this end (see the World Bank, 2013) trying to bring women together within their business social networks, they may have to work individually and strategically very hard to obtain the third dimension (knowing whom) of the intelligent career capital model.

Although nowadays it is possible to contact anyone by virtual means of communication, prestigious and influential contacts may require a local and long-term relationship. This virtually connected trend will require that, similarly to men in global careers, women leave their homes and move geographically for meetings to build further business knowledge and networks.

ORGANIZATIONS AND GLOBAL CAREER CHALLENGES FOR WOMEN

Organizations tend to disregard women for expatriation roles though evidence suggests that women expatriation tends to be successful (Caligiuri and Tung, 1999) in both their performance and career outcomes. The view and values about 'appropriateness' of women to take on global assignments, or even to take on managerial roles, varies considerably in different cultures. Schwartz (2006) and Hofstede (2001) show how people from different nations hold different views on a number of issues and dimensions. For example, Hofstede (2013) sees the US and the United Arab Emirates dimensions of femininity and masculinity similarly, rating these countries high in masculinity. Yet, although US and UAE women need social and professional networks for the development of their careers, the barriers women face are different; these barriers are contextual, with legal implications, and the realities for women to engage in a global career in the two countries are very different.

There are other cultural models, particularly for expatriation paths that started between the 1950s and 1970s and have been developed extensively from traditional expatriate assignments, mainly monitored by organizations. Altman and Baruch (2012) developed a model of work attractors, where the psychological contract between individuals, organizations and societies changed along time in two dimensions (Figure 21.2). One dimension sees expatriation as a 'calling' versus seeing it as vocational

		#1 TRADITIONAL PATH	#4 NEW PATH
Women work attractor	Women expat. as CALLING (wider career)	*Organizational commitment* Stress on organizational objectives/Strategic fit of assignment *Key aspects* Knowledge transfer Business development Aligned with firm's expat. type: EMISSARY	*Self-development* Stress on non-career focus; personal development *Key aspects* Life experience enrichment Aligned with firm's expat. type: PERIPHERAL
	Women expat. as VOCATIONAL (generic career)	#2 TRADITIONAL PATH *Expat. structured career path* Stress on career development by gaining relevant experience (initiated by organization) *Key aspects* Long-term career development Continuous career Aligned with firm's expat. type: GLOBAL	#3 NEW PATH *Career centred* Stress on career development by gaining relevant experience (initiated by individual) *Key aspects* Continuous global career or generic career build-up Aligned with firm's expat. type: PROFESSIONAL
		Traditional; continuous RELATIONAL	Emerging; interrupted TRANSACTIONAL
		Psychological contract	

Source: Adapted from Altman and Baruch (2012).

Figure 21.2 Traditional and new expatriate career paths

progress. The other is about the psychological contract – is it relational or transactional? These two dimensions generate four quadrants of different possible career paths.

Organizations acknowledge the challenges of interdependency of the expatriate and spouse, in 'mobility work' in particular (Reis, 2004). The idea of mobility work has been developed by Reis (2004) and is the necessary work that wives of multinational company expatriates do for their husbands to help them get ahead in their careers (for example, in particular the relevance of the emotional, sexual,[3] coaching, counselling work, and business networking that is included in mobility work).

In this chapter we are not ignoring the fact that gender is also an issue for men's expatriation and we would like to mention other relevant work related issues regarding expatriation. There is considerable research on wives/partners of men expatriates (Eby, 2001; Selmer and Leung, 2003). Makela et al. (2011) studied the importance of the spousal support in dual-career couples during international assignments. Cole (2011) also focused on women spouses of expatriates and found that only a small minority received employer-provided career assistance when their husbands had to move, although this support has not generated a difference in employment status (being employed or not) between those who received it and those who did not. Lauring and Selmer (2010) studied female accompanying partners of expatriates and how they used social strategies through philanthropic work. Kupka and Cathro (2007) focus on the importance of spousal support, adjustment and well-being of the expatriate, whereas Konopaske et al. (2005) explore spouse willingness to relocate internationally and Eby (2001) found that spouses experienced lateral and downward inter-firm mobility.

CONCLUSION

Often, the motives for self-expatriation are learning more about the world and having unique experiences, not just career enhancement (Richardson and McKenna, 2002). The ethnography-based concept of 'rites of passage' (Van Gennep, 2011) can be useful in discussing and understanding the role of expatriation in careers, in particular within large multinational firms. Expatriation and, later, repatriation are boundary-crossing phases in the career, with associated risks in career progression to higher positions in the organizational structure (which implies, for example, better compensation, benefits and prestige). In certain firms, expatriation is a part of life and an anticipated career stage; in others, it is marginalized; yet in others, expatriation may be outsourced (Baruch and Altman, 2002). Thus, one should be aware that global assignments, while possibly being enablers of future career success, might also pose threats to such success. Reading the political map within the organization is critical to figuring out whether or not expatriation would be the right move if the aim is career progression to a higher position in the organizational structure.

This chapter contributes to both career theory and to global human resources management literature, in particular to the challenges of expatriation to women and self-initiated expatriation (Tharenou, 2008, 2009, 2010; Altman and Baruch, 2012), which opens new outlets but not with fewer burdens (for example, single women in academia). Richardson and McKenna (2002) studied the voluntary, self-initiated expatriate and found that the subject should be much more extensively researched. We employed the push-pull model to analyse reasoning and issues for the challenges involved in women opting-out of global career moves, the KCM of Mainiero and Sullivan (2005), and the intelligent career capital framework (Arthur et al., 1995) for additional perspectives. Future research may wish to look at how women develop their global careers by undertaking various types of self-initiated assignments (for example, global trotting for academics in their sabbatical year).

NOTES

1. An employee travels from the domestic location to other parts of the world to conduct global business and then returns home shortly thereafter, so no relocation is necessary.
2. Transferring from a foreign subsidiary to the corporation's headquarters in another country, or vice versa.
3. Assuming that spouses/partners do not always engage in sex for their own pleasure but because of an 'altruistic' self-giving gesture with sexual meanings and sometimes mystified by 'pure relationships of love' (Giddens, 1992), the variety of activities with sexual meanings for the sake of the survival of marriage, or what is believed to be love, asked of partners is endless.

REFERENCES

Adler, N.J. (1994), 'Competitive frontiers: women managing across borders', *Journal of Management Development*, **13**(2), 24–41.

Adler, P.S. and S.W. Kwon (2002), 'Social capital: prospects for a new concept', *Academy of Management Review*, **27**(1), 17–40.

Altman, Y. and Y. Baruch (2012), 'Global self-initiated corporate expatriate careers: a new era in international assignments?', *Personnel Review*, **41**(2), 233–55.

Altman, Y. and S. Shortland (2008), 'Women and international assignments: taking stock – a 25-year review', *Human Resource Management*, **47**(2), 199–216.

Antal, B.A. (2000), 'Types of knowledge gained by expatriate managers', *Journal of General Management*, **26**(2), 32–51.

Apter, T. (1993), *Professional Progress: Why Women Still Don't Have Wives*, London: Macmillan.

Arthur, M.B., P. Claman and R. DeFillippi (1995), 'Intelligent enterprise, intelligent career', *Academy of Management Executive*, **9**(4), 7–22.

Arthur, M.B., D. Inkson and J. Pringle (1999), *The New Careers: Individual Action & Economic Change*, London: Sage.

Baruch, Y. (1995), 'Business globalization – the human resource management aspect', *Human Systems Management*, **14**(4), 313–26.

Baruch, Y. and Y. Altman (2002), 'Expatriation and repatriation in MNC: a taxonomy', *Human Resource Management*, **41**(2), 239–59.

Baruch, Y., M. Dickmann, Y. Altman and F. Bournois (2013), 'Exploring international work: types and dimensions of global careers', *International Journal of Human Resource Management*, **24**(12), 2369–93.

Borgatti, S.P. and R. Cross (2003), 'A relational view of information seeking and learning in social networks', *Management Science*, **49**(4), 432–45.

Bossard, A. and R.B. Peterson (2005), 'The repatriate experience as seen by American expatriates', *Journal of World Business*, **40**(1), 9–28.

Burt, R.S. (1992), *Structural Holes*, Boston, MA: Harvard University Press.

Cabrera, E.F. (2006), 'Opting out and opting in: understanding the complexities of women's career transitions', *Career Development International*, **12**(3), 218–37.
Caligiuri, P. and V. Di Santo (2001), 'Global competence: what it is, and can it be developed through global assignments?', *Human Resource Planning*, **24**(3), 27–35.
Caligiuri, P.M. and R. Tung (1999), 'Comparing the success of male and female expatriates from a US based company', *International Journal of Human Resource Management*, **10**(5), 763–82.
Carpenter, M.A., W.G. Sanders and H.B. Gregersen (2000), 'International assignment experience at the top can make a bottom-line difference', *Human Resource Management*, **39**(2–3), 277–85.
Catalyst (2013), 'Quick take: statistical overview of women in the workplace', accessed 17 April 2013 at www.catalyst.org/knowledge/statistical-overview-women-workplace.
Cole, N.D. (2011), 'Managing global talent: solving the spousal adjustment problem', *International Journal of Human Resource Management*, **22**(7), 1504–30.
DeFillippi, R. and M. Arthur (1994), 'The boundaryless career: a competency-based perspective', *Journal of Organizational Behavior*, **15**(4), 307–24.
Dickmann, M. and H. Harris (2005), 'Developing career capital for global careers: the role of international assignments', *Journal of World Business*, **40**(4), 399–408.
Eby, L.T. (2001), 'The boundaryless career experiences of mobile spouses in dual-earner marriages', *Group & Organization Management*, **26**(3), 343–68.
Eby, L.T., M. Butts and A. Lockwood (2003), 'Predictors of success in the era of boundaryless careers', *Journal of Organizational Behavior*, **24**(6), 689–708.
Giddens, A. (1992), *The Transformation of Intimacy: Sexuality, Love and Eroticism in Modern Societies*, Cambridge, UK: Polity Press.
Granovetter, M. (1973), 'The strength of weak ties', *American Journal of Sociology*, **78**(6), 1360–80.
Gregersen, H.B., A.J. Morrison and J.S. Black (1998), 'Developing leaders for the global frontier', *Sloan Management Review*, **40**(1), 21–33.
Groth, A. (2011), 'Sheryl Sandberg: the most important career choice you'll make is who you marry', *Business Insider*, accessed 5 December 2014 at http://www.businessinsider.com/sheryl-sandberg-career-advice-to-women-2011-12?IR=T.
Hakim, C. (2000), *Work–Lifestyle Choices in the 21st Century: Preference Theory*, Oxford: Oxford University Press.
Hakim, C. (2006), 'Women, careers, and work–life preferences', *British Journal of Guidance and Counselling*, **34**(3), 279–94.
Hakim, C. (2010), 'Erotic capital', *European Sociological Review*, **26**(5), 499–518.
Hall, D.T. (1976), *Careers in Organizations*, Glenview, IL: Scott Foresman.
Harris, H. (2004), 'Global careers: work–life issues and the adjustment of women international managers', *Journal of Management Development*, **23**(9), 818–32.
Harvey, M. and D. Wiese (1998), 'The dual career couples: female expatriates and male trailing spouses', *Thunderbird International Business Review*, **40**(4), 359–88.
Haslam, S.A. and M.K. Ryan (2008), 'The road to the glass cliff: differences in the perceived suitability of men and women for leadership positions in succeeding and failing organizations', *The Leadership Quarterly*, **1**(5), 530–46.
Hearn, J. and D. Morgan (1990), *Men, Masculinities and Social Theory*, London & New York: Routledge.
Hofstede, G. (2001), *Culture's Consequences: Comparing Values, Behaviors, Institutions, and Organizations Across Nations*, Beverly Hills, CA: Sage.
Hofstede, G. (2013), website, accessed 25 May 2013 at http://geert-hofstede.com/national-culture.html.
Inkson, K. and M. Arthur (2001), 'How to be a successful career capitalist', *Organizational Dynamics*, **30**(1), 48–58.
Jones, C. and R. DeFillippi (1996), 'Back to the future in film: combining industry and self-knowledge to meet the career challenges of the 21st century', *Academy of Management Executive*, **10**(4), 89–104.

Jones, C. and B. Lichtenstein (2000), 'The "architecture" of careers: how career competencies reveal firm dominant logic in professional services', in M. Peiperl, M. Arthur, R. Goffee and T. Morris (eds), *Career Frontiers*, Oxford: Oxford University Press, pp. 153–76.

Konopaske, R., C. Robie and J.M. Ivancevich (2005), 'A preliminary model of spouse influence on managerial global assignment willingness', *International Journal of Human Resource Management*, **16**(3), 405–26.

Kossek, E.E., S. Lewis and L.B. Hammer (2010), 'Work–life initiatives and organizational change: overcoming mixed messages to move from the margin to the mainstream', *Human Relations*, **63**(1), 3–19.

Kupka, B. and V. Cathro (2007), 'Desperate housewives – social and professional isolation of German expatriated spouses', *International Journal of Human Resource Management*, **18**(6), 951–68.

Lauring, J. and J. Selmer (2010), 'The supportive expatriate spouse: an ethnographic study of spouse involvement in expatriate careers', *International Business Review*, **19**(1), 59–69.

Levinson, D.J. (1978), *Seasons of a Man's Life*, New York: Knopf.

Levinson, D.J. (2011), *The Seasons of a Woman's Life*, New York: Ballantine Books.

Linehan, M. (2002), 'Senior female international managers: empirical evidence from Western Europe', *International Journal of Human Resource Management*, **13**(5), 802–14.

Mainiero, L.A. and S.E. Sullivan (2005), 'Kaleidoscope careers: an alternative explanation for the opt-out evolution', *Academy of Management Executive*, **19**(1), 106–23.

Makela, L., M. Kansala and V. Suutari (2011), 'The roles of expatriates' spouses among dual career couples', *Cross Cultural Management: An International Journal*, **18**(2), 185–97.

Markus, A.P. (2013), 'Global moves from and to Brazil', in C. Reis and Y. Baruch (eds), *Careers Without Borders: Critical Perspectives*, New York: Routledge.

Mayrhofer, W. and H. Scullion (2002), 'Female expatriates in international business: empirical evidence from the German clothing industry', *International Journal of Human Resource Management*, **13**(5), 815–36.

McKenna, S. and J. Richardson (2007), 'The increasing complexity of the internationally mobile professional: issues for research and practice', *Cross Cultural Management: An International Journal*, **14**(4), 307–20.

Merton, R.K. (1968), *Social Theory and Social Structure*, New York: Free Press.

Miller, E.L. and J. Cheng (1978), 'A closer look at the decision to accept an overseas position', *Management International Review*, **19**(3), 25–33.

Nahapiet, J. and S. Ghoshal (1998), 'Social capital, intellectual capital and the organizational advantage', *Academy of Management Review*, **23**(1), 242–66.

Ollier-Malaterre, A. (2009), 'Organizational work–life initiatives: context matters – France compared to the UK and the US', *Community, Work and Family*, **1**(2),159–78.

Omair, K. (2009), 'Typology of career development for Arab women managers in the United Arab Emirates', *Career Development International*, **15**(2), 121–43.

Parker, H. and M.B. Arthur (2000), 'Careers, organizing, and community', in M.A. Peiperl, M.B. Arthur, R. Gofee and T. Morris (eds), *Career Frontiers: New Conceptions of Working Lives*, Oxford: Oxford University Press.

Raider, H.J. and R.S. Burt (1996), 'Boundaryless careers and social capital', in M.B. Arthur and D.M. Rousseau (eds), *The Boundaryless Career: A New Employment Principle for a New Organizational Era*, Oxford: Oxford University Press.

Reis, C. (2004), *Men Working as Managers in a European Multinational Company*, Munich and Mering: Rainer Hampp Verlag.

Richardson, J. and S. McKenna (2002), 'Leaving and experiencing: why academics expatriate and how they experience expatriation', *Career Development International*, **7**(2), 67–78.

Richardson, J. and J. Zikic (2007), 'The darker side of an international academic career', *Career Development International*, **12**(2), 164–86.

Roberts, K., E.E. Kossek and C. Ozeki (1998), 'Managing the global workforce: challenges and strategies', *Academy of Management Executive*, **12**(4), 93–119.

Ryan, M.K. and S.A. Haslam (2007), 'The glass cliff: exploring the dynamics surrounding

the appointment of women to precarious leadership positions', *Academy of Management Review*, **32**(2), 549–72.
Sandberg, S. (2013), *Lean In*, New York: Random House.
Schwartz, S.H. (2006), 'A theory of cultural value orientations: explication and applications', *Comparative Sociology*, **5**(2), 136–82.
Seidler, V.J. (1994), *Unreasonable Men: Masculinity and Social Theory*, London and New York: Routledge.
Selmer, J. and A.S.M. Leung (2003), 'Provision and adequacy of corporate support to male expatriate spouses – an exploratory study', *Personnel Review*, **32**(1–2), 9–21.
Shortland, S. and Y. Altman (2011), 'What do we really know about corporate career women expatriates?', *European Journal of International Management*, **5**(3), 209–34.
Sima, C. (2000), 'The role and benefits of the sabbatical leave in faculty development and satisfaction', *New Directions for Institutional Research*, No. 105, 67–75.
Stahl, G.K., E.L. Miller and R.L. Tung (2002), 'Toward the boundaryless career: a closer look at the expatriate career concept and the perceived implications of an international assignment', *Journal of World Business*, **33**(2), 11–24.
Stroh, L.K., A. Varma and S.J. Valy-Durbin (2000), 'Why are women left at home: are they unwilling to go on international assignments?', *Journal of World Business*, **35**(3), 241–55.
Sullivan, S.E., M. Forret, S.C. Carraher and L. Mainiero (2009), 'Using the kaleidoscope career model to examine generational differences in work attitudes', *Career Development International*, **14**(3), 284–302.
Suutari, V. (2003), 'Global managers: career orientation, career tracks, life-style implications, and career commitment', *Journal of Managerial Psychology*, **18**(3), 185–207.
Tharenou, P. (2008), 'Disruptive decisions to leave home: gender and family differences in expatriation choices', *Organizational Behavior & Human Decision Processes*, **105**(2), 183–200.
Tharenou, P. (2009), 'Self-initiated international careers: gender difference and career outcomes', in S.G. Baugh and S.E. Sullivan (eds), *Maintaining Energy, Focus & Options over the Career: Research in Careers Vol. 1*, Charlotte, NC: Information Age, pp. 197–226.
Tharenou, P. (2010), 'Women's self-initiated expatriation as a career option and its ethical issues', *Journal of Business Ethics*, **95**(1), 73–88.
Tung, R.L. (1998), 'American expatriates abroad: from neophytes to cosmopolitans', *Journal of World Business*, **33**(2), 125–44.
Van Gennep, A. (2011), *The Rites of Passage*, Chicago, IL: University of Chicago Press.
World Bank (2013), 'World development report', accessed 4 December 2014 at http://siteresources.worldbank.org/EXTNWDR2013/Resources/8258024-1320950747192/8260293-1322665883147/WDR_2013_Report.pdf.

22. Pursuing partnerships: flexible work arrangements in US accounting and law firms
Leslie A. Levin, Mary Mattis, Andrea Tsentides and Jill Choate Beier

This chapter examines the perceptions of female accountants and attorneys employed in US accounting and law firms regarding their possibilities of becoming partners in their firms, and specifically, what strategies may be most useful in terms of reaching that goal. A mixed-method approach was used including a review of secondary source data on characteristics of the US workforce and work schedules, publications from law and accounting professional membership organizations and advocacy groups, and interviews with key informants from law and accounting firms.

The research focused on middle- and upper-level female managers who constitute the pipeline to partnership positions in their firms. The focus of the study is availability, use of, and experiences with flexible work arrangements (FWAs) in key informants' firms. We do not attempt to definitively link the use of FWAs and women's promotion to partnership (or lack thereof) in accounting and law firms, rather, we use the research to explore perceptions and suggest best practices.

THE BUSINESS IMPERATIVE FOR WORKPLACE FLEXIBILITY

Between the 1960s and the 1990s two remarkable interdependent trends in the US labour force were observed by demographers. The first was the enormous increase in women graduating from colleges and universities prepared to enter managerial and professional careers. By the 1980s (Mattis, 1990) women represented the most highly educated segment of the US labour pool, and more women than ever before were committed to careers rather than the intermittent workforce participation of earlier generations of women (Mattis, 1994). Consequently, by 1985, more than 70 per cent of women between the ages of 20 and 44 were in the US labour force (O'Connell and Bloom, 1987). The second trend was the increase in the age of marriage and childbearing in the USA and the rapid return of women to the workplace after childbirth. In 1987, approximately 50 per cent of children under the age of one had mothers in the labour force, up from 31 per cent in 1976 (Catalyst, 1988). In that same year, the US Department of Commerce reported that mothers of preschool-aged children were, and would continue to be, the fastest-growing segment of the US labour force (Bachu, 1988).

In keeping with these trends, female accounting graduates had steadily increased from 28 per cent of all graduating Certified Public Accountants (CPAs) in 1976–77 to 52 per cent in 1991–92. The demand for all accounting graduates also grew during the same period. In 1976–77, 24 per cent of graduates recruited by public accounting firms were women; in 1992, it had grown to 46 per cent (Catalyst, 2000). However, firms' success in recruiting women was not matched by success in retaining them. J. Michael Cook, Chairman and CEO of Deloitte LLP, Chairman of the American Institute of Certified Public Accountants (AICPA), and a noted champion of women's advancement, frequently talked about the 'leaky pipeline' in accounting. He noted that his firm and the accounting industry generally would not be able to sustain continued growth while losing talented women after five or more years of learning the business and cultivating clients. In 1993 the Families and Work Institute reported the average cost of turnover of high-potential managers and professionals was 150 per cent of the average annual salary for this group (Families and Work Institute, 1993); another study put the cost at 193 per cent (Galinsky, 1993). Cook's high-profile role in advocating for women's development in accounting was not matched by a champion for women's retention and advancement in the legal profession.

Along with accounting firms, most US business organizations were increasingly interested in how they could retain valued female employees, leverage their investment in women's recruitment and training, and reduce turnover costs. During the 1970s and 1980s the business programmes designed to help women manage work and family expanded from providing on-site childcare or subsidizing off-site programmes, to implementing flexible work arrangements (FWAs), including flextime within the traditional eight-hour day, telecommuting, compressed work periods, part-time arrangements, and job-sharing. By 2001 more than a fourth (28.8 per cent) of full-time and salaried workers in the USA were using FWAs (US Bureau of Labor Statistics, 2004). Over time, men also took advantage of these arrangements.

What, specifically, was happening in accounting and law firms during this period of growth regarding availability and use of FWAs? In May 2004, US government data, including business and professional firms, showed a small, but insignificant, difference in the use of FWAs by male (46.2 per cent) versus female workers (43.7 per cent) in accounting firms. In legal services, by contrast, a majority of men (58.6 per cent) were using FWAs compared to 34.1 per cent of women (McMenamin, 2007).

How should we interpret these statistics on the differing use of FWAs? Here, it is important to note the difference between *formal* and *informal* flexibility. The availability and use of formal FWAs is widely publicized in companies and firms that offer them. Flexible scheduling arrangements for individual employees are openly negotiated and documented in employees' terms of employment. Ongoing monitoring and management of such arrangements is typically handled by human resources departments in consultation with employees' supervisors. In order for companies/firms to use FWAs as a tool for recruitment and retention, they have to be approved by the organization, broadly publicized, and equitably distributed among employees who meet the organization's criteria for use. In contrast, informal flexibility flies under the radar in companies and firms. It is not documented and historically has been available only to corporate/firm elites – high-level employees, usually men, who have a great deal of flexibility because they are evaluated on their success in generating business and bringing in clients rather than on time spent in the office. More will be said about this later.

The positive environment for workplace flexibility in the early years of the twenty-first century lost much of its lustre during the 2007–09 recession in the US economy. Although goods-producing industries experienced steeper declines than service-producing industries, the number of employees in professional and business services declined by 1.6 million employees, or 8.9 per cent. Service industries responded in different ways to their labour needs during this period. Some maintained headcount by cutting employees' hours, whereas others shed employees. The prevailing strategy, to cut employees rather than hours, resulted in widespread layoffs and reduced hiring of business and professional workers (Kroll, 2011).

The effects of the recession on human resources strategies demonstrated that it is more difficult to make the business case for workplace flexibility in a buyer's market than in a seller's market. In a buyer's market, employees are hesitant to ask for accommodations, and employers have fewer reasons to consider these requests. The recession demanded a face-time work environment; employees could not take significant time away from work without jeopardizing their ongoing employment.

From 2010–12, the importance of access to flexibility in organizations seems to have diminished; this is not surprising given the continued weakness of the US economy. This period was characterized by two trends in companies/firms' use of FWAs: (1) an increase in arrangements that enabled employees to continue working full-time using various forms of flexible scheduling, (2) a decrease in FWA options involving significant time away from full-time work, including temporary part-time options and career breaks (Families and Work Institute, 2012).

Although most measures of corporate support for flexibility did not change significantly between 2005 and 2012, fewer employers reported rewards for those in the organization who supported flexibility: 12 per cent in 2012 compared to 31 per cent in 2005 (ibid.). Management of flexibility was no longer considered a criterion for reward in managers' performance appraisals and compensation decisions. The Society for Human Resource Management (SHRM) *2012 Employment Satisfaction and Engagement* report also reflected some erosion in the importance to employees of access to workplace flexibility. On a comparison of 26 'Very Important Aspects of Employee Job Satisfaction' between 2002 and 2011 (2003 data are omitted), flexibility to balance life and work issues dropped out of the top five satisfaction criteria for the first time in 2008. Prior to that year, flexibility had been considered the third most important aspect of job satisfaction for four years out of five. In 2008 flexibility fell to sixth place and continued downward to eleventh place in 2012.

SHRM's 2013 report, *Workplace Forecast: The Top Workplace Trends According to HR Professionals*, surveys human resource professionals on their views of key issues that will affect the future workplace, and what actions their organizations are planning to address these issues. Neither flexibility nor specific family needs were mentioned by the approximately 400 HR respondents to questions of top trends from 2003 to 2011 or for 2013 and beyond. Nevertheless, when asked about most effective tactics for attracting, retaining and rewarding their best employees over the next ten years, flexible work arrangements came up first in 2010 and 2012. Although this response declined from 2010 (58 per cent) to 2012 (40 per cent), it still surpassed responses for higher total rewards packages and career advancement. The emphasis on most talented employees seems to imply that these are employees targeted for high-level positions who will need to manage work/life responsibilities throughout their working lives.

THE IMPACT OF USING FWAs ON WOMEN'S CAREER ADVANCEMENT

Much of our research has focused on the cultural and economic factors that led to development of workplace flexibility and the positive impact of such arrangements on recruiting and retaining employees in a seller's market, particularly women. Findings from a ten-year retrospective study on FWAs conducted by Catalyst in 2000 confirm that flexibility is a valuable tool for promoting employee retention and commitment to an organization. However, the following quote suggests that the findings are less conclusive about FWAs as valuable tools for women's advancement:

> [E]ven though working mothers may reduce career involvement for a period – with the support of the right company – career advancement does not have to be sidelined. While half [of working mothers] continued to work part-time schedules, half have returned to full-time schedules. Most still work for the same company where they initiated their flexible work arrangements a decade ago, demonstrating that when business holds on to talented women when they want flexibility, business can retain valued employees . . . Most women in this study reported satisfaction with the career trade-offs they made in order to gain better work/life balance. (Catalyst, 2000, p. 48)

How do we interpret the seemingly contradictory messages in this quote that 'career advancement does not have to be sidelined' and most women 'reported satisfaction with the career trade-offs they made in order to gain better work/life balance?' It is clear that when companies/firms are in a growth mode and the economy is booming, FWAs are an important tool for recruiting and retaining women (and, increasingly, men). The question remains whether women who use FWAs can avoid being sidelined when it comes to career advancement. Does using an FWA severely limit women's access to networking, mentoring, lateral moves (for example, moving from staff to line positions, or from marketing to sales) and other important opportunities for career development? Does use of flexibility preclude women from ever catching up with their colleagues who invested more in 'face time'? Can women who use FWAs avoid being stereotyped as less committed to their organization and to their own career advancement? Will they be viewed as stayers rather than players in the field of candidates on track for leadership roles in their company/firm? In short, are organizations able to allow for flexible scheduling without penalty? In the sections that follow, we discuss the experiences of several women in accounting and law firms about their organizations' responses to these questions.

ACCOUNTING

Male Dominated or Not?

Accounting has traditionally been a male-dominated profession. Although approximately 50 per cent of new Certified Public Accountants (CPAs) entering the profession are women, only about 21 per cent of partners in

CPA firms nationwide are women according to the American Institute of Certified Public Accountants (AICPA, 2011). Even more dramatic, unpublished data from Catalyst reports that less than 9 per cent of all business and industry CFOs are women (AICPA, 2013). The disparity between the number of women entering the profession and the number of women in leadership positions indicates problems in their advancement. The AICPA recognizes the significance of women's advancement within the profession and its ties to organizational growth. Accounting has been one of the first fields to undertake formal steps to study and promote women's representation and advancement to leadership positions. In 1989 the AICPA created the Upward Mobility of Women Task Force, which evolved into the Women's Initiatives Executive Committee (WIEC). Through a series of workshops, webinars, articles, a speakers' bureau, women's network, and research, WIEC promotes opportunities for women's advancement into leadership positions through integration of their personal and professional lives (ibid.). According to its mission statement, WIEC educates men and women on the gap in advancement of women in the accounting profession, and, through research, develops policies and programmes aiming to influence the culture. Furthermore, WIEC designs and helps firms implement strategies for advancing women while providing women with visible examples through successful role models.

The remainder of this section addresses the following interrelated questions. Since women enter the profession in approximately equal numbers as men, where do they go? What retention policies do accounting firms have in place, and how do flexible work arrangements in particular affect women's retention and advancement? Findings from the AICPA *WIEC Benchmarking Survey of Firms* (Single, 2010) may shed some light on the subject. The survey indicates that at junior levels women make up the majority of professionals in smaller firms and just below 50 per cent in the largest firms, a percentage that is maintained through the manager level. The percentages begin to decrease at the senior manager level, and they fall to even lower numbers at the equity partner level. There is parity in these percentages among different size firms, however, with the proportion of women at the full equity partner level at 21 per cent for the largest firms, 14 per cent for mid-size firms, and 25 per cent for the smallest firms. A similar trend can be observed in firm ownership. Only 7 per cent of larger CPA firms (10–49 CPAs) are owned by women, as compared to 23 per cent of smaller CPA firms (fewer than ten CPAs). These numbers, in combination with an increase in the number of men starting at a senior/ manager level, may suggest a drift of women from larger to smaller firms (Single, 2012).

Why do women prefer smaller firms? A possible explanation may be that women who exit the workforce for a period of time find it easier to return to a smaller firm because of the simpler organizational and hierarchical structures of these firms, as well as their more flexible policies. Furthermore, women who are dissatisfied with their current work arrangements may choose to start their own practice. Robyn Mick decided to do just that when she had the 'realization that the traditional culture of "work above all else" in the CPA profession was not going to work for her vision of her life' (Bennett, 2012a). The firm currently has six team members and two partners and is built around flexibility. Robyn attributes the firm's success to good communication, technology utilization, and careful teambuilding around each client. Similarly, based on a personal interview we conducted, a female CPA who initially started at a Big Four firm found that the expectations regarding working hours did not fit her lifestyle, and she quit her job for a position at a smaller firm. Following her maternity leave, she considered not returning to the workforce, but a four-day flexible work arrangement at the smaller firm convinced her to stay. She is currently a director in that firm, and she remains satisfied with her position: 'I feel that having a CFO who is female and follows a flexible work schedule makes it a lot easier.'

Big Four Flexibility Strategies

According to the *WIEC Benchmarking Survey of Firms* (Single, 2010), accounting firms have adopted many policies aimed at improving retention. The policies most frequently in place are flextime hours, flexible spending accounts, part-time hours, work-at-home options, and special holiday hours. Notably, few firms offer such retention policies specifically to women, whereas the majority of firms make them available to all employees. Figure 22.1 depicts certain policies and practices aimed specifically at the advancement of women.

There are two schools of thought regarding the availability of such policies to employees. On the one hand, the few firms that offer them only to women do so as an affirmative policy to benefit the disadvantaged group. On the other hand, firms that make these policies available to all employees believe that the social changes in gender roles and expectations dictate making these opportunities equally available to men and women. Although the survey indicates women drifting towards smaller firms, the Big Four accounting firms have, in fact, invested heavily in offering and promoting flexibility in an attempt to respond to changing needs of the workforce and to decrease their employee turnover rates. The following short overview of the Big Four's retention policies provides an indication of their commitment to flexibility.

364 *Handbook of gendered careers in management*

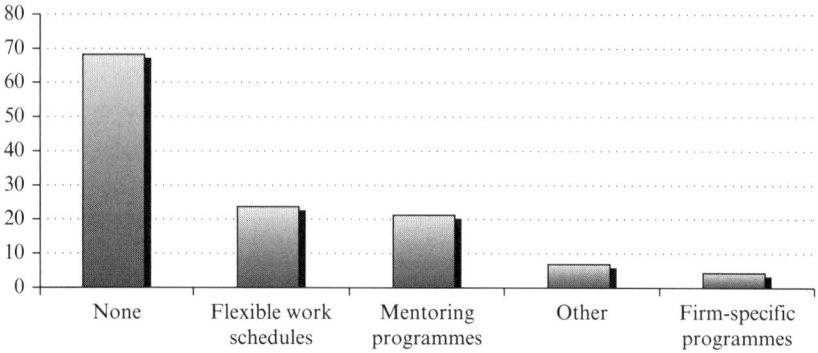

Source: *WIEC Benchmarking Survey of Firms* (Single, 2010).

Figure 22.1 Initiatives aimed at female advancement

According to its website, Deloitte LLP offers its employees both day-to-day informal flexibility as well as formal flexible arrangements (Deloitte, 2013). Informal flexibility refers to options allowing individuals and teams to design certain aspects of their work schedule according to their needs. Formal flexible arrangements refer to formal modification and reduction of the work schedule, and they are built around Deloitte's 'Mass Career Customization' framework. The company has also introduced a sabbatical programme that allows employees to take time off for a specified period. Deloitte has issued two publications on workplace flexibility: *Mass Career Customization: Aligning the Workplace to Today's Nontraditional Workforce* (Benko and Weisberg, 2007) and *The Corporate Lattice: Achieving High Performance in the Changing World of Work* (Benko and Anderson, 2010). Ernst & Young considers flexibility an 'ongoing focus'. The firm provides informal day-to-day flexibility and formal flexible work arrangements as well as family support services such as child- and elder-care resource and referral, daily life services, adoption assistance policy, lactation programme, legal consultation services, and maternity/paternity leaves. According to its website, Ernst & Young has focused on flexibility and work/life balance policies for a number of years, and it was featured in *Fortune* magazine's '100 Best Companies to Work For' for 15 consecutive years and *Working Mother*'s '100 Best Companies for Working Mothers' for 16 years (Ernst & Young, 2013). Similarly, PricewaterhouseCoopers, under its 'Flexibility^2' (Flexibility Squared) framework, offers informal flexibility including an 'unprescribed number of sick days' and referral resources (PricewaterhouseCoopers, 2013). Formally, it offers a number of flexible work arrangements including reduced hours, flextime, telecommuting, job-sharing, compressed work week, and sabbaticals. The company actively tries to cultivate a flexible culture and urges senior managers and partners to lead by example. Finally, according to its website, KPMG offers similar formal flexible work arrangements including an option to purchase up to 35 additional holiday days (KPMG, 2013). The option to obtain additional time off may contribute to the improvement of the work–life balance, which can in turn influence women's decisions to stay in the profession.

Impact on Women's Careers

So how do women perceive these initiatives, and how do they affect their careers? The existence of such programmes seems to be generally welcomed, and they are perceived as a trend towards the retention and advancement of women (Single, 2010) (Figure 22.2).

In our interviews, a senior associate at a Big Four firm stated, 'The firm offers several flex options which can be beneficial to women who want to balance their professional lives with their family responsibilities.' In response to a question about whether men take advantage of such policies she said, 'I am not aware of any men in my department who use formal flexible arrangements. I know men who use informal flexibility on a day-to-day basis, but I don't know anyone with an actual formal flexible schedule.' She also indicated that informal flexibility becomes more 'politically acceptable' with seniority. In regard to the impact of flexible work arrangements on women's advancement she said:

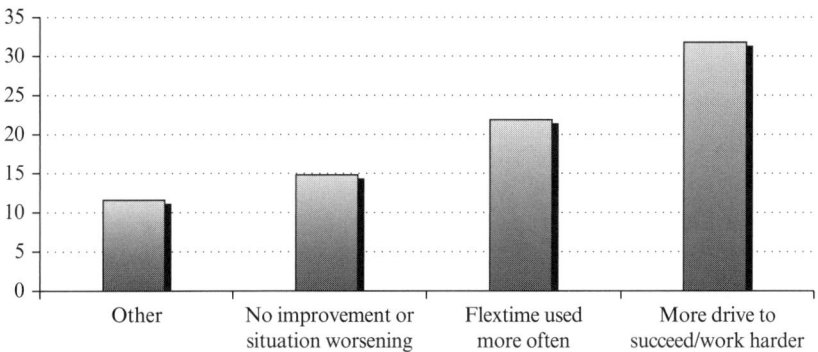

Source: WIEC Benchmarking Survey of Firms (Single, 2010).

Figure 22.2   Trends in retention/advancement of females

> They definitely do not help in the long run! There are two women in my team who use them. One uses a reduced-hours (and salary) option. She has just been promoted to manager, but she believes that her promotion was delayed. To tell you the truth, though, I think it just took a little longer for her to complete the number of hours at the firm. The other woman, however, works full time with extended hours and a day off. She has been in the firm for more than fifteen years, and she has not made partner yet. Everyone believes it's because of the flexible hours.

In fact the findings from the AICPA *WIEC Benchmarking Survey of Firms* (Single, 2010) indicate that although flexible work arrangements have contributed to retaining women at accounting firms, they have not helped in their advancement. One of the reasons identified is the difficulty that many firms face in promoting reduced-hour professionals, most of whom are women, within their existing firm policies and contracts. It seems necessary that such existing policies be reconsidered. Unfortunately, this may be a slow process for the large, often bureaucratic, organizations.

However, it is not all bad news as some women have successfully combined flexibility and advancement. In her interview featured on AICPA's 'Flexibility at the Partner Level Series' (Bennett, 2012b) Melissa Harman, a partner at Moss Adams, a medium-sized national firm with 22 locations, said that in her initial interview she made her expectations and intentions regarding flexibility known to the hiring partner. Throughout her tenure at the firm, clear communication has been central to her success, and she has been using flexibility in a variety of ways including reduced hours, extended days, and working from home, selecting an arrangement that best meets the client's needs and her own. Sometimes she worked fewer than 40 hours per week while at other times she had to work more. Important elements for integrating flexibility with a successful career have been her efforts to 'maintain adequate firm and client activities to ensure she was getting the necessary experience to stay on the partner track'. Finally, support from her partner at home and her formal mentoring relationship at work were also fundamental to her success.

The accounting profession in general, and accounting firms in particular, have been investing heavily in retention policies and programmes that support a healthy work/life balance. Despite an increase in the overall number of women in the field and their retention at higher rates, it does not appear that these programmes have positively affected women's advancement to leadership positions. Although this may be due to a combination of factors, a shift to a culture that more openly embraces flexibility as well as mentorship programmes would be steps in the right direction.

The Future of Accounting

Rapid advancements in technology and the evolution of cloud computing have made it possible for many public accounting firms to close their brick-and-mortar offices and go virtual. Cloud computing enables users to use programmes and applications and store data over the Internet rather than on their local drives. This can facilitate work-from-home arrangements. An estimated 5–10 per cent of all accounting firms are currently operating without a physical location (Drew, 2013). This new form of flexibility – if utilized correctly – may be key to women's advancement in the accounting profession.

LAW

Will Women Catch Up?

Law firms present a different picture than accounting firms with respect to women's advancement. While women have made small gains in their representation among law firm partners as a whole, the percentage of women associates continues to fall compared to their male counterparts. The latest findings on law firm demographics published by the National Association for Law Placement (NALP) reveal that in 2012 the percentage of women partners across the nation – 19.9 per cent – was up by a small amount compared with 2011 – 19.5 per cent (NALP, 2012). While any increase in the number of female partners is positive, it is important to note that the total change in the number of women partners since 1993 (when NALP first began to compile the data) has increased only 7.5 per cent – a rather marginal increase over a span of almost 20 years (ibid.).

Recent data suggest that some of these gains may have come from promotions to non-equity partnerships. A current trend in law firm management is to create multi-tiered partnerships in which partners are divided into two groups: equity and non-equity. Although no official definition exists, non-equity partners typically do not have an ownership stake in the firm, do not participate in profit sharing, and often do not have voting rights on important partnership matters. NALP reports that only 15.3 per cent of equity partners are women, while 27.3 per cent of non-equity partners are women (NALP, 2013b). 2012 is only the second year in which NALP has gathered such data, thus any conclusions are tentative at best. Nevertheless, it appears that women at the non-equity partnership rank are not involved in the leadership and management of the law firm in the way that equity partners are.

Table 22.1 Women law students and associates

	2011–12	2010–11	2009–10
% of women law students[a]	46.8	46.1	47.1
% of women summer associates	46.3	47.7	47.3
% of women associates	45.1	45.4	45.4

Note: a. Represents women enrolled as first-year law students.

Source: ABA (2012).

At the associate rank, women are not faring as well. Representation of women declined slightly for the third year in a row and has continued its small but steady slide from 45.7 per cent in 2009 to 45.1 per cent in 2012. Looking at the pipeline of women entering law firms reflects a similar downward trend (ABA, 2012). Table 22.1 shows the percentage of women in law school, as summer associates, and as associates from 2009 through 2012. The number of female summer associates is closely correlated to the number of female law students. However, the number of female associates is substantially lower compared to the number of summer associates, indicating some 'leakage' in the ranks of women as they journey from law school to law firm. Further, the percentage of women partners is starkly different from the percentages in Table 22.1. While almost one out of every two associates is a woman, only one in seven equity partners is a woman. The obvious inquiry is why women are not being promoted to the ranks of partner in similar proportions to when they entered the profession. In addition, with dwindling numbers of female law students and associates, how will the number and percentage of women at the rank of partner increase in law firms? Law firms are grappling with these questions and, in response, are trying to create new and innovative ways to attract and retain women. One such method is by offering FWAs to law firm associates.

Flexible Work Arrangements: A Deal Breaker?

One study suggests that the advent of FWAs to promote a healthy work/life balance is the key to improving retention and promotion of female attorneys (Calvert et al., 2009). The same study emphasizes that client service cannot suffer as a result of using FWAs. In fact, according to the study, many women who began working a reduced schedule quickly realized that being unavailable for one or two days per week was simply not feasible to maintain a vibrant law practice, and they went back to working five days per week with shorter scheduled work hours each day. However, many women reported that during certain periods (trial preparation or closing of a corporate transaction), they worked just as many hours per day or week as those attorneys who did not participate in an FWA programme (ibid.). This leads to the questions of what it really means for law firms to provide FWAs, whether these arrangements really help retain female lawyers, and what is really the impact on those who use them?

Law firms have increasingly made FWAs available to their experienced lawyers. In 2012, roughly 98 per cent of all law firm offices had an FWA policy, either as an affirmative policy or on a case-by-case basis. Overall, however, the number of lawyers utilizing FWAs continues to be very small, and in 2012 the percentage of lawyers utilizing FWAs (approximately 6 per cent) remained unchanged compared to 2011 (NALP, 2013a). The paucity of lawyers using FWAs distinguishes law firm practice from the rest of the USA workforce. The Bureau of Labor Statistics reports that in 2012, 13.1 per cent of professionals – such as architects, engineers and physicians – worked on a part-time schedule, more than double the 6.2 per cent of lawyers working part-time (ibid.). Additionally, most of the lawyers utilizing FWAs – over 70 per cent – were women, while only 2.7 per cent of all male lawyers reported using FWAs. Among female partners, 11.7 per cent utilized FWAs, and among associates 10.1 per cent used them (ibid.). Clearly, women are much more likely than men to take advantage of FWAs. The interviews conducted for this chapter reflect results that are consistent with NALP's study. The attorneys interviewed may shed some light on the realities of FWAs. The respondents, all women, represent a wide range of firm sizes (from less than 100 attorneys to more than 700) and a variety of ranks (from associate to counsel to partner).

All but one of the respondents reported that their employers allowed FWAs. Most of the firms allowed an attorney to work four or even three days per week, and some worked part of the time from home. With the exception of one, the respondents agreed that an attorney who utilized FWAs has little or no prospect of rising to the level of partner. The main reason is the perception that an attorney who is working part-time cannot work the requisite number of hours to provide adequate service to clients and/or bring in business, which is the principal criterion for determining promotion to partnership. One respondent suggested that, perhaps, the general perception that women are not capable of generating revenue persists in law firms. Another respondent suggested that the negative perception of attorneys who use FWAs may be generational. Partners who are older and have not faced the same socioeconomic challenges as today's legal workforce are less supportive of FWAs. One interviewee (not utilizing a FWA) reflected on a discussion she had with an older partner regarding her progression at the firm and her ability to generate as many billable hours as some of her colleagues due to childcare issues:

> The partner looked at me and said, 'Well, we all want to go to the dance recital and the little league game, but work does not always allow it.' I realized at that moment that I had little or no chance of changing his perception of me or my ability to be a productive partner because I was not talking about being able to attend 'fun' events. I was talking about having to leave work early because my child is sick or having no access to childcare on certain holidays or during severe weather events.

Other respondents disagree with the generational divide and suggest that the issue is really a cultural issue specific to each law firm. Whatever the reason behind the FWA bias, all respondents agree that partners who are also trying to balance the responsibilities of family and building a career are more likely to support female lawyers facing the same challenges. In those situations, the women reported feeling much more satisfied with career and promotion possibilities.

Where Can Women Go From Here?

Law firms have begun taking steps to help women progress through the ranks by providing more mentoring and creating women's affinity groups. *Working Mother* magazine teams up with Flex-time Lawyers consulting firm to identify the '50 Best Law Firms for Women' each year; since 2007 the number of law firms with affinity groups for women has grown from 86 per cent to 100 per cent (Henry, 2013). In addition, almost 100 per cent of law firms on the list provide management and leadership training, women's mentoring circles, programmes to help senior associates transition to partner, and networking events with female lawyers and female clients. It remains to be seen whether these initiatives, particularly when used in conjunction with FWAs, will help propel women to partner ranks in significant numbers.

BEST PRACTICES FOR ACCOUNTING AND LAW FIRMS

Best practices identified during this study are much more likely to be found in accounting than in law firms. For accounting they include the following:

- Culture that embraces flexibility through 'lead by example' practices from partners and upper management, clearly communicating

expectations and establishing a culture of accountability for making flexibility work.
- An infrastructure that facilitates FWAs: use of technology and cloud computing.
- Establishment of objective performance measures.
- Mentorship programmes and advocates and personalized plans/ roadmaps for advancement of employees using FWAs.
- FWAs carefully designed around organizational goals that reinforce the business case for workplace flexibility. This could entail different types of arrangements for different positions.

For law firms, best practices that were identified include the following:

- FWAs offered for specific family situations instead of a case-by-case determination.
- Mentoring and affinity groups for attorneys using FWAs.
- Promotion track, which may be slower, for attorneys using FWAs.

CONCLUSIONS

From the 1970s through approximately 2006, a sellers' market existed for new entrants to the workforce, especially women. Robust economic conditions and changes in the status of women, as well as concern about retention of talented female employees and the high cost of turnover, contributed to the emergence and use of FWAs in professional firms. Accounting was one of the first fields to take formal steps to study and promote women's hiring and advancement as J. Michael Cook, Chairman and CEO of Deloitte LLP, articulated in the business case for companies using FWAs.

Accounting firms continued to grow through the recession and to invest heavily in offering and promoting flexibility. However, while FWAs have contributed to retaining women in accounting firms, they have not promoted women's advancement. Although this may be due to a combination of factors, a shift in culture that openly embraces flexibility and mentorship programmes would be steps in the right direction. Rapid advances in technology, particularly the evolution of cloud computing, could make workplace flexibility more the norm than the exception.

Women's recruitment, retention and advancement, as well as use of FWAs, have been quite different in law firms than in accounting firms. Law firms were slow to adopt FWAs. Today, roughly 98 per cent of firms report that they have a FWA policy, whether as an affirmative policy or on a case-by-case basis. However, the number of lawyers utilizing FWAs continues to be very small – less than half of professionals in other industries.

The percentage of women associates continues to fall compared to their male counterparts, and by 2012 representation of women in law firms had declined for three years running. While women have made small gains in their representation among law firm partners as a whole, these gains have been largely at the non-equity level. The culture of law firms does not seem to have changed despite the large increase in women pursuing careers in law and in the availability of alternative work arrangements. It is not surprising then that all but one woman interviewed for this study said that using an FWA would be a 'deal breaker' in pursuit of partnership.

More research is needed to determine whether, over time, flexibility and other strategies will help or hinder women's attainment of partnerships in law and accounting firms.

REFERENCES

American Bar Association (ABA) (2012), 'Enrollment and degrees awarded', accessed 1 July 2013 at http://www.americanbar.org/content/dam/aba/administrative/legal_education_and_admissions_to_the_bar/statistics/enrollment_degrees_awarded.authcheckdam.pdf.
American Institute of Certified Public Accountants (AICPA) (2011), '2011 trends in the supply of accounting graduates and the demand for public accounting recruits', accessed 4 December 2014 at http://www.aicpa.org/InterestAreas/AccountingEducation/NewsAndPublications/DownloadableDocuments/2011TrendsReport.pdf.
American Institute of Certified Public Accountants (AICPA) (2013), 'Gender issues and business case', accessed 27 June 2013 at http://www.aicpa.org/Career/WomenintheProfession/Pages/GenderIssues.aspx.
Bachu, A. (1988), *Fertility of American Women (Current Population Reports)*, Series P-20, No. 436, Washington, DC: US Department of Commerce.
Benko, C. and M. Anderson, for Deloitte (2010), *The Corporate Lattice: Achieving High Performance in the Changing World of Work*, Boston, MA: Harvard Business School Press.
Benko, C. and A. Weisberg, for Deloitte (2007), *Mass Career Customization: Aligning the Workplace to Today's Nontraditional Workforce*, Boston, MA: Harvard Business School Press.
Bennett, M.L., for AICPA (2012a), 'Interview with Robyn Mick, CPA', *Flexibility at the Partner Level Series*, accessed 5 December at http://www.aicpa.org/Career/WomenintheProfession/DownloadableDocuments/RobynMickInterview.pdf.
Bennett, M.L., for AICPA (2012b), 'Interview with Melissa Harman, CPA', *Flexibility at the Partner Level Series*, accessed 20 June 2013 at http://www.aicpa.org/Career/WomenintheProfession/DownloadableDocuments/MelissaHarmonInterview.pdf.
Calvert, C., L. Chanow and L. Marks (2009), 'Reduced hours, full success: part-time partners in US law firms – the project for attorney retention', September 2009, accessed 4 December 2014 at http://amlawdaily.typepad.com/files/part-timepartner.pdf.
Catalyst (2000), *Cracking the Glass Ceiling: Catalyst's Research on Women in Corporate Management, 1995–2000*, New York: Catalyst.
Deloitte (2013), 'Benefits and rewards: leading from the front', accessed 25 June 2013 at http://mycareer.deloitte.com/us/en/life-at-deloitte/worklifefit/benefits/life-and-family.

Drew, J. (2013), 'How to open new doors by closing your office', *Journal of Accountancy*, **216**(1), 24–9.

Ernst & Young (2013), 'Flexibility makes a difference', accessed 30 June 2013 at http://www.ey.com/US/en/About-us/Our-people-and-culture/Diversity-and-inclusiveness/Flexibility-makes-a-difference.

Families and Work Institute (1993), *An Evaluation of Johnson & Johnson's Work–Family Initiative*, New York, NY: Families and Work Institute.

Families and Work Institute (2012), '2012 national study of employers', accessed 4 December 2014 at http://familiesandwork.org/site/research/reports/NSE_2012.pdf.

Galinsky, E. (1993), *Thirteen Consistent (and Sometimes Surprising) Findings from Work–Family Evaluations*, New York: Families and Work Institute.

Henry, D.E. (2013), '50 best law firms for women', *WorkingMother.com*, December/January 2013.

KPMG (2013), 'Who we are: work life balance', accessed 1 July 2013 at http://www.kpmgcareers.co.uk/who-we-are/work-life-balance.

Kroll, S. (2011), 'The decline in work hours during the 2007–09 recession', *Monthly Labor Review*, April, 53–9.

Mattis, M.C. (1990), 'Flexible work arrangements for managers and professionals: myths and realities', *Human Resource Planning*, **13**(2), 133–46.

Mattis, M.C. (1994), 'Organizational initiatives in the USA for advancing managerial women', in M.J. Davidson and R.J. Burke (eds), *Women in Management Current Research Issues*, London: Paul Chapman Publishing Ltd, pp. 261–76.

McMenamin, T.M. (2007), 'A time to work: recent trends in shift work and flexible schedules', *Monthly Labor Review*, December 2007, 3–14.

National Association for Law Placement (NALP) (2012), 'Representation of women among associates continues to fall, even as minority associates makes gains', news release, 13 December, accessed 4 December 2014 at http://www.nalp.org/2012lawfirmdiversity.

National Association for Law Placement (NALP) (2013a), 'Rate of part-time work among lawyers unchanged in 2012 – most working part-time continue to be women', 21 February 2013, accessed 4 December 2014 at http://www.nalp.org/part-time_feb2013.

National Association for Law Placement (NALP) (2013b), 'The demographics of equity – an update', *Bulletin*, February 2013, accessed 4 December 2014 at http://www.nalp.org/demographics_of_equity_update.

O'Connell, M. and D.E. Bloom (1987), *Juggling Jobs and Babies: America's Child Care Challenge*, Washington, DC: Population Reference Bureau.

PricewaterhouseCoopers (2013), 'Flexibility', accessed 29 June 2013 at http://www.pwc.com/us/en/about-us/diversity/pwc-work-life-balance.jhtml.

SHRM (2012), '2012 employment satisfaction and engagement', accessed 4 December 2014 at http://www.shrm.org/LegalIssues/StateandLocalResources/StateandLocal}StatutesandRegulations/Documents/12-0537%202012_JobSatisfaction_FNL_online.pdf.

SHRM (2013), 'Workplace forecast: the top workplace trends according to HR professionals', accessed 4 December 2014 at http://www.shrm.org/Research/FutureWorkplaceTrends/Documents/13-0146%20Workplace_Forecast_FULL_FNL.pdf.

Single, L.E., for AICPA (2010), 'WIEC 2010 benchmarking survey results', accessed 20 June 2013 at http://www.aicpa.org/Career/WomenintheProfession/DownloadableDocuments/2010WIECSurvey.pdf.

Single, L.E. (2012), 'The advancement of female professionals', *Career Insider*, 16 February 2012, accessed 25 June 2013 at http://www.cpa2biz.com/Content/media/PRODUCER_CONTENT/Newsletters/Articles_2012/Career/FemaleProfessionals.jsp.

US Bureau of Labor Statistics (May 2004), 'Flexible schedules of wage and salary workers, by occupation and industry', Table 1 in *A Time to Work: Recent Trends in Shift Work and Flexible Schedules*, Washington, DC: BLS, accessed 4 December 2014 at http://www.bls.gov/opub/mlr/2007/12/art1full.pdf.

23. Back to the future: a gendered analysis of 'getting on' in the professional services firm
Savita Kumra

This chapter discusses career advancement from a gendered perspective by presenting evidence in respect of the gendered issues evident in women's ability to advance their careers in the professional services firm (PSF). Though the increasing number of women entering the professional services has been remarked upon for a number of years, their ability to 'get on', particularly to the most senior levels in their firms, that is, partner level, remains stubbornly low. This chapter explores why this is the case. It begins with a reflection on key issues in the field as the number of women within PSFs began to rise. At the time, little attention had been paid to the promotion to partner process and its potentially gendered nature. Analysis of the available literature revealed that career advancement within professional services was presented in a straightforward and seemingly rational manner – those with the appropriate human capital to enter the profession, who worked hard and performed to the appropriate level, would be rewarded with advancement. However, it was evident that this representation of advancement could not adequately account for the lack of progress of the increasing numbers of women entering PSFs, unless we were to believe that the women entering such firms were as a group somehow deficient in their performance, less able than their male counterparts to meet the standards required of them and thus unable to progress to the senior levels of their firms.

It was clear this was not the case and so other explanations of why it might be that women were unable to access senior positions were explored. These explanations examined the phenomenon from two main perspectives: person-centred and situation-centred. This work is revisited and the chapter presents an overview of them both. The chapter then proceeds to assess progress made in respect of these issues and the focus of work that has sought to assess this. In the final section, the challenges that remain are discussed, focusing on contemporary issues occupying researchers in the field. It is evident and encouraging that the field has developed into a vibrant one, with studies covering a broad range of professional services contexts and examining an increasingly sophisticated range of issues.

However, also evident and not a little disappointing is the fact that little numerical progress has been made. The number of women in senior positions within PSFs remains low and thus the gendered nature of 'getting on' in the professional services continues to remain a central and pertinent issue.

INCREASING PARTICIPATION OF WOMEN IN THE PROFESSIONAL SERVICES FIRM: THEN AND NOW

When discussing professional service firms, it is clear that a number of occupational areas are being referred to (for example, law, investment banking, accountancy, consultancy, etc.), each with their own particular profession-related issues, labour market characteristics and internal organizational structural dimensions. When looking at women's participation in the professional services, it is evident that it is an arena to which women are increasingly attracted, but are not making significant inroads into senior positions. Back in the 1990s the position in accounting, for example, was that women were increasingly entering the field of accountancy as they benefitted from the ability to obtain the educational qualifications necessary for entry resulting from increased access to academic study, once denied to them through social stereotyping (Gammie and Gammie, 1995). Membership figures from the Institute of Chartered Accountants in England and Wales (ICAEW) showed female membership increasing: by 2000, women comprised 42 per cent of all ICAEW students and represented 18 per cent of its membership. This figure had increased from 11 per cent in 1990, and 4 per cent in 1980 (Perrin, 2000). A similar picture was evident in the membership statistics of other institutes, for example, the Scottish ICA's membership was split 75 per cent male and 25 per cent female and students were split 51 per cent male and 49 per cent female (ibid.).

The phenomenon was not restricted to the UK. Figures from the USA and Australia evidenced a similar trend. In the USA, more than half the graduating students were women, and there was gender equity at entry-level staff positions (Heard, 2001). The Australian CPA reported a steady increase in female members, from 5 per cent in 1978 to 15 per cent in 1990 to 31 per cent in 2000. In the under-30 age group, the majority of members were women (56 per cent), and a majority of the candidates enrolled in postgraduate Certified Public Accountant (CPA) programmes were women (Anonymous, 2001).

In seeking to assess why women were increasingly opting for careers in professional services, Crompton and Sanderson (1986) suggest that the dual pressures of supply-side constraints and cultural orientations may combine to steer women towards careers in professional practice rather than general managerial positions. They argue that professional practice, structured as it is around the attainment of objectively measured qualifications and experience, presents women with a 'level playing field' in which their achievements will be recognized as a matter of course and they in turn will reap the rewards. They also point to the structure of professional practice, organized as it frequently is around smaller units of private practice. They view such firms as being more accessible to women, and gender segregation may not be as evident as is perhaps the case when the occupation is based around employment in large complex organizations.

However, such a view is contested, as the success of women once they enter professional service firms is a subject of some interest. An important criterion for measuring achievement is to assess status within the firm. In Britain, by the age of 30, most accountants will have reached the level of assistant manager. By their mid-30s, those who have stayed within the profession will expect to become partners or to have their own firms. In 1987, 28 per cent of men in practice were partners by the age of 36, whilst only 14 per cent of women of the same age had reached this position (Grosvenor, 1989). Women's partnership prospects improve in smaller firms. Thus, in firms with fewer than five partners women constitute 25 per cent of partners, they represent 28 per cent of partners in firms with five to nine partners, but the number falls to only 3 per cent in firms with more than 100 partners (Silverstone, 1990). This is perhaps unsurprising when it is considered that partnership for women in the then (Big 5) accountancy firms is a fairly recent phenomenon: Price Waterhouse (now PricewaterhouseCoopers) appointed its first female partner as recently as 1983.

As with accounting, the number of women entering law has also increased. In 2000, an England and Wales Law Society poll showed that the number of female solicitors had more than quadrupled over the past decade, and the percentage of women in the profession more than doubled, from 15 per cent in 1980 to 38 per cent in 2000. Universities also reported an increase in numbers, with women comprising 51 per cent of law students (McDougall, 2001). A similar position was reported in the USA. There, women comprised 49 per cent of law students (compared to just 10 per cent in 1970) (Glater, 2001) and 41 per cent of associates (Eckberg, 2001). However, when looking at the more senior positions within the profession women comprise only 15 per cent of partners in US law firms (Eckberg, 2001).

The reasons women are attracted to the law include high salary, respect, job security and rewarding challenges (ibid.). Women see law as a future career due to the decline in real and perceived barriers to the profession.

It was not so long ago that judges would not hire women as law clerks, and their recruitment into major law firms was improbable (Glater, 2001). However, whilst entry-level positions began to be occupied by increasing numbers of women, inroads had yet to be made at more senior levels.

Coming up to date, we see unfortunately that little has changed. Comment is still made in respect of increasing numbers of women entering professional services, but the low number 'getting on' and attaining partner positions also remains the subject of much comment and analysis. For example, Bolton and Muzio (2008, p. 282) note: 'There seems little doubt that women have made huge progress; numerically dominating areas of the labour market and entering and succeeding in previously male dominated occupations and professional groups.' The past 30 years has seen high growth rates in women's participation in the legal profession, where their membership has increased by an unprecedented 1800 per cent (Law Society, 2006a) and women represent over 40 per cent of practising solicitors (Law Society, 2006b). There is also evidence that this trend is likely to continue: the percentage of female students enrolling with the Law Society of England and Wales has been around 62 per cent in the years from 2001 to 2009 (Law Society, 2010). Accounting has shown similar growth rates. Women comprise 48 per cent of worldwide female student members of the six major UK accounting bodies (Professional Oversight Board for Accountancy, 2010) and in management consulting firms women typically represent between 30–40 per cent of the intake.

However, it remains evident that the rise in women's participation in the professional services has not been accompanied by gender equality at senior levels. Figures show that increased entry by women into these areas of the labour market has resulted in vertical stratification and horizontal segmentation (Hagan and Kay, 1995; Sommerlad, 2002; Stake et al., 2007). Attainment of partner status remains the key indicator of career success, with those unable to reach this level moving on to other forms of work outside the firm, in what is often termed the 'up-or-out' system of promotion. At the partner level, we see that only 14–17 per cent of women make partner in the 'Big 4' (Spence, 2012), and in law firms in the UK, across private practice as a whole, only 21 per cent of women are partners, compared with 49 per cent of men (Law Society, 2010).

'GETTING ON' IN THE PROFESSIONAL SERVICES FIRM: EARLY RESEARCH CONSIDERATIONS

The literature in relation to promotion within the professional services back in the late 1990s and early 2000s indicates the centrality of the process for the effective future functioning of such firms. The 'up or out' rule is used to expel those unsuitable for higher positions within the firm in a timely manner, leaving the way clear for the retention of talented and uniquely experienced organizational members to stay. The 'up-or-out' system also ensures a constant flow of newcomers into the organization so the firm remains in touch with the market, and is able to continually attract and have a place for the brightest and the best. In relation to the partner promotion process, what becomes apparent is that technical skill is a given, as those without it would have been excluded at an early stage in their careers (McLean, 1998). However, what is also clear is that of those remaining, not all can become partners, as only a few openings are available and it is here that other criteria beyond objective measures of technical competence become important. What these criteria are have been alluded to, but not fully articulated as empirical studies of promotion processes within professional service firms, particularly outside the USA, were at the time rare (Morris and Pinnington, 1998), and rarer still was research considering the promotion to partner process and the effect of gender.

Some exceptions include the work by Spurr (1990) and Spurr and Sueyoshi (1991), who studied promotion processes within law firms, with particular emphasis on women lawyers' promotional outcomes. Spurr (1990) found substantial differences between the employment and promotion experiences of male and female lawyers, with women half as likely as men to be promoted to partner positions. In addition, Spurr and Sueyoshi's (1991) study found women were more likely to leave their firms without being promoted. In seeking to explain these findings Spurr and Sueyoshi (1991) suggest that perhaps a self-fulfilling prophecy is in place. It is possible, they assert, that women exert less effort in their work than their male peers, in the (correct) belief that increased effort on their part is unlikely to lead to promotion, but perhaps they are less likely to be promoted because they exert less effort. Other factors considered included the perception that women are more likely to relocate for a spouse's change in career and hence leave the firm, than men, and that clients may not be willing to work with female partners, as they are reluctant to invest large organizational resources in projects headed up by female partners (Spurr and Sueyoshi, 1991).

In her study seeking to explain the paucity of women at partnership level in accounting practice, particularly in larger firms, Maupin (1993) suggests that one of two levels of analysis are usually employed: a person-centred approach or a situation-centred approach. Person-centred explanations focus on characteristics of the women themselves, which results in their being perceived as unable to accept the challenges presented by the partnership role. The focus of study in this approach will therefore be issues such as female socialization, personality traits, behavioural patterns, and so on. For example, Mainiero (1994) interviewed senior female executives to determine the factors contributing to their success. She found women achieving high organizational positions shared a number of key organizational experiences. They had supervisory experience early on in their careers, with supervisory responsibility continuing throughout: line rather than staff positions, time spent in headquarters, time spent either assisting a senior manager or forming part of a high-profile task force, and later in their careers, general management experience was crucial to make the move into executive positions. Mainiero (1994) then queries what the personal characteristics are that are possessed by those identified as promotable that differentiate them from those who are not. She like others believes it to be a combination of timing, opportunity, contacts and competence. However, what is clear is that once identified as promotable, access to opportunities becomes available and progress through the ranks can be rapid.

Situation-centred explanations present an alternative paradigm, with the emphasis on the nature of the work environment and the effect this has on women aspiring to partnership positions. This perspective suggests that it is the characteristics of the organizational situation, rather than inner traits or skills possessed by women, that may shape and define women's behaviour at work. So, for example, Lyness and Thompson in their 1997 study of a matched sample of male and female executives sought to find the similarities and differences in their career experiences. In their view, career experiences would differ by gender, with the key influencing situational variable being sex-role stereotyping. In relation to sex stereotyping, which is defined as widely shared beliefs about the attributes possessed by men and women (Heilman, 1983), a number of organizational consequences may ensue. Women are not chosen for traditionally male roles due to the risk of their failure (ibid.). The result of such practice, as labour economists have observed, is occupational segregation by sex (Bielby and Baron, 1986). Even where women do manage to achieve jobs at the same level as men, they are frequently not provided with comparable authority, status or advancement potential (Baron et al., 1986; Eagly and Johnson, 1990).

Despite the attempt to match the male/female samples as closely as possible, there was evidence that the women's jobs had less authority, based on numbers of subordinates. Gender differences were not found in relation to either salary or bonus, but women were in receipt of fewer stock options than their male counterparts. Stock options in this organization were given as an incentive to individuals considered organizationally critical to encourage them to stay, thus the absence of this aspect from female executives' remuneration packages calls into question the organization's view of their criticality to its operation (Lyness and Thompson, 1997).

In attempting to assess which of these approaches is most relevant, Maupin's (1993) study presents some revealing findings. In seeking to explain the lack of women partners, a sample of male and female US accountants were asked for their views. Female respondents emphasized the situation-centred variables, such as the difficulty of combining the demands of being a partner with those of being a wife, mother, and so on; male respondents tended to attribute fewer women reaching partnership level to the women themselves (person-centred explanations), indicating that women's personal characteristics prevented their promotion.

A survey commissioned by the American Women's Society of CPAs (AWSCPA) (Heard, 2001) echoes some of these findings. The report indicated that women in the profession perceive lack of gender acceptance to be a key barrier to attaining senior positions within firms. Respondents also felt that access to high-visibility job assignments was unequally shared, with the majority of such assignments being allocated to men. This was an area closely studied by Deloitte and Touche in its programme to address the imbalance of men and women in partnership positions (McCracken, 2000). It was common knowledge in the firm that advancement was achieved by involvement on key, high-visibility projects. The process by which such work was assigned, however, remained largely unexplored.

In analysing the process, it emerged that women frequently missed out on key opportunities because partners (usually male) made erroneous assumptions about what they could and could not do – for example, women were not allocated to assignments in so-called masculine environments, such as manufacturing. Women were also denied opportunities because it was felt that the travelling involved on particular projects would be too taxing, or that husbands would be unwilling to relocate (ibid.). Further, an audit was undertaken to assess the type of assignments women were typically offered; it revealed that women were to be found working on accounts in non-profit, retail and health care – sectors generally lacking large high-profile global accounts. Assignments in manufacturing, finance and mergers and acquisitions, highly visible areas, were allocated to men. Deloitte and Touche took steps to address these issues, and through these interventions achieved the highest number of female partners (14 per cent) of any of the 'Big 5' accounting firms at the time (ibid.).

A Catalyst report *Women in Law: Making the Case* (2000) found that women lawyers consistently believe they are excluded from informal networks (53 per cent of women compared to 21 per cent of men) and have few mentoring opportunities, although these relationships can have a significant effect on who is viewed as having leadership potential and can positively impact how welcome women feel. Fifty-two per cent of women reported lack of mentoring opportunities compared with only 29 per cent of men. They are also more likely to report that commitment to family will negatively affect their career advancement (67 per cent of women compared to 49 per cent of men), with the consequence that women report planning to stay with their current employer for three years less than their male counterparts.

Having analysed the early literature it becomes apparent that once the impact of gender on the promotion process is acknowledged and accepted, a number of approaches have been adopted to understand the effect of this variable on organizational practice and process of promotion. Some researchers have sought to explain the impact of gender through examination of individual characteristics and their link with promotability. In this area studies have sought to show that organizational processes reflect bias against individuals not deemed promotable either through their lack of certain characteristics generally linked to promotability, or perceived lack of such characteristics (for example, Mainiero, 1994). Further examination of the promotion process has focused on organizational mechanisms operating to exclude certain groups from the ranks of the promotable. Such studies adopt as their focus institutionalized discriminatory processes serving to perpetuate existing gender power structures to the detriment of groups outside the norm (for example, Ohlott et al., 1994; McCracken, 2000). Also discussed were studies seeking to explain why women do not reach their full organizational potential; these include the effects of sex-role stereotyping (Lyness and Thompson, 1997) and lack of access to key developmental opportunities (for example, Ruderman and Ohlott, 1992; McCaulay et al., 1994; Ohlott et al., 1994; Tharenou, 1994; Slocum et al., 1997).

Whilst contributing greatly to our understanding of the factors that collectively make the promotion process for women one in which complex social processes cloud the picture of female advancement, what these studies share is their view that various socially constructed views around the gender 'female' combine to produce discriminatory practices, the result of which are the observable organizational phenomena. An increasing number of women are entering professions and professional organizations, yet failing to advance through the ranks in the numbers expected given their qualifications and skills.

DEVELOPMENT OF THE FIELD: WHERE ARE WE NOW?

As the field has developed, a number of alternative perspectives have been adopted. Most usefully, a number of studies have sought to combine both person- and situation-centred explanations within the same study in order to gain a more holistic understanding of advancement processes within PSFs and the impact of gender upon these. Thus, we see that some work has been done on the nature of the professions themselves and the way in which the 'professional' is conceptualized prevents women's advancement. It is argued that professions are historically masculine arenas inscribed by men and masculinities. Professionalism has traditionally been predicated on a masculine ideology (Witz, 1992; Davies, 1996), embodied through the ideal of the unencumbered man (Acker, 1990). As some have argued, it is specifically this aggressive form of masculinity that has significantly contributed to the recent financial crisis (Walby, 2009; Sauer, 2010; Nelson, 2011). The continued association of professionals with manly images supports perceptions that particular occupations are not 'natural' for women or racial 'others' (Hall et al., 2007; Czarniawska and Sevón, 2008). Those who are able to gain access to white masculine professions frequently find themselves re-segregated into 'softer' (that is, feminized and generally devalued) areas of the work (Crump et al., 2007). Thus, whilst inclusion has been gained, women's incorporation into the professions has been on unequal terms, with the result that both sex segregation and exploitation have occurred. Numerous studies document this demographic shift in professional and other organizational settings (Kanter, 1977; Acker, 1990; Witz, 1992; Sommerlad and Sanderson, 1998; Ashcraft et al., 2012). For example, the literature on the legal profession (Hagan and Kay, 1995; Wilkins and Gulati, 1996; Bolton and Muzio, 2008) assesses the way in which women have been positioned in the economics of law firms in the role of a 'transient proletariat' (Sommerlad, 2002, p. 217) whose labour efforts are expropriated by male elites. The position of women and black and minority ethnic (BME) professionals becomes paradoxical as they become essential human resources in the dominant economic models of professional services firms and a necessity for their increasingly leveraged business models, thus their absence is no longer cause for comment, but their presence has not gained them equality (Ashcraft et al. 2012).

Walsh (2012) looks at the choices made by women in PSFs. She concludes that their lack of advancement does not seem to lie in human capital explanations, as when comparing women's law school performance to that of their male counterparts, they do just as well (Hull and Nelson, 2000). Indeed, there is evidence to suggest that, in order to establish their partnership potential, women are in fact demonstrating higher standards of performance than men, as evidenced by law school grades, hours worked per week, number of professional activities and client development (Kay and Hagan, 1998; Noonan and Corcoran, 2004). However, when factoring in the organizational context and assessing subjective evaluations of eligibility for promotion she found there are a number of factors that can impede women's chances of promotion. The role of cultural capital has been particularly emphasized. Thus, with regard to cultural capital, Wass and McNabb (2006) argue that the importance of exceptional client service in legal practice demands high-level relational skills that include introducing new clients to the firm, marketing the firm's services and generally developing the business potential of the practice. Of particular significance to women is that these activities tend to take place outside normal working hours and are often focused around male-oriented social pursuits (Eagly and Carli, 2007). Such capital is more difficult and thus more costly for women to acquire, particularly for women with care-giving responsibilities.

Social interactions with senior lawyers in both work and non-work settings can also improve lawyers' chances of promotion (Walsh, 2012). It has been found, however, that women are less likely than men to engage in such social activities (Dinovitzer et al., 2009). The consequence is that women may find themselves excluded from social networks with the result that they lack the social and cultural capital resources that typify men's experiences in law firms (Sommerlad and Sanderson, 1998, p. 124). These deficits become particularly problematic as it is estimated that social and cultural factors can account for up to one-third of the impact of gender on lawyers' partnership promotion chances (Kay and Gorman, 2008, p. 310).

Further work has considered the position from within PSF firms and sought to identify the gendered nature of advancement processes. For example, Kumra and Vinnicombe (2008) sought to identify whether the promotion to partner process as it operated within a global consulting firm disadvantaged women. They found that it did, focusing attention on the *self*-managed nature of the career development process prevalent in the firm and also the single model of career success reflecting hegemonic masculine characteristics. Thus, for example, the self-managed nature of the career development process discussed by interviewees as a key requirement within the firm was shown to pose particular problems for women who have been socialized to collaborate rather than compete and who are more used to advocating on behalf of others rather than operating from an individually self-interested position. However, the nature of the PSF environment necessitates a self-managed approach to career management due to its flat structure, relatively unmanaged environment in which it is unusual for managers to directly work with those they manage and there are constant absences from any central office as individuals are frequently working on assignments at client sites, often for extended periods.

Exploring the phenomenon through a social capital lens, Kumra and Vinnicombe (2010) found that, when seeking to advance their careers by building and developing social capital, participants in their study utilized impression management techniques (Rosenfeld et al., 1995) as a defensive strategy to assist them in overcoming negative gender-based stereotypes they perceived evident in the firm. In the study these were related to ambition, likeability and availability. These were all characteristics identified in the study as highly desirable of those wishing to advance, but recognized by female participants as particularly problematic for women. It was thus evident that women not only had to work hard in order to meet the stringent requirements of excellent job performance, they also had to overcome additional hurdles related to negative stereotypes attaching to them because of their gender.

Studies have thus focused on understanding the nature of the PSF environment and how gender impacts the ability to 'get on' within it. We have moved from early work that sought to examine each of the approaches separately, to work that explores the gendered nature of professionalism (for example, Czarniawska and Sevón, 2008), the nature of promotion processes (for example, Kumra and Vinnicombe, 2008) and the impact of seemingly 'family-friendly' policies on women's career outcomes within the PSF environment (for example, Lupu, 2012). However, more needs to be done to continue this work and it is to a discussion of key areas of interest for future research that our attention turns in the next section.

DEVELOPING THE FIELD: WHERE TO NEXT?

Reflecting on where we are now, it is evident that much progress has been made. As can be seen from the array of work presented above, the issue of gender in PSFs and specifically 'getting on' in the PSF is one that is of interest to a number of researchers. The field is also a vibrant one as reflected by the number of special issues dedicated to the topic, for example, Gender, Work & Organization (2012), symposia at key conferences (for example, 'Gender in PSFs', Academy of Management, 2012) and representation at key conferences in general gender tracks. For example, at the recent British Academy of Management conference (2013) in Liverpool no less than six papers in the 'Gender in Management' track utilized PSF settings as their contextual background.

There is also clearly activity and energy directed at these issues from within the firms themselves. Professional services firms are frequently listed as 'Employers of Choice', or 'Best Places to Work' and are publicly vocal about their diversity initiatives, such as flexible work policies. Indeed, the Law Society of England and Wales recently convened an 'International Women in Law Summit' at which the issue of the lack of progress in women's advancement to partner positions was the core topic of discussion. Contributors from the profession itself, academia and key policy bodies discussed diversity from a number of perspectives. In the subsequent report produced by the Law Society (2012), a summary of three key messages arising from the event were provided. One concerned a fundamental change through the adoption of a flexible working culture that would ensure that women in the profession remained engaged on the right career track. Superficially the recommendation appears to be constructive, enabling those with caring responsibilities outside the workplace to combine work they value with other facets of their lives. On closer inspection, however, the recommendation is indicative of a well-rehearsed response that continues to place those unwilling or unable to work in hitherto accepted or expected ways as 'other', requiring of 'special' treatment and unable to meet the prevailing standard of the 'ideal' worker (Acker, 1990). The evidence of those opting for 'alternative' career tracks in the PSF is clear. In Kumra (2011), participants in the study expressed their disappointment in the firm's lack of commitment to its own stated and highly publicized flexible working policy, as well as the lack of perceived support and recognition of their contribution from superiors and peers. Also, in Lupu's (2012) work we see that the construction of 'alternative' feminized routes rather than 'approved' traditional routes, in the French 'Big 4' accounting firms, serve to derail women's careers from a very early stage, with the result that their opportunities for 'getting on' are circumvented early on.

As Crompton and Lyonette (2011) caution, by crowding women into family-friendly occupations or sections of occupations, not only is occupational sex segregation reproduced, but the gendered nature of the division of labour in a wider sense also remains unchallenged and unchecked – that is, a continuation of the normative expectation that women undertake the majority of domestic and caring work.

In future work the author would agree with Kornberger et al. (2010) who call for studies that seek to understand how gender relations are inscribed into the culture of firms, their strategic policy decisions and day-to-day practices that all combine to constitute the phenomenon of gender inequity. Also necessary are studies adopting a holistic and integrated position, such that we study not just the phenomenon, but the multiple factors that combine to produce it.

This is a call to those of us in the field to be mindful when we undertake our studies, that we ensure we do not separate the phenomenon from its context, or seek to over-simplify the complex. Studies that draw on varied themes, working on a broad canvas, ambitious in their aims and searching in their methods of enquiry are necessary to advance the field and move us to a position where the 'evidence' is incontrovertible and organizational action and response moves beyond obvious mechanisms that have previously proven ineffective and yet continue to be vaunted as the panacea to all ills. For women to 'get on' in the professional services, we need to move beyond the rhetoric of diversity to one of inclusion. There is little doubt that the PSF environment looks a lot more diverse than it did 30 years ago; what is also incontrovertible is that diversity reduces the higher up the hierarchy we go. Inclusion at senior levels eludes women entering the professional services and it is our responsibility as researchers in the field to continue to ask the question 'Why?' and not stop until all barriers have been uncovered and the playing field is as level as we would all wish it to be.

REFERENCES

Acker, J. (1990), 'Hierarchies, jobs, bodies: a theory of gendered organizations', *Gender and Society*, **4**(2), 139–58.
Anonymous (2001), 'Genders on CPA agenda', *Australian CPA*, April, 10–12.
Ashcraft, K.L., S.L. Muhr, J. Rennstam and K. Sullivan (2012), 'Professionalization as a branding activity: occupational identity and the dialectic of inclusivity–exclusivity', *Gender, Work & Organization*, **19**(5), 467–88.
Baron, J.N., A. Davis-Blake and W.T. Bielby (1986), 'The structure of opportunity: how promotion ladders vary within and among organizations', *Administrative Science Quarterly*, **31**(2), 248–73.
Bielby, W.T. and J.N. Baron (1986), 'Men and women at work: sex segregation and statistical discrimination', *American Journal of Sociology*, **91**(4), 759–99.
Bolton, S. and D. Muzio (2008), 'The paradoxical process of feminization in the professions: the case of established, aspiring and semi-professions', *Work, Employment and Society*, **22**(2), 281–99.
Catalyst (2000), *Women in the Law: Making the Case*, New York: Catalyst.
Crompton, R. and C. Lyonette (2011), 'Women's career success and work–life adaptations in the accountancy and medical professions in Britain', *Gender, Work & Organization*, **18**(2), 231–54.
Crompton, R. and K. Sanderson (1986), 'Credentials and careers: some implications of the increase in professional qualifications amongst women', *Sociology*, **20**(1), 25–42.
Crump, B.J., K.A. Logan and A. McIlroy (2007), 'Does gender still matter? A study of the views of women in the ICT industry in New Zealand', *Gender, Work & Organization*, **14**(4), 350–70.
Czarniawska, B. and G. Sevón (2008), 'The thin edge of the wedge: foreign women professors as double strangers in academia', *Gender, Work & Organization*, **15**(3), 235–87.
Davies, C. (1996), 'The sociology of professions and the profession of gender', *Sociology*, **30**(4), 661–78.

Dinovitzer, R., N. Reichman and J. Sterling (2009), 'The differential valuation of women's work: a new look at the gender gap in lawyers' incomes', *Social Forces*, **88**(2), 819–64.
Eagly, A.H. and L.L. Carli (2007), *Through the Labyrinth: The Truth About How Women Become Leaders*, Boston, MA: Harvard Business School Press.
Eagly, A.H. and B.T. Johnson (1990), 'Gender and leadership style: a meta-analysis', *Psychological Bulletin*, **108**(2), 233–56.
Eckberg, J. (2001), 'Female lawyers make their case: percentages changing – except at the uppermost levels', *The Cincinnati Enquirer*, 26 February.
Gammie, E. and R. Gammie (1995), 'Women chartered accountants – progressing in the right direction?', *Women in Management Review*, **10**(1), 5–13.
Glater, J.D. (2001), 'Women are closer to being majority of law students', *The New York Times*, 26 March.
Grosvenor, J. (ed.) (1989), *Ivanhoe Guide to Chartered Accountants*, Oxford: The Ivanhoe Press.
Hagan, J. and F. Kay (1995), *Gender in Practice: A Study of Lawyers' Lives*, Oxford: Oxford University Press.
Hall, A., J. Hockey and V. Robinson (2007), 'Occupational cultures and the embodiment of masculinity: hairdressing, estate agency and firefighting', *Gender, Work & Organization*, **14**(6), 534–51.
Heard, M. (2001), 'Is the glass ceiling cracking for women?', *Practical Accountant*, July, 56.
Heilman, M.E. (1983), 'Sex-bias in work settings: the lack of fit model', in B. Staw and L. Cummings (eds), *Research in Organizational Behavior*, Greenwich, CT: JAI Press.
Hull, K.E. and R.L. Nelson (2000), 'Assimilation, choice or constraint? Testing theories of gender differences in the careers of lawyers', *Social Forces*, **79**(1), 229–64.
Kanter, R.M. (1977), *Men and Women of the Corporation*, New York: Basic Books.
Kay, F. and E. Gorman (2008), 'Women in the legal profession', *Annual Review of Law and Social Science*, **4**, 299–332.
Kay, F. and J. Hagan (1998), 'Raising the bar: the gender stratification of law firm capitalization', *American Sociological Review*, **63**(5), 728–43.
Kornberger, M., C. Carter and A. Ross-Smith (2010), 'Changing gender domination in a Big Four accounting firm: performance and client service in practice', *Accounting, Organizations and Society*, **35**(8), 775–91.
Kumra, S. (2011), 'The social construction of merit in a professional services firm: guardian of equality or veil for inequity', conference paper presented at British Academy of Management, Aston, UK.
Kumra, S. and S.M. Vinnicombe (2008), 'A study of the promotion to partner process in a professional services firm: how women are disadvantaged', *British Journal of Management*, **19**(S1), S65–74.
Kumra, S. and S.M. Vinnicombe (2010), 'Impressing for success: a gendered analysis of a key social capital accumulation strategy', *Gender, Work & Organization*, **17**(5), 521–46.
Law Society (2006a), *Trends in the Solicitors' Profession: Annual Statistical Report 2005*, London: The Law Society of England and Wales.
Law Society (2006b), *Number of Solicitors Since 1950* [Fact Sheet Information Series], London: The Law Society of England and Wales.
Law Society (2010), *Trends in the Solicitors' Profession: Annual Statistical Report 2009*, London: The Law Society of England and Wales.
Law Society (2012), *International Women in Law Summit 2012: Setting the Agenda for Change*, London: Law Society of England and Wales.
Lupu, I. (2012), 'Approved routes and alternative paths: the construction of women's careers in large accounting firms. Evidence from the French Big Four', *Critical Perspectives on Accounting*, **23**(4–5), 351–69.
Lyness, K.S. and D.E. Thompson (1997), 'Above the glass ceiling? A comparison of matched samples of female and male executives', *Journal of Applied Psychology*, **82**(3), 359–75.
Mainiero, L.A. (1994), 'Getting anointed for advancement: the case of executive women', *Academy of Management Executive*, **8**(2), 53–67.

Maupin, R.J. (1993), 'Why are there so few women accounting partners? Male and female accountants disagree', *Managerial Auditing Journal*, **8**(5), 10–18.
McCaulay, C.D., M. Ruderman, P. Ohlott and J. Morrow (1994), 'Assessing the development components of managerial jobs', *Journal of Applied Psychology*, **79**(4), 544–60.
McCracken, D.M. (2000), 'Winning the talent war for women: sometimes it takes a revolution', *Harvard Business Review*, January, accessed 11 December 2011 at https://hbr.org/product/winning-the-talent-war-for-women-sometimes-it-take/an/R00611-PDF-ENG.
McDougall, D. (2001), 'Women now joining the legal profession in record numbers', *The Scotsman*, 11 September.
McLean, C. (1998), 'It's not what you know, it's who you know: an agency theory and network theory approach to explaining why individuals receive promotions within professional service firms', paper presented at the Academy of Management Meeting, San Diego, CA.
Morris, T. and A. Pinnington (1998), 'Promotion to partner in professional service firms', *Human Relations*, **51**(1), 3–24.
Nelson, J. (2011), 'Would women leaders have prevented the global financial crisis? Implications for teaching about gender and economics', Working Paper No. 11-03, Global Development and Environment Institute.
Noonan, M. and M. Corcoran (2004), 'The mommy track and partnership: temporary delay or dead end?', *Annals of the American Academy of Sociology and Political Science*, **596**(1), 130–50.
Ohlott, P.J., M.N. Ruderman and C.D. McCauley (1994), 'Gender differences in managers' developmental job experiences', *Academy of Management Journal*, **37**(1), 46–57.
Perrin, S. (2000), 'Jobs for the boys', *Financial Director*, June, 33–4.
Professional Oversight Board for Accountancy (2010), *Key Facts and Trends in the Accounting Profession*, London: Financial Reporting Council.
Rosenfeld, P., R.A. Giacalone and C. Riordan (1995), *Impression Management in Organizations: Theory, Measurement and Practice*, London: Routledge.
Ruderman, M.N. and P.J. Ohlott (1992), 'Managerial promotions as a diversity practice', paper presented at the 52nd annual meeting of the Academy of Management, Las Vegas.
Sauer, B. (2010), 'Speedy cars, perky women, champagne and striptease bars: neo-liberal masculinity in crisis?', accessed 5 December 2014 at http://www.eisa-net.org/be-bruga/eisa/files/events/stockholm/Sauer-Stockholm_SGIR.pdf.
Silverstone, R. (1990), 'Women in accountancy: ten years on', *Accountancy*, September, 70–73.
Slocum, J., A. Hurley, E. Fagenson-Eland and J. Sonnenfeld (1997), 'Does cream always rise to the top?', *Organizational Dynamics*, **26**(2), 65–71.
Sommerlad, H. (2002), 'Women solicitors in a fractured profession: intersections of gender and professionalism in England and Wales', *International Journal of the Legal Profession*, **9**(3), 213–34.
Sommerlad, H. and P. Sanderson (1998), *Gender, Choice and Commitment: Women Solicitors in England and Wales and the Struggle for Equal Status*, Aldershot, UK: Ashgate.
Spence, A. (2012), 'Big Four firm juggles the numbers to address lack of diversity', *The Times*, 2 October.
Spurr, S.J. (1990), 'Sex discrimination in the legal profession: a study of promotion', *Industrial and Labor Relations Review*, **43**(4), 406–17.
Spurr, S.J. and P. Sueyoshi (1991), 'Turnover and promotion of lawyers', *Journal of Human Resources*, **29**(3), 813–42.
Stake, J.E., K.G. Dau-Schmidt and K. Mukhopadhaya (2007), 'Income and career satisfaction in the legal profession: survey data from Indiana Law School Graduates', *Journal of Empirical Legal Studies*, **4**(4), 939–81.
Tharenou, P. (1994), 'Going up? Do traits and informal social processes explain advancing to increasingly higher levels in the managerial hierarchy?', unpublished paper, Management Department, Monash University.
Walby, S. (2009), 'Gender and the financial crisis', UNESCO report, accessed 5

December 2014 at http://www.lancaster.ac.uk/fass/doc_library/sociology/Gender_and_financial_crisis_Sylvia_Walby.pdf.
Walsh, J. (2012), 'Not worth the sacrifice? Women's aspirations and career progression in law firms', *Gender, Work & Organization*, **19**(5), 508–31.
Wass, V. and R. McNabb (2006), 'Pay, promotion and parenthood amongst women solicitors', *Work, Employment and Society*, **20**(2), 289–308.
Wilkins, D. and G. Gulati (1996), 'Why are there so few black lawyers in corporate law firms?', *California Law Review*, **84**(3), 493–525.
Witz, A. (1992), *Professions and Patriarchy*, London: Routledge.

24. What's 'woman's work'? Work–family interface among women entrepreneurs in Italy

Silvia De Simone and Vincenza Priola

Women's self-employment has experienced a significant growth in the last few decades (Gohmann, 2012; Koellinger et al., 2013) and the importance of its contribution to national economies has been recognized across the continents (see for example, Bruin et al., 2006; Huarng et al., 2012). This chapter focuses on women's self-employment in relation to work–family interface within the Italian context. By the end of 2011, 23.5 per cent of Italian enterprises were owned by women, however, while these constitute approximately a quarter of the total number of privately owned businesses, they contribute a third of the small business economy. Furthermore, female entrepreneurship is growing at a higher rate than the general enterprise growth (0.5 per cent versus 0.3 per cent in 2012),[1] and women entrepreneurs correspond to 16.3 per cent of women employed in the country (Osservatorio sull'imprenditoria femminile, 2013). While women entrepreneurs have been recognized as a 'major force for innovation and job creation' (Organisation for Economic Co-operation and Development (OECD), in Orhan and Scott, 2001, p.232), research has highlighted that the experiences and difficulties encountered by women when starting and operating a business are considerably different than those confronted by men (Neider, 1987; Kappler and Parker, 2011). Moreover, applying knowledge emerged from studies based on male-owned enterprises or men entrepreneurs to female entrepreneurship is inadequate in further understanding of the area (Carter and Cannon, 1992; Bird and Brush, 2002; Gupta et al., 2009; Minniti, 2009; Hughes and Jennings, 2012; Haus et al., 2013).

The study of gender and entrepreneurship is relatively new, although recently more consistent attention is placed on several aspects linked to women-owned businesses. Among these, scholars have investigated the masculine, and generally patriarchal, construction of entrepreneurship in the Western world (for example, Bruni et al., 2004; Aidis and Wetzels, 2007), the different motivations and barriers encountered by women and men entrepreneurs (for example, Fischer et al., 1993; Moore and Buttner, 1997; Shane et al., 2003) and the efforts and influences on entrepreneurs' work–life balance (for example, DeMartino and Barbato, 2003; Jennings and McDougald, 2007; Gimenez-Nadal et al., 2012). The literature on work–family interface and work–life balance among business owners reveals antithetical fields of study that, on the one hand, focus on the tension that exists between family life and entrepreneurial work (for example, Stoner et al., 1990; Williams, 2004), and on the other hand, postulates the attractiveness that self-employment has for women in providing greater flexibility and work–life balance (Presser, 1989; Brush, 1992; Loscocco, 1997; Caputo and Dolinsky, 1998; Boden, 1999; Hundley, 2000; Lombard, 2001; Arai, 2008), particularly in the case of mothers of small children (Caputo and Dolinsky, 1998; Taniguchi, 2002).

While the review of studies focusing on work–life balance and work–family interface expose contradictory arguments, Parasuraman and Simmers (2001) reject the idea that self-employment allows a greater balance between work and life and argue that when the high levels of job commitment, which characterize self-employment, are combined with high levels of family demands, incompatible pressures will be experienced by the self-employed entrepreneur. In such a context, the view that self-employment appears to warrant autonomy and flexibility can no longer be sustained, thus supporting the work–family conflict thesis.

The main aim of this chapter is to illustrate the ways in which Italian women entrepreneurs experience and manage the relation between the demands of their work and those of their family. Specifically, the analysis will focus on understanding whether the perceptions of work–family interface are constructed as conflicts and/or whether they are also viewed as opportunities for professional and personal enrichment. In exploring these experiences of work–family interface the chapter will also discuss the specific factors that affect the balance between work and life.

This chapter is organized as follows. The next section provides an overview of the current literature on the work–family interface, with an emphasis on the 'conflict' and the 'enhancement' perspectives. The outline of the research methodology is then presented before discussing the findings of the study based on 31 interviews with female entrepreneurs in Italy. The concluding section summarizes the findings and discusses the implications of the study for women entrepreneurs and policy-makers.

WOMEN, ENTREPRENEURSHIP AND WORK–FAMILY INTERFACE

While there has been growing interest in understanding the role that family responsibilities play in the work and career of women (and men) (see for example, Byron, 2005; Ford et al., 2007; Amstad et al., 2011), such research has mainly focused on salaried employees and little attention has been paid to the interface between work and family among women business owners. Most of the initial research on the relation between work and family focuses on the conflict perspective and suggests that conflict between work and family exist because there are competing demands from both roles that cannot be easily fulfilled simultaneously. The different roles undertaken by individuals as parents, carers, partners and workers lead them to complex situations in which they need to make choices, prioritize matters, make decisions and apply coping strategies on a daily basis (Mäkelä and Suutari, 2011). The tensions between family and work are thus viewed as a form of inter-role conflict in which the role pressures from work and family domains are incompatible (Greenhaus and Beutell, 1985). Greenhaus and Beutell (1985) differentiate among three sources of conflict between work and family, referring to the time, strain and specific behaviours required by one role that affect the fulfilment of the other. Conceptually, work–family conflict has been recognized as consisting of two distinct concepts: work interference with family and family interference with work (Kossek and Ozeki, 1998; Frone, 2003). Furthermore, it has been argued that individuals experience greater work interference in their family roles (Frone, 2003; Bellavia and Frone, 2005).

A large body of research has examined the antecedents and consequences of work–family conflict. The antecedents of work–family conflict are generally viewed as characteristics of the individual (for example: personality, behaviour), the family (for example: housework and childcare needs) or the job (for example: pressure, task demands) (see the reviews of Eby et al., 2005; Zhang and Liu, 2011). Similarly, the outcomes of work–family conflict have also been generally divided into three distinct categories (Bellavia and Frone, 2005; Amstad et al., 2011): work-related, family-related, and domain-unspecific outcomes. Researchers have also investigated the roles that gender, work and family support, time spent at work, childcare responsibility, dual-earner status and personality factors play in the relationship between work and family and their outcomes (see Eby et al., 2005; Ford et al., 2007; Amstad et al., 2011).

Increasingly, research on the relation between work and family focuses on the positive aspects that can emerge from the intersection of work and non-work roles. According to the enhancement perspective the relationship between work and family, in fact, may have positive consequences. Specifically, individuals occupying multiple roles in different life domains acquire social and psychological resources, new opportunities and enriching experiences that can be reinvested in other roles, contributing to their enhancement (Rothbard, 2001; Ruderman et al., 2002). Such interaction has been defined as: '*positive spill-over*' (Staines, 1980; Grzywacz and Marks, 2000; Carlson et al., 2006), indicating that the two domains positively influence each other (for example, happiness at work can lead to enhanced happiness in the family context and vice versa); '*work–family facilitation*' (Grzywacz et al., 2002), suggesting that engagement in one domain bears gains that enhance the functioning of the other; and '*work–family enrichment*' (Greenhaus and Powell, 2006), specifying that support, resources, skills, positive moods and emotions from one domain can improve the quality of life in the other domain. In an attempt to integrate the conflict perspective with the enhancement perspective and account for the complexity of the interaction between work and family roles, recently researchers (for example, Frone, 2003; Geurts et al., 2003; Kinnunen et al., 2006) have proposed the integration of positive and negative aspects of work to family influence and family to work influence, suggesting the definition of the relationships between work and family as 'interface'.

In applying the research on work–family interface to the specific experiences of women entrepreneurs, scholars (for example, Watson, 2003; Bruni et al., 2004; Winn, 2004; Ahl, 2006; Kock, 2008) have focused on the demands of both work and family roles as a source of conflict and/or as a positive challenge. Shelton (2006) argued that mitigating work–family conflict is an important condition for growth in entrepreneurial ventures and that women who successfully develop businesses will use the strategies learned in order to manipulate the different roles and manage the work–family conflict. Research (for example, Jamali, 2009) has shown that the highest level of work–family conflict is generally experienced by working mothers with young children, who often experience feelings of guilt because they fail to comply with prevailing gender standards, based on traditional gender and family models. While female entrepreneurship significantly contributes to Western economies, its significance may also be positioned as an opportunity and a potential challenge for society to contest the traditional division of gender roles (Ahl, 2006) and develop schemes that support dual-career families.

RESEARCH METHODOLOGY

This study is based on 31 biographical interviews with women entrepreneurs within the same region of Italy. The interviews were carried out during summer and autumn 2011 and participants were recruited via a self-employment association: AIDDA (Association of Women Entrepreneurs and Company Leaders). Initially, 50 business owners agreed to participate, however, for 19 of them finding the time to partake in the interviews proved difficult. Participants were mainly small-business owners operating in a variety of sectors. In terms of their socio-demographic profile, their ages ranged between 30 and 77 years, 16 of them within the age bracket '30–49' and the remainder within the '51 and older' group; 90 per cent were married or cohabiting and almost 90 per cent had children (two on average). In terms of education attainment, half had a university degree. Table 24.1 provides further details on length of self-employment, business size (five are micro-businesses with five or less employees while seven have between 50 and 360 employees) and business sector (26 per cent service sector; 23 per cent retail; 13 per cent tourism; 13 per cent manufacturing; 9 per cent health and social services; 9 per cent construction; and 7 per cent farming).

Topics covered in the interviews included work and educational background, routes into self-employment, reasons for becoming self-employed, experiences of work and life interactions and work–life balance. The face-to-face interviews were conducted by a research assistant, lasting between 60 and 90 minutes; they were digitally recorded and transcribed verbatim. The two authors and the research assistant independently examined the transcripts for emerging themes. In an initial stage the researchers read the transcripts independently in order to categorize the texts into the main themes emerging from the data. Subsequently the researchers worked together in order to agree on the identified themes, their denomination and the illustrative key quotes drawn from the different interviews. Several themes emerged from the data analysis. For the purposes of this chapter we will explore two of them: the participants' experiences of work–family interface and the perceptions of fairness and inequality in the distribution of housework and family care.

WORK–FAMILY RELATIONSHIP: CONFLICT OR ENHANCEMENT?

Although some authors have postulated that self-employment is attractive because it facilitates work–life balance (for example, DeMartino and Barbato, 2003; Arai, 2008), none of the entrepreneurs interviewed said that they chose self-employment as an opportunity to achieve work–family balance. While most interviewees highlighted the difficulties they experience/d in balancing work and family commitments, they also referred to the tools and strategies used to achieve a sense of stability between their work and family responsibilities. Family commitments and young children are viewed as stumbling blocks in the development of women's careers and their enterprises (for example, Stoner et al., 1999),

Table 24.1 Research participants (listed in alphabetical order)

Participants	Age	No. of Children	Family Status	Business Sector	Type of Activity	No. of Employees	Length of Self-employment (Years)
Altea	38	2	Married	Farming	Farm	6 (plus seasonal labour)	7
Alyssa	64	2	Married	Manufacture	Commercial products	64	33
Angelica	36	3	Married	Retail	Food store	21	9
Artemisia	61	1	Married	Retail	Food store	66	24
Brionia	60	2	Married	Business service	Cleaning company	4	28
Camelia	73	3	Married	Manufacture	Commercial products	60	31
Cassia	43	2	Married	Health and social services	Health consulting, therapies or counselling	7	16
Clivia	67	5	Married	Construction	Construction company	44	40

Table 24.1 (continued)

Participants	Age	No. of Children	Family Status	Business Sector	Type of Activity	No. of Employees	Length of Self-employment (Years)
Dafne	62	2	Separated	Health and social services	Retirement home	7 (with additional seasonal workers as needed)	29
Dalia	47	1	Married	Business service	Cleaning company	360	16
Erica	53	3	Married	Retail	Flooring store	7	30
Gardenia	30	2	Married	Manufacture	Home products	10	4
Gelsa	45	1	Married	Tourist services	Hotels	25	4
Gigliola	49	2	Married	Retail	Furniture store	20	30
Iris	53	1	Married	Business service	Consulting	6	13
Lavanda	32	0	Cohabitant	Retail	Agricultural machinery store	4	12
Lilia	37	1	Cohabitant	Farming	Farm	2 (plus seasonal labour)	6
Lina	33	1	Cohabitant	Business service	Consulting	5	4
Magnolia	67	2	Married	Construction	Construction company	27	30

Margherita	54	0	Married	Business service	Consulting	19	26
Melissa	64	7	Widow	Retail	Food store	20	39
Mimosa	77	3	Married	Tourist services	Hotels	220	40
Mirtilla	46	2	Married	Business service	Accounting	9	22
Orchidea	71	1	Married	Tourist services	Hotel	60	51
Peonia	51	2	Married	Health and social services	Health consulting, therapies or counselling	17	20
Pina	37	0	Separated	Manufacture	Commercial products	8	16
Primula	67	2	Married	Retail	Agricultural machinery store	14	22
Rosa	46	0	Married	Tourist services	Tourist services	23	16
Sabina	61	2	Married	Construction	Construction company	3 (plus additional workers when needed)	27
Viola	44	1	Cohabitant	Business service	Accounting	4	22
Violetta	43	3	Married	Business service	Cleaning company	50	15

particularly during the early years of childhood: 'When my children were babies, it was very hard to keep up with the practice' (Peonia, 51); 'Once children arrive, all becomes much more complicated' (Angelica, 36). However, 'now things are much better than in the early years because the children are adult. When they were babies it was very problematic and demanding, both work and family were arduous with three children' (Erica, 53). In spite of the perceived autonomy and flexibility that self-employment allows, high levels of job commitment combined with high levels of family demands generate incompatible pressures and conflict in these women entrepreneurs (Parasuraman and Simmers, 2001). The time and the strain of work commitments engender tensions between family and work domains that are, to an extent, constructed as incompatible (see Greenhaus and Beutell, 1985). Below, Clivia (67) views the work responsibilities as a source of conflict in relation to the needs of her family. Equally, she implies that when there are pressing work commitments it is the family time that has to be sacrificed:

> As a woman, I have always tried to tend to my children, particularly when they were babies, but work has deprived me of significant time that I could spend with my children; sometimes there are too many and urgent responsibilities. There isn't a secret solution to conciliate the two things, it's just very hard.

While several other respondents emphasize the fact that managing multiple roles creates strain and conflicts between the demands of work and family, and that participation in the work role is made more difficult by virtue of participation in the family role and vice versa, they have also confirmed that, with compromise, one learns to balance work with family obligations. The interviewees also suggested that combining an entrepreneurial career with the care of children is more difficult for women than it is for men, and that only a support network makes it possible. In fact, family and domestic support were recognized as extremely important in maintaining a level of work–family balance. Most women interviewed acknowledged the support of their extended family such as parents, parents-in-law and grandparents in providing childcare. As Fagnani et al. (2004) reported, in Italy, the provision for extended childcare[2] is less developed than in North European countries and the family network (particularly grandparents) generally plays a major role: 'At home I had my mother and grandmother's help, so the extended family helped me so much. To be able to entrust the children to reliable people who are close to you and to them allows you to do that extra something' (Altea, 38). When the support of extended family did not exist, paid staff were hired to provide childcare and housework. As Brionia (60) suggested: 'I had a governess at home for 30 years; without her I wouldn't have been able to develop the business as I did, because unfortunately there are no local services available.'

The issue of the lack of efficient government and local government services has also been highlighted by Artemisia (61) and Peonia (51), who spoke about the need to change social policies and services in order to make available good childcare and care for the elderly that fit the working hours of most working women: 'efficient services, places where to take the children and care services for the old are needed, otherwise it all falls on the shoulders of women' (Artemisia, 61):

> Then there is another problem that derives from the social organization of work: the structure of the working hours in the city doesn't allow workers to reconcile work with the family. When you finish work after eight in the evening, what time is left for the family? Only public sector offices close in the late afternoon, shops and private offices close at the same time at 8 in the evening, so it is difficult for both parents to be at home after school or pre-school. (Peonia, 51)

While most participants described the practical and emotional difficulties in reconciling work and family, several interviewees voiced the opinion that they were willing to forego the family to invest more time and effort in their work. Such 'inclination' was not constructed as a 'choice' or as a lack of commitment to the family but rather as a necessity. Neglecting one's own business is something that one cannot afford: 'I worked up to the day before giving birth' (Lina, 33); 'I work from Monday to Sunday without a day off, mine is not a job where you can take time off' (Lilia, 37); 'I personally take care of all things at home and at work' (Gigliola, 49).

According to the work–family 'interface' model both positive and negative influences of work to family and family to work characterize the experiences of work–family relations (Frone, 2003; Geurts et al., 2003; Kinnunen et al., 2006). However, most of the participants emphasized the conflicting element of the work–family domains, asserting that negative work experiences such as fatigue, worries, problems of various nature, do spill into the family life. Most of the interviewees voice with conviction that they bring their work troubles home. The extracts below show, in the words of two of them, how work concerns are constant in the mind of entrepreneurs, particular when there are pressing work issues to be addressed: 'When you have a worry at work, whatever that is, you never take a break, you bring the work home, you always think about the problem because you have to find a solution' (Angelica, 36):

> I believe that the work life always reflects itself in the family life, like the family life reflects itself in the work life. If you feel stressed at work you bring home the stress, if you have troubles at home, you take them with you to work . . . so

each sphere depends on the other. It's difficult to keep them separate; I don't believe that anyone can be successful at maintaining independent work and family lives. If at home you have a son who has the fever you can't be relaxed and smiling at work; in the same way if you have a urgent issue at work even when you are at home you fret because you must solve that matter; it doesn't go away until it's tackled. (Sabina, 61)

While the focus of most participants has been on the conflict between the two domains a few women constructed their experience highlighting the positive spill-over between work and family (Grzywacz and Marks, 2000; Carlson et al., 2006): 'If you have a peaceful and satisfactory family life, surely this is reflected in your work life' (Dafne, 62); 'Certainly the serenity that a person has at home is reflected in the work environment' (Viola, 44). The interaction between work and family roles is revealed in its complexity and reciprocity. However, while some elements of positive spill-over have emerged in the discourses of our participants, conflicts, pressures, commitments, time spent at work and in housework or childcare and the need for support have emerged as the fundamental pillars of entrepreneurial life for women with children (Amstad et al., 2011; Zhang and Liu, 2011).

IS THIS FAIR? PERCEPTIONS OF INEQUALITIES AND FAIRNESS IN THE DIVISION OF FAMILY WORK

Another fundamental issue that emerged in the interview conversations refers to the perceptions of the unequal distribution of family work (household labour and childcare) between the couple. Participants have reported that usually, as women, they carry the burden of family work as well as the responsibility to organize childcare and household help, no matter what their work schedule is (Coltrane, 2000; Greenstein, 2000): 'The tasks are unequally allocated: I personally do most things such as doctors' appointments, bills, grocery shopping and all other things that women do, such as cooking lunch and dinner. My husband is interested in the garden and he accompanies our son to the gym' (Gigliola, 49).

As widely discussed by participants, the division of housework follows the traditional gender division, in spite of the fact that these women work as much, or more, than their male partners. Most of the interviewees report that their partners' contribution to the household is generally limited to traditional male activities, such as gardening, DIY and taking the children to school or to their recreational activities. When men cook or help with domestic chores, this is seen as a concession, as something that men are not expected to do (see also Mannino and Deutsch, 2007) because taking care of the house is still conceived as 'woman's work' (Coltrane, 2000; Greenstein, 2000) by both men and women.

Although these women have challenged traditional work models, they appeared to conform to traditional roles in relation to their family life. While they realize the unjust distribution of family work, they do not appear to directly challenge it: 'It is never equal because all the house responsibilities, the lunch and the dinner are my concerns. When household help is bought in it's me who needs to organize it; but I'm from the old generation, so I loyally follow the traditional role of women of the old generation' (Primula, 67).

These testimonies echo the literature that reports that women entrepreneurs bear more family responsibilities than men, particularly with regard to childcare and household chores (Loscocco, 1997; Boden, 1999; Hundley, 2000; Anthias and Mehta, 2003; Heilbrunn, 2004). In fact, despite more recent social and cultural changes, research evidence still shows that the time that men and women spend on household work is biased against women, with women, on average, bearing approximately two-thirds of the family work, even when they are engaged in paid work (Coltrane, 2000; Greenstein, 2000; Aliaga, 2006). The division of family work plays an important role in the performance of women entrepreneurs and the growth of their businesses (Aidis and Wetzels, 2007; Jennings and McDougald, 2007). In fact, when observing growth patterns to women's businesses as compared to men's businesses, evidence shows that the profit and growth of women's enterprises decline in correspondence to periods of childcare responsibilities (Winn, 2005; Jayawarna et al., 2013). In describing the work–family conflict and the need to dedicate more time to the business than to the family, Erica and Mimosa, below, implicitly embrace the concept of sacrifice, inferring that career success can only be achieved to the detriment of the family (Broadbridge, 2009):

> I have always had work responsibilities in the morning and in the afternoon until the evening. I don't have a memory of my children growing up, I have never been to a school play; but I realize that now they are grown up, at that time I just got on with the work that had to be done, there wasn't an alternative. (Erica, 53)

> I have made a life choice. I have never taken my daughter to school; when she started at nursery school my daughter cried every day for a while because I wasn't there. I remember that it was hard but I didn't want to give up. I have devoted my life to work really. (Mimosa, 77)

Among the 31 women interviewed only Iris, Erica and Artemisia (see below) depict an equal distribution of family work. It is also worth noting that these three women are in their 50s and 60s and have grown-up children: 'My husband and I are sufficiently equal in the house, he does support, he generally washes the dishes, he irons his shirts' (Iris, 53); 'We are used to collaborating, we are equal, we both share the work in the house' (Erica, 53); 'My husband helps me so much, and he did when my son was young. We always had an equal relationship, equality in the distribution of the tasks at home and in the family' (Artemisia, 61).

It is interesting to highlight that although Artemisia recognizes the equal share of work between her and her husband, she still does not challenge the gender stereotype of housework as woman's work. In fact, she constructs her husband's housework contribution as help to her rather than as his own share of house and family care. While some authors focusing on the enrichment perspective appear to minimize the work–family conflict (Greenhaus and Powell, 2006), our participants have experienced more work interference in their family roles than family interference in their work (Frone, 2003; Bellavia and Frone, 2005). While many admitted that a satisfactory job will bring a more positive mood to the family, most of the interviewees have recognized the significant sacrifice that their children had to bear for their career. While pragmatism characterized these women's narratives, experiences of guilt (see also Guendouzi, 2006) were also evident in their talk:

> When I gave birth to my children I experienced the most difficult periods of my life because I had difficult pregnancies and then I had to be back to work 15 days after the birth. That was so difficult because you feel very guilty; I had to give them to a baby sitter. When they went to school and I had to pick them up at four o'clock, I was often late and the teachers were furious and they often left my children with the janitors. I was anxious, anguished and uncomfortable because I seemed to be the wicked mum who forgot her children. That was a very difficult phase in my children's growth and for me personally because I physically and psychologically suffered; I felt very stressed. (Gigliola, 49)

The above extract reveals the dialectical dilemma involved in balancing professional and maternal roles. Feelings of guilt towards the children are accompanied by psychological stress, also deriving from neglecting the self, which has to come after the work and the family: 'I trample on myself a little, because first I must satisfy the family's need and then the job; by doing so I neglect myself' (Dalia, 47). While acknowledging the difficulties experienced, these women rarely questioned their society's culture. Instead they represent dialogical dilemmas (Billig et al., 1988) in order to define and justify the organization of the family and the unequal distribution of housework. While Mirtilla (46) says that it is 'never equal', she justifies the unfairness by admitting that this is 'also because I'm very house-proud and possessive of my home, and I prefer to do the things myself. Never equal isn't a criticism to my husband, because it's me who wants to do it'. Similarly, other participants construct the unequal divisions of house chores as motivated by their desire to have things under control rather than by cultural norms.

CONCLUSIONS

The chapter has discussed the generally conflicting features of the work and family relation as experienced by female entrepreneurs. Self-employment allows limited flexibility of time and other resources and, as such, our participants admit to having had to neglect their family needs, particularly those of their young children, who had to be looked after by other family members or paid carers (whether nannies or nursery schools) while they had to bring the business's needs to the fore. It is interesting to note that the younger participants seem to accept the struggles they experience in balancing the needs of the family with the needs of the business as part of their career/life choices and do not necessarily challenge it or see any alternatives (if any would be available!). Equally in their interviews they do not appear to spend too many words discussing their sense of guilt or their difficulties in finding time to dedicate to the family. Most of the older participants with grown-up children, on the other hand, appear to linger on their memories, constructing their earlier role as young mothers as associated with guilt and, to an extent, inadequate parenting, privileging business needs over childcare.

While the literature provides support for organizational and individual measures that can be successful in improving work–life balance (for example, Thompson, 2002; Beauregard and Henry, 2009), this research generally focuses on large organizations and their employees. In these contexts resources are generally available to be allocated to employees' support services such as in-house childcare and extended parental leave. Our study, however, focusing on small businesses with limited resources, where generally the business owner also corresponds to the main decision-maker, highlights the specific needs of these women. The most pronounced complication surrounds the issue of maternity leave and early childcare. In fact, although the statutory period of parental leave in Italy is six months (five-month maternity leave is compulsory for employees), this in reality is often limited to a few weeks after the birth for small-business owners, because the prolonged absence of the main decision-maker can have negative consequences for the company (see, for example, Gigliola above). The Italian government has introduced a measure aimed at addressing this issue (Law No. 53 of 2000 – Article 9^3) that allows women entrepreneurs

404 *Handbook of gendered careers in management*

to be replaced by another entrepreneur or a self-employed individual during absences through a funded project called 'Figure of Exchange' (Art. 9, L.53/2000). In this way the entrepreneur can benefit from the full period of statutory maternity or parental leave without having to completely stop the activity of the business. While such action represents a step in the right direction, it is also replete with practical difficulties, in fact even when such a project can be put in place it is unlikely that the individual providing supply work (generally a self-employed person currently out of work or semi-retired) will have full knowledge of the business. Initiatives such as this, based on legislation, should be integrated by schemes acting at several levels. First, an infrastructure aimed at increasing and diversifying childcare supply is needed as well as a system of taxation that supports women labour market participation. Second, a coherent and comprehensive model of family-friendly policies, developed at both central and local levels, which involve the employed and the self-employed, would help in reconciling a higher fertility rate (currently 1.41) and a higher women's employment rate (currently 47 per cent compared to 67 per cent of men) in the Italian context.

Another issue highlighted by this study is the unequal distribution of household chores among women entrepreneurs and their male partners. It is evident that such inequalities are embedded in cultural traditions that still construct housework as 'woman's work'. The specific national culture influences the meaning and priorities of work and life (Lewis, 1999) and has an impact not only on the division of house/family labour among the genders but also on the meaning and willingness to accept support and by whom. In fact, while all interviewees recognized the support of the extended family and paid staff, some of them suggest that they want to be in control of household-related matters, rather than sharing this responsibility with their partners. This aspect could be the result of cultural traditions that not only construct housework as woman's work but are also embedded in the matriarchal society that characterized the indigenous inhabitants of this region for many centuries and thus may still influence the way in which women are positioned within the household.

NOTES

1. Considering only women-owned organizations, since 2011 in Italy there are 7298 more women-owned businesses. The sectors that have experienced the highest growth are: hospitality industry (+3640), construction (+1172), other services (+1102), estate agencies and parallel services (+951) and business-to-business services (+935). On the other hand, the sectors that have experienced recession are: agriculture (−5257), manufacturing (−832) and retail (−743) (Osservatorio sull'imprenditoria femminile, 2013).

2. In terms of early years education the Italian state provides, through local authorities, childcare and education from the age of 30/36 months in a pre-school environment, which generally runs between 8.30 and 16.30. On the other hand, the provision of public crèche facilities (from three months to three years of age) is limited. Furthermore, most services and retail sector (excluding public administration) have working hours that run between 9.00 and 13.00 and between 16.00 and 20.00, making the extended family the 'implicit partner' in childcare (Giovannini, 2013).
3. See http://www.unirc.it/documentazione/regolamenti_circolari/2000-53.pdf, accessed 5 December 2014.

REFERENCES

Ahl, H. (2006), 'Why research on women entrepreneurs needs new directions', *Entrepreneurship Theory and Practice*, **30**(5), 595–621.
Aidis, R. and C. Wetzels (2007), 'Self-employment and parenthood: exploring the impact of partners, children and gender', *IZA Discussion Paper*, No. 2813.
Aliaga, C. (2006), 'How is the time of women and men distributed in Europe?', *Statistics in Focus, Population and Social Conditions*, No. 4/2006, EUROSTAT.
Amstad, F.T., L.L. Meier, U. Fasel, A. Elfering and N.K. Semmer (2011), 'A meta-analysis of work–family conflict and various outcomes with a special emphasis on cross-domain versus matching-domain relations', *Journal of Occupational Health Psychology*, **16**(2), 151–69.
Anthias, F. and N. Mehta (2003), 'The intersection between gender, the family and self-employment: the family as a resource', *International Review of Sociology*, **13**(1), 105–16.
Arai, B. (2008), 'Self-employment as a response to the double day for women and men in Canada', *Canadian Review of Sociology*, **37**(2), 125–42.
Beauregard, T.A. and L.C. Henry (2009), 'Making the link between work–life balance practices and organizational performance', *Human Resource Management Review*, **19**(1), 9–22.
Bellavia, G.M. and M.R. Frone (2005), 'Work–family conflict', in J. Barling, M.R. Frone and K. Kelloway (eds), *Handbook of Work Stress*, London: Sage Publications, pp. 113–48.
Billig, M., S. Condor, D. Edwards, M. Gane, D. Middleton and R. Radley (1988), *Ideological Dilemmas: A Social Psychology of Everyday Thinking*, London: Sage.
Bird, B. and C. Brush (2002), 'A gendered perspective on organizational creation', *Entrepreneurship Theory and Practice*, **26**(3), 41–65.
Boden, R.J. (1999), 'Flexible working hours, family responsibilities and female self-employment: gender differences in self-employment selection', *American Journal of Economics and Sociology*, **58**(1), 71–83.
Broadbridge, A. (2009), 'Sacrificing personal or professional life? A gender perspective on the accounts of retail managers', *The International Review of Retail, Distribution and Consumer Research*, **9**(3), 289–311.
Bruin, A., C.G. Brush and F. Welter (2006), 'Introduction to the special issue: towards building cumulative knowledge on women's entrepreneurship', *Entrepreneurship Theory and Practice*, **30**(5), 585–93.
Bruni, A., S. Gherardi and B. Poggio (2004), 'Doing gender, doing entrepreneurship: an ethnographic account of intertwined practices', *Gender, Work & Organization*, **11**(4), 406–29.
Brush, C.G. (1992), 'Research on women business owners: past trends, a new perspective and future directions', *Entrepreneurship Theory and Practice*, **16**(4), 5–30.
Byron, D. (2005), 'A meta-analytic review of work–family conflict and its antecedents', *Journal of Vocational Behavior*, **67**(2), 169–98.
Caputo, R.K. and A. Dolinsky (1998), 'Women's choice to pursue self-employment: the role of financial and human capital of household members', *Journal of Small Business Management*, **36**(3), 8–17.
Carlson, D., K.M. Kacmar, J.H. Wayne and J.G. Grzywacz (2006), 'Measuring the positive

side of the work–family interface: development and validation of a work–family enrichment scale', *Journal of Vocational Behavior*, **68**(1), 131–64.
Carter, S. and T. Cannon (1992), *Women as Entrepreneurs*, London: Academic Press.
Coltrane, S. (2000), 'Research on household labor: modeling and measuring the social embeddedness of routine family work', *Journal of Marriage and the Family*, **62**(4), 1208–33.
DeMartino, A. and R. Barbato (2003), 'Differences between women and men MBA entrepreneurs: exploring family flexibility and wealth creation as career motivators', *Journal of Business Venturing*, **18**(6), 815–32.
Eby, L.T., W.J. Casper, A. Lockwood, C. Bordeaux and A. Brinley (2005), 'Work and family research in IO/OB: content analysis and review of the literature (1980–2002)', *Journal of Vocational Behavior*, **66**(1), 124–97.
Fagnani, J., D. Giovannini, L. Højgaard and H. Clarke (2004), *Fathers and Mothers: Dilemmas of the Work–Life Balance – A Comparative Study in Four European Countries*, Social Indicators Research Series, Vol. 21, Dordrecht, the Netherlands: Kluwer Academic Publishers.
Fischer, E.M., R.A. Reuber and L.S. Dyke (1993), 'A theoretical overview and extension of research on sex, gender, and entrepreneurship', *Journal of Business Venturing*, **8**(2), 151–68.
Ford, M., B. Heinen and K. Langkamer (2007), 'Work and family satisfaction and conflict: a meta-analysis of cross-domain relations', *Journal of Applied Psychology*, **92**(1), 57–80.
Frone, M.R. (2003), 'Work–family balance', in J. Campbell and L.E. Tetrick (eds), *Handbook of Occupational Health Psychology*, Washington, DC: American Psychological Association, pp. 143–62.
Geurts, S.A.E., M.A.J. Kompier, S. Roxburgh and I.L.D. Houtman (2003), 'Does work–home interference mediate the relationship between workload and well-being?', *Journal of Vocational Behavior*, **63**(3), 532–59.
Gimenez-Nadal, J.I., J.A. Molina and R. Ortega (2012), 'Self-employed mothers and the work–family conflict', *Applied Economics*, **44**(17), 2133–48.
Giovannini, D. (2013), 'Parenting and reconciling work and private life in Italy', *Exchange of Good Practices on Gender Equality. Comments Paper – Italy*, Brussels: European Commission.
Gohmann, S.F. (2012), 'Institutions, latent entrepreneurship, and self-employment: an international comparison', *Entrepreneurship Theory and Practice*, **36**(2), 295–321.
Greenhaus, J.H. and N.J. Beutell (1985), 'Sources of conflict between work and family roles', *Academy of Management Review*, **10**(1), 76–88.
Greenhaus, J.H. and G.N. Powell (2006), 'When work and family are allies: a theory of work–family enrichment', *Academy of Management Review*, **31**(1), 72–9.
Greenstein, T.N. (2000), 'Economic dependence, gender, and the division of labor in the home: a replication and extension', *Journal of Marriage and Family*, **62**(2), 322–35.
Grzywacz, J.G. and N.F. Marks (2000), 'Reconceptualizing the work–family interface: an ecological perspective on the correlates of positive and negative spillover between work and family', *Journal of Occupational Health Psychology*, **5**(1), 111–26.
Grzywacz, J.G., D.M. Almeida and D.A. McDonald (2002), 'Work–family spillover and daily reports of work and family stress in the adult labor-force', *Family Relations*, **51**(1), 28–36.
Guendouzi, J. (2006), 'The guilt thing: balancing domestic and professional roles', *Journal of Marriage and Family*, **68**(4), 901–9.
Gupta, V.K., D.B. Turban, S.A. Wasti and A. Sikdar (2009), 'The role of gender stereotypes in perceptions of entrepreneurs and intentions to become an entrepreneur', *Entrepreneurship Theory and Practice*, **33**(2), 397–417.
Haus, I., H. Steinmetz, R. Isidor and R. Kabst (2013), 'Gender effects on entrepreneurial intention: a meta-analytical structural equation model', *International Journal of Gender and Entrepreneurship*, **5**(2), 130–56.
Heilbrunn, S. (2004), 'On the impact of gender upon difficulties faced by entrepreneurs', *The International Journal of Entrepreneurship and Innovation*, **5**(3), 159–67.

Huarng, K.H., A.M. Tur and T.H.K. Yu (2012), 'Factors affecting the success of women entrepreneurs', *International Entrepreneurship and Management Journal*, **8**(4), 487–97.

Hughes, K.D. and J.E. Jennings (2012), *Global Women's Entrepreneurship Research: Diverse Settings, Questions and Approaches*, Cheltenham, UK and Northampton, MA, USA: Edward Elgar Publishing.

Hundley, G. (2000), 'Male/female earnings differences in self-employment: the effects of marriage, children, and the household division of labor', *Industrial and Labor Relations Review*, **54**(1), 95–114.

Jamali, D. (2009), 'Constraints and opportunities facing women entrepreneurs in developing countries: a relational perspective', *Gender in Management: An International Journal*, **24**(4), 232–51.

Jayawarna, D., J. Rouse and J. Kitching (2013), 'Entrepreneur motivations and life course', *International Small Business Journal*, **31**(1), 34–56.

Jennings, J. and E. McDougald (2007), 'Work–family interface experiences and coping strategies: implications for entrepreneurship research and practice', *Academy of Management Review*, **32**(3), 747–60.

Kappler, L.F. and S.C. Parker (2011), 'Gender and the business environment for new firm creation', *The World Bank Research Observer*, **26**(2), 237–57.

Kinnunen, U., T. Feldt, S. Geurts and L. Pulkkinen (2006), 'Types of work–family interface: well-being correlates of negative and positive spillover between work and family', *Scandinavian Journal of Psychology*, **47**(2), 149–62.

Kock, A. (2008), 'A framework for the development of women entrepreneurship in the Ekurhuleni district', unpublished MBA mini-dissertation, Potchefstroom: North-West University.

Koellinger, P., M. Minniti and C. Schade (2013), 'Gender differences in entrepreneurial propensity', *Oxford Bulletin of Economics and Statistics*, **75**(2), 213–34.

Kossek. E.E. and C. Ozeki (1998), 'Work–family conflict, policies, and the job–life satisfaction relationship: a review and directions for organizational behavior/human resources research', *Journal of Applied Psychology*, **83**(2), 139–49.

Lewis, S. (1999), 'An international perspective on work–family issues', in S. Parasuraman and J. Greenhaus (eds), *Integrating Work and Family: Challenges for a Changing World*, Westport, CT: Praeger, pp. 91–103.

Lombard, K. (2001), 'Female self-employment and demand for flexible, non-standard work schedules', *Economic Inquiry*, **39**(2), 214–37.

Loscocco, K.A. (1997), 'Work–family linkages among self-employed women and men', *Journal of Vocational Behavior*, **50**(2), 204–26.

Mäkelä, L. and V. Suutari (2011), 'Coping with work–family conflicts in the global career context', *Thunderbird International Business Review*, **53**(3), 365–75.

Mannino, C. and F. Deutsch (2007), 'Changing the division of household labor: a negotiated process between partners', *Sex Roles*, **56**(5), 309–24.

Minniti, M. (2009), 'Gender issues in entrepreneurship', *Foundations and Trends in Entrepreneurship*, **5**(7–8), 497–621.

Moore, D.P. and E.H. Buttner (1997), *Women Entrepreneurs: Moving Beyond the Glass Ceiling*, Newbury Park, CA: Sage.

Neider, L. (1987), 'A preliminary investigation of female entrepreneurs in Florida', *Journal of Small Business Management*, **25**(3), 22–9.

Orhan, M. and D. Scott (2001), 'Why women enter into entrepreneurship: an explanatory model', *Women in Management Review*, **16**(5), 232–47.

Osservatorio sull'imprenditoria femminile (2013), *Impresa-donna: 7mila in più le imprese rosa nel 2012* [Women's Enterprises – 7000 More Businesses in 2012], accessed 5 December 2014 at http://www.unioncamere.gov.it/P42A1377C160S123/Impresa-donna--7mila-in-piu-le-imprese--rosa--nel-2012-.htm.

Parasuraman, S. and C.A. Simmers (2001), 'Type of employment, work–family conflict and well-being: a comparative study', *Journal of Organizational Behavior*, **22**(5), 551–68.

Presser, H.B. (1989), 'Can we make time for children? The economy, work schedules, and child care', *Demography*, **26**(4), 523–43.
Rothbard, N.P. (2001), 'Enriching or depleting? The dynamics of engagement in work and family roles', *Administrative Science Quarterly*, **46**(4), 655–84.
Ruderman, M.N., P.J. Ohlott, K. Panzer and S. King (2002), 'Benefits of multiple roles for managerial women', *Academy of Management Journal*, **45**(2), 369–86.
Shane, S., E.A. Locke and C.J. Collins (2003), 'Entrepreneurial motivation', *Human Resource Management Review*, **13**(2), 257–79.
Shelton, L.M. (2006), 'Female entrepreneurs, work–family conflict, and venture performance: new insights into the work–family interface', *Journal of Small Business Management*, **44**(2), 285–97.
Staines, G.L. (1980), 'Spillover versus compensation: a review of the literature on the relationship between work and non-work', *Human Relations*, **33**(2), 111–29.
Stoner, C.R., R.I. Hartman and R. Arora (1990), 'Work–home role conflict in female owners of small businesses: an exploratory study', *Journal of Small Business Management*, **29**(1), 30–38.
Taniguchi, H. (2002), 'Determinants of women's entry into self-employment', *Social Science Quarterly*, **83**(3), 875–93.
Thompson, C.A. (2002), 'Managing the work–life balancing act: an introductory exercise', *Journal of Management Education*, **26**(2), 205–20.
Watson, J. (2003), 'Failure rates for female controlled businesses: are they any different?', *Journal of Small Business Management*, **41**(3), 262–77.
Williams, D.R. (2004), 'Effects of child-care activities on the duration of self-employment in Europe', *Entrepreneurship Theory and Practice*, **28**(5), 467–85.
Winn, J. (2004), 'Entrepreneurship: not an easy path to top management for women', *Women in Management Review*, **19**(3), 143–53.
Winn, J. (2005), 'Women entrepreneurs: can we remove the barriers?', *International Entrepreneurship and Management Journal*, **1**(3), 381–97.
Zhang, J. and Y. Liu (2011), 'Antecedents of work–family conflict: review and prospect', *International Journal of Business and Management*, **6**(1), 89–103.

PART 3

GETTING OUT

25. Playing, quitting or changing the game? A discussion of women managers' responses to organizational conditions
Yvonne Due Billing

> I thought how unpleasant it is to be locked out; and I thought how it is worse perhaps to be locked in.
>
> (Virginia Woolf, *A Room of One's Own*, 1929, p. 29)

Organizations were originally constructed and developed according to expectations that men were the breadwinners, and careers were arranged on the presumption that only men would make a career (Witz and Savage, 1992). Career structures were reserved for men who could spend most of their time in the organization as they were often supported by a partner who took care of everything else, including perhaps a part-time job. The work practices and norms reflected men's life situation (Meyerson and Kolb, 2000) and the competences required in the career positions were often those that were ascribed to men (Billing and Alvesson, 1994; Collinson and Hearn, 1996; Benschop and Doorewaard, 1998).

The long-time dominance of men in managerial positions made it harder for women to be regarded as competent for these positions (Kerfoot and Knights, 1993) and when women tried to get in they could be excluded by what Kanter (1977, p. 22) described as the 'masculine ethic'. They would have to learn 'the games mother never taught you' (Harragan, 1977). Organizations were clearly gendered in the sense that Acker (1992) has described them. There was a gender division of labour, a construction of symbols/images/discourses (of masculinities and femininities), which promoted a gendered image (for example, of the top manager) and the interactions between individuals were based on some already constructed ways of behaving. Finally, there was a dominant belief in a bodiless ideal worker.

The picture has changed somewhat today. First of all, women are highly educated – in the West, more so than men (Fine et al., 2009). And many women have made progress – they have careers. Second, the expansion of service and knowledge work is reducing the number of jobs with a very strong masculine image, thus paving the way for women. Third, management and leadership have for sometime now required the not so traditional masculine qualities of creativity, emotions, intuition, ethics, and relations (Alvesson and Sveningsson, 2003; Fletcher, 2004) along with empathy, communication (Fondas, 1997) and social responsibility. There is a de-masculinization of leadership and dissolution of the symbolic cultural connection between men and leadership. More and more women are getting into management.

This does not mean that organizations are gender neutral – the majority are still gendered. There is still a pronounced gender division of labour, horizontally and vertically, with women often occupying the less prestigious and powerful areas (Kottke and Pelletier, 2013). In most organizations work is still organized such that there is no consideration of family responsibilities (Lewis, 1997). And in many organizations 'management . . . has often been assumed to be consistent with characteristics traditionally valued in men' (Broadbridge and Hearn, 2008, p. 44). But there has been an increase in women's presence in higher positions and clearly organizations differ. They have different rules and norms, developed over time, and they have recruited 'players' with different symbolic capital and perspectives. People who might fit very well into one organization might not even want to apply for a position in another – different personalities are attracted to different cultures (Alvesson and Billing, 2009). This does not mean that there is a perfect match between organizations and their (women) managers, and that Acker's description is obsolete, but it is getting more complicated to understand what is reproducing gender inequalities.

This chapter is not concerned with the recruitment of women managers but with how they respond to the conditions in their organizations. As it is difficult to understand the complexities using dichotomous terms like either/or (for example, managerial career or family) because one easily slips into subjectivism and (or) structuralism, this chapter juggles with three possibilities developed by Hirschman (1970) (exit, voice and loyalty), which will be introduced in the following sections. It is then shown how and when loyalty is difficult to maintain and reactions such as voice and exit are set in action as a response to organizational conditions.

EXIT, VOICE AND LOYALTY

Although these concepts – exit, voice and loyalty – were originally developed to describe the processes and options available for the market to react to, this chapter uses them to demonstrate women managers' possible reactions to organizational conditions. Hirschman (1970) shows alternative ways of reacting to dissatisfaction with organizations, using exit, for example, in the sense that members quit the organization because of disagreeable conditions, or that customers cease to buy the goods and choose a competing product. Exit (quitting the organization) is the option available when the other possibilities have been used; voice is the possible critique that may lead to changes in the organization rather than exit. When a person chooses voice it is an attempt to change practices in the organization rather than leave. If this fails the person may choose to, or even have to, exit. But 'as a rule, then, loyalty holds exit at bay and activates voice' (Hirschman, 1970, p. 78), 'The *loyal* member does *not* exit, *but something happens to him*' (ibid., p. 88; emphasis in the original).

Loyalty implies that there is a strong connection to the organization, and the person may adapt to the expectations in the organization although it may be at unforeseen cost. Loyalty also has the function of retarding exit and of permitting voice to play a role, and it is the role of voice that is crucial for understanding organizations. It is the interplay of these three concepts that can illuminate different social phenomena and is useful to show the complexity in women managers' responses to organizational conditions.

ADAPTATION AND VOICE

Many organizations have some prestructured ideas and norms that are more in line with the first players – men – and women may have to adapt to live up to these (Billing and Alvesson, 1994). There are often, for example, already established ideas about managerial behaviour and ideas about work norms (Carli and Eagly, 2011). For a long time, modern management has largely been a masculine activity. Women and men have identified with masculinity and the advantages it offers (women in upper management have been shown to be masculine; Eagly and Karau, 2002) whereas those who identified with the feminine tended to be marginalized.

Women managers who entered the organizations some decades ago and were promoted in the organization often had no other choice than to assimilate themselves into the cultures and the conditions of the managerial jobs (see Hennig and Jardim, 1977). They increased their similarity with the male group of power in order to be accepted and included. In Billing's study (2006) they talked about the necessity to learn 'the rules of the game', men's 'lobbying methods' (networking), working within men's conditions (emphasizing strategy and efficiency), and making decisions fast without trying to get consensus first. There is considerable literature that shows that female and male leaders are or had to be similar (for example, Butterfield and Powell, 1981; Bayes, 1987).

The first women in management often had a token status, which means heightened visibility (Kanter, 1977; Billing and Alvesson, 1994; Benschop and Doorewaard, 1998) and therefore they did not have much choice other than to blend in or exit the organization. Voice may not have been seen as an option and was not activated; instead they have chosen to assimilate and stay in the organization, although it may have had some personal consequences. Whereas some women saw themselves as 'almost men' (Billing, 2006) a woman manager in Pini's (2005) study saw herself as being a member of a 'third sex': 'Women suggested that they were not just different from their male counterparts, but also from other women' (ibid., p. 81). They had to 'overcome the tension between their positions as "agricultural leader" and "women"' (ibid.).

In organizations, there may, however, also be a force and gendered expectation for women managers that pull in another direction than for them to be 'almost men' or a 'third sex' – that is, that they should be more gender appropriate in their leadership. They may experience that they are expected to exercise a different leadership style than men, more in accordance with their gender (Carli and Eagly, 2011). There is a tendency to capitalize on what are believed to be essentially women's skills – whether they are present or not (Fletcher, 2004). In Billing's (2006) study there is an example of a woman manager who found out that she had been hired to do the dirty work, to fire hundreds of employees with a soft touch. When she found out that she had to be the 'executioner', she quit the job.

Women managers may be constrained to certain management positions where they are supposed to do more of the tasks believed to be natural for women and they may not even be acknowledged for their efforts (Fletcher, 2004). Women in management tend to be in human resources and other support functions. For example, human resource management seems to be female dominated, and has even been described as a 'female ghetto' (Brewis and Linstead, 2004). There is a gender division of labour in management where some areas are believed to fit women better than men, thus leading to areas that are defined as masculine, favouring male leaders, and feminine areas that favour female leaders (Eagly and Karau, 2002).

Many women seem to adjust themselves to normative gender conceptions of appropriate positions and behaviour for women managers; that is, they accept being held accountable for their performance not just as managers but as women managers. For example, they may accept being expected to be softer, understanding and caring (Billing, 2006) – expectations that are not directed towards male managers. Some women in the study complained about this. One of them said that she saw herself as a manager not a woman manager. The effect of the expectations is, in the end, a matter of what the women do with the pressures, and how they define themselves – as gendered (women) managers or just as managers.

Even though women are willing to set high stakes and adapt, they may be faced with a paradoxical situation: they may be judged unfavourably by their subordinates for not being womanly enough, and by the male managers for not being managerial enough (see Gherardi, 1995; Carli and Eagly, 2011) and this may activate voice or exit. Women have different personalities and interact differently with their subordinates. Some of them may feel they have to live up to expectations, whereas others may not, not caring if they are seen as 'soft' or too tough, and here again voice will often be an option rather than exit.

Leadership and management are dependent on the structural conditions (including organizational cultures and social norms) and the positions the managers have (Ely and Padavic, 2007) rather than on psychological dispositions (see Billing and Alvesson, 2014). Consequently, the scope for action (and voice) is then limited. If there are differences in leadership this seems to be correlated with the congruity of their sex and leadership positions (Eagly and Karau, 2002). For example, Eagly and Johnson (1990, p. 248) found that 'leaders of each sex emphasized task accomplishments when they were in a leadership role regarded as congruent with their gender'. The style was then a function of their leadership role, although women were often evaluated as more task-oriented than men (Butterfield and Grinnell, 1999).

Gender expectations differ in organizations and so do organizational goals, structures, norms and challenges (Alvesson and Billing, 2009). Different cultures offer different possibilities for being loyal. Women are also at different stages in their lives and for some it is fine to adapt to the norms of the organization, changing their style into being more 'male' or alternatively to something more appropriate for their gender. Loyalty means, as Hirschman says, that 'something happens to them', and this is the cost of adaptation.

Younger women managers may interact differently with their colleagues (see Billing, 2006), regard their colleagues more as friends, and they may voice their concerns and dissatisfaction much more than older women managers. A young woman manager said that in her former organization she realized that she was paid less than her male counterpart. After her protest (voice) she was paid the same as him, some time after she left the organization anyway for a better alternative (ibid.). These women did not understand or accept unfair treatment and exit is always a possibility if things do not change and there is a better alternative.

TIME CONSTRAINTS AND EXIT

If organizational norms are to stay late, to travel a lot and work more than a normal work week, this may collide with women's family care responsibilities (and also for men who are caring fathers[1]). Women have often accepted their role as the primary caregiver and their care commitments will influence how far it is possible to keep up loyalty to the organization, but also how much energy can be invested in the social aspects of the organization. Women often 'underinvest in social capital' (Eagly and Carli, 2007, p. 68), which means they may miss out on networking that some see as essential for career success (Wolff and Moser, 2009). As long as family is seen as a woman's issue (Rhode, 2003) women pay a disproportionate price and they may find that they have to drop off the managerial track if they have substantial family commitments. Men may, however, also feel unfairly treated because it may be difficult for them to justify a reduced schedule. Lack of time is a major problem and will affect how much, for example, it is possible to travel (Davidson and Burke, 2000).

Many feel tensions between private life and work (see Billing, 2013) and private life does not function as a buffer against stress. Women (middle) managers report more stress than men (Frankenheuser, 1993; Fielden and Cooper, 2001) often because of a double burden, as unpaid work often remains the responsibility of women (Liss, 2013). For some it is possible to combine career and family because of the family-friendliness of the organization or because of a helpful partner or hired help. But full-time availability and travelling do not integrate well with small children if parents also want to be with them. Carli and Eagly (2011) refer to a study of 25 000 managers that shows that women more often than men quit their job for family reasons.

Commitment may, however, be based on loyalty primarily to the organization rather than to family as it is difficult to compromise. Exit then of the family becomes a possibility, that is, divorce or not starting a family. Many more women managers than men seem to have problems coping with having both a managerial job and family or they may not want both. Statistics show that female managers are often single and childless (Davidson and Burke, 2000; Højgård, 2002; Guillaume and Pochic, 2007), while this is not the case for men. This could be interpreted as women managers being over-committed and too loyal to the organization as they abstain from having children (and exit family), which male managers do not. On the other hand we do not know if the women who get to the top are just less interested in children and traditional family life. In between quitting totally and loyalty there may be a transition period where the woman is discovering what she wants.

AMBIVALENCE AND EXIT

Women managers may be ambivalent about accepting a managerial position not solely because of problems balancing private life and work. In Billing's study (2006) women managers stated that they feared they would lose contact with their former non-managerial job, and they saw exit as always being a possibility as they had an acceptable alternative. There were also parts of the managerial job they disliked. For example, they were not happy about managing former colleagues and making decisions on behalf of them, and they were afraid of not being able to keep up their friendships with them. They also felt that they had to distance themselves from parts of the job. The managerial role was seen as a part they had to play, and if the script did not fit them they would either leave the organization or exit the job as a manager and return to a non-managerial position. It was important for them to dis-identify with the managerial role. For example, in their free time when they were together with colleagues they did not see themselves as managers. These women were well educated and they had a positive alternative, going back to their former job. They had set a limit to how long they wanted to be in a managerial position. A common saying was, 'I give it three years'. For many of them it seemed to be a question of time before they would exit the managerial job to remain loyal and committed to themselves (and their colleagues). Some of the interviewees complained that they had changed into something they did not quite like about themselves. The loyal women felt that 'something had happened to them' but these women did not see voice as a possibility.

However, as stated, there may be many good reasons for women managers to exit the job, but before this happens there may have been attempts to make their voices heard in order to change the organizational cultures and norms.

CHANGING NORMS AND CULTURES

There are many people who are willing to accept what is often called 'the rules of the game' (Billing, 2006) and therefore it is not so easy to change the organization from within, but there may be other ways – organizations are not immune to what goes on in society and pressures for change may come from the outside (Billing, 2011). For example, in relation to the missing balance between family and work, if laws are passed that grant (and demand) that fathers take parental leave, then organizations will have to adapt to these changed circumstances and men will hopefully see themselves as equally committed to childcaring, and women would then be able to invest more in 'social capital', which is seen as so important for career success (Eagly and Carli, 2007).

Changes in organizations may sometimes be initiated by top management and may be crucial for creating gender equality (Meyerson and Kolb, 2000; Wilson, 1998) and for changing the organizational culture (Billing and Alvesson, 1994), thus paving the way for new ideas and ways of interacting. For example, in one Scandinavian organization some decades ago the new CEO wanted to get rid of the hierarchies in favour of a more flat structure with decentralized decision-making. He also announced that the best leadership should consist of feminine and masculine elements and started recruiting new managers from areas that were female dominated. This change meant that women started seeing themselves as managerial candidates and some applied for and got these positions. The 'cultural revolution' meant that nothing was the same any more and it opened up to new ideas, ways of interacting, and so on. For example, a woman manager found that meetings in her work groups were more efficient if they started with small talk about personal matters.

It is, however, not so easy to change cultures as there may be values and underlying assumptions that go against changes – when women have become managers they may be seen as violating the game by not playing according to the norms and they may be seen as not managing in a gender-appropriate way (Carli and Eagly, 2011). The ideas of the CEO might not necessarily be accepted and/or implemented in the rest of the organization, and therefore women may find some resistance anyway, which is also shown in research by Roper (1996). Everyone does not automatically back up a cultural revolution; there may be inertia in the structures.

To change anything it is, of course, important to voice concerns but also to know what is going on and where it is possible to get to. For example, in one organization there seemed to be very unclear promotion patterns, which resulted in the fact that no women got promoted (Billing and Alvesson, 1994). There were some taken-for-granted ideas about women and men, and gendered conceptions of managerial jobs. At a subconscious level women were believed to be unable to do the job as manager and there was no awareness of this gender stereotyping. Such perceptions of women undermine their positions and the only way to change things is to change these stereotypes (Deutsch, 2007) and make gender irrelevant. Gendered practices (and subconscious expectations) can only be changed if there is an awareness that they exist, and even then it may be difficult to change things. But even small changes may be incremental and affect larger changes (Meyerson and Fletcher, 1999). Martin (2003) provides an example of voice, a minor incident of a woman manager complaining about her being treated like a secretary and not as a 'Vice President' and how her complaint started a gender group in the company, which eventually led to greater gender awareness in the organization.

The changes of the discourse of management – and a demand for more social skills and emotional awareness – de-masculinize management (Billing and Alvesson, 2000) and diminish the connotation between leadership and masculinity, and thus it will also affect the symbolic connection between men and leadership. This will widen the targeted group for managers, as it will attract not just more women but also perhaps different people, men and women who have not earlier seen themselves as potential managers and who may have some different ideas about work–life and gender norms. At least, according to Fletcher (2004), this is the case if this more participatory (post-heroic, shared), non-hierarchical flexible style of leadership keeps its feminine image, but she also suggests that there are reasons to be sceptical about new leadership as there may only be superficial changes behind the rhetoric.

CONCLUSIONS

The significant change in women's role in higher education – now exceeding that of men – has meant that for many women it is obvious to work full-time, careers are important, and family is for many not regarded as the main priority. Some also earn more than their husbands/partners (Billing, 2006) with whom they share housework or they have hired help. Many of these women are more aware of their rights and will thus influence expectations to how women are (supposed to be) and what they will accept.

Organizations may still be run according to norms that may be hard to live up to. But for norms to exist they have to be acted out as norms, and the question is how much women contribute to the construction of norms in their daily interactions. There is an interplay between loyalty, change and exit, and during these practices norms may be supported or challenged. Organizational contexts and the local work cultures influence how women and men are constructed, what people think and believe and are decisive for how women can be as managers and which values, norms and ideas are prevalent.

The tendency of more men being interested in taking fatherhood seriously may change the way we work and create more balance between work and family. On the other hand, organizations that have to deal with tougher competitive pressures will primarily be interested in those they can take advantage of. Organizations and management 'need' what is necessary to be able to survive in a competitive, sustainable world and therefore people are hired who are willing to, and are capable of, accepting these demands and they may not be family friendly. Accelerating demands may be hard to live up to, especially for those with care commitments. This is, of course, a problem and may hit women more if they have not been able to negotiate an equal sharing of house- and caring work with their partners.

Cultural changes seem to affect personalities and according to Twenge (1997) women increasingly endorse masculine-stereotyped traits and men seem not to endorse feminine-stereotyped traits. There is a decrease in sex differences; men and women have become increasingly similar. This is not difficult to understand, as younger women have had to develop those characteristics that are necessary for success in a professional world, for example, to be more instrumental and goal oriented. Women and men can, of course, display masculine and feminine behaviour depending on the people they interact with and the demands of the context (Binns, 2008; cf. Martin, 2003).

Exit, voice, and loyalty all demand practices of some sort: they are practices within settings of constraints. Some rules and norms and gender expectations may match the ideas of the women managers – others may be so much in conflict that they will leave if things are not changed. In between the possibilities of exit and loyalty there may have been attempts to change the culture, the work conditions, the gendered discourses, but voicing these concerns may result in the organization sanctioning and 'exiting' the person. Changing organizations means changing dominant belief systems (and undermining stereotypical gender regulation norms) and constructing new beliefs and practices.

CHANGES?

Organizations are not stable and rational with fixed structures but are processes where change is possible (Acker, 1992). We have to look at these processes and see if and how work is divided, evaluated, and gendered, and that meanings are created through symbols, ideology, and relations. Hierarchies cannot totally be avoided. More research shows that workplaces for only women or only men also create hierarchies (Lindgren, 1996; Alvesson and Billing, 2009). There are competing masculinities in male-only organizations (Connell, 1995; Collinson and Hearn, 1996), and competing femininities in female-only organizations, and these are related to other subjectivities, like age, class, professions, and even nations (for example, Tienari et al., 2005).

It is easier to make changes if there is a will to change in the organization and that we know what the purpose of the change is. Is it a change of the gender composition in management – or is it about retaining women in management – for example, doing something about the stress level – and what is the purpose believed to be, more efficiency, justice, a different more humane inclusive culture, or is a 50:50 distribution the common goal? All these goals assume differences between men and women and that women have to be helped to a better situation or that a change of the gender order is needed. But what about the consequences of gendered socialization, often leading to what is believed to be gender-appropriate jobs? Although there is no agreement across cultures about what is gender-appropriate work, within the monolithic culture there have been strong ideas about what is women's and men's work, and this counts for work in the household as well. It is the deep-seated ideas of perceptions of men/women in the culture that must be changed, and we have to acknowledge that for many women, their 'ability to devote time to paid work is the outcome of a complex and highly gendered set of negotiations and compromises within the household' (Probert, 2005, p. 70).

Structures become visible if one goes against the norm, if a man wants to work in a female-dominated area and vice versa or when a woman does not want to take care of her child and leaves it to the father. Instead of holding on to ideas of women/men as biological creatures with essentially different experiences and eradicate these or celebrate them, it is better to focus on the complexity of everyday organizational processes. The focus is then on ongoing processes and on how meaning and subjectivity is constructed in daily discursive processes and how different constructions take place.

The problem is that in our contemporary society there is a tendency to support the discourse of the ideal employee who is willing to sacrifice his or her personal interests in favour of the interests of the organization. This belief in a bodiless idealized worker (Acker, 1992) with no other commitments than work needs to be questioned. Hopefully, the continuing demasculinization of leadership and the weakening of the traditional norms in management will have the effect that there will be more demands for life balance, not just a balance between career and family/personal life but also for the individual between mind and body.

NOTE

1. In the Nordic countries (except Denmark) legislation on paternity leave (reserved for males) has meant that it is now more common for fathers to take leave in relation to childbirth, as these months will be lost if not taken by the fathers. This increases the possibility of questioning the traditional image of men as the ideal workers.

REFERENCES

Acker, J. (1992), 'Gendering organizational theory', in A. Mills and P. Tancred (eds), *Gendering Organizational Analysis*, London: Sage.

Alvesson, M. and Y.D. Billing (2009), *Understanding Gender and Organizations*, 2nd edition, London: Sage.

Alvesson, M. and S. Sveningsson (2003), 'Managers doing leadership. The extraordinarization of the mundane', *Human Relations*, **56**(12), 1435–59.

Bayes, J. (1987), 'Do female managers in public bureaucracies manage with a different voice?', paper presented at the 3rd International Interdisciplinary Congress on Women, Dublin, 6–10 July.

Benschop, Y. and H. Doorewaard (1998), 'Covered by equality: the gender subtext of organizations', *Organization Studies*, **19**(5), 787–805.

Billing, Y.D. (2006), *Viljan till makt?* [The Will to Power?], Lund: Studentlitteratur.

Billing, Y.D. (2011), 'Are women victims of a male norm phantom in management?', *Gender, Work & Organization*, **18**(3), 298–317.

Billing, Y.D. (2013), 'Happily working until they drop: when there is no longer a balance between stress and fun – a task for leadership', in J. Lemmergaard and S.L. Muhr (eds), *Critical Perspectives on Leadership: Emotion, Toxicity, and Dysfunction*, Cheltenham, UK and Northampton, MA, USA: Edward Elgar Publishing.

Billing, Y.D. and M. Alvesson (1994), *Gender, Managers and Organizations*, Berlin/New York: De Gruyter.

Billing, Y.D. and M. Alvesson (2000), 'Questioning the notion of feminine leadership. A critical perspective on the gender labelling of leadership', *Gender, Work & Organization*, **7**(3), 144–57.

Billing, Y.D. and M. Alvesson (2014), 'Leadership – a matter of gender?', in S. Kumra, R. Simpson and R.J. Burke (eds), *The Oxford Handbook of Gender in Organizations*, Oxford: Oxford University Press.

Binns, J. (2008), 'The ethics of relational leading: gender matters', *Gender, Work & Organization*, **15**(6), 600–20.

Brewis, J. and S. Linstead (2004), 'Gender and management', in S. Linstead et al. (eds), *Management and Organization: A Critical Text*, New York: Palgrave Macmillan.

Broadbridge, A. and J. Hearn (2008), 'New directions in research and continuing patterns in practice', *British Journal of Management*, **19**(S1), S38–S50.

Butterfield, D.A. and J.P. Grinnell (1999), 'Re-viewing gender, leadership, and managerial behaviour: do three decades of research tell us anything?', in G.N. Powell (ed.), *Handbook of Gender & Work*, Thousand Oaks, CA: Sage.

Butterfield, D.A. and G.N. Powell (1981), 'Effect of group performance, leader sex, and rater sex on ratings of leader behavior', *Organizational Behavior and Human Performance*, **28**(1), 129–41.

Carli, L. and A. Eagly (2011), 'Gender and leadership', in A. Bryman et al. (eds), *The SAGE Handbook of Leadership Studies*, London: Sage.

Collinson, D. and J. Hearn (1996), 'Breaking the silence: on men, masculinities and managements', in D. Collinson and J. Hearn (eds), *Men as Managers, Managers as Men*, London: Sage.

Connell, R.W. (1995), *Masculinities*, Cambridge, UK: Polity Press.

Davidson, M. and R.J. Burke (2000), *Women in Management*, London: Sage.

Deutsch, F.M. (2007), 'Undoing gender', *Gender & Society*, **21**(1), 106–27.

Eagly, A. and L. Carli (2007), 'Women and the labyrinth of leadership', *Harvard Business Review*, September, 62–71.

Eagly, A. and B. Johnson (1990), 'Gender and leadership style: a meta-analysis', *Psychological Bulletin*, **108**(2), 233–56.

Eagly, A.H. and S.J. Karau (2002), 'Role congruity theory of prejudice toward female leaders', *Psychological Review*, **109**(3), 573–98.

Ely, R. and I. Padavic (2007), 'A feminist analysis of organizational research on sex differences', *Academy of Management Review*, **32**(4), 1121–43.

Fielden, S.L. and C.L. Cooper (2001), 'Women managers and stress: a critical analysis', *Gender, Work and Health*, **20**(1/2), 3–16.
Fine, P., W. Sawahel and M. Jarjour (2009), 'Global women no longer the second sex', *University World News*, **98**, 25 October.
Fletcher, J. (2004), 'The paradox of postheroic leadership: an essay on gender, power and transformational change', *The Leadership Quarterly*, **15**(5), 647–61.
Fondas, N. (1997), 'Feminization unveiled. Management qualities in contemporary writings', *Academy of Management Review*, **22**(1), 257–82.
Frankenheuser, M. (1993), *Kvinnligt, manligt, stressigt* [Female, Male, Stressful], Höganäs: Bra Böcker/Nike.
Gherardi, S. (1995), *Gender, Symbolism and Organizational Cultures*, London: Sage.
Guillaume, C. and S. Pochic (2009), 'What would you sacrifice? Access to top management and the work–life balance', *Gender, Work & Organization*, **16**(1), 14–36.
Harragan, B.L. (1977), *Games Mother Never Taught You*, New York: Rawson Associates.
Hennig, M. and A. Jardim (1977), *The Managerial Woman*, New York: Anchor Press.
Hirschman, A.O. (1970), *Exit, Voice and Loyalty. Responses to Decline in Firms, Organizations, and States*, Cambridge, MA: Harvard University Press.
Højgård, L. (2002), 'Tracing differentiation in gendered leadership: an analysis of differences in gender composition in top management in business, politics and the civil service', *Gender, Work & Organization*, **9**(1), 15–38.
Kanter, R.M. (1977), *Men and Women of the Corporation*, New York: Basic Books.
Kerfoot, D. and D. Knights (1993), 'Management, masculinity and manipulation: from paternalism to corporate strategy in financial services in Britain', *Journal of Management Studies*, **30**(4), 659–77.
Kottke, J.L. and K.L. Pelletier (2013), 'Advancing women into leadership. A global perspective on overcoming barriers', in M. Paludi (ed.), *Women and Management. Global Issues and Promising Solutions*, Santa Barbara, CA: ABC-Clio.
Lewis, S. (1997), '"Family friendly" employment policies: a route to changing organizational culture or playing about at the margins?', *Gender, Work & Organization*, **4**(1), 13–23.
Lindgren, G. (1996), 'Broderskapets logic' [Brotherhood logic], *Kvinnovetenskaplig tidskrift*, **17**(1), 4–14.
Liss, M. (2013), 'Inequality in the division of household labour and child care: causes, consequences, and how to change', in M.A. Paludi (ed.), *Women and Management. Global Issues and Promising Solutions*, Santa Barbara, CA: ABC-Clio.
Martin, P.Y. (2003), '"Said and done", versus "saying and doing". Gendering practices, practicing gender at work', *Gender and Society*, **17**(3), 342–66.
Meyerson, D. and J. Fletcher (1999), 'A modest manifesto for shattering the glass ceiling', *Harvard Business Review*, January–February, 127–36.
Meyerson, D. and D. Kolb (2000), 'Moving out of the "armchair": developing a framework to bridge the gap between feminist theory and practice', *Organization*, **7**(4), 553–71.
Pini, B. (2005), 'The third sex: women leaders in Australian agriculture', *Gender, Work & Organization*, **12**(1), 73–88.
Probert, B. (2005), '"I just couldn't fit it in": gender and unequal outcomes in academic careers', *Gender, Work & Organization*, **12**(1), 50–72.
Rhode, D. (2003), 'The difference "difference" makes', in R. Ely et al. (eds), *Reader in Gender, Work, and Organization*, London: Blackwell.
Roper, M. (1996), '"Seduction and succession": circuits of homosocial desire in management', in D. Collinson and J. Hearn (eds), *Men as Managers, Managers as Men*, London: Sage.
Tienari, J., A.-M. Søderberg, C. Holgersson and E. Vaara (2005), 'Gender and national identity construction in the cross-border merger context', *Gender, Work & Organization*, **12**(3), 217–41.
Twenge, J.M. (1997), 'Changes in masculine and feminine traits over time: a meta-analysis', *Sex Roles*, **36**(5/6), 305–24.

Wilson, F. (1998), 'Gendered career paths', *Personnel Review*, **27**(5), 396–411.
Witz, A. and M. Savage (1992), 'The gender of organization', in M. Savage and A. Witz (eds), *Gender and Bureaucracy*, Oxford: Blackwell.
Wolff, H.G. and K. Moser (2009), 'Effects of networking on career success. A longitudinal study', *Journal of Applied Psychology*, **94**(1), 196–206.

26. Encore careers: motivating factors for career exit and rebirth
Wendy Marcinkus Murphy and Elizabeth Hamilton Volpe

Career success has been the focus of decades of research, yet few researchers have explored career transitions, particularly at mid-life. Often referred to in the popular press as 'encore careers' these are career transitions individuals make from a primary to a secondary career – a second act that increasingly, although not exclusively, occurs for individuals in the mid- to late stages of their careers (Alboher, 2012; Freedman, 2012). This chapter investigates why people who have achieved objective success in their career voluntarily choose to leave, and even more interestingly, why they leave not to retire but to become fully engaged in a different occupation.

After exiting their primary careers, individuals experience the birth of a second career often motivated by the desire to contribute to society or one's community, pursue work that is deemed personally interesting or meaningful, or achieve balance between their professional and personal lives (Freedman, 2006; Goggin, 2009). Individuals who pursue encore careers are less motivated by status or compensation-based career outcomes and more interested in exploring a passion, keeping their mind active, having flexibility in employment, and engaging in work that is an authentic representation of their identity and priorities (Bank, 2009).

Popular press discussions of encore careers identify this type of career transition as a primarily Baby Boomer (individuals born in the USA between 1946 and 1964; Twenge et al., 2010) phenomenon driven by the desire to combine financial security with personal meaning and social impact during the mid- to late stages of life (Freedman, 2006; Bank, 2009; Goggin, 2009). In this chapter we focus less on the quantitative age of individuals who make substantive career transitions as a defining feature of encore careers and more on the qualitative reasons motivating individuals who have achieved objective success in their career to voluntarily leave, not to retire, but to become fully engaged in a different occupation.

Existing research has not focused on encore careers or how the motivations for these career transitions are unique from other career decisions individuals make. Drawing on existing theory and preliminary interviews, this chapter identifies factors that motivate individuals to transition into encore careers as well as those that facilitate (or impede) this type of career transition. Gender is highlighted as a moderating variable that influences the saliency of motivating factors and the conditions that enable encore career transitions. We conclude the chapter by discussing considerations for future research surrounding encore career transitions.

EXISTING THEORY

We integrate research on voluntary turnover, careers, and positive organizational scholarship to delineate the motivations driving men and women to make the significant transition from a primary to a secondary career. We begin with the voluntary turnover literature as the background for our research.

Researchers discuss three prevailing rationales for why individuals leave organizations, namely turnover induced by affect (March and Simon, 1958), 'shocks' (Lee and Mitchell, 1994), and an array of forces from calculative to normative (Maertz and Campion, 2004). March and Simon (1958) proposed that negative affect (mostly in the form of job dissatisfaction) coupled with the perception of available job alternatives causes individuals to leave organizations, implying an affect-induced, linear and rational approach to turnover. Lee and Mitchell (1994) highlighted that factors other than affect prompt voluntary turnover by proposing an unfolding model of turnover that uses the existence (or non-existence) of 'shocks' – for example, value, goal or behavioural mismatches or misfits between an individual and organization, along with the degree of psychological analysis involved in quitting to outline decision paths individuals follow when making turnover decisions (Lee et al., 1996, 1999). Maertz and Campion's (2004) model integrates these to propose eight forces (see the Appendix at the end of the chapter for definitions) related to different decisions to quit. However, none of these forces fully explain why people are leaving for encore careers. Calculative forces, that is, anticipated future satisfaction with a job, may play a role in that people sense a potential to be more satisfied doing something else. In fact, those pursuing encore careers are likely to fulfil the conditions of pre-planned quitters (ibid.), with few possibilities for the organization to avoid the loss. At the root of these theories is the interaction between the individual and the nature of the job (Holtom et al., 2008).

Research on women's turnover has primarily focused on push or pull factors, including work–family demands, lack of advancement opportunities, or unfavourable working conditions (for example, unsupportive boss, stress, and burnout). These factors most often result in 'opting out', that is, leaving the paid workforce entirely (Mainiero and Sullivan, 2006; Cabrera, 2007; Stone, 2007; Percheski, 2008). In contrast, popular press accounts of encore career transitions describe an intentional desire to make a positive change into a different occupation, most often during mid- to late life following considerable success in a primary career (Alboher, 2012; Freedman, 2012).

The existing research on turnover focuses on why individuals leave organizations or the workforce, not on why individuals voluntarily exit one career to become fully engaged in an encore career. Furthermore, the existing literature takes a negative view of turnover (for an exception see Holtom et al., 2008), focusing on what drives individuals away from organizations or paid employment, rather than highlighting positive aspects by focusing on what attracts or entices individuals to pursue alternative career paths. Although intuitively one may think that alternative forces (Maertz and Campion, 2004) may be high in this kind of change, the job alternatives available in encore careers are often unknown and call for a period of exploration and reflection.

In this chapter we introduce new antecedents that are specific to individuals' turnover into encore careers. We first describe our exploratory research design. Based on our interviews and the extant literature, we then focus on motivating factors – meaningful work, fun, novelty, work flexibility, and occupational characteristics – that drive both men and women to pursue encore careers and highlight how the saliency of these antecedents varies by gender. Finally, we examine how gender, financial resources and interpersonal support serve as moderating conditions that facilitate (or impede) individuals' transitions to encore careers.

RESEARCH DESIGN

Our sample includes six full-time college professors, three men and three women, who are actively engaged in encore careers. Participants were equally divided in job status, three with tenure and three full-time lecturers, although all seen as senior faculty. At the time of their transition into an encore career, participants were on average 44 years old, married with children (average age 10.8 years old). Participants' first careers represented a wide range of industries including accounting, banking, biomedical devices, healthcare services, and military. Each had achieved a high-status position (for example, CEO, partner, top manager) and was in a financially rewarding and/or prestigious role.

Teaching has been identified as the most popular occupational choice for encore careers (Freedman, 2006), therefore our focus on academics is an appropriate representation of individuals pursuing this type of career transition. We used a snowball sampling technique to identify participants, which is useful when researching a unique population that is difficult to access through traditional means (Heckathorn, 1997; Salganik and Heckathorn, 2004).

We conducted one-hour semi-structured interviews that included the following questions: 'Could you describe your career and how you got to the position you are in today?' 'Could you elaborate on how you made the decision to leave [name of organization], what were your considerations?' 'What has been the result of this change [to encore career]?' All interviews were voice recorded and professionally transcribed. Data was coded using content analysis (Fontana and Frey, 2000), identifying patterns in responses and generating themes, which were triangulated across several participants. In the presentation of our framework, we provide exemplary quotes to represent the range of responses and illustrate relevant factors most clearly.

FACTORS MOTIVATING ENCORE CAREERS

We propose five factors that motivate individuals to leave their primary careers and launch encore careers (Figure 26.1). These motivating factors are individually based – that is, the desire for meaningful work, fun, and/or novelty –and structurally based – that is, the desire for increased work flexibility and different occupational characteristics. While the latter are classic work–life pull and organizational push factors in the turnover and women's careers literature respectively, research shows that men may reasonably fear the stigma of such rationale (Vandello et al., 2013). The first three individual factors are new contributions to the conversation on turnover and career success.

Meaningful Work

Positive organizational scholarship literature around the meaning of and meaningfulness of work focuses on individual perceptions and implies positive meaning derived from work. Thus, 'meaningful work' is perceived and experienced as significant by the individual (Rosso et al., 2010). This parallels the careers literature focus on the subjective career and the experience of work as a calling (Hall, 2002; Hall and Chandler, 2005). Individuals can experience meaningfulness or a sense of calling toward any career domain (Hall and Chandler, 2005). Scholars in both areas have discussed values and motivations grounded in an agentic perspective of 'the

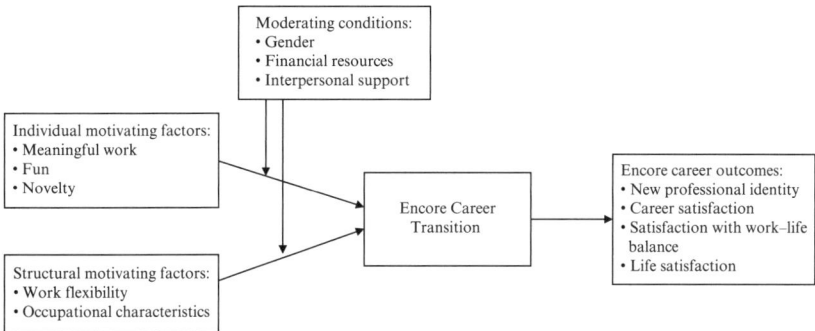

Figure 26.1   Factors motivating encore careers

self'. One of the ways that values contribute to meaningfulness is through the fulfilment of personal potential (Super and Sverko, 1995) or through a values-driven career (Hall, 2002).

Popular press discussions highlight the desire for personal meaning and social impact as reasons individuals pursue encore careers (Freedman, 2006; Bank, 2009; Goggin, 2009). In mid- to late life individuals often experience a reordering of priorities, shifting focus from more traditional success to engaging in work that has greater personal significance. Encore careers offer individuals the opportunity to live their values and use their talents to contribute to community and society while continuing to earn an income. For that reason work in the non-profit sector, education, and healthcare fields is often the target of encore careers (Freedman, 2006, 2012; Bank, 2009; Goggin, 2009). Participants described meaningful work as a factor motivating them to pursue encore careers. One participant revealed how meaningful he found his encore career upon reflection: 'If you find a place like I have, it's a very purposed life.' Similarly, participants talked about feeling fulfilled by their choice to pursue a second act career and loving what they do:

> I tell people a lot of times that decision [to transition into an academic career] was probably the best thing that ever happened to me. I love the career that I have. I feel really fulfilled. It does keep me learning, which I really enjoy. It's just a very stimulating environment intellectually, I really enjoy it.

As another participant described:

> It's the ability to work, not because you have to, but because you want to. And I come here every day, not because I have to; I come here because I love coming here and there's something about getting up in the morning and wanting to beat it out the door to get to someplace.

Fun

Fun at work is defined as any social, interpersonal, or task activities that provide an individual with enjoyment or pleasure (Fluegge, 2008). Research on fun at work has focused on 'packaged' or management-led activities such as socializing (for example, bowling, picnics), celebrating (for example, holidays, birthdays, award ceremonies), and policies (for example, relaxed dress code) that make the work environment 'fun' (Karl et al., 2005; Bolton and Houlihan, 2009). However, scholars are increasingly interested in how intrinsic characteristics of a job, rather than only extrinsic factors, influence fun at work (Tews et al., 2012).

Scholars view global fun or an attitude toward workplace fun as a more general work attitude (for example, Karl et al., 2005; McDowell, 2005; Fluegge, 2008). Unlike specific activities that infuse fun at work, an attitude toward fun means that fun is viewed as appropriate, salient, and with positive perceived consequences (that is, good for productivity rather than a waste of time) (Karl et al., 2005). The idea is that the work itself is fun or that fun is an essential component of working. This global concept of an attitude toward fun aligns with positive organizational scholarship that emphasizes the positive energy from work that enables individuals to thrive (Cameron et al., 2003).

Fun at work is related to positive affect (Fluegge, 2008), a predictor of human flourishing that connotes goodness, generativity, and growth (Fredrickson and Losada, 2005). Studies of fun at work have linked it to job satisfaction (Karl et al., 2005, 2007) and have shown that intrinsic characteristics, such as collegial co-worker interactions and engaging job responsibilities, significantly influence applicants' attraction to a job (Tews et al., 2012). Thus, it is the attitude toward fun that is likely to trigger the appeal of an encore career. Participants described the desire to do something fun as a motivation for changing careers and the importance of fun to their satisfaction in their encore careers. For example: 'I really like this job – it's a fun job – and I like teaching the students, and they like the combination; they like the practical experience and the applied knowledge. It's a fun job; life is good.' Similarly, another participant commented: 'I like the energy around the young folks, and the people that are inquisitive about what I did in my [first] career. It really is fun.'

Novelty

In *Composing a Further Life*, Bateson (2010, p. 26) describes a second stage of adulthood when 'the use of skills seems to be a central component in the satisfaction people find in their work, especially the kind of skills that involve a measure of improvisation, addressing problems that call for specific and often creative solutions rather than repetition of standard solutions'. Theories of intrinsic motivation have long included learning driven by curiosity or interest as a defining characteristic. Eccles and Wigfield (2002) describe this as central to the idea of intrinsic motivation. Intrinsically motivated individuals have a preference for hard or challenging tasks and strive for competence or mastery (Dweck, 2000). Both interest and challenge underlay a sense of novelty in the work itself.

Hall (2002) identifies learning cycles as critical for appreciating the potential of later career stages. He argues that individuals move through stages of exploration, trial, establishment, and mastery through each position or role in their career. Similarly, popular press accounts highlight intellectual stimulation and exciting new challenges as factors driving engagement in encore careers (Freedman, 2006; Bank, 2009). As such, the desire for novelty in their work motivated participants, for example:

> There was this recipe that I was applying each time and it was starting to get too similar, meaning I knew what I needed to do. I could go in with my eyes closed in many of these environments and do precisely a version of what I'd done before and that was probably the biggest element. I would use the word 'recipe'. It wasn't quite that specific, but the approach was very, very similar. And I felt like I needed more variety.

Another participant described prior work as 'mundane', stating that it 'wasn't all that creative', which motivated the pursuit of a second act career. Similarly, another participant highlighted the opportunity to 'keep learning and up to date' as a driving force in the decision to pursue an encore career.

Work Flexibility

Work flexibility, or the lack thereof, has long been a consideration of work–family researchers because of its potential to decrease work–family conflict and increase productivity (Greenhaus and Beutell, 1985; Allen et al., 2013). The importance of flexibility is rooted in resource theory on the basis that individuals have limited time, attention and energy to allocate across work and non-work domains (for example, Marks, 1977; Kirchmeyer, 1992; Allen et al., 2013). Flexible work arrangements generally provide flexibility in terms of 'when' work gets done (for example, flextime or flexible scheduling) or 'where' work gets done (for example, flexplace or telecommuting) (Hill et al., 2001; Allen et al., 2013).

Research shows that employees who perceive more work flexibility, in terms of having personal control and autonomy in their work environment, report lower levels of work-to-family interference and intentions to quit

(Porter and Ayman, 2010). Work flexibility also positively contributes to employee engagement (Richman et al., 2008) and organizational commitment (Ng et al., 2006). In talking about factors motivating their decision to pursue encore careers, participants highlighted their desire to have more control over where and when they worked. For example: 'I thought of this as being more flexible and conducive to having a family.' Similarly: 'I wanted to be home, to see my wife a lot more. Now, I'm able to exercise more too.' Furthermore, when being asked about some of the best aspects of their encore careers, participants talked about their ability to be more autonomous:

> I work harder than I worked in public accounting, but things are much more under my control. That's what I like about this job. So it's much more flexible and you know what, they pay me to think about whatever it is that I would like to learn. That's incredibly privileged.

Occupational Characteristics

Some occupational characteristics may be seen as less desirable by those in mid- to late life stages regardless of an individual's particular job or role. There is evidence for this in studies of early retirement, whereby age has been shown to impact one's ability or desire to conform with certain occupational characteristics, for example, intense physical demands or substantive complexity, the degree to which work requires thought and independent judgement (Hayward, 1986). Holtom and colleagues' (2008) comprehensive model identifies characteristics specific to the job itself as antecedents to turnover, including routinization, job scope, autonomy, and role states.

Whereas some characteristics are specific to a particular job, the characteristics we highlight are a part of the occupation or industry and therefore simply changing jobs would not change these demands. Such characteristics include travel, relocation requirements, and the consequences of an organization's product or services. Examples are public accounting careers that require extensive travel to client sites, military careers requiring extended individual deployment every one to two years, and the biomedical device industry where product development and production requires both intense accuracy and time sensitivity. Such aspects of an occupation could be viewed as exciting or exhilarating in earlier career stages. In contrast, these characteristics were associated with feelings of stress or pressure by our participants and aspects of their careers that wore them down over time. It is notable that participants also described these characteristics as stressful because of the negative impact on how they engaged in their work and non-work lives. As one participant whose first career was in the military described:

> The intensity and lifestyle of an officer in the military is that you are on the job 24/7 so your time is always accounted for. You earn 20 days per year of paid leave, not vacation. And as you become more senior, you always have to be reachable, so you never feel like you are away from it, you're always 'on duty'. I started looking for new positions where my wife's family is from. We wanted to set down roots, we had moved 20 times in 20 years.

The stressors of travel were salient to several participants, for example: 'Best thing is I'm home. I was on the road a total of 17 years. And in that time I was on the road no less than half of my time, two weeks per month.' In contrast, the stressor of the product itself was pressure that a former biotech executive was happy to leave behind:

> I am more relaxed. One of the things that is hard to portray about the [biomedical device] business is not only do you have day-to-day numbers you're worried about, but what we're dealing with is life-supporting, life-sustaining and there's always that elevated level of intensity around it and I don't miss that.

Finally, the changing nature of the occupation itself was reason to leave: 'The [banking] industry had changed a great deal during deregulation ... I found my autonomy was really getting less and less ... I didn't feel that you could be as involved and do as much decision-making, and you couldn't work as independently.'

MODERATING CONDITIONS FOR ENCORE CAREER TRANSITIONS

Career decisions are made in the context of individuals' broader life. Thus, the motivating factors identified above interact with gender, financial resources, and interpersonal support, which serve to either facilitate (or inhibit) individuals' transition into an encore career.

Gender

Although all respondents discussed several motivating factors impacting their decision to pursue encore careers, work flexibility was the most salient motivator for the women we interviewed. In contrast, it was secondary or tertiary concern (if mentioned at all) for the men, generally seen as an additional benefit that came along with a different set of occupational characteristics. Research has identified family demands as a classic work–life pull factor causing women to leave the workforce (March and Simon, 1958; Cabrera, 2007; Bagger et al., 2008). The popular press also focuses on professional women opting out of the workforce (for example,

Belkin, 2003; Wallis, 2004; Story, 2005). What makes this research unique is that engagement in encore careers is not about opting out, or leaving the workforce, but instead about multiple factors that motivate voluntarily leaving careers in which one has achieved objective success in order to become fully engaged in a different occupation.

Research has shown that both the protean and kaleidoscope career models are conceptually useful in understanding women's career decisions and transitions (Cabrera, 2009). Specifically, the protean career model provides additional support for work–life dynamics as a salient factor influencing women to pursue encore careers. Under the protean career model careers are self-guided by personal values and subjective measures of success (Hall, 1976, 2004). Women who pursue protean careers act as self-agents who customize their careers in response to their personal values and particular life situations, for example, the desire to achieve work–life balance, and redefine the meaning of career success (Valcour et al., 2007; Valcour and Ladge, 2008; Cabrera, 2009). Since positive work–life dynamics are highly prioritized by women, pursuing an encore career allows women to act as self-agents, directing their own careers by engaging in a new career field that helps them to find success both at work and home. As one female participant commented:

> My kids went to daycare so I saw both sides – I saw the working parents that have their kids in there for 60 hours a week and I saw the stay-at-home moms. I always felt like, who am I comparing myself to? You want to compare yourself to everything the stay-at-home mom was doing, the playdates, whatever. And so that was just really hard for me. And I still feel like I did a good job with that but I never felt in either place . . . I had other people around me giving 120 per cent, and I couldn't give 120 per cent because of my family and I wasn't willing to give 120 per cent.

Furthermore, according to the kaleidoscope career model, decisions made at the mid-point of women's careers are primarily driven by a desire for balance, or the satisfying integration of work and non-work life (Mainiero and Sullivan, 2006; Sullivan and Mainiero, 2008). As one participant noted: 'I wanted to teach at this [college] level, so that I could be home with my children more. That was a big part of it.'

According to another female participant:

> I think it [encore career] lets me max out in both areas [work and life]. My schedule would have been more regular [in first career], but I wouldn't have had the access to all the kids' activities. I manage my own schedule; I think the degree of autonomy we have in this career is just tremendous. I feel really very fortunate.

Financial Resources

Popular press accounts suggest financial resources play a role in the decision to pursue encore careers. Encore careers provide an opportunity for individuals to engage in fulfilling work while ensuring financial stability and consistency, even if the objective compensation does not match that earned in previous employment (Freedman, 2006; Bank, 2009; Goggin, 2009). Thus, financial resources are a condition that may facilitate the transition to encore careers.

In early retirement research the lack of a financial need to work and retirement of one's spouse are conditions that have been identified as 'pull' factors for career exit. It is notable that pull factors are perceived positively and with voluntary exit, whereas push factors (for example, poor health, disliked work, employer policies) are perceived as negative and more involuntary (Shultz et al., 1998). Encore careers are voluntary turnover decisions, theoretically consistent with retirement research. However, financial resources moderate the encore career motivations rather than serve as pull factors toward no longer working.

We see a distinct difference between genders in how financial resources are conceptualized, whether individually or as a family unit. Our male participants described their individual financial resources as a condition facilitating their entry to encore careers. In contrast, our female participants described finances in conjunction with their spouse's work status, discussing their financial resources as a family unit.

All male participants described financial resources as necessary for 'entertaining' encore career factors. For example: 'I am sceptical whether I would let my mind entertain this if I didn't have that financial comfort. So if I had month-to-month bill-paying pressure, then I don't think I would have taken the risk. I would have looked from afar and said gee, it would have been fun, but I don't know if I would have done it, just for those reasons.'

For female participants, financial resources were viewed holistically, including their spouses' earnings and their broader life circumstances. One, in particular, described this relationship most clearly:

> My husband has a job. I don't have to be a bazillionaire. We have a nice house, we go on a nice vacation. I want my kids to go to college. But we're not extravagant people, so I think some of those people have much more extravagant lifestyles than we did. I took a huge pay cut to come here, but that wasn't what it was about. I never think about my paycheck here. I don't care if I'm working at midnight on something because it's ok and I'm coming up with something fun for class the next day.

Interpersonal Support

According to social cognitive career theory, relationships facilitate or hinder individuals' career choices at all life stages (Lent et al., 1994, 2002). Support from relationships at work and home have long been viewed as buffers to negative events, moderating the effects of stress (Viswesvaran et al., 1999) and work–life conflict (Martins et al., 2002) on career outcomes. We suggest that interpersonal relationships moderate the factors motivating encore careers thus serving to facilitate (or impede) this transition.

Researchers have also identified both work and personal relationships as influences on the meaning of work (Rosso et al., 2010). Family members are often the most salient non-work relationships that provide support (Murphy and Kram, 2010) and confirmation that the work is right for the individual (Brief and Nord, 1990). The interaction between the individual's positive perceptions and affirmation from key relationships, particularly spouses and friends, was highlighted by several participants, consistent with extant research on career transitions (for example, Motulsky, 2010). For example: 'My wife was supportive. She had enjoyed traveling with the military and meeting people but was ready to settle down too.' Another participant stated: 'I had a lot of support for my decision. My colleagues at the bank thought I was very lucky and my family and friends all thought it was a great decision.'

One participant's spouse was not supportive, which made the transition more challenging and demonstrates the importance of interpersonal support. Fortunately, she had other sources of non-work support from family and friends. This is notable because family members become a larger proportion of social networks during childrearing years, even more significantly for women whose overall social networks tend to contract in size (Munch et al., 1997; Volpe and Murphy, 2011). She explained: 'My husband was extremely angry when was I making up my mind about what I was going to do in my career; I wanted to go back to school, he did not bargain for me to go back to school . . . he didn't like that. He got an associate's degree, but that's as far as he went. My mother was supportive. My friend was supportive, so friends were fine.'

Since all of our participants were valued employees, their direct supervisors tended to be against this transition, for example: 'My boss tried to talk me into staying in the Marine Corps. Most Marines leave when they can no longer be promoted, but that was not my case.' Other colleagues were more willing to offer support, for example: 'The last couple of years I didn't love my boss. I had a better relationship with my boss's boss, so I had to have a talk with him. He knew me for 20 years. And he had definitely seen the transition of my passion for what I did, to maybe not as passionate.'

ENCORE CAREER OUTCOMES

Careers scholars define career success in terms of objective or subjective outcomes. Objective success frequently includes salary, salary growth, and/or promotions, whereas subjective success is operationalized as job or career satisfaction (Hall, 2002; Heslin, 2005). By definition, encore careers are initiated after achieving some degree of objective success. Breaking away from traditional career metrics is part of the motivation itself, thus outcomes of this transition do not have a clear linkage with objective success. As a result, the outcomes of encore careers are mainly subjective, including a new professional identity, career satisfaction, satisfaction with work–life balance, and life satisfaction.

Overall, participants were proud and enjoyed their new professional identity. They expressed satisfaction with the outcomes of their encore career transition in both work and non-work domains. One participant commented: 'There's the pride of being an educator; it's a good life. I love what I do, so when I go talk to students there's a great pride in telling them about the school.' Another participant remarked: 'I don't reference the bank career very often. It's kind of odd now that I think about it. At this point this is the one [academic career]. It's the envy of my friends.'

Of particular importance is the idea that participants reflect on their career satisfaction in terms of others' reactions to their careers, rather than solely self-referent criteria (that is, compared to their own aspirations), an implicit assumption in many assessments (Heslin, 2005). In addition, they enjoy discussing their new careers:

> Before, I would say I worked in an accounting firm and I had been there for 20 years. Anybody who knew the industry would know that I would have to be a partner. But it was uncomfortable for me to say I was a partner, does it sound like I'm bragging? It's easy for me to say now that I'm a faculty member. What's really odd is people want to talk more about that than they ever wanted to talk about accounting.

DISCUSSION

Our research develops a foundation for conceptualizing encore careers by exploring predictive motivating factors and conditions that facilitate this transition. When individuals are influenced by a desire for increased meaning, fun, novelty or flexibility in their work, or a change in occupational characteristics, they seek opportunities to pursue encore careers by fully engaging in work that is completely different and outside the comfort zone of their previous career. Enacting encore careers leads individuals to develop a new professional identity, and results in revived career and life satisfaction, as well as a greater sense of work–life balance.

By introducing the concept of encore careers into the academic literature, this chapter moves the conversation beyond popular press accounts focused primarily on defining this career transition and advocating community and programme support for encore careers (Freedman, 2006; Bank, 2009; Goggin, 2009). We expand the discussion of voluntary turnover, moving beyond the traditional push/pull factors that drive individuals to move from one organization to another (for example, March and Simon, 1958; Lee and Mitchell, 1994; Maertz and Campion, 2004) by focusing on antecedents that attract individuals who are successful, high achievers in their current occupations, to make substantive transitions from a primary to a secondary career path.

Popular press accounts have framed encore careers as a Baby Boomer or retirement career phenomenon pursued by individuals during their 'golden years' as a way to enhance financial security and engage in work that promotes the 'greater good' (see, for example, the premise behind the encore.org organization). Contrastingly, our participants never mentioned age as a factor driving them to pursue encore careers. For these individuals pursuing an encore career was a conscious decision to develop a new professional identity often requiring periods of trial and exploration as well as self-investment in additional training such as graduate education.

The women in our sample transitioned into their second career act at an earlier age than did the men. On average, the women we interviewed pursued encore careers at 38 years old, though it is notable that all had achieved considerable success in their industries (for example, partner in firm, senior management) and thus made significant financial sacrifices to do so. This life stage difference (earlier mid-career versus later mid-career for men) may help explain our finding of work flexibility as an especially salient factor driving women to transition to encore careers since it is likely that mid-career women experience the overlap of intense family and professional demands that often motivates them to seek alternative career paths. Existing career research further supports the notion that career decisions made toward the mid-point of women's careers are often driven by the desire for the satisfying integration of work and non-work life (Mainiero and Sullivan, 2006; Sullivan and Mainiero, 2008) and points to switching organizations, reducing hours, or completely disengaging from the paid workforce as key career transitions women make. Our research found that rather than simply switching organizations, going part-time, or 'opting out', women who became fully engaged in a different occupation by pursuing encore careers were able to more satisfactorily integrate work and non-work life. The question of why women are willing to make such a significant change earlier in their lives than men is worthy of further exploration.

The motivating factors identified here may also interact with one another to magnify the positive outcomes of encore career transitions. For example, Ng et al. (2006) found that a three-way interaction among supportive management communication, opportunity for learning, and work flexibility increased organizational commitment. Likewise, individuals' simultaneous experience of multiple motivational factors (meaningful work, fun, novelty, work flexibility, occupational characteristics) in encore careers would likely act in conjunction to heighten their experience of career satisfaction or other subjective measures of career success. Finally, this research uncovered moderating conditions that affect the salience of these factors and facilitate the transition to encore careers including gender, financial resources, and interpersonal support. Gender differences in the conceptualization of financial resources were particularly important. Men discussed finances in individual terms whereas women assessed their finances in terms of family resources. This may reflect societal stereotypes of the male breadwinner as well as gender expectations around careers (DeArmond et al., 2008; Broadbridge and Simpson, 2011; Vandello et al., 2013). In addition, non-work and non-supervisory sources of interpersonal support were often more supportive of encore career transitions. This complex interplay of resources, relationships and career development also reflect gender differences in opportunities and constraints in the extant literature (for example, Volpe and Murphy, 2011).

LIMITATIONS AND FUTURE RESEARCH

Participants were identified through an exploratory convenience sample consisting of six full-time college faculty members. Although this limits the generalizability of this research, it is important to note that the most popular job choice for encore careers is teaching (Freedman, 2006). In addition, referral-based sampling is a well-established and statistically validated technique for accessing hard to reach populations (Salganik and Heckathorn, 2004). Future research should include individuals outside of higher education to confirm and potentially revise or expand the factors found as motivating individuals to pursue encore careers. Future research should include participants of various relationship statuses, with and without children, as it is likely that both impact the role of financial resources and interpersonal support we found to moderate factors motivating encore career decisions.

Future quantitative studies are needed to confirm the qualitative factors identified as motivating individuals' decisions to pursue encore careers. Collecting quantitative data would also enable examination of the relationships among these motivating factors and subjective career success outcomes such as career satisfaction, satisfaction with work–life balance, and life satisfaction. In addition, quantitative data would allow a more fine-grained analysis of gender differences in the salience of motivating factors.

Future qualitative research should focus on the process that individuals move through when transitioning from a primary to a secondary career, in order to expand and delineate the current 'black box' of the encore career transition in our model. A more comprehensive understanding of encore careers would be gained by studying the activities involved and sequencing of this career transition process. This kind of analysis would also provide practical insights for advising individuals interested in pursuing encore careers.

The trend towards encore careers began as a Baby Boomer phenomenon and thus it is unknown how this may unfold for future generations. Contrary to popular press accounts, empirical research on generational value differences shows an increase in leisure and extrinsic (status and money) values between Baby Boomers and later generations (Twenge et al., 2010). Millennials (born 1978–2000) do not have higher altruistic work values (for example, helping, societal worth) than previous generations (ibid.) although they came of age when multiple career transitions were more common (for example, Arthur and Rousseau, 1996) and the idea of values-based work is more frequently expressed (Hall, 2002). Clearly, there are many opportunities for future research and practical insights into encore careers.

REFERENCES

Alboher, M. (2012), *The Encore Career Handbook: How to Make a Living and a Difference in the Second Half of Life*, New York: Workman Publishing Company.
Allen, T.D., R.C. Johnson, K.M. Kiburz and K.M. Shockley (2013), 'Work–family conflict and flexible work arrangements: deconstructing flexibility', *Personnel Psychology*, **66**(2), 345–76.
Arthur, M.B. and D.M. Rousseau (1996), *The Boundaryless Career*, Oxford: Oxford University Press.
Bagger, J., A. Li and B.A. Gutek (2008), 'How much do you value your family and does it matter? The joint effects of family identity salience, family-interference-with-work, and gender', *Human Relations*, **61**(2), 187–211.
Bank, D. (2009), 'Encore careers and the economic crisis', *Generations*, **33**(3), 69–73.
Bateson, M.C. (2010), *Composing a Further Life: The Age of Active Wisdom*, New York: Knopf.
Belkin, L. (2003), 'The opt-out revolution', *New York Times Magazine*, 26 October, 42.

Bolton, S.C. and M. Houlihan (2009), 'Are we having fun yet? A consideration of workplace fun and engagement', *Employee Relations*, **31**(6), 556–68.

Brief, A.P. and W.R. Nord (1990), *Meanings of Occupational Work*, Lexington, MA: Lexington Books.

Broadbridge, A. and R. Simpson (2011), '25 years on: reflecting on the past and looking to the future in gender and management research', *British Journal of Management*, **22**(3), 470–83.

Cabrera, E.F. (2007), 'Opting out and opting in: understanding the complexities of women's career transitions', *Career Development International*, **12**(3), 218–37.

Cabrera, E.F. (2009), 'Protean organizations: reshaping work and careers to retain female talent', *Career Development International*, **14**(2), 186–201.

Cameron, K.S., J.E. Dutton and R.E. Quinn (2003), *Positive Organizational Scholarship: Foundations of a New Discipline*, San Francisco, CA: Berrett-Koehler.

DeArmond, S., M. Tye, P.Y. Chen, A. Krauss, A. Rogers and E. Sintek (2008), 'Age and gender stereotypes: new challenges in a changing workplace and workforce', *Journal of Applied Social Psychology*, **36**(9), 2184–214.

Dweck, C.S. (2000), *Self-theories: Their Role in Motivation, Personality, and Development*, Lillington, NC: Psychology Press.

Eccles, J.S. and A. Wigfield (2002), 'Motivational beliefs, values, and goals', *Annual Review of Psychology*, **53**(1), 109–32.

Fluegge, E.R. (2008), 'Who put the fun in functional? Fun at work and its effects on job performance', unpublished doctoral dissertation, University of Florida.

Fontana, A. and J. Frey (2000), 'The interview: from structured questions to negotiated text', in N. Denzin and Y. Lincoln (eds), *Handbook of Qualitative Research*, 2nd edition, Thousand Oaks, CA: Sage, pp. 645–72.

Fredrickson, B.L. and M.F. Losada (2005), 'Positive affect and the complex dynamics of human flourishing', *American Psychologist*, **60**(7), 678–86.

Freedman, M. (2006), 'The social-purpose encore career: baby boomers, civic engagement, and the next stage of work', *Generations*, **30**(4), 43–6.

Freedman, M. (2012), *The Big Shift*, New York: PublicAffairs.

Goggin, J. (2009), 'Encore careers for the twenty-first-century aging-friendly community', *Generations*, **33**(2), 95–7.

Greenhaus, J.H. and N.J. Beutell (1985), 'Sources of conflict between work and family roles', *Academy of Management Review*, **10**(1), 76–88.

Hall, D.T. (1976), *Careers in Organizations*, Pacific Palisades, CA: Goodyear.

Hall, D.T. (2002), *Careers In and Out of Organizations*, Thousand Oaks, CA: Sage.

Hall, D.T. (2004), 'The protean career: a quarter-century journey', *Journal of Vocational Behavior*, **65**(3), 1–13.

Hall, D.T. and D.E. Chandler (2005), 'Psychological success: when the career is a calling', *Journal of Organizational Behavior*, **26**(2), 155–76.

Hayward, M.D. (1986), 'The influence of occupational characteristics on men's early retirement', *Social Forces*, **64**(4), 1032–45.

Heckathorn, D.D. (1997), 'Respondent-driven sampling: a new approach to the study of hidden populations', *Social Problems*, **44**(2), 174–99.

Heslin, P.A. (2005), 'Conceptualizing and evaluating career success', *Journal of Organizational Behavior*, **26**(2), 113–36.

Hill, E.J., A.J. Hawkins, M. Ferris and M. Weitzman (2001), 'Finding an extra day a week: the positive influence of perceived job flexibility on work and family life balance', *Family Relations*, **50**(1), 49–58.

Holtom, B.C., T.R. Mitchell, T.W. Lee and M.B. Eberly (2008), 'Turnover and retention research: a glance at the past, a closer review of the present, and a venture into the future', *Academy of Management Annals*, **2**(1), 231–74.

Karl, K.A., J.V. Peluchette and L. Harland (2007), 'Is fun for everyone? Personality differences in healthcare providers' attitudes toward fun', *Journal of Health and Human Services Administration*, **29**(4), 409–47.

Karl, K.A., J.V. Peluchette, L. Hall and L. Harland (2005), 'Attitudes toward workplace fun: a three sector comparison', *Journal of Leadership and Organizational Studies*, **12**(2), 1–17.

Kirchmeyer, C. (1992), 'Nonwork participation and work attitudes: a test of scarcity vs. expansion models of personal resources', *Human Relations*, **45**(8), 775–95.

Lee, T.W. and T.R. Mitchell (1994), 'An alternative approach: the unfolding model of employee turnover', *Academy of Management Review*, **19**(1), 51–89.

Lee, T.W., T.R. Mitchell, L. Wise and S. Fireman (1996), 'An unfolding model of voluntary employee turnover', *Academy of Management Journal*, **39**(1), 5–36.

Lee, T.W., T.R. Mitchell, B.C. Holtom, L.S. McDaniel and J.W. Hill (1999), 'The unfolding model of voluntary turnover: a replication and extension', *Academy of Management Journal*, **42**(4), 450–62.

Lent, R.W., S.D. Brown and G. Hackett (1994), 'Towards a unifying social cognitive theory of career and academic interest, choice, and performance', *Journal of Vocational Behavior*, **45**(1), 79–122.

Lent, R.W., S.D. Brown and G. Hackett (2002), 'Social cognitive career theory', in D. Brown and Associates (eds), *Career Choice and Development*, 4th edition, San Francisco, CA: Jossey Bass, pp. 255–95.

Maertz, C.P. and M.A. Campion (2004), 'Profiles in quitting: integrating process and content turnover theory', *Academy of Management Journal*, **47**(4), 566–82.

Mainiero, L.A. and S.E. Sullivan (2006), *The Opt-out Revolt: Why People Are Leaving Companies to Create Kaleidoscope Careers*, Mountain View, CA: Davies-Black Publishing.

March, J. and H. Simon (1958), *Organizations*, New York: John Wiley.

Marks, S.R. (1977), 'Multiple roles and role strain: some notes on human energy, time and commitment', *American Sociological Review*, **42**, 921–36.

Martins, L.L., K.A. Eddleston and J.F. Veiga (2002), 'Moderators of the relationship between work–family conflict and career satisfaction', *Academy of Management Journal*, **45**(2), 399–409.

McDowell, T. (2005), 'Fun at work: scale development, confirmatory factor analysis, and links to organizational outcomes', unpublished doctoral dissertation, Alliant International University, California.

Motulsky, S.L. (2010), 'Relational processes in career transition: extending theory, research, and practice', *The Counseling Psychologist*, **38**(8), 1078–114.

Munch, A., J.M. McPherson and L. Smith-Lovin (1997), 'Gender, children, and social contact: the effects of childrearing for men and women', *American Sociological Review*, **62**(4), 509–20.

Murphy, W.M. and K.E. Kram (2010), 'Understanding non-work relationships in developmental networks', *Career Development International*, **15**(7), 637–63.

Ng, T.W.H., M.M. Butts, R.J. Vandenberg, D.M. DeJoy and M.G. Wilson (2006), 'Effects of management communication, opportunity for learning, and work schedule flexibility on organizational commitment', *Journal of Vocational Behavior*, **68**(3), 474–89.

Percheski, C. (2008), 'Women's employment, family structure, and social inequality', unpublished dissertation, Princeton, NJ: Princeton University.

Porter, S. and R. Ayman (2010), 'Work flexibility as a mediator of the relationship between work–family conflict and intention to quit', *Journal of Management and Organization*, **16**(3), 411–24.

Richman, A.L., J.T. Civian, L.L. Shannon, J. Hill and R.T. Brennan (2008), 'The relationship of perceived flexibility, supportive work–life policies, and use of formal flexible arrangements and occasional flexibility to employee engagement and expected retention', *Community, Work and Family*, **11**(2), 183–97.

Rosso, B.D., K.H. Dekas and A. Wrzesniewski (2010), 'On the meaning of work: a theoretical integration and review', *Research in Organizational Behavior*, **30**, 91–127.

Salganik, M.J. and D.D. Heckathorn (2004), 'Sampling and estimation in hidden populations using respondent-driven sampling', *Sociological Methodology*, **34**(1), 193–240.

Shultz, K.S., K.R. Morton and J.R. Weckerle (1998), 'The influence of push and pull factors

on voluntary and involuntary early retirees' retirement decision and adjustment', *Journal of Vocational Behavior*, **53**(1), 45–57.
Stone, P. (2007), *Opting Out? Why Women Really Quit Careers and Head Home*, Oakland, CA: University of California Press.
Story, L. (2005), 'Many women at elite colleges set career path to motherhood', *New York Times*, 20 September, A1.
Sullivan, S.E. and L.A. Mainiero (2008), 'Using the kaleidoscope career model to understand the changing patterns of women's careers: designing HRD programs that attract and retain women', *Advances in Developing Human Resources*, **10**(1), 32–49.
Super, D.E. and B. Sverko (1995), *Life Roles, Values, and Careers*, San Francisco, CA: Jossey-Bass.
Tews, M.J., J.W. Michel and A. Bartlett (2012), 'The fundamental role of workplace fun in applicant attraction', *Journal of Leadership and Organizational Studies*, **19**(1), 105–14.
Twenge, J.M., S.M. Campbell, B.J. Hoffman and C.E. Lance (2010), 'Generational differences in work values: leisure and extrinsic values increasing, social and intrinsic values decreasing', *Journal of Management*, **36**(5), 1117–42.
Valcour, M. and J.J. Ladge (2008), 'Family and career path characteristics as predictors of women's objective and subjective career success: integrating traditional and protean career explanations', *Journal of Vocational Behavior*, **73**(2), 300–309.
Valcour, M., L. Bailyn and M.A. Quijada (2007), 'Customized careers', in H. Gunz and M. Peiperl (eds), *Handbook of Career Studies*, Thousand Oaks, CA: Sage, pp. 188–210.
Vandello, J.A., V.E. Hettinger, J.K. Bosson and J. Siddiqi (2013), 'When equal isn't really equal: the masculine dilemma of seeking work flexibility', *Journal of Social Issues*, **69**(2), 303–21.
Viswesvaran, C., J.I. Sanchez and J. Fisher (1999), 'The role of social support in the process of work stress: a meta-analysis', *Journal of Vocational Behavior*, **54**(2), 314–34.
Volpe, E.H. and W.M. Murphy (2011), 'Married professional women's career exit: integrating identity and social networks', *Gender in Management*, **26**(1), 57–83.
Wallis, C. (2004), 'The case for staying home', *Time*, 22 March, 51–9.

APPENDIX

Turnover Forces and Definitions Outlined by Maertz and Campion (2004, p. 570)

Affective – current affective response (negative emotional response) to an organization.

Contractual – psychological contract obligations to an organization and violations of contract.

Constituent – commitment to people or groups in an organization.

Alternative – perceived alternatives to current job.

Calculative – anticipated future satisfaction associated with continued organization membership.

Normative – pressures to stay or leave an organization derived from expectations of others.

Behavioural – behavioural commitment to an organization (value of tenure and membership).

Moral – moral/ethical values about quitting.

27. Senior women, work–life balance and the decision to quit: a generational perspective
Deirdre A. Anderson and Susan Vinnicombe

The work–life balance debate has shifted from the emphasis on family, and particularly those with young children, to a broader perspective that encompasses wider sections of the workforce (Casper et al., 2007; Ransome, 2007; Darcy et al., 2012). In this chapter we examine the experiences of an elite group of women who have reached the top echelon of their organization, and therefore could be described as career-focused, and yet for whom life outside of work, including family, extended family and friends, is highly salient.

Our focus in this chapter is to address how the search for balance between the work and non-work domains affects the decision-making of a sample of women when they choose to leave their organization. The women had all achieved the level of partner within a major international consulting firm and will henceforth be referred to as 'women partners'.[1] The research was carried out on behalf of the firm who were committed to developing and retaining a diverse workforce and wanted to understand more about what would encourage senior female executives to stay within the firm. The firm had supported women's progression into partnership roles over a number of years. They had been successful in achieving a relatively large percentage of women partners. However, in the few years previous to the research request, the proportions of women partners exiting the firm had been significantly higher than the male partners. The firm and the researchers were therefore interested in finding out why these women partners had chosen to leave the organization.

We will begin with an examination of what is known about work–life balance in the context of women's careers. This will be followed by considering the concept of the ideal worker and the impact of family on career. We will explore generational differences with regard to work–life balance. After outlining the methodology we will present empirical evidence from the women themselves, comparing the perspectives through the lens of generational differences. Finally we will discuss the implications and make suggestions for future research.

CAREERS AND WORK–LIFE BALANCE

Women's professional and managerial careers have increasingly come under the spotlight as researchers have recognized that these do not fit the models derived from studies of men working in male-dominated organizations. New forms of careers have emerged, often labelled protean (Hall and Mirvis, 1996) or boundaryless (Arthur, 1994), requiring adaptability and flexibility but these did not give explicit attention to the differences between men's and women's typical careers. Similarly, more recent work examined work–life balance at different career stages as defined by age but, again, did not address the gendered aspects (Darcy et al., 2012). Further work identified the need to include relational elements in order to understand the greater complexities of the paths of women's careers (Gilligan, 1982; White, 2000; Mainiero and Sullivan, 2005; O'Neil and Bilimoria, 2005) and it is on this area that we will focus.

Women's careers have to be considered within the context of their whole lives, recognizing the challenges and stresses, choices and constraints that affect women's lives uniquely. Women experience balance, connectedness, interdependence, achievement and motivation in ways that encompass both their career and their relationships with family and friends (Gilligan, 1982). For instance, the kaleidoscope model (Mainiero and Sullivan, 2005) focuses on the 'fit' of work and family. Women talk about opportunities and possibilities as well as the blocks experienced in creating their own path that provide challenge and allow specific needs to be met. Just as a kaleidoscope presents a different pattern as the pieces move and are reflected in three mirrors, women face the three issues of challenge, balance and authenticity, which have to be addressed as they shape their career. So in the early career stage the model suggests that women are often concerned with challenge and achievement of goals, as they establish themselves in their career. Balance and authenticity are relevant but remain in the background. In mid-career, which is the time when many professional women tend to have children, the issue of balance comes to the fore as women face the often conflicting demands of work and family, which may be resolved by compromise. The model suggests that women are freed from such demands in the late career stage and they are then more able to make career choices that fit with their value systems, thus addressing the challenge of authenticity.

Similarly, O'Neil and Bilimoria (2005) suggested that women's careers develop through the three phases of idealistic achievement, pragmatic endurance and reinventive contribution. In the first phase, classified as between the ages of 24–35, women are likely to have an internal career locus, driven by the desire for job satisfaction, achievement and success.

Strategic decisions will be proactively made to ensure career progress. In contrast, the second phase (ages 36–45) is characterized by a more pragmatic approach during a time when there are greater demands in both professional and personal roles, calling into question the dominance of career within their lives. Frustration and dissatisfaction may be evident with regard to the workplace and career progress may have stalled. Following this phase, a more ordered career pattern emerges, with acknowledgement of the input of others into the direction their career has taken. During this phase of reinventive contribution (ages 46–60), there is a greater emphasis on giving to communities, organizations and families.

The theme of authenticity was highlighted by Ruderman and Ohlott (2004) in their framework for developing high-achieving women and was referred to as the desire to have healthy alignment between inner values and beliefs and outer behaviours. As with the two models above, this framework also identified age as being significant with regard to the importance of different factors in women's careers. The need for 'wholeness' was suggested to be relevant for those in their mid- to late thirties and is similar to the balance of work and other interests indicated in the mid-phases of the models above. Job performance is positively related to interests outside of the workplace and this framework includes the development of an organizational culture that recognizes and supports the demands from the non-work domain. Ironically, the flexible working initiatives that are often introduced as part of work–life balance initiatives in an attempt to create such a culture can result in imposed work intensification when workloads do not decrease in line with a contractual reduction in working hours (Kelliher and Anderson, 2010).

So a picture emerges of transitions throughout the career trajectory, which may be more of an unconscious and subtle recalibration over time rather than active shifts (Gordon et al., 2002). This is particularly relevant for women as the important years in moving up hierarchically in one's professional life often occur at the same time as the desire for, and the experience of, family life with children: 'It is clear that the early professional career is structured for maximum conflict with the family career' (Bailyn, 2004, p.1514). With this in mind, Moen and Sweet (2004) argue the case for policy-making and research to move from a focus on the work and family dichotomy to a more integrated approach to careers.

IDEAL WORKER

Despite the increasing recognition of the differing approach to career adopted by women, managers and professionals of both sexes are particularly susceptible to the 'ideal worker' norm of domesticity (Wharton, 2006) and the subsequent doubt over their commitment to their employer and their career if they stray from that ideal by adopting a pattern of work that involves less face time (Van Dyne et al., 2007). Face time refers to time spent in the workplace during more standard working hours when one is therefore available to work with colleagues on a face-to-face basis. The ideal worker has historically been seen as someone who can give their time unstintingly and willingly to their employing organization and have no conflicting demands on their time (Pitt-Catsouphes et al., 2006). Alongside this is the assumption of the existence of another adult based full-time in the home to attend to domestic and caring responsibilities. In the twenty-first century many families do not have such a structure of full-time breadwinner and full-time homemaker (Marks, 2006) and households may consist of different mixes of number of adults, age and number of children or no children, and presence or absence of elderly dependents (Ransome, 2007).

Two overlapping work–life balance discourses have been identified that fail to acknowledge these gendered assumptions (Lewis et al., 2007). The first one refers to personal control of time, suggesting that individuals are able to make their own decisions about priorities in their lives around work, career and family. Similarly, workplace flexibility, which ostensibly offers choices about where, when and how much to work, may also not challenge the gendered constraints to the adoption of flexible work arrangements, which are often seen as incompatible with senior management positions. This is particularly critical at early career stages when both women and men may be reluctant to avail themselves of flexibility because of the concern over perceived lack of commitment to their role and the organization (Darcy et al., 2012). Other studies clearly demonstrate the dissatisfaction of employees with the work–life initiatives that are available to them (Kossek et al., 2011).

IMPACT OF FAMILY

Men and women experience work–life conflict differently, with men regretting not seeing more of their children, whereas women express exhaustion at trying to maintain two roles (Liff and Ward, 2001). Much media attention resulted from Belkin's (2003) article in the *New York Times* about professional women leaving the workforce due to the pull of motherhood. The combination of such pull factors, combined with the push of job dissatisfaction, was suggested as an explanation for increasing numbers of women exiting. There has subsequently been a debate about whether motherhood is the primary factor in such a decision. Realistically women take career breaks or 'off-ramp' and organizations have been encouraged to make better provision for women to 'on-ramp', supporting their endeavours to rejoin organizational life (Hewlett and Luce, 2005). Of course, motherhood is not the only caregiving activity and provision of eldercare is increasingly a demand that has to be met and can be more unpredictable than the relatively routine arrangements that can be put in place for young children. Finding high-quality after-school care for older children (six+) also presents challenges (Moore et al., 2007). These many factors contribute to the belief by junior managers that motherhood would result in the 'end of their career' and this was linked to the small numbers of women with children in senior organizational positions (Liff and Ward, 2001).

GENERATIONAL LENS

A generation is commonly defined as an 'identifiable group that shares birth years, age location and significant life events at critical developmental stages' (Kupperschmidt, 2000, p.66). Differences are attributed to generational cohorts because of the potential influence of major events within the wider environment that affect the formation of personality, values and beliefs at critical stages in development (Macky et al., 2008). For the purposes of this study we used the classification given by Mainiero and Sullivan (2005) that describes those born between 1946 and 1960 as Baby Boomers and those born between 1961 and 1982 as Generation X (or GenXers).

The limited findings about generational differences with regard to work–life balance provide mixed conclusions. GenXers are generally regarded as valuing work–life balance more highly than Baby Boomers (Howe and Strauss, 2000; Callanan and Greenhaus, 2008; Sullivan et al., 2009) yet other studies confirm that Baby Boomers also value work–life balance highly (Beutell and Wittig-Berman, 2008; Cennamo and Gardner, 2008), referring to work–life balance as freedom.

METHOD

This chapter draws on findings from a qualitative study designed to explore why women partners had decided to leave a global professional services firm over the previous few years. Forty-seven women were contacted by the client to ask if they would participate in the study and the contact details of those who responded positively were passed on to the researchers. Thirty-one interviews were subsequently conducted representing a response rate of 66 per cent. Because of the global locations of the women, only one interview could be conducted face-to-face. The remaining 30 took place by telephone across eight different time zones during a period of three weeks. The interviews were semi-structured in nature and interview questions were emailed to respondents the day before the interview. The researchers gained permission from each respondent to record the interviews, which were then transcribed. For the purposes of this chapter a thematic approach to analysis was undertaken, supported by the use of NVivo software.

FINDINGS

Twenty-one women had most recently worked for the firm in North America and the remaining ten had been based in Africa, Australia, Asia or Europe. The women's period of attachment to the firm ranged from 4 to 29 years, with 18 having been there for more than 15 years. At the time of the interview 20 of the women were married or living with a partner; 4 had children who were grown up, 16 had children under the age of 18 years, and 11 did not have children.

In presenting the findings we examine the importance of the search for balance in the women's decision to leave the firm. They ranged in age from 34 to 57 at the time of leaving and we adopted a generational lens to analyse the data, comparing the Baby Boomers (who were the same age as O'Neil and Bilimoria's phase 3 women [46–60 years]) with the GenXers (who were the same age as O'Neil and Bilimoria's phase 2 women [36–45 years]). The career stages mentioned in the literature imply that women are in different places due to the link with age, whereas all of the women in this sample had reached the top of their career, hence our use of generation over career stage. In addition we contrasted those who were mothers and those who did not have children (Table 27.1) in order to explore any differences in terms of seeking work–life balance.

We found that many of the women in our sample had decided to give up their high-powered jobs to do something entirely different, to do voluntary work or to set up their own business. They described their decision

Table 27.1 Number of women partners by generation and parental status

	Those Without Children	Those With Children
Baby Boomers	6	10
GenXers	5	10

to leave as the culmination of many factors, not wishing to attribute the decision to any one particular incident. However, aspects of work–life balance featured in many of the interviews. Interestingly, nearly all of the women were keen to reflect back on their admiration and affection for the firm where they had worked happily for many years. This provided a positive context for the negative experiences that had triggered their departure from the firm.

Baby Boomers With No Children

These six women who did not have children talked about reaching an age where they were keen to move on in their lives. This was an age at which it was common to retire within their firm and at that particular time the option to do so was financially very attractive, offering future security. So it was portrayed as part of the normal course of events. Yet the interviews revealed other factors that had played a part in that decision. Several talked about the opportunity to get involved with voluntary work, for instance, which would benefit others:

> I turned 50 in September and just am feeling very strongly that the second half of my life has got to be worth more, it's got to be more meaningful, it's got to have a broader impact than just being a partner in (the firm), right? So I really have been very strongly thinking that I need to be doing something more valuable with my life. (Sherri)

Others talked of being ready to walk away from a pressured lifestyle and a couple of women specifically talked about wanting to spend time with elderly relatives, indicating that family demands from the non-work domain were important. For one woman such demands unexpectedly arose immediately following her retirement:

> My father became ill as well as my father-in-law and so we spent the first year after I retired just really caring for our families so we really turned into being caregivers at that time. And then we . . . let's see, we caught up with people and caught up with life. (Jacqui)

Beyond that need to provide care, was the idea of 'catching up' or being able to spend time on things other than work, something that another woman talked about when explaining her response to a request that she make a fundamental change in her role:

> I said well I don't think I can continue with that kind of life where I don't have time for myself because . . . if you move over to the other group where your client is on the other side of the world, your work hours are really stretched

quite a bit, so I said no, I don't think that will ever be an option for me, I don't want to even start considering that. I need to start having [pause] I want to have my evenings when I can do my own stuff. (Jamilah)

For this group of women balance was something that they had lived without but there were changing demands on their time, both within the workplace and from family. At the same time, they were questioning their own needs and desires to live their lives in a different way.

Baby Boomers With Children

The ten women in this category had children of varying ages up to 18 years and beyond. Again there were many factors involved in their decision to leave. For instance, they talked about the changes that were then taking place in the firm that were adversely affecting relationships as the leadership and strategic direction changed. There was an acknowledgement of a lack of challenge in the opportunities that were available to them, leaving them with a lack of passion and energy that was previously unfamiliar to them in their career at this firm. Many of them had thrived for years on such challenges and when those challenges were no longer there, they felt it was time to take stock and to reassess their life goals. For instance, the excessive level of travelling was questioned when other aspects of their job were no longer satisfactory with one woman talking of having reached a 'tipping point'.

Such ongoing travel demands, although long accepted as an essential part of their roles, became particularly unacceptable for some who were facing major changes in their family lives. One woman explained the limited roles offered to her while she was going through a divorce:

> They offered me three different roles, leadership roles, all of which would be travelling four to five days a week and I just felt I couldn't do that to my children. . . . The divorce was very unexpected and it was very hard for them and emotionally they needed me there . . . and so I just made a decision to stay with my family. (Aileen)

The main issue was the lack of flexibility on offer as it was presented as an 'all or nothing' situation with no sense of compromise or of balance. The firm did not recognize the women as 'whole persons' with other responsibilities. This short-sighted approach allowed little room for negotiation: 'I think if they had said to me . . . maybe we can work out something where you're only travelling two days a week . . . I might have stayed and I think today I would have been back full time' (Aileen).

Several of these women talked about wanting to spend time with their children and interestingly, they were particularly the ones with teenagers, wanting to have that time while they still had the chance to be involved in their lives. The issue of balance was not one of providing care for young children but the chance to share quality time with older children, having 'missed out' due to the demands of their roles when the children were younger:

> Primarily I left so that I could spend more time with my family. I was doing quite a bit of travelling at the time and my daughter was beginning high school and I felt that if I was going to spend time with her this was the time. And I wanted to spend the time with her before she went to college. (Kirsten)

Just one woman had children under the age of five years and she described a combination of wanting to care for her young children at the same time as an elderly relative had become very ill, presenting further demands from the non-work domain, demands that she wanted to be able to attend to. Others had grown-up children and yet they expressed the strong desire to be geographically close to them, especially when their role had previously taken them to a different continent for a number of years. Again, there was sense of inflexibility when negotiating with the firm: 'The problem for me was, even though my children were grown up, I had been away from my children for a long time and I wanted to get back to where my family was' (Lyddie). So the pull of family is clearly not just about the need to provide childcare for young children but a much more encompassing factor.

Generation X With No Children

These five women also described changes in the leadership of the firm and the changing expectations of the type of work that they would be expected to undertake. This caused them to re-evaluate their own career aspirations, questioning whether the firm could offer them opportunities that they would value. Several expressed a lack of support in their career going forward:

> The region was going through some reorganizations, some leadership changes and I decided it wasn't really potentially where I wanted to be. . . . There was little support for growing a new client base locally. It was everybody for themselves. Some of the people I worked with were leaving, so the people that I truly valued were no longer going to be around. (Amy)

The demands of the role of partner were relentless and the women talked of continuous pressure with no time to be able to recover, just the expectation that they could continue delivering at the same pace regardless of the toll it was taking on them. One woman described a particularly demanding role involving terminating the contracts of many employees at different locations:

> I'd spend all week doing this and I'd be in tears every Friday night driving home as I'd spent the week firing people and I was so exhausted that I was just emotionally drained and I spent the weekend sleeping because I just couldn't sleep during the week because I was so upset over it but there was never anybody that I felt that I could talk to about this. (Jolanda)

For her, the option to leave when the firm was seeking to shed partners provided much needed relief from a life that was completely out of balance. Additionally, there was recognition that she had actually met all of her career goals and that her aspirations were focused on personal, non-work issues.

As with the older women who did not have children, family considerations were still mentioned as driving forces in the decision to leave and travel continued to emerge as a critical theme in the ability to lead a balanced life. One woman talked of getting married relatively late in life and reassessing how she wanted to spend her time:

> It wasn't [pause] well yes it was the travel, but for me it was just that I was working for all those years and I had nothing to do and then I got married and it was like, hey, I can actually have a life. . . . All of a sudden I had a reason to be home every night. (Caitlin)

The extended family were factors for this group also, and in particular, the wish to be involved in caring for sick or elderly relatives. Such factors were acknowledged to be part of the myriad issues that contributed to their decision:

> I actually had some things in my personal life, a relative who was terminally ill, that made me also think about life and what I had not done and what I wanted to do and maybe realize how short life was. There were numerous reasons; it was a lot of small things. (Jolanda)

Generation X With Children

Six of the ten women in this group had children under five years and they spoke of the challenges of working in such a time-consuming role and at the same time trying to meet the needs of parenting young children. The issue was not about childcare per se, as these women earned high salaries, which allowed them to utilize the care of their choice, often a nanny. This group used the word 'balance' most often when talking about the demands from the work and non-work domains, referring of course to the lack of balance and the constant striving for such an elusive concept: 'Every once in a while I just came to the realization that you want to have this great career that requires a tremendous amount of

Senior women, work–life balance and the decision to quit 455

time and commitment and you just can't balance everything sometime' (Kim).

There was no sudden decision to leave but an increasing sense of the relentless nature of their role. They talked of 'not leading a life, but merely running a schedule' as they sought to find some way not just to meet the demands but also to be able to enjoy both 'job and mothering'. As one woman explained:

> Not only had my commute gotten longer but there was mounting frustration on my part with respect to being able to spend time with my children; I work many of the weekends and it's been until late at night, sometimes until 2 in the morning, sometimes at work and sometimes coming home and finishing up what I didn't get to do in the office. (Laura)

One woman painted a particularly vivid picture of the practical difficulties that may confront mothers of young children, explaining how she was asked to cut short her maternity leave when her child was three months old to take on a particular project in a different state. In order to maintain breastfeeding of her young baby she employed a nanny to accompany them both during their regular Monday to Friday spent away from home:

> The baby got on the flight with me every Monday morning at 6 am, up at 4 and on the flight at 6 and flew down to [name of place] when she was three months to nine months. I flew my nanny down too, she would stick with her during the day and I breastfed for nine months, you see, that whole thing. I would be in the middle of a meeting and I'd have to go out and express milk. The craziness of it, I would have to stand, there was no place to do this. Sometimes I'd have to lock the conference room and people would be like 'We have this conference room booked' and I'd be sitting there pumping away or even in the bathroom that had no combination and they'd open the door and I'd be standing right there boobs exposed, expressing milk, you know what I mean? It's things like that, it would be great if they were just thought through, simple things like that, that stuff we could do a lot for but we don't do. It got to the point where I said actually I'm leaving the firm. (Lisa)

The other contributing factors that emerged for three of the women in this group were medical issues of conceiving and bearing children. Complications after the birth of a child prevented one woman from being able to fly, severely limiting the options available to her. She also wanted to work flexibly, a request that was not looked upon favourably, although other women did talk of having done so for relatively short periods of time. Getting older was mentioned with regard to conceiving as well as the stress of the continuous travel demands:

> I wanted to try for a child and we'd been trying for five years. I was travelling an awful lot and it made it difficult so I thought that, well if I was going to have

a chance to have a baby this was the time that I'd have to try and do it. It was hard just getting pregnant and it would also be very hard to have a baby with the firm. I'd have to see and if I didn't get pregnant and have children, then I would reconsider and go for the high career model. Then I was headhunted, and I actually got pregnant pretty much one month after I started my new job. (Agnes)

This woman was concerned, not only that it was getting harder to conceive as she got older, but also that she would not be able to meet the demands of the role of partner in this firm if/when she had a baby/young child. At the time of the interview, aged 42, her child was almost a year old and she was successfully established in the senior role that she had moved to in a different organization.

The four women with older children (aged between 5 to 18 years) talked of wanting time and flexibility to be with their children, again describing a mounting sense of frustration, as the demands and pressures never eased with very long working hours, including weekends. Many of these ten women did not want to become 'stay at home moms' and several moved into senior roles within other organizations where they were able to use their skills and expertise and continue to develop and progress their careers. At the same time, the cultures of these new organizations with different work practices and an absence of extreme working hours resulted in their being able to spend the time with their families that they craved.

DISCUSSION AND CONCLUSIONS

In this chapter we have attempted to demonstrate how the search for balance was part of the decision to leave the organization for women who are Baby Boomers or Generation X, with or without children. It is not the preserve of the 36–45-year-old women. These women often felt that the changes in the direction of the firm had resulted in them being treated as commodities. They were dealing with the continual tensions of balancing a very demanding senior role and the needs of family in the wider sense of the word but those changes, brought about by major restructuring within the firm, broke the fragile equilibrium of their lives.

Different pictures emerged for these four groups of women partners. The Baby Boomers who did not have children were ready to move into retirement but they were defining retirement in multidimensional ways. By definition they had been working for many years, in relentlessly pressurized jobs, and they were keen to make time for both self and others and were striving to find greater meaning in their life, thus linking to the 're-inventive contribution' phase of O'Neil and Bilimoria's (2005) model.

The Baby Boomers with children displayed more of an attitude of frustration and irritation with the way they had been treated over what had often been a long career with the firm. They talked of a lack of energy and of the passion no longer being alive and they disliked the changes in the strategic direction of the firm. Perhaps because they were mothers, they did not have the freedom or the desire to move into complete retirement but talked of wanting to do different work in cultures that were more accepting of the realities they faced from the non-work domain.

The GenXers without children talked much more about work–life balance and were looking to the future, wanting to re-evaluate their career aspirations and the unfolding nature of their career. The fourth group of GenXers with children wanted to maintain challenging careers but also to have a sense of control over their lives, working in a culture more attuned to achieving a sense of balance.

A picture emerged of women above the glass ceiling who were facing a range of 'pull' and 'push' factors at a time in their lives when financial security offered them true choices. It appeared that the 'push factors' such as excessive travel demands, lack of support, feeling undervalued and unwelcome role changes, all in a masculine culture and career structure, were often the starting point for re-assessment of their position, in career and in life. If those 'push' factors are managed, then women may not turn to the 'pull' factors, such as family and alignment with values that often completed the decision process. The family and caregiving responsibilities and desires of women have to be part of the context for examining aspects of women's careers. The continual emphasis on competition, of fighting for clients, continual self-promotion and little teamwork does not sit comfortably with women's preferences for building and developing relationships.

It is interesting to consider the career phases and stages with respect to the level of seniority achieved. Inevitably, women achieve senior positions at different times in their lives and many of the women in this study achieved partnership in a professional services firm in their thirties. At the time of leaving the firm many had completed that role for more than 20 years whereas the youngest participant had been a partner for just four years. The career phase models fail to address the complexity of the lives of these senior women.

The demands of the role have an effect on the way they are able to live their lives. So we would argue that the level of seniority affects the salience of the factors identified in the literature at different ages or stages. What is interesting about this study are the ways in which the search for balance remains salient. However, the use of cross-sectional data is a limitation and does not allow for accurate interpretation of generational differences.

Similarly, the cross-national aspect of this study, while interesting, is not sufficient to examine potential contextual differences. A time lag study examining people at the same ages at different points in time would enable such differences to be separated from the age/career stage differences (Twenge, 2010).

NOTE

1. Where appropriate, we will also refer to 'male partners' to refer to men in consulting firms who have reached the level of partner.

REFERENCES

Arthur, M.B. (1994), 'The boundaryless career: a new perspective for organizational enquiry', *Journal of Organizational Behavior*, **15**(15), 295–306.

Bailyn, L. (2004), 'Time in careers – careers in time', *Human Relations*, **57**(12), 1507–21.

Belkin, L. (2003), 'The opt out revolution', *New York Times*, 26 October.

Beutell, N.J. and U. Wittig-Berman (2008), 'Work–family conflict and work–family synergy for generation X, baby boomers, and matures: generational differences, predictors, and satisfaction outcomes', *Journal of Managerial Psychology*, **23**(5), 507–23.

Callanan, G.A. and J.H. Greenhaus (2008), 'The baby boom generation and career management: a call to action', *Advances in Developing Human Resources*, **10**(1), 70–85.

Casper, W.J., D. Weltman and E. Kwesiga (2007), 'Beyond family-friendly: the construct and measurement of singles-friendly work culture', *Journal of Vocational Behavior*, **70**(3), 478–501.

Cennamo, L. and D. Gardner (2008), 'Generational differences in work values, outcomes and person–organisation values fit', *Journal of Managerial Psychology*, **23**(8), 891–906.

Darcy, C., A. McCarthy, J. Hill and G. Grady (2012), 'Work–life balance: one size fits all? An exploratory analysis of the differential effects of career stage', *European Management Journal*, **30**(2), 111–20.

Gilligan, C. (1982), *In a Different Voice: Psychological Theory and Women's Development*, Cambridge, MA: Harvard University Press.

Gordon, J.R., J.E. Beatty and K.S. Whelan-Berry (2002), 'The midlife transition of professional women with children', *Women in Management Review*, **17**(7/8), 328–41.

Hall, D.T. and P.H. Mirvis (1996), 'The new protean career: psychological success and the path with a heart', in D.T. Hall (ed.), *The Career is Dead – Long Live the Career*, San Francisco, CA: Jossey Bass, pp. 15–45.

Hewlett, S.A. and C.B. Luce (2005), 'Off-ramps and on-ramps', *Harvard Business Review*, **83**(3), 43–54.

Howe, N. and W. Strauss (2000), *Millennials Rising: The Next Great Generation*, New York: Vintage.

Kelliher, C. and D.A. Anderson (2010), 'Doing more with less? Flexible working practices and the intensification of work', *Human Relations*, **63**(1), 83–106.

Kossek, E., B.B. Baltes and R.A. Matthews (2011), 'Innovative ideas on how work–family research can have more impact', *Industrial and Organizational Psychology*, **4**(3), 426–32.

Kupperschmidt, B.R. (2000), 'Multigeneration employees: strategies for effective management', *Health Care Manager*, **19**(1), 65–76.

Lewis, S., R. Gambles and R. Rapoport (2007), 'The constraints of a "work–life balance" approach: an international perspective', *International Journal of Human Resource Management*, **18**(3), 360–73.

Liff, S. and K. Ward (2001), 'Distorted views through the glass ceiling: the construction of women's understanding of promotion and senior management positions', *Gender, Work & Organization*, **8**(1), 19–36.

Macky, K., D. Gardner and S. Forsyth (2008), 'Generational differences at work: introduction and overview', *Journal of Managerial Psychology*, **23**(8), 857–61.

Mainiero, L.A. and S.E. Sullivan (2005), 'Kaleidoscope careers: an alternate explanation for the "opt-out" revolution', *The Academy of Management Executive*, **19**(1), 106–23.

Marks, S.R. (2006), 'Understanding diversity of families in the 21st century and its impact on the work–family area of study', in M. Pitt-Catsouphes, E.E. Kossek and S. Sweet (eds), *The Work and Family Handbook: Multi-disciplinary Perspectives and Approaches*, Hillsdale, NJ: Lawrence Erlbaum Associates, pp. 41–65.

Moen, P. and S. Sweet (2004), 'From "work–family" to "flexible careers": a life course reframing', *Community, Work and Family*, **7**(2), 209–26.

Moore, S., P. Sikora, L. Grunberg and E. Greenberg (2007), 'Managerial women and the work–home interface: does age of child matter?', *Women in Management Review*, **22**(7), 568–87.

O'Neil, D. and D. Bilimoria (2005), 'Women's career development phases: idealism, endurance, and reinvention', *Career Development International*, **10**(3), 168–89.

Pitt-Catsouphes, M., E.E. Kossek and S. Sweet (2006), 'Charting new territory: advancing multi-disciplinary perspectives, methods and approaches in the study of work and family', in M. Pitt-Catsouphes, E.E. Kossek and S. Sweet (eds), *The Work and Family Handbook: Multi-disciplinary Perspectives and Approaches*, Hillsdale, NJ: Lawrence Erlbaum Associates, pp. 1–16.

Ransome, P. (2007), 'Conceptualizing boundaries between "life" and "work"', *International Journal of Human Resource Management*, **18**(3), 374–86.

Ruderman, M.N. and P.J. Ohlott (2004), 'What women leaders want', *Leader to Leader*, **31**, 41–7.

Sullivan, S.E., M.L. Forret, S.M. Carraher and L.A. Mainiero (2009), 'Using the kaleidoscope career model to examine generational differences in work attitudes', *Career Development International*, **14**(3), 284–302.

Twenge, J.M. (2010), 'A review of the empirical evidence on generational differences in work attitudes', *Journal of Business and Psychology*, **25**(2), 201–10.

Van Dyne, L., E.E. Kossek and S. Lobel (2007), 'Less need to be there: cross-level effects of work practices that support work–life flexibility and enhance group processes and group-level OCB', *Human Relations*, **60**(8), 1123–55.

Wharton, A.S. (2006), 'Understanding diversity of work in the 21st century and its impact on the work–family area of study', in M. Pitt-Catsouphes, E.E. Kossek and S. Sweet (eds), *The Work and Family Handbook: Multi-disciplinary Perspectives and Approaches*, Hillsdale, NJ: Lawrence Erlbaum Associates, pp. 17–40.

White, B. (2000), 'Lessons from the careers of successful women', in M.J. Davidson and R.J. Burke (eds), *Women in Management: Current Research Issues, Vol. 2*, London: Sage.

28. Exploring the career decisions of professional women with dependent children
Helen M. Woolnough and Jane Redshaw

Figures suggest that in the UK today there are more women with dependent children in the workforce than ever before (Office for National Statistics, 2013). Since 1996 when comparable records were first kept, the number of working mothers has increased by almost 800000 to 5.3 million (ibid.). This increase is due to changes in societal attitudes, legislation and family-friendly policies that have positively impacted on the ability of many women to enter into and remain in the workforce. Research has shown that professional women in the UK (that is, those who have acquired professional knowledge through high levels of experience and/ or extensive study), are likely to return to work after having children, and recent figures, for example, suggest that approximately nine in ten professionals or associate professionals and over eight in ten managers returned to work after childbirth (Chanfreau et al., 2011). It is important to note, however, that not all women have experienced these changes equally and research has revealed that mothers from disadvantaged backgrounds are less likely to return to work after childbirth (Smeaton, 2006).

For mothers who do return to work after having children, the figures highlighted above mask the realities many face in reconciling work and home life (McRae, 1993; Hilbrecht et al., 2008; Greenhaus et al., 2012). Also, such figures do not reveal the factors influencing a mother's decision to return to work and the extent to which decisions made are a result of personal choice or external pressures, for example, financial. For example, given the extensive research that has documented how career interruptions to have a family result in wage penalties for women, the need to return to work within a certain time frame to financially support the family is, for many women, a very real concern (Theunissen et al., 2011). This chapter addresses conceptual and theoretical arguments in relation to the career decisions of working mothers, particularly professional women in the workplace. The chapter also presents initial results from an exploratory comparative qualitative study to investigate career decisions and satisfaction with career decisions made among two cohorts of professional women with dependent children at different stages of the lifespan (Woolnough and Redshaw, 2013). Finally, recommendations are offered to support professional women with dependent children.

In the UK, women are now entitled to strengthened legislation concerning maternity benefits and entitlements and there is welcome emerging recognition of the role of fathers in the form of paternity rights. Mothers take an average of 39 weeks' maternity leave, whilst 71 per cent of men take two weeks' paternity leave or less (Chanfreau et al., 2011) and the Equality Act introduced in 2010 in the UK (Gov.uk, 2010) provides guidance for flexible working rights for parents who want to adapt their working pattern due to childcare responsibilities. Until recently in the UK, parents of children younger than six (18 in the case of disabled children), had the right to apply for flexible working providing they have completed 26 weeks' continuous service with their employer. From June 2014, however, this right to request flexible working has been extended to all employees (Department for Business Innovation and Skills, 2014). Employers are not obliged to accept requests, but they do have a statutory duty to take the request seriously. Flexible working may take the form of changes to the hours worked, changes to the times when those hours are worked (for example, term-time only working), and/or an ability to work from home.

Research has reported, however, that workplace flexible working is far from widespread. A study conducted by the Equality and Human Rights Commission (2007) found that an estimated 6.5 million people in Britain are not fully using their talents in the labour market, but might be enabled to do so if better flexible working practices were available. Of this 6.5 million, 56 per cent were women, suggesting that many more women could make valuable contributions to the workforce if provided with improved opportunities to balance work and home life. Furthermore, research has reported the implicit and explicit prejudice experienced by many women (and men) who take advantage of family-friendly work initiatives (Burke and Nelson, 2002). Often, engaging in such initiatives is regarded by managers and fellow colleagues as a lack of commitment to work (Brown, 2010).

Clearly not all women who worked before having children want to return to work (Lovejoy and Stone, 2012). This may be a decision women make before leaving work for maternity leave or a mother who previously intended to return to work may decide to remain at home following the birth of her child (Woolnough and Redshaw, 2013). Popular media in the UK and USA have highlighted the 'opt out' trend where well-educated, married professional women choose to leave their careers either temporarily or permanently to become full-time mothers (Grant-Vallone and Ensher, 2011; Lovejoy and Stone, 2012). The decisions professional women make once having children have received academic attention and the extent to which a woman's decision to exit the workforce is a subjective choice or a consequence of anticipated 'push and pull factors', including, for example, tensions reconciling the demands of work and family, is the subject of academic discourse (Kumra, 2010; Carlson et al., 2011; Greenhaus and Powell, 2012).

According to Hakim's (1996) preference theory, women differ in their attachment to work. These differences influence the decision about whether to return to work or not and if so, in what capacity. Prior to having children, women generally work full-time and this reflects their work-centred attitudes and behaviour (ibid.). Upon having children, however, their priorities change and many women either reduce hours at work or leave the workforce altogether. For Hakim (1996), this represents a lack of commitment to paid work and a career. Subsequent research has contested Hakim's work, highlighting myriad factors that may need to be taken into consideration when deciding whether or not to return to work and indeed the capacity in which to return (Houston and Marks, 2003; Kumra, 2010). Houston and Marks's (2003) longitudinal study of 349 first-time mothers, for example, revealed that almost a quarter of the women in their sample were unable to return to work as they had originally planned during their pregnancy, providing support for the idea that career decisions made are likely to be a combination of preference and circumstance.

A considerable number of mothers who return to work in the UK change their working pattern from full-time to part-time employment. The Office for National Statistics (2012) shows that in the second quarter of 2011, 37 per cent of mothers with dependent children were working part-time (compared to 6 per cent of fathers). Although in recent times fathers have requested flexible working patterns to fulfil their childcare responsibilities, part-time workers are still predominantly women. Working part-time may be a realistic solution for women (and men) who wish to remain in the workforce but combine this with caring for children. Hakim's (1996) work again considers that mothers who work part-time are likely to do so to accommodate their domestic needs, reflecting a lack of commitment to their career. Empirical work investigating the career of female part-time nurses in the National Health Service (NHS) has, however, challenged this theory (Lane, 2004; Davey et al., 2005). Respondents in Lane's survey of over 600 qualified nurses working part-time in the NHS reported a high degree of under-achievement in their career advancement. Lane (2004) argues that the very fact the nurses in her study reported under-achievement in their career progression means that they did value their careers. Subsequently, what theorists have mistaken for a lack of commitment may actually reflect people channelling efforts into social and family issues because their career opportunities working part-time are significantly limited.

Certainly, literature has revealed that part-time posts tend to result in a downgrading of the role and studies have shown that women who return to work after having children have had to accept demotion in order to work part-time hours (Houston and Marks, 2003; Grant et al., 2006). Consequently, women may find themselves unable to utilize the full range of skills and talents they possess. Female part-time workers face disadvantage with regard to lack of access to training and development, being less likely to gain promotions, and less likely to be provided with opportunities to supervise others (Burke and Nelson, 2002). Also, there is a distinct lack of provision for part-time workers at senior organizational levels (Tomlinson, 2006). This means that women may be forced to act in lower-level roles due to the absence of more senior part-time positions they would be capable of filling, given the opportunity (Equality and Human Rights Commission, 2007; Las Heras and Hall, 2007).

The transition back to work after having children can be a difficult time for women and faced with real or perceived lack or organizational support and potential prejudice for engaging in family-friendly work initiatives, it is not surprising that many talented women face difficulties in the workplace and beyond (Millward, 2006; Cabrera, 2009; Carlson et al., 2011). Certainly, it is well documented that, frustrated by lack of career opportunity and the demands of balancing work and home, women leave the workplace to start their own business (Hewlett and Luce, 2005; Hunt and Fielden, 2006). In summary, the academic literature and popular discourse highlights that, although mothers now enjoy strengthened legislation concerning maternity benefits and entitlements, progress in relation to supporting women reconcile work and home life when they return to work is somewhat limited.

Based on a review of the issues discussed in the literature, the authors conducted an exploratory qualitative study to investigate anticipated and real career decisions made by two cohorts of professional women in the North of England at differing stages of the lifespan. Consistent with previous empirical work, the study addressed the relationship between intention and subsequent behaviour (Houston and Marks, 2003). The study also examined the factors that influenced these career decisions and how women felt about the career decisions they had made in retrospect. Specifically, the study investigated comparisons between two cohorts of professional women with children. Cohort 1 consisted of 15 women whose first child was born between 2011 and 2006: essentially these were women whose first child was five years old or younger (pre-school age in the UK). Cohort 2 consisted of 15 women whose first child was born between 1990 and 1995: for these women, their first child was approximately 18 years old and therefore either nearing or at the age when he or she would no longer be considered a 'dependent child' in the UK. The research compared the two cohorts to identify the extent to which the experiences of women have changed (or not) in the past 15–20 years.

Interviewees were accessed through contacts using a snowballing approach (Mason, 1994) and data were collated through semi-structured, face-to-face interviews to facilitate the ability to explore salient issues and themes. Specifically, factors influencing career decisions and satisfaction with the career decisions made in retrospect were addressed at two stages: (1) during late pregnancy with first child and (2) when returning to work (or not). Interviews lasted approximately one hour. They were recorded (with permission) and transcribed for data analysis, which followed a thematic approach (Ritchie and Spencer, 1994).

Demographic data revealed that the average age of women in cohort 1 when they had their first child was 32 and the average age of women in cohort 2 was 30. Before falling pregnant with their first child, all women in both cohorts were working full-time. Furthermore, at this time all women in both cohorts were married or living with their partners and all husbands or partners were earning a comparable or higher salary. No restriction was placed on area or type of professional role to elicit the experiences of women within an array of professions. Women in both cohorts were employed in areas of work including accountancy, teaching, medicine, human resources, retail and project management. The following discussion presents an overview of the main themes emanating from the data in relation to the stages addressed in the interviews.

STAGE 1: DURING LATE PREGNANCY

Thematic analysis of the interview materials revealed that during late pregnancy, all but one of the women in cohort 1 (women whose first child was born between 2011 and 2006) planned to return to work after the birth of their first child. There was a sense that returning to work was a fait accompli and as such the possibility of leaving the workforce to care for their child on a full-time basis was not generally discussed with husbands or partners. Essentially, women in cohort 1 disclosed that there was not much of a decision to make. Women in cohort 1 expected to return to work and they considered that their spouse or partner also expected them to return. Women in cohort 1 reported that during late pregnancy they planned to return to work within the same organization on a part-time basis to combine motherhood with maintaining their careers. No women in this cohort expressed a desire to return to full-time employment whilst their child was a baby. Generally, women in cohort 1 were satisfied with their anticipated arrangements at this time. Two respondents explained: 'I always absolutely knew I would go back to work. I didn't question it at all, not for a second! I knew that I would go back but I always assumed that I would go back part-time. I didn't even see an issue with that. [Husband] and I didn't even discuss it. We just both assumed that I would work part-time' (Sarah, age 35, cohort 1); 'I never really thought about it. I always knew I'd go back [to work] after having [child]. Ideally three days' (Hannah, 35, cohort 1).

Analysis of the interview materials, however, revealed that a few women in cohort 1 anticipated that they would either have to leave their organization or return to work at a lower grade to facilitate part-time work: 'I couldn't do my role part-time so I knew that I'd have to leave work. I didn't want to work full-time after having [child]', (Gemma, 36, cohort 1), and: 'There were other people who had come back and done three days so I didn't envisage that would be a problem but I knew I couldn't come back to the same role on a three-day basis so I'd have to be demoted' (Emily, 36, cohort 1).

Women in cohort 1 revealed that at this stage perceived financial pressure was the main factor influencing their anticipated decision to return to work. Whilst the financial rewards of working appeared paramount, it became clear through the interviews that the sense of personal fulfilment and self-identity derived from their working life also influenced their career decisions at this time. The following quotes highlight these factors: 'My husband said that he wouldn't fund my lifestyle. We needed my salary to contribute towards the mortgage. He pretty much expected me to go back to work. I think he would have resented me if I hadn't' (Frances, 34, cohort 1), and: 'I always enjoyed work and I just couldn't imagine staying at home with a child for five days, it's just not what I wanted to do' (Sarah, 35, cohort 1).

Similarly to cohort 1, most women from cohort 2 (women whose first child was born between 1990 and 1995) also planned to return to work after the birth of their first child. Again, many women in cohort 2 anticipated that they would return to work within the same organization and it was interesting to note that in contrast to cohort 1, several women in cohort 2 stated that they planned to return to work full-time. Analysis of the interview data revealed a difference in the main factor influencing the decision to return to work. Women in cohort 2 reported concerns relating to the detrimental impact time away from work would have on their career progression. Respondents commented: 'My expectation was that I would return to work. I had worked so hard at my career. It would have been difficult to keep my career at that level and take time off. I was the only woman at that time who had a child' (Mary, 55, cohort 2), and: 'The profession moves on so quickly, I thought it would be harder to go back at a later date' (Rosie, 48, cohort 2).

Women in cohort 2 did, however, express similar comments to cohort 1 in relation to the personal fulfilment and self-identity derived from their working life. The following respondent commented: 'Everyone worked, it was part of their identity, I wanted to have both' (Annie, 53, cohort 2). Some women in cohort 2 expressed a desire to exit the workforce when their baby was born. These women either commented on a lack of financial pressure and therefore more freedom to decide whether to return to work or not, or acknowledged that they were unable to combine both motherhood and work in their preferred capacity and suggested that: 'We were in a position that we could manage without my income. I had an image of a stay at home mum, I wanted to look after my daughter, I thought I would find it difficult to leave my baby with someone else' (Jenny, 52, cohort 2), and: 'I couldn't do the work I was doing on a part-time basis, I wanted to have children and spend time with them so I stopped work' (Amy, 56, cohort 2).

Thematic analysis of the interview materials revealed similarity between the cohorts at stage 1 in that women in both cohorts 1 and 2 generally anticipated that they would return to work after their first child was born. However, the main reason offered for this differed. For women in cohort 1 the decision to return to work or not was primarily influenced by perceived financial pressures. For women in cohort 2, more concerns were expressed relating to the detrimental impact time away from work would have on career progression. Interestingly, more women in cohort 2 at this stage highlighted that they considered several options before deciding whether to return to work or not and if so, in what capacity. This is in contrast to the women in cohort 1 who at this stage were more definite in their assumption that they would return to work, albeit on a part-time basis.

STAGE 2: RETURNING TO WORK AFTER THE BIRTH OF THE FIRST CHILD (OR NOT)

The vast majority of women in cohort 1 disclosed that they had taken between 9 and 12 months' maternity leave and then returned to work within the same organization, in the same role, on a part-time basis after having their first child. This is consistent with the anticipated arrangements that women in cohort 1 outlined in stage 1: during late pregnancy. One respondent stated: 'Yes I did return to my previous role once [child] was about a year old. I went back three days a week' (Mary, 36, cohort 1). Again, women in cohort 1 generally highlighted financial pressures and the personal fulfilment and self-identity that work afforded them as the main factors influencing their career decisions. The following quotes reflect these findings: 'We can't afford for me not to work. I think when you're used to having money you don't realize the impact of not having money' (Suzanne, 31, cohort 1), and: 'I enjoy work. I went back for some adult conversation!' (Maddy, 32, cohort 1). Several women, however, commented that they decided not to return to work as previously planned. This was due to emotions associated with leaving their baby. As one respondent said: 'I just couldn't bear to leave her' (Olivia, 36, cohort 1).

The extent to which women in cohort 1 were able to manage their work and family demands appeared to influence whether they were satisfied with the career decisions they had made. Women in cohort 1 outlined numerous key organizational and personal factors influencing whether or not they felt they could make their professional lives work. These included: the extent to which work can be flexible, a supportive boss and colleagues, a supportive and 'hands on' partner and satisfaction with the childcare they had in place either in the form of family support and/or private nursery. In the words of one respondent: 'The extent to which work can be flexible is key. I've managed to negotiate hours that mean I can drop off [child] at nursery and back to collect [child]. When [child] is well and we've all slept it's fine. When [child] is poorly it can be a nightmare trying to reorganize things so I can look after [child]' (Ruby, 31, cohort 1).

Interestingly, several women who had returned to work on a part-time basis expressed dissatisfaction and indicated that there was a difference between the rhetoric and reality of working part-time. One respondent suggested that: 'I think working part-time you get the worst of both worlds. The organization demands more of you than you can do in the hours you're supposed to work and children demand more from you than you have the time or energy to give' (Grace, 35, cohort 1). Furthermore: 'Officially I work part-time but often I feel like I'm trying to shoe-horn a full-time role into part-time hours' (Mary, 36, cohort 1). Despite this, some women in cohort 1 reported a sense that employers and colleagues considered them to be less committed to their careers because they were working part-time.

Analysis of interview materials revealed that the majority of women in cohort 2 had taken between three and five months' maternity leave and then returned to work as planned after their child was born. Similarly to women in cohort 1, women in cohort 2 returned to work but in a much shorter period of time. Again, women in cohort 2 highlighted the same organizational and personal factors as women in cohort 1 influencing the extent to which they could make their professional lives work. As with cohort 1, a few women in cohort 2 decided not to return to work due to emotions associated with leaving their child. However, women in cohort 2 reported that difficulties arose over a period of time once they returned to work and consequently there was a mismatch between initial intention and subsequent behaviour. For these women managing work and family demands proved problematic, as outlined in the following quotes: 'My full-time job didn't fit with regular childcare. Nurseries closed at 6 pm and I couldn't always make it back for then. I had to reduce my hours, which meant changing the nature of my job. There was a sense of having taken a step backwards' (Mandy, 49, cohort 2), and: 'Working and looking after children was far more tiring and complex than I thought' (Ami, 51, cohort 2). It is important to note that all women in cohort 2 went on to have subsequent children. Just over half of women in cohort 2 had two children in total and the other half ultimately went on to have three children. Interestingly, analysis of the data materials for cohort 2 revealed the impact of the second child on career decisions. Within two years of the birth of the second child almost all respondents in cohort 2 had reduced their working hours further or had withdrawn from the workforce entirely. Respondents offered a variety of reasons for this, including difficulties managing childcare for two children and the cost implications of childcare for more than one child that made work prohibitive, highlighted by the following respondent: 'I just about coped with one child but when my second child came along it became impossible to maintain the same hours. It was just too complicated to organize childcare and work those hours in that role with two children' (Janet, 52, cohort 2). Many of these women ultimately returned to the workforce after, on average, a seven-year break but they generally returned to less demanding roles requiring fewer skills and qualifications. There was a clear sense that exiting the workforce had impacted on their career. Some women were accepting of this; others expressed dissatisfaction and commented, for example, that: 'Ultimately my career just fizzled out' (Orla, 51, cohort 2). These issues were not reported by cohort 1 due to returning to work more recently than cohort 2 and many not experiencing a return to work with more than one child. It may be the case that women in cohort 1 who go on to have more children encounter these issues in future.

CONCLUSION

This chapter first addressed conceptual and theoretical arguments in relation to the career decisions of working mothers, particularly professional women in the workplace. Second, the chapter also presented initial results from an exploratory comparative qualitative study to investigate career decisions, and satisfaction with career decisions made between two cohorts of professional women with dependent children at different stages of the lifespan. Cohort 1 consisted of 15 women whose first child was five years old or younger. Cohort 2 consisted of 15 women whose first child was approximately 18 years old. The research compared the two cohorts to identify the extent to which the experiences of women have changed (or not) in the past 15–20 years. Main findings from the study along with recommendations to support professional women with dependent children are discussed.

First, it is important to acknowledge the limitations of the study. The study involved a small number of professional women who were demographically very similar limiting external validity. Additionally, the study relied on self-reported data (Mason, 1994). It would, for example, be useful to include husbands and partners in future research. Furthermore, there may have been issues with memory recall, particularly for cohort 2 who were asked to reflect on experiences 15–20 years ago. Despite its limitations the study revealed some interesting results. Consistent with previous research, most women in cohort 1 planned to return to work on a part-time basis after their first child was born (Houston and Marks, 2003; Grant et al., 2006). For women in cohort 1, intention to return to work was often linked to perceived financial pressures. It would appear that, for cohort 1, financial planning and lifestyle prior to pregnancy depended on two salaries, meaning that to maintain this, women were required to return to work. This was not, however, the only factor influencing their decision to return to work or not. Personal fulfilment and a self-identity acquired through work also influenced the decision to return. Although the financial implications of not working were frequently mentioned, thematic analysis of the interview materials revealed that work was about much more than this for many women.

Again, women in cohort 2 generally considered that they would return to work after their first child was born. Most women in cohort 2 reported that they planned to return to work on a part-time basis but some intended to return full-time and a few planned to leave work after their child was born. For women in this cohort, financial pressures did not appear to figure as much in their decision-making. Rather, women in cohort 2 reported concerns relating to the detrimental impact taking time away from work would have on their careers, that if they stepped out of their profession they would be unable to return. Again, this was not the only factor influencing their decision to return to work. Women in cohort 2 also discussed the sense of personal fulfilment and self-identity work afforded them.

Interestingly, women in cohort 1 appeared to express an expectation that they would return to work after having children. This is arguably a positive finding, suggesting that improvements in legislation and advances in flexible working mean that professional women now feel able to return to work (Chanfreau et al., 2011). However, it could be argued that improved legislation and advances in flexible working may have increased the expectation of professional women to return to work. This study revealed that women in cohort 1 did not generally discuss returning to work with their husbands or partners. Rather, there appeared to be an implicit understanding that these women would return to work and that, for the majority, this would be on a part-time basis. For women in cohort 2 there was much more variability around the decision to return to work or not, which may be indicative of less protective legislation and limited opportunities for flexible working at the time but may also reflect the exploration of alternative options.

A further revealing finding suggested that a shift in career decision-making came within a few years of a subsequent child being born. Within two years of a second child being born all women in cohort 2 had further reduced their working hours or withdrawn from the workforce entirely. Many women in cohort 2 then returned to the workforce an average of seven years later but to roles requiring fewer skills and qualifications. As a result, such women often reported underachieving in their careers. This shift in career decision-making was not reported by women in cohort 1, as generally these women had not experienced a return to work with two or more children. This is an important finding in relation to the impact of multiple children on managing work and family life. It is likely that both personal and organizational factors need to be addressed to retain talented professional women with any number of children but particularly multiple children. For example, although flexible working was theoretically available for many husbands and partners, particularly in cohort 1, it was exclusively mothers as opposed to fathers who made the necessary adjustments to their working patterns once their child was born. Expanding opportunities for and encouraging fathers to also adopt flexible working may impact on the ability of professional mothers and indeed the whole family to reconcile work and home life. Future research is required to address the extent to which the women in cohort 1 who return to work with subsequent children face increasing conflict in reconciling work and home life.

Both cohorts outlined limitations associated with part-time working. Women from both cohorts commented on the lower status of part-time work and difficulties of managing to complete professional roles within part-time hours and this is consistent with previous research (Burke and

Nelson, 2002; Las Heras and Hall, 2007). The similarity between the cohorts is an interesting finding and suggests that despite increased availability and acceptability of professional women returning to work part-time, such women face penalties for doing so. Further work is needed to redress the status of part-time work and for many professional roles there appears to be a need to develop an increased understanding of what constitutes part-time work.

Additionally, both cohorts outlined similar key organizational and personal factors influencing the extent to which they were satisfied with the career decisions they made. These included: the extent to which work can be flexible, a supportive boss and colleagues, a supportive and 'hands on' partner and satisfaction with the childcare they had in place. Again this similarity is an interesting finding. Over time, women in cohort 2 were frequently forced to make career adjustments because of dissatisfaction with one or more of these factors, often precipitated by returning to work after having multiple children, thereby causing a mismatch between what they would have liked to have achieved in their careers and the reality of their situation. Consequently, for women in cohort 2 their careers often slowed down or even stagnated. It is yet to be determined whether or not women in cohort 1 will encounter the same barriers.

In conclusion, the study revealed much similarity between the two cohorts despite the 15–20 year gap. Although there were reported differences in the primary motivating factor for returning to work, ultimately women in cohort 1 who decided to return to work appeared to be facing many of the same issues reconciling work and home life as their counterparts in cohort 2, despite the 15–20 year gap. Although mothers now experience strengthened legislation concerning maternity benefits and entitlements and there have been advances in flexible working, progress in relation to supporting women reconcile work and home life when they return to work is somewhat limited. Women may be more inclined to return to work after childbirth but the extent to which they feel supported and valued once they return is questionable. Additional research is required to help families and employers find solutions to retain female talent in the workforce following childbirth, thereby contributing to the development of a diverse workforce capable of meeting the challenges of the ever-changing world of work.

REFERENCES

Brown, L.M. (2010), 'The relationship between motherhood and professional advancement: perceptions versus reality', *Employee Relations*, **32**(5), 470–94.

Burke, R.J. and D.L. Nelson (2002), *Advancing Women's Careers: Research and Practice*, Oxford: Blackwell.

Cabrera, E. (2009), 'Fixing the leaky pipeline: five ways to retain female talent', *People and Strategy*, **32**(1), 40–46.

Carlson, D.S., J.G. Grzywacz, M. Ferguson, E.M. Hunter, C.R. Clinch and T.A. Arcury (2011), 'Health and turnover of working mothers after childbirth via the work–family interface: an analysis across time', *Journal of Applied Psychology*, **96**(5), 1045–54.

Chanfreau J., S. Gowland, Z. Lancaster, E. Poole, S. Tipping and M. Toomse (2011), *Maternity and Paternity Rights and Women Returners Survey 2009/10*, Department for Work and Pensions Research Report No. 777.

Davey, B., T. Murrells and S. Robinson (2005), 'Returning to work after maternity leave: UK nurses' motivations and preferences', *Work, Employment and Society*, **19**(2), 327–48.

Department for Business Innovation and Skills (2014), *Making the Labour Market More Flexible, Efficient and Fair*, accessed 8 December 2014 at https://www.gov.uk/government/policies/making-the-labour-market-more-flexible-efficient-and-fair/supporting-pages/encouraging-modern-workplaces-and-flexible-working.

Equality and Human Rights Commission (2007), *Sex and Power: Who Runs Britain?*, Manchester, UK: EHRC.

Gov.uk (2010), *Equality Act 2010*, London: HMSO, accessed 8 December 2014 at http://www.legislation.gov.uk/ukpga/2010/15/contents.

Grant L., S. Yeandle and L. Buckner (2006), 'Working below potential: women and part time work', working paper, Centre for Social Inclusion, Sheffield Hallam University, UK.

Grant-Vallone, E.J. and E.A. Ensher (2011), 'Opting in between: strategies used by professional women with children to balance work and family', *Journal of Career Development*, **38**(4), 331–48.

Greenhaus, J.H. and G.N. Powell (2012), 'The family-relatedness of work decisions: a framework and agenda for theory and research', *Journal of Vocational Behavior*, **80**(2), 246–55.

Greenhaus, J.H., J.C. Ziegert and T.D. Allen (2012), 'When family-supportive supervision matters: relations between multiple sources of support and work–family balance', *Journal of Vocational Behavior*, **80**(2), 266–75.

Hakim, C. (1996), *Key Issues in Women's Work*, London: Athlone Press.

Hewlett, S.A. and C.B. Luce (2005), *Off-ramps and On-ramps: Keeping Talented Women on the Road to Success*, Boston, MA: Harvard Business School Press.

Hilbrecht, M., S.M. Shaw, L.C. Johnson and J. Adrey (2008), '"I'm home for the kids": contradictory implications for work–life balance of teleworking mothers', *Gender, Work and Organization*, **15**(5), 454–76.

Houston, D.M. and G. Marks (2003), 'The role of planning and workplace support in returning to work after maternity leave', *British Journal of Industrial Relations*, **41**(2), 197–214.

Hunt, C.M. and S.L. Fielden (2006), 'Online coaching for female entrepreneurs', in D. McTavish and K. Miller (eds), *Women in Leadership and Management*, Cheltenham, UK and Northampton, MA, USA: Edward Elgar Publishing.

Kumra, S. (2010), 'Exploring career "choices" of work centred women in a professional service firm', *Gender in Management: An International Journal*, **25**(3), 227–43.

Lane, N. (2004), 'Women and part-time work: the careers of part-time NHS nurses', *British Journal of Management*, **15**(3), 259–72.

Las Heras, M.L. and D.T. Hall (2007), 'Integration of career and life', in D. Bilimoria and S.K. Piderit (eds), *Handbook on Women in Business and Management*, Cheltenham, UK and Northampton, MA, USA: Edward Elgar Publishing.

Lovejoy, M. and P. Stone (2012), 'Opting back in: the influence of time at home on professional women's career redirection after opting out', *Gender, Work & Organization*, **19**(6), 631–53.

Mason, J. (1994), 'Qualitative interviewing: asking, listening and interpreting', in M.B. Miles and A.M. Huberman (eds), *Qualitative Data Analysis*, 2nd edition, Thousand Oaks, CA: Sage.

McRae, S. (1993), 'Returning to work after childbirth: opportunities and inequalities', *European Sociological Review*, **9**(3), 317–38.

Millward, L.J. (2006), 'The transition to motherhood in an organizational context: an interpretative phenomenological analysis', *Journal of Occupational and Organizational Psychology*, **79**(3), 315–33.

Office for National Statistics (2012), *Gender Working Patterns*, accessed 8 December 2014 at http://www.ons.gov.uk/ons/about-ons/what-we-do/publication-scheme/published-ad-hoc-data/pre-june-2012/gender/index.html.

Office for National Statistics (2013), *Women in the Labour Market: Full Report 2013*, accessed 11 April 2014 at http://www.ons.gov.uk/ons/dcp171776_328352.pdf.

Ritchie, J. and L. Spencer (1994), 'Qualitative data analysis for applied policy research', in A. Bryman and B. Burgess (eds), *Analysing Qualitative Data*, London: Sage, pp. 173–94.

Smeaton, D. (2006), 'Work return rates after childbirth in the UK trends, determinants and implications: a comparison of cohorts born in 1985 and 1970', *Work, Employment & Society*, **20**, 5–25.

Theunissen, G., M. Verbruggen, A. Forrier and L. Sels (2011), 'Career sidestep, wage setback? The impact of different types of employment interruptions on wages', *Gender Work & Organization*, **18**(S1), 110–31.

Tomlinson, J. (2006), 'Routes to part-time management in UK service sector organizations: implications for women's skills, flexibility and progression', *Gender, Work & Organization*, **13**(6), 585–605.

Woolnough, H.M. and J. Redshaw (2013), 'An exploratory study to investigate career choice and satisfaction among two cohorts of professional women with children at different stages of the lifespan', in Proceedings of the British Psychological Society Annual Conference, 9–11 April 2013, Harrogate, UK.

29. Retirement – a new beginning or the beginning of the end?
Adelina M. Broadbridge and Agneta Moulettes

Planning for retirement is a complex process influenced by personal preferences, resources, economic factors, institutional policies, and social norms (Szinovacz et al., 2013). Retirement has been described as a distinct stage in the life course, and one that in the twentieth century has been linked with an infrastructure of support (Phillipson, 2013). However, at the beginning of the twentieth century few people formally retired; this was reserved for the rich middle classes. Even though some countries had already introduced state-made provision for people to retire (for example, Sweden in 1913), it did not reach full maturity until the middle of the twentieth century, and it was not until then a set retirement age in Europe became the norm. In the UK this was set to 65 for men and 60 for women, while the official retirement age in Sweden was set to 65 for both men and women (Henkens and Schippers, 2012; Werner, 2013). With life expectancy rates being around 70 the meaning of retirement was clearly some respite before death.

Today many more people are living longer and various macro-level factors have led to a series of changes regarding policies for retirement and, as Phillipson (2013, p.144) points out, retirement is a 'desirable new stage in life', providing choices rather than waiting for death. Towards the end of the twentieth century in response to environmental factors, there were provisions made for early retirement. For example, in the UK, voluntary redundancy packages became attractive to those who could retire in their fifties yet be able to draw on a company pension. Of course, this was a privileged state for only some (mainly men), and a very much middle-class view; many working-class people were not afforded these choices and because of various constraints had no alternative than to work on until the official state retirement age. They did not have private pension schemes to enable them to retire early and have a standard of living that allowed them to enjoy their retirement at a certain standard of living. Depending on external circumstances the attitude towards older workers and their place in the organization and retirement has changed over the years. For example, while early retirement was introduced as a strategy to lower unemployment caused by economic crises and technological development in the 1970s, retirement today is often perceived as an unaffordable luxury (McManus et al., 2007; Phillipson, 2012).

Shultz and Henkens (2010) note that the sustainability of the pensions systems in Western countries are under question, and today we see that European laws are changing regarding retirement policies. For example, Norway and Sweden have moved the retirement age from 65 to 67. In the UK, official retirement ages have been equalized between women and men, while the drawing of the state pension will be raised between 2044 and 2046 to 68 (Gov.uk, 2014). With an ageing population, the proportion of older workers in the European labour force is increasing, and the notion of retirement and what it means to individuals is set to change again. In some European countries (for example, France, Germany and the UK) age discrimination laws also mean that people can carry on working once they have reached the official retirement age, and some people are selecting this option (Sargent et al., 2013). Moreover, as Phillipson (2013) reminds us, retirement and its place in post-industrial economics has currently been called into question. Issues of how to incorporate older workers fully into the labour market and expectations of values and benefit of the post-retirement period have led to claims of a reinvention, including new pathways, new meanings and new arrangements (Beehr and Bennett, 2007; Sargent et al., 2013).

The meaning and process of retirement can signify different things to different people depending on their individual, household and societal circumstances, and it has increasingly been seen as part of self-management (Sterns and Kaplan, 2003; De Vos and Segers, 2013). Szinovacz et al. (2013) argue that in planning their retirement, employees consider the state of the economy (macro), firm climates and conditions (meso), and their own personal ability and willingness to retire at a certain age (micro).

Based on the preceding paragraphs, this chapter explores what retirement means to women about to retire, or having recently retired, in the current economic climate. It examines the choices perceived available to pre-retirement and retired people and their attitudes towards retirement. From our findings we are able to deduce that not everyone approaches retirement in the same way. Davies and Jenkins (2013) categorize individual-level experiences of the retirement transition into five positions: clean breakers; continuing scholars; opportunists; the reluctant; avoiders. We also categorize retirees depending on how they view themselves and their overall attitudes to retirement. However, our typology differs from theirs, which partly may be due to the fact that that we, instead of using a matched sample (which in their case consists of academic staff), include people with a variety of professions and who either have retired or are still working.

WORK AND RETIREMENT TRANSITIONS

Several researchers have considered people's decisions for retirement and show it is not a straightforward move from being in work to being in retirement, nor is it one that engenders the same feelings for people. Post et al. (2013) suggest that retirement is influenced by career stage, surfacing the case for different approaches to retirement planning, depending on career stage and organizational context. They found that high work centrality is associated with retiring later and those with positive attitudes to retirement seek to retire earlier. Ekerdt et al. (1996) also show the heterogeneity of people's retirement by drawing attention to the five categories used to describe their plans, that is, plans to retire completely, partially, change jobs, never retire, and being uncertain about retirement. Warren and Kelloway (2010) show how work attitudes predict people's own perceptions of their life, age and hence retirement, while Ekerdt (1998) identified a phase of remote anticipation when people begin to organize their lives and work with a view to future retirement. Three stages of retirement have been identified by Szinovacz (2013), from pre-retirement planning to retirement transition to full retirement. Retirement patterns have changed over the years and there are more phased retirement schemes available nowadays or people taking 'bridge' jobs (Cahill et al., 2006; Phillipson, 2013; Pleau and Shuman, 2013). Hall (2002) reconceptualized careers and suggested people may experience personal and professional growth in the later stages of their careers and engage in a new learning cycle, rather than disengage altogether.

Retirement is seen as a process (see August, Chapter 30 in this handbook) rather than a singular event determining the end of paid work, a process that Loretto and Vickerstaff (2013, p. 65) describe as 'messy and disruptive'. While Zaniboni et al. (2010) describe it as lengthy and complex, various aspects, both internal and external to the individual, impinge on retirement decisions. These will include the current demographic and economic labour market conditions, as well as an individual's (or household's) social background, financial circumstances (including pension provision and expectations) and characteristics, their health, their occupation, work conditions, career values and self-concept and social networking (De Vos and Segers, 2013; Loretto and Vickerstaff, 2013; Münderlein et al., 2013; Pleau and Shuman, 2013; Post et al., 2013; Szinovacz et al., 2013). Loretto and Vickerstaff's (2013) work with 57 couples in middle- and lower-income status reveal that women's retirement trajectories depend on their partner's pathway and circumstances, and that men's decisions and circumstances dominate. Similar conclusions were arrived at by Moen and Spencer (2006) in their study on micro and macro aspects of life after retirement. Others were influenced by parents and friends; some were influenced to retire as they had seen contemporaries dying, thus recognizing their own mortality. Other people, they argue, drift into retirement owing to ill health or unemployment.

All these factors present themselves as either choices or constraints to each person concerned, and are likely to impact the person's perceptions and experiences of retirement. Factors such as the ability to retire, the influence of others and the centrality of work all play a part in a person's perception of retirement (Loretto and Vickerstaff, 2013; Post et al., 2013). With regard to retirees themselves there are those who would like to retire, but are afraid of the unknown (known as 'hesitant retirees') and 'reluctant retirees' comprising those who have been thrown into retirement owing to factors out of their control (such as redundancy, restructuring, ill health). For these people the experience and meaning of retirement might be seen as less positive than for those who have retired on their own terms. Hendricks and Russell Hatch (2009) argue that today's increased number of choices may come with unknown consequences. Older people, they claim, are often on their own and dependent on their own creativity and resources. So retirement may also be a scary thought for all those who are short of family and friends and lack social skills.

GENDER DISCOURSES

Davies et al. (2013) noted that although retirement can be gender specific, relatively little research has been conducted on the impact of gender on retirement decisions. Han and Moen (1999) argue that gender differences towards retirement reflect gendered stereotypes and structures, while women's dual roles impact on their retirement decisions (Post et al., 2013). Loretto and Vickerstaff (2013) also acknowledge the role that gender plays in decisions to retire, retirement planning and retirement itself. They argued that individuals' expectations and behaviours reflect a complicated, dynamic set of interactions between domestic environments and gender roles. They found that joint planning of retirement was much less common than might have been expected. Men were influenced by market-driven pathways (linked to pensions and work issues) while women were driven by a domestic pathway (linked to caring). Likewise, they found that the responsibility for financial retirement planning was often highly gendered; pensions were regarded as part of the man's world. They also found there was no desire for working longer; rather, people wanted freedom (from deadlines and work pressures), with women seeing it as a freedom from juggling work and home responsibilities but not a freedom from domestic work (describing themselves as semi-retired), yet for men this freedom was regarded as a time to pursue leisure interests. Nevertheless, the employment context was important for some women; for those with boring jobs, retirement provided a reason to leave the workforce. Other women, who have had career breaks to raise children, may see this as a time for progressing their careers, rather than a time for giving up work. As Liechty et al. (2012, p. 390) assert, 'research suggests that, for women later years are increasingly viewed as a time of opportunity and self-reinvention'. Married women were more likely to give social reasons for intending to carry on working, whereas men gave financial ones. Job quality and job satisfaction were important incentives to carry on working, especially for women. Thus, Loretto and Vickerstaff (2013, p. 79) conclude that the traditional division of labour has a 'profound impact on retirement timing, meaning and planning'.

METHOD

For this research, 14 Swedish women participated in the study. The sample was based on convenience sampling techniques and constituted people with various professional backgrounds – educators, controller, physician, veterinarian, nurse, salesperson, self-employed persons, and health consultant. The interviews were conducted during spring and summer 2012. To find out whether their attitude to retirement had changed when approaching or reaching retirement four follow-up interviews were carried out two years later. Table 29.1 provides an overview of the respondents.

The main purpose of the research was to conduct an exploratory investigation to find out in some depth about people's attitudes to retirement generally. Because the research was exploratory in nature we very much wanted the interviews to be respondent driven rather than interviewer driven. Although we had some general themes to guide our research, we wanted to keep the interviews as open as possible, and allow respondents to answer as freely as they wished. The reason for this was that we wanted to avoid leading questions and instead capture their stories without too much interference and preconceived understandings of retirement. Each interview took between 30 and 90 minutes (averaging an hour) and was conducted by the Swedish author. The interviews were transcribed in the native language. They were later translated into English and categorized into preliminary themes. Both authors read the text and then discussed and made changes along the analytical process. Drawing on these exploratory qualitative interviews and in line with the aims of the book, this chapter particularly draws on some of the women's accounts to illustrate the range of attitudes to, and reasons for, retirement.

Retirement – a new beginning or the beginning of the end? 479

Table 29.1 Demographic background of the respondents

Name	Age	Marital Status	Family Situation	Retired	How Long
Irene	63	W	None	Yes*	2 years
Sara	62	RM	2 Ch	No**	
Cecilia	67	M	3 Ch/5GCh	Yes*	3 years
Amanda	66	M	2Ch/2GCh	Yes*	3 years
Karoline	65	C	2Ch	No**	
Nina	63	C	1Ch/2GCh	No*	
Eva	63	M	2Ch	No	
Anna	63	M	None	Yes	4 months
Louisa	57	C	2Ch	No	
Sue	59	M	1Ch/1GCh	No	
Agnes	56	M	4Ch/5GCh	No	
Mary	63	M	1Ch	No**	
Betty	63	M	2Ch	No**	
Amy	67	M	4Ch/3GCh	Yes	8 years

Notes:
M = married, RM = remarried, C = cohabiting, W = widow, Ch = children, GCh = grandchildren.
Follow-up interviews have been conducted with participants marked with *. Those marked ** had also retired since they first were interviewed.

EMOTIONAL NOTIONS OF RETIREMENT – A NEW BEGINNING OR THE BEGINNING OF THE END?

The themes 'new beginnings' and 'the beginning of the end' provide a useful framework for analysing some of the most salient interview accounts that emerged in the study. The former refers to respondents who thought of retirement as something positive and vividly declared that they looked forward to a life as a retiree, while the latter refers to respondents who had a harder time to envision a life without a job or a meaningful occupation.

New Beginnings

The participants in this category tended to be eager retirees, that is, they regarded retirement positively and as an opportunity to leave paid work. For some about to retire this meant a life on the move travelling the world and spending time at the golf course and with friends. These are the kind of responses we might expect from those about to retire – a new-found freedom to do things they can only dream about currently. For others, retirement meant an opportunity for creating more family time. They did not always envision any major adventures, but rather longed for the days they would be free from the worries and obligations that working life forced upon them. Several of the women's stories suggest that their careers to date were all consuming, leaving them little time for an optimal balance between their work and non-work. Thus, they craved some freedom to allow them to dispose of their time as they please.

Irene, who had worked as a teacher most of her life, explained: 'Retirement means that you aren't forced to leave for work every morning . . . you can hide under the cover as long as you please.' For those about to retire, they spoke about spending their time doing ordinary things like reading, clearing away old papers, tidying up the contents of wardrobes, putting old photos in order – precisely the kinds of activities that they do not have enough time to do while they are still working. When asking Sara who had not yet retired, if she did not fear she would be bored staying home all day she immediately objected: 'No, I would have things to do . . . clean out . . . go through all the photos and albums, cooking, go mushrooming . . . get time for myself . . . help my mother . . . I would have some time to visit my daughters.' So rather than taking up new adventures, Sara saw this as time to attend to her domestic obligations. Since both her mother and daughters lived far away she seldom had the opportunity to see them. She also admitted that she had a bad conscience about her 85-year-old mother who lived alone in the country and who she knew needed help. Thus, although Sara expressed her longing to be free from the obligations that paid work brings, she is still prepared to take on new responsibilities as a retiree. The fact that life after retirement brought about other duties was also illustrated by Cecilia who had retired at the age of 63 and together with her husband she was now spending much of the time looking after the grandchildren:

> I have never felt the urge to sail the Caribbean. We decided not to do as my parents did who lived far away when our children grew up. We decided instead to devote our time to the grandchildren. We didn't have grandparents to turn to for help when our children grew up since they had moved to Spain.

In contrast to Sara, who provides the impression that it is her duty to take care of her mother, Cecilia provides an idealistic view of the family and what the family is for. She appears to feel it is her obligation to be there to help raise the grandchildren. She recounts the time when their own children grew up and how they had missed the presence of grandparents and points out that they decided not to make the same mistake. 'We could have followed my parents' example and moved to Spain,' she says, 'but we wanted to be here for our children and grandchildren.' Cecilia's emphasis on 'we' gives the impression that she is particular about affirming that her husband enjoys looking after the grandchildren as much as she does. As most fathers of the Baby Boomer generation he worked hard to support the family and as a retiree and grandfather he has now the opportunity to compensate for not being there for his own children. He was not alone in his actions: Amanda's husband also takes care of the grandchildren when she is not at home.

Despite wanting to retire, some people's stories showed how complex this decision process might be. Sara's story was a case in point. During the first interview, she longed for retirement but so far had not been on the redundancy list when the company was downsizing and this affected her decision more than her dreams of retiring. She had received the news shortly before the first interview that she was not included among those offered to leave with a redundancy payment:

> I had hoped they would offer me a redundancy payment this time when they got rid of people... but I didn't get it. I didn't get it the last time they got rid of people and I didn't get it this time either even though I have asked for it. I was so disappointed. But that's life... there's no justice.

Even though in the first interview she had emphasized that she did not worry about money she obviously is not prepared to leave before 65 without being financially compensated. Knowing that she had been loyal to the company for many years she did not want to leave without the reward that her colleagues had received when they left. She was not concerned about the money per se because they did not have any bank loans to worry about and she knew that she would get enough to live on the day her mother was gone. What she wanted was justice and as long as she was not offered a redundancy payment she kept on working even if she had lost all her motivation.

Before retiring the women talked about an easy-going life where they have the time to do ordinary things. This is also what they initially do when they retire, but once they have tidied up their home and got rid of everything that reminded them of work they engage in various other activities including pastimes and travelling.

Although there is an inevitable period of adjustment, the creation of a new identity as a pensioner seemed to be fairly easy for all the respondents. They commented on their present life in the positive by explaining: 'I really enjoy life and would not dream of going back [to work]' (Amanda) and 'I cannot understand how I had the time to work' (Amy). To illustrate how much they have to do as pensioners Eva provides the following example from a board meeting in the tenant-owners' group of which she is one of the younger members:

> There I was at this board meeting where we were discussing a new chairman and one of the guys who still works says: 'I have a lot of work so I honestly don't think I have the time' whereupon another person who's a pensioner replies: 'I don't have the time either . . . my calendar is full.'

Once retired they talk about themselves in an outgoing, active and expressive way by including social networks and leisure activities. They are all busy going to lunches with friends and former colleagues, to concerts, playing golf, and going abroad on vacations. Cecilia eventually bought a house in Spain where she spends part of the year and takes Spanish language courses to ameliorate her communication skills. Cecilia was one of the respondents interviewed twice (once before she retired and then again after her retirement). Interestingly, now she has retired her attitude has changed somewhat. She seems to have started to think about herself and what she appreciates in life, not just about her family. Anna takes night courses in geography at the university and even though she no longer has any use for her studies she takes them seriously. Sara finally got her name on the redundancy list and left the company 18 months before her 65th birthday with a redundancy payment. At the time of the last interview she had already attended to her domestic obligations and tidied up the wardrobes, organized her photos and visited her mother and children on several occasions; now, as she said, she was 'enjoying life'. Together with her husband, who had also retired, they have already made several holiday trips.

Another common characteristic among those who were eager to retire was that they had spent most of their working life in the same organization and had experienced several organizational changes over the years. Approaching retirement they no longer felt motivated to take part in any more reorganization and adjust to new organization practices. Amanda, for instance, who had worked as a teacher for adult education most of her life explained:

> I had decided to retire when the new national programme of study was going to be implemented. I would be 64 by then. . . . I had no motivation to start anew and take in all these new courses and a new grading system. Besides, my husband had already retired and it wasn't that fun for him to stay home all day and wait for my retirement.

This demonstrates how Amanda's views appear to reflect Moen et al. and Loretto and Vickerstaff's findings that a husband's position dominates and might determine a woman's decision. However, we need to consider that the same views might be taken by men who retire before their partners. As it happened, events took a further change for Amanda: 'But when the government drew back their financial support to adult education things changed ... those who wanted out could apply for a redundancy payment ... and so I did. This meant that I left at 63 instead of 64.' Amanda was not the only one of the respondents who retired when offered a redundancy payment. On the contrary, most of those who left before they had turned 65 (the official retirement age in Sweden) did so because they were offered a redundancy payment.

What characterizes the respondents in the 'new beginnings' group is that they all talk about retirement in a very positive way. The only negative thing they could think of was the loss of social contact with colleagues. However, even though none of those who have retired visit the workplace, many nonetheless keep in contact with some of their colleagues. Others found social contact in different ways. After retirement, Mary found some temporary work as a receptionist in a fitness centre. This is in accordance with Cahill et al. (2006), Pleau and Shuman (2013) and Phillipson's (2013) findings that some people choose to take a bridge job instead of full-time retirement. Even though it means that she sometimes works from seven in the morning until six or seven at night she enjoys the job: 'I meet a lot of people and you don't think about time.' Betty has found other activities and is happy not having to go to work every morning. 'I've joined two choirs and we practise a lot. We had a concert last spring and it was hard work. To take part in the concert we had to learn all songs by heart and that was hard. But I managed.'

Beginning of the End

Although the majority of the respondents associate retirement with freedom and claim they look forward to the day that they no longer have to worry about work, there are those to whom the words 'retirement' and 'pensioner' evoke negative emotions. Like Louisa, for instance, who explains retirement as 'just a step closer to death', and Nina, who associates the words to 'someone who's dependent on others ... illness and misery', and underscores that even though she is in good health she does not like the word pensioner. Their association to illness, misery and death implies that there might be a fear of stigma connected to retirement. Hence, from their perspectives as long as you are alive and healthy enough you should work instead of being dependent on society. Also, when asking Nina how long she is planning to work for she explains that she is at least going to work until she turns 67, and justifies her plan by adding that 'there are people who work until they are 70 and work night shifts ... because they love their job. I love my job and my colleagues.' Louisa expresses similar thoughts about work, but while Nina seems to lay stress on her own well-being Louisa seems more concerned about being useful and keeping busy:

> I don't think I will stop working. I will probably devote my time to charity because I have many projects. I will for instance work for Red Cross, or . . . well some kind of charity. I know that I need to feel useful, but I don't care about earning money.

What Nina and Louisa have in common is that they both work in the health care sector – Nina as a nurse in mental health and Louisa as head of a project on social sustainability. They are both committed to their careers and have no plans to retire in the near future. Furthermore, it may also be that work is such an important part of their identity that they cannot imagine creating a new identity as a retiree. Some obviously find it difficult imagining a life without work and seem to fear a future where they risk being dependent on society. Perhaps their enthusiasm to continue to work in fact might be a way of avoiding thoughts of becoming old and ill and even being mortal (Moen and Spencer, 2006). Hence, as long as they are working they feel young and active. However, it also supports Luchak et al.'s (2008) finding that employees with higher levels of affective work commitment are more likely to plan to retire later.

The following statement from Karoline indicates that there may be other reasons for continuing to work:

> I have not decided when I will retire. I'm 66 next year . . . but I will continue working. I think it's better to work because it diverts my thoughts . . . especially after my daughter died. If I would stay home I would think of her all the time. I do think of her every day, but it helps to work. And what would I do if I stopped working? I haven't had the time or the mental strength to cultivate any hobbies, since our minds were always set on our daughter. I'll take one semester at a time and finish working when I feel the time is right . . . if I still have the health to work.

Bearing in mind that Karoline had lost her daughter a couple of years earlier it is evident that she is a special case and that her motive to continue working not only differs from Louisa's and Nina's but to most people within the Baby Boomer cohort. Considering also her statement that work diverts her thoughts about her daughter she obviously thinks of it as a kind of therapy that she needs to cling on to until she feels better. So contrary to Moen and Spencer's (2006) suggestion that people are influenced to retire as they have experienced someone close dying, Karoline preferred to continue working. What is interesting about her statement is that when she thinks about her future she seems to substitute work with a hobby and belief that one has to have a livelihood that is as time consuming as work in order to enjoy retirement. Furthermore, she seems to imagine that retirement implies a life in isolation. Hence, without a social network and a meaningful livelihood that replaces work she apparently fears she would lose her spark. However, even though Louisa, Nina and Karoline's overall motives differ they seem to share a tacit understanding that one should not be a burden to society as long as one is healthy enough to work.

The desire to retire by the women in this group partly contradicts Loretto and Vickerstaff's (2013) findings that people want their freedom and do not have a desire to work longer. They do seem to want their freedom, but it is rather related to control and other people's power to govern their life. One of the findings revealed about those who continue to work in some form after officially retiring is the fact they (not their organization) are in control of their working conditions. Respondents who chose to remain in work after reaching pension age either changed employer and work task or continued working as self-employed.

CONCLUSION

In this chapter we have tried to gain a contemporary understanding of people's attitudes towards retirement. We have seen that attitudes to retirement are not a straightforward process and, for some, can be lengthy and complex (Zaniboni et al., 2010). Women perceive of retirement in different ways, especially before they retire.

For those still working, freedom from obligations and the liberty to govern their own life proves to be the two most important motives for retiring. While there was some evidence of respondents wanting to retire fully, some were somewhat indecisive, which was also in line with Zaniboni et al.'s (2010) findings. In accordance with Henkens and Leenders (2010), retirement intentions were mainly explained by work-related factors, and like Szinovacz et al. (2013), the respondents showed evidence of considering macro, meso and micro factors in planning their retirement.

Those women who fell into the 'new beginnings' category (the majority of the respondents) all generally regarded retirement in a positive light. Like Szinovacz (2013) they parallel the three stages of retirement in their narratives, with some taking on 'bridge' jobs (Cahill et al., 2006: Pleau and Shuman, 2013; and Phillipson, 2013) in their transition to the retirement period. Others' experience of transition involved them undertaking all the general tasks they have been unable to attend to whilst working. They saw retirement as enabling them to do normal things outside of the working environment like catching up on domestic tasks and caring responsibilities and providing a new-found freedom. What is apparent from some respondents' (for example, Sara and Cecilia) view of this freedom is that it is less about money and leisure and more about substituting paid work for non-paid work. Their accounts resemble Loretto and Vickerstaff's findings that women want a freedom from juggling work and home responsibilities although they continue to undertake domestic work and caring responsibilities. Where our findings might differ from Loretto and Vickerstaff's is that some of our respondents obviously change their opinion once they have retired. After retiring they start to think more about their own life and how to make the most of it as long as they can. What further characterizes the 'new beginnings' respondents is that various women were further motivated to retire by being offered a financial incentive to leave employment or in order to avoid further organizational changes. They were no longer motivated in their careers, being tired of organizational changes. None of the women in this category appeared to show signs of experiencing professional growth in the later stages of their career (Hall, 2002). Most of the women could afford to take an early pension because they were offered a redundancy payment and were financially independent or partially supported by their husbands. The women in this group generally indicated that they did not or had not worried much about money in retirement. The common answer to issues about money was that 'It's a matter of adjustment' and 'You do not have to spend so much money on clothes or on travelling back and forth to work'. The women in this category easily adjusted to their retirement possibly owing to their positive interpretation on the subject area, and so did not appear to suffer from issues of taking on a new identity as a pensioner.

The women falling into the other category of retirees approached retirement more reluctantly and with more trepidation. They took a more negative view of retirement, associating it with negative emotions such as dependency/burden, fear, isolation, misery, illness and death. They spoke about keeping on working for as long as feasibly possible. They did not see their careers so much as progressing but nevertheless talked of continuing to work in positive terms such as being useful, busy, therapeutic and maintaining well-being. They did experience issues of their future identity as a retired person and this spurred them to continue some form of employment, whether it be with their current employer, a new employer or via charity work. Continuing to undertake some form of work after formal retirement helped them remain socially integrated with other people and also provided those in professional careers a means of continuing to provide their skills and be seen as making a worthy contribution to society. To this end, these women might somewhat adhere with Hall's (2002) claim that people can experience personal and professional growth in the later stages of their career.

This exploratory study has demonstrated the complexity of examining women's retirement views and how macro, meso and micro factors might all have bearings on an individual's attitude and experience towards retirement. Further research is being undertaken to explore in more depth the effects of readjustment to a new way of life on people's identities as pensioners and what this means to them and how it impacts how they live their lives. One of the characteristics of the respondents in this study is that they represent the Baby Boomer generation and thus belong to a privileged group who are reaping the benefits of increased prosperity of the post-war era. Contrary to women 100 years earlier who had a difficult time surviving, this group of respondents represents a carefree and independent group who are not necessarily financially dependent on others. We are acutely aware that this sample of women could be deemed as fortunate and that this position is not afforded to all women (or men).

Given the longevity and decreasing birth rate in Europe future generations are most likely to have to work far longer. Nevertheless, politicians' vision of an extending working life may not be an easy achievement considering that neither people taking part in this study nor mid-career people taking part in Post et al.'s (2013) study seem attracted to this thought. There will need to be a major shift in thinking about the way we approach retirement. Opportunities for earlier retirement in the future are potentially less likely and organizations need to consider how they ought to incorporate older workers. Further research needs to be conducted on attitudes to retirement and the opportunities it presents. For example, it would be interesting to study women who live alone, low-paid workers and those who entered the labour market late in their career and consider what attitude they might have towards retirement and how they are likely to differ. Reflection of the men from this Baby Boomer era also needs to be considered. With changing attitudes, it would be interesting to see to what extent Baby Boomer men and their identities are distinguished. Another study that is warranted is how young women and men think about retirement. One of the authors has conducted focus groups with undergraduate students on their views of retirement and this has uncovered some interesting findings. For example, for many they do not see themselves retiring until at least their seventies owing to the changes in the macro-environment. They also see themselves as needing to save for retirement much earlier than those from the Baby Boomer cohort. By the same token this might be why many young people from the Generation Y era equally view their work–life balance equally as important as their careers (Broadbridge et al., 2007). Thus, more research needs to be conducted to examine the potential differences in attitudes to retirement between people from different generations.

REFERENCES

Beehr, T.A. and M.M. Bennett (2007), 'Examining retirement from a multi-level perspective', in K.S. Shultz and G.A. Adams (eds), *Aging and Work in the 21st Century*, New York: Psychology Press, pp. 277–302.
Broadbridge, A., G. Maxwell and S. Ogden (2007), '13_2_30: expectations, perceptions and experiences of retail employment for Generation Y', *Career Development International*, **12**(6), 523–44.
Cahill. K., M. Giandrea and J. Quinn (2006), 'Retirement patterns from career employment', *The Gerontologist*, **46**(4), 514–23.
Davies, E. and A. Jenkins (2013), 'The work-to-retirement transition of academic staff: attitudes and experiences', *Employee Relations*, **35**(3), 322–38.
Davies, E., K. Dhingra and J. Stephenson (2013), 'The role of line managers in retirement management and their perceptions of their role of the timing of employee retirement', Netspar Discussion Papers, May 2013, Network for Studies on Pensions, Aging and Retirement.
De Vos, A. and J. Segers (2013), 'Self-directed career attitude and retirement intentions', *Career Development International*, **18**(2), 155–72.
Ekerdt, D. (1998), 'Workplace norms for the timing of retirement', in K.W. Schaie and C. Schooler (eds), *Impact of Work on Older Adults*, New York: Springer, pp. 101–23.
Ekerdt, D.J., S. DeViney and K. Kosloski (1996), 'Profiling plans for retirement', *Journal of Gerontology: Social Sciences*, **51B**, S140–S149.
Gov.uk (2014), 'State pension age timetables', accessed 12 December 2014 at https://www.gov.uk/government/uploads/system/uploads/attachment_data/file/310231/spa-timetable.pdf.
Hall, D.T. (2002), *Careers In and Out of Organizations*, Thousand Oaks, CA: Sage.
Han, S.K. and P. Moen (1999), 'Clocking out: temporal patterning of retirement', *American Journal of Sociology*, **105**(1), 191–236.
Hendricks, J. and L. Russell Hatch (2009), 'Lifestyle and aging', in R.H. Binstock, L.K. George, S.J. Cutler, J. Hendricks and J.H. Schulz (eds), *Handbook of Aging and the Social Sciences*, San Diego, CA: Elsevier.
Henkens, K. and M. Leenders (2010), 'Burnout and older workers' intentions to retire', *International Journal of Manpower*, **31**(3), 306–21.
Henkens, K. and J. Shippers (2012), 'Active ageing in Europe: the role of organisations', *International Journal of Manpower*, **33**(6), 604–11.
Liechty, T., C. Yarnal and D. Kerstetter (2012), '"I want to do everything!": leisure innovation among retirement-age women', *Leisure Studies*, **31**(4), 389–408.
Loretto, W. and S. Vickerstaff (2013), 'The domestic and gendered context for retirement', *Human Relations*, **66**(1), 69–90.
Luchak, A.A., D.M. Pohler and I.R. Gellatly (2008), 'When do committed employees retire? The effects of organizational commitment on retirement plans under a defined-benefit pension plan', *Human Resource Management*, **47**(3), 581–99.
McManus, T., J. Anderberg and H. Lazarus (2007), 'Retirement – an unaffordable luxury', *Journal of Management Development*, **26**(5), 484–92.
Moen, P. and D. Spencer (2006), 'Converging divergences in age, gender, health and well-being. Strategic selections in the third age', in R.H. Binstock, L.K. George, S.J. Cutler, J. Hendricks and J.H. Schulz (eds), *Handbook of Aging and the Social Sciences*, San Diego, CA: Elsevier.
Münderlein, M., J.F. Ybema and F. Koster (2013), 'Happily ever after? Explaining turnover and retirement intentions of older workers in the Netherlands', *Career Development International*, **18**(6), 548–68.
Phillipson, C. (2012), 'Globalisation, economic recession and social exclusion: policy challenges and responses', in T. Scharf and N.C. Keating (eds), *From Exclusion to Inclusion in Old Age: A Global Challenge*, Bristol: Policy Press, pp. 17–32.
Phillipson, C. (2013), 'Commentary: the future of work and retirement', *Human Relations*, **66**(1), 143–53.

Pleau, R. and K. Shauman (2013), 'Trends and correlates of post-retirement employment, 1977–2009', *Human Relations*, **66**(1), 117–45.
Post, C., J.A. Schneer and F. Reitman (2013), 'Pathways to retirement: a career stage analysis of retirement age expectations', *Human Relations*, **66**(1) 87–112.
Post, C., J.A. Schneer, F. Reitman and d.t. ogilvie (2013), 'Pathways to retirement: a career stage analysis of retirement age expectations', *Human Relations*, **66**(1), 91–116.
Sargent, L.D., M.D. Lee, B. Martin and J. Zikic (2013), 'Reinventing retirement: new pathways, new arrangements, new meanings', *Human Relations*, **66**(1), 3–21.
Shultz, K.S. and K. Henkens (2010), 'Introduction to the changing nature of retirement: an international perspective', *International Journal of Manpower*, **31**(3), 265–70.
Sterns, H.L. and J. Kaplan (2003), 'Self-management of career and retirement', in G.A. Adams and T.A. Beehr (eds), *Retirement: Reasons, Processes, and Results*, New York: Springer, pp. 188–212.
Szinovacz, M.E. (2013), 'A multilevel perspective for retirement research', in M. Wang (ed.), *The Oxford Handbook of Retirement*, Oxford: Oxford University Press, pp. 152–73.
Szinovacz, M.E., L. Martin and A. Davey (2013), 'Recession and expected retirement age: another look at the evidence', *The Gerontologist*, published online, accessed 25 March 2014 at http://gerontologist.oxfordjournals.org/content/early/2013/02/26/geront.gnt010.short.
Warren, A.M. and E.K. Kelloway (2010), 'Retirement decisions in the context of the abolishment of mandatory retirement', *International Journal of Manpower*, **31**(3), 286–305.
Werner, E. (2013), of Människors upplevelser av pensionssystem och pensionsförberedelser. De första 100 åren – svensk välfärdspolitik mellan historia och framtid [Human Perception of Pension and Retirement Preparation. The First 100 Years – Swedish Welfare Policy Between Past and Future], Rapport från forskarseminariet i Umeå, 16–17 January 2013, *Försäkringskassan*.
Zaniboni S., G. Sarchielli and F. Fraccaroli (2010), 'How are psychosocial factors related to retirement intentions?', *International Journal of Manpower*, **31**(3), 271–85.

30. Transitioning with Grace: women's post-retirement needs and adjustment
Rachel A. August

Grace was my modern dance teacher. I adored her style and finesse, though she was very old, at least in my eyes and those of my grade school dance classmates. Her face was full of wrinkles and her hair was thinning and grey. Her hands had age spots and even her feet were wrinkly and gnarled, which we all knew since modern dancers like us wore bare feet as we twirled across the floor. Nevertheless, she was fabulously creative, energetic, and in tune with the world. Much later I discovered that Grace had actually been retired when I knew her, having been a dancer for an international, well-known modern dance company many years before. As a dancer, of course, she had retired somewhat young, though by the time I knew her she was quite advanced in age. She spent over two decades in her retirement years teaching young girls like me about the love of movement.

Grace may have been unusual for her time. This was, after all, 40 years ago, when fewer women belonged to the workforce at all, much less worked into their retirement years. These days her situation might not have been so unusual. The massive Baby Boomer generation not only brought widespread female participation to the workforce, but also a dramatic increase in the number of women who are now reaching stereotypical retirement age. Women compose almost 47 per cent of the United States labour force overall and those over age 55 now work in almost comparable rates to men. Women comprise 46.9 per cent of the total US labour force age 55 and over, or 12.6 million people (United States Government Accountability Office, 2010). Comparable female labour force participation rates for women aged 55 and over are seen in many European countries, including Germany, the United Kingdom and France (Organisation for Economic Co-operation and Development, 2013).

Those figures have risen dramatically in recent decades. In the USA, women over age 55 had a workforce participation rate of only 22.3 per cent as recently as 1988 and 33.9 per cent in 2008. Additionally, a sizable proportion of the women aged 55 and over, approximately 40 per cent, are employed in management, professional, and related occupations (United States Department of Labor, 2008). Many also extend their careers beyond traditional retirement age. Upon self-identifying as retired, 43 per cent of women actually transition into post-retirement work situations, most typically within two years of retirement (Pleau, 2010).

How do women fare in the post-retirement period in terms of their well-being and adjustment? That question is addressed in this chapter, using the resource-based dynamic perspective on retirement adjustment (Wang et al., 2011) in the analysis. Additionally, this chapter elaborates upon the resource-based perspective by incorporating into it a model developed specifically to understand women's careers, the kaleidoscope career model (Mainiero and Sullivan, 2005, 2006). In doing so, it is suggested that the gendered context of post-retirement adjustment is a topic worthy of attention, and may be better studied by more directly incorporating the unique elements of women's work experiences into more general models of retirement adjustment.

POST-RETIREMENT ADJUSTMENT

Szinovacz (2013) suggests that the full retirement process as experienced by individuals can be divided into three stages beginning with a pre-retirement planning period, followed by a retirement transition period, and ending with complete status as a full retiree. This last stage is the 'post-retirement stage' with the major task being adaptation or adjustment to retirement: it is this post-retirement stage that is of most interest here. This time period is sometimes overlooked in reference to general models of career development, yet is an important and connected piece of the career cycle as well.

Describing adjustment in the post-retirement period is complicated by changes in the nature of retirement itself. It is now well accepted that retirement is not a singular event demarcating the end of paid work, but rather a process. Employees may undergo multiple entries and exits from the workforce as workers use various forms of bridge employment as a way of slowly transitioning out of paid work (Kim and Feldman, 2000; Wang et al., 2008). Moreover, how to identify what counts as 'retirement' is complex, since multiple measures have been used for the concept, including non-participation in the labour force, reduction in hours worked, hours worked or earnings below a minimum cut-off, receipt of retirement or pension income, exit from one's main employer, a later-life career change, self-assessed retirement, and some combination of the preceding list (Denton and Spencer, 2009). The concept of retirement itself is under reinvention, with changes in the timing, the types of activities pursued, the meanings associated with this period of life, and even rejection by some of the concept altogether as unrealistic or at least unappealing (Sargent et al., 2013).

Post-retirement adjustment is an important concern for many professional women on the brink of retirement. Some have argued that professional women may hold very strong work-related identities (Volpe and Murphy, 2011), even stronger than those of non-professional women (Price, 2002); such identities have the potential to make adjusting to retirement particularly challenging. However, there is mixed evidence concerning that adjustment. For instance, a study of Dutch employees at a multinational company demonstrates that women tend to have more problems adjusting to retirement than men (Van Solinge and Henkens, 2008). On the other hand, a qualitative study of professional women reveals consensus among the women about the relative 'ease' of the retirement transition (Price, 2003).

There is a sizable body of literature concerning the quality of post-retirement adjustment and the concept refers to 'psychological comfort regarding the retirement life' (Wang et al., 2011). A review of the key predictors of the quality of retirement adjustment (Wang and Shultz, 2010) suggests five major categories of predictors: individual attributes (for example, physical, mental, and financial health), pre-retirement job-related variables (for example, job stress, job satisfaction, and work role identity), family-related variables (for example, marital status, marital quality, and number of dependent children), retirement-transition-related variables (for example, retirement planning, retiring earlier than expected, and retiring for health-related reasons), and post-retirement activities (for example, bridge employment, volunteering, leisure activities).

Recently, Wang et al. (2011) have introduced a resource-based dynamic perspective on retirement adjustment, which admirably brings together the wide array of predictors influencing retirement adjustment into a coherent theoretical model. This perspective also recognizes the inherent process-based nature of retiring and the potential for intra-individual changes in adjustment over time. The model suggests that retirement adjustment is driven by access to and utilization of a number of resources, including physical, cognitive, motivational, financial, social, and emotional resources. Those resources, in turn, have as antecedents the various categories of predictors described above as well as potential others such as societal norms and government policy. Adjustment for any one individual is conceptualized as a longitudinal process, and may fluctuate as a function of increasing or decreasing resources.

WOMEN AND POST-RETIREMENT ADJUSTMENT

The role of gender in post-retirement adjustment is not made entirely apparent in the resource-based dynamic model, though it certainly is a point of interest given predictors such as individual and family-related variables. Van Solinge (2013) has noted that gender is typically used as a control variable in studying retirement adjustment; this appears to be the case in the resource-based dynamic perspective as well. However, many researchers have argued that gender should be more directly incorporated into models of retirement adjustment, given potential differences in the retirement experience due to structural differences in the labour market according to gender (Moen, 1996), different work and background experiences related to job type, career progression, and longevity (Griffin et al., 2013), differences in the history of opportunities (August and Quintero, 2001) and differences in family roles and obligations (Everingham et al., 2007).

The gendered context of retirement adjustment has been addressed in some research. Though many variables suggested by Wang et al. (2011) are relevant to women's retirement adjustment, among the unique predictive factors for women include the continuity of their employment history (Price and Dean, 2009), the extent of their role expansion in retirement (Price, 2003), electronic communication with extended social networks (Waldron et al., 2005), pre-retirement social contacts (Kubicek et al., 2011) and the quality of retiring women's female friendships (Wingrove and Slevin, 1991).

The body of literature on women's retirement adjustment has faced the same challenge as the general literature on retirement adjustment; it also constitutes a mass of predictors without grounding in a theoretical, coherent whole. Consequently, an examination of the gendered context of retirement adjustment would also benefit from a theoretical lens permitting systematic examination of women's retirement adjustment.

PRESENTATION OF THE THEORY

One potentially helpful theoretical model is the kaleidoscope career model (KCM) introduced by Mainiero and Sullivan (2005, 2006). This model of career development suggests that women constantly concern themselves with three major needs as their careers evolve over time: (1) authenticity, defined as being true to oneself and making decisions that suit the self above others; (2) balance, defined as making decisions so that the various aspects of one's life, including work and non-work, form a coherent whole; and (3) challenge, defined as engaging in activities allowing one to pursue autonomy, responsibility, and control while learning and growing. The model was originally developed to describe the 'opt-out phenomenon' in which a growing number of women with high-powered corporate executive careers choose to 'downshift' their careers into less highly demanding jobs and consequently create new career trajectories. However, the needs described in the KCM are applicable in various patterns for women at all career stages (ibid.). Moreover, their relevance has recently been demonstrated for women's career development in the post-retirement years, whether they are involved in part-time work, bridge employment, or significant volunteer activities (August, 2011a).

At its heart, the KCM is essentially a motivational theory of women's career development, given that it rests on the idea that career choices and trajectories are motivated (at least in part) by the needs of authenticity, balance, and challenge. Need-based theories abound in organizational and management psychology (for example, McClelland's 1985 needs for achievement and power; Hackman and Oldham's 1975 job characteristics model and the need for growth), and are well-accepted as fundamental in driving work-related behaviour. Research on the KCM demonstrates that gender contextualizes the importance of those particular needs over time. Men typically follow a pattern of focusing on challenge in the early career, followed by authenticity, and then balance. Women, on the other hand, generally evolve from an early career focus on challenge, to a middle-career focus on balance, to a late-career focus on authenticity (Mainiero and Sullivan, 2006). Cabrera's (2007) test of the KCM for a cross-sectional sample of women in different age groups confirms those outcomes for women, and August's (2011a) examination of the model for women in their retirement years underscores the distinctive importance of authenticity as well as challenge.

Wang et al. (2011) suggest that the resource-based dynamic perspective could be further developed by integrating motivational theory and research (among other theoretical perspectives) to elaborate upon knowledge of retirement adjustment. Since the KCM is both grounded in motivational theory and developed specifically to explain women's work lives, it seems particularly fitting to use it as a lens for viewing of women's retirement adjustment. Doing so may shed light on how women's unique motivational needs can become satisfied and consequently act as resources for positive retirement adjustment. This chapter aims to illustrate those issues, using as touchstones two cases of retired women. The use of qualitative data based on case studies seems especially valuable in the study of retirement adjustment; in doing so, researchers are able to account for the extensive, complex, and interlinked array of contextual variables pertaining to each unique individual's adjustment (Price, 2003; Kloep and Hendry, 2006; Nuttman-Shwartz, 2007).

RETIREMENT STORIES

The cases used to illustrate motivational needs of retired women and consequent adjustment are drawn from a larger project on women's later-life career development. That project involved a 12-year longitudinal study, for which women in human service professions were interviewed in depth both shortly prior to their retirement and then again following their official retirement from the workforce. Approximately two-thirds of the women studied held supervisory or managerial positions. The methodological details, sampling information and procedures involved in conducting those semi-structured face-to-face interview studies can be found in August and Quintero (2001) and August (2011a, 2011b). The cases presented here depict Audrey and Elizabeth,[1] who were first introduced in the 2001 study prior to their retirement. The information reflects their lives in the post-retirement period, during the second phase of the longitudinal study.

Audrey

Audrey officially retired ten years ago, having worked as a nurse's assistant for most of her career. She spent the last few years prior to her retirement working as a hospital orderly, since the hospital she worked for downsized and her former position was cut. She was not happy about her demotion to orderly. She loved her duties as a nurse's assistant and 'cried every day, but stuck it out as long as I had to'. She made peace with the situation because it continued to allow her to work until she was eligible for retirement. While she did not spend her career in management or as a professional, her retirement experiences offer important contrasts, and yet remarkable similarities, to Elizabeth's experiences depicted in the next case.

Audrey defines herself as 'retired', though she continues to bring in some regular income, both by babysitting the children of physicians at her former employing hospital and by regularly collecting and returning the recyclable cans and bottles she gathers in a wide walking route adjacent to her neighbourhood. Her financial resources are not vast; she estimates her annual income, including her retirement pension, to be somewhat less than $20 000. This is approximately $15 000 per year less than the median income for households headed by people age 65 and over, though it is not entirely unusual. Median incomes for retirees who draw income from Social Security alone are approximately $15 600 per year. Audrey's income puts her somewhat above the US Federal poverty guidelines of $11 670 for a family of one person, though she is by no means financially 'comfortable'. However, she notes that she does not have major financial debt, as she paid off the mortgage on her small tract home near the local raceway and has no need to move anywhere else. Her health is relatively good, all things considered. Audrey is diabetic, which she controls through 'better cooking' and has high blood pressure, for which she takes regular medication. She also has arthritis in her hip, though as she notes: 'I'm 74 years old, so all of that just goes with age.'

Her days are relatively predictable. When she first gets up, she takes her three small dogs for a walk, which she remarks is 'really important exercise'. After that, she watches her favourite television shows for an hour or two each morning. In the afternoon she 'visits the thrift shops' and sometimes goes to the grocery store. Normally she walks to each location, as she does not have a car. This is, of course, time consuming, given her arthritis. She was divorced, re-married, and subsequently widowed many decades ago, so Audrey is used to living alone and doing things on her own. As she says, 'I like being by myself.' She has a few friends she sees at the Senior Centre periodically, though she does not feel especially close to them because of her differing values. Many of them, she explains, 'are on the County' welfare roll, and that situation does not suit her. She also goes to church regularly and sees friends and neighbours there. She places great value on her independence. As she notes, 'Everybody thinks I'm independent, and I am. I don't ask for anything and I don't have to borrow anything. My brother and sister, they live out of state (over 800 kilometres away), and if they want to give me something I won't accept stuff.'

None of these things – a late-life job demotion, minimal financial resources, the aches and pains of ageing, widowhood and few social connections, bother her in the present; they are just a part of her life. In her view, she is one of the lucky few. As she says, every morning the first thing she thinks of is that she is 'just thankful that I'm alive, that I have been able to retire, and that I'm blessed'. Retirement, she says, 'is fantastic. I'm enjoying every bit of it.' She elaborates that it signifies that she worked her whole life, and that she has 'earned it'. Further, she has structure to her day that makes her happy and a place to put her energies. Collecting recyclables is an important part of her week 'because it keeps me going. It's like getting up and going to a job; I know I have to do this on Monday, or Tuesday, or whichever day.' As she says, 'For me, I'm happy. I don't need any more than what I have.'

As for her future, what does she see? She says she has a dream some day that she'll become a grandmother, though she indicates that is not likely given her grown children's current circumstances. Other than that, she says, 'If I continue health-wise the way I am, I'll live a long life. And I get a lot of joy out of my dogs. They're like my children.'

Elizabeth

Elizabeth also retired ten years ago and like Audrey is also 74 years old. Her retirement trajectory was much more complicated, as is typical in the lives of many professionals who do not retire in one single move. She retired from a long career as a private-practice psychotherapist, during which she worked in an office setting with many other mental health professionals. She actually began the retirement process by phasing out her practice, shifting it to part-time and then eventually to seeing clients on only three days, every other week. This allowed her to move with her husband to a resort town along the coast of the Western United States about 240 kilometres from her work, where they converted their former vacation home into a regular residence for their retirement. During this initial period of retirement she lived in a hotel three days per week in her former town while winding down her practice, with her main home being in the resort town. During this period she also began a new career as a newspaper advice columnist and was syndicated in several papers around the country.

Eventually, however, she shifted from her therapy and advice columnist work into real estate. She did not do this for the income potential, she notes, as her annual household income is 'well over $100 000'. She did it because it 'sounded fun'. She got the idea from her brother-in-law, who said he was looking for a vehicle in which to place a recent inheritance, and she suggested real estate and began looking into it. She did not take any classes in real estate, but 'ordered the books and studied out of them' teaching herself the relevant information. She passed the real estate licensure test a few years into her retirement and now works for a local commercial realty office. She loves this work as it 'turned out to be a nice way to make friends and deal with people in business'. In addition, she enjoys the inherent challenge of the work itself. As she puts it, 'the most thrilling is when you're working on a deal, and you have to put together the buyer and the seller and make it work. And after, it's like winning a race you've trained for your whole life.' In addition, she says, it is 'always a learning experience'.

Her days are busy and varied. Like Audrey, she begins with early morning exercise to protect her 'pretty good health'. The rest of the day is usually filled with activities related to her real estate career, though she mostly works from home and if she does go to the office she leaves by 5 pm, unlike her earlier career years. The evenings regularly involve visits with new friends she and her husband made following their later-life move, and often include small parties or spontaneous gatherings. She says, 'we have probably more fun now than we've ever had, since we were first married, because we don't have a lot of responsibilities'. Her family, too, is important to her. She sees them frequently, for family trips, birthdays, and various occasions. As she says, they give her 'enormous satisfaction and I'm speaking of the children and grandchildren. I mean, just enormous pleasure and fun. Now I have the freedom to do things like go to my grandchildren's Open House at school.'

She feels much better about her life than she did in the early retirement years, during which she struggled with her work-related identity. In winding down her therapy practice, she says: 'I lost my contact with my office and friends and clients. I look back and think I was grieving and looking at a whole change in lifestyle. It's only been since I've morphed into real estate and also connected with the friends that we've met here, that now I think it's just a great life.'

The transition period was difficult. She says, 'I was doing both and I was a little bit conflicted about which "hat" I was really wearing. I didn't tell my academic colleagues I was selling real estate and I didn't talk a lot about psychology in my real estate career. And so I had to really get comfortable, changing careers.'

Now, however, she says that retirement 'couldn't be any better now. I'm happy with what I have. I'm happy now to be past the phase of my life as a psychologist. I'm very content.' As for her future, she sees 'life going along much like it is for the next several years. I enjoy my real estate work and would continue for some time.' She says that at some point 'I would retire again and spend more time gardening. My garden gives me great comfort and beauty.'

DISCUSSION

Audrey and Elizabeth clearly lead very different lives in terms of work, social activities, family connections, and day-to-day living. However, both report being happy, fulfilled, and currently appear to be well adjusted. Using typical definitions of retirement adjustment (Wang et al., 2011), both Audrey and Elizabeth report being psychologically comfortable with their retirement life and feel at peace regarding the changed circumstances of their lives.

It also appears that Audrey and Elizabeth have met their main needs as specified in the KCM, that is, they have met their needs for authenticity, balance, and challenge, though they have done so through mostly different vehicles. Authenticity refers to being 'genuine and true to oneself' (Mainiero and Sullivan, 2006, p.115) and can be manifested in many ways in later life, including taking care of oneself and developing self-acceptance (August, 2011a). In that regard, both women exercise without fail each morning, and remark on its importance to their health and well-being. They are taking care of their physical selves, a growing concern with advancing age. Perhaps more importantly, they have clearly become self-accepting. Elizabeth struggled with this issue for some time early in her retirement transition, unsure if her new professional path was the right choice and worried about what her friends would think. However, in the end, she remarks upon how comfortable she is now, and happy to have moved beyond her former occupation into something new. Audrey struggled less with the transition, though she seems to have felt a bit pushed into retiring. She may have waited somewhat longer to retire had she remained in her higher-paying and more enjoyable nurse's assistant position and not been demoted. Nevertheless, she has adjusted to her situation in retirement and clearly accepts her life as is, remarking that her first thought upon waking is being 'thankful that I'm alive, that I have been able to retire, and that I'm blessed'.

Balance refers to the need to arrange the various pieces of life, including work and non-work, into one coherent picture. Research on the KCM (Mainiero and Sullivan, 2005; Cabrera, 2007; August, 2011a) suggests that this need is a less pressing one in later life, likely because achieving balance is typically not as complicated during this time period when women are less likely to act as primary caretakers for young children. This circumstance is the case for Audrey and Elizabeth; additionally, neither is in the situation of needing to care for a spouse or other ageing relative. They also seem to have fallen into an easy balance with regard to integrating friends and family members into their lives. Elizabeth easily and happily does so, and feels good that she has the time to arrange visits and occasions with new friends as well as many members of her extended family. Audrey appears less interested in social connectivity in the first place, and as she remarks, likes being by herself. Nonetheless she seeks and finds social activity when she wants it, particularly at church and sometimes at the Senior Centre, as well as staying in touch with her siblings by telephone.

Challenge refers to a person's need to learn and grow in their jobs. It can be manifested in many ways in later life for women, including engaging in activities that demonstrate competence, provide intrinsic interest or intellectual stimulation (August, 2011a). Elizabeth clearly has met this need in her real estate career, which is inherently interesting or 'fun' for her. In addition, it provides many opportunities for her to demonstrate competence through arranging and closing deals, which is an aspect of the job that she loves. Audrey, too, has found a way to meet the need for challenge, though perhaps not in a way traditionally described in management theory. Collecting recyclables 'keeps her going', as she says, and is 'like a job'. It pushes her to do something productive, and certainly must be even more challenging given the long walking route required and her arthritis. However, she is committed to it and makes sure she does it every week. In addition, it is very important to her that she demonstrates her emotional and financial independence, and that her brothers and sisters are aware of this. The small income she earns seems to make her feel competent, able to live on her own without help.

The resource-based dependency model (Wang et al., 2011, p. 206) indicates that retirement adjustment revolves around the 'total capability an individual has to fulfill his or her centrally valued needs'. In other words, people who have more resources available to fulfil their needs will experience less difficulty in adjusting to retirement. Both Audrey and Elizabeth have managed to find ways to satisfy the central needs outlined by the KCM, though clearly in quite different ways. In the end, meeting these psychological needs becomes a resource for well-being and positive adjustment in retirement. It may be that over time, those resources change and they are no longer able to meet their motivational needs, but for now, their retirement is just as they like it.

The resource-based dynamic perspective offers an important advancement in understanding retirement adjustment. Women's retirement adjustment, in particular, can be best understood by taking into account the unique configurations and manifestations of resources likely to be held by women. Doing so requires theory and data driven by women's workplace experiences. The KCM is one such helpful theory, and appears to help elaborate upon women's retirement adjustment according to their ability to satisfy the key motivators of authenticity, balance, and challenge. There are likely other theories involving work-related motivation (for example, goal-setting theory, expectancy theory, equity theory) that might help explain retirement adjustment as well, though none of them derive directly from nor are meant to apply specifically to women's work experiences.

It is telling that both Audrey and Elizabeth felt positive about their retirement experiences and well adjusted to the situation. Women, professional and non-professional alike, retire under and enter into a wide range of circumstances, some of which are positive and probably advantageous and some of which are not. Women retire voluntarily, are forced to leave jobs due to limited organizational resources, poor health, family needs and everything in between. Women retire with large pensions, small pensions, or no pension at all, much less face simple and easy home life situations or challenging ones in their later years. As with the distinctive pathways of women's careers in general (Gersick, 2013) women's retirement pathways can be remarkably unique. Despite this, the markedly different cases of Audrey and Elizabeth suggest that all such circumstances can foster positive adjustment, given the resources individuals subsequently gather to promote adjustment. Audrey and Elizabeth both appear to have gathered key resources in that they have fulfilled needs for at least authenticity, balance, and challenge. Further, the interrelatedness of those and other resources is likely at issue as well. It may be that resources accumulate exponentially together, essentially feeding off each other, and a serious loss of resources in one area can have negative implications for resources in other areas (Kloep and Hendry, 2006).

CONCLUSIONS

In this chapter, motivation-related resources have been the focus, though the resource-based dependency model also includes physical, cognitive, financial, social and emotional resources. The gender-specific content and/or context of those resources are topics worthy of future exploration, with many woman-centred or gender-related theories to consider. For instance, Gilligan's (1982) formative work on the centrality of relationships in women's lives and the many subsequent workplace studies related to this topic (Gallos, 1989; Richardson, 1999; O'Neil and Bilimoria, 2005) would likely be particularly useful in understanding women's social resources. Taylor et al.'s (2000) work on women's tend-and-befriend coping response to stressful situations is likely to be instructive in terms of understanding women's emotional resources. Feminist economic theory (Ferber and Nelson, 2003) may provide a useful lens for understanding the unique aspects of women's financial resources.

Van Solinge (2013) points out that people can adjust to new situations like retirement without actually enjoying it, though Audrey and Elizabeth did not seem to report that state of affairs. However, this points to the complex nature of adjustment, in general. There are likely many dimensions of adjustment (for example, emotional, physical, social, etc.), and any single individual's adjustment is likely to vary across dimensions. It may be that certain aspects of adjustment are either more or less difficult for women than men, given the available resources.

Additionally, adjustment may not mean the same things to all people regardless of gender groupings, and may be a somewhat relative concept by nature. Adjustment within certain realms may be more important to specific individual's well-being than other areas of adjustment, and underscore the importance of understanding individual pathways into retirement and subsequent adjustment (Kloep and Hendry, 2006). Further, what might appear to be poor or undesirable retirement adjustment from one individual's point of view may be perfectly acceptable and desirable from another's, so long as that person's unique needs are fulfilled. Teasing apart all of these nuances in adjustment, too, may be worthy avenues of study, taking into account the high likelihood that the meanings of positive adjustment will be conditioned by social class, religion, cultural background and other important social identities.

PRACTICAL IMPLICATIONS

An understanding of retirement adjustment and its antecedents most directly helps retirees, as it can provide insight into how to improve the quality of one's own retirement. Such insight might also assist those who create career counselling interventions, social programmes, government legislation, and initiatives on ageing designed to improve retirees' lives. Additionally, understanding the unique contributions of authenticity, balance, and challenge to retirement adjustment may offer special advantages. As motivations, they are driven at least in part by personal agency, or people's active attempts to anticipate and shape outcomes and to plan ahead for future actions. In other words, women can make choices to seek situations that offer opportunities for meeting authenticity, balance, and challenge needs. Theoretically, enacting those choices should improve capacity for retirement adjustment.

The women in the cases described here seemed naturally high in personal agency; they clearly made active attempts to shape their lives. Others may not naturally hold these qualities. However, there is growing evidence from the field of positive organizational behaviour that hope, self-efficacy, and resilience, and the connected and underlying construct of agency, are actually motivational states that can be trained and improved upon through relatively brief interventions (Luthans et al., 2008). If so, organizations that serve retirees, such as community centres, retirement communities or employing organizations themselves, might offer training to improve upon retirees' capacity to perform goal-directed behaviour that would enable them to meet needs for authenticity, balance and challenge.

More directly, organizations can assist with post-retirement adjustment by offering employment opportunities to retirees who seek it, as such employment may provide opportunities to fulfil needs for authenticity, balance, and challenge. Additionally, as Sullivan and Mainiero (2007, 2008) have pointed out, organizations can develop progressive human resource policies to meet the needs for authenticity, balance and challenge. These include wellness programmes focused on health and the whole person, workshops on spirituality and finding purpose in work, corporate social responsibility programmes, multiple flexible scheduling options, time banks for paid eldercare leave, and creating organizational cultures that emphasize lateral moves for learning and skills development. Women working in such organizations in their post-retirement years – whether part-time, in phase out situations, or in new post-retirement careers – are likely to better adjust to retirement if they access such resources.

Many companies would in fact benefit from employing retired women, as several studies show that older workers have many qualities advantageous to organizations. For instance, as compared to younger employees, older employees in general feel a stronger psychological contract with their employing organizations. Older workers also feel especially obligated to work extra hours if necessary, to work well with others, and to provide quality products and services (Schalk, 2004). Older employees also show greater proactivity (that is, initiative related to work tasks) than younger employees (Van Veldhoven and Dorenbosch, 2008). Experienced older workers also may have unique talents and skills developed through longevity (Greller and Stroh, 2004) that are necessary for organizations to remain competitive in restricted economic times and/or due to intense global competition.

POST-SCRIPT

Our language has not yet caught up with theoretical and empirical advances in our understanding of retirement. Clearly retirement is not a discrete event, nor is it a static moment in women's lives. Perhaps we should avoid the words 'retired' and 'retirement' altogether, as they imply an inertness that does not reflect the evidence of retirees experiencing a dynamic, ongoing period of living, not unlike other developmental periods. As many (cf., Everingham et al., 2007; Jones et al., 2010; Moulaert and Biggs, 2013; Sargent et al., 2013) have recently suggested, the meaning and idea of retirement itself is under reconstruction with multiple possibilities for its reformation. In the future, we might turn our attention to 'retiree development and adjustment' with a focus on all of the associated developmental changes, and shifting motivations, needs, and environments that come with living a full life. The retiree would then become the centre of the experience, rather than the period of time.

Finally, what about Grace? I still wonder, was she happy? Was she a well-adjusted retiree? I did not have the maturity at the time to wonder, and when I came of age, never got the chance to ask. I am not sure I would have been happy, running around barefoot with a bunch of giggling elementary schoolgirls, after an illustrious career as an international dancer. However, she sure looked happy. She must have found what she needed.

NOTE

1. Both names are pseudonyms chosen by the research participants. Elizabeth, however, chose two different pseudonyms (Elizabeth and Kristen) for each of the two phases of the longitudinal study. For consistency with the 2001 study, her original pseudonym is used here.

REFERENCES

August, R.A. (2011a), 'Women's later life career development: looking through the lens of the kaleidoscope career model', *Journal of Career Development*, **38**(3), 208–36.

August, R.A. (2011b), 'Women's retirement meanings: context, changes, and organizational lessons', *Gender in Management: An International Journal*, **26**(5), 351–66.

August, R.A. and V.C. Quintero (2001), 'The role of opportunity structures in older women workers' careers', *Journal of Employment Counseling*, **38**(2), 62–81.

Cabrera, E.F. (2007), 'Opting out and opting in: understanding the complexities of women's career transitions', *Career Development International*, **12**(3), 218–37.

Denton, F.T. and B.B. Spencer (2009), 'What is retirement? A review and assessment of alternative concepts and measures', *Canadian Journal on Aging*, **28**(1), 63–76.

Everingham, C., P. Warner-Smith and J. Byles (2007), 'Transforming retirement: re-thinking models of retirement to accommodate the experiences of women', *Women's Studies International Forum*, **30**(6), 512–22.

Ferber, M.A. and J.A. Nelson (2003), *Feminist Economics Today: Beyond Economic Man*, Chicago, IL: University of Chicago Press.

Gallos, J.V. (1989), 'Exploring women's development: implications for career theory, practice, and research', in M.B. Arthur, D.T. Hall and B.S. Lawrence (eds), *Handbook of Career Theory*, New York: Cambridge University Press, pp. 110–32.

Gersick, C. (2013), 'Getting from "keep out" to "lean in": a new roadmap for women's careers', *Yale SOM Working Paper*, accessed 8 December 2014 at http://papers.ssrn.com/sol3/papers.cfm?abstract_id=2315013.

Gilligan, C. (1982), *In a Different Voice: Psychological Theory and Women's Development*, Cambridge, MA: Harvard University Press.

Greller, M.M. and L.K. Stroh (2004), 'Making the most of "late career" for employers and workers themselves: becoming elders not relics', *Organizational Dynamics*, **33**(2), 202–14.

Griffin, B., V. Loh and B. Hesketh (2013), 'Age, gender, and the retirement process', in M. Wang (ed.), *The Oxford Handbook of Retirement*, New York: Oxford University Press, pp. 202–14.

Hackman, J.R. and G.R. Oldham (1975), 'Development of the Job Diagnostic Survey', *Journal of Applied Psychology*, **60**(2), 159–70.

Jones, I.R., M. Leontowitsch and P. Higgs (2010), 'The experience of retirement in second modernity: generational habitus among retired senior managers', *Sociology*, **44**(1), 103–20.

Kim, S. and D.C. Feldman (2000), 'Working in retirement: the antecedents of bridge employment and its consequences for quality of life in retirement', *Academy of Management Journal*, **43**(6), 1195–210.

Kloep, M. and L.B. Hendry (2006), 'Pathways into retirement: entry or exit?', *Journal of Occupational and Organizational Psychology*, **79**(4), 569–93.

Kubicek, B., C. Korunka, J.M. Raymo and P. Hoonakker (2011), 'Psychological well-being in retirement: the effects of personal and gendered contextual resources', *Journal of Occupational Health Psychology*, **16**(2), 230–46.

Luthans, F., J.B. Avey and J.L. Patera (2008), 'Experimental analysis of a web-based training intervention to develop positive psychological capital', *Academy of Management Learning & Education*, **7**(2), 209–21.

Mainiero, L.A. and S.E. Sullivan (2005), 'Kaleidoscope careers: an alternate explanation for the "opt-out" revolution', *Academy of Management Executive*, **19**(1), 106–23.

Mainiero, L.A. and S.E. Sullivan (2006), *The Opt-out Revolt: Why People Are Leaving Companies to Create Kaleidoscope Careers*, Mountain View, CA: Davies-Black Publishing.

McClelland, D.C. (1985), *Human Motivation*, Glenview, IL: Scott Foresman.

Moen, P. (1996), 'A life course perspective on retirement, gender, and well-being', *Journal of Occupational Health Psychology*, **1**(2), 131–44.

Moulaert, T. and S. Biggs (2012), 'International and European policy on work and retirement: reinventing critical perspectives on active ageing and mature subjectivity', *Human Relations*, **66**(1), 23–43.

Nuttman-Shwartz, O. (2007), 'Is there life without work?', *International Journal of Aging and Human Development*, **64**(2), 129–47.

O'Neill, D.A. and D. Bilimoria (2005), 'Women's career development phases: idealism, endurance, and reinvention', *Career Development International*, **10**(3), 168–89.

Organisation for Economic Co-operation and Development (2013), 'Labor force statistics by sex and age – indicators', accessed 1 May 2013 at http://stats.oecd.org/Index.aspx?DatasetCode=LFS_SEXAGE_I_R.

Pleau, R.L. (2010), 'Gender differences in post-retirement employment', *Research on Aging*, **32**(3), 267–303.

Price, C. (2002), 'Retirement for women: the impact of employment', *Journal of Women and Aging*, **14**(3/4), 41–57.

Price, C. (2003), 'Professional women's retirement adjustment: the experience of re-establishing order', *Journal of Aging Studies*, **17**(3), 341–55.

Price, C.A. and K.J. Dean (2009), 'Exploring the relationships between employment history and retired women's social relationships', *Journal of Women & Aging*, **21**(2), 85–98.

Richardson, V.E. (1999), 'Women and retirement', *Journal of Women and Aging*, **11**(2/3), 49–66.

Sargent, L.D., M.D. Lee, B. Martin and J. Zikic (2013), 'Reinventing retirement: new pathways, new arrangements, new meanings', *Human Relations*, **66**(1), 3–21.

Schalk, R. (2004), 'Changes in the employment relationship across time', in J.A.M. Coyle-Shapiro, L.M. Shore, M.S. Taylor and L.E. Tetrick (eds), *The Employment Relationship: Examining Psychological and Contextual Perspectives*, Oxford: Oxford University Press, pp. 284–311.

Sullivan, S.E. and L.A. Mainiero (2007), 'Benchmarking ideas for fostering family-friendly workplaces', *Organizational Dynamics*, **36**(1), 45–62.

Sullivan, S.E. and L.A. Mainiero (2008), 'Using the kaleidoscope career model to understand the changing patterns of women's careers: designing HRD programs that attract and retain women', *Advances in Developing Human Resources*, **10**(1), 32–49.

Szinovacz, M.E. (2013), 'A multilevel perspective for retirement research', in M. Wang (ed.), *The Oxford Handbook of Retirement*, Oxford: Oxford University Press, pp. 152–73.

Taylor, S.E., K.C. Klein, B.P. Lewis, T.L. Gruenewald, R.A. Gurung and J.A. Updegraff (2000), 'Biobehavioral responses to stress in females: tend-and-befriend, not fight-or-flight', *Psychological Review*, **107**(3), 411–29.

United States Department of Labor (2008), 'Older women workers, age 55 and over, 2008', accessed 29 March 2013 at http://www.dol.gov/wb/factsheets/Qf-olderworkers55-08.htm.

United States Government Accountability Office (2010), 'Analysis of female managers'

representation, characteristics, and pay', accessed 29 March 2013 at http://www.gao.gov/products/GAO-10-892R.
Van Solinge, H. (2013), 'Adjustment to retirement', in M. Wang (ed.), *The Oxford Handbook of Retirement*, New York: Oxford University Press, pp. 311–24.
Van Solinge, H. and K. Henkens (2008), 'Adjustment to and satisfaction with retirement: two of a kind?', *Psychology and Aging*, **23**(2), 422–34.
Van Veldhoven, M. and L. Dorenbosch (2008), 'Age, proactivity and career development', *Career Development International*, **13**(2), 112–31.
Volpe, E.H. and W.M. Murphy (2011), 'Married professional women's career exit: integrating identity and social networks', *Gender in Management: An International Journal*, **26**(1), 57–83.
Waldron, V.R., R. Gitelson and D.L. Kelly (2005), 'Gender differences in social adaptation to a retirement community: longitudinal changes and the role of mediated communication', *The Journal of Applied Gerontology*, **24**(4), 283–98.
Wang, M. and K.S. Shultz (2010), 'Employee retirement: a review and recommendations for future investigation', *Journal of Management*, **36**(1), 172–206.
Wang, M., K. Henkens and H. van Solinge (2011), 'Retirement adjustment: a review of theoretical and empirical advancements', *American Psychologist*, **66**(3), 204–13.
Wang, M., Y. Zhan, S. Liu and K. Shultz (2008), 'Antecedents of bridge employment: a longitudinal investigation', *Journal of Applied Psychology*, **93**(4), 818–30.
Wingrove, C.R. and K.F. Slevin (1991), 'Samples of professional and managerial women: success in work and retirement', *Journal of Women and Aging*, **3**(2), 95–117.

Index

acceptance 2, 5, 21, 24, 44, 68, 75, 161, 196–201, 204, 270, 380
accuracy goals 101
Acker, J. 184–5, 190–91
Adams, Susan 6
adaptation 161, 165, 345, 413–15, 491
adaptive
  preferences 49, 182, 276
  women 51–2, 342
Adler, P.S. 265
advancement process 382–3
affinity groups 159, 168, 370–71
affirmative action 96, 326
Agars, Mark 6–7, 166, 281
age 8, 108, 130, 133–4, 140–41, 143–4, 147–51, 183, 276, 311, 376, 420, 432, 438, 446–7, 450–51, 490, 499
  discrimination 147, 475
agency 44, 48, 54, 56, 65, 68, 91, 180, 186, 191, 293–5, 298, 313, 315–18, 502
agency–communion paradigm 293
agentic 91–3, 194, 293–5, 299, 428
Allen, Kim 36–7, 40–41
Allen, T.D. 231
Altman, Y. 341, 350
ambiguity 96–100
ambivalence 417
Americans with Disabilities Act (ADA) 148
Anderson, Deirdre 8
Anker, R. 179
applicant pool 99
appreciative inquiry 161, 165–6
Armstrong, C. 230
Arts & Labor Occupy group 35
Ash, R.A. 233
assignments 3, 6, 21, 136, 143–4, 159, 167, 209, 214, 233, 244, 278, 280, 298, 341–4, 346–8, 350, 352–3, 380, 384

Association to Advance Collegiate Schools of Business (AACSB) 16–17
attention 93
attributes 2, 4, 16, 36, 45, 63, 91–2, 96, 194, 363, 369, 492
Auer, P. 112
August, Rachel 8, 495
authentic 311–12, 314, 318, 425
authenticity 18, 276, 317–18, 345–6, 446–7, 493–4, 498–503
awareness 316–18
Ayman, R. 230

Baby Boomers 8, 276, 284, 425, 438, 440, 449, 452–4, 456–7, 481, 484, 487, 490
backlash 307, 315
Barrett, Mary 5
Barsh, J. 3, 160
Bartunek, J.M. 164
Baruch, Yehuda 7, 260, 350
Bateson, M.C. 430–31
Baxter, Judith 252
Becker, G.S. 181
Beckett, Andy 33–4
Beier, Jill Choate 7
beliefs 194–205
Belkin, L. 448
Bendl, Regine 5, 140–41, 146–50
Bergman, B. 195
Bergmann, T.J. 140
bias 5, 16, 69–70, 90–102, 107, 159–64, 166, 168–70, 209, 244, 255, 261, 281, 297, 370, 381, 401
Bickel, J. 237
Bilimoria, D. 446–7, 450, 456
Billing, Yvonne Due 8, 413–14, 417
biological classification 66
boardroom diversity 326
Bolton, S. 377
boundary crossing 352
boundary management 259, 283

boundaryless careers 276, 446
Bourdieu, Pierre 6, 48, 112, 179–80, 186–91
Bowles, H.R. 233
Braun, Susanne 5
Broadbridge, Adelina 4, 6, 8, 225, 260
Broderick, Elizabeth 326
Brown, C. 182
Bruyère, S.M. 148
Bryans, Patricia 7, 17
Brzezinski, Mika 255
bullying 279–81
Burke, S. 231
burnout 199, 426
business education 15–17
business schools 4, 16–17, 25, 83, 209
Butler, J. 61
Butterfield, D.A. 293
Buzzanell, M. 119

Cabrera, E.F. 494
Cahill, K. 483
Cameron, Deborah 106, 120
Campbell, S. 5, 105, 110–14, 116, 118, 120
Campion, M.A. 426
capital 6, 38, 179–80, 187–8, 191, 412
  career framework 341, 345–7, 349–50, 353
  cultural 37, 50, 187, 192, 383
  economic 187
  human 6, 36, 98, 181–2, 185, 188, 191, 215, 259, 264–5, 275, 291–2, 374, 382
  psychological 205
  social 6, 20, 40, 187, 260, 265–7, 278–9, 298–9, 346–7, 383–4, 416, 418
capitalism 31, 124, 190
career
  aspirations 453, 457
  breaks 182, 292, 360, 449, 478
  category 203
  coach 218, 246
  commitment 22, 228
  decisions 57, 425, 433–4, 438–9, 460–71
  early 57, 249–50, 346, 446, 448, 494
  enhancement 222, 228, 352
  functions 233–4

history 76, 305, 309
impact 215–16
mid 30, 245, 346, 438, 446, 487
models 7, 259, 276, 285, 341, 343–5, 434, 456, 491, 493
opportunity 3, 20, 99, 136, 255, 278, 327, 346, 463
progression 6–7, 21, 24, 187, 251, 345, 352, 462, 465–6, 493
prospects 348
satisfaction 199–202, 204, 228, 275, 280, 429, 437, 439–40
self-management 259–60, 268, 270, 383, 475
signposting 246–7, 254
strategy 219
success 6–7, 21, 158, 198–200, 203–4, 217, 246, 268, 270, 275–8, 280, 282–4, 305, 309, 352, 377, 383, 401, 416, 418, 425, 428, 434, 437, 439–40
support 6, 22, 51, 246–7, 249–50, 253
values 476
Career Pathway Survey 6, 195, 197–205
Carli, Linda 7, 197, 244, 252, 416
Carroll, Lewis 270
Carter, N. 15–16
Carver, C.S. 199
Cathro, V. 352
Chambers, John 254
change cultures 202, 418
change models 161–6
Chesterman, C. 305
Chia, R. 67
childbirth 358, 421, 460, 471
childcare 51, 53, 62, 116, 168, 279, 291, 293, 358, 370, 392, 398–401, 403–5, 453–4, 461–2, 467–8, 471
choice feminism 5, 46–7
Churchill, Winston 195
Cialdini, R.B. 166
Clair, J.A. 151–2
Cohen, D.S. 167
Cole, M.S. 75, 77, 145
Cole, N.D. 352
Collins, K.M. 231
Collins, N.W. 229
Colyvas, J. 65

commitment 6, 22, 38, 47, 51, 58, 85, 118, 164, 168, 175, 182, 196, 198, 202, 211, 228, 235, 245–6, 269–71, 290, 315–18, 329, 351, 361, 363, 381, 385, 391, 394, 398–400, 416, 420–21, 432, 439, 448, 455, 461
communal 91, 194, 293–6, 299
communication 16–20, 24–5, 39, 77, 97, 111, 129–30, 134, 163, 218, 221, 230, 234, 334, 349–50, 363, 366, 412, 439, 482, 493
conflict 49, 51–2, 105–6, 118, 124, 168, 215, 217, 232, 245, 283–4, 342, 346, 391–4, 398–403, 420, 431, 436, 446–8, 470, 498
Connell, R.W. 308
constructionist paradigm 107
continuous change 161, 164–5
conversation analysis (CA) 105, 108–11, 118
conversations 5, 105–13, 115, 118, 149, 160, 175, 214, 237, 261, 264, 335, 400, 428, 438, 467
Cook, A. 267
Cook, J. Michael 358, 371
Cooperrider, D.L. 165
corporate boards 7, 90, 99, 158, 166, 170, 290, 323
corporate governance 322, 324, 326–7, 329
cost mitigation 210–11
counter-stereotypical information 16
Cox, T. 163, 165, 167
credibility 17, 313–14, 317–18, 349
Crompton, R. 53, 277, 375–6, 385
cross-cultural 140, 213, 221, 348
cultural capital 37, 50, 187, 192
cultural conditions 44, 58
cultural feminization 39
cultural knowledge 128, 187
cultural orientations 376
cultural stereotypes 111
curriculum 16–17, 25
culture 3, 7, 22, 34–5, 38, 58, 79, 106, 114, 116, 118, 127–8, 131, 133, 135, 149–50, 159–60, 162–3, 183–4, 187, 195, 201–2, 220–21, 253, 255, 259, 281, 283, 290, 297, 326, 336, 343–4, 362–3, 365–6, 370–72, 385, 402, 404, 418, 420–21, 447, 457

Dart, Beatrix 254
Davies, E. 475, 477
De Oliveira, E.T.V.D. 75
De Simone, Silvia 7
decision-makers 96–7, 123, 131, 133, 145, 159, 208, 278, 403
Decker, Diane 4, 16–17
demasculinize management 421
denial 196–7, 199–202, 204, 271
Dent, F.E. 244
dependent children 460–71
disability 144, 148–50
discourse 477–8
dispositional optimism 199, 203
distributive negotiating style 18
diversity checklist 327
diversity dimensions 140–41, 144–5, 147, 149–52
diversity initiatives 96, 168, 175, 324, 385
diversity training programmes 159
Doldor, E. 140
domestic support 398
double-bind 68
double-loop learning 168
downshift 494
doxic order 189–90
Dreher, G.F. 233
dual-earner 392
dualistic gender concept 61, 66, 70
Duffy, M. 191
Dunn, P. 336
Dworkin, T.M. 233

Eagly, A.H. 194–5, 197, 244, 252, 416
early retirement 432, 435, 474
Eberherr, Helga 5
Eby, L.T. 352
Eccles, J.S. 431
Eckert, P. 118
education 15–25
Ekerdt, D.J. 476
Elacqua, T.C. 195
elite networks 137
elite women 305, 348
Ellemers, N. 305

Elliott, C. 309
emergent change 164–5
Emirbayer, M. 180, 188
employee resource groups 159, 165
employment decisions 48, 74–5, 93
encore career 8, 425–40
enhancement 151, 228, 352, 391–4
Ensher, E.A. 232
essentialist paradigm 106–7, 117
ethnicity 51, 108, 117, 125, 128, 135–7, 140–41, 143–4, 146–8, 150–52, 191–2
European Commission 148–9, 244
evaluation 97–8
Everett, J. 180
exclusion 5, 62, 69, 75, 123, 136–7, 140–47, 151–2, 231, 258
executive search consultants 5, 123, 126, 132, 134–6, 140–44, 147–50, 152, 258
executive search development 5, 123–37, 140–52
exit 363, 412–17, 419–20, 427, 435, 462, 466, 491
expatriates 7, 341–4, 346–52
explanatory style optimism 199, 202–4

face time 359, 361, 448
Faludi, S. 54
family commitments 6, 38, 245–6, 394, 416
family matters 311, 317–19
family responsibilities 116, 133–4, 161, 181, 245, 277, 282, 292, 311, 365, 391, 394, 401, 412
family roles 291, 316, 392–3, 398, 400, 402, 493
family support 252, 349, 364, 392, 467
fatherhood 419
fathers 80, 135, 265, 269, 291, 416–17, 421, 451, 461–2, 470, 481
female directors 305, 322, 331, 333
female entrepreneurship 7, 390–404
femininity 30, 39, 44, 47, 54, 66, 76, 87, 95, 107, 179, 187, 189–90, 306–7, 310–11, 350
feminist economic theory 501
feminist language 107
feminized occupations 30–31, 38–40, 57, 179–92, 382

financial pressure 465–7, 469
financial rewards 465
Fiorina, Carly 254
Fletcher, J.K. 231, 234, 419
flexible work 36, 39, 283, 349, 385, 447, 461–2, 470–71
    arrangements 7, 165, 357–72, 431, 448
    options 160, 168
    policies 382
    programmes 160
    rights 461
formal mentoring programmes 22, 228, 251, 281, 366
Fortune 500 companies 1–2, 15, 24, 214, 290
Fowler, Jane 6, 234
Frankel, L.P. 109
Fullan, M. 225
fun 8, 370, 427–30, 435, 437, 439

Gardner, Howard 167
Gardner, Phil 39
Garfinkel, H. 77
gatekeepers 5, 68, 123
gender binary 150, 189, 306–7, 310–11, 316, 318
gender diversity 17, 159, 161, 169, 175, 225, 297, 324, 327–9, 337
Gender Equality Act 120, 125
gender gaps 16, 62, 124, 291–2, 296
gender hierarchies 61–3, 69, 259
gender inequalities 4, 30–42, 53, 55–7, 123, 125, 134, 137, 147, 180, 184–7, 189–91, 194, 255, 281, 298, 412
gender neutral/neutrality 2, 19, 44, 57–8, 61, 76, 80–81, 183–5, 190, 208, 212–13, 221, 292, 310
gender roles 24, 47, 61, 63, 69, 160, 277–8, 281, 363, 393, 477
gender segregation 61–2, 68, 125, 191, 298, 376
gender sensitivity 81–2
gendered expectations 87, 219, 308, 318, 414
gendered institutions 181, 184–5
gendered practices 85, 229, 418
gendered scripts 65–6, 77, 82
gender-typed 92, 95–6, 98, 100

Generation X (GenXers) 8, 284, 449–50, 453–7
Generation Y 284, 487
Giddens, A. 142–4
Gill, R. 54–5
Gilligan, C. 501
Gladwell, Malcolm 170
Glass, C. 267
glass ceiling 6–7, 22, 185, 194–205, 210, 259, 305, 342, 457
glass cliff 166, 298, 342
glass escalator 181, 185–6
Glatt, Eric 35
Gleicher, David 164, 167
global assignments 342, 344, 346, 348, 350, 352
global careers 7, 341–53
  virtual 349–50
goal-directed behaviour 502
goal-setting 229–30, 500
Godshalk, V.M. 230
Gorman, E.H. 145
Gouvier, W.D. 148
Graves, L.M. 20, 22–3, 110
Gumperz, J.J. 110
Gupta, Vipin 6

habitus 6, 62, 67–8, 179–80, 186–91
Hackman, J.R. 494
Hakim, Catherine 5, 45, 47–56, 58, 182–3, 342–3, 462
Hall, D.T. 431, 476, 486
Han, S.K. 477
Hanappi-Egger, Edeltraud 5, 62, 65–8, 258–9
handicap script 81, 86
harassment 3, 35, 196, 278–81
Hardin, J.R. 145
Hareli, S. 76
Hargreaves, A. 225
Harman, Melissa 366
Harris, F. 53
Haslam, S.A. 342
Hass, Susan 6
headhunters 123–4, 126, 132–6, 140, 142
headhunting 5, 141, 202, 456
hegemonic gender 61
hegemonic masculinity 2, 307–8, 383
Heilman, Madeline 5, 95

Hendricks, J. 477
Henkens, K. 475, 485
heterogeneity 48–9, 51, 53, 128, 476
heterosexual matrix 61
hierarchical dualities 147
Hirschman, A.O. 412–13, 415
Hirsh, W. 316
Hofstede, G. 350
Hole, Arni 326
Holgersson, Charlotte 5, 75, 133
Holmes, O. 150
Holtom, B.C. 432
Holton, Viki 6, 244
home-centred women 49–52, 182
homosociality 75, 134, 258, 269
Hopkins, J. 64
horizontal segmentation 134, 187, 377
household labour 400
housework 291, 392, 394, 398, 400, 402, 404, 419
Houston, D.M. 462
human capital 6, 36, 98, 181–3, 185, 188, 191, 215, 259, 264–5, 267, 275, 291–2, 346, 374, 382
human resource management (HRM) 57–8, 74, 77, 95, 101, 129
human resources 70, 95, 101, 129–30, 134, 147, 175, 179, 199, 215, 359–60, 382, 414, 464
Huppatz, Kate 6
Huskins, W.C. 232, 237
Hwang, H. 65
Hytii, Ulla 5

ideal worker 2, 8, 38, 268, 385, 411, 421, 445, 447–8
idealistic achievement 446
identity 51, 64–9, 108, 115–16, 130, 151, 275, 345, 425, 429, 437–8, 465–7, 481, 484, 486, 492, 498
  managerial 65, 68–9
impersonality 112, 114
imposter syndrome 24
incivility 279–80
indigenous groups 146
inequality
  division of family work 400–403
  gender 4, 30–42, 53, 55–7, 123, 125, 134, 137, 147, 180, 184–7, 189–91, 194, 255, 281, 298, 412

information
    interpretation 93–4
    processing 93–4
    recall 94
initiatives 76, 96, 159, 161, 166, 168, 170, 220, 243, 248, 253, 280, 327, 349–50, 362, 364–5, 370, 385, 404, 447–8, 461, 463, 502
    diversity 175, 324
insecure work 32, 41
institutional language 112
intelligent career capital model 341, 350
intercultural issues 111
Intern Aware 34
Intern Bridge 39
Intern Labor Rights 35
internship 4, 25, 30–42
interpersonal attraction 230
interpersonal support 427, 429, 433, 436, 439
interpretive schemes 142–4, 146–7, 149, 151–2
inter-role conflict 392
interview
    interaction 105, 118
    technique 119
intrinsic motivation 431

Jackson, C. 316
Jackson, J.C. 195
Jackson, Margaret 325–6
Jamali, D. 393
Jenkins, A. 475
job applications 74, 77–8, 85
job assignments 144, 380
job dissatisfaction 426, 448
job profiles 142–4, 148
job satisfaction 22, 158, 229, 276, 360, 430, 446, 478, 492
Johnson, Jessica 35–6, 40, 210
Johnson, V. 180, 188
Jones, L. 182
judgement criteria 97

kaleidoscope career 7, 276, 341, 343–7, 434, 446, 491, 493
Kanter, R.M. 4, 183–4, 187
Karau, S.J. 194–5
Kelloway, E.K. 476
Khurana, R. 133

King, J.E. 150
Kirkpatrick, J. 46
Kniveton, B.M. 75
Konopaske, R. 352
Kornberger, M. 385
Kotter, J.P. 162, 167
Kottke, Janet 6–7, 166, 281
Kouzes, J. 209–10
Kram, K.E. 225, 233–4
Kumra, Savita 7, 383–5
Kupka, B. 352
Kwon, S.W. 265

labour force 45–6, 62, 125, 258, 357–8, 390, 475, 490–91
lack of fit 5, 90–102, 187
Lahey, Katy 325
Lane, N. 462
language 5, 33, 100, 105–8, 111, 114–20, 146, 184, 208–9, 221, 253, 264, 478, 482, 503
Lawrence, T. 65
leadership goals 200
leadership potential 313, 381
leadership programmes 159, 243, 254
leadership style
    autocratic 295–6
    democratic 295–6
    directive 296
leaky pipeline 69, 245, 358
learning 25, 32–3, 35–8, 40, 161, 163, 168–9, 210, 212, 227, 230, 235–6, 238, 248, 271, 309–10, 312, 319, 349, 429, 431, 439, 503
    cycles 431, 476
Ledbetter, Lilly 279
Lee, T.W. 426
Leenders, M. 485
legislation 1, 41, 70, 111, 114, 125, 148–9, 170, 258, 404, 460–61, 470–71, 502
Levin, Leslie 7
Lewin, Kurt 161–2, 165
Lewis, Patricia 4–5
Liechty, T. 478
life satisfaction 275, 429, 437–8, 440
life stage 57, 305, 311, 318–19, 345, 432, 436, 438
lifestyle preferences 48, 53, 182
Linder, Karen 254–5

Lindorff, M. 195
Linell, P. 110, 119
Lirio, P. 284
listing 129–31
Llewellyn, N. 77
long-distance commuting couples 252
Lord, Linley 7
Loretto, W. 476–8, 482, 485–6
loyalty 22, 269–71, 412–13, 415–16, 419–20
Luchak, A.A. 484
Lupton, B. 190
Lupu, I. 385
Lyness, K.S. 95, 379
Lyonette, C. 277, 385

Maertz, C.P. 426
Mainiero, L.A. 318, 345, 379, 493, 502–3
Makela, L. 352
Malcahy, Anne 252
male dominated positions 130
Managerial Attitudes Towards Women Executives Scale 195
managerial identity 65, 68–9
Manzi, Francesca 5
Marks, G. 462
Martin, B. 66
Martin, P.Y. 418–19
masculine professions 382
masculinity 2, 66–9, 75–6, 107, 181, 189, 208–10, 213, 299, 306–8, 311, 347, 350, 382, 413, 419
masculinity construction 65, 68–9
Matchar, Emily 46
matching 133, 230
maternity benefits 461, 463, 471
maternity leave 248, 251–2, 311, 363, 403, 455, 461, 466–7
Mattis, Mary 7, 245
Maupin, R.J. 378, 380
Mavin, Sharon 7, 17
Maxfield, Sylvia 6
Mayer, Marissa 251
McConnell-Ginet, S. 118
McDowell, L. 45
McKenna, S. 352
McMurray, A. 146
McNabb, R. 383
McRae, S. 53, 182–3

meaningful work 427–9, 439
mentees 6, 23, 225–38, 334
mentoring 4, 6, 20–23, 25, 33, 40–41, 140, 201, 245, 247, 249–51, 253–4, 268, 278–9, 312, 336–7, 361, 366, 370–71, 381
  benefits 228–9
  functions 233–6
  opposite sex 22–3, 229–31, 233
  outcomes 230
  programmes 22, 228–9, 251, 260, 281, 299, 326–7, 333–6, 364, 366, 371
  psychosocial 21
  relationships 16, 21–3, 225–38
mentors 3, 6, 21–3, 176, 196, 198, 225–38, 248–50, 266–71, 278–9, 281, 298–9, 334
mentorship 21, 23, 278–9, 366, 371
merit 44
meritocracy 44, 58, 326
meta-analysis 95, 158, 291–3, 295–7
Meyerson, D. 336
Mick, Robyn 363
Millennials 284, 440
Miller, Lisa 45
Mincer, J. 181
mindsets 3, 19, 159–61, 176
Mitchell, T.R. 426
mobility work 351
Moen, P. 447, 476–7, 482, 484
Morales-López, E. 112
Morrish, L. 151
motherhood 45, 51, 198–9, 292, 448–9, 464, 466, 471
mothers 3, 45–6, 51, 80, 87, 169, 187, 198, 244, 251–2, 265, 276, 291, 358, 361, 364, 391, 393, 403, 450, 455, 457, 460–63, 468, 470–71
Moulettes, Agneta 8
multiple roles 314, 392, 398
Murphy, S.E. 232
Murphy, Wendy Marcinkus 8
Muzio, D. 377

narrativized speech 105, 117
needs 36, 51, 63, 114, 127, 160, 163, 184, 211, 226, 235, 251, 276, 281, 343, 359, 364, 390, 403, 446
  clients' 133, 366

family 360, 398, 403, 454, 456, 462
post-retirement 8, 490–504
women's 8, 170, 315, 403, 490–504
Neergaard, A. 137
negative expectations 96, 98–100
negative performance 93–5, 99–101
negotiated resignation 196
negotiating 18–20, 227–8, 232–4, 236, 453
neoliberalism 31, 33, 36–7, 40, 124, 185–6
networking 6, 20–23, 38, 41, 196, 198, 217, 228, 249, 259–60, 278–9, 281, 299, 312, 351, 361, 370, 413, 416, 476
networks
  family 217
  opposite sex 21
  professional 217, 298, 350
Ng, I. 158, 439
non-executive posts 258
non-work domains 431, 437, 445, 447, 451, 453–4, 457
non-work experience 76, 78, 87
not-for-profit organizations 123, 330, 332–4
novelty 8, 427–31, 437, 439

occupational characteristics 427–9, 432–3, 437, 439
occupational segmentation 180
occupational segregation 2, 48, 179, 184–5, 189, 278, 379
O'Gorman, J.G. 234
Ohlott, P.J. 447
older workers 147, 474–5, 487, 503
Oldham, G.R. 494
O'Mara, K. 151
O'Neil, D. 446–7, 450, 456
Opportunity Now 243
opting out 45–6, 353, 433–4, 438
organization development 163–4
organizational discourse 110, 160
organizational fit 116
organizational ideologies 112
organizational politics 314
Oxfam 32
Ozbilgin, M. 68, 179

Parasuraman, S. 391
parental leave 79–82, 85–8, 125, 134, 292
Paris, Lori 4, 16–17
part-time working 3, 32, 39, 41, 51, 125, 182, 245, 251–2, 292, 309, 311, 358, 360–61, 363, 369, 411, 438, 462–7, 469–71, 494, 497, 503
pathways 276, 278, 280–84, 330, 332–3, 335–7, 475–7, 501–2
  Career Pathway Survey 6, 195, 197–205
patriarchal cultures 159, 344
patriarchy 49, 54, 307–8
Patterson, Nicola 7
Paule, A. 146
pay 16, 30, 32, 35, 159, 167–8, 170, 233, 255, 435, 499
pay gap 48, 258, 291–2
pay rises 158
Pearson, C. 146
pensions 474–7, 481, 486, 491, 495, 500
Percheski, C. 46
performance 3, 22, 24, 30, 34, 39, 96–101, 105, 118–19, 163, 190, 202, 216, 230, 260, 268–9, 281–2, 290, 293, 296–7, 314–15, 318, 327, 350, 360, 364, 371, 374, 382–4, 401, 414, 447
  negative 93–5, 99–101
Perlin, Ross 31, 33–5, 41–2
personal agency 502
personal brand 313
personal disclosure 105, 112, 114–16
personal fulfilment 465–7, 469
personality 108, 111, 129–31, 203, 259, 262–3, 292, 379, 449
person-centred explanations 374, 378, 380
Phillipson, C. 474–5, 483
physical attractiveness 50, 95
Pinar, M. 145
planned change 161–5
Pleau, R. 483
positional advantage 36–8
positive organizational scholarship 426, 428, 430, 502
positive spillover 393, 400
Posner, B. 209–10
Post, C. 476, 487

postfeminism 44–7, 54–8
post-retirement 8, 490–504
post-structuralist perspectives 107–8, 114, 117
Powell, G.N. 20, 22–3, 110, 202, 293
Powell, P.I. 210
pragmatic endurance 446
predictors 158, 492–3
preference theory 5, 45, 47–56, 58, 181–3, 342, 462
pregnancy 183, 462, 464–6, 469
prejudice 101, 146, 194–5, 202, 293, 461, 463
pre-planned quitters 426
primary careers 425, 427–8
Priola, Vincenza 7
privilege 4, 34, 36–7, 46, 56, 134, 190, 259, 432, 474, 487
Probyn, E. 56
Proença, M.T.V.C. 75
professional services firms 7, 123, 332, 374–86, 449, 457
professionalism 132, 232, 382, 384
profiling 127–9
projective agency 68
promotion 7, 21–2, 38, 65, 158–9, 163, 167, 182, 187–8, 190, 196–8, 201–2, 210–11, 218–19, 229, 233–4, 244, 250–51, 255, 260, 262, 275, 291–2, 294, 298, 310, 346, 357, 366–71, 374, 377–8, 380–81, 383–4, 418, 437, 463
  policies 5, 69
  processes 70, 168
protean careers 259, 276, 346, 434
psychosocial functions 231, 233–4
push-pull model 7, 341, 343–5, 352
Puwar, Nirmal 38

queen bee syndrome 295
Quinn, R.E. 165
Quintero, V.C. 495
quotas 70, 158, 290, 322, 324–6, 329

Ragins, B.R. 231, 234
recognition-based processes model 16
recruiters 5, 74–8, 84–7, 145, 150
recruitment decision-making 75–6, 78, 87
Redshaw, Jane 8

redundancy 474, 477, 481–3, 486
Reis, Cristina 7, 260, 348
reluctant retirees 477
retirement 4, 8, 435, 438, 451, 456–7, 474–85, 490–91
  age 474, 483, 485, 490–91
  early 432, 435, 474
  planning 474, 476–8, 485
  trajectories 476–7
  see also post-retirement
Riach, K. 147
Rice, J. 162–3
Richardson, J. 348, 352
risk aversion 208–22
risk-taking 6, 208–11, 213, 215–22, 260, 271
Roberts, C. 5, 105, 110–14, 116, 118, 120
Rometty, Virginia 250
Roper, M. 418
Rose, C. 65
Rosenthal, S.L. 237
Ross, Andrew 31
Ross-Smith, Anne 7
Ruderman, M.N. 447
Russell Hatch, L. 477
Ryan, M.K. 342

Sandberg, Sheryl 15, 22, 165, 251, 254–5, 267, 315, 347–9
Sanderson, K. 375–6
Scharff, C. 54
Schegloff, E.A. 108
Scheier, M.F. 199
Schein, V.E. 293
Schmidt, Angelika 5
scholarship 38, 329, 335–6, 426, 428, 430
Schwarz, Madeline 39, 350
Scott, R.W. 70
scripting behaviour 74, 77, 85
Sealy, R. 244
second acts 425, 429, 431
secondary careers 425–6, 438, 440
sectorial segmentation 179
segregation
  gender 61–2, 68, 125, 191, 298, 376
  horizontal 134, 187, 377
  occupational 2, 48, 179, 184–5, 189, 278, 379
  vertical 6, 125–6, 134, 179–92

selection criteria 142–5, 149
self-acceptance 499
self-belief 262–4, 267–8, 270, 312–13
self-confidence 194, 202, 229, 262–3, 265, 267–8, 345
self-construction 66, 69–70
self-control 131
self-efficacy 6, 16, 19, 23–5, 213, 215–17, 262–4, 311–13, 318, 502
self-employment 7, 390–91, 394, 403–4, 478, 485
self-fulfilment 342, 346, 378
self-management 259–60, 268, 270, 383, 475
self-promotion 210–11, 457
self-reported behaviour 231
self-surveillance 54
Seligman, P. 200
sexism 24, 54–5, 107, 166, 184
sex-role stereotyping 64, 244, 379, 381
sexual harassment 35, 196, 279
sexual orientation 140–41, 143–4, 148–51
Shapiro, Mary 6, 260
Sheffield, J. 146
Sheker, Geeta 254
Shelton, L.M. 393
Sheridan, Alison 7
Shortland, S. 341
Shultz, K.S. 475
Shuman, K. 483
Silva, C. 15–16
Simmers, C.A. 391
Simpson, Ruth 4–5, 225
single-loop learning 168
Skeggs, Beverley 37
Smith, Paul 6, 195–7, 199, 201, 203–4
social capital 6, 20, 40, 187–8, 260, 265–7, 278–9, 298–9, 346–7, 384, 416, 418
social class 6, 48, 186, 190–91, 345, 348, 502
social exchange theory 269
social identities 502
social inequalities 31, 34
social media 35
social networks 20, 137, 188, 350, 383, 436, 476, 482, 485, 493
social resources 501
social space 188–9

social stereotyping 375
social-cultural context 36, 44, 124, 137
societal perspectives 135
societal power structures 125
socio-cultural 20, 54, 124, 133, 135, 137
sociolinguistics 105–20
Sosik, J.J. 230
speech 105–8, 112, 114–15, 117
speech patterns 18
Spence, L. 77
Spencer, D. 476, 484
spirituality 150, 503
spouses 81, 131, 198, 217–18, 292, 298, 342–3, 347, 349, 351–2, 378, 435–6, 464, 499
Spurr, S.J. 378
Stead, V. 309
stereotypes
  descriptive 293–4
  prescriptive 293–4
structural framework 5, 62, 68
structuralism 67, 412
structuration theory 143
Sueyoshi, P. 378
Sullivan, S.E. 318, 345, 493, 502–3
supportive leadership 281, 283
Sweet, S. 447
symbolic violence 189–91
Szinovacz, M.E. 475, 485, 491

talents 19, 93, 166, 170, 229, 270, 429, 461, 463, 503
Tanguary, D.M. 76
Tannen, D. 106
Tatli, A. 68, 179
Taylor, S. 140, 501
think manager–think male paradigm 7, 64, 74, 293, 305
third sex 414
Thompson, D.E. 379
Thunqvist, D. 110, 119
Tienari, Janne 5, 140, 145, 258
time constraints 416
token 4, 81, 86, 96, 181, 183–5, 187, 191, 297, 414, 487
tokenism 86, 183–5, 329
Tompkins, M. 336
trade unions 32, 34, 41, 124
transformational leadership 64, 296, 299

transitions 4, 36, 78, 214, 238, 246, 333, 370, 416, 425–9, 433–40, 447, 463, 475–7, 485, 491–2, 498–9
triple-loop learning 168
trust 22, 111, 127, 230, 232, 236, 248, 266, 313, 398
Tsentides, Andrea 7
Tsoukas, H. 67
turning around projects 247
turnover 358, 363, 371, 426–8, 432, 435, 438, 444
Twenge, J.M. 420

UK Centre for Policy Studies 54
unemployment 137, 474, 477
unions 32, 34, 41, 124
up-or-out system 377–8
Ursell, Gillian 38

validity 110, 195, 199, 201, 203–4, 469
values 36, 38, 48–9, 53, 57–8, 64, 66, 69–70, 76, 107, 114, 127, 150, 159, 163, 170, 235, 259, 276, 281, 306, 311, 316, 336, 343, 345, 349–50, 418–19, 428–9, 434, 440, 444, 447, 449, 457, 475–6, 496
van Solinge, H. 493, 501
vertical segregation 6, 125–6, 134, 179–92
vertical stratification 377
Vickerstaff, S. 476–8, 482, 485–6
Vinnicombe, Susan 8, 260, 383–4
virtual global careers 349–50
voice 4, 49, 53, 58, 111, 120, 170, 214, 312, 412–15, 417–18, 420
Volpe, Elizabeth Hamilton 8
voluntary redundancy 474
voluntary turnover 426, 435, 438
Voydanoff, P. 283

wage parity 19
Wages for Housework 41
Wajcman, J. 66
Walsh, J. 382
Wang, M. 492–4
Warren, A.M. 476
Warren, T. 245
Wass, V. 383
Weick, K.E. 165

well-being 8, 21, 101, 125, 199–200, 202–4, 284, 352, 484, 486, 491, 499–501
Welsh, E.T. 231
West, C. 306
Whelehan, I. 54
Whitney, D. 165
wholeness 447
Whole-Scale™ Change method 164, 167–8
Wigfield, A. 431
Williams, C. 185–6, 190–91
Williams, Jannine 7
Willmott, H. 68
Wingfield, A. 191
women
  academics 348–9
  on boards 1, 322–37
  entrepreneurs 7, 390–404
  expatriates 7, 341–4, 346–52
  partners 367–8, 380, 445, 449–50, 456
  successful 2, 52, 165, 198, 259–60, 319
Women as Managers Scale 195
Women Workplace Culture Questionnaire 195
Wood, G.J. 195
Woolnough, Helen 8
work
  assignments 21, 278, 280, 298
  engagement 158, 199–202, 204, 263
  part-time 3, 32, 39, 41, 51, 125, 182, 245, 251–2, 292, 309, 311, 358, 360–61, 363, 369, 411, 438, 462–7, 469–71, 494, 497, 503
  placement 37–8, 41
work-centred attitudes and behaviour 462
work-centred women 49, 51
work–family balance 182, 196, 394, 398
work–family conflict 217, 283, 391–3, 401–2, 431
work–family enrichment 393
work–family facilitation 393
work–family interface 390–405
working history 80, 84

working mothers 51, 169, 244, 251–2, 361, 393, 460, 468
work–life balance 8, 62, 169, 253, 259, 275, 277, 283, 344–5, 361, 364–6, 368, 391, 394, 403, 429, 434, 437–8, 440, 445–58, 487
Workplace Explanation Survey 202
work-related identities 492, 498
WorldatWork 160
Wrigley, B.J. 196

Yee, L. 3, 160
young family years 202

Zaniboni, S. 476, 485
Zikic, J. 348
Zimmer, L. 184
Zimmerman, D.H. 306